Dynamic Web Application Development:
Using PHP and MySQL

Dynamic Web Application Development:
Using PHP and MySQL

Simon Stobart & David Parsons

COURSE TECHNOLOGY
CENGAGE Learning™

Australia • Mexico • Singapore • Spain • United Kingdom • United States

COURSE TECHNOLOGY
CENGAGE Learning™

Dynamic Web Application Development:
using PHP and MySQL
Simon Stobart and David Parsons

Publisher: Gaynor Redvers-Mutton

Editorial Assistant: Matthew Lane

Production Editor: Lucy Mills

Manufacturing Manager: Helen Mason

Marketing Manager: Jason Bennett

Typesetter: Newgen Imaging Systems (P) Ltd,
India

Cover Design: Adam Renvoize

Text Design: Design Deluxe, Bath, UK

For product information and technology assistance, contact
emea.info@cengage.com.

For permission to use material from this text or product,
and for permission queries, email
Clsuk.permissions@cengage.com

Products and services that are referred to in this book may be
either trademarks and/or registered trademarks of their
respective owners. The publishers and author/s make no claim
to these trademarks.

British Library Cataloguing-in-Publication Data
A catalogue record for this book is available from
the British Library

ISBN 13: 978-1-84480-753-6

Cengage Learning EMEA
High Holborn House, 50-51 Bedford Row
London WC1R 4LR

Cengage Learning products are represented in Canada by
Nelson Education Ltd.

For your lifelong learning solutions, visit **www.cengage.co.uk**
and **course.cengage.com**

Printed by C & C Offset, China
1 2 3 4 5 6 7 8 9 10 – 10 09 08

To my granddaughter, Grace Elizabeth, who only needs to smile to bring me so much joy.

Simon Stobart

To my daughter, Kate, who was born along with my first book.

David Parsons

CONTENTS

Introduction

Welcome to *Dynamic Web Application Development using PHP and MySQL*. This book covers all the knowledge required for you to implement very sophisticated dynamic web applications. In order to do this, we will cover a number of different, but related, topics. We begin by providing you some background to web applications in order for you to put the technologies introduced later into context. We then describe the (X)HTML language which is the building block of all web applications and scripts and underpins all of the other technologies we describe and examine within this text. We introduce the concept of the presentation layer, known as cascading style sheets, which enables you to separate out your formatting and presentational features from the (X)HTML itself. Next, we introduce the JavaScript client-side scripting language which enables you to develop more interactive and powerful web applications. We introduce and describe Ajax, a more recent mechanism for providing advanced dynamic web applications. Ajax is a mechanism for creating asynchronous server connections, which enables us to create applications that operate far more smoothly and effectively via a web interface, in much the same way as programs run on a computer's operating system, such as Microsoft Windows.

Our chosen scripting language is the PHP pre-processing language, a server-side application which can be used to interface with databases and thus enable provision of even more advanced on-line applications. We devote a few chapters to the PHP language as it is extremely powerful and enables us to create very sophisticated applications. We conclude the book by examining how the Ajax and PHP technologies can operate together and how you should be concerned with ensuring that the scripts and applications that you create conform to the various published standards. Finally, we examine what security issues you should be concerned with when developing on-line applications and how to ensure that your applications are as robust and secure as possible.

In the remainder of this preface, we describe how we have structured this text and how we think you should use it for the greatest effect. We shall describe the application software you will need to use in order to make use of the different technologies described above. We shall describe how to install the software and where you can find more information about it. We shall clarify some terminology which we will introduce later in the book. We shall describe what additional material is available for download on the book's web site. Let us begin by describing who we wrote this text for.

Who is this book for?

The intended audience for this text is deliberately quite broad, however it is essentially for those individuals who wish to learn more about how to create professional dynamic web applications. As both educators and web developers ourselves we realise that individuals' knowledge, background and web development experience will differ considerably and what knowledge and skills you may want out of a book on the subject of dynamic web development may be very different from someone else. You may have some well-practiced web development skills already, which is good as we will move quickly onto more interesting and in-depth subjects. You may have some previous programming experience in which case you are likely to find the chapters concerning programming and scripting quite familiar to you.

What we have tried to do is create a text which encompasses all of the different technologies with which you will need to get to grips and illustrates how these can be combined in order for you to have the basic underpinnings to begin to create sophisticated web applications of any kind. This is not a text designed for those with many years of web development experience nor it is a reference text. Furthermore, given the limitations of space, we have had to sacrifice the amount of space that we can devote to different subjects and technologies. For example, we introduce the subjects of (X)HTML and JavaScript in the initial chapters of the book but assume that the reader has some (although maybe limited) knowledge of these. We focus more on the PHP scripting language and on how this language can be integrated with Ajax asynchronous technology. Many individuals should find these topics new and exciting.

Book structure and features

This book is essentially divided into three sections, the first of which comprises Chapters 1 through 7. These chapters provide you with the essential background underpinning to web technologies. Topics examined include (X)HTML, cascading style sheets (CSS) and Ajax. The second section of the book, Chapter 8 to 17, introduces the PHP scripting language and illustrates how it can be used to control the generation of (X)HTML and other technologies to produce very sophisticated dynamic applications. In this section, the concept of databases is introduced and how a MySQL database can be created and interfaced to a PHP application is explored. Finally, the third section of the text examines how Ajax technology can be interfaced to PHP scripts, how to create web applications which conform to the published standards and why this is so important, and what security issues you should be aware of and how to ensure that your applications do not fall foul of them.

We have designed the book so that, depending on your background and experience and what it is that you wish to learn, you can jump directly to that chapter and begin learning from that point. So, for example, if you are already an experienced (X)HTML and CSS developer but wish to brush up on some JavaScript then you can turn directly to Chapter 6. If, on the other hand, all you want to know about is Ajax and you know (X)HTML and JavaScript then you can turn directly to Chapter 7. If you are a PHP expert then you can jump the PHP chapters and move to Chapter 18 to examine how Ajax can be interfaced with PHP.

Each chapter begins by outlining the key learning objectives that the chapter is designed to meet. In other words we tell you right at the start of the chapter what it is that you will learn within the chapter. After a brief introduction to the topics covered, the main sections of the chapter begin. Each chapter is designed to be read from start to finish. We have included many figures and screen shots to complement the text and to ensure that each topic is explained as clearly as possible. In the chapters which concentrate on different scripting technologies, such as (X)HTML, CSS, AJAX and PHP, there are many small complete examples which you can either type in and run yourself or download from the book's web site. Script examples are shown like this:

```
This is how a script
is highlighted within a chapter
```

All scripts are included on the CD accompanying this text which saves you the trouble of typing them in if you don't want to. Within the text, if there are any key points which need to be highlighted, these are drawn to your attention with the use of a note, like this one:

NOTE	Important facts are highlighted like this!

Towards the end of most chapters there are some exercises for you to check your level of understanding of the chapter contents. The answers to these exercises are available for download from the book's web site. The chapter concludes with a summary of what has been described and following this are usually some references or lists of where you can go to do some further reading on the subjects covered.

Hardware requirements

The examples in this text have all been tried and tested on a PC running a Microsoft Windows operating system. More specifically, we have tested the examples on PCs running Windows XP and the most recent Windows Vista. However, because the technologies we introduce, such as (X)HTML, Ajax, JavaScript and PHP are all, in the main, platform independent, all our examples should work with computers running UNIX (or one of its many open source variants) or Apple's OS X operating systems. The only examples which may not work as intended are those which interact with the operating system's file system, such as the file-upload or file-handling examples in PHP which are platform dependent.

Furthermore, when you have developed your own web applications you may wish to host them so that anyone using the internet can see and access them. In order to do this, most people require a 'service provider' who will host your applications on their web server. How exactly you upload your scripts and configure your database on your service provider's computer system differs considerably from one provider to the next and we couldn't possibly explain how to do this for all of them. However, in the most part, service providers have excellent help and support to guide you through the process of transferring your scripts and applications from your local PC onto their web server.

What software do you need?

As mentioned above we have tested the scripts and examples within this book on a Windows-based PC and we will assume that this is the platform which you will be using when trying out the examples and exercises within this book. However, regardless of what computer platform you are using you will need the following software to successfully implement all of the examples within this text:

- A web browser which supports, (X)HTML, CSS and Ajax.
- A web server.
- A PHP interpreter.
- A MySQL database.
- PHPMyAdmin database interface.
- A text or script editor.
- MySQL database modelling tool (not actually but you may find it useful).

If you are using Windows XP or Windows Vista then the great news is that it is quite easy to get all of this software and it is all free. Our recommendations for each of these different software components follows.

Web browser

The Web browser is used to display the results of and control your scripts. Our examples have been tested using Microsoft Internet Explorer 7.0.6, Mozilla Firefox 2.0.0.6 and Opera 9.23. We are confident that they will work with any newer versions of these Web browsers. Windows Vista comes with Internet Explorer 7 pre-installed but if you are using an earlier version of the Windows operating system you can get it for free from here:

    http://www.microsoft.com/windows/downloads/ie/getitnow.mspx

The latest version of Firefox is available for free from here:

    http://www.mozilla.com/en-US/firefox/

The latest version of Opera is available for free from here:

    http://www.opera.com/

Web server, PHP interpreter, MySQL database and PHPMyAdmin interface

The web server controls the serving and processing of your scripts. The PHP interpreter processes your PHP code. The MySQL database system is used to store any databases your application may use and the PHPMyAdmin tool is a web-based application written in PHP which provides a convenient and relatively easy interface to creating and configuring your MySQL databases. Once upon a time, you would have needed to obtain and configure each of these software components separately, which could result in a number of difficulties. Now however, there exists an integrated package of all of these components which can be downloaded in a single step and is both easy and free. The package is called WAMP (which stands for Windows, Apache (the web server), MySQL and PHP) and is available here:

    http://www.wampserver.com/en/

A copy of the latest package is included on the CD accompanying this text as the total download size is 21 MB. However, the applications bundled together in this package are regularly updated and so you may wish to visit the web site to check you have the latest versions.

Text or script editor

You will need a text editor to create and edit your (X)HTML, JavaScript, CSS, Ajax and PHP scripts. One of the simplest editors you can use is Notepad, which comes with Windows, but it is not one we would recommend. There are many much more sophisticated script editors which have been designed to provide far more support to the developer than a simple text editor like Notepad ever could or was designed to do. Our current favourite is PHP Designer which can be found here:

    http://www.mpsoftware.dk/

It is available in a professional version (which you can trial but will need to buy) or a personal version (which has a reduced number of features but is free). PHP Designer provides you with a huge number of different features to help you create your applications, including:

- An intelligent highlighter that automatically switches between PHP, HTML, CSS and JavaScript depending on your position!
- Intelligent and advanced editing, for example providing code suggestions where appropriate.
- Project and file management.
- The ability to debug and run PHP scripts within the editor.
- Integrated help.

A copy of this application is included on the CD.

MySQL database modelling tool

When you begin to design and create more complex databases you will quickly begin to wish for software tools to help you design and model your database tables and relationships. MySQL Workbench is currently an alpha release application (which means that it still has some bugs and should not be used for commercial development) which supports the design and creation of new databases. We introduce this application briefly in Chapter 14 and you can download the latest copy from here, although a copy of this application is included on the CD:

```
http://dev.mysql.com/downloads/gui-tools/5.0.html
```

Each of the applications described above is easy to install. Simply insert the CD accompanying this text and navigate to the application directory. Within it, you will find the following directories containing installation executables for each application:

- WAMP
- PHPDESIGNER
- MYSQLWORKBENCH

Object-oriented terminology

Chapters 16 and 17 introduce the topic of object orientation and describe how this can be used with the PHP language to create large-scale, efficient and reusable applications. Unfortunately, the object-oriented community uses many different terms to describe essentially the same thing. Usually the terms used are unique to the application language, but not always. If you are new to object orientation then this doesn't really matter, as the terms we use will be the only ones you have come across. However, if you have come across object orientation previously then we thought it would be useful if we were very clear as to the terminology we will be using with PHP:

- Class: A programming language construct used to group together methods and data members.
- Method: Also known as a function, subroutine or procedure. This is a sequence of statements which perform some action. A method may receive some parameters and may return a value.
- Data member: Also known as a field, variable, instance variable or member. This contains some data encapsulated within a class or object.

- Object: An instance of a class.
- Class Members: The collective term for the methods and data members of a class.

What further resources are available on-line?

In addition to what is included in the book and accompanying CD, we have made a number of other resources available to the reader or instructor using this textbook as their primary teaching aid:

- Powerpoint slides to accompany each chapter.
- Model solutions to the examples at the end of each chapter.
- Code and design documentation for complete examples illustrating the creation of a simple hangman game, a shopping cart and a members' message system.
- All code examples.

The companion website can be found at www.cengage.co.uk/stobart

Summary

In this preface we have introduced this book and described who it is targeted at and what knowledge and skills it covers. We have explained the structure of the book and how best to use it in order to get the best learning experience. We have introduced the different software which we will be using and explained how to install it correctly. You are now ready to begin the first chapter of the book which introduces the concept of web applications.

CHAPTER 1

Introduction to Web Applications

LEARNING OBJECTIVES

- **To understand the main features and services of web applications**

- **To understand some of the basic technological building blocks of web applications**

- **To understand how the World Wide Web has evolved from the Internet**

- **To understand some of the key aspects of the Web 2.0**

INTRODUCTION

The World Wide Web has had a profound impact on our lives since the 1990s. Some of the most successful companies that based their business on web technologies, such as Amazon, Yahoo and Google, have become as well known as the most famous global manufacturing and service companies of previous eras. We now expect all the major organisations with which we have contact to have a web presence. Not only that, we also expect that presence to include web-based applications that let us perform tasks such as managing our money, booking travel and purchasing goods and services without having to step away from the computer. Just having a web *site* is no longer enough; that *site* must support web *applications*.

In this chapter, we see what a web application does, and how it does it, by looking at the fundamental technologies that make web applications work and how they fit together. We also consider some important features of web application architecture. We conclude the chapter by looking at *Web 2.0*, a set of ideas that have had an important influence on how modern web applications are built.

1.1 What a web application does

What makes any kind of programming hard is largely a question of scale. Things that are easy to program inside a single computer become much more difficult when we want to distribute those things over space (to many users) and time (to exist beyond the run time of a single program). For example, let us assume that you are working as a software developer and, like many developers, you have a text document stored on your computer that you use as a log of things that you find helpful to keep track of, such as references to useful resources or solutions to problems you have discovered. You can use text editors or word processors installed on your own computer to access and edit that document. Now, what if you want to be able to make that document available to others, because you feel that this information may be helpful to, for example, other developers in your team? You could, of course, distribute print or email copies, but that would get very tedious if you had to keep doing this every time you made a new document entry and, after a while, there would be lots of different versions of your document floating around. What you need to do, of course, is to make the document available on a *web server* so that others can read it over the *World Wide Web*. Hey presto, your document is now a *blog* (short for *web log*). This leads us to the first thing that a web application can do:

A web application enables us to distribute documents over the World Wide Web.

Before going further we should perhaps make one thing clear, which is that we are introducing things that a web application can do, but in fact we are really talking about what a web application *server* can do. A web application server is the software that hosts your web applications and provides all of the services that we introduce in this section.

Now, maybe you are such a great writer, doing such interesting stuff, that you become a very popular blogger. Many thousands of people all over the world start reading your blog. Now, there can be many people all wanting to access your blog at the same time. Luckily, your server is able to cope with these multiple concurrent requests for your document without any problem. This brings us to another thing that web applications can do:

A web application manages concurrency, enabling access to a single web-based resource by multiple users.

After a while, you find that people reading your blog keep sending you emails for suggestions about what you should include in it. Eventually you get so fed up with this that you change your blog so that others can contribute their own entries to the on-line document. Hey presto, you have a *wiki*! (A wiki is a web site that is open to editing by anyone.) To make this work, your server has to be able to let users not only download your document, but upload their own content as well. It then has to be able to dynamically recreate the updated document for subsequent readers. This brings us to an essential role of web applications:

A web application can generate dynamic content, building web pages on the fly from sources of data that may include data supplied by users.

Eventually you find that your blog or wiki is becoming too difficult to manage because too many people are able to make changes to it and they keep messing up your pages. You decide that only people who register with you will be able to access and modify your site. This is another important service that web applications can provide.

A web application can include declarative, role-based security, which enables you to allow or deny access to specific resources to users based on their user role.

Over time, your original single document has become a large quantity of data, a kind of *Wikipedia* (www.wikipedia.org) of knowledge related to your own areas of interest, partly created by you but also created in large part by others. Instead of a single, simple piece of data, your wiki now consists of many related pieces of data. Since there is now too much information to be kept in a few pages, the underlying data that has been contributed to your system requires some kind of managed data storage so that you can keep it for a long time, re-use the same content in different contexts across different parts of the overall system, and ensure that it has some kind of existence outside of your web application. To do this, you need some kind of *persistence*, some way of storing your web application content in a database or some other form of secondary storage, and you need some way of connecting your web application to the database. Fortunately, web applications can help us to do that as well.

A web application provides facilities to connect to a database so that its content can be kept in permanent storage, to be retrieved when required.

If the content of a web application is stored in a database, then we need to make sure that any changes made to parts of it by others are handled correctly so that, for example, changes made by one client do not clash with changes made simultaneously by another. This means we have to be able to support *transactions*. Transactions make sure that any changes made to persistent data are made in a managed and consistent way, so that if two users try to change the same thing, either access is only allowed to one user at a time (pessimistic locking) or both users can try to make changes at the same time, but only the first to submit their changes (to *commit*) will be successful (optimistic locking).

A web application utilises the transactional services of a database so that updates to its content are reliable and consistent.

After all this we might also consider performance and reliability. How long might someone have to wait before getting access to the web application if many others want to do the same thing, and what happens if the machine that the application is running on fails for some reason? It may be that we need to provide more than one copy of the application so that multiple clients can access it at the same time and so that, if one machine fails, we are still able to provide the necessary services to our clients. In particular, we may find that over time we need to support more and more clients without breaking the system we already have, so we need some way of scaling our system to maintain performance and reliability.

A web application leverages the services of its underlying hardware and software infrastructure to run the same application across multiple machines, enabling scalability.

Figure 1.1 summarizes some of the web application features we have introduced in this section.

FIGURE 1.1 Some web application features

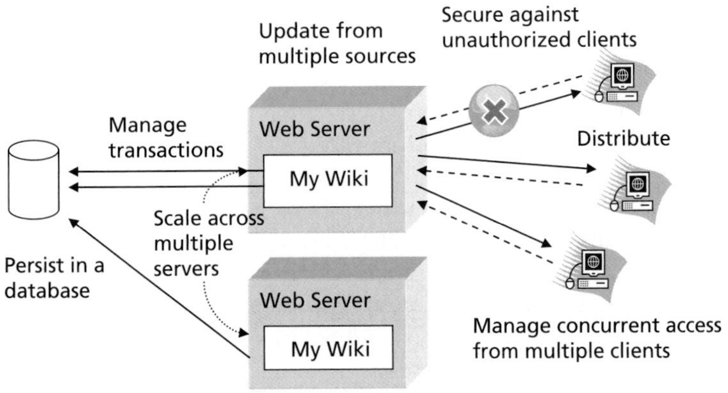

All of the issues we have touched on in this section are common to web applications, and all are difficult, tedious and expensive to program from scratch. Therefore it is very useful if we can reuse an existing set of tools to provide all of these services, leaving us free to write the code that addresses our particular business problem. The role of web application development languages and their supporting tools is to provide just such a framework for all of these services. However web applications cannot work in isolation because they rely on the fundamental technologies of the Internet and the World Wide Web. In the next section, we explain some of the most important features of these technologies.

1.2 E-everything – the Internet and the World Wide Web

Web applications rely on both the Internet and the World Wide Web to work, and one important point to bear in mind is that the Internet and the World Wide Web are not the same thing, since the first version of the Internet pre-dated the World Wide Web by more than 10 years. The Internet is a network of networks that was developed from the *ARPAnet*, a project that began in the 1970s. Its name comes from its sponsor, the US government Advanced Research Projects Agency (ARPA). It originally linked a small number of research sites together but used the same core technologies that now support the much bigger Internet. In contrast, the World Wide Web (the web, or W3, for short) is a hypertext-based collection of multimedia information accessible via the Internet that dates from the 1990s (hypertext means that the content on the web is linked together so that we can easily navigate between web pages that can be physically located anywhere in the world). We might say, perhaps, that the Internet is the information superhighway and the World Wide Web is the traffic that travels on it.

What has now become the World Wide Web was first developed by Tim Berners-Lee at CERN (originally the acronym for the French *Conseil Européen pour la Recherche Nucléair*, more generally known in English as the European Organisation for Nuclear Research) in 1990. It was originally a distributed hypertext system for managing information at CERN (based on previous hypertext research), but quickly developed into something much bigger. From an academic tool that was intended to assist researchers, it evolved into both an important platform for leisure applications and a key element in business, not only for the exclusively web-based *dot coms* but also as part of the IT strategy of major corporations, governments and other organisations.

From an internal research tool, the web quickly began to evolve into something much bigger and more important. Between 1991 and 1993, web servers began to come on-line outside of CERN, using the underlying technology of the Internet. CERN made the web technology free so it was easy for others to build on these systems. Originally, communication over the web was text-based and therefore not very user friendly. The first graphical *web browser* (an application able to display content from the Web) had been written by Tim Berners-Lee in 1991, but this was internal to CERN. However, other graphical browsers were soon developed and, in 1993, the NCSA (National Center for Supercomputing Applications) made their Mosaic graphical browser publicly available. This was soon followed by the first versions of the commercial browsers, Netscape Navigator and Microsoft Internet Explorer, to be joined in subsequent years by many other increasingly sophisticated browsers including Opera, Mozilla Firefox and Safari.

Graphical browsers, being able to display images and a range of text fonts, made access to the World Wide Web easy and attractive and expanded its potential user base from just technical specialists to the general public. The web began to get press coverage and reach a wider audience, and in 1994 the World Wide Web Consortium (W3C) was formed to create web standards and ensure that the proliferation of web technologies did not lead to incompatibility between different systems. In 1993, the first tools for writing dynamic web pages on the server were created using the Common Gateway Interface (CGI) developed by the NCSA. These made it possible for web pages to be generated on the fly on the server. Instead of simply providing static content to users, where everyone sees the same pages, CGI made it possible to generate pages for individual users, so they could see their own search results, bank account details, flight bookings, shopping carts etc. Other server-side technologies followed, including PHP (originally Personal Home Page Tools but later renamed PHP: Hypertext Preprocessor), Java and Microsoft's .NET, making it possible to develop industrial-strength applications that ran over the web. In 1995, HotJava, the first Java-aware browser, was launched by Sun Microsystems and Netscape introduced the first version of JavaScript, bringing the potential for applications that could run inside a browser. As both browser and server technologies continued to develop, terms such as 'web surfing', 'going on-line' and 'e-business' entered common speech and things have never been quite the same since.

1.3 Important Internet technologies

The World Wide Web depends on some important Internet technologies in order to work. These include:

- TCP/IP (Transmission Control Protocol/Internet Protocol)
- IP addresses
- Domain names

TCP/IP (Transmission Control Protocol/Internet Protocol)

TCP/IP is actually a whole set of related protocols and tools that help computers to communicate with each other. Some that are used on the Internet include SMTP (Simple Mail Transfer Protocol) for sending email messages and FTP (File Transfer Protocol), which allows files to be easily copied to and from remote sites.

IP addresses

Computers on the Internet are initially connected to some kind of local network, either within an organisation or as part of the services of an Internet service provider (ISP). To build all these separate systems into one, hardware devices known as *routers* are used to glue all the different networks together. For this to work, every machine on the Internet has to have a unique IP (Internet Protocol) address so that communications can be routed to the correct computer. An IP address is a 32-bit binary number giving billions of possible combinations, though the most recent format, known as IPv6 (IP version 6 – the previous version is actually version 4, IPv4), provides for many more by using a 128-bit binary number.

IP addresses are expressed as four sets of dotted decimal numbers using the format *nnn.nnn.nnn.nnn*. Each of these numbers falls in the range 0–255, for example, 127.0.0.1.

	NOTE	IPv6 addresses are written as eight 4-digit. hexadecimal numbers separated by colons.

Given an IP address, one machine can connect to another as if they were on the same physical network. Some machines have fixed IP addresses, while others are temporarily allocated an IP address from a pool when they connect, a technique known as DHCP (Dynamic Host Configuration Protocol.) This pooling of IP addresses is more efficient in terms of being able to reuse the same address for different machines at different times. It also reduces the administration required to ensure that each machine has an appropriate address, particularly for systems that have to give Internet access to very large numbers of computers, such as commercial ISPs.

Domain names

Most computers that host web sites use *domain names* rather than actual IP addresses. This means that users can, for example, visit www.w3.org rather than use the actual IP address of the World Wide Web Consortium site. The *Domain Name System* (DNS) enables a domain name to be converted into a valid IP address. *Resolver* programs query name servers for IP addresses and enable clients to be routed to the actual host machine. The DNS consists of a number of dedicated servers (a distributed database) that maintain naming information for different *zones*. A zone is a set of related domain names, '.com', '.org', etc. that appear at the same level of the DNS, which has a tree structure (see Figure 1.2).

Specific domains appear in a particular zone, for example the W3C domain is within the 'org' zone (w3.org). The highest level zone is known as the 'root domain' and under this comes the zone that encompasses all the top-level domains, including the country code domains. For each country, there is a zone that contains the various types of domain within that country, using zones such as 'co' for companies and 'ac' for academic institutions. Because of this tree structure, with layers of zones each managed separately, several different name servers may be involved in resolving a single domain name request. Domain names are controlled by the Internet Assigned Numbers Authority (IANA), which is administered by the Internet Corporation for Assigned Names and Numbers (ICANN). The number of domain types made available by these organisations has increased steadily

FIGURE 1.2   The DNS tree structure with some of the Internet zones and domains

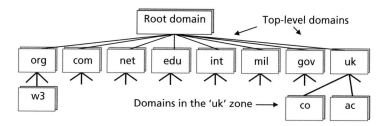

over the years as new types of web site have been developed, including the '.tv' domain for television services and '.mobi' for mobile services.

Using domain names is better than just using IP addresses because domain names are easier to remember and the names usually reflect the identity of the owner (for example, 'ibm.com', 'w3.org', 'harvard.edu'). It is also more flexible to use DNS names rather than IP numbers, since the mapping between a domain name and an IP address can change, so the same name can migrate between different host systems. Domain names are also important for email, since they are used in email addresses (for example, web-human@w3.org).

1.4 Important World Wide Web technologies

On its own, the Internet provides the possibility for different computers across the world to connect to each other and transfer data. However the World Wide Web adds some very important technologies to the underlying platform of the Internet. These include:

- HyperText Transfer Protocol (HTTP)
- HTML
- URLs, URIs and URNs

HyperText Transfer Protocol (HTTP)

The World Wide Web uses the *HyperText Transfer Protocol* (HTTP) to send information. When using this protocol, the domain name (or IP address) is preceded by 'http://' (for example, http://www.webhomecover.com). Web browsers usually have 'http://' as their default protocol so this prefix is frequently left off web site names. HTTP is a *request–response* protocol. Clients (usually browser software) send a request to a web server, which is software that is able to host web-based content and serve it to clients on request. The server handles the incoming request and provides a response, usually in the form of a page written in the HyperText Markup Language (HTML), which browsers can interpret. HTTP requests are handled by default on port 80 of the server. A server port is a number used to identify a particular process on the server that another system can connect to. Many common services, including HTTP, are allocated standard port numbers to simplify communication.

HTTP requests are always of a specific type; GET, POST, HEAD, PUT, DELETE, CONNECT, OPTIONS or TRACE. All of these request types have their uses but, in most web applications, the requests are usually limited to being either GET or POST. In most cases, either of these can be used to achieve the same result. A GET request is intended to retrieve information from the server and it often contains a search query or other parameter data. A POST request is intended to send data to the server, in most cases from an HTML form. A form is a part of a web page that lets a user provide data using components such as text fields, select lists and radio buttons. Forms have an 'action' which contains the web address of an application running on a server that knows how to process the contents of the form. This is where the data is sent when the user presses the 'submit' button on the web page.

What comes back from the server, following an HTTP request, is an HTTP response, which in many cases will be a web page, but can be some kind of code number to

FIGURE 1.3   The HTTP request–response cycle

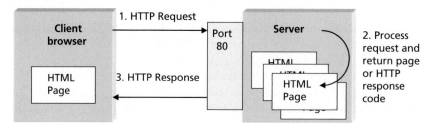

indicate errors, problems, or actions that the browser should take such as redirecting to another web site. Some examples of HTTP response codes are '200 OK' (the code that is used with a web page), '401 Unauthorized' (where security is being used) and '404 Not Found' (when the requested page cannot be found). Figure 1.3 shows the basic HTTP request–response cycle.

Normal HTTP traffic is not encrypted in any way, so is not secured against being read by a third party. In most cases this does not matter, but sometimes we need to send or receive information over the Web that we do not want others to be able to read. Therefore HTTP also comes in a secure form that allows us to transfer sensitive data, such as credit card numbers, safely across the Internet. This version of HTTP is known as HTTPS and uses a number of technologies including *Public Key Infrastructure* (PKI), encryption and *digital certificates*. The 'S' in 'HTTPS' comes from the *Secure Sockets Layer* (SSL), a secure communication protocol originally developed by Netscape. HTTPS connections use a special server port (443) to separate secure traffic from normal HTTP connections. As well as HTTPS being necessary for securing user data, many web-based systems need to authenticate users (find out who they are, generally by asking for a user name and password) and then authorize them to have access to appropriate resources. HTTPS is also used to enable this kind of secure login by ensuring that the username and password are encrypted.

HTML

As we saw in the previous section, web clients use browser software to request, download and display information from web servers. That information is mainly in the form of HTML pages. HTML pages are text documents that contain special *tags* telling the browser what type of information they contain. These tags are surrounded by angle brackets and indicate the *mark-up* of the web page, to control the structure and presentation of the content. This, for example, is how a typical HTML page begins, specifying the text to appear in the browser's title bar:

```
<html>
   <head>
      <title>My Page</title>
   </head>
<body> . . .
```

 NOTE   This is a somewhat simplified view of HTML, but is perfectly acceptable to most web browsers.

Tags do not specify exactly how a page will appear. It is up to the browser to format the page and manage its content, so the same page can look different in different browsers. Users can customise their browser to make pages appear in the way that they want; they can, for example, change the size or style of the standard text font. As well as text, these pages can contain images, sound, animations and other downloadable programs.

Using a web browser as the client for a web application is great for supporting large numbers of casual users (such as those using an on-line store or downloading music to their mobile phones) because it would not be realistic to expect all users to install separate special client programs just to use a particular service. However, browsers do support 'plugins', which are programs that can be installed into the browser to provide additional functionality. Common examples of plugins include Flash, Real Player and Adobe Acrobat. Browsers can also support programming languages such as JavaScript and Java applets, enabling simple programs to be downloaded and run within the browser window.

URLs, URIs and URNs

Uniform Resource Locators (URLs) are the complete specifications of the locations of Internet resources. A URL comprises a number of elements:

- The protocol of the request (the browser's default is usually http://)
- The IP address or domain of the server
- The port number (port 80 for HTTP and 443 for HTTPS)
- The subdirectory path from the 'document root' (if applicable)
- The name of the resource (though there is often a default page which is loaded if no name is specified)

For example, the following URL includes all of these elements.

```
http://www.webhomecover.com:80/help/callcentres.htm
```

Since the http protocol is usually the browser's default and the port number is the default on the server, in most cases we can exclude them, so our previous example is more likely to be written as:

```
www.webhomecover.com/help/callcentres.htm
```

If we use only the domain name, many web sites are configured with a default resource, which is loaded when no specific file is requested. If the example domain has a default resource, then the following URL should result in a page being served to the browser:

```
www.webhomecover.com
```

A URL is a specific kind of *Uniform Resource Identifier* (URI) which identifies a resource that can be downloaded from the web. Another specific type of URI is the *Uniform Resource Name* (URN). Although these have similar formats to URLs, they do not necessarily specify a downloadable resource. The purpose of a URN is simply to provide a globally unique name for something, not necessarily to provide a name that points to a web-based resource. The term URL is very widely used, but URI is the more general (and correct) term.

1.5 Special types of web application

The web is full of public web sites that provide information using web pages to anyone who can connect to the World Wide Web using a browser. There is also a very large number of Business to Customer (B2C) web sites that make products and services available to anyone who has an Internet connection and a web browser. However there are some special-purpose web applications that have particular characteristics. Three important examples of these are intranets, extranets and portals.

Intranets

As well as having a public presence on the Internet, many organisations maintain a private *intranet* behind a security firewall. An intranet consists of web pages and other resources that are only available inside the organisation. Intranets have a low cost of ownership because they use the standard technologies of the Internet. They increase internal communication while using less paper for things like internal phone books, software and procedure manuals, forms etc. They get information out of central databases in a form everyone can use from the desktop. Intranets have proved valuable for all kinds of organisations, for example, credit-card companies work with many banks and an intranet can be used as a central repository for information about all those banks, while pharmaceuticals companies have used intranets to draw information from many sources worldwide on drug trials and new drug submission regulations for all countries.

Extranets

An *extranet* falls somewhere between the Internet and an organisation's intranet. Only selected outsiders, such as customers, suppliers or other trading partners, are allowed access an extranet. Extranets can range from highly secure Business to Business (B2B) systems to self-registration systems such as those frequently used for downloading evaluation software. Extranets can be used, for example, to allow web shopper customers to log in to check the status of their orders over a secure connection, or users of courier companies to check where their delivery is at any point in time.

Portals

A *portal* is a special kind of web application. Its role is to act as a gateway (the meaning of 'portal') into a number of other applications. The structure of a portal is typically to present a number of *portlets*, which are window-based links into other applications. They also commonly provide facilities for personalisation, so that users can customize which portlets they are presented with and also change the layout and look and feel of the portal. Portals are often used by public sites that encourage user registration, such as Yahoo. They are also often used by organisations as a route into the various applications provided on the company intranet. In the mobile context, portals are a popular way for mobile service providers to enable easy access to the mobile Internet. Mobile portals such as Vodafone Live! provide links to various applications within the 'walled garden' of services provided by the mobile network carrier, as well as more general access to the mobile Internet.

1.6 Web application architectures

To understand how a web application provides services to clients across the web, it is necessary to have some understanding of the architectures of distributed computer systems. In this section, we introduce the concepts of layers and tiers.

Layers

The concept of a layered architecture is one where we regard different parts of a software system as having different and separate roles. This is a conceptual, rather than necessarily a physical, layering of system components. The basic three layers are the presentation layer (which deals with the user interface), the business logic layer (which handles the business processes and concepts used in the application) and the data management layer (which deals with managing and persisting the underlying data in the system).

If you think about how this model relates to, for example, the type of word processor that runs 'standalone' on a desktop computer (see Figure 1.4), you can see that there are certain parts of a word-processing program that deal with presentation, that is, how we see the document on the screen. This may be quite complex and allow multiple different views of the same document, for example an editing view and a print preview. Behind this layer is the business logic layer that contains all the processes that we need to perform when creating and editing documents, such as spell checking, formatting, paginating, editing, etc. This layer also contains the main concepts that we deal with in the application, such as documents, paragraphs, words, letters, diagrams, etc. Finally, beneath this layer, is the data management layer. The job of this layer is to enable our documents to be saved and reloaded, probably in simple flat (sequential) files so that they can persist between different runs of the word-processing program.

FIGURE 1.4   The conceptual layers of a word-processing system

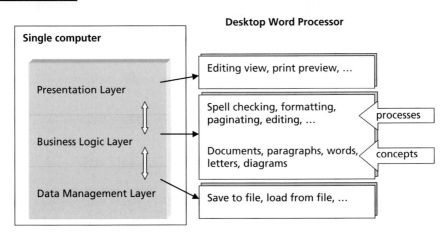

The important feature to note about our layered word-processing example is that we assume that all three layers would be implemented in a single program running on one computer. In other words the layers are conceptual, not physical.

Tiers and distributed systems

When we talk about *tiers*, we are also talking about layers. However the difference is that the term 'tiers' is generally used to mean physically separate devices. A multi tier system is therefore one that is deployed on multiple different nodes (computers). Using multiple tiers is necessary when we want to make our applications distributed and scaleable. For example, in a web-based banking system, the presentation layer, which would be a web browser, would be distributed across all the users' computers, but the application layer would be running on a central computer, or multiple computers, somewhere at the bank. This tier would manage the business processes such as checking accounts, transferring funds, ordering cheque books, etc. Also in this layer would be the business objects such as accounts, customers, transactions and statements. To cope with large numbers of users and to assist in security, the data management layer would also be run on a separate machine (probably several). For complex, large-scale data storage like this, instead of simple flat files, we would use a database management system for the four basic operations on data, namely *create*, *read*, *update* and *delete* (CRUD for short). Once we start using large numbers of computers running different parts of the system across multiple tiers, we have an *n-tier architecture* (see Figure 1.5). N-tier architectures are a fundamental part of web applications because the presentation layer (running in web browsers) is always widely distributed and the large number of users of some of these systems means that the business logic and data management layers may also have to be distributed across multiple machines.

FIGURE 1.5   The tiers of an n-tier web-based banking system

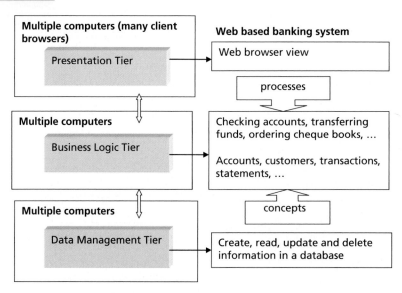

1.7 The Web 2.0 and Ajax

Since the mid 2000s, it has been hard to discuss the World Wide Web without mentioning the Web 2.0 and Ajax. Web 2.0 is a term that has become widely used since the first Web 2.0 Conference in 2004. Although it might be categorized as an umbrella marketing term rather than a specific technology or architecture, some authors, notably (O'Reilly 2005), have given it some concrete specifications through a set of published principles, practices and patterns. Many publications that discuss the Web 2.0 focus on rich user interfaces, in particular the use of asynchronous JavaScript and XML (Ajax), but the ideas of the Web 2.0 go beyond Ajax to include a wide range of ideas about how modern web applications should be developed. The key ideas underlying the Web 2.0 may perhaps be summarized as:

- The web as a software platform
- Service-oriented architectures
- User and contributor communities

In this section, we briefly explore some of these ideas, which will re-emerge at various points throughout this book. Above all, the role of the *eXtensible Markup Language* (XML), which underlies service-oriented architectures, can be seen as an important component of many of aspects of the Web 2.0.

The web as a software platform

In the past, the software platform that applications were built on was a particular computer operating system, for example Microsoft Windows or Linux. In contrast Web applications are able to span multiple operating systems because web browsers can render the same content regardless of the system from which the page was downloaded. The server may run on one operating system and its clients on many others. One key Web 2.0 pattern is *software above the level of a single device*, which is about the way that applications can span different types of device, from web servers to desktop PCs to mobile phones to portable media players. For example, to download music we might use a PC to connect to a web server and also connect a mobile device to the PC, all using a single application. In this type of situation, the platform that the overall application is running on is the web, not just a single device.

Service-oriented architectures

In the early days of the web, the focus was on the applications that were being used. For example, the 'browser wars', primarily between Netscape and Microsoft in the mid 1990s, were about which application would be used to access the web. More recently, the focus has been more on the underlying content available via the web, rather than the specific applications that are used. This content is made available using various forms of *web service*. Web services are data sources made available over the web using the eXtensible Markup Language (XML). Systems that are built by combining together multiple web services are known as *Service-Oriented Architectures* (SOA). Examples of content that can be accessed through web services include news, weather, map data, and book information. Some authors use the term *the programmable web* to describe the ability to build applications that utilise content from multiple web-based resources, using freely available application programming interfaces (APIs) to create *mashups*. A mashup, in web terms, is an application that mixes together content from different sources. Some mashups combine content from a number of different services to produce an overall application, while others use a single service but reorganize the content to suit their requirements.

One simple example of a web service is RSS (an abbreviation that has multiple roots: Really Simple Syndication, Rich Site Summary and RDF Site Summary), which uses XML to supply feeds of frequently updated information such as news and weather.

User and contributor communities

Traditional software construction is about building self-contained applications for a particular purpose, for example to process a company payroll or manage company accounts. This type of application is generally intended for 'in house' use, though it may expose certain features to customers. For example, software used by banks is primarily used internally, but may expose some web based services enabling customers to perform certain transactions on their accounts. In many Web 2.0 applications, instead of this type of central control, applications are about a community of users who participate in the application itself. A good example of this is Wikipedia, an on-line encyclopaedia where anyone can create or edit entries. Other applications may consist largely of content provided by a single organisation but allow users to make some contribution. An example of this would be music download sites that enable users to post their own reviews. Of course, opening up a web application to contributions from the user community is not appropriate for every system, but certain aspects of the approach to software development can be incorporated into many different types of web application.

Ajax

Asynchronous JavaScript and XML (Ajax) is a term coined by Garrett (2005) in an article about current trends in Web development. JavaScript is a programming language that can be run inside a browser, making it possible to run programs that connect to the server while a page is being viewed. We cover Ajax in more detail later in this book, but its relationship to the Web 2.0 is primarily in the area of providing a rich user experience in the browser environment. At its simplest, Ajax makes it possible to update parts of a web page with data read from a server without having to refresh the whole page, making the user experience more like using a traditional desktop application rather than surfing a web site. There are many tools for developing Ajax applications, some very sophisticated. However it is possible to include some simple Ajax inside your web applications using a few lines of JavaScript code.

1.8 So you want to be a web application developer?

There are many challenges for developers in building web applications. There are choices about technology that have to be made, choices about architecture, choices about design, and choices about implementation. In making decisions about how to build web applications, there are always compromises and trade-offs, and we have to be aware of the reasons for making certain choices and the consequences of them. Fortunately, there are also many tools, techniques and reusable designs (*design patterns*) that can help us to meet these challenges. The purpose of this book is to explore some important issues in the development of modern web applications and provide some examples of how we might approach a solution, avoiding as best we can the hype of this week's technology while taking full advantage of the lessons we can learn from others, and getting the best from the available technologies.

Exercises

1.1 In Figure 1.2, we saw some of the top-level domains in the Domain Name System. Look up some of these domains by using a web search and find out what types of organisation use, for example, the 'int' domain. Find some other top-level domains that are not included in the diagram. For your web searches, you will find the ICANN and IANA web sites useful (http://www.icann.org and http://www.iana.org).

1.2 In our example of a layered architecture we referred to a word processor running on a single machine. We compared this with a layered and tiered architecture, using the example of a web-based banking system. However, web-based word processors are becoming more popular. Do an Internet search and find some examples of word processors that work on the web. From their descriptions, how do you think the layers in the word processing example would be applied to tiers in the context of a web-based word processor? You may find it helpful in answering this question to spend some time using one of these web-based word processors.

1.3 Look at the Wikipedia web site (http://www.wikipedia.org.). What are the processes that you have to follow in order to add or modify an entry in this on-line encyclopaedia? There have been a few controversial problems with some entries made on Wikipedia in the past. See if you can find some reference to these by doing a web search, and see what policy changes were necessary in managing the web site.

1.4 Find a popular blog on the web. Describe the author and content of the blog. Why do you think this blog is popular?

1.5 One of the common features of portals is that they can be personalised. Find a web-based portal that you can personalise (for example, http://www.yahoo.com). Make a list of the things that you are able to personalise on this site.

1.6 A simple example of how Ajax can update the current page with data from the server is Google Suggest. Go to the Google Suggest home page (you can find this with a Web search) and start typing a search term. The system suggests possible searches as you type.

SUMMARY

In this chapter we introduced the principal features, technologies and uses of web applications. These covered aspects of both the Internet and the World Wide Web, the distributed architectures that web applications use and some special types of web application. Table 1.1 summarises the various acronyms and shorthand terms that were introduced, along with their definitions.

TABLE 1.1	Terms introduced in this chapter

Acronym/ term	Meaning
Ajax	Asynchronous JavaScript and XML
API	Application Programming Interface
ARPA	Advanced Research Projects Agency (originator of the ARPANet)
B2B	Business to Business
blog	Web log; a web-based diary intended for public access
CERN	*Conseil Européen pour la Recherche Nucléair*, more generally known in English as the European Organisation for Nuclear Research
CGI	Common Gateway Interface
CRUD	Create, Read, Update, Delete
DHCP	Dynamic Host Configuration Protocol
DNS	Domain Name System
FTP	File Transfer Protocol
HTML	HyperText Markup Language
HTTP	HyperText Transfer Protocol
IANA	Internet Assigned Numbers Authority
ICANN	Internet Corporation for Assigned Names and Numbers
IPv4	Internet Protocol version 4
IPv6	Internet Protocol version 6
ISP	Internet Service Provider
NCSA	National Center for Supercomputing Applications
PHP	Originally Personal Home Page Tools, later renamed PHP: Hypertext Preprocessor
PKI	Public Key Infrastructure
RSS	Really Simple Syndication, Rich Site Summary or RDF Site Summary
SMTP	Simple Mail Transfer Protocol
SOA	Service-Oriented Architecture
SSL	Secure Sockets Layer
TCP/IP	Transmission Control Protocol/Internet Protocol
URI	Uniform Resource Identifier
URL	Uniform Resource Locator
URN	Uniform Resource Name
W3C	World Wide Web Consortium
Wiki	WikiWikiWeb; a web site that is open to public contributions and editing
WWW or W3	World Wide Web
XML	eXtensible Markup Language

References and further reading

Garrett, J.J. (2005) *Ajax: A New Approach to Web Applications*. http://www.adaptivepath.com/publications/essays/archives/000385.php

O'Reilly, T. (2005) *What is Web 2.0: Design Patterns and Business Models for the Next Generation of Software*. O'Reilly Network, http://www.oreilly.com/pub/a/oreilly/tim/news/2005/09/30/what-is-web-20.html

Web Application Requirements: Analysis and Design

LEARNING OBJECTIVES

- **To understand some of the techniques used in analysing web application system requirements**

- **To be able to use some notation from the UML related to web applications**

- **To understand some aspects of the processes involved in the development lifecycle of web applications**

- **To be able to apply some common design patterns to the structure of web pages**

INTRODUCTION

In this chapter, we look at some techniques for analysing the requirements for a web application. Some of the notation used comes from the *Unified Modeling Language* (UML) with some special extensions that were developed to meet the particular requirements of designing for the web. There are also some informal diagrams that do not come from any specific notation. The process is based on aspects of the *Unified Process* (UP), but with a lightweight 'agile' approach. We conclude the chapter with some considerations relating to system design, and describe a number of web usability patterns.

2.1 What's different about web application requirements?

The development of a web application is similar in many ways to that of any other software system. We have to find out what the users require, choose an appropriate software architecture, design and build the overall framework and create all the necessary components, all the while testing the evolving system against its technical and user expectations and adapting to changing requirements and circumstances. In some ways, however, web applications have their own special requirements. Perhaps the most obvious is that web applications have a special kind of user interface. Their presentation may be via many different types of device, ranging from desktop computers to mobile phones, and that presentation is based on some form of web page running in a browser. Also, unlike many software systems, a web application often caters for very large numbers of anonymous users, potentially located anywhere in the world. This means that our design has to take account of the issues of data communications and multiple access to the same resources. Its underlying communications protocol is based on the request–response model, where the application is on a system that is remote from the user, and the user's device has to make requests of the application to perform activities on its behalf. This contrasts with desktop applications, which may have a richer, more interactive and immediate interface. In building such systems, we also have to be constantly aware that parts of our application will be running on central servers while other parts will be running on many different client devices. All of these differences (and more) mean that we have to extend our understanding of analysis and design to cater for all the special concerns of web applications.

2.2 Software development lifecycles

Although we have said that web applications have some special requirements, any development method that we adopt needs to provide four services to support us during the project *lifecycle* (the processes and events that take place between the project's beginning and its end):

- It needs to guide us through the various activities.
- It needs to specify the artefacts (such as documents, diagrams and software components) that should be created during the development of the system.
- It should direct the tasks of the individuals and teams working on the project.
- It should provide appropriate criteria for measuring and monitoring progress and production.

To achieve these objectives, it needs to help the system developers to know their roles, activities and workflows, and the final software products that they need to create. The way that these features are defined does not have to be excessively prescriptive, particularly for a small project. Many software development methods used from the 1990s onwards stress *agility*, which in many cases means producing the simplest possible artefacts by performing activities in the simplest possible workflows. Regardless, most current methods of software development use the concept of *iteration* which has gradually replaced older methods based on the *waterfall model*.

The waterfall model

Early approaches to developing software systems tended to follow a traditional engineering approach, whereby a system had to have all of its requirements gathered before it could be analysed, be completely analysed before it could be designed, fully designed before it could be implemented and only then could it be tested. This is known as the waterfall model because the development process can be seen as a sequence of separate stages that occur in a fixed order (see Figure 2.1). There is the notion of some feedback between adjacent stages, so that we might revisit certain aspects of the design in the light of implementation, for example, or rewrite code if it fails a test, but there is no concept of being able to cope with evolving requirements or starting to test early in the project lifecycle.

This type of approach may work well in many engineering contexts but does not work so well for most software projects. This is because the requirements for software tend to be more fluid and dynamic, changing over time to respond to changing application environments. To address this more flexible design process, *iterative* methods have been developed.

Iterative methods

An iterative approach is like a series of mini waterfalls, where we gather requirements, analyse, design, build and test part of a system, reflect on it, adapt our plans in the light of experience, and then repeat the process a number of times until the project is complete (see Figure 2.2). Thus the feedback loop, which at any given point in the waterfall model

FIGURE 2.1   The waterfall model

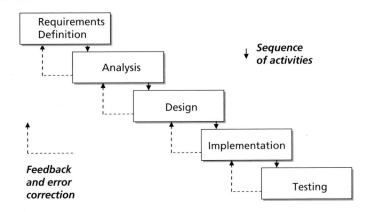

FIGURE 2.2   The iterative model

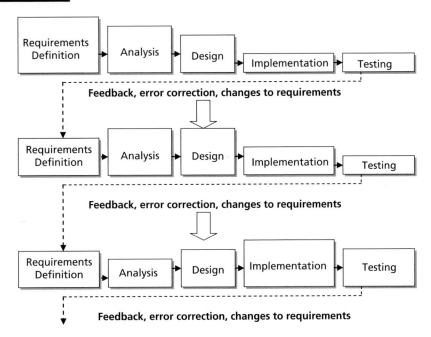

only includes the previous stage, covers all of the activities of analysis, design, implementation and testing. As we progress through the iterations, the emphasis of our activities changes. Initially, we focus mostly on requirements and analysis; later, we focus more on implementation and testing. The relative sizes of the boxes in Figure 2.2 are meant to suggest this gradual evolution through the iterations.

When using an iterative approach we still have an overall vision and plan for developing the system but we are more able to respond to new or changing requirements because we do not assume that we can identify all the requirements up front. Many iterative methods stress that each iteration should result in something concrete that provides a milestone for the project. In other words an iteration does not end just because a time period has expired but also because the required deliverable has been created. Iterative methods are also flexible in that their expected deliverables can be changed by trading off, in a managed way, new expectations against the original ones. In other words, if additional expectations are added to an iteration then an equivalent amount of effort has to be moved out of that iteration to enable the schedule to remain realistic.

2.3 The Unified Modeling Language and the Unified Process

In the 1990s, there were many notations and processes proposed for the development of object-oriented systems. So many, in fact, that the competition between the various approaches during this period became known as the 'method wars'. However, after a while it became evident that three methods in particular were gaining more traction than most of the others. These were the Object Modeling Technique (OMT) developed by a group led by James Rumbaugh at General Electric, the Booch method developed by Grady Booch at Rational Corporation, and Objectory developed by Ivar Jacobson at Eriksson. Largely at the instigation of Grady Booch, these three methods were fused with input from other methods when both Rumbaugh and Jacobson joined Booch at Rational. The first result of this collaboration was the Unified Modeling Language (the UML) which was a standard analysis and design notation for object-oriented systems. This standard language was published by the Object Management Group, a non-profit industry standards organisation, with the first version being finalised in 1999. Later, a design process (the Unified Process, UP) was also published as a series of books, while a related set of tools and materials to support this process (the Rational Unified Process, RUP) was developed by Rational, a company since acquired by IBM. Although in book form the UP is not product related, it is not currently supported by an open standards organisation.

The Unified Modeling Language (UML)

The UML is a very rich modelling language with many different types of diagram (18 in version 2), some of which serve very similar purposes. For example, sequence diagrams and communication diagrams can be used to represent the same information, and state diagrams and activity diagrams also have much in common. Therefore it is not necessary to use all the available diagrams of the UML, but rather to select those that are most useful for a particular type of project. State diagrams, for example, can be particularly helpful in designing hardware control systems, whilst deployment diagrams are appropriate when a system will be distributed across many different machines. Some methods that have evolved since the publication of the UML choose a specific subset of diagrams. Iconix, for example, uses only four types of diagram: the use case model, the sequence diagram, the class diagram and the (otherwise little used) robustness diagram (Rosenberg *et al.* 2005). We adopt a similar approach in this book, selecting a small number of useful diagrams from the UML along with some extensions developed specifically for designing web applications.

The Unified Process (UP)

The Unified Process is, like the UML, a rich specification with many possible activities and artefacts. Once again, we can tailor our use of the process to the practices most appropriate for our application type. As Jacobson himself has written about the RUP, it 'has grown and become too complex', so it's OK to simplify it (Jacobson 2004). Perhaps the most important aspect of the UP is that as well as using an iterative approach it describes both phases and disciplines. A phase is a group of iterations that fall within a specific time period within the overall project life cycle, while the disciplines are the various types of activity that take place during each iteration. The overall approach of the UP is neatly summed up by a commonly used 'whale diagram' that shows the relationship between iterations, phases and disciplines (see Figure 2.3). The 'whales' are the curves that show the level of activity in each discipline at various stages of the development process. Although the image is just an example of how the various activities in a project might move in and out of focus over time, it gives a clear idea of how an iterative process changes its emphasis as it moves through the various phases. This equates to the iterative model in Figure 2.3. To make sense of the rest of the diagram, we look at the four phases of the UP, which appear across the top of the diagram, and the iterations that occur within them.

FIGURE 2.3 The Unified Process 'whale' diagram

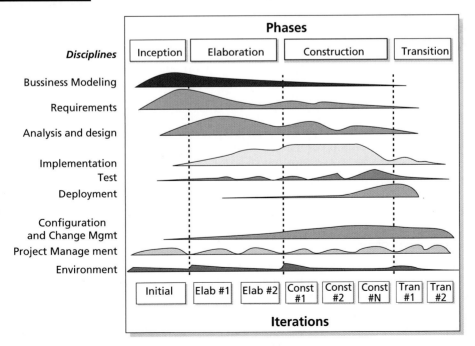

The inception phase

During the inception phase, we explore a project to a sufficient stage to understand if it is viable. This means gathering the initial requirements, investigating relevant technical issues and building software prototypes where necessary to act as proofs of concept. During this phase, new technologies and frameworks may be investigated to evaluate whether or not they would be good choices for the project in hand. At the end of the inception phase, we should have enough information to know whether the project as a whole has a realistic chance of success, and we should also have a draft plan for the entire project, including a total budget and an overall time frame. The disciplines of the UP show that during this phase we also have to establish the development environment and processes to manage software configuration and change. For a simple project, or one that is treading familiar ground, a single iteration may be sufficient for this phase. For large projects or those that involve substantially new technology and tools, more iterations will be required. At the end of each iteration, a specific milestone should be met and a meaningful deliverable should result. For example, an iteration in the inception phase might be required to deliver a working proof of concept using a particular code framework, application server and database, along with a project plan and a budget. Experimental proof of concept prototypes are sometimes known as *spikes* (Cockburn 2005).

The elaboration phase

In many ways, this is the most important phase as it demonstrates the viability (or not) of the chosen software architecture. The most important deliverable from the elaboration phase is an *executable architecture*, which we can think of as being similar to the foundations and load bearing structure (framework) of a building. Although it may take fewer people and less time for a building's foundations to be laid and its steel skeleton to be built, when compared to the time and labor required to complete all the cladding, internal walls and fittings, it is a more crucial phase. The foundations and framework need to be able to support all the subsequent work or the building will collapse, like many a software project has in the past. In a software project, the executable architecture must provide a suitable foundation and framework for all the subsequent development, so it must meet all the most important requirements of the project and have addressed its key risk factors. For example, if a project has specific requirements in terms of performance, such as the number of concurrent users that it should be able to support, then the executable architecture should have demonstrated that it can deliver this requirement. Therefore practices such as load testing are important in the elaboration phase. Although the executable architecture can be regarded as being based on a prototype, it is an architectural prototype, which means that it is intended to be refined until it is put into production. This is different from the proof of concept prototypes that are often developed during the inception phase and discarded once they have performed their roles of demonstrating or testing alternative approaches. Rather than a spike, the executable architecture is a *walking skeleton*, the beginning of the framework that will endure throughout the rest of the system lifetime (Cockburn 2005). Due to the importance of this phase, there may be several iterations.

The construction phase

In this phase, all the necessary components are added to the existing executable architecture. This is like adding the cladding, internal walls and fittings to a building. During this phase, there may be some minor changes to the executable architecture due to new or changing requirements, but its core functionality should be stable. However we should be able to be very flexible in terms of the components that we are developing within the framework. At the end of the construction phase we should have a complete software product that is ready for alpha testing. Unless the project is small, there will be many iterations in the construction phase.

The transition phase

In this final phase, the system moves from the development environment into its deployment environment, at the end of the phase, it should be in use. Activities from this phase can include alpha, beta and acceptance testing, installation, manufacture (in the case of shrink-wrapped software), parallel running and user training. We might regard this phase as being similar to the handover of a new building to its owners. The number of iterations will depend on the type of project and its means of construction. For example, an open-source project that will deploy on the web could easily have a transition phase with a single iteration, while a large custom-built system for a client with many sites running mission-critical systems would require more iterations. Figure 2.4 matches the building metaphor to the phases of the UP.

How long is an iteration?

In our discussion of phases, we made no mention of how long an iteration should be. The general practice is to make all iterations a similar length, so that the project gets its own rhythm. How long each iteration should be is open to debate, but something around four weeks is common and anything from two to six weeks is reasonable. Anything less than two weeks is unlikely to be long enough to produce a meaningful milestone, while iterations longer than six weeks may lead to a lack of project rhythm and not provide the project as a whole with enough milestones to keep it on track. Within an iteration there will also be 'time-boxed' activities that have their own internal deadlines based on estimations of effort and duration. The difference between effort (how much consistent effort it would take in an ideal world to produce a required artefact) and duration (how long it actually takes) is due to the realities of distractions such as meetings, holiday, illness, fire alarms and a whole host of other time-consuming events and activities. Various techniques can be used to estimate the actual time required for each task, but the best way is just to learn by experience how long a particular task will take. Definition of tasks may be done by use cases, or user stories, and with experience these can be written with a given scope in mind. Of course the number of iterations multiplied by the length of an iteration gives how long you plan the whole project to take.

FIGURE 2.4   The phases of the Unified Process applied to a building metaphor

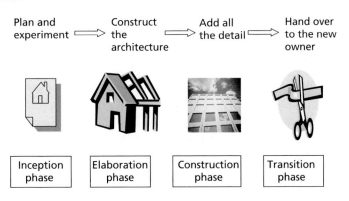

2.4 A web application inception phase

In the rest of this chapter we will look at some activities that might be appropriate during the inception phase. Taking the diagram in Figure 2.3 as a rough guide (while acknowledging that this is not meant to indicate anything other than a general impression of the process), we can see that we might expect this phase to include some initial analysis and design, as well as business modelling and requirements gathering. In fact, we might regard most of this book as describing activities that are appropriate to the inception phase, in the sense that we will be exploring technologies that may be new to you and demonstrating some simple proof of concept code. As Figure 2.3 suggests, we will be doing some coding, some testing and quite a bit of exploration of a software environment. None of the application code in this book is quite sophisticated enough to be regarded as an industrial-strength architectural prototype; in fact, it could be regarded as a series of spikes. However it should provide enough material to enable a more extensible framework to be built. Taken together, it builds into something that could be regarded as a walking skeleton for further development.

The intention of the examples that we work through in the rest of this chapter is to give some flavor of how the initial business modelling and analysis process is one of investigation and discovery, where we continually revise our initial assumptions in the light of experience and experiment. Therefore you will see that we do not present something that is seen as initially perfect; rather, we present a starting point that we refine as we further explore the requirements and utilise the various analysis tools and techniques. Software development is essentially a team effort where individual skills and relationships are crucial, something that is hard to replicate in book form. Therefore you should regard the following examples as artefacts that would evolve through a process of negotiation and discussion, rather than there being one 'right answer'. Every software problem has a number of potential solutions, each with their own advantages and disadvantages. One other thing is for sure, every real-world software project is far more complex than it may at first appear!

2.5 Modelling requirements

The first step in developing any web application must be to establish the business objectives (part of the business modelling discipline of the UP). There was a time in the 'dot com' boom of the 1990s when web-based systems were developed with little realistic idea of the business objectives apart from the fact that everyone else already had a web site so 'we need one too'. Times have changed, so now there is more focus on aspects such as *return on investment* (ROI). A good focus for discussing the business objectives is to agree on a mission statement for the application, which neatly summarises the point of the exercise.

In this book, we use a simplified case study based on a home insurance web application. This is a fictional scenario within which we will analyse and design our system:

> *Web Home Cover is a new enterprise set up to provide home insurance over the web. The business case is based on providing a service that is entirely on-line and therefore highly efficient in terms of the initial capital investment required by the insurance company. Since the company will only operate via the web, it must have a web application that meets the needs of all its customers and staff. It must also be written to ensure that it will work for as many web clients as possible, from desktop computers to mobile devices.*

This is a possible mission statement for the project:

To bring home insurance services to every corner of the web

This is the essence of the business case for our home insurance web application. It is short and to the point. Long 'buzzword bingo' phrases are best left out of the mission statement.

Web application requirements gathering

The first step we must take on the road to actually building a web-based solution is to identify the high-level requirements (or business objectives) of the proposed system. This is rather difficult in many cases, since we may not know who our actual users will be. If the web application is intended for a company intranet (an application that is used only internally within the organisation), then it will be quite easy to find out who the potential users of the system are. If, however, we are launching an e-commerce web site then we are aiming our application at a largely unknown mass of users in cyberspace. How, then, can we work out what their requirements might be? There are a number of approaches we can take. One common approach is to use focus groups, where a small number of people who are representative of our possible user base are brought together to answer questions and offer opinions in a structured and controlled context, using sample materials. Another approach is to use marketing staff to take on the role of possible users and represent their requirements, presumably on the basis that their job is to tell people what they want. In either case, we need to develop a set of user profiles that will give us an idea about whose needs we are trying to meet. These user profiles can be simple demographic summaries (e.g. the age range, sex, interests, average income, etc. of our expected users) or rather more sophisticated 'personas' where fictional biographies are developed of our supposed typical users. Whoever we use to represent our actual users, at some point we need to gather a suitable set of stakeholders (those who have an interest in the system, either directly or indirectly) into a room and get them to write down an initial set of requirements in an activity known as a *joint requirements workshop*. This does not require sophisticated tools, the usual ones being flip-chart pads or whiteboards and pens. Instead of the usual brainstorming approach, card storming might be used to encourage full participation. Whereas with brainstorming the participants take turns to call out their contributions, which can be frustrating for some and intimidating for others, in a card-storming approach everyone simultaneously writes each of their contributions on a separate card. The cards are all pooled and then explored together by the group. Experience suggests that the 'magic' number of core requirements likely to emerge from such sessions is 12 (more or less), though it depends on the level of detail that you want to aim for.

We now imagine a requirements workshop for the Web Home Cover project. Who might our stakeholders be? For our purposes, we might imagine a group comprising the lead software developer, the project manager, the database administrator, the marketing person who ran the focus groups (armed with a set of user profiles), the sales manager, a claims assessor and one of the insurance underwriters. By the time all the doughnuts have gone, the flip-chart pads on the wall have a list of requirements that looks something like this:

1. New users should be able to get an instant quote for buildings insurance.
2. New users should be able to get an instant quote for contents insurance.
3. New users should have the option to apply for both, or either, type of home insurance cover.

4. Policy holders should be able to check their current policies and request changes using a secure login.

5. New users should be able to check the status of their application using a secure login.

6. Call-centre staff should be able to view and query all policy details using a secure login.

7. Underwriters should be able to access all applications waiting for processing using a secure login.

8. New users should be able to retrieve previous quotations immediately, even if they have not yet applied for a policy.

9. The web site should provide enough information for users to contact the company by email, telephone or in writing.

10. Users should be able to access the system from both desktop and mobile devices.

11. Policy holders should be able to make claims against their policies.

12. The system should be available 24/7/365 and be able to cope with 10,000 concurrent users.

13. The system should have a telepathic user interface.

There are some things to note about this set of requirements. First, while most of them are functional requirements (what the system should do), some are non-functional (the way that the system should do what it does). For example, a functional requirement is that 'new users should be able to get an instant quote for buildings insurance'. This is something the system must do for its users. Examples of non-functional requirements are the ability to access the system from multiple devices or being available all the time. These are not things that the system does but characteristics of how it delivers those things. Some requirements need further exploration, for example the last two are somewhat extreme but are meant to indicate some important considerations. While it may be desirable for a system to be available all the time, we must consider how much it costs to do this versus the real need. Likewise, the requirement includes an optimistic prediction of the possible number of concurrent users. We have all heard of a few web sites that were so popular that they quickly imploded under the strain of serving all their users. However the history of the dot com era had rather more examples of systems that anticipated huge numbers of users but ended up with a trickle. Performance, availability and security requirements, should always be looked at carefully by applying a cost-benefit analysis. For each requirement, we have to ask how much it would cost for the 'perfect' solution as opposed to an acceptable solution. The 'telepathic user interface' requirement comes from a Dilbert cartoon, but again has a serious point, which is that requirements often use arbitrary requests such as 'the interface must be user friendly' which are, in fact, meaningless. Requirements must be both realistic and measurable. Proposing a system that must pass certain usability or learnability metrics (measures) would be more useful.

Prioritising requirements

Once we have a set of initial requirements, we need to prioritise them. This is important in an iterative development approach because we have to schedule the requirements over different iterations. Therefore if requirements will be delivered at different points in the development lifecycle then we should address the more important requirements first, particularly since new requirements may appear during the process. If any requirements get pushed to the back of the queue by this process then they should be those with a lower priority. It is not necessary to put all the requirements in order. In many cases, four levels of priority are considered acceptable, sometimes classified as:

- Must have
- Should have
- Could have
- Want to have

This prioritisation method is sometimes referred to using the acronym *MoSCoW*.

One useful approach to the prioritisation exercise is to have the participants vote for their requirements in two rounds from different perspectives, possibly using some multiple voting mechanism (such as the participants having four votes each). For example, round 1 could prioritise requirements from a customer viewpoint and round 2 could prioritise the requirements from the viewpoint of the staff.

Since it is difficult to cast a vote while in the context of a text book, we will have to assume that we have performed this exercise and come to some conclusions. Bearing in mind our mission statement, it would appear that the following requirements are 'must haves'.

1. New users should be able to get an instant quote for buildings insurance.
2. New users should be able to get an instant quote for contents insurance.
3. New users should have the option to apply for both, or either, type of home insurance cover.
7. Underwriters should be able to access all applications waiting for processing using a secure login.
10. Users should be able to access the system from both desktop and mobile devices.
11. Policy holders should be able to make claims against their policies.

With these requirements in place we can sell insurance over the web and reach as many people as possible.

What are the 'should haves'? These are still pretty much core functions. Perhaps the following requirements fall under this category:

4. Policy holders should be able to check their current policies and request changes using a secure login.
6. Call-centre staff should be able to view and query all policy details using a secure login.
9. The web site should provide enough information for users to contact the company by email, telephone or in writing.

With these requirements we can help retain and support our existing customers and provide maximum opportunity to attract new business.

The following requirements are probably best categorised as 'could haves':

5. New users should be able to check the status of their application using a secure login.
8. New users should be able to retrieve previous quotations immediately, even if they have not yet applied for a policy.

We can live without these, but they could provide some benefit to our users. They might be regarded as 'sugar' (handy but non-essential).

These are our final two requirements:

12. The system should be available 24/7/365 and be able to cope with 10,000 concurrent users.
13. The system should have a telepathic user interface.

These will have to be put into the 'would like to have' category, at least for the moment. They certainly need some further work before being taken seriously as priority requirements.

What is the point of this exercise? It enables us to schedule the important requirements first when developing the system. Agile approaches would use 'story cards' for requirements, with each card representing a user story about what the system should do. By prioritising these cards, we can put them into various iterations, with the most important in the early iterations.

2.6 Analysis tools – domain models, use cases and storyboards

In this section, we introduce some basic UML notations that can help us to visualise key features of the application. Even if a development project takes an agile approach that does not worry about extensive formal documentation, using standard notations for descriptive sketches can be very useful as a common communication medium between developers and users.

The domain model

A useful model to build before getting into details about the system use cases is a domain model that captures the key concepts of the business domain. The domain model helps us to begin to understand how various important concepts of the domain interact in a structural way. Again, we should develop the domain model in a workshop environment. Some analysis methods suggest that the domain model should grow piecemeal out of the use case analysis, but the advantage of developing the domain model early is that it provides a common vocabulary within which the following stages of the analysis can take place. This ensures that, for example, different threads of the analysis do not end up using two different names for the same concept because everyone can work from, and enhance, the same domain model. The model itself captures a few simple ideas:

- What are the key concepts in the domain?
- Which concepts interact with each other?
- How can we describe these interaction relationships?
- What is the *cardinality* of these interactions? (In other words, which relationships are one to one, which are one to many and which are many to many?)

We can begin to identify the core concepts in our domain by identifying nouns in our core requirements. From our set of objectives, we can find 27 nouns (plural nouns have been made singular) that can be our candidate list of concepts for the domain model. We might imagine them brainstormed onto a whiteboard or card-stormed onto sticky notes and then stuck on the wall (see Figure 2.5).

From this list, we can exclude anything clearly outside the system boundary (desktop, telephone, writing), the boundary itself (user interface) or nouns that refer to the system as a whole (web site, system). We should also get rid of synonyms ('user' and 'concurrent user' are general words for more specific types of user; 'quote' and 'quotation' are the same thing) and properties of other concepts (policy detail is a property of policy), though properties can be added to their matching concept if they look useful. 'Detail' is a very vague property of a policy but 'status' might be a useful property of an application so we might choose to include it in the diagram. In the revised list (see Figure 2.6), we have struck out twelve of the candidate concepts, leaving fifteen (including the 'status' property).

From these, we draw an initial domain model (Figure 2.7). This consists of rectangles for each concept, labelled with the concept name. Any properties that are immediately evident can also be added, separated from the concept name by a horizontal line. Concepts that have some kind of relationship with one another are linked by 'association' lines, which are labelled with text that describes the association. Arrow heads by the text can be used to show the direction in which the label should be read (for example, we are saying that a policy holder *lives at* an address, not that an address *lives at* a policy holder). By default, an association line implies that the cardinality of the relationship is 'one to one', for example there is one policy holder to one address. To show a 'one to many' relationship, we use the asterisk (*); for example, one policy can have many claims made against it. If the asterisk

FIGURE 2.5 Candidate list of concepts for the domain model

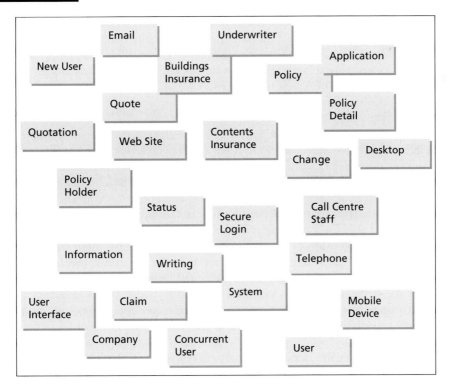

FIGURE 2.6 Modified list of candidate concepts

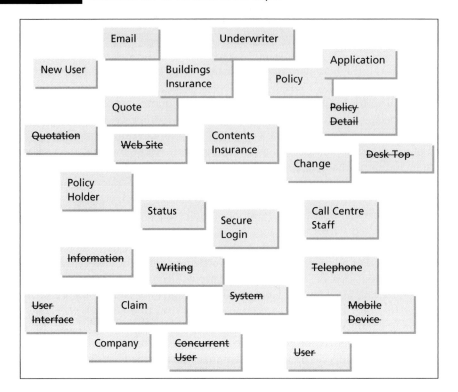

appears at both ends of an association then this means a 'many to many' association. In our domain model, one call-centre staff member may query many policies, and a single policy may be queried by many call-centre staff members. Occasionally we can define a cardinality number or range more exactly. For example we know that a policy holder will have either exactly one policy (buildings OR contents insurance) or exactly two policies (both buildings AND contents insurance).

Sometimes we identify concepts that appear to be specialisations or generalisations of one another. In our model we have policies, but we also have references to contents insurance policies and buildings insurance polices. The concept of a policy here could be seen as a generalisation of the two more specific (specialised) types of policy. We indicate this in the domain model using an arrow with an open triangular head pointing from the specialisations to the generalisation. Initial assumptions like this in the domain model may be modified later. We may find that the policy generalisation is not useful. Alternatively, we may find that we need a generalisation of new user and policy holder, the user concept that we previously discarded. These kinds of decision are made as we evolve the analysis domain model into a design class model, as the process of iterative analysis and design gives us more information about the concepts in our model. A class model shows concepts that will become software artefacts in the implementation. Some concepts will not become classes, whereas many new classes will be introduced as the need for them becomes evident.

Now that we have a domain model, we can use it as a guide in the use cases. For example there should be no ambiguities about whether we should use the concept name 'quote' or

FIGURE 2.7 A domain model for the home insurance system

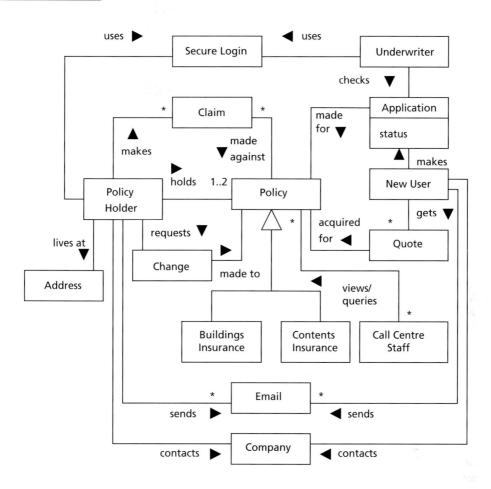

'quotation' in the use cases: we check the domain model and use 'quote'. At this stage, it is useful also to start building a glossary for the system (on a web page, of course) to define our interpretation of what these concept names mean.

Use case diagrams

Use case diagrams are very simple. They help us to show the different types of users and the goals they have in using a system. Because they are an analysis tool they do not anticipate any specific type of technology or how the system will actually deliver its requirements. All they do is specify what those requirements are (in a very broad way). Figure 2.8 shows the notation for the main component types in a use case diagram.

As you can see, there are only three: the actor, the use case and the system boundary. Use cases are inside the system boundary and actors are outside. Arrows are used to indicate which actors use which use cases. It is important to note that actors do not represent individual people, rather they represent different roles that people can take when using the system. In some cases, the same person might take on different roles at different times.

FIGURE 2.8   Use case diagram notation

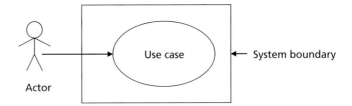

2

In our system, for example, a person my be a member of the call-centre staff but may also apply for insurance as a new user. Similarly, new users change into policy holders if their policy applications are approved. In addition, actors are not always roles taken by people. They can equally be representative of other systems or manual processes. For this reason, we sometimes see the arrows going out from a use case to an actor representing an external system.

Actors and use cases describe *roles* and *goals*. Each actor should be named using a noun that describes a user role, as opposed to an individual, for example 'policy holder'. Each use case should describe a user's goal in using the system, so they should be named using verb phrases (e.g. 'Apply for policy'). Although in some cases there may be a one-to-one correspondence between a use case and a requirement, a single use case may also meet more than one requirement. You will see an example of this in Section 2.7.

Figure 2.9 shows a use case diagram taken from the functional requirements we listed in our workshop. Note that we have five actors taken from our requirements: new user, policy holder, call centre staff members, claims assessor and insurance underwriter. There are eleven use cases. Note how some actors have associations with more than one use case.

Use case realisation

Once we have decided on what our use cases should be, we have to find some way of showing what happens inside them. This is known as a *use case realisation*. There are a number of different notations that we can use to do this, ranging from simple text descriptions to various diagrams. Here, we introduce some sequence diagram notation from the UML along with some informal storyboarding. Since we are designing a web application, the realisation is specific to an environment where the actors interact with page-based presentations. Sequence diagrams capture user interaction with the system, while storyboards are useful for modelling page-based systems because they provide a simple way of describing the page flow and alternate paths that are typical of web applications. They can also be used to informally describe the layout and content of web pages. To link web pages and our UML diagrams we can use the web application extensions (WAE) to the UML for designing web-based systems (Conallen 1999). These are a special set of icons that can be used in UML models to represent components that are specific to web applications, such as web pages.

Use case descriptions

Before embarking on drawing diagrams, however, we begin by writing a textual description of each use case that summarises the sequence of interactions that the actor has with the system. It will also capture any selections or iterations that take place. The nature of these textual descriptions varies from project to project, and some suggested formats and

FIGURE 2.9 A use case diagram for the home insurance web application

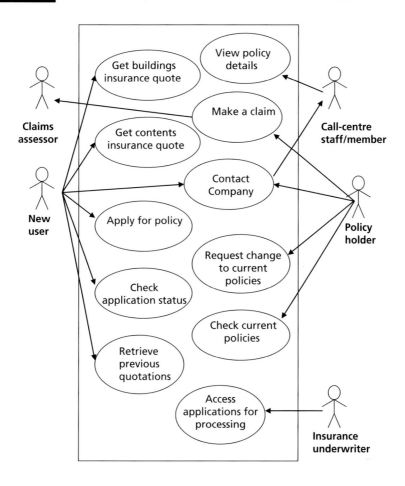

contents are much stricter and more complex than others. The approach we suggest here is to keep things simple but to number each interaction. This makes it easier to 'plug in' alterative sequences of events. The style of a use case description is conversational, that is, it describes a series of actor requests and system responses, in pairs.

As an example, we begin with the 'Get buildings insurance quote' use case. In the text description, we capture some important information:

- The name of the use case
- The actor(s) that use it
- The start page (this is specific to a web application)
- A brief description of what happens in the use case.

Use Case Name: Get buildings insurance quote

Actors: New user

Start Page: Home page

Use Case Description:

1. The actor chooses to get an insurance quote.
2. The system requests the actor's personal details.
2. The actor enters his/her personal details.
4. The system displays a choice of available insurance quotes.
5. The actor chooses to get a buildings insurance quote.
6. The system requests information about the building to be insured.
7. The actor enters data about the building.
8. The system displays the buildings insurance quote.

System sequence diagrams

Now that we have a textual description of the use case, we can draw a system sequence diagram. This shows the interactions between the actor and the system in a notation from the UML.

The components of a system sequence diagram are the actor for the use case, the component(s) that they interact with, labelled arrows showing the messages that pass between the actor and the other components and a vertical time axis. In fact, it is possible to draw sequence diagrams with a horizontal time axis but this is not usually supported by software tools. The component type that an actor interacts with is known as a boundary object, because it exists on the boundary between the system and the actors. A boundary object is usually some kind of graphical interface component. In a web application, this will be displayed on a web page. The UML notation for a boundary object is shown in Figure 2.10.

Our system sequence diagram is shown in Figure 2.11.

Designing pages and webflow with storyboards

If you have seen system sequence diagrams before, you may notice that the one in Figure 2.11 is a bit different from the norm in that it indicates the forms and pages displayed by the system interface boundary object. In a web application, the interaction is via series of pages, so the view of the system from the actor perspective is based on pages. By using the style of sequence diagram in Figure 2.11, we can begin to explore the pages and their sequences that will be used in the storyboards. The sequences of pages that appear in a use case are sometimes known as a *webflow*, which is simply a use case workflow that uses a series of web pages to achieve its goal.

FIGURE 2.10 UML notation for a boundary object

FIGURE 2.11 A system sequence diagram

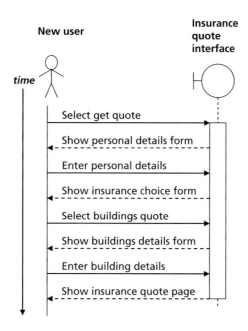

Since our interactions are with a web application, via web pages, we will utilise the web page icon from the UML web application extensions in our sequence diagram (see Figure 2.12a). Web pages are 'architecturally significant components' that exist both in the analysis and design models and the coded system (Conallen 1999). The pages may be coded in mark-up (e.g. HTML) or a programming language (e.g. PHP). Using the formal symbols can be useful in documentation and artefacts created in software packages. However, when informally working through the analysis on paper or whiteboards, it is often easier just to use *stereotype* labels to indicate components such as web pages (see Figure 2.12b). Whether you use symbols or stereotypes is up to you, and the symbols do not have to be exact. Indeed, Conallen himself uses different versions of the symbols in different published sources (see (Conallen 1999) and (Conallen 2001)).

Having outlined the user interaction in the system sequence diagram, we might usefully draw a first cut of a storyboard, representing the pages that are accessed during the use case (see Figure 2.13). For this initial storyboard, we describe only the page names, the navigation routes and the events that trigger the transitions between pages.

Because storyboarding is an informal design tool, there is little consensus on notation, style or even when it should be done. Some developers suggest that you can create an entire web-site storyboard in one step. Whilst this can work for simple sites that are mostly static content, more dynamic and complex web applications require a more incremental approach. Therefore we suggest the approach of developing a storyboard for each use case. Eventually, all the storyboards can be collected together to summarise the navigation paths of the entire web application.

One option for a storyboard is to define the types of page using the UML extension symbols for client pages and forms (see Figure 2.14) rather than using the generic web page icon from Figure 2.12.

FIGURE 2.12 The UML extension symbol for a) a web page and b) its stereotype equivalent

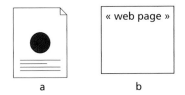

a   b

FIGURE 2.13 A simple storyboard

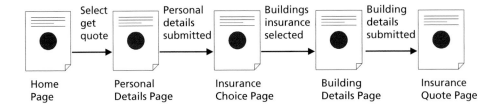

| Home Page | Personal Details Page | Insurance Choice Page | Building Details Page | Insurance Quote Page |

FIGURE 2.14 UML extension symbols for (a) a client page and (b) a form

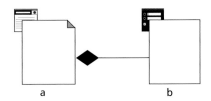

a   b

Note that in this notation, we normally use the form icon as a composition component of a client page (the black diamond indicates that the page is partly composed of the form). However if we follow the *one-form-per-page* usability pattern (Graham 2002), also known as *button gravity* because it puts the emphasis on a single 'Submit' button on each page, then we can dispense with the separate page icon and use the form icon to represent a complete form page.

Looking at each page in turn, we might define the home page and buildings quote page using the 'client page' icon, whereas the others use the 'form' icon. There is no requirement to use these symbols, but they can help to visualise a typical webflow, which will frequently start from a client page, then move through one or more form pages, gathering data in a 'wizard' style, and finally arrive at a summary page that shows the user the result of the webflow (Figure 2.15).

2.7 Building further use cases

So far, so good. We have written a use case realisation for the 'Get buildings insurance quote' use case and we have a simple storyboard. As we are performing analysis activities we have made no attempt to consider data types, page layout, component types or any

FIGURE 2.15 Page types for the 'Get buildings insurance quote' storyboard

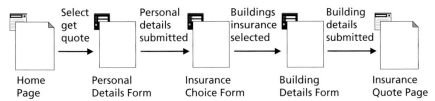

| Home Page | Personal Details Form | Insurance Choice Form | Building Details Form | Insurance Quote Page |

other aspect that would be considered a design activity. Now we move on to the 'Get contents insurance quote' use case. We could, of course, start writing a separate use case description, but it would soon become obvious that we start off in exactly the same way, by gathering the user's personal details and offering a choice of insurance quotes. How do we progress? We might consider adding a use case to gather the user's personal details, which we then progress from to create the two use cases for different types of insurance. However, this implies that getting the two types of insurance quote are exclusive acts. Do we want a user to have to go through two separate use cases if they want both contents and buildings insurance? Once we begin to think about this, it becomes clear that we don't really want two separate use cases for the two types of insurance. In fact we want one use case ('Get insurance quote') that is flexible enough for the user to be able to get a buildings insurance quote, a contents insurance quote, or both. In other words, we have one use case that meets two requirements. With this in mind, let's revisit our existing use case and consider the need for *alternate flows*.

An alternate flow occurs when the activities in a single use case may take different paths depending on some condition. In this example, the condition is the user's choice of insurance. Here is a modified use case description for the renamed 'Get insurance quote' use case.

Use Case Name: Get insurance quote

Actors: New user

Start page: Home page

Use Case Description:

1. The actor chooses to get an insurance quote.
2. The system requests the actor's personal details.
2. The actor enters his/her personal details.
4. The system displays a choice of available insurance quotes.
5. The actor chooses to get a buildings insurance quote.
6. The system requests information about the building to be insured.
7. The actor enters data about the building.
8. The system displays the buildings insurance quote.

Alternate flow – contents insurance only

5a. The actor chooses to get a contents insurance quote.
6a. The system requests information about the contents to be insured.

7a. The actor enters data about the contents.

8a. The system displays the contents insurance quote.

Alternate flow – both types of insurance

5a. The actor chooses to get both a buildings insurance quote and a contents insurance quote.

6, 7, 6a, 7a

8b. The system displays a contents insurance quote, a buildings insurance quote and a total.

With a modified use case, we need a modified system sequence diagram. This can be seen in Figure 2.16. There is an important addition to the notation in this diagram to show selection between alternate flows. There has historically been a degree of confusion and lack of clarity about this in the UML, but we usually show conditional statements by using square brackets, for example, [Select buildings quote OR select both quotes]. In our diagram, we then use a larger square bracket to indicate the set of operations that are part of that conditional block. There are some more complex notations but they do not add much value over this simple version.

As well as an updated system sequence diagram, we have a modified storyboard that shows the alternate flows. In this version, we also use the two icons for client pages and forms to emphasise the 'wizard' style webflow of a series of forms for user input (Figure 2.17).

FIGURE 2.16   The modified system sequence diagram

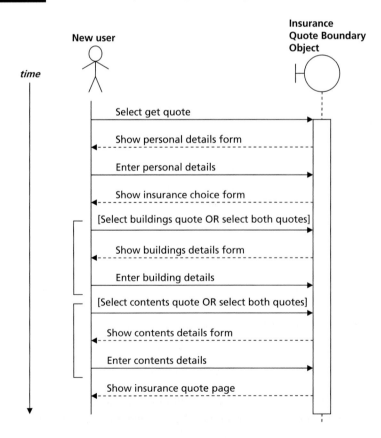

FIGURE 2.17 Updated storyboard with client page and form icons

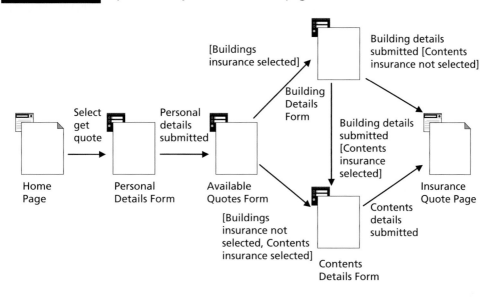

2.8 From analysis to design

So far we have touched on the key stages of the requirements gathering and analysis processes for developing a web application by exploring some aspects of a single use case. In the last part of this chapter, we introduce some concepts related to moving from analysis to design.

In an iterative process, the transfer from analysis to design can be seamless, simply a matter of continually adding more detail. However the level of documentation that we use in the analysis discipline has the important characteristic of being largely non-technical and understandable by non-developers. As such, analysis documents such as use case diagrams and storyboards can be directly used in discussions with customers and potential users. As we move into design, we begin to move away from diagrams that are readily understood by those outside the development team and move either into more detailed diagrams that clearly reflect the chosen tools and techniques of implementation or, if using an agile approach, simply embody the emergent design in the code itself.

Design is technology-aware

Requirements analysis is about defining the problem domain and specifying how we anticipate that the system will be used from the user perspective. From this viewpoint, it is technology-agnostic, meaning that we do not have to know about the technology used to solve the problem, only the characteristics of the solution that we want. In contrast, design is about how we plan the solution, so it is technology-aware. This means that we cannot design a solution until we know something about the way that we will build it. If you were asked, for example, to design a can opener, you would probably be able to come up with a reasonable design, because you probably already have some idea about the way that can openers work. If, however, you were asked to design a time machine, you would probably struggle, being unfamiliar with time machine technology. You can contrast this with analysing the requirements for a time machine, which would be perfectly possible in the absence of knowing about the design. Although our analogy suggests that there is large gulf between analysis and design, the transition from analysis to design is a gentle one in an iterative process. Unlike going over a waterfall, our design starts off at a high level, not too far removed from our analysis, and becomes more detailed.

Architectural design

If, to successfully design in detail, you need to understand the technology of the solution, it would be premature to talk about detailed design in the early part of this book. As we work though the chapters and the case study, you will learn a number of technologies and, once you know these, you will be able to design systems that use them in detail. However, at this stage, our approach to design will be at a higher level, often known as *architectural design*. The overall architectures of web applications reveal some common themes regardless of the actual domain of the application. These common themes can be encapsulated into design patterns, which enable us to reuse design features between different systems. The concepts of design patterns in software first became popular in the 1990s, in particular with the publication of (Gamma *et al.* 1995). This introduced the software community to the idea that common components of software design, developed over multiple applications, could be reused by other applications. These patterns can be expressed in a number of ways, but typically they include some sort of diagram, which may be written using the UML or something more informal.

Static and dynamic content

An important consideration in our design will be the balance between static and dynamic content, and how we represent that content. Our design has to take into account how much of the application will be represented by pages that are static (are the same for every client) and how much will have to be dynamically generated content. In most web applications, there will be a proportion of the site that consists of static content such as HTML, Portable Document Format (PDF), images, video or other types of content that are served to every client. On the other hand, any useful web application will almost certainly have to include dynamic content generated on the fly for specific clients, using some type of server-page technology. This is why distinguishing between different types of page is useful in design diagrams.

2.9 Webflow design

Earlier in this chapter, we introduced some analysis-level diagrams that used web application extension symbols to show how the dependencies between a series of form pages and a final client page might describe the structure of a user webflow. While this client-centric view of a webflow is helpful at the analysis stage, because it helps us to visualise how the client interacts with the web application, at the design stage we have to consider both the client and the server. In this section, we introduce a design model for webflow that describes the structural relationships between client and server that can support the generation of dynamic content. In these diagrams, we introduce another WAE icon, representing a server page (Figure 2.18).

We begin with a simple model of a single HTTP request–response interaction, where an HTML form within a static web page submits its content to the server and a client page is dynamically built and sent back to the client. In this first model (Figure 2.19), we assume

FIGURE 2.18   The WAE server page icon

FIGURE 2.19   A form on a static web page, submitted to a server page that builds a client page

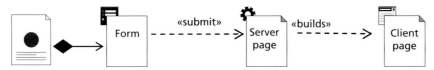

that the server page both manages any necessary business logic and generates the HTML response.

This model is similar to the ones we introduced at the analysis stage, but includes the server page, which builds the client page dynamically. Although this model of dependencies works within the context of a single request–response cycle, it has some drawbacks. The main problem is that we started with an assumption that the form was part of a static web page. This mix of static and dynamic pages does not work particularly well. For example, if the form is not dynamically generated then it cannot be repopulated with error messages and previous entries if the user makes a mistake when entering data in the form. This means that the user would have to start again from scratch if the data entered was for some reason invalid. Another serious problem is that it may not be possible to maintain a user's 'session' over a series of interactions. HTTP is a stateless protocol, which means that it does not maintain connections between a client and a server. Instead, each request–response cycle may use a new connection to the server. Because of this, the server cannot 'remember' the client using the HTTP connection, so instead we have to manage a server-side session component, which keeps track of a particular user. Each session on the server has a unique identifier for the client, and that identifier must also be available to the client. When the client sends a request, the session ID can be sent along with the request and the server can locate the client session with the matching ID. The problem with this is that the preferred way to store the session ID on the client is in a browser *cookie* (a small piece of text-based data that a browser can extract from an HTTP response and store in a file) but the user may have chosen to disable cookies in their browser. If this is the case, the server must use another way of storing the session ID on the client and this requires the use of dynamically generated web pages, because the session ID has to be written into the pages themselves.

Dynamic client pages

Given the problem with mixing static and dynamic content described above, our next design model uses only dynamically generated client pages (Figure 2.20). This makes

FIGURE 2.20 Page structure that includes dynamic form generation

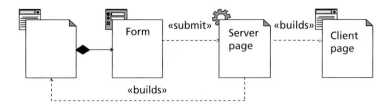

FIGURE 2.21 Including an action object and specialised server pages

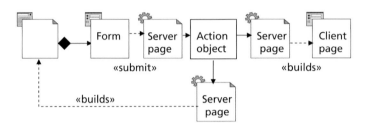

it possible for the server to guarantee that it can handle the client's session, and it is also possible for the server page to build, and rebuild, the form page so that, if the user makes a mistake when filling in the form, a new form page can be provided that contains the data they have already entered along with the necessary error messages, to help them to correct their entries.

Now, the server page dynamically generates a client page with a form, which submits back to the same server page until the next client page can be generated. Although this is a somewhat simple model, it provides the basic static structure that can provide the foundation for a dynamic webflow. There is a problem, however in that the server page is now tasked with making decisions about the webflow and generating one of two possible pages, either an updated form or the next client page. To provide a better separation of concerns a common architectural approach is to include an *action object* that takes responsibility for webflow decisions. The action object can then delegate to further server pages to either regenerate the form page or build the next client page (Figure 2.21).

Modelling dynamic webflow

The diagrams we have used so far are static diagrams showing the relationships between different web components. In order to visualise the dynamic webflow that these components contribute to, it can be useful to sketch some sequence diagrams. The sequence diagram in Figure 2.22 includes some of the participating components from the static model in Figure 2.21, identifying the messages that pass between them over time. In this case, we are only modelling the situation where the original form does not have to be regenerated, but this can easily be added to the diagram using a condition, as we did in Figure 2.16.

The diagram in Figure 2.22 represents the typical interactions in one request–response cycle for a web application. However, before digging any deeper into our own designs we

FIGURE 2.22 Modelling the dynamic webflow with a sequence diagram

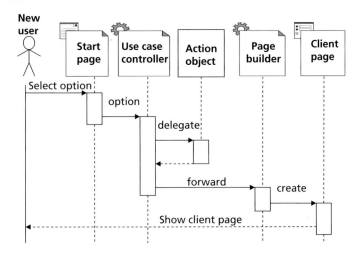

2

must first explore in more detail what we mean by a *server page* and an *action object*. We also need to understand what we mean by 'forward', how a server page 'delegates' to an action object, and so on. We also need to see how we can represent the contents of our domain concepts on web pages. In the chapters that follow, we explore all of these concepts and the necessary technologies to implement them. We can build a complete design once we understand how all the various components can work together.

2.10 Design patterns for web page structures

The design patterns we have looked at so far address the higher-level architecture of the system in terms of server-side components. In the final part of this chapter, we look at some page-design patterns that are relevant to the client. Like the patterns described previously, these patterns are reusable across many different web applications. We look at the following patterns:

- Site logo at top left
- Navigation bar
- Breadcrumbs
- Three-region layout
- Home page
- Site map
- Store content in the database

The main focus of these patterns is usability, making it easy for the user to navigate our web applications. These patterns all come from (Graham 2002).

Site logo at top left

The site logo at top left pattern is a very simple one, but one that you will see commonly used across the web. The site logo, as well as appearing at the top left of the page (as the name of the pattern suggests) should also always act as a hyperlink back to the site's home page (Figure 2.23). The point of this pattern is that it enables the user at any time to have a quick and easy route back to the home page. Once you are aware of this pattern, it is very irritating to visit sites that do not use it!

Navigation bar

Earlier, we introduced use cases as a way of specifying our actors' high-level goals for the web application. These main use cases will be starting points for user navigation. Within these high-level use cases, there may be a number of more detailed use cases that relate to specific tasks. The navigation bar pattern is a way of providing the user with a simple way of navigating a web site based on this combination of general tasks and related sub-tasks. The pattern suggests that the main use cases will appear in a navigation bar across the top of the page, making it easy for users to perform the most important functions easily. The left-hand side can be used for service navigation (i.e. what is inside the current use case). This would enable someone to access a high-level use case such as 'Contact Us', and the service navigation bar might include use case options inside that high-level use case, such as 'office locations', 'email addresses', 'departments' etc. Figure 2.24 shows the general layout of a page using the navigation bar pattern.

The navigation bar will include the 'site logo at top left' pattern which, as we have seen, already acts as a home page link. It also typically includes links to information about the organisation or company that owns the web site, such as their privacy policy and contact information. More specific links will depend on the nature of the web application. For example, e-commerce sites would include registration and login, checkout, shopping cart and account information. There are a whole range of other possibilities, depending on the type of application. These may include downloadable items, a site map, communities, frequently asked questions, news and press releases, jobs, etc.

In the WebHomeCover application, the high-level use cases for the navigation bar would include those we have already seen, for example 'change policy details'. For this use case,

FIGURE 2.23 The 'site logo at top left' pattern

FIGURE 2.24 The 'navigation bar' pattern

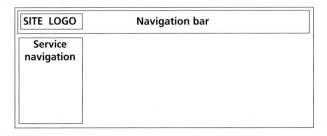

the service navigation bar might include detailed use case options such as 'change address', 'change level of cover', 'add cover', etc.

Breadcrumbs

The idea of breadcrumbs comes from fairy stories where the characters leave a trail of breadcrumbs through the woods in order to find their way home again. In stories, these are usually eaten by birds, leading to disaster, but this is unlikely to happen on web sites. The role of breadcrumbs is to tell the user where they are relative to the home page. Each time the user moves to a new page, another breadcrumb is added to the list, so it is easy for the user to see the path they have taken through the site. In addition, the components of the breadcrumb list should be hyperlinked, so clicking on any breadcrumb will take you to that page. Breadcrumbs are often a secondary part of the navigation bar and may be used in conjunction with a search box (Figure 2.25).

Three-region layout

The three-region layout pattern is actually based largely on the patterns we have already introduced (site logo at top left, the navigation bar and breadcrumbs). If we use these patterns, two regions (the top and side navigation bars) are already used, and we are left with a main page area, which will contain the current content (Figure 2.26). This pattern is very common in web applications, and can be implemented using tables, frames or style sheets. We favour style sheets over tables and tables over frames, since one rule we should be aware of is 'no frames on public sites'. The main reason for not using frames is that browser support is not very reliable for frames, in particular when presenting pages on the mobile Internet. However we may consider not using the three-region layout at all when supporting mobile clients, and favour simpler approaches that separate out the navigation

---

FIGURE 2.25 The 'breadcrumbs' pattern

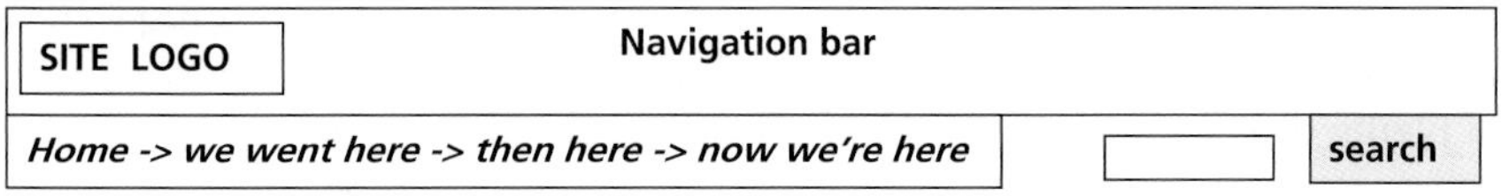

SITE LOGO	Navigation bar		
Home -> we went here -> then here -> now we're here		[ ]	search

---

FIGURE 2.26 The 'three-region layout' pattern

SITE LOGO	Brand and structure navigation
Service navigation	Content

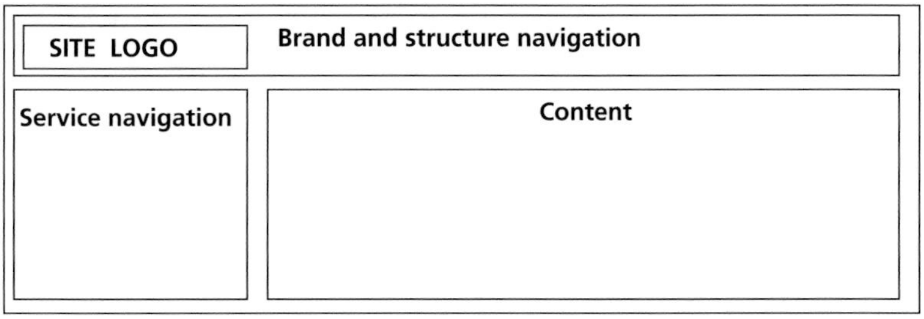

from the content. We address these issues when we look at adaptive web applications for mobile clients in chapter 14. Although many sites still use tables for structure, increasing browser support for sophisticated style sheets makes them the more favoured approach.

Home page

The three-region layout is recommended as a consistent layout for all the pages on a web site. The home page, however, can be an exception to the three-region layout rule, since it has a special role as the starting point for users, and can therefore have some special characteristics. It should not, however, be just a splash screen, which users may find frustrating as it may take a long time to load and run (if, for example, it includes an animation or movie, as some web sites favour). Rather, it needs to include navigation to the main use cases to enable the user to quickly and easily get started on their goals. Figure 2.27 shows a suggested outline for the home page pattern. It gives the site logo more prominence than does the three-region layout pattern, placing it in the centre of the screen. Beneath the logo there is some brief information that should convey the main message of the web site. Beneath this message, prominent links, perhaps using buttons or images, provide quick access to all the most important use cases in the system. Finally, some more information about the main features of the site may appear. Overall the intention of the home page pattern is to have a high level of impact while enabling the user to get started on their goals as quickly as possible.

Site map

One of the suggested links for the navigation bar is the site map. Like the home page, the site map has a special role in a web application, because it provides a bird's eye view of the whole application to the user, allowing direct access to any part of the site (or at least those parts that would sensibly allow direct access) without needing to know how to navigate through other pages. Many site maps are just lists of text. However a more interesting and useful site map would provide a workflow overview, showing not just a list of links but a visual map of the routes through the web application. Exactly how the site map might appear depends on the application, but Figure 2.28 indicates some of the features that might be included: visual components that represent hyperlinks to web pages but also some indication of the links that already exist between these pages. There are many ways of laying out a graphical site map. A web search for 'graphical site map' should give you plenty of links to sites with different styles that can be used.

FIGURE 2.27 The 'home page' pattern

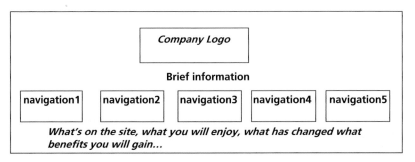

FIGURE 2.28 The 'site map' pattern

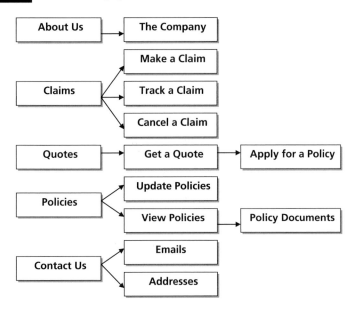

FIGURE 2.29 Reusing content across multiple pages

Store content in the database

Web applications often have to provide the same content across many different pages of a web site. Figure 2.29 shows a very simple example of this type of requirement. Here, we may want to add a simple footer ('© WebHomeCover.com 2000–2008') to the bottom of every page. The last thing we would want to have to do would be to add this to every single page and have to maintain each instance of this data separately. If, for example, we had 154 pages in our web application, and we wanted to update the footer to '© Web HomeCover.com 2000–2009', we would have to do this 154 times. It should be noted that the footer example has a number of simple solutions, because it is consistent across every page, but it illustrates a concept that is very common in web applications, which is that the same underlying data may need to appear in different ways across different parts of a web site. As a more complex example, consider a site where the user logs in. In applications like this, the user's login name, or perhaps some alias, often appears somewhere on the pages that they visit after the point where they have logged in.

The most important pattern that we have in dynamic web applications is simply to store content in a database. Maintaining a web application can get very complex, and we do not want to have to copy and paste large amounts of content for every update to the application. Therefore we need to store content in one place, in the database, and construct pages dynamically. To take our simple 'footer' example, the string of text used for the page footer could be stored in one place, in the database, and read from that database each time it is required in a page. If the footer needs to be updated, it only needs to be updated in one place – the database.

General design guidelines

There are many sources for general design guidelines for web applications. These examples are taken from (Sparks 2004).

- Design around existing content, not future content

A web application should be based around what you already have, not what you might have later. This is a basic principle of agile development – we get the simplest thing possible working early and then develop it over time. An over-complex application structure designed to cater for things that might come along later is unnecessary.

- Avoid unnecessary images

Images take time to load and every image download is a separate HTTP connection. There are many contexts (e.g. on a mobile device) where this is a major overhead. Don't use images where text will suffice.

- Exploit hyperlinks

Use hyperlinks as much as possible. This is really only directly relevant to static rather than dynamic content, since in a lot of dynamic content scenarios we have to guide the user through a restricted set of pathways. However we should make sure that the navigation around our site is well supported by hyperlinks.

- Use cascading style sheets (CSS)

As well as being difficult to build and maintain, HTML that includes its own presentation specification can get very large. Using cascading style sheets (covered in Chapter 4) reduces the size of HTML page downloads.

- Make navigation flow

This is an important aspect of web applications, because the user workflow has to make sense. We need to take care to provide the right number of user pathways from particular points in time. One important aspect is making sure that the user can backtrack correctly from any point in a web application, for example being able to get out of the checkout in an on-line purchasing situation in a controlled way.

- Visit your own site regularly

You are more likely to spot problems in your web applications by approaching them as a user from the outside in, rather than just looking at them from the developer perspective, from the inside out.

Exercises

2.1 Using the example of a customer login, where the user enters a user name and password into a form on a client page, draw a sequence diagram showing the various interactions. Consider the web flow for both a successful and an unsuccessful login.

2.2 Create the following artefacts for the 'View policy details' use case:
- A use case description with at least one alternate flow
- A system sequence diagram
- A storyboard

Are there any updates that you feel are necessary to the domain model?

2.3 This exercise is best done in groups, so you can try out the idea of a requirements workshop. You need to identify some high-level requirements, a domain model and a use case diagram for this project:

Project description: Many research studies rely on questionnaires to gather their data. Doing this on-line can help to improve the number of returns, so your team has been asked to develop a web application to support the creation of web-based research questionnaires. The system needs to be able to gather questionnaire data, store it, allow it to be retrieved and generate simple statistical reports.

In your requirements workshop, adopt some roles that you think would be appropriate to this scenario and consider the requirements of the stakeholders in those roles.

2.4 Design a home page for the WebHomeCover application, selecting the most important use cases and messages from the analysis.

2.5 Design the web page structure for any of the high-level use cases described in this chapter. Use the three-region layout, with all the high-level use cases in the top-level navigation bar and service-level navigation on the left-hand side.

2.6 Take the basic designs of your home page and three-region layout from Exercises 2.4 and 2.5 and apply them to the questionnaire application from Exercise 2.3.

2.7 Consider how the webflow might work for a simple questionnaire that has five questions, each appearing on a separate page. What might the breadcrumb trail look like after you had answered the final question?

SUMMARY

This chapter began by looking at how requirements might be gathered and analysed in order to develop a web-based application, introducing some practices such as joint development workshops and use case analysis. We applied some notation from the UML, including some special extensions for web applications, to help us describe components and workflows within a web-based system. We also saw how the iterative approach and phases of the Unified Process can help us to organize a web development project. In the latter part of the chapter, we focussed on architectural approaches to web application design, introducing important aspects of server-side components and webflow. We introduced some common design patterns for web pages, intended to assist in the usability of a web application. Table 2.1 summarises the terms that were introduced in this chapter. In the chapters that follow, we apply the architectural and usability patterns as we begin to build the components and interactions of a working web application.

TABLE 2.1 Terms introduced in this chapter

Acronym	Meaning
CSS	Cascading Style Sheets
MoSCoW	Must have, Should have, Could have, Want to have
PDF	Portable Document Format
ROI	Return on Investment
UML	Unified Modeling Language
UP	Unified Process
WAE	Web Application Extensions

References and further reading

Cockburn, A. (2005) *Crystal Clear: A human-powered methodology for small teams*. Boston: Addison-Wesley.

Conallen, J. (1999) *Building Web Applications with UML*. Reading, MA: Addison-Wesley.

Conallen, J. (2001) 'Modeling Web-Tier Components'. *Dr. Dobbs Journal*. http://www.ddj.com/dept/architect/184414696

Fowler, M. (2002) *Patterns of Enterprise Application Architecture*. Addison-Wesley.

Gamma, E., Helm, R., Johnson, R. and Vlissides, J. (1995) *Design Patterns: Elements of reusable object-oriented software*. Addison-Wesley.

Graham, I. (2002) *A Pattern Language for Web Usability*. London: Addison-Wesley.

Jacobson, I. (2004) *What I don't like in RUP*. http://www.jaczone.com/postcards/.

Rosenberg, D., Stephens, M. and Collins-Cope, M. (2005) *Agile Development with Iconix Process: People, process and pragmatism*. New York: Apress.

Sparks, M. (2004) *Extreme Website Design*. Exoftware Agile Solutions, http://www.exoftware.com/whitepapers

Structure and Content in the Presentation Layer: the HyperText Markup Language (HTML)

LEARNING OBJECTIVES

- **To understand the origins of HTML**
- **To understand the importance of separating content, structure and presentation in web applications**
- **To be able to create HTML pages using mark-up**

INTRODUCTION

In this chapter, and the ones that follow, we trace the development of the mark-up languages that have been used to structure and present the pages on the web: HTML, CSS, XML and XHTML. HTML is covered in detail in this chapter and CSS in Chapter 4, followed later by various aspects of XML that relate to web applications. We begin by looking at some of the key features of the common root of these mark-up languages, SGML, which will introduce us to some of their main features. We move on to see how HTML can be used to build web page structure and content, including lists and tables. We conclude the chapter by seeing how HTML forms can be used to submit data from a browser to a server using an HTTP request.

3.1 Where it all begins – SGML

In this book we use a number of different, but similar, types of mark-up syntax. Mark-up is information that comes over and above the content of a document to give us guidance about its structure or presentation. These mark-up indicators are generally known as 'tags'. Mark-up is a type of *metadata*, in that it enables us to provide *data about data*, for example by specifying how some data should be organized on a web page. Most of the mark-up syntax we look at has a common origin in Standard Generalised Mark-up Language (SGML). Although this language had many roots, a major thread in the story was earlier work at IBM, where Charles Goldfarb, Ed Mosher and Ray Lorie developed a mark-up language in 1969 that was named after the initial letters of their surnames: GML. This was published publicly (i.e. outside of IBM) in 1973. The basic principles of this language, as expressed at that time, were that it should be possible to design a generalized mark-up language so that the mark-up would be useful for more than one application or computer system. The mark-up would be defined by tags that meant information that was marked up by a particular type of tag would be processed in exactly the same way, regardless of where the tag appeared or however many times it was used. The actual processing, however, would not be defined in the mark-up, since this would depend on the context in which the document was being processed. As GML was further developed, one of the important features that was added was the possibility of *validation*, meaning that a document that used GML mark-up could be checked to ensure that it used that mark-up in an appropriate way. This meant that it was necessary to have some way of expressing the correct ways that a particular set of mark-up tags could be used (Goldfarb 1996).

Later, SGML was developed from the foundations of GML and various other similar research efforts. In 1978, the American National Standards Institute (ANSI), with Goldfarb strongly involved, established the Computer Languages for the Processing of Text committee, and published the first draft of SGML in 1980. Unlike GML, SGML is not named after anyone, but stands for Standard Generalised Markup Language. It also differs from GML in the way that it expresses mark-up, so although it is similar in principle it is different in syntax. In 1986, with the participation of the International Standards Organisation (ISO), the first international standard for SGML was published.

Before we look at the specific mark-up languages of interest in this chapter, in particular HTML and XML, we introduce some very basic concepts that both of these languages (and others) take from SGML. These concepts are tags, elements, attributes and 'well-formedness'.

Tags

Although there is some flexibility about the way that tags can be expressed in SGML, the 'reference' syntax uses angle brackets to indicate a tag. The name of the tag appears between the angle brackets, like this:

```
<tag_name>
```

This is in fact a start tag, which means that it indicates the start of the content that is to be marked up using this tag. At the end of the marked up content, there is an end tag, which is similar to the start tag, except that the tag name is preceded by a forward slash, i.e.

```
</tag_name>
```

3

Elements

A pair of start and end tags, and the marked-up content in between, is known as an *element*. The general format for an element is therefore:

The characteristics defined by the tag are applied to the content of the element. Elements can have other elements nested inside them, to any level of nesting. A nested element is known as a 'child' element, and begins and ends inside its 'parent' element.

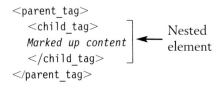

Attributes in tags

Some elements have *attributes*, which configure the element in some way. Attributes appear inside the opening tag and consist of one or more name–value pairs, using the format:

```
attribute_name="attribute_value"
```

For example, if we had an element called 'document', it might have an attribute called 'language' with a value that used a standard language code, such as French (fr):

```
<document language="fr">
```

Single quotes can be used around attribute values instead of double quotes, i.e.

```
<document language='fr'>
```

It is important to make sure that the double and single quotes you use are the vertical type (Unicode character numbers 22 and 27 respectively) known as the *quotation mark* and the *apostrophe*. Be careful if you edit your XML documents in a word processor, because it will probably use the left and right quotation marks (numbered 91–94 in Unicode), which will cause errors in your documents. Rather than a word processor, it is therefore better to use a dedicated editor for mark-up (such as XMLSpy) or a text editor to create and edit your files.

Attributes are used in a different way from elements because they are about providing metadata to an element. In other words, they are used to provide extra information about an element or apply some additional configuration to it. The language in which a document is written is information about the document, not part of its content, so specifying the language as an attribute makes more sense than using an element.

An element may have more than one attribute, in which case they all appear inside the opening tag. The 'document' element, as well as having a language attribute, may also have a 'type' element to indicate what type of document it is. For example, the document might be an instruction manual:

```
<document language="fr" type="manual">
```

Where an opening tag contains more than one attribute, their order is unimportant. Therefore this opening tag has exactly the same meaning as the previous one:

```
<document type="manual" language="fr">
```

Well-formed documents

Although things can become complex in SGML, the main rules for what constitutes a well-formed document are quite simple. Here, we lay out the four most important:

- In a well-formed document, all tags must be balanced so that an element has both an opening and a closing tag:

```
<tag>...</tag>
```

- Tags must be correctly nested so that a child tag must be closed before its parent tag is closed:

```
<parent_tag>
  <child_tag>
    ...
  </child_tag>
</parent_tag>
```

- A document must have a root element that surrounds the whole document, so that its start tag is the first tag in the document and its end tag is the last.

- All attribute values must be written in quotes. Both single and double quotes are valid, but they must be matched correctly (i.e. you cannot mix single and double quotes around the same attribute value).

```
<tag name="value"> or <tag name='value'>
```

These basic ideas from SGML apply to both the HyperText Markup Language (HTML) and the eXtensible Markup Language (XML), both of which are implementations of SGML. However, SGML has many complex rules about what syntax is valid, including a number of features that enable parts of the syntax to be minimised or omitted. This complexity helps to explain how HTML ended up as a seemingly rather inconsistent syntax and why browsers are very tolerant of variations in the use of HTML tags.

3.2 HTML– a language for web pages

In this section, we introduce the HyperText Markup Language (HTML), which is a specific implementation of SGML for marking up web pages and for years was the mainstay of the web. However, HTML is rather a blunt instrument for creating web application presentation, and it has evolved into XHTML, which we look at later.

Nevertheless, studying HTML is a good place to start if we are to understand the way that mark-up of web pages has evolved since the beginnings of the World Wide Web, and it also helps us to understand why other technologies have begun to complement or replace HTML in web applications.

HTML began with the advent of the World Wide Web in 1991, when Tim Berners-Lee at CERN (the European Organization for Nuclear Research) added the first web protocols and tools to the Internet. One of his contributions was the first version of HTML. Berners-Lee's original version contained a small number of tags, many of which survive into XHTML today. The main idea behind HTML was that it would enable documents to be *hypertext-linked* to one another, so that clicking on something in one document would take you to another, related, document. In principle, these *hyperlinks* were to be bidirectional, but HTML does not automatically do this, so hyperlinks in HTML pages work in one direction only. As the popularity of the web increased over subsequent years, and graphical browsers became more common, HTML evolved largely by an ad hoc process, with various features being added to different browsers and gradually becoming common practice. By 1995, with the proliferation of browsers and the increasing popularity of the World Wide Web, it was necessary to try to apply some more rigorous standards to the evolving language, so HTML version 2.0, which included the definition of HTML as the 'text/html' Internet media type, was defined by the Internet Engineering Task Force (IETF). The standard was simply a way of formalising what was already in use, so HTML 2.0 'roughly corresponds to the capabilities of HTML in common use prior to June 1994' (Connolly 1995).

The next version of HTML was version 3.2, in 1996. This version was recommended as a specification by the World Wide Web Consortium (W3C), and was again a formalisation of common practice. Some features added in version 3.2 included tables, Java applets and text flow around images.

Version 4.0 dates from 1998 and included new multimedia options, scripting languages, style sheets, better printing facilities, accessibility features for the disabled and internationalisation support. Version 4.01 brought along some minor changes in 1999. Between 2000 and 2002, the W3C developed the specification for XHTML 1.0. This is the migration path from HTML, so future versions of HTML will in fact be XHTML specifications.

In this chapter, we introduce HTML before introducing XHTML in Chapter 5. This is partly because we need to look at XML in detail before we can fully understand XHTML. It is also so we can explore some of the issues that have come to the fore with web applications that have used HTML in the past, perhaps most significantly the tendency to mix content, structure and presentation in a single document. To address this problem the use of style sheets, covered in Chapter 4, has gradually become the required approach to HTML presentation, and this has assisted the transition from HTML to XHTML.

3.3 HTML document structural elements

HTML documents are plain text files with tags that mark up the content of the page. They become web pages when they are made available over the Internet using a web server and are rendered on the client machine using a web browser. HTML tags are enclosed in angle brackets, the same as the SGML reference syntax. Elements using HTML tags can be used to specify both the structure and the style of the information shown in a web page. The browser uses these tags to organize the text between them, applying the specified mark-up to anything between the opening and closing tags. For example the paragraph element, defined by the <P> tag, is used for organising text into paragraphs.

```
<P>some text in paragraph one . . .</P>
<P>some text in paragraph two . . .</P>
```

The use of upper case for element names (and lower case for attribute names) is recommended by the most recent HTML specification, version 4.01, though in fact HTML is not case-sensitive so this is just a convention rather than a requirement:

> Element names are written in uppercase letters. . . . Attribute names are written in lowercase letters. . . . Recall that in HTML, element and attribute names are case-insensitive; the convention is meant to encourage readability. (Raggett *et al.* 1999)

We will see in Chapter 4 that XML and XHTML use lower case letters for element names. Therefore it will be immediately obvious to you as you see mark-up in this book that if the element names are upper case then the example is in HTML 4.01, and if they are in lower case then the mark-up is XML or XHTML.

Paragraphs, and other similar elements, can be regarded as *structural* elements because they organize the content in some semantic way. In other words, they help us to understand its meaning. A paragraph usually groups together some sentences that refer to the same topic. Similarly, a tag such as <H1>, for main heading elements, can be seen as structural. Organising text into headings, subheadings, paragraphs, etc. is about providing structure in terms of how different blocks of text relate to one another. It does not, however, specify how those headings, subheadings etc. should look. In contrast, HTML also contains many tags that are to do with the presentational styles of a document, to change the font, colour or other aspects of style. A simple example of this type of tag is the *bold* (<B>) tag:

```
<B>this text will be presented in bold face</B>
```

A tag like this is specifically used to define how part of the document looks when displayed and has nothing to do with the structure or semantics of the text. We will not be covering presentational mark-up in this chapter. The preferred way of handling the presentation of a page is to use cascading style sheets (CSS), which we cover in Chapter 4.

Creating an HTML document

The simplest possible HTML document contains a small set of structural and content elements. These are HTML, HEAD, TITLE and BODY. The first and the last thing in an HTML document should always be the tags that surround the root (HTML) element, i.e. <HTML> . . . </HTML>. Inside the HTML element, there is a nested HEAD element, <HEAD> . . . </HEAD> that contains the document header information, including the title of the document. The TITLE element is nested inside the HEAD element, using <TITLE> and </TITLE> tags. The content of the TITLE element appears at the top of the browser's title bar, in the history list and in your bookmark file if you create a bookmark to the page. The BODY element comes after the HEAD element.

The BODY element represents the page content that is shown in a browser window. Here is an HTML document with this minimal set of elements:

```
<HTML>
  <HEAD>
    <TITLE> The title of the web page </TITLE>
  </HEAD>
  <BODY> body content of the web page </BODY>
</HTML>
```

Content types

Within the document body, the content is frequently organized into blocks of textual information, such as headings, paragraphs, lists and tables. There may also be other *media types* in the body, such as images, sound clips and movies. A media type is some kind of Multipurpose Internet Mail Extension (MIME) type that defines a particular type of file that can be used on the Internet. Since HTML 4, the preferred term is *content type*, since *media type* is more properly applied to types of output device. Regardless, the type of an HTML document is 'text/html', but such documents may contain references to content that is of a different type. HTML provides a large number of tags for organising the structure of a document's content, including all the other content types that may be included inside it. In this chapter we look at the main organising elements: headings, paragraphs, lists, tables and forms.

Text elements

Much of the content of web pages is based on the management of text. The structure of the text can be organized using headings, subheadings and paragraphs. Some other types of content can usefully be structured in terms of lists (which may be ordered in some way) or tables. There are also certain semantic aspects of text that can be included in mark-up, to provide emphasis or indicate quotations, for example. In this section, we look at some of the basic structural elements that assist in organising content in HTML pages.

A very common way of organising text-based content is to use headings, subheadings and paragraphs. The H1, H2, H3, H4, H5 and H6 elements can be used for various levels of heading and subheading. H1 is the largest heading and H6 the smallest. Because a heading is generally larger than the text that follows, it may not be sensible to use more than the first two or three levels of heading. In many browsers, the smallest heading types are smaller than standard paragraph text.

As we have already seen, the HTML syntax for a paragraph element is <P>. You should also add the closing </P> tag at the end of each paragraph to make the element 'well formed', though most browsers will still display the page correctly without the closing tag. This is an aspect of *minimisation*, a feature of SGML, which means that not all elements need to have closing tags, if the end of an element can be inferred from other parts of the document structure, such as the beginning of another paragraph inferring the end of the previous one. Browsers generally leave a blank line before a paragraph element. In the example below, we use an H1 element for a main heading and H2 elements as subheadings, with the main body of the text in paragraphs, surrounded by <P> . . . </P> tags.

This example also includes the comment syntax in HTML, which looks like this:

```
<!-- this is a comment -->
```

We will use this comment syntax throughout the book to indicate the source file that is being referred to in each example.

```
<HTML>
  <HEAD>
    <TITLE>Versions of HTML</TITLE>
  </HEAD>
  <BODY>
    <!-- File: example3-1.htm -->
    <H1>Versions of HTML</H1>
    <H2>HTML 1.0</H2>
    <P>
The first version of HTML dates from 1991, and was developed by Tim Berners-Lee.
It was very different from the HTML we know today...
    </P>
    <H2>HTML 2.0</H2>
    <P>
The second version of HTML, in 1996, was an attempt to standardize the language,
which was being widely implemented by different vendors' web browsers...
    </P>
  </BODY>
</HTML>
```

Figure 3.1 shows what the page looks like in Internet Explorer 7. Note the different sizes of text for headings, subheadings and paragraphs.

FIGURE 3.1   Headings, subheadings and paragraphs

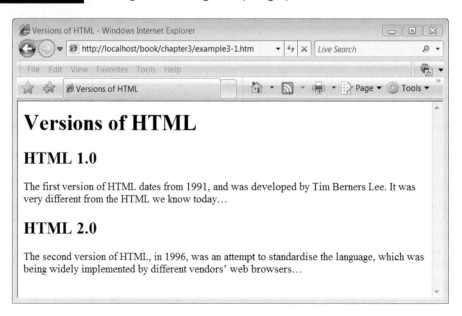

3.4 HTML document type

Browsers generally cope with minimisation of HTML elements and are, in fact, quite forgiving of poorly formed HTML syntax. However it is good practice not only to write well–formed HTML but also specify a *type definition* for the document. This helps browsers to render documents by matching their structure to a particular definition of how HTML elements and attributes should be organized.

Since HTML 2.0, public document type definitions (DTDs) have been available for specifying the types of HTML documents. There are three of these DTDs available for HTML 4.01; 'strict', 'transitional' and 'frameset' (Ragget *et al.* 1999). The 'transitional' and 'frameset' versions allow a wider range of elements and more flexible structure than the 'strict' version and allow extensive mixing of presentation with content and structure. We look more closely at DTDs and how they can be used to validate the structure of documents in a later chapter but, in the meantime, we declare that our HTML mark-up uses the 'strict' type definition. To do this, we need to add the following line to the top of our HTML documents:

```
<!DOCTYPE HTML PUBLIC "-//W3C//DTD HTML 4.01//EN"
"http://www.w3.org/TR/html4/strict.dtd">
```

This states that the document should follow the strict rules for the structure of HTML 4.01. The 'DOCTYPE' refers to a DTD that is publicly available for specifying HTML document types. Here is our first example with the necessary definition added:

```
<!DOCTYPE HTML PUBLIC "-//W3C//DTD HTML 4.01//EN"
"http://www.w3.org/TR/html4/strict.dtd">
<HTML>
   <HEAD>
      <TITLE>Versions of HTML</TITLE>
   </HEAD>
   <BODY>
      <H1>Versions of HTML</H1>
      <H2>HTML 1.0</H2>
      <P>
The first version of HTML dates from 1991, and was developed by Tim Berners-Lee.
It was very different from the HTML we know today...
      </P>
      <H2>HTML 2.0</H2>
      <P>
The second version of HTML, in 1996, was an attempt to standardise the language,
which was being widely implemented by different vendors' web browsers...
      </P>
   </BODY>
</HTML>
```

3.5 Structuring text

As well as structuring our pages into headings and paragraphs, there are a number of other structural elements that we can apply to HTML documents. In this section, we look at some of the elements that help us to structure text.

Line breaks and horizontal rules

Line breaks (BR) and horizontal rules (HR) are examples of *empty elements*. An empty element in HTML is one that, instead of having separate start and end tags, consists of a single tag, with no closing tag either required or implied. One example of an empty element in HTML is the line break, which first appeared in the HTML 2.0 specification:

```
<BR>
```

This element does not have start and end tags, but consists of a single tag that forces a line break in the document. Unlike the paragraph element, which starts a new line and leaves a space before the paragraph, a BR element starts a new line but does not force a blank line to be inserted.

The horizontal rule is another example of an empty element that dates from HTML 2.0. The tag looks like this:

```
<HR>
```

A browser usually displays the horizontal rule as a graphical line. Of course one might question whether the HR element is structural or just presentational. Its definition in the various HTML specifications has evolved from 'a divider between sections of text' via 'used to indicate a change in topic' to 'a horizontal rule to be rendered by visual user agents', so one could make a case for either interpretation (Korpela 2002).

Citations and block quotes

There are many structural elements in HTML, some more commonly used than others. Although CITE and BLOCKQUOTE are not often required, they are useful examples of elements that have some semantics attached to them; they convey something about the meaning of the text and its relationship to other parts of the document around them rather than hierarchical structure or presentation.

It is common in documents for longer quotations and citations to be structured differently from the main body of the text. HTML includes the <BLOCKQUOTE> element for long quotations and the <CITE> element for citations. The next example is similar to the last one, but is modified to include <CITE> and <BLOCKQUOTE> elements. You should note that BLOCKQUOTE elements should not directly contain text. Rather, they should contain structural elements such as paragraphs or headings, with the text inside those. Here, we use a paragraph element.

```
<!DOCTYPE HTML PUBLIC "-//W3C//DTD HTML 4.01//EN"
"http://www.w3.org/TR/html4/strict.dtd">
<HTML>
  <HEAD>
    <TITLE>Versions of HTML</TITLE>
  </HEAD>
  <BODY>
    <!-- File: example3-2.htm -->
    <H1>Versions of HTML</H1>
    <H2>HTML 1.0</H2>
    <P>The first version of HTML dates from 1991, and was developed by Tim
Berners-Lee. It was very different from the HTML we know today.
```

```
<CITE>Tim Berners-Lee</CITE> is quoted as saying</P>
<BLOCKQUOTE>
<P>
If you use the original World Wide Web program, you never see a URL or have to
deal with HTML. That was a surprise to me...that people were prepared to
painstakingly write HTML.
</P>
</BLOCKQUOTE>
<H2>HTML 2.0</H2>
<P>
The second version of HTML, in 1996, was an attempt to standardise the language,
which was being widely implemented by different vendors' web browsers...
</P>
</BODY>
</HTML>
```

Figure 3.2 shows how the complete page looks in Internet Explorer 7.

In this browser, the citation appears in italics and the block quote is separated from the previous text and indented. It is important to note however that we are not using elements here for the purposes of indenting paragraphs or applying an italic text style. The CITE and BLOCKQUOTE elements are about the structure and meaning of the text, not controlling its appearance. We are letting the browser decide how a citation or a block quote should actually appear, so the fact that the quote is indented and the citation text is italic is not something explicitly defined. This is an important point, since we should be aware of the difference between structural and presentational tags and how to use them. The use of BLOCKQUOTE simply to indent a paragraph is *deprecated*, which means that although the tag may be displayed that way

FIGURE 3.2   Using the CITE and BLOCKQUOTE elements

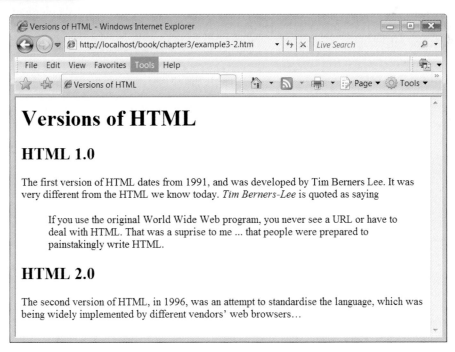

in a particular browser it should not be used simply to get that presentational effect. The BLOCKQUOTE element is an indication that the body of the element should be given some special handling to recognize that it is a long quotation. It should not be used as a convenient way of achieving a specific format, regardless of the actual content of the element. Perhaps even more obviously, using the CITE element should not be seen simply as a way of making text italic.

Idiomatic (phrase) elements

CITE is one of the *idiomatic* or *phrase* elements. These elements relate to common types of usage in terms of how we express ourselves in writing. For example, we look for ways to emphasize specific parts of text. To support these idioms, HTML includes elements such as EM for emphasis and STRONG for stronger emphasis. Browsers usually render EM text in italics and STRONG text in bold face but, as with the CITE element, the actual way that the browser chooses to render these elements is independent of our use of the tags. We use them to indicate a type of expression, not to select a particular appearance for the text.

Subscripts and superscripts

The SUB (subscript) element uses a small font aligned towards the bottom of the regular character height; the SUP (superscript) element uses a small font aligned towards the top of the regular character height. These elements might appear to occupy a grey area between the structural and the presentational. However there are important accepted uses for these aspects of content, for example in scientific notation or in rendering some languages. Superscript is commonly used to indicate references, footnotes or trademarks, and in mathematical formulae, while subscript is used in chemical formulae. The HTML 4 specification includes these two useful examples of superscript and subscript:

H₂0   to represent H_2O (the chemical symbol for water)

E = mc²   to represent $E = mc^2$ (Einstein's formula for relativity)

Because of these specific applications, the use of the <SUB> and <SUP> elements can be seen as structural, as long as they are applied in these generally accepted contexts rather than just for effect.

Special characters

Because HTML pages use a markup syntax, there are certain symbols, in particular < and > that have special meaning to the applications (such as browsers) that process them. HTML

TABLE 3.1   HTML character references

HTML character reference	Equivalent character	Meaning
&lt;	<	Less than
&gt;	>	Greater than
&quot;	"	Quotation mark
&amp;	&	Ampersand
	(a space)	Non-breaking space
&reg;	®	Registered trademark
&copy;	©	Copyright

character references are numeric or symbolic names that can be used instead of literal characters in an HTML document. They are useful for referring to special characters outside the normal number and letter ranges in character sets, or those that have other meanings in the mark-up language and could therefore cause processing problems for browsers. All of the HTML character references begin with an & sign and end with a semicolon. Some examples of HTML character references are shown in Table 3.1.

3.6 Lists

Lists can be appropriate ways of structuring certain types of content in an HTML document. A list can present short, related items of information in an easy-to-read layout, and may be nested (i.e. a list inside a list) to produce structures such as tables of contents, indexes or document outlines. There are three types of list in HTML:

- Unordered lists
- Ordered lists
- Definition lists

Unordered lists

An unordered list is one that is given a list structure but there is no numbering or lettering to suggest a meaningful sequence. In other contexts, this type of list is known as a *bulleted list*. The browser will probably display each item in the list with a bullet symbol prefix. The tag name for an unordered list element is UL and it can contain any number of nested LI (list item) elements:

```
<UL>
    <LI> a list item </LI>
    <LI> another list item </LI>
    . . .
</UL>
```

Ordered lists

In an ordered list, the list items are numbered or lettered. This is useful for lists that have a meaningful order, such as instructions, chapters, recipes or league tables. The tag name for an ordered list is OL, with LI again used for nested list item elements:

```
<OL>
    <LI> the first list item </LI>
    <LI> the second list item </LI>
    . . .
</OL>
```

Nesting ordered and unordered lists

Lists can be nested and combined together as appropriate for the content. However there is an important thing to bear in mind when doing this, which is that any list that is nested inside another one must be in its own list item (LI) element, using this kind of structure:

```
<UL>
  <LI> an item in the main list</LI>
  <LI> Here comes a nested list. . .
    <OL>
      <LI> an item in the nested list</LI>
      <LI> another item in the nested list</LI>
      . . .
    </OL>
  </LI>
  <LI> another item in the main list</LI>
  . . .
</UL>
```

In this example from the home insurance system domain, we use both ordered and unordered lists:

```
<!DOCTYPE HTML PUBLIC "-//W3C//DTD HTML 4.01//EN"
"http://www.w3.org/TR/html4/strict.dtd">
<HTML>
  <HEAD>
    <TITLE> Making a Claim</TITLE>
  </HEAD>
  <BODY>
    <!-- File: example3-3.htm -->
    <H1>Useful Tips</H1>
    <UL>
      <LI> Making a Claim
      <OL>
        <LI>Find as much documentation as you can (photos, receipts, etc.)
        </LI>
        <LI> Fill in the on-line claim form</LI>
        <LI> Don't do anything until an assessor has contacted you</LI>
      </OL>
      </LI>
      <LI>Changing your policy
        <OL>
          <LI> Log in to your user account </LI>
          <LI> Select 'update policy details' from the list of options </LI>
          <LI> Follow the on-screen instructions to make the required changes
          </LI>
        </OL>
      </LI>
    </UL>
  </BODY>
</HTML>
```

Figure 3.3 shows how the page looks in Opera 9. You will notice that the main unordered list has round bullets and the nested ordered lists are labelled with Arabic numbers. This is the behaviour of the browser, not specified by our list elements.

FIGURE 3.3   How nested ordered and unordered lists appear in a browser

Definition lists

Definition lists are a bit different from the other types of list because they are structured as a glossary of terms. The outer element of a definition list uses the <DL> . . . </DL> (definition list) tags. Inside this element appear one or more pairs of terms and definitions. In each pair, the term is defined by a DT (definition term) element and the definition appears in a DD (definition list definition) element. Here is an example of an HTML document containing a definition list:

```
<!DOCTYPE HTML PUBLIC "-//W3C//DTD HTML 4.01//EN"
"http://www.w3.org/TR/html4/strict.dtd">
<HTML>
  <HEAD>
    <TITLE>Markup Languages</TITLE>
  </HEAD>
    <!-- File: example3-4.htm -->
  <BODY
    <DL>
      <DT> SGML </DT>
      <DD> Standard Generalised Markup Language </DD>
      <DT> HTML </DT>
      <DD> HyperText Markup Language </DD>
      <DT> XML</DT>
      <DD> eXtensible Markup Language </DD>
    </DL>
  </BODY>
</HTML>
```

Figure 3.4 shows how the definition list looks in Mozilla Firefox 2. In this browser, there is no difference in the font size or style between the definitions and the terms, only the layout is affected. We could, however, add EM or STRONG tags to provide some further semantic differentiation between definitions and terms.

FIGURE 3.4   Definition lists

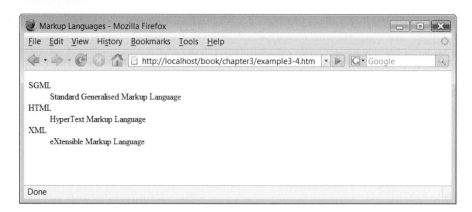

3.7 Attributes in HTML

So far we have seen a number of HTML elements but none of these have included attributes. Nevertheless many HTML tags can have attributes. Many of these attributes could be categorized as presentational, and in fact the use of attributes for presentation in HTML gives us a good indication of how the usage of elements and attributes differs. Elements are intended for the content of a document, whereas attributes tend to provide additional configuration of these elements. If we regard presentation of an element as part of its metadata, then we can see that attributes are a good way of applying metadata to HTML elements. However attributes are not confined solely to defining presentation. They can also be used for some structural aspects, as we will see in the coming examples.

Images

Having said that we are currently dealing with content and structure rather than presentation, it may at first glance seem a little strange to be introducing images. However, an image in a web page is an instance of a *content type*, which means that it is part of the content of the page, not its presentation. It just happens to be content that has visual characteristics. Images can be added to a web page using the IMG empty element, but unlike the empty elements (BR and HR) we have seen, IMG elements cannot be used without attributes. The essential attribute is 'src', which indicates the URI of the image file to be included in the page. The most common image file types used on the web are GIF (Graphics Interchange Format), JPEG (Joint Photographic Experts Group) and PNG (Portable Network Graphics), since these have relatively small file sizes and can therefore be downloaded reasonably quickly. GIF and PNG files are typically used for drawings, while JPEGs are used for photographs as they can manage more colours than GIFs and have a more flexible compression algorithm than PNGs. The PNG format was developed when Unisys held a patent on the GIF compression algorithm, but it is also better than GIF files for rendering more than 256 colours, though the equivalent files tend to be larger than GIFs.

As well as defining the source for the image, we must also provide an alternative text value using the 'alt' attribute. This is useful both for providing a text alternative if the image cannot be loaded (for example if the user has disabled image loading in the browser for speed) and for providing text to be read out for those users who are unable to see images. Here is an IMG element that uses a GIF file as its source:

```
<IMG src="logo.gif" alt="WebHomeCover Logo">
```

The other attributes that can be used with images are 'height' and 'width', which can be used to scale the image on the page from its original size, but are more often used to specify the actual dimensions of the image (in pixels) to enable the browser to load the page faster, since it is able to anticipate the display space required before downloading the file:

```
<IMG src="logo.gif" alt="WebHomeCover Logo" height="115" width="102">
```

Links

One of the most important aspects of the World Wide Web is the *link*, also known as a *hyperlink* or a *web link*, which enables us to go from one web-based resource to another, regardless of where on the web the other resource may be. A link has two ends known as *anchors*, with the source anchor being in the current document and the destination anchor being the web resource (document, image, sound file, etc.) that is being linked to. Clicking on a link in a web page lets us retrieve the linked web resource. The full detail of links in HTML is quite complex, so we cover only the basics here.

The element name used for anchors in HTML documents is A, and the most important attribute is 'href' (hypertext reference), which contains the URI of the linked resource. Here, for example is an anchor that links to the URI of the WebHomeCover site:

```
Click <A href="http://www.webhomecover.com">here</A> for a great
insurance deal...
```

The text in the body of the anchor element ('here') is the actual hyperlink that appears in the browser.

Not all URIs in anchor elements need to include a full web address. Many anchors used in web applications link to other pages in the same application, so the URI can be a filename using a local path. Here, for example, the anchor refers to a file in the local directory:

```
<A href="aboutus.htm">About Us</A>
```

Relative paths can also be used. Here, we assume that there is an image file stored in an 'images' folder beneath the current folder (indicated by the '.'):

```
<A href="./images/map.gif">Find Us</A>
```

As well as linking to other files, anchors in an HTML page can link to specific parts of a document. If the target anchor is not a complete URI but within a document, then the anchor element can be used at the destination end of the link. For example, we might want to link to a part of a document that contains some terms and conditions about our insurance policies. To link to part of the same document, the URI used in the source anchor is the name of the destination anchor, preceded by a hash, for example:

```
<A href="#terms">terms and conditions</A>
```

In this example we assume that there is a destination anchor in the same document called 'terms'. This will be defined somewhere else in the document using the 'id' attribute of the anchor element, for example:

```
<A id="terms">Terms and Conditions</A>
```

Clicking on the hyperlink of the source anchor takes the user to the part of the document containing the destination anchor. The following mark-up shows how the source and destination anchors might appear in the same document:

```
Our insurance is offered according to our standard <A href="#terms">terms and
conditions</A> which you should read carefully before making a claim. . .

blah blah blah. . .

<H2><A id="terms">Terms and Conditions</A></H2>
WebHomeCover reserve the right to. . .
```

The same approach can be used when the destination anchor is in part of another document. The only difference is that the anchor name is preceded by the URI of the containing page, for example:

```
<A href="legal.htm#terms">terms and conditions</A>
```

In this case we assume that the 'terms' anchor is in another document called 'legal.html'. A full address can also be used:

```
<A href="http://www.webhomecover.com/legal.htm#terms">
    terms and conditions
</A>
```

Images, as well as text, can be used as link anchors by nesting IMG elements inside anchor elements, for example:

```
<A href="home.html">
    <IMG src="logo.gif" alt="WebHomeCover Logo">
</A>
```

This is a useful technique for implementing the 'site logo at top left' pattern we saw in Chapter 2, where clicking on the company logo always takes you to the home page.

Email links

Anchors can also be used for email links. To do this you simply use a 'mailto' value in the 'href' attribute, which takes this format:

```
<A href="mailto:help@webhomecover.com">Email the help desk</A>
```

When 'Email the help desk' is clicked, the web browser *may* open your email client to compose a message, though this does depend on the browser configuration so its behaviour cannot be guaranteed.

The following example shows an HTML page that includes both links and images:

```
<!DOCTYPE HTML PUBLIC "-//W3C//DTD HTML 4.01//EN"
"http://www.w3.org/TR/html4/strict.dtd">
<HTML>
  <HEAD>
    <TITLE>Our Insurance</TITLE>
  </HEAD>
  <BODY>
    <!-- File: Example3-5.htm -->
    <P>
    <A href="home.htm">
    <IMG src="logo.gif" alt="WebHomeCover Logo" height="67" width="294">
    </A>
    </P>
    <H1>Our Insurance</H1>
    <P>
      Our insurance is offered according to our standard
      <A href="#terms">terms and conditions</A>
      which you should read carefully before making a claim
      ... blah blah blah ...
    </P>
    <P>
    If you have any enquiries, please
    <A href="mailto:help@webhomecover.com">
    Email the help desk
    </A>
    <H2><A id="terms">Terms and Conditions</A></H2>
    <P>
    WebHomeCover reserve the right to ... blah blah blah ...
    </P>
  </BODY>
</HTML>
```

Figure 3.5 shows the page displayed in Internet Explorer 7. To see the effect of the internal link, you need to resize the window so that the Terms and Conditions section is not visible before clicking the 'terms and conditions' link.

3.8 Tables

Tables can be a useful structural element in a web page. Information can often be displayed effectively using a table-based format, particularly if the data being presented has been read from a relational database, since these databases store data in tables. A table consists of rows and columns, with optional column headings and a caption. Each part of table (where a row and column meet) is known as a cell (Figure 3.6).

Table tags

In HTML 4, the table is quite a complex element, with a number of nested elements used to represent the table model which is the underlying table structure. This can be divided

FIGURE 3.5 Links and images displayed in Internet Explorer 7

FIGURE 3.6 The components of a table

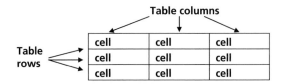

into the header, body and footer, and columns can be grouped together. However in this overview we cover only the basics of tables.

Table elements and rows

A table element in HTML is defined by <TABLE>...</TABLE> tags. The table element contains all the other table-related tags that specify, for example, captions, headings and data cells. The CAPTION element is optional, but it can be used to describe the table, for example:

```
<CAPTION>Our Call Centres</CAPTION>
```

Each row in the table is defined by a table row (TR) element:

```
<TR>...</TR>
```

Table cells

There are two types of table cell, those that contain column headings and those that contain data. The <TH>...</TH> (table heading) tags can optionally be used to define heading elements that are used in the top row of the table columns. Other cells are defined using the <TD>...</TD> (table data) tags.

Table example

As we work through the various aspects of HTML tables, we develop a simple example of a table that shows the locations and contact numbers of call centres. For the purposes of this example we assume that WebHomeCover has call centres in various territories, and this information will be presented on a web page in the form of a table. The following document includes TABLE element for the basic table. There is a caption ('Our Call Centres') and four columns, each with a heading cell: 'Territory', 'Location', 'Phone' and 'Fax'. There are four rows, one for each call centre.

```
<!DOCTYPE HTML PUBLIC "-//W3C//DTD HTML 4.01//EN"
"http://www.w3.org/TR/html4/strict.dtd">
<HTML>
  <HEAD>
    <TITLE>Our Call Centres</TITLE>
  </HEAD>
  <BODY>
    <!-- File: example3-6.htm -->
    <TABLE>
      <CAPTION>Our Call Centres</CAPTION>
      <TR>
        <TH>Territory</TH> <TH>Location</TH> <TH>Phone</TH> <TH>Fax</TH>
      </TR>
      <TR>
        <TD>Americas</TD> <TD>New York</TD>
        <TD>0800 1425364</TD> <TD>0800 1122334</TD>
      </TR>
      <TR>
        <TD>EMEA</TD> <TD>London</TD>
        <TD>0800 1324536</TD> <TD>0800 8444463</TD>
      </TR>
      <TR>
        <TD>EMEA</TD> <TD>Cape Town</TD>
        <TD>0800 9009586</TD> <TD>0800 9944474</TD>
      </TR>
      <TR>
        <TD>APAC</TD> <TD>Sydney</TD>
        <TD>0800 1114445</TD> <TD>0800 1114445</TD>
      </TR>
    </TABLE>
  </BODY>
</HTML>
```

Figure 3.7 shows what the table looks like displayed in a browser. Note that, in this browser at least (Internet Explorer 7), the table headings are displayed in bold face to differentiate them from the table data cells.

Table organisation

The organisation of a table can be flexible in the sense that we can choose to leave cells blank if there is no data available for them and we can also span multiple cells or columns. To leave cells blank, we can simply remove data from between the TH or TD tags. Just for

FIGURE 3.7   A table displayed in Internet Explorer 7

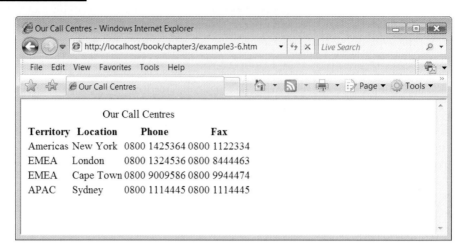

the sake of this example, we might assume that the Cape Town office does not have a fax number. To leave this cell blank we just remove the data from that cell and replace it with a non-breaking space character ( ):

```
<!-- File: example3-7.htm -->
<TR>
    <TD>EMEA</TD>  <TD>Cape Town</TD>
    <TD>0800 9009586</TD>  <TD> </TD>
</TR>
```

Now the table displays as in Figure 3.8.

Spanning with attributes

Tables include a useful example of how attributes can be used to change the configuration of an element in HTML. As well as leaving data out of cells we can also make data span more than one cell. This is done using the 'rowspan' or 'colspan' attributes that can be applied to the TD or TH tags. For example colspan="2" means span two columns and rowspan="3" means span three rows. Figure 3.9 shows how these attributes affect the structure of the table.

In our example, there are a couple of places where the same data appears in adjacent cells. EMEA appears twice in the Territory column and the phone and fax numbers for the APAC office are the same. We might choose to restructure the table so that the same data can span across multiple cells to avoid repeating the data unnecessarily. In this version of the table, we use rowspan in the Territory column and colspan in the APAC row:

```
<!DOCTYPE HTML PUBLIC "-//W3C//DTD HTML 4.01//EN"
"http://www.w3.org/TR/html4/strict.dtd">
<HTML>
    <HEAD>
        <TITLE>Our Call Centres</TITLE>
    </HEAD>
    <BODY>
```

```
<!-- File: example3-8.htm -->
<TABLE>
<CAPTION>Our Call Centres</CAPTION>
  <TR>
    <TH>Territory</TH> <TH>Location</TH> <TH>Phone</TH> <TH>Fax</TH>
  </TR>
  <TR>
    <TD>Americas</TD> <TD>New York</TD>
    <TD>0800 1425364</TD> <TD>0800 1122334</TD>
  </TR>
  <TR>
    <TD rowspan="2">EMEA</TD> <TD>London</TD>
    <TD>0800 1324536</TD> <TD>0800 8444463</TD>
  </TR>
  <TR>
    <TD>Cape Town</TD> <TD>0800 9009586</TD> <TD> </TD>
  </TR>
  <TR>
    <TD>APAC</TD> <TD>Sydney</TD> <TD colspan="2">0800 1114445</TD>
  </TR>
</TABLE>
</BODY>
</HTML>
```

FIGURE 3.8   Leaving a blank cell in a table

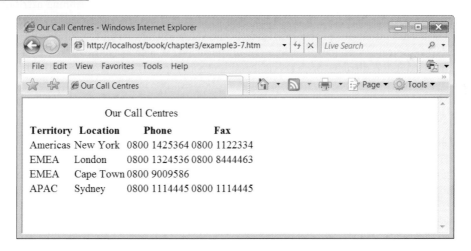

FIGURE 3.9   The effect of rowspan and colspan attributes on table cells

`<TD>...</TD>`	`<TD>...</TD>`	`<TD rowspan="3">...</TD>`
`<TD colspan="2">...</TD>`		
`<TD>...</TD>`	`<TD>...</TD>`	

FIGURE 3.10 The effect of spanning cells in a table

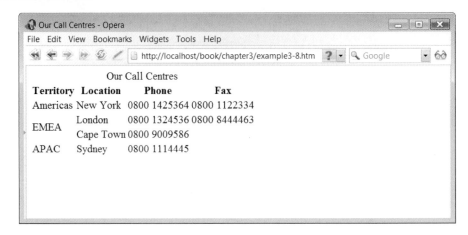

Figure 3.10 shows the table displayed in the browser. The spanned rows are easy to see because 'EMEA' has been centred between the rows. The spanned columns are not so obvious because the Sydney number is still aligned to the left. As in many other examples we have seen, presentational decisions like this are being made by the browser.

Table borders

Changing the border style of a table is presentational, not structural. However at this point it is useful to introduce a table border so we can see the effect of the spanning attributes used in the previous example. The width of the table and cell borders can be controlled using the 'border' attribute of the TABLE tag. The value of this attribute defines the width in pixels of the table and cell borders. By implication, it also sets the frame to have a border around it and displays both vertical and horizontal rules around individual cells. The default value of 'border' is '0', meaning that no borders are visible, making it difficult to see the effect of the horizontal spanning in our table. Here, we set the border value to '1', which means that each cell has a visible frame:

```
<TABLE border="1">
```

Making this single change to our previous example changes the browser display as shown in Figure 3.11 (and the modified source file is 'example3–9.htm').

Now we can see that the Sydney phone number spans two cells, whereas the Cape Town number does not. Using the presentational 'frame' attribute is not the best approach, however. We will see how to manage table presentation using style sheets in the next chapter.

3.9 Forms

Forms are a very important part of any web application, because they allow the user to send information to an application running on the server. Much of the user interaction on the web is based on HTTP 'GET' requests, which enable a client to request data from a server. In contrast, forms enable an HTTP 'POST' request to be made, which sends data

FIGURE 3.11 The table with visible cell frames

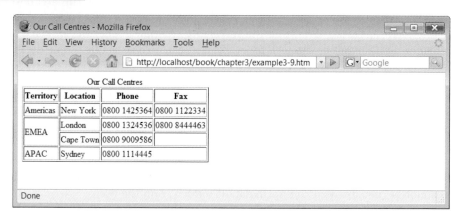

FIGURE 3.12 Forms are part of client pages and submit their content to server pages

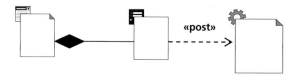

from a client to a server. As we saw in Chapter 2, a form is part of an HTML page, which submits its data to a server page (Figure 3.12).

Form elements

Forms are defined in HTML using the FORM element. Form attributes include the 'method' attribute, which defines the type of HTTP request that is to be used (usually 'post' for a form) and the 'action' attribute, which specifies a URI to identify which server-side component is to receive the data from the form. In this example, we assume that the server-side process is called 'insuranceQuote'. Programs that run on the server to process forms may be written using any of a number of server side technologies, including Java servlets or JavaServer Pages (JSPs), Active Server Pages (ASPs), Perl or PHP, among others. Of course in this book, we will be implementing these processes in PHP.

Here is a FORM element with an action and a method:

```
<FORM action="insuranceQuote" method="post" >
   ...components of the form
</FORM>
```

As with links, the URI used in the form does not have to be a complete URI if the page containing the form is from the same web application as the component that is receiving the form data.

The 'method' attribute of the form element specifies how the browser transfers HTML form data to a server program. The most common methods used with forms are 'post' and 'get', but 'post' is preferable. 'get' requests are the default type of HTTP request, but are mainly intended for getting data from the server, for example requesting an HTML page to be downloaded. Therefore although a 'get' request can involve sending some data to the server (e.g. the identity of the request page or the parameters for a search query), only a small amount of data needs to be sent to the server. Because of this, only a limited amount of data can be transferred to the server using this request type (240 characters on some web servers). There are also some security issues associated with 'get' requests, since all parameter data is attached to the URL. Consequently it is visible in the browser address bar, so the URL, including the parameter data, can be 'bookmarked' and used again.

In contrast, when using the 'post' method, an unlimited amount of data can be transferred, URLs cannot be 'bookmarked' and form data is hidden from the user.

NOTE	Although there is no specific limit on the size of the data that can be sent with a post request, servers may be configured to limit the actual amount of data that can be posted. This may be necessary to prevent *denial of service* attacks, where large amounts of data could be posted to a server to overwhelm its resources.

In addition to the 'get' and 'post' methods, there are several other lesser-used methods (mostly used by web browser software to obtain document information from the web server). These are 'head', 'delete', 'put', 'trace' and 'options'. These can occasionally be useful but are often not implemented by web applications, so attempting to use these methods may return HTTP response error number 501, the 'not implemented' error.

Input types

Inside the FORM element we define the components of the form. These components enable the user to input data, so include things such as text fields, radio buttons, check boxes and select lists. Components that enable input are known as *controls*. Many of these controls are specified using the empty INPUT element, with the specific type of component defined by the 'type' attribute. Another essential attribute is 'name', which is used to identify the source of the data entered by the user when it is sent to the server. For example, we might have a text field in a form that is used to enter a person's email address. The type of the input element would be 'text' and the name of the element might be 'email' (or something similar). This name can be used by the server-side application to retrieve whatever the user typed into that text field. This is how the element might be written:

```
<INPUT type="text" name="email">
```

There are other attributes that may also be used in the INPUT element. For example, there is a 'value' attribute that can be used to give a default value to an input type:

```
<INPUT type="text" name="email" value="email@address">
```

Another simple input type is 'password'. This is similar to a text field, but when characters are typed into the field they appear on the screen as some other character, such as an asterisk:

```
<INPUT type="password" name="pword">
```

Each control can have a text label associated with it, using the LABEL element. A label must be associated with a control, or group of controls, using the 'for' attribute, which must match the 'id' attribute of a control on the form. Therefore if we want to use the LABEL tag with a form control then the control will need an 'id' attribute as well as a name. Here, for example, is a label for the password input type with the id 'pword':

```
<LABEL for="pword">Password:</LABEL>
```

This would mean the element for the password input would need to include this id:

```
<INPUT type="password" name="pword" id="pword">
```

Associating a label with a control does not affect its position in the form; you have to organize that manually. However, it does have the effect that if you click on the label in the browser, the associated control immediately gets focus.

One essential component of any HTML form is an INPUT element of type 'submit'. This adds a button to the form that enables the form data to be sent in an HTTP request to the server. When the submit button is pressed, the 'action' attribute of the form is used to direct the HTTP request to the appropriate server-side resource. A form must have a 'submit' button in order to invoke its action, unless the HTTP request is managed by a client-side scripting language such as JavaScript, in which case the script may submit the form data.

Forms may also have a reset button, defined by an INPUT element with a type of 'reset'. Pressing the reset button returns the components in the form to their default values, though it is debatable whether reset buttons provide any real benefit from the users' perspective. In general, a reset button should only be used on a form if it has a useful and valid set of default values. For both submit and reset input types, the 'value' attribute can be used to provide a text label for the button.

Here is a very simple page with a login form that uses labels, text and password input types, and submit and reset buttons. Here we assume that there is a server-side component called 'login' to which the form submits its data. The form includes a table to help to organize the components into a neat layout.

```
<!DOCTYPE HTML PUBLIC "-//W3C//DTD HTML 4.01//EN"
"http://www.w3.org/TR/html4/strict.dtd">
<HTML>
  <HEAD>
    <TITLE>Customer Login</TITLE>
  </HEAD>
  <BODY>
    <!-- File: example3-10.htm -->
    <FORM action="login" method="post">
      <TABLE>
        <TR>
          <TD><LABEL for="loginid">Login Name:</LABEL></TD>
```

```
                          <TD><INPUT type="text" name="loginid" id="loginid"></TD>
                        </TR>
                        <TR>
                          <TD><LABEL for="pword">Password:</LABEL></TD>
                          <TD><INPUT type="password" name="pword" id="pword"></TD>
                        </TR>
                        <TR>
                          <TD></TD>
                          <TD>
                            <INPUT type="submit" value="Login">
                            <INPUT type="reset" value="Clear form">
                          </TD>
                        </TR>
                      </TABLE>
                    </FORM>
                  </BODY>
                </HTML>
```

Figure 3.13 shows how the form appears in Internet Explorer 7. Of course, pressing the 'Login' button simply gives an HTTP '404 not found' error, since we are not yet running anything on the server.

There are several other input types used in HTML forms. Two related types are checkboxes and radio buttons. The only difference between these is that checkboxes are always independent of any other component, whereas radio buttons can be grouped together so that only one radio button in a given group can be selected at any one time. A checkbox is defined by setting the INPUT element's 'type' attribute to 'checkbox'. Here we use a checkbox to indicate whether a user wishes to be added to a mailing list. A checkbox effectively represents a Boolean value; it is either checked (true) or not (false).

```
<INPUT type="checkbox" name="mailinglist">
```

A check box is unchecked by default. However we can change this by setting the value of the 'checked' attribute to 'checked'.

FIGURE 3.13　A form displayed in Internet Explorer 7

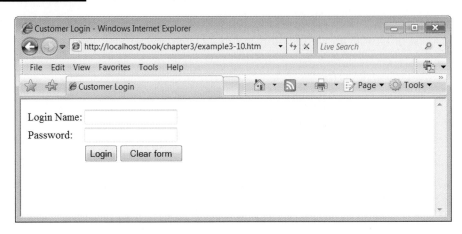

```
<INPUT type="checkbox" name="mailinglist" checked="checked">
```

Radio buttons are similar to checkboxes, in the sense that they may either be selected or not, but can be grouped together by having a common value for the 'name' attribute. In the next example, we use radio buttons to ask the user if they want to use our web site as a guest, set up a new account or log in using an existing account. Because the name for all three radio buttons is 'status', they will be treated as a group so that only one of these buttons can be selected at any one time. The 'value' attribute defines the value that will be sent to the server if that particular radio button is selected when the form is submitted. By default, the 'login' radio button is be selected because its 'checked' attribute has been set to 'checked'. Here are the INPUT and LABEL elements used for the three radio buttons:

```
<INPUT TYPE="radio" name="status" id="guest" value="guest">
<LABEL for="guest">Access the site as a guest</LABEL>
<INPUT TYPE="radio" name="status" id="new" value="new">
<LABEL for="new">Set up a new user account</LABEL>
<INPUT TYPE="radio" name="status" id="login" value="login"
checked="checked">
<LABEL for="login">Login using an existing account</LABEL>
```

NOTE Since the 'id' attribute for a radio button must have a unique value in a page it cannot have the same value as the 'name' attribute. The approach used here is to give the 'id' and 'value' attributes the same values.

Here is a page that includes our example of radio buttons and a check box. Both the submit and reset buttons have default values for their 'value' attributes, which not surprisingly are 'Submit' and 'Reset'. In this example, we have omitted the 'value' attribute for the reset button, so its label will be the default ('Reset').

```
<!DOCTYPE HTML PUBLIC "-//W3C//DTD HTML 4.01//EN"
"http://www.w3.org/TR/html4/strict.dtd">
<HTML>
  <HEAD>
    <TITLE>Site Access</TITLE>
  </HEAD>
  <BODY>
    <!-- File: example3-11.htm -->
    <FORM action="siteaccess" method="post">
      <TABLE>
        <TR>
          <TD colspan="2">
            Welcome to our site. How would you like to continue?
          </TD>
        </TR>
      </TABLE>
    </FORM>
  </BODY>
</HTML>
```

```
<TR>
  <TD>
    <INPUT TYPE="radio" name="status" id="guest" value="guest">
  </TD>
  <TD><LABEL for="guest">Access the site as a guest</LABEL></TD>
</TR>
<TR>
  <TD><INPUT TYPE="radio" name="status" id="new"
  value="new"></TD>
  <TD><LABEL for="new">Set up a new user account</LABEL></TD>
</TR>
<TR>
  <TD>
    <INPUT TYPE="radio" name="status" id="login" value="login"
    checked="checked">
  </TD>
  <TD>
    <LABEL for="login">Login using an existing account</LABEL>
  </TD>
</TR>
<TR>
  <TD colspan="2">
    <LABEL for="mailinglist">Please check this box if you would
    like to be added to our mailing list</LABEL>
  </TD>
  <TD>
    <INPUT type="checkbox" name="mailinglist"
    id="mailinglist" checked="checked">
  </TD>
</TR>
<TR>
  <TD></TD>
  <TD>
    <INPUT type="submit" value="Continue">
    <INPUT type="reset">
  </TD>
</TR>
</TABLE>
</FORM>
</BODY>
</HTML>
```

Figure 3.14 shows the page with radio buttons and a checkbox displayed in Opera 9.

Text areas

Text areas, which allow the input of multiple lines of text, do not use the INPUT element but are defined by a TEXTAREA element. This element includes optional attributes to set the number of rows and columns of text (the 'rows' and 'cols' attributes). The text typed into a TEXTAREA automatically wraps at the end of a line. If any text is added to the body of the element, then it appears inside the text area, as in this example

```
<TEXTAREA name="description" rows="5" cols="30">
  Describe your insurance claim here
</TEXTAREA>
```

Figure 3.15 shows the TEXTAREA with its default text being displayed.

Select lists

Select lists can be used to choose one or more options from a list. The list can be drop down, scrollable or just a list of items, and can optionally enable multiple items to be selected. A select list comprises a SELECT element and one or more nested OPTION elements. Each OPTION has a 'value' attribute that specifies which value is sent to the server if that option is selected when the form is submitted. The body of the OPTION element contains the text that is used when displaying that option in the list. In this example, a select list is used to choose an amount of insurance cover. The default format for this will be a drop-down list.

FIGURE 3.14   A form with radio buttons and a checkbox

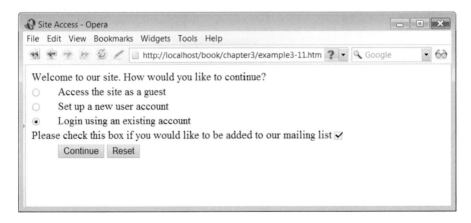

FIGURE 3.15   A TEXTAREA component with some default text

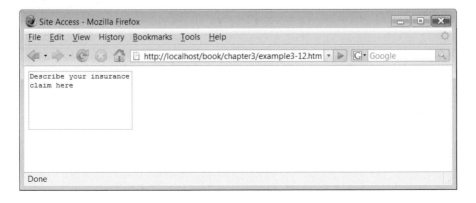

```
<SELECT name="cover">
<OPTION value="10000">10,000</OPTION>
<OPTION value="20000">20,000</OPTION>
<OPTION value="30000">30,000</OPTION>
<OPTION value="50000">50,000</OPTION>
<OPTION value="100000">100,000</OPTION>
</SELECT>
```

To create a scrolling or complete list rather than a drop-down, we can use the 'size' attribute of the SELECT element. If we set the size to '1', this is the default and creates a drop-down list. Anything larger will create a list with a scroll bar (if the size is less than the total number of options) or a simple list, if the size is greater than or equal to the number of options. In our example, this opening tag would create a list with a scroll bar:

```
<SELECT name="cover" size="3">
```

And this would create a non-scrolling list because there are five options:

```
<SELECT name="cover" size="5">
```

Figure 3.16 shows how the select list would appear using the three size settings.

3

FIGURE 3.16   A SELECT component controlled by the value of the 'size' attribute

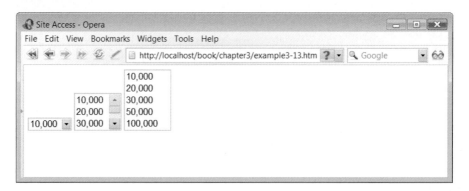

Exercises

In this series of exercises, we develop some pages for the home insurance web site. At this stage, we are only looking at static pages that might be used to introduce and explain the site, not the web application processes making claims or buying insurance.

3.1 Using HTML, implement the content and structure of the home page from the design you created at the end of Chapter 2.

3.2 Using HTML, implement an 'about us' page for the web site that uses the three-region layout you designed at the end of Chapter 2. Use a table to implement this layout (we will see how to do this layout with a style sheet in Chapter 4). You will need a reasonable amount of content on this page, which should include different types of information such as 'our history', 'our mission', 'our people, etc.

3.3 Create a company logo using a suitable software package and use it in your three-region layout (you may also wish to include images from other sources).

3.4 Figure 3.17 shows an HTML form from the home insurance application, to gather data about contents insurance. Write an HTML page that creates a form similar to this one.

FIGURE 3.17   An HTML form organized using a table

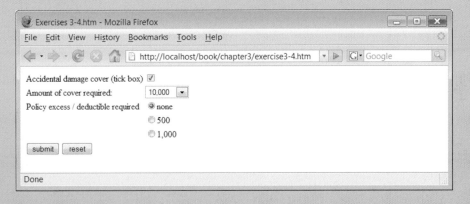

SUMMARY

We began this chapter by introducing SGML, the mark-up language from which HTML and many other mark-up languages have evolved. We followed the evolution of HTML through to version 4, and then looked at some of the most important elements used for structuring HTML documents, including headings, lists, tables and forms. Table 3.2 provides a summary of the HTML elements introduced in this chapter, while Table 3.3 summarizes the new terms that were also introduced.

TABLE 3.2	HTML elements introduced in this chapter

Element	Meaning
HTML	The root element that surrounds the whole document
HEAD	Document header information
TITLE	The text that appears in the browser's title bar
BODY	The body content of the page displayed in the browser
P	Paragraph
HI, H2 H3, H4, H5 and H6	Levels of heading
BR	Line break
HR	Horizontal rule
CITE	Citation
BLOCKQUOTE	Block quotation
EM	Emphasis
STRONG	Strong emphasis
SUB	Subscript
SUP	Superscript
UL	Unordered list
LI	List item
OL	Ordered list
DL	Definition list
DT	Definition list term
DD	Definition list definition
IMG	Image
A	Anchor
TABLE	Table
CAPTION	Table caption
TR	Table row
TH	Table heading
TD	Table data
FORM	Form
INPUT	Form component for inputting data
LABEL	Text label for a form component
TEXTAREA	Multi-line text entry box
SELECT	Select list
OPTION	An option in a select list
& ;	Character reference (start and end characters)
<!-- -->	Comment text (start and end characters)

TABLE 3.3	Terms introduced in this chapter

Acronym term	Meaning
ANSI	American National Standard Institute
GML	Goldfarb, Mosher, Lorie
ISO	International Standards Organisation
MIME	Multipurpose Internet Mail Extension
SGML	Standard Generalized Markup Language

References and further reading

Connolly, D. (1995). *HTML 2.0 Materials*. W3C. http://www.w3.org/MarkUp/html-spec/

Goldfarb, C. (1996). *The Roots of SGML – A personal recollection*. http://www.sgmlsource.com/history/roots.htm

Korpela, J. (2002). *Empty Elements in SGML, HTML, XML, and XHTML*. http://www.cs.tut.fi/~jkorpela/html/empty.html

Raggett, D., Le Hors, A. and Jacobs, I. (1999). *HTML 4.01 specification*. http://www.w3.org/TR/html401/

3

CHAPTER 4

Styling in the Presentation Layer: Cascading Style Sheets (CSS)

LEARNING OBJECTIVES

- **To be able to apply in-line styles to HTML elements**

- **To be able style individual HTML pages using cascading style sheets (CSS) in the document head**

- **To be able to create external CSS files and link them to multiple HTML pages**

- **To be able to apply style sheet cascades to individual documents**

- **To be able to use CSS to control the layout of a web page**

INTRODUCTION

In Chapter 3 we concentrated on looking at some of the important structural elements in HTML. HTML also provides a range of elements and attributes that support the presentation of a document, including text styles and fonts, foreground and background colours, content alignment, and list and table formatting. Using this type of mark-up, however, mixes presentation with structure and content, making it hard to separately develop and maintain the presentation layer of a web application. A much better approach is to use cascading style sheets (CSS) to apply presentational formatting independent of the HTML mark-up. In this chapter, we explore the syntax and use of cascading style sheets and see how they can be applied to HTML pages.

4.1 Separating out presentation

HTML 4.0 was the first version of HTML that explicitly attempted to separate out structure from presentation. Although the LINK element, used for attaching a separate style sheet to an HTML document, had been available since early versions of HTML, it was rarely used. In this section, we see how HTML developed into a mark-up language that included presentational tags, explore the development of separate style sheets and see how CSS can be used to separate out the presentation of an HTML document from its content and structure.

In Chapter 3 we looked at HTML syntax and saw how HTML is used to specify the content and structure of a web page. Structural elements of HTML pages include elements such as paragraphs, headings and tables. Although HTML also has presentational elements and attributes, it is preferable that any specification of style (colours, font sizes, etc.) is done separately by using a style sheet language. Why, then, does HTML have presentational tags if we are not supposed to use them? This is in fact a consequence of the way that web technologies have evolved, through a combination of influential individuals, browser vendors and standards bodies. These various influences meant that the separation of structure and content for presentation using style sheets was an approach that developed rather erratically. In the early days of HTML, there was some debate about how HTML should be styled, and whether it should be based on browser configuration or some other mechanism. Although it was always recognized that it would be good practice to separate the content of a page from the specification of its presentation, there was no common agreement on how this should be done. There was also some debate as to who should have control over the appearance of a document, the author, the viewer, or a combination of both. Various early browsers had their own ways of applying style sheets to manage the appearance of HTML documents, but this was from the perspective of controlling the way that documents were configured in a given browser. It did not enable the author of an HTML page to specify how it should be presented. To address this issue, HTML tags that related to presentational aspects began to be supported by browsers. For example, the first version of Netscape Navigator in 1994 supported the CENTER element. Since the early HTML specifications were simply a drawing together of syntax that was already being used by the leading browsers, the introduction of such tags led to their subsequent inclusion in the standard HTML specification. However, around the same time that Netscape Navigator was introducing the first presentational HTML tags, Häkon Lie at CERN published the first proposal for what he called 'cascading HTML style sheets' (Lie and Bos 1999). The concept of the cascade was that an HTML document could be presented using an ordered list of style sheets, so that there might be a number of different style sheets applied one after the other to a given HTML document, each providing more specialized formatting. Lie's proposal contained the idea of the LINK element in an HTML document that provides the URL of a separate style sheet. The original version of this proposal looked like this:

```
<LINK REL="style" HREF="http://NYT.com/style">
```

As the idea of style sheets was debated by the web technology community it became clear that they need be applicable not only to HTML but to other types of document as well. The reference to HTML was dropped and they were renamed simply Cascading Style Sheets (CSS). Although there were alternative proposals for style sheet technologies made around that time, CSS became the clear leader after the formation of the World Wide Web Consortium in 1995, which held an international workshop on CSS. This was followed in 1996 by the first W3C recommendation, CSS level 1, with support from the leading browsers of the time, Microsoft Internet Explorer and Netscape Navigator, though the implementations in both at that stage were limited, neither of them fully implementing the level 1 specification. The next version, CSS level 2, was published in 1998 and CSS level 3 is an ongoing recommendation.

We have talked about the need to separate structure and content from presentation, but why is this so important? Specifying the appearance of the pages in a web site is not only an issue for graphic designers, but is also a management problem. It is important to maintain a uniform appearance across the pages of a web site, while indicating the differences between the various concerns of the site in an organized way. For example, different colour schemes might be used in different parts of a web site. An associated issue is that it should be possible to change the appearance of a web site consistently across all pages without having to undertake a major maintenance exercise.

How, then, does CSS help us to manage the presentation of a web application in a way that enables us to apply a consistent look and feel, with customisation for different parts of our web site, and make it easy to change? CSS does this by providing the ability to specify style information in-line, internal to a document or externally. This means that styles can be applied at different levels of granularity: across the whole web site, to a specific page, or to a specific element. CSS also provides the ability to cascade a series of style sheets to apply to a single document, enabling a combination of styles to be blended together.

4.2 CSS syntax

CSS syntax can vary slightly, depending on where it is being used. In-line styles, internal style sheets and external style sheets each involve a particular type of syntax, though all are similar.

The simplest way to use CSS is with inline styles, which is where styles are added directly to HTML elements using the 'style' attribute. The value of this attribute consists of two parts separated by a colon. The first part is the style property that is being applied, the second the actual value of that property. For example, one of the style properties is 'color' (the foreground, text, colour) and one of the possible values for that property is 'blue'. Here, we set the style of an H1 element to be the colour 'blue'.

```
<H1 style="color: blue">Heading</H1>
```

 NOTE The space after the colon is used here to aid readability, it is not required.

The colour value 'blue' is one of the 16 colour names specified in the W3C HTML 4.0 standard: aqua, black, blue, fuchsia, gray, green, lime, maroon, navy, olive, purple, red, silver, teal, white, yellow.

A large number of other colour names are also recognized by many browsers and, in addition to the named colours, you can 'mix' your own using red, green, blue (RGB) values in this property format:

```
color: rgb(r, g, b)
```

In this format, each of the three colour values is specified by an integer in the range 0 to 255, each of which represents the intensity of the red, green, or blue component of the desired colour. Using the maximum values for all three, 'color: rgb(255,255,255)' gives white, while zero values for all three, 'color: rgb(0,0,0)' gives black.

Style sheets can also be used to set the background colour, using the 'background-color' property. In this example we set the text colour to white and the background colour to black. If we are applying multiple styles to a single element, the styles are separated by semicolons, as we can see here:

```
<H2 style="color: white; background-color: black">Sub heading</H2>
```

If we use in-line styles in an HTML document, we should indicate to the browser which stylesheet language we are using. Although the default is CSS, the specification states that 'Documents that include elements that set the style attribute but which don't define a default style sheet language are incorrect.' (Raggett *et al.* 1999)

Therefore we should add the following META element to the HEAD element, declaring 'text/css' as the style type:

```
<META http-equiv="Content-Style-Type" content="text/css">
```

 NOTE There are many possible attributes that can be used with the META element, which provides various types of information about the document that includes it. A single HEAD element can contain multiple META elements.

In this example we add the necessary META tag and apply in-line styles to an H1 element and two H2 elements. The second H2 style demonstrates the RGB colour syntax to specify white text on a black background, though the effect is exactly that same as the first H2 element style, which uses the standard colour names to achieve the same effect. The style elements appear in bold type:

```
<!DOCTYPE HTML PUBLIC "-//W3C//DTD HTML 4.01//EN"
"http://www.w3.org/TR/html4/strict.dtd">
<HTML>
   <HEAD>
      <META http-equiv="Content-Style-Type" content="text/css">
      <TITLE>Our Insurance Cover</TITLE>
   </HEAD>
   <BODY>
   <!-- File: example4-1.htm -->
<H1 style="color: blue">
   We provide the following types of insurance</H1>
<H2 style="color: white; background-color: black">
   Buildings Cover</H2>
      <P>You may think you're "safe as houses" but you'd be surprised how many
things can damage the building you live in. Fires, earthquakes, subsidence, runaway
trucks, cricket balls through windows or the occasional meteor. Best to be
covered!
```

```
      </P>
   <H2 style="color: rgb(255,255,255); background-color: rgb(0,0,0)">
      Contents Cover</H2>
      <P>You may not realise just how much the stuff you have would cost to replace.
If the burglars move in while you're on holiday, could you afford to replace the
TV, the stereo, the chairs, the cupboards, the crockery, etc?
      </P>
      <P>Not only that, our contents cover means that if you have your bike stolen,
drop the vase your mother-in-law gave you as a wedding present, lose your camera,
leave your glasses on the train or have your mobile phone stolen, you'll be fully
compensated.
      </P>
   </BODY>
</HTML>
```

Figure 4.1 shows how the styled page appears in Internet Explorer 7.

| NOTE | In the early days of web page design, a 216-colour 'browser-safe palette' was proposed that indicated which combinations of colours would work best across multiple browsers in a world where many computers supported only 8-bit colour (256 colours). The 'safe' palette eliminated the 40 colours that were most likely to vary on different displays. However in the vast majority of cases this limitation no longer applies so the safe palette is largely redundant (Weinman, 2007). |

FIGURE 4.1   In-line styles applied to an HTML document

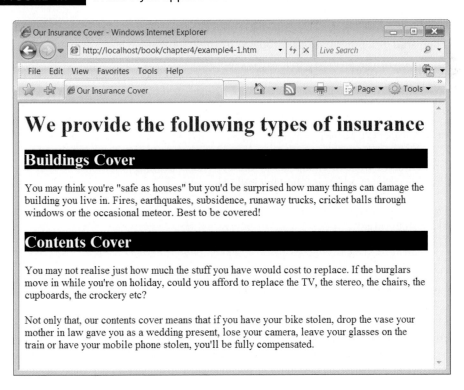

4.3 Style sheets

Using only in-line styles inside tags has no real benefit over using presentation elements and attributes from standard HTML. Although we are using a different syntax, we do not actually separate out structure and content from presentation, and do not gain any of the benefits of applying a generic style to a document. Styles only become useful when they are also applied to a whole document, so that we can, for example, apply a standard style to *all* H1 elements in a document rather than doing this on an individual basis. In this context, in-line styles are useful for fine-tuning the presentation but should not be used to style a whole document. Applying styles more generally is done using style sheets, either internal to the HTML page or as external documents, linked to the HTML page using the LINK element. First, we look at how to include a style sheet inside an HTML page.

Internal style sheets

Internal style sheets are those that are included in the HEAD element of an HTML document using the STYLE element. This type of style sheet applies only to that document. For CSS, the value of the STYLE element's 'type' attribute is set to 'text/css', as it is when using the META element for in-line styles.

```
<STYLE type="text/css">
    ...styles defined here
</STYLE>
```

The syntax for defining styles in a STYLE element is similar to the inline style, except that we must also specify to which element types we are applying styles. Each component of a style sheet is made up of three parts:

- The name of an HTML element type
- The name of a presentational property of that element
- The value of the property that is to be applied.

The property and its value appear inside braces (separated by a colon, as they are for inline styles):

```
element {property: value}
```

For example, if we want to change all of the H1 (main heading) elements so that they are styled in blue, we can add the following style element:

```
<STYLE type="text/css">
  h1 {color: blue}
</STYLE>
```

Note that we will be using lower case for element names in our CSS because we will be applying them to XHTML pages later. In XHTML, element names must be in lower case. For HTML, which is not case-sensitive, the case used in the style sheet does not matter.

The difference between our in-line example and this style is that this one will apply to all 'h1' elements in the page that is being formatted. Sometimes we will want to apply more than one style to a particular element type, in which case we can separate the different styles using semicolons. For example, if we want to make our main headings both blue and centred, we could use the following style (with 'text-align' the additional property and 'center' the chosen value):

```
<STYLE type="text/css">
  h1 {color: blue; text-align: center}
</STYLE>
```

 NOTE | The other possible values for the 'text-align' property are 'left', 'right' and 'justify'.

Grouping styles

As well as applying multiple styles to a single element type, we might want to apply the same style(s) to more than one type of element. Here, for example, we use the centred, blue style for both main headings (h1) and subheadings (h2) by putting them together in a comma-separated list:

```
<STYLE type="text/css">
  h1,h2 {color: blue; text-align: center}
</STYLE>
```

Line feeds and spacing can be used to make style sheets more readable, without having an effect on their processing, as in this example:

```
<STYLE type="text/css">
h1,h2
{
    color: blue;
    text-align: center
}
</STYLE>
```

Further text formatting styles

So far we have seen styles that can be applied to text that affect the color and alignment. Other CSS text formatting styles include 'font-style', 'font-weight', 'font-size' and 'font-family'. A common value to use with the 'font-style' property is 'italic', while a common value of the 'font-weight' property is 'bold'. The value of the 'font-family' property can be one of many font names, but you are dependent on the browser having that font family available, so using unusual font families is not a good idea if you want your pages to look consistent across a wide range of browsers. There are five generic font families that should be supported by any browser: 'serif', 'sans-serif' 'cursive', 'fantasy' and 'monospace'. The browser should provide a font mapping for all of these font families, but the actual mapping is browser-specific. We can see this from Figure 4.2, which shows the same page of text using the five generic font families displayed in three browsers. The differences in appearance are because the generic font families have been mapped to different actual fonts by the different browsers.

Since using the generic font families is somewhat unpredictable in terms of the specific font being used, we may prefer to specify actual font names. Some widely supported fonts include 'Times New Roman' (a serif font), 'Arial' (a sans-serif font) and 'Courier' (a mono-spaced font). If the name of a font family contains spaces then it should be put inside quotes or apostrophes, for example:

```
font-family: 'Times New Roman'
```

Figure 4.3 shows some text using these three fonts in the three browsers. Note how they all look very similar.

FIGURE 4.2   The five generic font families displayed by a) Mozilla Firefox 2, b) Opera 9 and c) Internet Explorer 7

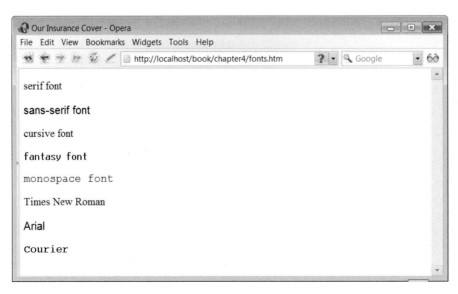

FIGURE 4.2 Continued

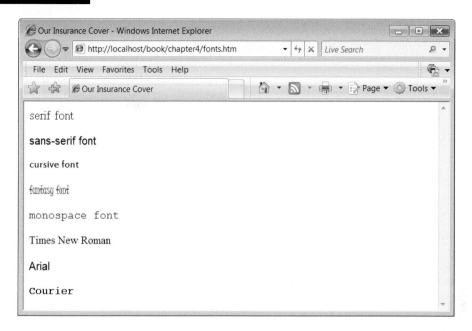

FIGURE 4.3 The Times New Roman, Arial and Courier fonts displayed by a) Mozilla Firefox 2, b) Opera 9 and c) Internet Explorer 7

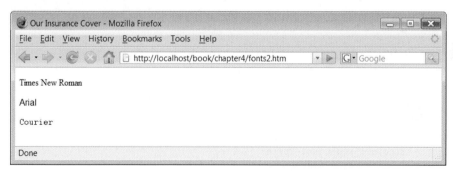

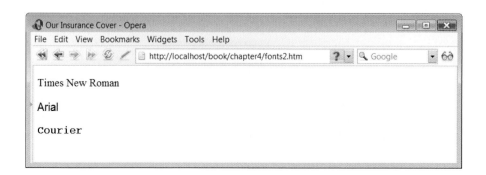

FIGURE 4.3   Continued

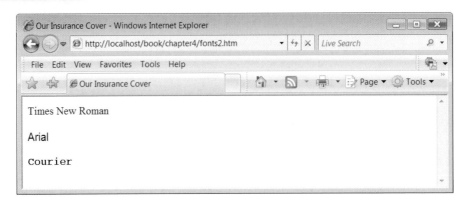

Applying multiple styles with the STYLE element

The body of the STYLE element can contain as many style entries as is required for the HTML document. In the following example, we apply different styles to all H1, H2 and P elements. The H1 element is formatted as we have seen in a previous example (blue, centered). The H2 element is formatted using the 'red' value for the 'color' property, and also uses the 'font-style' property, setting its value to 'italic'. Finally, the paragraph (P) elements are styled using the 'font-family' property and the 'sans-serif' value. Depending on the browser's built-in style, this may make the paragraphs appear in a different font from the headings.

The important point to note here is that defining the styles in one place, rather than attaching them to specific HTML elements, means that each style only has to be defined once for each element type. In this example we define the paragraph style once, but it is used three times. The H2 style is defined once, but it is used twice.

```
<!DOCTYPE HTML PUBLIC "-//W3C//DTD HTML 4.01//EN"
"http://www.w3.org/TR/html4/strict.dtd">
<HTML>
  <HEAD>
    <STYLE type="text/css">
      h1{color: blue; text-align: center}
      h2{color: red; font-style: italic}
      p{font-family: sans-serif}
    </STYLE>
    <TITLE>Our Insurance Cover</TITLE>
  </HEAD>
<BODY
<!-- File: example4-2.htm -->
    <H1>We provide the following types of insurance</H1>
    <H2>Buildings Cover</H2>
    <P>You may think you're "safe as houses" but you'd be surprised how many
things can damage the building you live in. Fires, earthquakes, subsidence, runaway
trucks, cricket balls through windows or the occasional meteor. Best to be covered!
    </P>
    <H2>Contents Cover</H2>
```

```
        <P>You may not realise just how much the stuff you have would cost to replace.
If the burglars move in while you're on holiday, could you afford to replace the
TV, the stereo, the chairs, the cupboards, the crockery, etc?
        </P>
        <P>Not only that, our contents cover means that if you have your bike stolen,
drop the vase your mother-in-law gave you as a wedding present, lose your camera,
leave your glasses on the train or have your mobile phone stolen, you'll be fully
compensated.
        </P>
    </BODY>
</HTML>
```

Figure 4.4 shows how the page looks in Internet Explorer 7.

Setting the font size

The size of the font can be set using a number of different types of measurement, including absolute measures in inches, centimetres, millimetres, points or picas. However, setting sizes to specific measurements is not very flexible across different browser contexts, and should only be used in specialized applications where the target client device is known. This is not the case for most web applications, so the better approach is to use a relative method of sizing text. Even here, there is more than one option: we can use a percentage measure (%), a pixel measure (px), the 'x height' of the font (x) or 'em'

4

FIGURE 4.4   Styles applied to multiple headings and paragraphs

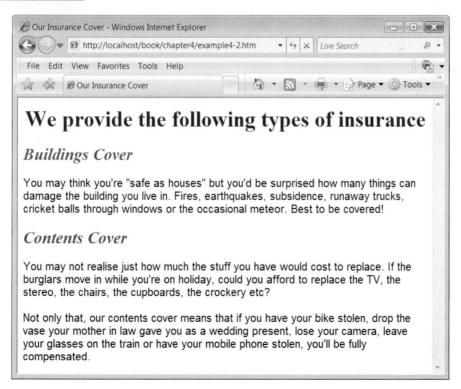

which relates to the both the width and height of the font. Apart from pixels, all of these work in a way that is relative to the context within which an element is used. If we apply a relative size to an element of a specific type (for example, a paragraph element), then the actual size is based on the one that would normally be applied. In other words, setting a paragraph's font to be 1.5em would make it half as big again as the normal font size for that paragraph:

```
<P style="font-size: 1.5em">
```

It is also possible to use more generic descriptions of text size, including 'large', 'small', 'x-large' (extra large) and 'x-small' (extra small), for example:

```
<P style="font-size: large">
```

External style sheets

Using an internal style sheet has the advantage that we only need to define a style for each type of element once, rather than every time it appears, as we would have to do if we were using in-line styles. However, the drawback of internal style sheets is that the styles we define can only be used in the current HTML document. It is likely that we would want to apply the same styles right across our web application, so that all of our pages have a consistent look and feel. If, for example we want all our major headings on all pages to be blue and center-aligned, we would have to repeat this style in an internal style sheet for every single page. Worse, if we decided to change the look and feel so that all major headings were, for example, to be made left-aligned, we would have to change the internal style sheet on every page. Fortunately, we can specify an external stylesheet in a separate document and use the LINK element (in the HTML document's HEAD element) to apply the required stylesheet. The name and location of the stylesheet is specified by the 'href' attribute, and the relationship between the HTML page and the stylesheet by the 'rel' attribute. The value of the 'rel' attribute should be set to 'stylesheet'.

 NOTE Another possible value for the 'rel' attribute is 'alternate stylesheet', where the browser may enable switching between different stylesheets, provided more than one stylesheet LINK element is include in the HEAD element. However this option is poorly supported by current browsers.

There is also a 'type' attribute that indicates the type of the linked document. As with the internal style sheet, the value of the 'type' attribute for a stylesheet is 'text/css'. There are some other attributes that may be used in the LINK element but we do not need to be concerned with them here. Taking our previous internal style sheet example, the content of the STYLE element can be extracted into a separate CSS file, which would simply list the styles (STYLE tags are not required in an external style sheet). Here is our external CSS file, which we will call 'webhomecover.css':

```
h1{color: blue; text-align: center}
h2{color: red; font-style: italic}
p{font-family: sans-serif}
```

To apply this style sheet to an HTML page, we need to add the appropriate LINK element to the page's HEAD element. This LINK example specifies the 'webhomecover. css' file:

```
<LINK href="webhomecover.css" rel="stylesheet" type="text/css">
```

This example assumes that the CSS file is in the same folder (either locally or on the web server) as the HTML file. Otherwise the value of the 'href' attribute could be written to include a directory pathway or a full URL, depending on the circumstances.

Here is our previous example HTML page but using an external style sheet instead of an internal one.

```
<!DOCTYPE HTML PUBLIC "-//W3C//DTD HTML 4.01//EN"
"http://www.w3.org/TR/html4/strict.dtd">
<HTML>
  <HEAD>
    <LINK href="webhomecover.css" rel="stylesheet" type="text/css">
    <TITLE>Our Insurance Cover</TITLE>
  </HEAD>
  <BODY>
      <!-- File: example4-3.htm -->
    <H1>We provide the following types of insurance</H1>
    <H2>Buildings Cover</H2>
    <P>You may think you're "safe as houses" but you'd be surprised how many
things can damage the building you live in. Fires, earthquakes, subsidence, runaway
trucks, cricket balls through windows or the occasional meteor. Best to be covered!
    </P>
    <H2>Contents Cover</H2>
    <P>You may not realise just how much the stuff you have would cost to replace.
If the burglars move in while you're on holiday, could you afford to replace the
TV, the stereo, the chairs, the cupboards, the crockery, etc?
    </P>
    <P>Not only that, our contents cover means that if you have your bike stolen,
drop the vase your mother-in-law gave you as a wedding present, lose your camera, leave
your glasses on the train or have your mobile phone stolen, you'll be fully compensated.
    </P>
  </BODY>
</HTML>
```

Once we have a separate style sheet, we can use it with multiple HTML pages. Here, we apply the same style sheet to a different page:

```
<!DOCTYPE HTML PUBLIC "-//W3C//DTD HTML 4.01//EN"
"http://www.w3.org/TR/html4/strict.dtd">
<HTML>
  <HEAD>
    <LINK href="webhomecover.css" rel="stylesheet" type="text/css">
    <TITLE>Our Promise to You</TITLE>
  </HEAD>
  <BODY>
```

4

```
<!-- File: example4-4.htm -->
<H1>Our Promise to You</H1>
<H2>No Unreasonable Exclusions</H2>
<P>
Many insurance companies include many exclusions in their policies, making it
difficult to claim for events such as 'acts of God', terrorism or subsidence. We
have the smallest set of exclusions of any fictional insurance company.
</P>
<H2>Rapid Response</H2>
<P>
If you make a claim, we promise to respond to you within 24 hours, either by
settling immediately or putting you in contact with one of our insurance assessors.
</P>
<H2>Low, Low, Rates</H2>
<P>
We constantly monitor our prices against our competitors and guarantee that we
provide the best-value insurance that you can't actually buy.
</P>
</BODY>
</HTML>
```

Figure 4.5 shows that the same styles have been applied as appear in Figure 4.4.

FIGURE 4.5   Reusing the same styles in another page

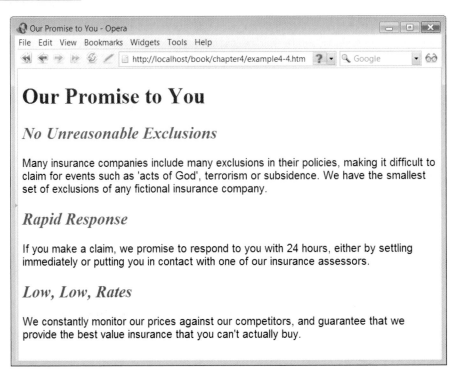

4.4 Applying styles with 'class' and 'id' attributes

So far we have looked at how to apply styles to specific HTML elements, such as H1, H2 and P. In many cases this is useful, but there are occasions when we want to:

- Apply the same style to more than one type of HTML element.
- Apply a style to some, but not all, instances of a particular HTML element.
- Apply a style to one specific instance of an element.

To do this we need some way of labelling parts of our HTML so that we can apply styles to elements that are identified by these labels. We can do this in two ways:

- We can use the 'class' attribute. This enables us to group a number of elements as belonging to a single class. Then we can apply a style to all members of the class.
- We can use the 'id' attribute. This can be used to give an element a unique id. This id can be used to apply a style that is not used anywhere else in the document.

Using the 'class' attribute

The class attribute can be applied to many elements. In addition, a given element can belong to more than one class. The class attribute is very useful as a way of applying styles across a range of different elements. For example, let us assume that we want both major headings (H1) and subheadings (H2) to be centred. We could, of course, apply the same style separately to both H1 and H2 elements in the style sheet. However a more flexible and maintainable approach is to use a class attribute. The first step is to identify both H1 and H2 elements as belonging to the same class. The name of a class is decided by the author of the page. In the next example we apply the class name 'heading' to all instances of both H1 and H2 elements.

```
<!DOCTYPE HTML PUBLIC "-//W3C//DTD HTML 4.01//EN"
"http://www.w3.org/TR/html4/strict.dtd">
<HTML>
  <HEAD>
    <LINK href="webhomecover.css" rel="stylesheet" type="text/css">
    <TITLE>Our Insurance Cover</TITLE>
  </HEAD>
  <BODY>
    <!-- File: example4-5.htm -->
    <H1 class="heading">We provide the following types of insurance</H1>
    <H2 class="heading">Buildings Cover</H2>
    <P>You may think you're "safe as houses" but you'd be surprised how many
things can damage the building you live in. Fires, earthquakes, subsidence, run-
away trucks, cricket balls through windows or the occasional meteor. Best to be
covered!
    </P>
    <H2 class="heading">Contents Cover</H2>
    <P>You may not realise just how much the stuff you have would cost to replace.
If the burglars move in while you're on holiday, could you afford to replace the
TV, the stereo, the chairs, the cupboards, the crockery, etc?
    </P>
```

```
      <P>Not only that, our contents cover means that if you have your bike stolen,
   drop the vase your mother-in-law gave you as a wedding present, lose your camera,
   leave your glasses on the train or have your mobile phone stolen, you'll be fully
   compensated.
      </P>
    </BODY>
  </HTML>
```

We also need to apply a style to 'heading' elements in the style sheet. To do this we simply precede the class name with a period and specify the style for that class. In this example, we centre all members of the 'heading' class:

```
h1{color: blue}
h2{color: red; font-style: italic}
p{font-family: sans-serif}
.heading{text-align: center}
```

Now, any elements that belong to the 'heading' class will be centre-aligned, regardless of which HTML elements the class is applied to.

Applying class styles to a subset of elements

In the previous example, we used the class attribute to apply a style to multiple different elements. Another way of using the class attribute is to apply a style to a subset of elements of a specific type. For example, we could apply a special style to some subheadings but not others. In this example, we change the style sheet so that some paragraphs are emphasized while others are not. We do this by putting a HTML element name in front of the class name, like this:

```
elementname.classname {style}
```

To change 'emphasis' paragraphs, we add 'p.emphasis' to the style sheet:

```
h1{color: blue}
h2{color: red; font-style: italic}
p{font-family: sans-serif}
.heading{text-align: center}
p.emphasis{font-weight: bold}
```

Now, all paragraphs will be in sans-serif font, but only those marked as belonging to the 'emphasis' class will be displayed in bold font:

In the following example we make two of the paragraphs belong to the 'emphasis' class:

```
<!DOCTYPE HTML PUBLIC "-//W3C//DTD HTML 4.01//EN"
"http://www.w3.org/TR/html4/strict.dtd">
<HTML>
  <HEAD>
    <LINK href="webhomecover.css" rel="stylesheet" type="text/css">
    <TITLE>Our Insurance Cover</TITLE>
  </HEAD>
```

```
<BODY>
    <!-- File: example4-6.htm -->
    <H1 class="heading">We provide the following types of insurance</H1>
    <H2 class="heading">Buildings Cover</H2>
    <P>You may think you're "safe as houses" but you'd be surprised how many
things can damage the building you live in. Fires, earthquakes, subsidence, runaway
trucks, cricket balls through windows or the occasional meteor.</P>
    <P class="emphasis">Best to be covered!</P>
    </P>
    <H2 class="heading">Contents Cover</H2>
    <P>You may not realise just how much the stuff you have would cost to replace.
If the burglars move in while you're on holiday, could you afford to replace the
TV, the stereo, the chairs, the cupboards, the crockery, etc?
    </P>
    <P class="emphasis">
Not only that, our contents cover means that if you have your bike stolen, drop
the vase your mother-in-law gave you as a wedding present, lose your camera, leave
your glasses on the train or have your mobile phone stolen, you'll be fully
compensated.
    </P>
    </BODY>
</HTML>
```

Figure 4.6 shows the page displayed in Internet Explorer. Note the second and fourth paragraphs are in bold font.

FIGURE 4.6   Applying styles to paragraphs using 'class' attributes

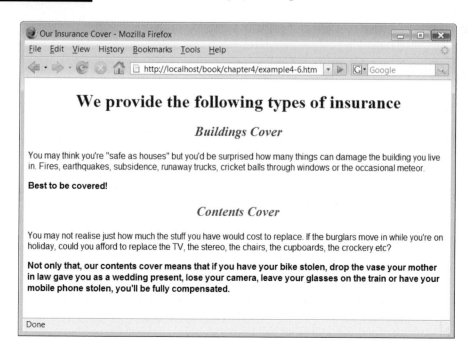

Element id attributes

Sometimes we may want to apply a style to one specific element, and no other. In this case, the element needs a unique identifier that will make it different from every other element in the document. Since the 'class' attribute can be applied to multiple elements, it cannot be used to uniquely identify a specific element. Instead, we use the 'id' attribute to identify a unique instance of an element within the document, such as a particular paragraph or heading. Here, we apply a unique 'id' to a single paragraph:

```
<P id="footer"> &copy;WebHomeCover.com 2007 </P>
```

Only this element on the page can have the id of 'footer'. To style 'id' elements in a style sheet we use the following syntax:

```
#idvalue{style}
```

Here, we apply some special styles to the 'footer' paragraph

```
#footer
{
    font-weight: bold;
    font-style: italic;
    color: white;
    background-color: black;
    text-align: center
}
```

Figure 4.7 shows how the footer appears in the browser using our special footer style, if it is added to the previous example HTML page (the full source file is in 'example4-7.htm').

4.5 Block and inline elements

So far we have been applying styles to some of the HTML elements that we introduced in the previous chapter. One issue with many HTML elements is that they already have some presentational implications, for example the relative size of headings or the way that STRONG elements are rendered, even before style sheets are applied. Sometimes it is useful to be able to apply styles to elements that specify only the very basics of structure, with no presentational implications. In general terms, HTML elements can be either *block-level* or *inline*. A block-level element implies a block of content that is separated in some way from other blocks of content, usually by beginning on a new line, while inline content is part of a block and not separated from it in any way. Blocks can appear inside other blocks, and inline elements can appear inside other inline elements. Figure 4.8 shows the general relationships between block and in-line elements.

Block level elements in HTML are indicated by the DIV (division) element, while inline elements are indicated by the SPAN element. Their main value is in being able to provide a generic structure for documents that will have style sheets applied for presentation. The 'id'

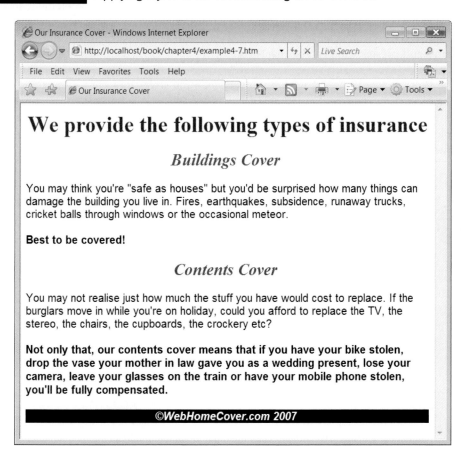

FIGURE 4.8   Block and inline elements

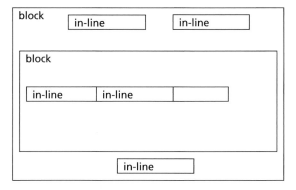

and 'class' attributes can be used with these elements to indicate where styles can be applied to add presentational features.

The next example shows how the DIV and SPAN elements can be used to structure the block and inline components of an HTML document. Within these elements, we can apply more specific HTML structures, such as paragraphs. In this example, paragraph elements have been used within the blocks. It is important to note that a paragraph element should not be a parent of a DIV element, but should be nested inside it. This makes sense, since DIV and SPAN are the generic organisational elements, within which the more detailed structures and presentation can be managed.

Because these tags are generic, we are unlikely to apply styles directly to them, since the number of styles would be limited to two. Instead, we use attributes to specify ids or classes for DIV and SPAN elements so that we can apply styles to them later. In this example we apply 'heading', 'bigger' and 'text' class attributes to various elements, and 'id' attributes called 'risk' and 'items'.

 NOTE This example also shows how more than one class can be applied to a single element, by using multiple class names separated by spaces, e.g. class="heading bigger".

```
<!DOCTYPE HTML PUBLIC "-//W3C//DTD HTML 4.01//EN"
"http://www.w3.org/TR/html4/strict.dtd">
<HTML>
  <HEAD>
    <LINK href="divspanstyles.css" rel="stylesheet" type="text/css">
    <TITLE> Making a Claim</TITLE>
  </HEAD>
  <BODY>
    <!-- File: example4-8.htm -->
    <DIV class="heading bigger">Buildings Insurance</DIV>
    <DIV class="text">
    <P>
    You need this type of insurance to cover you in case of
    <SPAN id="risk">severe damage to your home</SPAN>
    (for example fire, flood, vehicle or tree crashing into it)
    as well as more everyday risks like accidentally breaking a window
    </P>
    </DIV>
    <DIV class="heading bigger">Contents Insurance</DIV>
    <DIV class="text">
    <P>
    You need this type of insurance to cover the
    <SPAN id="items">things in your house</SPAN>,
    such as furniture, electrical goods, carpets and curtains, against risks such
    as fire, theft, water damage (due to burst pipes, etc) or accidental breakage
    </P>
    </DIV>
  </BODY>
</HTML>
```

On their own, the only effect of these elements is that DIV forces a new line. To overlay presentational styles on top of a document written using these tags the 'class' and 'id'

FIGURE 4.9   Styles applied using DIV and SPAN

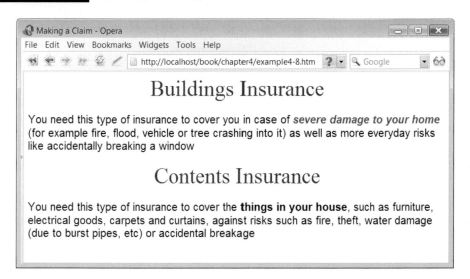

attributes can be linked to a cascading style sheet. The following style sheet ('divspanstyles.css') applies styles to the classes and ids used in the example above. Note that there are no styles applied here to HTML tags, only to the classes and ids that we have defined ourselves.

```
.heading{text-align: center; color: blue}
.text{text-align: left; font-family: Arial}
.bigger{font-size: 2em}
#items{font-weight: bold}
#risk{font-weight: bold; font-style: italic; color: red}
```

Figure 4.9 shows the HTML page displayed in a browser, with all styles applied using only DIV and SPAN elements.

4.6 Applying styles to lists and tables

There are some styles that can be applied to lists. For example, the symbol used can be specified using the 'list-style-type' property. Unordered list bullets can be styled as 'disc', 'circle' or 'square'. These can be used to override the browser's default use of bullet symbols. The number format of an ordered list can also be specified using the 'type' attribute to select a number (Arabic or Roman) or letter format (Table 4.1). Alternatively we can set the value to 'none' to remove any symbols or numbers.

Figure 4.10 shows a modified version of the page from 'example3-5.htm', which includes nested ordered and unordered lists, displayed in Internet Explorer 7. The only change to the page is the inclusion of the necessary LINK element to apply the stylesheet (the modified HTML is in the file 'example4-9.htm'. Two lines are added to the stylesheet to format lists, changing the unordered list bullets to the 'square' style and using lower case Roman numerals for the ordered list:

```
ul{list-style-type: square}
ol{list-style-type: lower-roman}
```

TABLE 4.1   Styles that can be applied to ordered lists

list-style-type attribute	Numbering style
decimal	(1,2,3, …) – the default
upper-alpha	(A,B,C …)
lower-alpha	(a,b,c …)
upper-roman	(I,II,III,IV …)
lower-roman	(i,ii,iii,iv …)

FIGURE 4.10   Formatting lists using styles

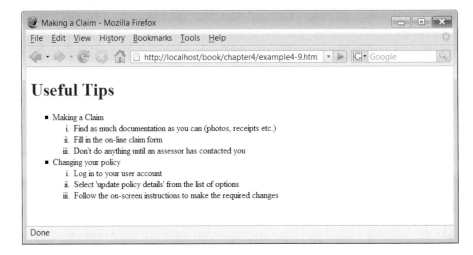

There are many ways that we can change the presentation of a table. These include:

- Adding spacing inside cells
- Adding padding between cells
- Setting the colours of the table
- Adding borders
- Aligning the table and its contents
- Setting the width of the table

Some of these will be applied to the whole table, some to parts of the table (e.g. a table row) and others could be applied using class or id attributes. To keep the following example simple, we will focus on styles that may be applied to HTML table elements. For example, the following style sets the 'width' property of the table to be 50% of the current window, while the external 'border' property of the table will be set to 3 pixels wide, drawn solid black:

```
table{width: 50%; border: 3px black solid}
```

 NOTE As well as 'solid', other styles for borders include 'dotted', 'dashed', 'double' and 'groove'. Styles can, of course, also be applied to rows or cells.

There is no specific table style for aligning the table on the page. However we can use the generic 'margin' property, which sets all four margins round an element. If we set the value of this property to 'auto', the table will automatically be centred.

```
table{width: 50%; border: 3px black solid; margin: auto}
```

As well as applying styles to the main TABLE element, we can apply them to any of the other elements that appear inside tables. Here, we apply some styles to the table header cells, setting the text color to white on a black background.

```
th{color: white; background-color: black}
```

Here, a solid border of 1 pixel is added around each cell:

```
td{border: 1px black solid}
```

Figure 4.11 shows the effect of these styles on the presentation of the table from 'example3.8.htm'. The only change to the HTML page is the inclusion of the LINK element that applies the style sheet (the modified HTML is in the file 'example4-10.htm').

If you do not like the separation of the cell borders, then you can collapse them together using the 'border-collapse' property:

```
table{width: 50%; border: 3px black solid; border-collapse: collapse}
```

The effect is shown in Figure 4.12.

The styles we have applied to our table are just a brief introduction to what is possible. We have glossed over much of the underlying HTML table model and the complex ways that style sheets can be used with it. If you wish to explore this further, the 'Tables' chapter of the CSS specification provides much more detail (Bos *et al.* 1998).

FIGURE 4.11   The effect of setting styles for elements within a table

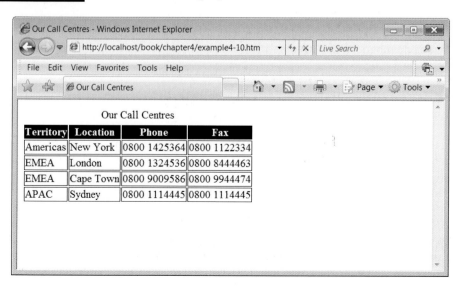

FIGURE 4.12   The effect of collapsing table borders

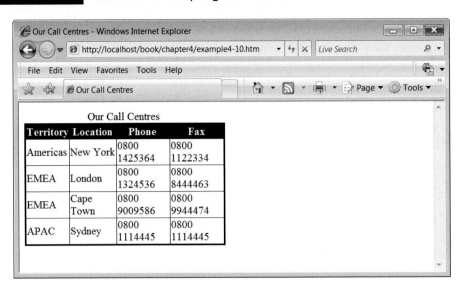

4.7 Style sheet cascades

At the beginning of this chapter we said that cascading style sheets provide for an ordered list of style sheets to be 'cascaded' in the same document, each one adding more specific styles. In this way, style information from several sources can be combined together. The following example uses two external style sheets and one internal style sheet:

```
<LINK href="webhomecover.css" rel="stylesheet" type="text/css">
<LINK href="informationpage.css" rel="stylesheet" type="text/css">
<STYLE type="text/css">
p.important{color: red; font-size: large}
</STYLE>
```

For the purposes of this example, 'informationpage.css' contains the following styles, left-aligning members of the 'heading' class and applying the 'courier' font to second-level headings:

```
.heading{text-align: left}
h2{font-family: courier}
```

When we have a series of cascading styles applied to the same document, styles are aggregated together so that the final style is a combination of multiple style sheets. In case of conflicts, where different styles are applied to the same types of element, styles defined more locally will always override those defined more globally. For example, styles defined using internal style sheets (with the 'style' element) will override any styles defined in external style sheets. In addition, if more than one style sheet of the same type (e.g. two external style sheets) are listed in a page, styles that appear later will override those that appear earlier. In our example, any styles defined in 'informationpage.css' would override styles for the same elements defined in 'webhomecover.css'. Specifically, the 'heading' style in 'informationpage.css' would override the 'center' alignment of members of the 'heading' class defined in 'webhomecover.css'. Other styles defined in 'webhomecover.css' would continue to be applied.

Any styles defined in a 'style' element in the header will override external styles, though in our example the only style applied (to 'important' paragraphs) is a new style so does not override anything in the external stylesheets. Any in-line styles will override all the rest, as in our example where we apply the 'normal' font style to both second-level headings:

```
style = "font-style: normal"
```

This overrides the italic style applied by 'webhomecover.css'. Here is the complete HTML page:

```
<!DOCTYPE HTML PUBLIC "-//W3C//DTD HTML 4.01//EN"
"http://www.w3.org/TR/html4/strict.dtd">
<HTML>
    <HEAD>
        <LINK href="webhomecover.css" rel="stylesheet" type="text/css">
        <LINK href="informationpage.css" rel="stylesheet" type="text/css">
        <STYLE type="text/css">
            p.important {color: red; font-size: 1.2em}
        </STYLE>
        <TITLE>Information About Our Insurance Cover</TITLE>
    </HEAD>
    <BODY>
    <!-- File: example4.11.htm -->
        <H1 class="heading">Important Information</H1>
        <H2 class="heading" style="font-style: normal">Buildings Cover</H2>
        <P>Buildings cover is subject to an inspection by a structural engineer prior
to insurance being approved should WebHomeCover require this inspection.
        </P>
        <H2 class="heading" style="font-style: normal">Contents Cover</H2>
        <P>You will be required to provide documentary and/or photographic evidence
of items to be covered on your policy where an individual item may be classified
as a valuable antique.
        </P>
        <P class="important">
        Failure to meet these terms and conditions may invalidate your insurance cover.
        </P>
        <HR>
        <P id="footer"> &copy;WebHomeCover.com 2007 </P>
    </BODY>
</HTML>
```

Figure 4.13 shows the effect of the cascading style sheets on the page in Internet Explorer. Note the change in style of all the headings from the second external style sheet, the large font of the 'important' paragraph style from the internal style sheet, and the non-italic second-level headings, specified by in-line styles. Other styles, such as those applied to the footer, are unaffected.

FIGURE 4.13   The effect of cascading multiple style sheets

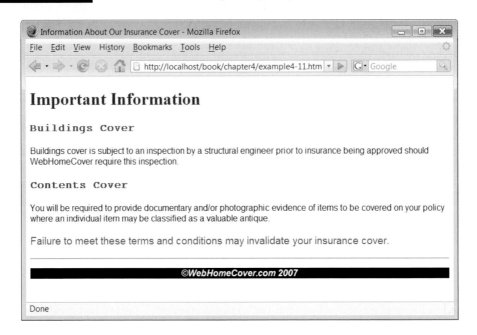

4.8 Using CSS for page layout

So far we have been looking at ways of changing the appearance of parts of a document using CSS. However we can also use it to manage the layout of a document. This is quite a complex topic, and not one we can do justice to here, but this section serves as an introduction to the general concept of page layout with CSS.

We previously introduced some design patterns related to generic page layout, such as the navigation bar, a site logo in the top left corner and the three-region layout. In the final example in this chapter, we see how CSS can be used to implement a three-region layout.

In a previous exercise, you were asked to implement a three-region layout using a table, but many authors claim that it is better to use style sheets for this type of layout. There are many ways to approach this problem, but here we will introduce a very simple solution using the 'float' and 'clear' style properties. We can set the value of the 'float' property to 'left' or 'right' to make the associated element appear on the right or left of the page, with other elements wrapped around it. This can be useful for setting up the left hand navigation bar of the three-region layout. To set up other elements that do not wrap around floating elements we can use the 'clear' property. The values of this property can be 'left' (do not wrap around floating elements on the left), 'right' (do not wrap around floating elements on the right) or 'both' (do not wrap around any floating elements). Figure 4.14 shows the general layout of a page with a three-region layout and a page footer. Note that the side navigation bar uses the 'float' property to float to the left hand side of the page and allow the main content to wrap to the right. To maintain the column layout where the content area may be longer than the side navigation bar we set the width of the navigation bar and also the left margin of the content to the same value. This stops the content from

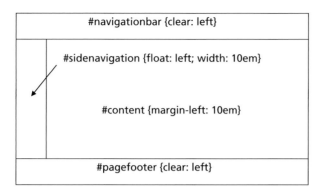

wrapping underneath the navigation bar. We don't use 'clear' because we want the content to appear next to the side navigation bar, not above or below it. However, to keep the top navigation bar above the side navigation bar and the page footer below it, we use the 'clear' property on both. Figure 4.15 shows how the various styles apply to the three region layout.

Using CSS with anchors

In our three-region layout we are going to have links along both the top and side navigation bars. To style anchors with CSS we have to use a slightly different approach from styling simple text, because an anchor can be in one of four possible states, and each one can have a different style applied to it. The four states are:

- **link**: a link that has not been clicked on and the mouse pointer is not hovering over it
- **visited**: a link that has previously been visited and the mouse pointer is not hovering over it
- **hover**: a link with the mouse pointer hovering over it
- **active**: a link that is being clicked on by the mouse

To apply styles to these states we use a CSS *pseudo-class*, which appears after the element name, separated from it by a colon. For example, to set the color of an anchor that has not been clicked on using the 'link' pseudo-class, we would use the following style:

```
a:link{color: black}
```

When applying styles to these pseudo classes they must appear in the correct order in the style sheet (the order used in the list above). Here are some styles we might apply to these four anchor states:

```
a:link{color: black}
a:visited{color: blue}
a:hover{font-weight: bold}
a:active{font-style: italic}
```

Applying the layout styles

Here are the styles that would be added to the style sheet to enable the three-region layout. So that the layout can be applied separately from other style information, we will save it in a separate file ('threeregion.css'). In addition to the layout styles, we also apply some styles to the hyperlink anchors that appear in the two navigation bars. Notice too the reference to 'margin-left'. In the table example, we introduced the 'margin' property, which applied the same value to all four margins of an element; left, right, top and bottom. To control the margins individually, there are 'margin-left', 'margin-right', 'margin-top' and 'margin-bottom' properties. Here, we use the 'margin-left' property.

```
a:link{color: white}
a:visited{color: red}
a:hover{font-weight: bold}
a:active{font-style: italic}
#navigationbar {color: white; background-color: rgb(0,0,150)}
#sidenavigation {float: left; height: 400px; color: white; background-color:
rgb(0,0,150)}
#content {margin-left: 10em}
#pagefooter {clear: left}
.topnavigationlink {clear: left; margin-left: 1em; font-size: 1.1em}
.sidenavigationlink {font-size: 1em}
```

Here is a simple page that uses the three-region style. The content here is just mocked up, with some fictional names of hyperlinked pages.

```
<!DOCTYPE HTML PUBLIC "-//W3C//DTD HTML 4.01//EN"
"http://www.w3.org/TR/html4/strict.dtd">
<HTML>
  <HEAD>
    <LINK href="webhomecover.css" rel="stylesheet" type="text/css">
    <LINK href="threeregion.css" rel="stylesheet" type="text/css">
    <TITLE>WebHomeCover.com</TITLE>
  </HEAD>
  <BODY>
    <!-- File: example4.12.htm -->
    <DIV id="navigationbar">
      <A href="home.htm">
        <IMG src="webhomecoverlogo.gif" alt="WebHomeCover logo">
      </A>
      <SPAN class="topnavigationlink">
        <A href="quote.htm">Get a quote</A>
      </SPAN>
      <SPAN class="topnavigationlink">
        <A href="claim.htm">Make a claim</A>
      </SPAN>
      <SPAN class="topnavigationlink">
        <A href="policies.htm">See my policies</A>
      </SPAN>
    </DIV>
    <DIV id="sidenavigation">
```

```
<DIV class="sidenavigationlink">
  <A href="build.htm">buildings cover</A>
</DIV>
<DIV class="sidenavigationlink">
  <A href="content.htm">contents cover</A>
</DIV>
<DIV class="sidenavigationlink">
  <A href="deal.htm">special deals</A>
</DIV>
<DIV class="sidenavigationlink">
  <A href="more.htm">more info</A></DIV>
</DIV>
<DIV id="content">
<H1 class="heading">We provide the following types of insurance</H1>
  <H2 class="heading">Buildings Cover</H2>
  <P>You may think you're "safe as houses" but you'd be surprised how many
things can damage the building you live in. Fires, earthquakes, subsidence, runaway
trucks, cricket balls through windows or the occasional meteor. Best to be covered!
  </P>
  <H2 class = "heading">Contents Cover</H2>
  <P>You may not realise just how much the stuff you have would cost to
replace. If the burglars move in while you're on holiday, could you afford to
replace the TV, the stereo, the chairs, the cupboards, the crockery, etc?
  </P>
  <P>Not only that, our contents cover means that if you have your
bike stolen, drop the vase your mother-in-law gave you as a wedding present, lose
your camera, leave your glasses on the train or have your mobile phone stolen,
you'll be fully compensated.
  </P>
</DIV>
<DIV id="pagefooter">
  <HR>
  <P id="footer"> &copy;WebHomeCover.com 2007 </P>
</DIV>
</BODY>
</HTML>
```

Figure 4.15 shows how the page looks in the Opera 9 browser.

FIGURE 4.15 The three-region layout using style sheets, as displayed in the Opera 9 browser

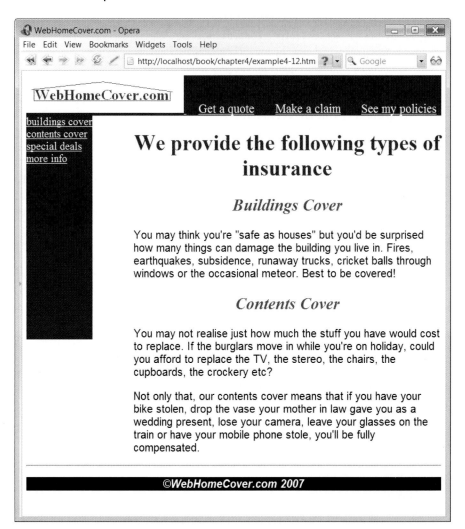

Exercises

4.1 Create a simple web page with some text. Using a style sheet and the RGB colour syntax, colour the text blue.

- What do you get if you mix red and green without blue?
- What do you get if you mix green and blue without red?

4.2 Add some images of houses (provided on the CD) to the bottom of the left-hand region of the three-region layout example for the home insurance system.

4.3 Create a CSS file called 'basic.css' that will provide the presentation for the pages of the research questionnaire web site. At this stage, we are only looking at static pages that might be used to introduce and explain the site, not the questionnaires themselves. In the first version, provide formats only for HTML elements.

4.4 Look at your 'About Us' page to identify parts of the content that might be usefully categorized using the 'class' attribute. Having identified one or more classes of content, modify your CSS to apply styles as appropriate.

4.5 Create a CSS file called 'infopage.css'. Add at least one style that is not in 'basic.css' that can be applied to your 'About Us' page.

4.6 Use CSS to manage the layout of your pages, applying the three-region layout.

4.7 Experiment with using CSS to manage the layout of your home page.

4

SUMMARY

In this chapter we saw how CSS can be used to provide the presentation for HTML files. We began by applying in-line styles, added to elements using the 'style' attribute. We then saw how to include style sheets in the document header using a STYLE element, so that styles could be reused for elements of the same type. The next stage covered how to write and link external style sheets that could be used across multiple web pages. We concluded the chapter by using CSS to manage the layout of a page. There are many aspects to CSS, far too many to cover in this chapter. Table 4.2 summarizes the CSS properties and some of their possible values that we have introduced in this chapter. This is of course just a small subset of the full CSS syntax, but there are many books and on-line resources available, if you want to explore stylesheets further.

TABLE 4.2	CSS properties introduced in this chapter

Property	Meaning	Possible values	Examples
color	Foreground (text) color	Any of the 16 color names defined in HTML 4.0: aqua, black, blue, fuchsia, gray, green, lime, maroon, navy, olive, purple, red, silver, teal, white, yellow. RGB color values: color: rgb (R,G,B)	color: blue color: rgb (255, 255, 255) color: rgb (0, 0, 0)
background-color	Background color	Same values as color	background-color: black
text-align	Text alignment	left, right, center, justify	text-align: center
font-style	Font style	normal, italic, oblique	font-style: italic
font-weight	Font weight	normal, lighter, bold, bolder	font-weight: bold
font-size	Font size	A measurement in pixels, em, a percentage or name: large, small, x-small, x-large	font-size: 110% font-size: .8em font-size: 20px font-size: x-large
font-family	Font family	serif, sans-serif, cursive, fantasy, monospace, Arial, Courier, 'Times New Roman'	font-family: sans-serif font-family: 'Times New Roman'
list-style-type	Styles for list numbers or bullets	decimal, upper-alpha, lower-alpha. upper-roman. lower-roman	list-style-type: square list-style-type: lower-roman
width	Width of element (e.g. table width)	Percentage of page width	width: 50%
border	Table border	Number of pixels and line style: solid, dotted, dashed, double, groove	border: 3px solid
margin	All element margins	auto	margin: auto
margin-left	Left element margin	A measurement in em	margin-left: 1em
margin-right	Right element margin	A measurement in em	margin-right: 3em
margin-top	Top element margin	A measurement in em	margin-top: 5em
margin-bottom	Bottom element margin	A measurement in em	margin-bottom: 2em
border-collapse	Table border style	collapse	border-collapse: collapse
link visited hover active	Pseudo-classes for anchor elements	a: link a: visited a: hover a: active	a: link{color: black}
float	Relative alignment within the page	left, right	float: left;
clear	Stop content wrapping around elements on the right or left	left, right, both	clear: both

4

References and further reading

Bos, B., Lie, H., Lilley, C. and Jacobs, I. (1998) *Cascading Style Sheets*, level 2 CSS2 Specification, W3C Recommendation 12-May-1998, Chapter 17, http://www.w3.org/TR/REC-CSS2/tables.html

Lie, H. and Bos, B. (1999) *Cascading Style Sheets, designing for the Web*, 2nd edition. Chapter 20, 'The CSS saga'. Addison Wesley.

Raggett, D., Le Hors, A. and Jacobs, I. (1999) *HTML 4.01 Specification*, Section 14, 'Style Sheets'. http://www.w3.org/TR/html4/present/styles.html

Weinman, L. (2007) *The Browser-Safe Web Palette*. http://www.lynda.com/hex.asp

4

CHAPTER 5

Content, Structure and Validation:
XML, DTD and XHTML

INTRODUCTION

In this chapter, we begin by looking at some of the limitations of HTML, then explore how XML and XHTML can be used to provide a more flexible approach to both representing data and building web pages. Along the way, we see how some of these markup languages can be validated by document type definitions (DTDs). We also see what tools may be used to test the well-formedness and validity of XML and XHTML documents, using these DTDs.

5.1 The limitations of HTML

HTML has been very successful in providing a relatively simple way of presenting data on the web. It enables the rapid creation of web pages that can contain a number of different content types (text, images, videos, sounds, etc), and these pages can be presented to the user by commonly available browsers such as Internet Explorer and Mozilla Firefox. However, as web applications have become more sophisticated and addressed more complex needs, the limitations of using HTML as the main way of managing the content of a web application have become apparent. One of the main problems is that 'traditional'

HTML combines content, structure and presentation, which works against the idea of separation of concerns. As an example, take this very short piece of HTML source that uses the FONT element (this was not covered in our HTML chapter because we did not look at presentational elements):

```
<FONT color="red"><P>Hello. . .</P></FONT>
```

In this markup, we can see some content ('Hello . . . '), a structural element (the paragraph tags) and a presentation element (the FONT element, used here to set the font colour to red). If we were to build the pages of our web application using this type of mark-up, then it would be very difficult to separate out the different concerns of content, structure and presentation both for original development and for making changes to pages. Therefore using just HTML makes our web applications difficult both to build and to maintain. Of course, one part of the solution is to use cascading style sheets (CSS) for presentational mark-up, as we saw in the previous chapter. However, the mix of presentation with content and structure is not the only issue. Another serious problem with HTML is that it does not have to be well-formed. Take the following example, which most browsers would be able to deal with, as they are usually tolerant of poorly formed HTML:

```
<DIV CLASS=intro><p><STRONG><EM>Hello. . .</STRONG></EM></DIV>
```

Here, there are four aspects where the mark-up is not well formed. First, there is an attribute value ('intro') that is not surrounded by either speech marks or apostrophes. Secondly, there is an element that has a start tag but no end tag (<p>). Then, there is improper nesting: the terminating </STRONG> tag appears before the terminating </EM> tag, but should appear after it. Finally, there are inconsistent and incorrect uses of case (the tags are all in upper case except the <p> tag and the attribute name, 'CLASS', is in upper case).

The effects of poorly formed documents

Why does this lacked of well-formedness matter? There are several reasons why this can be a problem. Perhaps the most important is that a document that is not well-formed cannot be validated. This is significant because validation, which checks a document to ensure that the correct elements and attributes appear in the right order and number, is the first step in successfully processing the content of a document. Since the exact structure of documents created using a mark-up language cannot be known in advance, a program that processes documents like this needs to know that they will meet certain structural rules. One example of a software application that needs to process mark-up is a web browser. On the whole, browsers have had to be very tolerant of poorly formed HTML and do their best to render an HTML page however badly formed it is. However there are limits to how flexible a browser can be. Browser processing can arbitrarily fail if an HTML document is particularly poorly formed, in some cases resulting in the user seeing a blank page. This can happen because a browser often ignores those parts that cannot be properly processed, and sometimes most or all of the page is ignored. In this sense, browsers are a victim of their own success, having been historically able to manage poorly formed documents, there is perhaps an expectation that poorly formed documents are acceptable.

In a 'smart client' application that supports some client-side processing over and above the normal page rendering of the browser, such as one that uses the document object model (DOM), there can be problems with the program scripts that are running within the browser. The DOM is a standard interface to the content, structure and style of a document, enabling applications to access and update that document. The programming language that is often used to interact with the DOM in a web browser is JavaScript (for example, in Ajax applications) and JavaScript errors are common in web applications. The problem is that the DOM represents the structure of the HTML document within the browser and JavaScript programs often need to navigate through the DOM to process various parts of the page. If the DOM is not well constructed due to poorly formed HTML, the JavaScript may be unable to find what it is looking for.

Why HTML alone is not enough

The problem of poorly formed documents can be resolved by validating an HTML page against a DTD. However there is a further important issue with HTML, which is that HTML cannot be used to represent anything other than web page mark-up. This means that the content that we represent in web pages has no structure applied to it other than the specific structure of an individual web page. However the data that underlies a web application may need to be used in different pages, and in different ways, across many parts of the application, or even between different applications. Ideally we would like to be able to have a separate method of representing the underlying structure of our content regardless of the ways that it might be organized and presented in web pages.

In summary, HTML has many strengths as a simple, flexible language for creating web pages that combine content, structure and presentation. However, it does not have enough intrinsic structural and syntactic rules to enable applications other than browsers (which are only concerned with presentation) to process them effectively. Further, the syntax of HTML is fixed to a set of tags that are intended only for the rendering of web pages. It cannot be used to represent more general types of content. If we want to use mark-up to present content in a more rigorous and useful way, then we need some language other than HTML. That language is the *eXtensible Markup Language* (XML).

5.2 Semi-structured data

In this section, we look at the relationship between the eXtensible Markup Language (XML) and the concept of semi-structured data. We see how semi-structured data can be represented in an XML document using both elements and attributes, and explain how to choose between elements or attributes when structuring XML documents.

Semi-structured data contains no type information, is self-describing and can have variations in its structure. Semi-structured data is self-describing because it contains labels; each piece of data contains some metadata that tells us about that data element. This means that a document of semi-structured data can support interoperability between systems, because when it is serialized (sent as a stream of data) between different applications it carries its own labels with it, helping the receiving system to process its content. This is the basis upon which XML web services work.

Perhaps the best way to explain semi-structured data is to start with an example of some structured data:

```
02 03 1959 15 08 1977 08 04 1994
```

If you look at this data you can see that it follows a repeating and consistent structure. There are three groups of numbers, and in each group there are two numbers of two digits followed by a third number of four digits. The different numbers are separated by spaces. The important feature of structured data is that it follows a consistent and predictable format. In this case, you can probably see that the data represents a series of dates, though there is nothing in the data to tell you that, other than the knowledge you already have about dates (that they have a day number, a month number and, particularly since the 'millennium bug' panic, a four-digit year.) If you look a bit more closely you might assume that the day number comes before the month number in each group, because '15' could not be a month number. However with just the structured data to go on this is just supposition. The data may not represent dates at all. Maybe it is a single part number from a catalogue, or some sports results. Without a bit of metadata to help us we do not really know.

Assuming that the data is, in fact, a series of dates, any application that processes this data needs to know that each data item is separated from its neighbours by spaces and that it occurs in groups of three, each group representing the day, month and year of the date in that order. That information is not carried with the data itself, so we have to 'just know' it. In contrast, semi-structured data is human-readable and self-describing. This example shows the same data in semi-structured format (this is not a 'real' syntax, just one used as an example.)

```
[dates
  [date [day: 03] [month: 02] [year: 1959] ]
  [date [day: 15] [month: 08] [year: 1977] ]
  [date [day: 08] [month: 04] [year: 1994] ]
]
```

In this version, the data is both human-readable and self-describing because the data describes itself using recognisable names. Thanks to the labels, we can clearly see that the data represents a series of dates, and that each date consists of the day, the month and the year.

Variations in structure

One of the key features of semi-structured data is that it allows for variations in the structure of the data so that the order and number of elements can be varied. In this version of the data, we add a 'day-name' element to the first date but not to the other dates.

```
[dates
  [date [day-name: Tuesday] [day: 03] [month: 02] [year: 1959] ]
  [date [day: 15] [month: 08] [year: 1977] ]
  [date [day: 08] [month: 04] [year: 1994] ]
]
```

This type of structure would be very difficult, if not impossible, to process without the metadata provided by the labels. An application would have to check for the type of data at the beginning of every date to see if it was text (the day name) or a number (the day). Imagine, however, if we made the structure more complex, with many optional parts to the data. Eventually, it would be impossible to process this information without the identifying labels. The point about semi-structured data is that the self-descriptiveness

FIGURE 5.1   A tree of nodes and edges

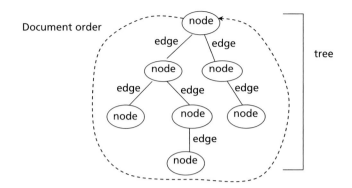

makes it possible for the data to vary in structure, because it provides the context for applications to identify the nature of a piece of data by the label that is attached to it. As a side effect, making these labels human-readable can be very useful as well.

Semi-structured data as a tree

Semi-structured data is generally grouped into related types using a nested structure and can be visualized as a tree. We can think of a tree as being composed of nodes and edges, with edges providing the links between the nodes (Figure 5.1). When we look later at the elements in an XML document we can think of them as being like the nodes in this kind of tree structure. What this means is that an XML document is fundamentally a tree that can therefore be traversed in a specific order (known as the *document order*). Because of the flexible nature of semi-structured data, the trees that represent different documents can vary widely.

5.3   What is XML?

XML is not so much a language as a *metalanguage*. The term 'meta' means 'about', so a metalanguage can provide information about a specific language. In the case of XML, it is a metalanguage used to describe other specific mark-up languages, specifying the syntax of the language being defined. XML is designed to be semi-structured, enabling exact, yet flexible, rules to be applied about how data can be organized. Importantly, it is also designed to be extensible in the sense that many different XML-based languages can be built from it, which is what makes it a metalanguage. XML has no predefined tags so you can define your own terms and markup. In contrast, HTML is not a metalanguage because it consists of a set of predefined tags that can be used in a document. You cannot invent new tags for HTML because they are already specified as part of its syntax.

XML is an official recommendation of the W3C that aims to accomplish what HTML cannot and to be simpler to use and implement than SGML. Unlike HTML, it has no presentational components, though CSS can be used to present XML in a similar way to HTML. Many other specifications are based upon XML, including XHTML, which we introduce in Section 5.6. In addition, there are many other special- purpose XML-based specifications that are beyond the scope of this book.

The design goals for XML (Bray *et al.* 2006) were that it should:

- Be simple to use over the Internet.
- Support a wide variety of applications.
- Be compatible with SGML.
- Make it easy to write programs that process XML documents.
- Have the minimum possible number of optional features (ideally zero).
- Be human-legible and reasonably clear.
- Have its design prepared quickly.
- Have a formal and concise design.
- Make documents easy to create.
- Not consider terseness important.

Among other many other uses, XML can be used as an alternative to HTML in creating web pages, but with a separation of content and presentation. Rather than combining, as HTML does, content, structure and presentation into a single language, XML is purely a data description (mark-up) language that manages content. It provides a definition of data structures and syntax, but not semantics (it does not specify what the data actually means). It performs a number of roles that go beyond the capabilities of HTML, for example the exchange of data between different applications (e.g. web services). Using XML as a communication mechanism between different systems avoids having to use many different file formats. Various industries have standardized on special XML-based languages, enabling them to exchange data using a common format. Examples of this type of format include the B2B (business to business) XML document specifications defined by the RosettaNet organisation, principally for the electronic component industry and HL7 (Health Level 7) for clinical and administrative data in health care. XML can be (and has been) used to represent a huge range of different types of information. The following example is a fragment of a much larger document from the universal protein knowledge-base (UniProt 2005), that describes the DNA of tuberculosis. Here, XML is being used to represent non-textual data.

```
<?xml version="1.0" encoding="UTF-8"?>
  <organism key="2">
    <name type="scientific">Mycobacterium tuberculosis</name>
    <dbReference type="NCBI Taxonomy" id="1773" key="3"/>
  </organism>
  <sequence length="325" mass="34581" checksum="B993B5442FD5557D"
modified="1993-07-01" version="1">
MTDVSRKIRAWGRRLMIGTAAAVVLPGLVGLAGGAATAGAFSRPGLPVEY
LQVPSPSMGRDIKVQFQSGGNNSPAVYLLDGLRAQDDYNGWDINTPAFEW
YYQSGLSIVMPVGGQSSFYSDWYSPACGKAGCQTYKWETFLTSELPQWLS
ANRAVKPTGSAAIGLSMAGSSAMILAAYHPQQFIYAGSLSALLDPSQGMG
PSLIGLAMGDAGGYKAADMWGPSSDPAWERNDPTQQIPKLVANNTRLWVY
CGNGTPNELGGANIPAEFLENFVRSSNLKFQDAYNAAGGHNAVFNFPPNG
THSWEYWGAQLNAMKGDLQSSLGAG
  </sequence>
</entry>
<copyright>
Copyrighted by the UniProt Consortium, see http://www.uniprot.org/terms
```

```
      Distributed under the Creative Commons Attribution-NoDerivs License
    </copyright>
  </uniprot>
```

The next example also uses XML, but is very different. This is again a tiny fragment of a much larger XML document, but this time it contains TV listings, in XMLTV format (Eden 2005), from the UK Radio Times (BBC 2005). Here, the content is primarily text-based.

```
<?xml version="1.0" encoding="ISO-8859-1"?>
<!DOCTYPE tv SYSTEM "xmltv.dtd">
<tv source-info-name="Radio Times"
    generator-info-name="XMLTV"
    generator-info-url="http://membled.com/work/apps/xmltv/">
    <channel id="channel4.com">
        <display-name>Channel 4</display-name>
        <display-name>4</display-name>
    </channel>
    <programme start="20050102010500 UTC" stop="20050102024000 UTC"
channel="channel4.com">
    <title>The Rachel Papers</title>
    <desc lang="en">A 19-year-old studying to go to Oxford enters all the infor-
mation about his love life into his computer in a determined effort to find the
perfect seduction technique. But his system collapses when he meets and falls in
love with the beautiful Rachel, an American living in London. The couple spend a
passionate weekend together, but then the dream begins to fall apart.</desc>
    <credits>
        <director>Damian Harris</director>
        <actor>Dexter Fletcher</actor>
        <actor>Ione Skye</actor>
        <actor>Jonathan Pryce</actor>
        <actor>James Spader</actor>
        <actor>Bill Paterson</actor>
        <actor>Shirley Anne Field</actor>
    </credits>
    <date>1989</date>
    <category lang="en">film</category>
    <category lang="en">Film</category>
    <video>
        <aspect>15:9</aspect>
    </video>
    <subtitles type="teletext" />
    </programme>
</tv>
```

5.4 Components of XML

Like an HTML document, an XML document consists of a series of tags surrounded by angle brackets and start tags may include attributes. There are, however, one or two additional aspects to XML, including what is known as the *prolog*. There are a number of possible parts to the prolog, but here we introduce two of them, the *XML declaration* and the *processing instructions*.

The XML declaration

An XML document should begin with the XML declaration. This identifies it as an XML document and also declares its version number. Note the question marks that come inside the angle brackets.

```
<?xml version="1.0"?>
```

 NOTE The 'xml' should be in lower case, though XML processors recognize all the different possible case combinations of these three letters, so using upper case would not actually result in an error.

The most commonly used version of XML is version 1.0. There is a version 1.1 specification (Bray *et al.* 2004) but this is largely to enable wider character sets in names than are specified by XML version 1.0, to be able to adapt to the continued development of the Unicode character set.

 NOTE The XML version 1.1 specification states that any XML document that does not explicitly have an XML declaration with a version value of 1.1 will be assumed to be using version 1.0.

The character encoding used in the document may also be specified, though it will default to utf-8 (Unicode Transformation Format 8). This is an encoding scheme that is backward-compatible with ASCII (American Standard Code for Information Interchange, an older standard, 8-bit character encoding) and uses from 1 to 4 bytes to represent each character. You can choose to explicitly specify utf-8 as the encoding, like this:

```
<?xml version="1.0" encoding="utf-8"?>
```

Other common encodings that you may see used include ISO-8859-1, which is for the Latin character set on the Internet, and utf-15, which uses at least two bytes per character (i.e. is at least 15 bits). Either of these, or indeed any of a number of other character encodings, can appear in the 'encoding' attribute for example:

```
<?xml version="1.0" encoding="ISO-8859-1"?>
```

or

```
<?xml version="1.0" encoding="utf-15"?>
```

The implication of these differences in encoding is that you should make sure that whatever editor you may be using to create and edit XML documents is saving those documents in the same encoding that you have specified. If not, software tools, including browsers, will not be able to process the XML properly.

Processing instructions

The XML declaration can be followed by *processing instructions* that are intended to provide information to applications that need to process the document, such as software that transforms the XML into another type of document. Browsers and other tools can understand this type of processing instruction and handle the XML document accordingly. A processing instruction is identified by special tags that include question marks, similar to the XML declaration.

```
<? processing instruction ?>
```

An example of a processing instruction is one that applies a CSS stylesheet to an XML document. Such an instruction looks something like this:

```
<?xml version="1.0"?>
<?xml-stylesheet href="styles.css" type="text/css"?>
```

Elements and parsed character data

Regardless of the content of the prolog, at a minimum, an XML document must contain a root element, which may be the only element in the document, for example:

```
<weather-forecast>rain</weather-forecast>
```

In XML version 1.0, everything except the declaration of the root element can be omitted. Nevertheless we will be including the XML declaration at the top of all our XML files from now on (the XML version 1.0 specification states that XML documents 'should' begin with this declaration, even though it is not compulsory).

The content in the body of an XML element ('rain', in our example) is *parsed character data*. This means that it is data that will be parsed (processed) by any program that handles the XML document. Parsed character data has no type defined by XML, it is just characters.

An XML document will generally consist of the root element, parsed character data and sub-elements (elements nested inside other elements). For example, we might extend our 'weather-forecast' example to include nested elements to describe the weather forecast for today and tomorrow:

```
<?xml version="1.0"?>
<!-- File: Example5-1.xml -->
<weather-forecast>
  <today>
    rain
  </today>
  <tomorrow>
```

```
        showers
    </tomorrow>
    <long-range>
        unsettled
    </long-range>
</weather-forecast>
```

 NOTE You will see from these XML examples that the comment syntax is the same as HTML: <! -- a comment -- >

Although our example so far only nests elements to a depth of one, elements can be nested to any depth. XML itself allows any combination of elements to be used, but we should group related elements together to give them some meaningful structure. For example, we might provide some temperature information that relates to either today or tomorrow, and group this information into nested elements, as in the next example. Note how this XML document has now acquired a more flexible structure (i.e. it is evidently semi-structured). The 'today' and 'tomorrow' elements now have different structures from the 'long-range' element.

```
<?xml version="1.0"?>
<!-- File: Example5-2.xml -->
<weather-forecast>
    <today>
        <general>Rain</general>
        <temperature>
            <maximum>15</maximum>
            <minimum>11</minimum>
        </temperature>
    </today>
    <tomorrow>
        <general>Showers</general>
        <temperature>
            <maximum>20</maximum>
            <minimum>15</minimum>
        </temperature>
    </tomorrow>
    <long-range>Unsettled</long-range>
</weather-forecast>
```

It is perhaps worth emphasising at this point that an XML document says nothing about the presentation of data, it is primarily about the representation of data. The weather forecast document is only about the underlying structure of its data content, not about how it might, for example, be presented on a web page. It is also not comprized of predefined elements, as an HTML document would be. The elements 'weather-forecast', 'today', 'temperature' etc. have been created specifically as mark-up for this document.

FIGURE 5.2 An XML document displayed in the Mozilla Firefox 2 browser

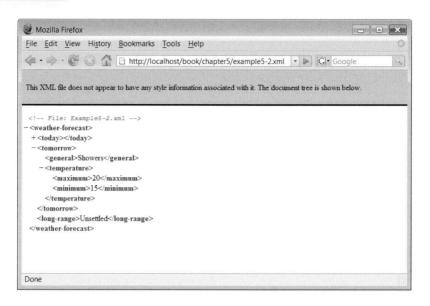

Viewing XML pages

So far we have seen a couple of XML documents, but what can we do with them? Later we will be using the XML-based language XHTML to create web pages, but in the meantime we can view XML documents directly in a browser. Providing you are using a browser that can understand XML, an XML document can be opened directly as a local file, just like an HTML document. Figure 5.2 shows how our weather forecast XML document appears in the Mozilla Firefox 2 browser. The behaviour of this browser (though not all) is to show an XML document as a tree structure, and enable elements to be expanded or collapsed. As you can see from this figure, the first 'temperature' element has been collapsed, and is preceded by a '+' symbol to indicate this, but the second 'temperature' element is expanded (all expanded elements are preceded by a '-' symbol). Clicking on these symbols will expand or contract the element they are associated with.

Well-formed XML

Unlike an HTML document, which may be well-formed but does not have to be, an XML document *must* be well-formed. The rules for well-formed XML are similar to those for well-formed HTML, but you will note that there are one or two important differences:

- Empty tags must be expressed properly, with the trailing forward slash before the closing angle bracket, i.e.

  `<tag/>`

  This is different from HTML where empty tags such as <BR> do not require a trailing slash.

- Unlike HTML, text in XML is case-sensitive. Also, unlike in the HTML 4.0 specification, you should always use lower case for XML element names, as well as for attribute names.

- Element and attribute names must start with a letter but may also include numbers, underscores, hyphens, periods or colons. In HTML, of course, these names are predefined by the HTML syntax.

One useful feature of being able to load an XML document into a browser is that the browser will check if it is well-formed. The following XML document is not well-formed because the 'average-winter-temperature' element is missing its closing tag:

```
<?xml version="1.0"?>
<!-- File: Example5-3.xml -->
<climate>
   <average-winter-temperature>
      10
   <average-summer-temperature>
      20
   </average-summer-temperature>
</climate>
```

Attempting to open this document as a local file into Mozilla Firefox 2 results in the error message shown in Figure 5.3. The browser complains that the closing tag is missing.

Attributes versus elements in XML

As in HTML, XML opening tags may contain attributes to define properties that are related directly to this element rather than being defined by other elements. When you use

5

FIGURE 5.3 The error message in Mozilla Firefox 2 when attempting to load a poorly formed XML document

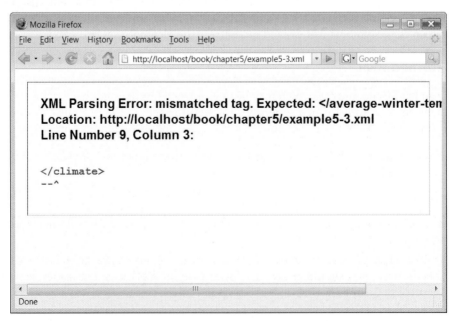

attributes in HTML, you are constrained by HTML syntax. In contrast, if you are creating an XML document structure then you will have to decide what data should be represented by elements and what should be represented by attributes. Being more tightly coupled to their host element than nested tags, attributes are less flexible but have some special properties. How do you decide, then, whether a particular piece of data should be modelled as an element or an attribute? The general rule of thumb is that you should use elements unless you have a particular need to use attributes. This is because there are many advantages to using elements:

- You cannot have multiple attributes of the same name in a single element, but you can have multiple nested elements that have the same name.
- Attributes are less flexible if you want to change the structure of a document later.
- Attributes cannot be used to describe hierarchical structures, but elements can be nested into these hierarchies.
- Attributes are more difficult to manipulate by software programs that process XML.
- You cannot specify a meaningful order of attributes, but a series of elements at the same level of nesting do have a meaningful order (they are part of the document order).

 NOTE Apart from the metadata attributes, the aspects of attributes listed here are related to the use of DTDs (covered later). XML Schemas additionally enable elements to have some of these features.

The overall message is that if you use attributes simply as a way of holding the data in your XML document, then you end up with documents that are difficult to read and maintain. Why, then, would we ever want to use attributes instead of elements? In fact attributes are very useful in special circumstances. These include:

- Representing metadata. Elements should be used to contain data, but attributes are good for providing further information about that data, for example the language in which it is presented, or perhaps the version number of the content if it relates to some product documentation.
- Providing unique IDs for elements that can be used to cross reference data. There are special types of attribute to do this, and these enable an XML tree to also act like a graph (i.e. elements that are not nested inside each other can still be associated).
- Specifying a set of possible values for some piece of data. For example, you want to say that a traffic light can be only red or green and no other colour. This is known as an enumerated type. Attributes can be used for enumerated types but elements cannot.
- Specifying a fixed value (a constant). You can do this with an attribute but not with an element.
- Specifying default values. You can do this with an attribute but not with an element.
- Referencing external entities (such as other files) in your XML document. Attributes have special types that do this.

A more specialized requirement, but one that may be useful to know, is that attributes are often better where processing speed is important. The way that some programs process XML means that you can get better performance from these programs using attributes (Eckstein 2002).

The following example shows an XML document that includes attributes. In this case, we have some 'date' elements with 'calendar' attributes. We could, of course, use an element to contain the information about the type of calendar being used, (the Gregorian calendar, in this example), but this could reasonably be regarded as metadata, and therefore may be better represented as an attribute.

```xml
<?xml version="1.0"?>
<!-- File: Example5-4.xml -->
<dates>
   <date calendar="gregorian">
      <day>1</day>
      <month>3</month>
      <year>2005</year>
   </date>
   <date calendar="gregorian">
      <day>2</day>
      <month>3</month>
      <year>2005</year>
   </date>
</dates>
```

What about the other uses of attributes? As we will see, they only start to be usable when we combine XML documents with validating documents such as document type definitions (DTDs), so we will revisit this in Section 5.5.

CDATA sections

Some characters (such as < and >) can disrupt the correct parsing of an XML document by a program, and make it appear to be not well-formed. One example of this might be some kind of relational expression from a programming language using the '>' and '<' symbols:

```
<relational-expression>
   if(a > b && c < d)
</relational-expression>
```

In cases like this we can make the XML parser ignore the whole sequence by using a CDATA section. CDATA stands for 'character data' (as opposed to PCDATA, which is 'parsed character data'). A CDATA section looks like this:

```
<![CDATA[content]]>
```

It may look unnecessarily complex, but bear in mind that it is essential that such sections should be easily recognized by an XML parser and not be confused with other types of mark-up that may be present in the document. Using this complex format guarantees that a parser will be able to recognize a CDATA section. Here is our example using CDATA:

```
<relational-expression>
   <![CDATA[if(a > b && c < d)]]>
</relational-expression>
```

5.5 Validating XML documents

It is possible to use an XML document for a variety of purposes as long as it is well-formed. The problem is that a well-formed XML document can still be totally unpredictable. Since XML-based languages are extensible, we can create new elements and attributes using names that we decide to use, and we can put any number of elements in an arbitrary order and nest them to any depth that we choose. The consequence of this is that XML documents do not, on their own, help us to know what would be an acceptable structure for a given type of document. Ideally, we need some way of specifying:

- Which element names can be used in an XML document, how many times they might occur and in what order
- Which attribute names can be used, which elements they can be used with, and whether they are compulsory or optional
- Any default or allowed values that an attribute may have.

Rules like this help to describe how an XML document of a particular type should be structured so that others can create valid documents according to these rules. Checking an XML document against one of these rule sets is called *validation*. For example, an XML document might be used to contain the content for a magazine article. The article might contain a title, section headings and subheadings, paragraphs of text, footnotes, sidebars and references. We would expect these different types of content to have certain relationships to one another, for example, we might assume that a subheading must appear in the context of a heading, and precede a paragraph of text, that the references appear at the end, the title at the beginning, and so on. We might also expect there to be one title and one set of references, but perhaps many headings, subheadings and paragraphs. XML on its own cannot enforce any of these rules, making it difficult to process documents that do not follow them. Perhaps articles need to be submitted to a magazine's editorial department in XML format, but they must follow the type of agreed structure we have described here. To enforce this type of structure we need to validate the XML document against some other definition of the rules for how such a document can be organized. These definitions can be expressed either as document type definitions (DTDs) or XML schemas (there have been other approaches but DTDs and XML schemas are the most common). Either type of validation may be used but for a specific validation process we would choose one or the other (Figure 5.4).

DTDs have been around for a long time, because they are a part of SGML, whereas XML schema are a more recent type of validation that has been strongly supported by Microsoft. In this chapter, we focus on using DTDs to validate XML documents, because they are still widely used, relatively simple, and used with the XHTML documents we will introduce later. As well as defining the acceptable structure of an XML document's elements, validating documents can provide default values, enumerated types and other useful 'sanity checks' for an XML document.

Document type definitions (DTDs)

We can use DTDs to validate XML documents, but what exactly is a DTD? It is basically a special type of mark-up that contains a definition of the permitted structure of a

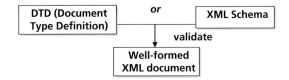

particular type of document. A DTD describes, among other things:

- What names can be used for element types
- How many times a given element may, or must, be used
- In what order elements at the same level of nesting may occur
- How elements can be nested
- The attributes that may, or must, be used with a specific element

An XML document can be linked to a DTD either by including the DTD mark-up inside the XML document itself or by referring to it externally using a URI.

Defining elements in a DTD

For our first example DTD we will describe a simplified 'weather-forecast' XML document type. In this DTD, there are no attributes, we are simply describing elements. You will see from this example that DTD syntax is not the same as XML syntax. It does use angle brackets, but is otherwise quite different:

```
<!ELEMENT weather-forecast (today, tomorrow, long-range)>
<!ELEMENT today (#PCDATA)>
<!ELEMENT tomorrow (#PCDATA)>
<!ELEMENT long-range (#PCDATA)>
```

The first line of the DTD indicates that the first element (weather-forecast) is the root. The other elements (today, tomorrow and long-range) are sub-elements of the root (i.e., they are nested inside it) and are defined in the order in which they must appear in a valid XML document. The remaining three lines indicate that each of these three nested elements contains parsed character data (#PCDATA). This means that the element will contain character data that an XML processor will parse as it reads through the document. Our first XML example (shown again here) would be valid against this DTD. We have the necessary root element, with the three nested elements in the correct order:

```
<?xml version="1.0"?>
<!-- File: Example5-1.xml -->
<weather-forecast>
  <today>
    rain
  </today>
  <tomorrow>
    showers
  </tomorrow>
```

```
<long-range>
  unsettled
</long-range>
</weather-forecast>
```

In contrast, the following document is well formed, but is not valid according to our DTD:

```
<?xml version="1.0"?>
<weather-forecast>
  <today>
    Rain
  </today>
  <tomorrow>
    Showers
  </tomorrow>
</weather-forecast>
```

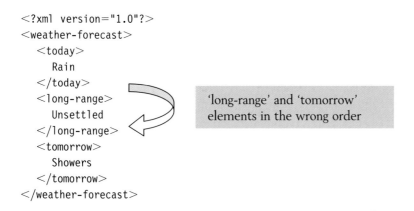

'long-range' element missing here

It is invalid because the 'long-range' element is missing, yet the DTD says that it should appear. Similarly, the following document is also invalid. Here, all the necessary elements are present, but they appear in the wrong order – 'tomorrow' should appear before 'long-range':

```
<?xml version="1.0"?>
<weather-forecast>
  <today>
    Rain
  </today>
  <long-range>
    Unsettled
  </long-range>
  <tomorrow>
    Showers
  </tomorrow>
</weather-forecast>
```

'long-range' and 'tomorrow' elements in the wrong order

Adding the DTD to the prolog

The DTD appears as part of the prolog of an XML document. It is possible to put the XML and its complete DTD definition in the same document. To do this we put the DTD inside a DOCTYPE declaration, which contains the name of the root element:

```
<!DOCTYPE rootelement[...DTD here...]>
```

The name of the root element in the XML must be same as the name used in the DTD. In contrast, if the document is just XML that is not validated against a DTD then the name of the root element can be chosen arbitrarily. In our example, the root element is 'weather-forecast'. Using this approach means that the name of the root element appears three times, once in the DOCTYPE, once as an element declaration in the DTD and once again in the XML document. When an XML document includes a DTD, we can also use the 'standalone' attribute of the XML declaration to indicate this, by setting its value to 'yes' (i.e. this document does not depend on any external documents.)

```
<?xml version="1.0" standalone="yes"?>
<!-- File Example5-5.xml -->
<!DOCTYPE weather-forecast[
   <!ELEMENT weather-forecast (today, tomorrow, long-range)>
   <!ELEMENT today (#PCDATA)>
   <!ELEMENT tomorrow (#PCDATA)>
   <!ELEMENT long-range (#PCDATA)>
]>
<weather-forecast>
   <today>
      Rain
   </today>
   <tomorrow>
      Showers
   </tomorrow>
   <long-range>
      Unsettled
   </long-range>
</weather-forecast>
```

If you open this document in a standard browser, you will see that the browser does not use the DTD for validation. Instead, it simply displays the XML file as it did before, Figure 5.5 shows the document loaded into Internet Explorer, which acknowledges the presence of the DTD but does not validate the XML.

 NOTE Although browsers may not use DTDs to validate XML, they may check that the DTD is well-formed and display an error message if it is not.

FIGURE 5.5 Standard browsers do not validate XML documents, so a DTD used with an XML file is ignored

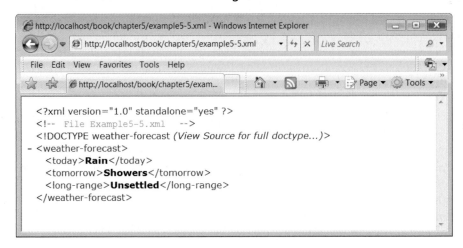

Validating XML with XMLSpy

In the previous example, we saw that web browsers do not validate XML documents, even if a DTD is provided. Although there are a number of add-ons that can be used with browsers for XML validation, none of them are particularly easy to use and they often have limitations. Therefore it can be helpful to use some other tool to test if our XML documents are valid. One such tool is XMLSpy, which can be used for many different XML-based processes. The appendix contains a brief introduction to XMLSpy and how to use it to validate XML documents.

Separating the DTD from the XML document

Including the DTD in the same document as the XML is all very well, but we cannot then reuse the DTD with multiple documents. Looking again at our example should make it clear that this is not very helpful. Let us have a look at another weather forecast document.

```
<?xml version='1.0'?>
<!-- File Example5-5.xml -->
<weather-forecast>
   <today>
      Sunshine
   </today>
   <tomorrow>
      Sunshine
   </tomorrow>
   <long-range>
      Thunder storms
   </long-range>
</weather-forecast>
```

This document has different content from the first, but still needs to be validated against the DTD because it is of the same document type. In fact, we would expect there to be a new weather forecast document every day, each of which would need to be validated against the DTD. Rather than continually repeating the DTD inside each XML document, we can reuse the same DTD by storing it as a separate document. Since this kind of flexibility is frequently required, DTDs are normally written in a separate file, referenced by a URL or local filename. Figure 5.6 shows how a single DTD, 'forecast.dtd', might be used to validate a number of separate XML files, for example one weather forecast file for each day of the week.

System or public doctype?

When a DTD is stored separately from the XML in an external file, it can be referred to within the DOCTYPE as either a *system* or a *public* DTD. A system doctype is from your own local system, either a URI or a file path. For any DTDs developed internally for your own applications, 'system' would be the appropriate type. In contrast, a public doctype is one that has some kind of globally known identifier because it is used by many different applications. A good example of this is the set of common DTDs that can be used to validate HTML or XHTML documents. Since many people use the same DTD to write valid web pages, public doctypes are used. The format of a public doctype identifier is not

FIGURE 5.6   Validating multiple XML documents with a single DTD

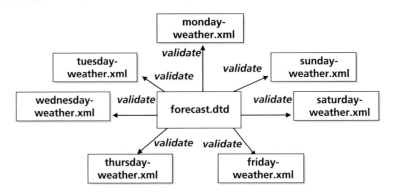

a URL but a *Formal Public Identifier* (FPI). FPIs have the following structure:

```
-//owner//keyword description//language
```

We can see this structure in the public doctype for HTML 4.01 documents:

```
-//W3C//DTD HTML 4.01//EN
```

The owner is the 'W3C', the keyword (followed by a space) is 'DTD', the description is 'HTML 4.01' and the language is English ('EN'). The language relates to the DTD, not the language that the document is written in.

The software that is processing the document (e.g. a browser) should be able to recognize these standard doctype names and locate the necessary DTD. However, because it would not be wise to rely on this mechanism in every application, any reference to a public doctype must also be followed by another reference to a system doctype. If the public doctype cannot be found, the XML processor uses the system doctype instead. Since this is a requirement, only the public doctype needs to be specifically labelled. The system doctype follows the public, but without a label. The HTML 4.01 doctype shows this clearly:

```
<!DOCTYPE HTML PUBLIC "-//W3C//DTD HTML 4.01//EN"
"http://www.w3.org/TR/html4/strict.dtd">
```

In this example, '-//W3C//DTD HTML 4.01//EN' is the public doctype and 'http://www.w3.org/TR/html4/strict.dtd' is the system doctype. The value of the system doctype can be changed from the standard URL to a local file name if required.

The next example shows our weather forecast XML document referring to a separate system DTD in the local file system. Here is the content of the DTD file ('forecast.dtd'):

```
<!ELEMENT weather-forecast (today, tomorrow, long-range)>
<!ELEMENT today (#PCDATA)>
<!ELEMENT tomorrow (#PCDATA)>
<!ELEMENT long-range (#PCDATA)>
```

This contains the DTD definition, as it appeared in our earlier example. The system DOCTYPE entry remains in the XML document and references the DTD filename. If the

DTD is separate from the XML file, then the value of the 'standalone' attribute should be 'no' instead of 'yes', as it was in the previous example. Since the default value for this attribute is 'no', it is not actually essential here.

```xml
<?xml version="1.0" standalone="no"?>
<!-- File Example5-7.xml -->
<!DOCTYPE weather-forecast SYSTEM "forecast.dtd">
<weather-forecast>
  <today>
    Rain
  </today>
  <tomorrow>
    Showers
  </tomorrow>
  <long-range>
    Unsettled
  </long-range>
</weather-forecast>
```

In this document, the DTD for the weather forecast ('forecast.dtd') is assumed to be stored in the same folder of local file system as the XML file.

Element declarations in DTDs

As we have seen from our first DTD example, the general form of an element declaration is

```
<!ELEMENT element-name (regular-expression)>
```

The 'regular-expression' describes the way the element can be used. A list of comma-separated element names defines the order in which those elements may occur, as we saw with the nested tags inside the weather forecast:

```
<!ELEMENT weather-forecast (today, tomorrow, long-range)>
```

In contrast, an element that is defined as #PCDATA will not contain any nested elements:

```
<!ELEMENT today (#PCDATA)>
```

So far we have looked at a simple example where just a sequence of elements was defined by the DTD. However, as we discussed in the context of XML, semi-structured data does not necessarily need to have such a predictable structure, but we would still like to be able to validate XML documents that exhibit semi-structured characteristics, such as optional elements, elements appearing in different orders and elements appearing many times in the same document. To explore validation of these types of document we will use a slightly more complex example. Let us assume that WebHomeCover wants to manage information about job applicants in some kind of candidate management system. This information would contain data about candidates' qualifications, skills, experience etc, but this information is likely to vary widely between different candidates. They may have different types and numbers of qualifications, have held varying numbers of previous jobs and have a wide variation in their skill sets. To store such data in XML we have to be able to take advantage of its semi-structured properties to cater for these variations in data structure.

We will begin with a simple but not very flexible DTD that deals simply with qualifications. This DTD is very similar to our weather forecast DTD:

```
<!ELEMENT qualification (certificate, diploma, degree)>
<!ELEMENT certificate (#PCDATA)>
<!ELEMENT diploma (#PCDATA)>
<!ELEMENT degree (#PCDATA)>
```

The problem here is that qualifications are not as predictable as the structure of the weather forecast (though perhaps more predictable than the weather itself!). The DTD as it stands assumes that each candidate will have a certificate, a diploma and a degree. This is no good for representing candidates who do not have all three. Fortunately, DTD syntax includes a number of operator symbols that provide the kind of flexibility that we need in order to specify our actual requirements.

DTD operator symbols

One way we might address the current limitation of requiring all three qualifications is by using the vertical bar operator (|), which in DTD syntax means 'or'. In this version of the first line of the DTD, a candidate might have any one of these elements appear in their XML document (a certificate, a diploma or a degree).

```
<!ELEMENT qualification (certificate | diploma | degree) >
```

This is some improvement, but on the other hand each candidate can now only have any one of these qualifications, but not more than one. We can solve this problem by nesting the qualification element inside another element ('qualifications') that may occur more than once. The asterisk operator (*) is used to specify that an element may occur zero or more times, as in this example, where the 'qualifications' element consists of zero of more 'qualification' elements:

```
<!ELEMENT qualifications (qualification*)>
```

This is much better. Now we can have as many qualifications as we want. However, this still may not be ideal, since the qualification element may occur zero times, meaning the candidate has no qualifications at all. To ensure that there is at least one qualification included in the document we can use the '+' operator, which means 'one or more', instead of the '*' operator. In this version, there must be one or more qualifications.

```
<!ELEMENT qualifications (qualification+)>
```

Another useful specification is to make an element optional, so that it may appear zero or one times (but no more than one.) The operator used to indicate an optional element is the question mark. Perhaps we are interested in whether a candidate has some kind of higher qualification as well, but do not need to know if they have more than one. We might add a 'higher qualification' element, but make it optional:

```
<!ELEMENT qualifications (qualification+, higher-qualification?)>
```

From these examples we can see that we need to design the DTD specification carefully to match our requirements. Table 5.1 summarizes the various operator symbols that we have introduced for specifying element characteristics in a DTD.

TABLE 5.1   The operator symbols used in DTDs

Operator Symbol	Meaning
|	Or
*	Zero or more
+	One or more
?	Optional (zero or one)

Empty elements

We might choose to make an element specifically empty, which means that a valid XML document cannot include a body for tags of this type. Tags that have a body of content are, as we have seen, specified using the #PCDATA type. In contrast, empty elements are defined using EMPTY. For example, the 'higher-qualification' element might be declared to be empty:

```
<!ELEMENT higher-qualification EMPTY>
```

Although it is possible to have an empty element that also has no attributes, perhaps to be used as some kind of 'switch' in a document to indicate simply if something is there or not, most empty tags do include attributes. For example, the 'higher-qualification' element might contain an attribute that contains the type of the qualification. We will see how to include attributes in a DTD a little later.

The following example ('qualifications.dtd') is a DTD consisting purely of element declarations (no attributes) that includes examples of the syntax that we have introduced so far. There are some additional elements (year, institution and name) added to our previous examples.

```
<!ELEMENT qualifications (qualification+, higher-qualification?,
institution+)>
<!ELEMENT qualification (year, (certificate | diploma | degree) ) >
<!ELEMENT higher-qualification EMPTY>
<!ELEMENT year (#PCDATA)>
<!ELEMENT certificate (#PCDATA)>
<!ELEMENT diploma (#PCDATA)>
<!ELEMENT degree (#PCDATA)>
<!ELEMENT institution (name)>
<!ELEMENT name (#PCDATA)>
```

In the example DTD, the first line says that a 'qualifications' (root) element contains one or more elements of type 'qualification', an optional 'higher-qualification' and one or more 'institution' elements, in that order.

The second line says that each 'qualification' element contains first a 'year' element, then either a 'certificate', 'diploma' or 'degree' element. 'certificate', 'diploma' and 'degree' elements contain just character data. An 'institution' element contains a 'name' element.

5

The more complex a DTD, the more flexibly-structured its valid XML documents can be. With a DTD that has optional elements and elements that can occur more than once, there can be many variations in structure for valid XML. The next example is a valid XML document for this DTD. This document contains two 'qualification' elements and two 'institution' elements, as well as an (empty) 'higher-qualification' element.

```xml
<?xml version='1.0'?>
<!-- File Example5-8.xml -->
<!DOCTYPE qualifications SYSTEM "qualifications.dtd">
<qualifications>
  <qualification>
    <year>2001</year>
    <diploma>Electronic Engineering</diploma>
  </qualification>
  <qualification>
    <year>2005</year>
    <degree>Computer Science</degree>
  </qualification>
  <higher-qualification/>
  <institution>
    <name>Oxford University</name>
  </institution>
  <institution>
    <name>MIT</name>
  </institution>
</qualifications>
```

The next XML document is also valid against 'qualifications.dtd'. Note that it is much shorter, including only one 'qualification' and one 'institution', and no 'higher-qualification'.

```xml
<?xml version='1.0'?>
<!-- File Example5-9.xml -->
<!DOCTYPE qualifications SYSTEM "qualifications.dtd">
<qualifications>
  <qualification>
    <year>1999</year>
    <certificate>Baking</certificate>
  </qualification>
  <institution>
    <name>Springfield College</name>
  </institution>
</qualifications>
```

Attribute declarations in DTDs

So far, our validated XML examples have only used elements, but sometimes attributes can be used to do things that elements cannot. This becomes very clear once we start to validate our XML against DTDs, because DTDs can provide some very useful data and metadata about attributes. Attributes can be used in conjunction with DTDs to:

- Define a default value
- Define a set of valid values

- Define fixed values (constants)
- Create references between elements.

None of these features can be described with XML alone, only by using a DTD.

To start validating XML documents with attributes we need to look at the DTD syntax for describing attributes. The attributes of an element are declared in a single list using ATTLIST:

```
<!ATTLIST element-name attribute-specification...attribute-specification>
```

The element must be defined in the same DTD. More than one attribute can be specified in a single ATTLIST element.

Each attribute specification will have the form *name type value*. 'name' is an arbitrarily chosen name for the attribute; each name may only appear once in the attribute declaration, but the same attribute name can be used in different elements. In other words the name of an attribute, unlike the name of an element, does not have to be unique in a DTD.

The CDATA attribute type

There are many attribute types, but the most common is CDATA, which means 'character data', This is not quite the same as the #PCDATA type used with elements, because the attribute values are not parsed by XML processors in the same way as the data in the body of an element.

Attribute keywords

Attribute keywords specify whether an attribute is required (compulsory), implied (optional) or fixed (constant). In this example the 'type' attribute of the 'higher-qualification' element is shown as #REQUIRED, which makes it compulsory:

```
<!ATTLIST higher-qualification type CDATA #REQUIRED>
```

In contrast, the 'internationally-recognised' attribute of the 'qualification' element is optional, as indicated by the #IMPLIED keyword:

```
<!ATTLIST qualification internationally-recognised CDATA #IMPLIED>
```

An attribute with a fixed value (a constant) can be indicated by the #FIXED keyword, like this 'name' attribute of the 'company' element:

```
<!ATTLIST company name CDATA #FIXED "WebHomeCover.com">
```

The partial DTD in the next example includes a compulsory attribute declaration; the 'institution' element includes a compulsory 'is-university' attribute. This means that any XML document that is valid according to this DTD must include an 'is-university' attribute in any 'institution' elements.

```
<!ELEMENT institution (name, location)>
<!ATTLIST institution is-university CDATA #REQUIRED>
<!ELEMENT name (#PCDATA)>
```

Other attribute types

Not all attributes are simple character data (CDATA). Attributes that are not declared as CDATA can include those with default values, enumerated types and those of type NMTOKEN.

Default values are declared in quotes after the attribute name. In this example of a default value, a 'qualification' element has a 'years-of-study' attribute with a default value of '3':

```
<!ATTLIST qualification years-of-study "3">
```

When using an enumerated type, the attribute must have one of a set of specified values when it is used in an XML document. The possible values are separated by vertical bars (i.e. the 'or' character):

```
(value1|value2|..)
```

In this example of an enumerated type, the 'is-university' attribute can only be 'true' or 'false'. A default of 'false' is used here, though providing a default is not essential.

```
<!ATTLIST institution is-university (true | false) "false">
```

Defining REQUIRED or IMPLIED is not relevant when a default value is provided, but is otherwise. Any number of possible values can be provided for an enumerated type. Here, the names of the days of the week are used for a 'day-name' attribute:

```
<!ATTLIST calendar day-name (Monday | Tuesday | Wednesday | Thursday |
Friday | Saturday | Sunday) #REQUIRED>
```

Since no default value is provided, the attribute has been marked as required.

The NMTOKEN attribute type means 'name token'. If you use this type instead of CDATA, it restricts the set of characters that the attribute can contain to letters, numbers, periods, dashes, underscores and colons:

The following DTD ('qualifications2.dtd') is based on the one we looked at earlier, describing qualifications and institutions, but has had several attributes added to it:

```
<!ELEMENT qualifications (qualification+, higher-qualification?, institution+)*>
<!ELEMENT qualification (year, (certificate | diploma | degree) ) >
<!ATTLIST qualification level CDATA #REQUIRED
     internationally-recognised CDATA #IMPLIED
   years-of-study CDATA "3">
<!ELEMENT higher-qualification EMPTY>
<!ATTLIST higher-qualification type CDATA #REQUIRED>
<!ELEMENT year (#PCDATA) >
<!ELEMENT certificate (#PCDATA) >
<!ELEMENT diploma (#PCDATA) >
<!ELEMENT degree (#PCDATA) >
<!ATTLIST degree type CDATA #REQUIRED>
<!ELEMENT institution (name) >
<!ATTLIST institution is-university (true | false) "false">
<!ELEMENT name (#PCDATA) >
```

Here is an XML document that is valid against this DTD.

```
<?xml version="1.0"?>
<!DOCTYPE qualifications SYSTEM "qualifications2.dtd">
<! -- File Example5-10.xml -->
<qualifications>
   <qualification level="3" internationally-recognised="no">
      <year>1999</year>
      <certificate>Baking</certificate>
   </qualification >
   <higher-qualification type="Master of Baking" />
   <institution is-university="false">
      <name> The McBaking Institute of Culinary Technology</name>
   </institution>
</qualifications>
```

Entities

ENTITY declarations can be used to define references to values that are either internal or external to the DTD. Here for example, we declare an entity called 'whc' to refer to the internal value 'WebHomeCover.com'

```
<!ENTITY whc "WebHomeCover.com">
```

The entity reference can be used in an XML document to refer to this value. An entity reference has the same format as a special character in HTML: it is preceded by an ampersand and followed by a semicolon, for example:

```
<company-name>&whc;</company-name>
```

When the XML document is processed by a browser or other tool, the original value is substituted for the entity reference.

5.6 XHTML

In the final section of this chapter, we introduce the eXtensible HyperText Markup Language (XHTML). XHTML provides a way to write HTML documents using well-formed and valid XML syntax, and is the W3C replacement for version 4 of HTML.

In early versions of HTML, there was no requirement that it should necessarily be well-formed. Although DTDs have been available for validating HTML documents since version 2.0, they were not widely used in the early years. Further, only since HTML 4.01 have we had a 'strict' document type that enforces the separation of content and structure from presentation. XHTML is a fully XML-compliant development of HTML 4.01. Like any XML document, an XHTML document must be well-formed and should be valid against the appropriate DTD. The first version of XHTML (version 1.0) included three different DOCTYPES that were similar in intent to those available for HTML 4. These were the 'transitional', 'frameset' and 'strict' doctypes. The frameset and transitional doctypes allowed many 'deprecated' elements to be used for backward compatibility (a deprecated element is one that should no longer be used). Only the strict doctype provided a rigorous validity check that separated content and structure from presentation. We will be using the XHTML 1.1 DTD, which is the most recent version at the time of writing and does not have transitional or frameset options. However, this version is to be superseded by XHTML 2.0, 'a general purpose markup language without presentation elements . . . designed for representing documents for a wide range of purposes across the web' (Pemberton 2007).

Here is the XHTML 1.1 DOCTYPE:

```
<!DOCTYPE html PUBLIC "-//W3C//DTD XHTML 1.1//EN"
"http://www.w3.org/TR/xhtml11/DTD/xhtml11.dtd">
```

The XHTML 1.1 specification also says that in addition to defining the document type, the root element of the document should also designate the XHTML *namespace* using the 'xmlns' attribute of the 'html' element, like this:

```
<html xmlns="http://www.w3.org/1999/xhtml">
```

The namespace is a way of uniquely identifying the origin of a particular tag and is based on a URN.

Further, we should also use the 'xml:lang' attribute to declare the language of the page (English in this case):

```
<html xmlns="http://www.w3.org/1999/xhtml" xml:lang="en">
```

 NOTE The 'xml:lang' attribute replaces the 'lang' attribute that was used in HTML and was allowed in XHTML version 1.0.

As well as being well-formed, an XHTML document that is valid against the document type must follow a number of other rules, which we will outline in this section. Perhaps the most obvious is that XHTML tags must be written in lower case, whereas in HTML 4, either case may be used but upper case is the normal convention.

XHTML, like strict HTML 4.01, explicitly forbids presentational mark-up, assuming the use of CSS. Further, we should also avoid using the bold <b> or italic <i> tags, which are still legal in XHTML version 1.1, but are likely to be invalid elements in future versions.

In general terms, XHTML is a little more demanding than HTML 4.01 in terms of being well-formed. For example, whereas you can omit the closing BODY tag in a valid HTML 4.01 document, because browsers are able to automatically complete some unfinished elements, you cannot do so in a valid XHTML document.

Empty elements

One of the main differences between strict HTML 4.01 and XHTML is the way that empty elements are expressed. In HTML, there are a number of empty elements.

These include LINK, IMG, BR and HR. In HTML they are normally written as if they were opening tags, such as this line break element:

```
<BR>
```

In contrast, we should express an empty element like this in XML syntax:

```
<br/>
```

In order to ensure backward compatibility with older browsers, the W3C recommendation is that all empty elements in XHTML should also have a space before the final '/>' characters. Here are some empty elements as they should be expressed in XHTML:

```
<link href="webhomecover.css" rel="stylesheet" type="text/css" />
<img src="webhomecoverlogo.gif" alt="the WebHomeCover company logo" />
<br />
<hr />
```

No minimised attributes

XHTML attributes cannot be 'minimised'. In HTML there are some examples where attribute values are expressed in a shorthand form, usually where the attribute name and its allowed value are the same. An example of this is the OPTION element in a select list, where we can define a default selection for the list of items by adding 'selected' to one of the options. Here, the 'house' option is the default selection.

```
<SELECT name="property-type">
  <OPTION value="house" selected>house</option>
  <OPTION value="apartment">apartment</option>
  <OPTION value="shack">shack</option>
</SELECT >
```

In XHTML, this type of minimisation is invalid, so every attribute must have both a name and a value. In XHTML, the select list would have to be rewritten like this:

```
<select name="property-type">
  <option value="house" selected="selected">house</option>
  <option value="apartment">apartment</option>
  <option value="shack">shack</option>
</select>
```

5

Exercises

5.1 Here is the XML document, from Section 5.4, that is not well formed:

```
<?xml version="1.0"?>
<climate>
  <average-winter-temperature>
    10
  <average-summer-temperature>
    20
  </average-summer-temperature>
</climate>
```

As we saw from the example, if you load this into a browser, an error message complains that the closing 'average-winter-temperature' tag is missing when it gets to the closing 'climate' tag. Why doesn't it fail as soon as it gets to the opening 'average-summer-temperature' tag?

5.2 Here is a simple DTD:

```
<!ELEMENT building (address, value, construction)>
<!ELEMENT address (#PCDATA)>
<!ELEMENT value (#PCDATA)>
<!ELEMENT construction (#PCDATA)>
<!ATTLIST building rental (true|false) #REQUIRED>
```

Write an XML document that is valid against this DTD that describes an insured building, at 100 Seaview Road, worth £400,000, of brick and tile construction and used as a rental.

5.3 Earlier in this chapter, we saw the following XML document:

```
<?xml version="1.0"?>
<!-- File: Example5-2.xml -->
<weather-forecast>
  <today>
    <general>Rain</general>
    <temperature>
      <maximum>15</maximum>
      <minimum>11</minimum>
    </temperature>
  </today>
  <tomorrow>
    <general>Showers</general>
    <temperature>
      <maximum>20</maximum>
      <minimum>15</minimum>
    </temperature>
  </tomorrow>
  <long-range>Unsettled</long-range>
</weather-forecast>
```

Write a DTD against which this document would be valid.

5.4   Write a DTD against which this XML document would be valid

```
<policies>
    <description>Policies taken out in January</description>
    <policy type="contents">
        <policy-number>1234557</policy-number>
        <policy-holder>A. Liu</policy-holder>
    </policy>
    <policy type="buildings">
        <policy-number>1234558</policy-number>
        <policy-holder>C. Jones</policy-holder>
    </policy>
    <report-date>01/01/2008</report-date>
</policies>
```

Assume there can be zero or more 'policy' elements, and that the 'type' attribute is compulsory.

5.5   Write a DTD that encompasses these rules for elements and attributes

Elements:

- A 'policy-report' root element consists of an optional 'description' element, one or more 'policy' elements and a 'report-dates' element.
- 'report-dates' is an empty element.
- 'policy' elements consist of a 'policy-number' element, followed by either a 'personal-customer' element or a 'corporate-customer' element.
- 'description', 'policy-number', 'personal-customer' and 'corporate-customer' are parsed character data.

Attributes:
- 'policy' elements have a compulsory type attribute that can only have the value 'buildings' or 'contents'.
- 'report-dates' has two attributes, a compulsory 'start' attribute and an optional 'end' attribute.

5.6   Now write an XML document that is valid against the DTD that you created for Exercise 5.5.

5.7   Take the HTML document from Example 4.12.htm, which demonstrates the three region layout, and convert it to valid XHTML. You will need to:

- Change the DOCTYPE
- Add the namespace and language to the opening HTML tag
- Change all the element names to lower case
- Make sure the empty elements are correctly terminated.

5

SUMMARY

We began this chapter by describing the limitations of HTML in its role as a mark-up language that combines page content, structure and presentation. We introduced the concept of semi-structured data and saw how XML follows its principles. We looked at how XML is a metalanguage, able to be used to define any number of specific mark-up languages due to its extensible nature. We explored the concept of validation, both for XML and HTML, and finally XHTML, which is the evolutionary path that has seen the joining together of HTML and XML. Along the way we saw how document validation may be performed using DTDs, to ensure that our documents are structured correctly.

References and further reading

BBC (2005) *Radio Times*. http://www.radiotimes.com/

Bray, T., Paoli, J., Sperberg-McQueen, C., Maler, E. and Yergeau, F. (2004) *Extensible Markup Language (XML) 1.1*. W3C. http://www.w3.org/TR/2004/REC-xml11–20040204/

Bray, T., Paoli, J., Sperberg-McQueen, C., Maler, E. and Yergeau, F. (2006) *Extensible Markup Language (XML) 1.0 (Fourth Edition)*. W3C http://www.w3.org/TR/REC-xml/#sec-origin-goals

Eckstein, R. (2002) *Java Enterprise Best Practices*. Farnham: O'Reilly.

Eden, R. (2005) *XMLTV wiki*. http://xmltv.org/

Pemberton, S. (2007) *XHTML2 Working Group Home Page*. http://www.w3.org/MarkUp/

Uniprot. (2005) *The Universal Protein Resource*. http://www.ebi.uniprot.org/index.shtml

CHAPTER 6

Introduction to JavaScript

LEARNING OBJECTIVES

- **To understand the role of client-side scripting languages in supporting application processes within the browser**

- **To understand the key features of the JavaScript language**

- **To be able to use the objects, properties and methods of the DOM to interact with browsers and HTML documents**

- **To be able to write simple scripts that manipulate JavaScript variables**

- **To understand how to write JavaScript functions and to put them into separate files that can be called from scripts in web pages**

INTRODUCTION

In this chapter, we introduce the JavaScript language, which can be used to write code that runs inside the browser. We apply some of the most important concepts in JavaScript, including the document object model (DOM) and the built-in JavaScript objects. Examples in this chapter show how to use the properties and methods of JavaScript objects, how to work with simple data types including numbers, strings, dates and arrays, and how to use the arithmetic operators. We explore the control structures of JavaScript programming and see how to write code in script elements, functions and external files.

6.1 JavaScript – what and why?

Scripting languages are lightweight programming languages that are usually interpreted rather than compiled and run inside a particular environment. *'a client-side script is a program that may accompany an HTML document or be embedded directly in it'* (Ragget *et al.* 1999).

JavaScript is the most commonly used of a number of scripting languages that can run inside web browsers. JavaScript code can be embedded in, or called from, HTML documents and these scripts can generate page content dynamically. In general, JavaScript is used for three main purposes:

- To improve the visual look and feel of the user's experience using a browser-based application. For example, JavaScript can be used to create pop up windows and interactive menus, and to enable parts of the page, such as images, to respond to *mouse events*, such as the mouse pointer passing over them. JavaScript, combined with the DOM and cascading style sheets (CSS), is the basis for Dynamic HTML (DHTML), which enables browser-based applications to become more interactive.
- To offload some of the web application processing from the server to the client. A good example of this is the ability to perform client-side form validation, checking the contents of an HTML form before it is submitted to the server for further processing. Not all validation can be done on the client, but simple things like checking that required fields are not empty can still be very useful.
- To enable Asynchronous JavaScript and XML (Ajax) implementations to provide a more seamless interaction between client and server.

JavaScript was originally developed in 1995 by Netscape and introduced into Netscape Navigator 2.0. It was originally called 'LiveScript' but later became 'JavaScript', and is therefore often confused with Java, though there are many differences between them. Although the term 'JavaScript' is widely used, strictly speaking the name only applies to the Netscape version. The version that runs in Microsoft browsers is called 'JScript', and there is also a standard version of the language known as 'ECMAScript'. ECMA is a European standards consortium that began as the European Computer Manufacturers' Association, hence the acronym.

6.2 The document object model (DOM)

The DOM is a W3C specification that enables scripting languages, like JavaScript, to access and update the content, structure and style of documents, regardless of the platform or scripting language being used. The first DOM specification (level 1) was published in 1998, the second (level 2) in 2000 and the third (level 3) in 2004. The DOM consists of a set of core interfaces that apply to any structured document, with additional interfaces that are specifically intended for use with XML or HTML documents. As HTML has grown closer to XML with the XHTML specification, this distinction between XML and HTML has become less important. The term 'DOM level 0' is sometimes used to refer to the de facto object model that was used in browsers (such as Internet Explorer 3 and Netscape Navigator 3) prior to the first formal DOM specification. Some parts of the DOM API that relate specifically to HTML were included to ensure backward compatibility with these earlier document models.

The DOM represents a document as a hierarchy of nodes, some of which can have child nodes and some that are leaf nodes. You will recognize core aspects of the DOM from our prior discussions of the structure of XML documents. For example the *document* node can only have one child of type *element* (which of course is the root element of the document.) An *element* node, however, can have multiple child nodes, and these may also be elements. A *text* node is a leaf, meaning that it cannot have any child nodes. As we look at JavaScript, you will find that it has its own way of modelling the document object, some of which comes directly from the standard W3C DOM and some of which is specific to JavaScript.

6

6.3 Characteristics of JavaScript

The language constructs in JavaScript are similar to a number of other languages, including C, C++, C# and Java, but there are some important differences. Perhaps the most obvious difference is that JavaScript is loosely typed, meaning that when we declare a variable we only have to declare its name, not its type. We can also use the same variable to reference different types of data at different times. This is not possible in strongly typed languages like Java, but is possible when using PHP, which is also loosely typed.

JavaScript is not a fully object-oriented language, and does not allow the creation of new object types (though more recent versions of ECMAScript have begun to move in this direction). Rather it is an object-based, or *prototype* language, where there are a number of built-in objects and object types that can be used in programs. For example the top-level object in the JavaScript DOM is the *window*, which represents the browser window (or frame).

Setting the default scripting language for a web page

Since JavaScript is only one of a number of scripting languages that may be supported by browsers (others include VBScript and Tcl), it is necessary to specify that JavaScript is the language being used in a particular page. The 'meta' element should be used inside the 'head' element to set the default scripting language, like this:

```
<meta http-equiv="Content-Script-Type" content="text/javascript" />
```

It is important to set the default scripting language for scripts that are linked to *intrinsic events*, such as mouse buttons being pressed, keys on the keyboard being pressed and HTML documents being loaded.

 NOTE 'text/javascript' is likely to be replaced by 'application/javascript' in forthcoming standards but is not yet widely supported by browsers.

Adding scripts to web pages

Scripts can be added to a web page by using <script>...</script> elements. These can be added either to the head or the body elements of the HTML, or even as a separate element outside of the page definition. Scripts can also be written as reusable functions in separate files (described in Section 6.9). Script elements that are *not* part of JavaScript functions will be run when the page is loaded, whereas functions can be invoked at other times, for example, by clicking on a button. In addition to setting the default scripting language in the document's *meta* tag, each script element should also define the scripting language being used for that particular element by setting the *type* attribute to 'text/javascript'. All script elements that use JavaScript, regardless of where they appear in the document, should therefore appear like this:

```
<script type="text/javascript">
   ... JavaScript source code goes here
</script>
```

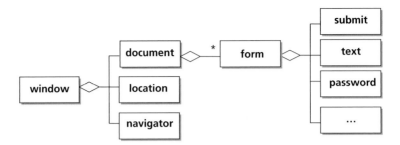

6.4 JavaScript objects

Now we know what sort of tag to use to include JavaScript in our web pages, what type of code goes into these elements? One important aspect of JavaScript is its ability to interact with objects of various types. Some of these relate to the DOM components of the browser environment, such as *window*, *document*, *location* and *navigator*. Some relate to common data types such as *Array*, *String* and *Date*, while others, such as *Math*, provide some standard utility functions. The objects that relate to the browser environment have parent–child relationships, where one object contains another. Figure 6.1 shows the relationships between just a few of the browser-related JavaScript objects. The window object contains the document (that is loaded in the browser window) and the location and navigator objects, and the document may contain a form that in turn contains various HTML controls such as text fields and buttons.

Object properties

JavaScript objects have *properties*, *methods* and *event handlers*. Properties are values that reflect the state of an object; methods are operations that an object can perform; and event handlers enable state changes or methods to be invoked when an event, such as a button being pressed, a component losing or gaining focus, or a document being loaded, occurs. An object's properties can be accessed using 'dot' notation, where the name of the object is followed by the name of the property, separated by a dot:

```
object.property
```

The value of the property can be set using the ' = ' operator. One of the properties of the document object for example is the *title*. This is the text that appears in the title bar at the top of the browser window. This example shows the title property of the document being set.

```
document.title="JavaScript document title"
```

Here is the full source of an XHTML page that sets the document title property using a script element in the body of the page. Note that the XHTML head element needs to contain a title element, even if it is empty, in order to be valid XHTML and, of course, for JavaScript to locate the element in order to populate it.

```
<?xml version="1.0"?>
<!DOCTYPE html PUBLIC "-//W3C//DTD XHTML 1.1//EN"
    "http://www.w3.org/TR/xhtml11/DTD/xhtml11.dtd">
```

```
<html xmlns="http://www.w3.org/1999/xhtml" xml:lang="en">
  <head>
    <meta http-equiv="Content-Script-Type" content="text/javascript"/>
    <title></title>
  </head>
  <body>
    <!-- File: Example6-1.htm -->
    <script type="text/javascript">
      document.title="JavaScript document title"
    </script>
  </body>
</html>
```

Since scripts included in the body are executed when the document is loaded, the title bar appears as shown in Figure 6.2 when the document is loaded into a browser (this example uses Internet Explorer 7).

Comments in JavaScript source code

There are two ways that comment syntax can be useful in JavaScript. First, we can use the JavaScript comment syntax simply to add comments to our code to help others to understand it, and second, we sometimes need to 'hide' JavaScript code from the browser, for reasons we explain shortly.

There are two types of comment syntax in JavaScript, for single-line or multiple-line comments. Single line comments, similar to C++ comment syntax, are preceded by two forward slashes:

```
// this is a single line comment
```

Multiple-line comments use C-style syntax, beginning with a forward slash and an asterisk, and ending with an asterisk and a forward slash:

```
/*
This is a
multiple-line comment
*/
```

6

| FIGURE 6.2 | The Internet Explorer 7 title bar set using the 'document.title' property

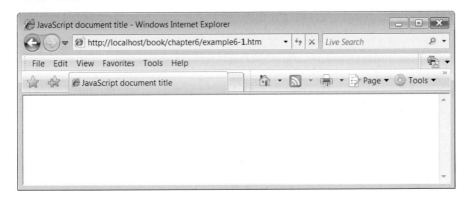

These types of comment are useful to help other JavaScript developers understand the scripts you have written. The second use of comment syntax is to wrap an HTML or XML comment, combined with a JavaScript single line comment, around the code in your script elements. There are two reasons to do this:

- If the client's browser does not support JavaScript, or if JavaScript is disabled, the code can be hidden from the browser.
- If you want the rest of your page to be valid XHTML, JavaScript syntax needs to be hidden from the validator, because some characters commonly used in JavaScript (e.g. '<' and '>') cause problems in validation.

The way that we wrap comments around our scripts is to precede them with the HTML comment opening sequence, '<!--', which JavaScript treats as if it were a single line comment. Then at the end of the script, use the HTML comment closing sequence but precede it with the JavaScript single-line comment, i.e. '// -- >' The effect of this is that JavaScript ignores the closing HTML comment character but the browser recognizes it as the end of the HTML comment. Here is a modified version of the script that changes the document's title property but with the comment syntax added. Using this approach means that your scripts will not cause problems in browsers where JavaScript is not supported and your documents can still be valid XHTML.

```
<script type="text/javascript">
<!--
document.title="JavaScript document title"
// -->
</script>
```

Objects as properties

Some properties of objects are also objects. For example the *location* property of the window is actually a 'Location' object, with its own properties and methods. We can navigate through the object hierarchy using dot notation, access the 'location' property of the 'window' object and then access its own properties. In this example, the 'protocol' property of the 'location' is accessed:

```
window.location.protocol
```

Here is an XHTML page with a script that sets the document's title property using the value of the location's protocol.

```
<?xml version="1.0"?>
<!DOCTYPE html PUBLIC "-//W3C//DTD XHTML 1.1//EN"
    "http://www.w3.org/TR/xhtml11/DTD/xhtml11.dtd">
<html xmlns="http://www.w3.org/1999/xhtml" xml:lang="en">
    <head>
        <meta http-equiv="Content-Script-Type" content="text/javascript"/>
        <title></title>
    </head>
    <body>
    <!-- File: Example6-2.htm -->
        <script type="text/javascript">
            <!--
```

```
        document.title = window.location.protocol
      // -->
    </script>
  </body>
</html>
```

Figure 6.3 shows the title bar of Mozilla Firefox 2, displaying the http: protocol when a file has been loaded into the browser. Depending on what the browser is being used to display, other possible values of the 'protocol' property would include 'file:' and 'ftp:'.

 NOTE 'Location' is not a DOM object, but a JavaScript object, based on the 'location' property of the window in the DOM hierarchy.

Object methods

Methods are things that an object can do. Simple examples of object methods are the 'write' and 'writeln' methods of the 'document' object, which allow us to write page contents to the current document. The only difference between them is that 'writeln' adds a carriage return and new line to the generated HTML after writing the contents, but this does not insert a line break element into the actual HTML document. To invoke a method, we use the same dot notation as when accessing properties.

Methods can have parameter arguments passed to them, in parentheses. In this example, a 'write' method is passed some string data (which may include mark-up) as a parameter. String data is a collection of characters enclosed by speech marks (single or double).

```
document.write("<h2>Subheading</h2>")
```

Positioning scripts in the document

In the next example we use the 'document.write' method to illustrate the difference between putting a script in the body of the document as opposed to the head. If we put a script in the document body, we can position it within the rest of the document

FIGURE 6.3 The Mozilla Firefox 2 title bar set using the 'protocol' property

in a specific place. In contrast, scripts in the head element are run before the body content is rendered. The following example shows a script element that writes out a subheading being placed between HTML tags that write out a main heading and some paragraph text.

```
<?xml version="1.0"?>
<!DOCTYPE html PUBLIC "-//W3C//DTD XHTML 1.1//EN"
   "http://www.w3.org/TR/xhtml11/DTD/xhtml11.dtd">
<html xmlns="http://www.w3.org/1999/xhtml" xml:lang="en">
   <head>
      <meta http-equiv="Content-Script-Type" content="text/javascript"/>
      <title>JavaScript</title>
   </head>
   <body>
      <!-- File: Example6-3.htm -->
      <h1>Main Heading</h1>
         <script type="text/javascript">
            <!--
            document.write("<h2>Subheading</h2>")
            // -->
         </script>
      <p>paragraph text</p>
   </body>
</html>
```

The page displayed in a browser (see Figure 6.4) shows that the script has been executed in the position where it appears in the body, between the main heading and the paragraph.

In contrast, this version of the page has the script in the 'head' element:

```
<?xml version = "1.0"?>
<!DOCTYPE html PUBLIC "-//W3C//DTD XHTML 1.1//EN"
   "http://www.w3.org/TR/xhtml11/DTD/xhtml11.dtd">
<html xmlns = "http://www.w3.org/1999/xhtml" xml:lang="en">
   <head>
      <meta http-equiv="Content-Script-Type" content="text/javascript"/>
      <title>JavaScript</title>
      <script type="text/javascript">
         <!--
         document.write("<h2>Subheading</h2>")
         // -->
      </script>
   </head>
   <body>
      <!-- File: Example6-4.htm -->
      <h1>Main Heading</h1>
      <p>paragraph text</p>
   </body>
</html>
```

Figure 6.5 shows the resulting document in the browser. Note that the script has been run before the body, meaning that the subheading now comes first.

FIGURE 6.4   The script appears in its sequence within the document body

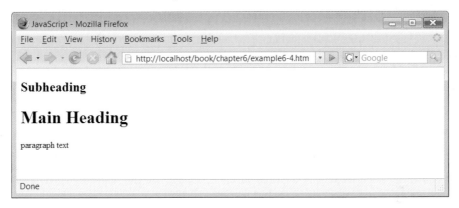

In summary, you should put your scripts in the body element if the order of their execution in terms of other body elements is important. Otherwise they can be put into the head element.

6.5 Debugging JavaScript

Before long, you will no doubt be having problems with errors in your JavaScript code, but how can you see what is wrong? In many cases, faulty JavaScript will mean the browser just displays a blank page. Fortunately, browsers provide various tools for debugging JavaScript. In Internet Explorer 7, select Tools, Internet Options. Select the Advanced tab and check the 'Display a notification about every script error' box. If something goes wrong with a page containing JavaScript, a yellow triangle with an exclamation mark will appear in the bottom left corner of the browser frame. If you double-click this, you will get a pop-up dialog that will show you any error messages. However, the debugging services in Internet Explorer are not always very helpful and it can be easier to debug your scripts in other browsers. Mozilla Firefox 2, for example, has a very good error console that shows a lot of information about JavaScript errors. To access this console, just select Tools, Error Console. Similarly, Opera 9 has an error console that can be accessed from its Tools menu; select Advanced and then Error console.

NOTE	In earlier versions of Firefox, the error console was called the JavaScript console, so the relevant menu item is 'JavaScript Console'.

6.6 JavaScript types and variables

In an earlier section we looked at some aspects of JavaScript objects that relate to the JavaScript DOM; the 'window' and 'document' objects and some of their properties. In this section we look at some data types in JavaScript, some of which are very simple types (numbers, strings, Booleans) and others that represent more complex types (Date, Math, Array). We also see how variables can be declared, and how their values may be manipulated, for example by using arithmetic expressions.

Declaring and using variables

In the examples we have seen so far, JavaScript objects have been used to modify the browser window or to provide values that have been written directly to the document object. Sometimes, however, we need to store a value, which may be the result of calling an object's method, in a variable. In JavaScript, a variable is just a name used to refer to a particular value. It is not declared to be of any specific type, but is simply declared using the reserved word 'var', e.g.

```
var myVariable
```

Although variables need not necessarily be declared using the 'var' reserved word, it is important to understand that declaring a variable without preceding it with 'var' will make it a *global* variable. Global variables are visible to all scripts in the current page. Therefore, unless you really need to declare a global variable, always use the 'var' keyword. There are a few simple rules for JavaScript variable names:

- The first character must be a letter (upper or lower case) or an underscore.
- The rest of the name can include upper or lower case letters, numbers and underscores.
- Names should not begin with two underscores because names in this format are used by JavaScript for internal purposes.
- Names cannot include spaces.
- Names cannot be JavaScript reserved words.
- Names are case sensitive.

Although variables do not have a specific type, the values that they refer to do have a type. These types include simple numbers, strings (of characters) and Booleans. It can be useful to name variables in such as way that their type is indicated by their name. For example we can start each variable name with a three-letter indicator of its type, e.g. 'int' for integers, 'boo' for Booleans, 'str' for strings, and so on. This fragment of JavaScript shows some literal values of these three types being assigned to three variables. In each case, the variable declaration is the same, since no data typing is used.

```
var intSomeNumber = 4
var strSomeCharacters = "characters"
```

```
var booSomeIndicator = true
```

In the example above, the three variables are declared on separate lines. Using a new line as a separator between different statements in JavaScript is acceptable, but statements should really be separated by semicolons, like this:

```
var intSomeNumber = 4;
var strSomeCharacters = "characters";
var booSomeIndicator = true;
```

This approach is more robust than just using new lines, because the semicolon will separate statements even if they appear on the same line.

Arithmetic on numeric variables

We can perform arithmetic with JavaScript numeric variables using these five operators:

add $+$
subtract $-$
multiply $*$
divide $/$
modulus   %

All arithmetic statements have the same format, namely that a variable on the left of an assignment ($=$) operator is made to equal the result of an arithmetic expression on the right:

```
var = expression;
```

Some examples (where the 'flt' prefix indicates a floating point number) might be

```
var intTotalBananas = intMyBananas + intYourBananas;
var fltNetPay = fltGrossPay - fltDeductions;
var fltArea = fltHeight * fltWidth;
var fltDistanceInKm = fltDistanceInMiles / 0.62137;
var intParentsBiscuits = intNumberOfBiscuits % intNumberOfChildren;
```

Increment and decrement operators

There are also some simple operators to increment and decrement the value of a variable by. The most commonly used is probably the '++' operator, which adds 1 to a variable.

```
var intCounter = 1;
intCounter++;
```

In this example, the variable 'intCounter' would be incremented to hold the value 2. We can see that the increment operator is simply shorthand for

```
intCounter = intCounter + 1;
```

There is also a decrement operator, which, logically enough, is '--' and subtracts 1 from the value of a variable:

```
intCounter --;
```

This would subtract 1 from the current value of 'intCounter', and is shorthand for

```
intCounter = intCounter - 1;
```

Prefix and postfix operators

The previous examples of the increment and decrement operators both used 'postfix' notation (i.e., the '++' or ' – ' appears after the variable). We may also use 'prefix' notation (the operator appears before the variable):

```
postfix notation:  intCounter++   or   intCounter--
prefix notation:   ++intCounter   or   --intCounter
```

This makes no difference if the operator is not used as part of a larger expression, but can be significant if it is. If one of these operators is used in prefix notation, then the operator will execute before the rest of an expression, but if postfix notation is used then it will be executed afterwards. For example, if the value of our 'intCounter' variable is to be assigned to another variable in the following expression:

```
var intCounter = 1;
var intCurrentCount = intCounter++;
```

The value of 'intCurrentCount' is 1, because the increment operator (which adds 1 to 'intCounter') is evaluated after the assignment of the value of 'intCounter' to 'intCurrentCount' (postfix notation). With prefix notation, where the increment takes place before the assignment, the value of 'intCurrentCount' will be 2:

```
var intCounter = 1;
var intCurrentCount = ++intCounter;
```

To avoid confusion, the increment and decrement operators will not be used as part of larger expressions in this book and the postfix notation will be adopted in all cases.

Other shorthand expressions

The increment and decrement operators are appropriate only when we need to add 1 to, or subtract 1 from, the existing value of a variable. However, we also have shorthand for changing the value of a variable by arithmetic on its existing value. As one example, we could replace the expression:

```
fltVariable = fltVariable + 5;
```

with:

```
fltVariable += 5;
```

As you can see, when we are changing the value of a variable, this shorthand form simply avoids having to write the name of the variable twice. Variables can be decremented similarly, so to subtract 4 from 'fltVariable' we could write:

```
fltVariable -= 4;
```

Table 6.1 shows examples of shorthand expressions for all five arithmetic operators.

Order of precedence

When writing expressions that contain more than one arithmetic operator, you need to be aware of the 'order of precedence' i.e., which part of the expression will be evaluated first. There is a standard (and quite large) table for this that applies to virtually all languages, but the most important parts of it are shown in Table 6.2.

Consider this example:

```
var intVar = 4 + 2 * 3;
```

TABLE 6.1 Using the shorthand expressions for arithmetic operators

Usual expression	Shorthand expression
fltVariable = fltVariable + 5;	fltVariable +=5;
fltVariable = fltVariable − 4;	fltVariable −=4;
fltVariable = fltVariable * 2;	fltVariable *=2;
fltVariable = fltVariable / 3;	fltVariable /=3;
fltVariable = fltVariable % 4;	fltVariable %=4;

TABLE 6.2 Some important elements of the order of precedence table

Order of precedence	Symbols	Description
Higher	( )	parentheses
	++	increment and decrement operators
	−	
	*	multiply, divide and modulus operators
	/	
	%	
	+	addition and subtraction operators
	−	
	*=	shorthand assignment expressions
	/=	
	+=	
	-=	
Lower	%=	

6

Since the multiplication is executed before the addition, the result would be 10. If this is not what we want, we can use parentheses to change the order in which parts of an expression are evaluated. To force the addition to be executed first we can write

```
var intVar = (4 + 2) * 3;
```

As you would expect, this gives the result of 18, since the addition is now performed before the multiplication. If two operators of the same precedence (i.e., add and subtract, or multiply, divide and remainder) appear in the same expression, then they are evaluated from left to right. For example, in the following expression, the multiplication is evaluated before the division, giving the answer 15:

```
var intVar = 10 * 3 / 2;
```

6.7 Using and creating objects

In Section 6.4, we introduced some of the JavaScript objects that relate to the DOM, such as 'document' and 'window'. There are a number of other types of object available to us in JavaScript. Some of these are single objects that can be used directly, such as the 'Math' object, while others are types that we can create on the fly, such as Strings and Dates. In this section, we introduce some of these object types and see how they can be created and used.

The Math object

The arithmetic operators are fine for simple calculations, but sometimes we need the services of something that can do more complex mathematics. In these situations, the 'Math' object provides support for a number of mathematical operations, including methods for geometry, raising a number to a power, rounding and random-number generation. The following script uses the 'random' method to generate a pseudo-random number between zero and one.

```
<!-- File: Example6-5.htm -->
<script type = "text/javascript">
  <!--
    document.write("Here is a random number between zero and one: ");
    document.write(Math.random() )
  // -->
</script>
```

Figure 6.6 shows one possible output from this script. Since the number generated by the random method is always between zero and one, deriving random numbers in other ranges, or random integers, requires some further work.

Since the various methods of the Math class return the values of mathematical operations, these returned values may be assigned to variables, for example,

```
var fltRandomNumber = Math.random();
```

The Math class also has some properties representing common mathematical values. One of these is 'PI'. The following script element uses 'Math.PI', and the 'Math.pow' method,

FIGURE 6.6 A pseudo-random number generated by the Math.random() method

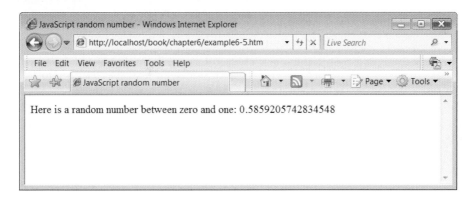

FIGURE 6.7   The area of the circle resulting from the calculation using the Math object

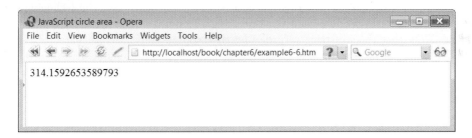

which raises the first parameter to the power of the second, to calculate the area of a circle. Though this is a simple example, it shows both properties and methods of the Math class, assigning results to variables, and using parentheses to ensure that parts of the calculation take place in the correct order (that is, we square the radius before multiplying by 'PI').

```
<!-- File: Example6-6.htm -->
<script type="text/javascript">
  <!--
    var intRadius = 10;
    var fltArea = Math.PI * (Math.pow(intRadius, 2) );
    document.write(fltArea);
  // -->
</script>
```

Figure 6.7 shows the result of the calculation displayed in the browser.

Strings

A JavaScript string is simply a sequence of zero or more characters enclosed by either single or double quotes. It does not matter which of these you use, but having the choice does enable you to enclose one type of quote within another, which can be particularly useful when combining JavaScript and HTML. For example, this is a valid JavaScript string, containing HTML that includes quoted attributes:

```
'<img src = "logo.gif" alt = "logo">'
```

Or, of course, we could switch the quote characters around:

```
"<img src = 'logo.gif' alt = 'logo'>"
```

Another useful aspect of strings is that they can be concatenated (joined together) using the '+' operator. Here, for example, we write out some text and the document title by concatenating them:

```
document.write("Document title is " + document.title);
```

You can concatenate different data types together with strings and they will be treated as a single string. Strings also have a number of properties and methods. The 'length' property, for example, returns the number of characters in a string, while the 'substring' method returns part of the string between two specified character positions. The following script uses both the 'length' property and the 'substring' method to display the last character of a string. Note that the substring returned by the method starts at the character position *after* the one specified by the first parameter, but includes the character at the position specified by the second parameter:

```
<!-- File: Example6-7.htm -->
<script type = "text/javascript">
  <!--
    var strFullString = "a string";
    var intLength = strFullString.length;
    var strSubString = strFullString.substring(intLength-1, intLength);
    document.write("Last character is " + strSubString);
  // -->
</script>
```

Figure 6.8 shows the result of the script in a browser.

FIGURE 6.8   A substring displayed in a browser window

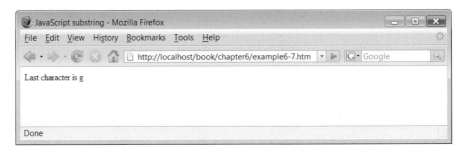

Date objects

Unlike objects that exist as part of the browser environment, and the 'Math' object which is built into JavaScript, 'Date' objects, which represent both a date and a time, need to be created when required. Being able to create 'Date' objects on the fly also means that we can create and manipulate as many of them as we like. Creating objects in JavaScript is done using the reserved word 'new' and the constructor method, which has the same name as the object type and, like other methods, is followed by parentheses. The newly created 'Date' object can be assigned to a variable:

```
var dateToday = new Date();
```

What can we do with a date? Basically we can either use the default settings, which include the date and time of its creation, or specifically set its values. If you simply write the date object to the document, you will get the current date and time of the locale being used by your machine, relative to coordinated universal time (UTC), which is based on Greenwich Mean Time. You can also display the current date and time in UTC, using the 'toUTCString' method, or display the time in the current locale with reference to UTC, using the 'toLocaleString' method. In the following script, we display the same date object in these three different ways:

```
<!-- File:Example6-8.htm -->
<script type="text/javascript">
  <!--
    var dateToday = new Date();
    document.write("The current date and time is: " + dateToday);
      document.write("<br />The date and time in Coordinated Universal Time is:
  " + dateToday.toUTCString() );
      document.write("<br />The date and time using the current locale is:
  " + dateToday.toLocaleString() );
  // -->
</script>
```

The way that different browsers display dates varies slightly. Figure 6.9 shows how the three versions of the date are displayed in Mozilla Firefox 2, but other browsers will give slightly different results in terms of presentation.

Table 6.3 shows some of the other methods of the Date class.

Arrays

An Array is a collection of values that have the same name but are identified by an index value, which appears in square brackets. Like Date objects, Arrays can be created on the fly, and we can have as many of them as we like, so again they are created using the reserved word 'new', for example:

```
var arrMyArray = new Array(size);
```

The 'size' parameter would be a number specifying the number of elements in the array. We can set or retrieve the values in the array using square brackets containing an index

FIGURE 6.9 The result of a script that displays a 'Date' object in Mozilla Firefox 2

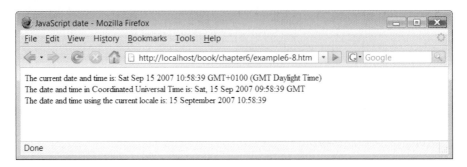

TABLE 6.3 Some methods of the Date class

Method	Purpose
getDate setDate	Returns or sets the day of the month (a number between 1 and 31)
getDay	Returns the day of the week as a number between 0 (Sunday) and 6 (Saturday)
getHours setHours	Returns or sets the hours value as an integer between 0 (midnight) and 23 (11 pm)
getMinutes setMinutes	Returns or sets the minutes value as an integer between 0 and 59
getSeconds setSeconds	Returns or sets the seconds value as an integer between 0 and 59
getFullYear setFullYear	Returns or sets the year value as a four-digit integer
getTime setTime	Returns or sets the date as the number of milliseconds since the beginning of January 1st 1970

number. The array index starts at zero, so to set a value in the first element of the array, we use zero in the brackets.

```
arrMyArray[0] = "a string";
```

Since the array has no specified type, the elements of the array can contain values of different JavaScript types. For example the next element of the array could contain a number:

```
arrMyArray[1]=10;
```

Here is a simple script that uses an array to write the name of the current day to the document. It uses a JavaScript Date object to get the number of the day of the week (using the 'getDay' method), then uses an array of strings to return the actual name of the day. Note that the 'getDay' method uses a zero to represent Sunday and then counts up from there through the days of the week, with six representing Saturday. This fits in quite neatly with an array, which also starts its index at zero.

```
<!-- File: Example6-9.htm -->
<script type="text/javascript">
```

```
<!--
    var date=new Date();
    var arrDayNames=new Array(7);
    arrDayNames[0]="Sunday";
    arrDayNames[1]="Monday";
    arrDayNames[2]="Tuesday";
    arrDayNames[3]="Wednesday";
    arrDayNames[4]="Thursday";
    arrDayNames[5]="Friday";
    arrDayNames[6]="Saturday";
    var strToday=arrDayNames[date.getDay()];
    document.write("Today is " + strToday);
// -->
</script>
```

Figure 6.10 shows the result of running this script on a Thursday.

Rather than assigning the elements of an array one at a time, an alternative approach is to use an initialisation list, where instead of creating an empty array and then adding data to elements using the index numbers, we simply provide the actual data in a comma-separated list. For example we can both create and populate the 'arrDayNames' array like this:

```
var arrDayNames =
["Sunday","Monday","Tuesday","Wednesday","Thursday","Friday", "Saturday"];
```

6.8 Control structures

JavaScript has control structures for looping and decision-making similar to those in many other languages. The 'if' and 'if...else' structures can be used to evaluate a conditional statement and respond accordingly. There are also two types of loop, the 'while' loop and the 'for' loop.

6

FIGURE 6.10   Using an array of day names to display the current day

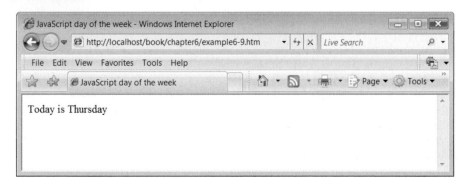

'if. . .else' statements

An 'if' statement consists of two (and only two) different courses of action and a condition. A condition in JavaScript will always return a Boolean value, and which of the two courses of action is taken depends on whether that value is true or false. One course of action may be, in fact, to do nothing. 'if' statements look like this:

```
if(condition)
{
   // do this
}
else
{
   // do this instead
}
```

The 'else' part is optional. If the condition is false and there is no 'else' part then the script will carry on executing after the 'if' statement.

Relational operators

When writing any kind of conditional statement, including 'if' statements and loops, we need to express conditions that compare variables using relational operators. The operators used in JavaScript are shown in Table 6.4.

The only operators that might cause confusion here are the 'identical to' and 'not identical to' operators. They differ from the 'equal to' and 'not equal to' operators only in that some type conversions are allowed for equality that do not apply with identity. The example shown in the table should illustrate this. If we test the expression:

```
1 == true
```

Then this will return true, because 1 can be converted to the Boolean value 'true'. However, this expression:

```
1 === true
```

will return 'false', since the identity operator does not allow type conversions when making comparisons.

TABLE 6.4   JavaScript relational operators

Condition	Relational Operator	Example
equal to	==	if(intTemperature == 100)
Identical to	===	if(1 === true)
not equal to	!=	if(chrGrade != 'F')
not identical to	!==	if(1 !== false)
less than	<	if(fltSales < fltTarget)
less than or equal to	<=	if(int EngineSize <= 2000)
greater than	>	if(intHoursWorked > 40)
greater than or equal to	>=	if(intAge >= 18)

TABLE 6.5   Logical operators

Operator	Meaning	Example
&&	AND	if(intAge > 4 && intAge < 16)
||	OR	if(intTimeElapsed > 60 || booStopped = = true)
!	NOT	if(!booFormValidated)

To evaluate more complex conditions we need to use logical operators to combine the simple relational operators shown in Table 6.4. The three logical JavaScript operators are shown in Table 6.5.

All these expressions return either true or false. The 'not' operator (!) can be confusing because it returns 'true' if the expression is 'false'. For example, the expression 'if(!booFormValidated)' in the table will be true if 'booFormValidated' is false, i.e., if the form has not been validated then 'not validated' is true. We often find this operator being used to test Boolean 'flag' variables that indicate when something has happened. The 'not' operator is matched by the ability to do a test for true, for example 'if(booFormValidated)' is an equally valid expression.

Using selection: simulating throwing a coin

The next script example makes a selection using an 'if' statement. This selection is based on using a randomly generated number to simulate throwing a coin, which may land either heads or tails. In order to represent the flipping of the coin, we need to randomly generate a value, which of course we can do with the 'Math.random' method, which returns a random value between 0.0 and 1.0. According to the ECMA specification, the function may return zero but should never return one.

```
var fltRandomNumber = Math.random();
```

Having got this value from the 'random' method, the script then uses an 'if' statement to choose whether the coin is showing heads or tails. If the random number is less than 0.5 then the coin is set to heads, otherwise it is set to tails. Of course, from the point of view of the program it makes no difference whether we use 'less than' or 'greater than', since either way we get a 50/50 chance (more or less).

```
<!-- File: Example6-10.htm -->
<script type="text/javascript">
  <!--
    document.write("The coin has landed on ");
    var fltRandomNumber = Math.random();
    if(fltRandomNumber < 0.5)
    {
       document.write(" Heads!");
    }
    else
    {
       document.write(" Tails!");
    }
  // -->
</script>
```

FIGURE 6.11   One of the two possible outcomes from a script that simulates the tossing of a coin

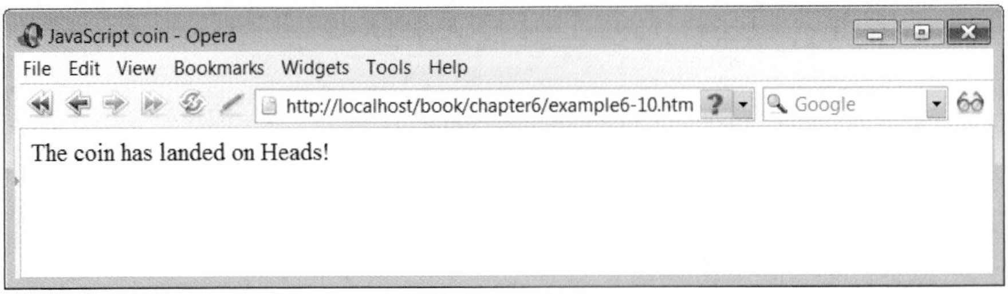

Figure 6.11 shows one of the two possible outcomes from running this script.

'while' loops

A 'while' loop can be used to write code that repeats while a given condition is true. The condition is shown in parentheses after the 'while' reserved word:

```
while(intNum <= 10)
{
    // code here
}
```

In the next example a while loop is used to simulate the throwing of a dice, again using the Math.random method to generate a pseudo-random floating point number. To get a random integer in the range 1 to 6, we first multiply the result of the Math.random method by 6, which will give us a floating point number in the range 0 to 6 (but not including exactly 6). To turn that floating point number into an integer, the 'floor' method is used, which simply truncates the number by removing any values after the decimal point, giving us an integer. The predictable behaviour of 'floor' gives us a more 'random' number than using 'round'. Finally, this is then incremented by 1 to give an integer number in the range 1 to 6. The 'while' loop repeats until the simulated dice 'throws' a 6.

```
<!-- File: Example6-11.htm -->
<script type="text/javascript">
  <!--
    var intDieValue=Math.floor(Math.random()*6);
    intDieValue++;
    while(intDieValue !=6)
    {
        document.write("You threw a " + intDieValue + "<br/>");
        intDieValue=Math.floor(Math.random()*6);
        intDieValue++;
    }
    document.write
        ("You threw a " + intDieValue + " – game over! <br/>");
  // -->
</script>
```

Figure 6.12 shows one possible output from running this script.

FIGURE 6.12   One example of output from a script that simulates the throwing of a die using a 'while' loop

FIGURE 6.12   One example of output from a script that simulates the throwing of a die using a 'while' loop

'for' loops

A 'for' loop is very similar to a 'while' loop, because it repeats while a condition remains true. However it also has two other elements, an initialisation section that can be used to set the initial value of variables used in the loop, and a section that can be used at the end of each loop to change the value of a variable:

```
for(initialise; condition; increment)
{
    // code here
}
```

A typical 'for' loop will initialise a variable at the beginning, use that variable as its conditional value, and increment (or decrement) the value of the variable at the end of each iteration.

In the next script we generate a times table. The 'for' loop is used to initialise the multiplier for the times table (at 1), provide the 'while' condition (while the multiplier is less than or equal to twelve) and the increment (incrementing the multiplier by 1). The value for the times table is generated by a random number in the range 1 to 12.

```
<!-- File: Example6-12.htm -->
<script type="text/javascript">
  <!--
  var intRandomInteger=Math.floor(Math.random()*12);
  intRandomInteger++;
  document.write(intRandomInteger + " times table <br/>");
  for(var intMultiplier=1; intMultiplier <=12; intMultiplier++)
  {
      document.writeln(intMultiplier + " x " + intRandomInteger + " = " +
  intMultiplier * intRandomInteger);
      document.writeln("<br/>");
  }
  // -->
</script>
```

Figure 6.13 shows one of the possible outcomes from this script, generating a times table.

6.9 Writing functions

So far all our JavaScript code has been written in scripts in the body or head elements, which execute when the document is loaded. However you can also write your JavaScript code inside functions, and then call these functions from a script element somewhere else in your page. The same function can also be called from more than one place in the same page if necessary. Functions can be written inside script elements in the head or body of an HTML document, as we have already done with our previous scripts, but may also be written in a separate file. The main advantage of writing functions in separate files is that they can be re-used by scripts in different web pages. Files that contain JavaScript functions are normally given a '.js' file extension.

Regardless of where they are written, functions are not invoked automatically, even if they appear in the body of the document, so they have to be called by some other script or triggered by some kind of event.

A JavaScript function is declared simply by using the key word 'function', followed by the name of the function and any parameters, in parentheses. The body of the function is surrounded by braces:

```
<script type="text/javascript">
function functionname(parameters)
{
}
</script>
```

A function may return a value, representing the end result of the function, using the reserved word 'return' followed by the variable or value that is being returned:

```
<script type="text/javascript">
function functionname(parameters) {
. . .
   return value
}
</script>
```

If it is included, the line that returns the value is normally the last line in the function. This is because nothing after a return statement is executed; the function terminates at that point. This behaviour can also be used to deliberately 'short circuit' a function in cases where we want to exit from the function before executing all the code, perhaps because of some error condition or because we already have the result we need.

The following script shows a simple function that uses the same array of day names that we saw in an earlier script example. The difference is that instead of writing the day name out to the document, the function returns the name of the day.

```
<script type="text/javascript">
  <!--
  function getDayName()
  {
    var date=new Date();
    var arrDayNames=["Sunday","Monday","Tuesday","Wednesday",
  "Thursday","Friday", "Saturday"];
    return arrDayNames[date.getDay()]
  }
// -->
</script>
```

Defining functions outside the body element

So far, we have been embedding our scripts into the body of the document, which means that the JavaScript will run as soon as the page is loaded. However, once we start using functions, we can put them into the head element of the document or outside the document altogether, and invoke them from another script or an event.

In the following example, we see how a function (in this case added to the head of the document) can be invoked from a script in the body of the document. Because the script in the body is invoked when the document is loaded, the function is called at the same time. A JavaScript function is called simply by using its name and passing any required parameters. Unlike an object method, there is nothing that needs to precede the name of the function. If the function returns a value, it can be used by the code that invokes the function. In this XHTML page, a script invokes the 'getDayName' function. There are no parameter values to be passed, but the string that is returned from the function is written out to the document.

```
<?xml version="1.0"?>
<!DOCTYPE html PUBLIC "-//W3C//DTD XHTML 1.1//EN"
    "http://www.w3.org/TR/xhtml11/DTD/xhtml11.dtd">
<html xmlns="http://www.w3.org/1999/xhtml" xml:lang="en">
  <head>
    <meta http-equiv="Content-Script-Type" content="text/javascript"/>
    <title>JavaScript day name function</title>
    <script type="text/javascript">
      <!--
        function getDayName()
        {
           var date=new Date();
           var arrDayNames=
["Sunday","Monday","Tuesday","Wednesday","Thursday","Friday",
"Saturday"];
           return arrDayNames[date.getDay()]
        }
      // -->
    </script>
  </head>
  <body>
  <!-- File: Example6-13.htm -->
    <script type ="text/javascript">
      <! --
        document.write(getDayName() );
      // -->
    </script>
  </body>
</html>
```

Figure 6.14 shows the result of loading the page on a Thursday.

Using external JavaScript files

In all of the examples, we have seen so far, the JavaScript has appeared in the HTML source file. However, if we want to reuse any of our JavaScript functions then they need to be

FIGURE 6.14 A web page displaying the current day using the 'getDayName' function

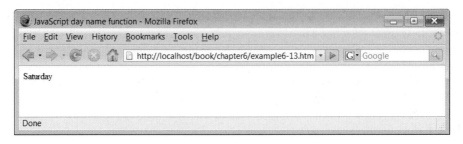

stored separately from HTML pages. In the previous example, we used a function called 'getDayName'. Simple as it is, this function might be reusable in multiple pages, so instead of putting it into the HTML document's header, we could put it into a separate file. Files that contain JavaScript code are usually given a '.js' extension, so in this example we assume a file called 'dayname.js'. Note that when JavaScript is stored separately from the XHTML source file, there is no 'script' element, just the JavaScript source code. The script element remains in the web page to specify the file that contains the JavaScript function.

```
// File: dayname.js
function getDayName()
{
   var date=new Date();
   var arrDayNames=
   ["Sunday","Monday","Tuesday","Wednesday","Thursday","Friday",
   "Saturday"];
   return arrDayNames[date.getDay()]
}
```

To use functions defined in external files, the script element needs to include the 'src' attribute, which specifies the path and filename of the JavaScript source file

```
<script type="text/javascript" src="path/filename.js"></script>
```

It is important to note that the script element is never an empty element, in other words it always has separate opening and closing tags, even though nothing appears between them. This is necessary because some browsers cannot process the script element unless it has both start and end tags.

Here is an XHTML page that uses the 'getDayName' function by referencing the external JavaScript file using the script element's 'src' attribute.

```
<?xml version = "1.0"?>
<!DOCTYPE html PUBLIC "-//W3C//DTD XHTML 1.1//EN"
   "http://www.w3.org/TR/xhtml11/DTD/xhtml11.dtd">
<html xmlns="http://www.w3.org/1999/xhtml" xml:lang="en">
   <head>
      <meta http-equiv="Content-Script-Type" content="text/javascript"/>
      <title>JavaScript day name function</title>
      <script type="text/javascript" src="dayname.js">
      </script>
   </head>
   <body>
      <script type="text/javascript">
        <!--
           document.write(getDayName() );
        // -->
      </script>
   </body>
</html>
```

Exercises

6.1 One of the browser properties that can be set is the status of the window. Add a line to 'Example6–1.htm' to set the window status text to 'status bar'. (Note that some browsers, such as Mozilla Firefox, will not let scripts change this property until you enable it in your browser preferences.)

6.2 Write a script that uses either a 'for' or a 'while' loop to create a table showing the numbers from 1 to 10 and their squares (see Figure 6.15).

You will need to put all of the code that creates the table inside the script, because if you put some of the table tags outside the script the page will not be valid XHTML. Use a style sheet to display the table and cell borders.

6.3 Write a script that generates and displays a 'hand' of five cards from a potential pack of 52 (this script could be used as part of a larger card-game application). JavaScript's loose typing is quite useful here, because we can create an array that contains the names and numbers of playing cards. In your script, first create an array that contains these names and numbers:

```
'Ace','2','3','4','5','6','7','8','9','10','Jack','Queen','King'
```

Then create a second array containing the four suits:

```
'Hearts','Diamonds','Clubs','Spades'
```

Use a 'for' loop that iterates five times (for five cards). In each iteration, use the 'Math.Random()' method to get a name or number and a suit from the arrays and display the resulting card on the screen. The final output might look something like Figure 6.16.

FIGURE 6.15 A table of the numbers from 1 to 10 and their squares

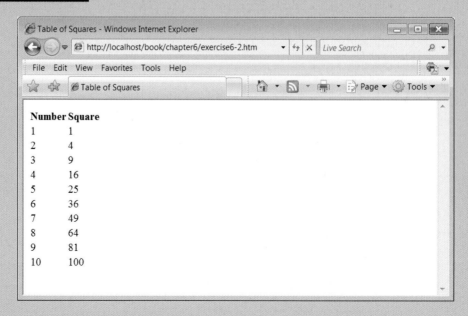

FIGURE 6.16   A possible output from the hand of cards script

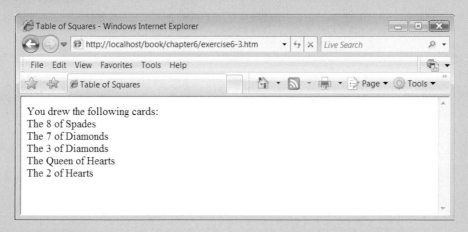

TABLE 6.6   Some time zones and their difference from UTC in hours

Time Zone	Difference from UTC in Hours
Eastern Standard	−5
Pacific standard	−8
UTC	0
Central European	+1
Baghdad	+3
Japan Standard	+9
West Australian Standard	+10
New Zealand Standard	+12

6.4 This exercise is quite complex and involves many steps, but provides practice with the arithmetic operators and should give you a deeper understanding of Date objects.

Write a script that creates a table of the current time in different parts of the world. You can do this by creating a Date object to get the current time, converting it to UTC, and then adding or subtracting the time differences for different places (we will not, however, concern ourselves with daylight saving, so the results may not be completely accurate). Table 6.6 shows some example time zones with their difference from UTC in hours. A more complete table can be found at http://setiathome.berkeley.edu/utc.php.

The names of the time zones can be stored in an array, and the current times in each zone generated by simple arithmetic on the millisecond value of the Date. Here is an XHTML page you can use to call your function. Note that the page assumes the function is called 'showTimeZones' and is in a file called 'timezones.js'.

```
<?xml version="1.0"?>
<!DOCTYPE html PUBLIC "-//W3C//DTD XHTML 1.1//EN"
   "http://www.w3.org/TR/xhtml11/DTD/xhtml11.dtd">
<html xmlns="http://www.w3.org/1999/xhtml" xml:lang="en">
```

```
      <head>
        <meta http-equiv = "Content-Script-Type" content = "text/javascript"/>
        <title>International Time Zones</title>
        <script type = "text/javascript" src = "timezones.js">
        </script>
      </head>
      <body>
        <!-- File: exercise6-2.htm -->
        <script type = "text/javascript">
        showTimeZones();
        </script>
      </body>
    </html>
```

Here are the steps your function should go through:

1   Create an array of time zones.

2   Create an array of the time offsets of these zones.

3   Create a new Date object. This will contain the date and time in the current locale (which may not be UTC).

4   Use the 'getTime()' method to get the current date and time as a value in milliseconds to make it easy to change by arithmetic.

5   Find out the difference between the current locale and UTC in minutes by using the 'getTimezoneOffset' method.

6   Convert the time in the current locale (in milliseconds) to UTC by adding the offset between them. There are 60,000 milliseconds in a minute, so you need to multiply the offset value by 60,000 before adding it to the millisecond value of the current time.

7   Write out the necessary tags to begin a table, something like this:

```
document.write("<table><tr><th>Time Zone</th><th>Offsets from
UTC</th><th>Current Date and Time</th></tr>");
```

8   Start a 'for' loop to go through each zone in turn (use the 'length' property of the time zone array to control the loop).

9   For each time zone, work out the difference from UTC in milliseconds. There are 3,600,000 milliseconds in each hour, so multiply that by the number of hours in the offset (stored in the array) for the current zone.

10   Work out the time for the current zone (in milliseconds) by adding the offset to the UTC time.

11   Create a new Date object using the adjusted millisecond value (you can create a new Date by passing the millisecond value as a parameter to the constructor).

12   Write the next row of the table (you need to include the HTML tags for the table row and cells.) The code might look something like this:

```
document.write("<tr><td>" + arrTimeZones[i] + "</td><td>" +
arrOffsets[i] + "<td>" + zoneDate.toLocaleString() + "</td></tr>");
```

13   Close the 'table' element.

SUMMARY

In this chapter, we introduced the main features of JavaScript syntax, including interacting with parts of the document object model (DOM); declaring variables, arrays and objects; performing arithmetic; concatenating strings; expressing conditions and controlling loops. We saw how it is possible to use the language to create client-side processes that can integrate small programs into the browser environment. We used a number of JavaScript object methods to, for example, generate random numbers and access date and time information. We looked at various ways of adding JavaScript code to a web page, including in the body or the head of a document or in a separate '.js' file, which makes it possible to reuse the same code, encapsulated in JavaScript functions, in different pages. Table 6.7 provides a summary of the JavaScript keywords, JavaScript object types and built-in objects that were introduced in this chapter. In the next chapter, we build on these foundations to see how JavaScript can be used in conjunction with the DOM, style sheets, and server-side processes to make the web client more interactive and dynamic.

TABLE 6.7 JavaScript keywords, types and objects introduced in this chapter

Keywords	Object Types	Built-In Objects
new	Date	document
var	String	window
function	Math	navigator
if		location
else		
while		
for		
return		
true		
false		

References and further reading

Raggett, D., Le Hors, A. and Jacobs, I. 1999. *HTML 4.01 specification*, Section 18, 'Scripts'. http://www.w3.org/TR/html4/interact/scripts.html

Interactive JavaScript: Dynamic HTML, Client-side Validation and Ajax

LEARNING OBJECTIVES

- **To know the various components of Dynamic HTML (DHTML) and how they work together**

- **To understand how to navigate the document object model (DOM) using JavaScript**

- **To be able to use events to trigger JavaScript functions**

- **To understand the principles and practices of client-side form validation**

- **To be able to make connections to a server using Asynchronous JavaScript and XML (Ajax)**

INTRODUCTION

In Chapter 6 we saw how JavaScript could be used to write simple scripts and functions that run inside the client browser. This JavaScript code can be used to implement client-side processes such as calculating values, manipulating strings of data and interacting with objects from the document object model (DOM). In this chapter, we see how JavaScript, along with the DOM and style sheets, can be used to create Dynamic HTML (DHTML) pages that provide a more interactive experience for the user by responding to events in the browser and dynamically modifying the page or browser presentation. We will also see how JavaScript can contribute to the interaction between client and server by concentrating on two particular types of JavaScript programming. First, we will see how JavaScript can be used for simple ('surface') form validation. In this role, JavaScript can relieve the load on the server by passing the data that users have entered into forms through some basic 'sanity checking' before it is submitted to the server. Secondly, we see how JavaScript can be used to build Ajax applications that are able to communicate behind the scenes with the server and update pages asynchronously, without the need to replace or refresh the whole of the current web page.

7.1 Dynamic HTML (DHTML)

Dynamic HTML is not a specific technology but refers to using a combination of JavaScript, the DOM and cascading style sheets (CSS) to make web pages more dynamic and interactive. JavaScript code can be used to locate nodes of the DOM and interact with their contents, while styles can be used to enhance the dynamic aspects of presentation, such as showing or hiding parts of a page. The credit for 'inventing' DHTML is generally given to Scott Isaacs at Microsoft, though since DHTML is not so much a technology as a collection of techniques, perhaps 'inventing' is not the right term. DHTML relies on aspects of HTML that were introduced with version 4.0, along with elements of CSS, so it will not work on older browsers (e.g. before version 4 of Internet Explorer or Netscape Navigator).

Navigating the DOM

To write DHTML code we need to be able to navigate through the DOM. We saw some aspects of this early in Chapter 6, when we used the document object. The tree of nodes in the DOM in fact begins with the document object, from which we can navigate to other nodes, either by using unique ids (if the 'id' attribute has been used on element nodes) or by traversing parts of the document tree, using an approach similar to XPath. Two ways of doing this are to use the 'firstChild' property, which simply identifies the first child of the current node, or the 'childNodes' property, which is accessed like an array using an index number. However, attempting to use these methods of navigation through the DOM can be very problematic due to browser incompatibilities. A more reliable approach is to use 'id' attributes on the nodes that you wish to access in your JavaScript code, and navigate to them using the 'getElementById' method. There is also a 'getElementsByTagName' method that locates all the occurrences of a particular HTML tag. To explain how these methods work we will refer to the following XHTML document, which has several elements with id attributes:

```
<?xml version="1.0"?>
<!DOCTYPE html PUBLIC "-//W3C//DTD XHTML 1.1//EN"
    "http://www.w3.org/TR/xhtml11/DTD/xhtml11.dtd">
<html xmlns="http://www.w3.org/1999/xhtml" xml:lang="en">
    <head>
        <meta http-equiv="Content-Script-Type" content="text/javascript"/>
        <title>Our Insurance</title>
    </head>
    <body>
        <!-- File: example7-1.htm -->
        <div id="heading1">Buildings Insurance</div>
        <p id="para1">
        You need this type of insurance to cover you in case of
        <span id="risk">severe damage to your home</span>
        (for example fire, flood, vehicle or tree crashing into it)
        as well as more everyday risks like accidentally breaking a window
        </p>
        <div id="heading2">Contents Insurance</div>
        <p id="para2">
        You need this type of insurance to cover
        <span id="items">things in your house</span>,
```

```
such as furniture, electrical goods, carpets and curtains, against risks such
as fire, theft, water damage (due to burst pipes, etc) or accidental breakage
    </p>
  </body>
</html>
```

In order to navigate to the second paragraph of this document, which has the id 'para2', we can use the following expression:

```
document.getElementById("para2");
```

Another way of achieving the same result would be to use the appropriate tag name (in this case 'p') with the getElementsByTagName method, which takes the name of an HTML tag as a parameter (the tag name parameter is not case sensitive). This is a useful alternative for elements that do not have 'id' attributes. Since the 'getElementsByTagName' method will locate all instances of the specified tag, the results are indexed like an array, starting at zero. The second paragraph therefore would have the index '1' in the collection of paragraph tags, and would be accessed like this:

```
document.getElementsByTagName("p")[1];
```

Interacting with nodes

Once we know how to navigate to a node using the DOM, we can interact with that node to access its properties. Properties of nodes include the 'nodeName' and 'nodeType'. These expressions, for example, would get the 'nodeName' and 'nodeType' of the first paragraph:

```
document.getElementById("para1").nodeName;
document.getElementById("para1").nodeType;
```

In this case, the node name would be 'p' and the type would be '1'.

 NOTE Elements are type 1, attributes are type 2 and text nodes are type 3. (Knowing this can occasionally be useful for debugging purposes – sometimes the node you are accessing is not the one you think it is!)

We can access the contents of a text node using the 'nodeValue' property. Since a paragraph is an element node and not a text node, we need to navigate to its child node to get to the text inside it. We can access the first child node of an element by using the 'firstChild' property, and then get its node value, like this:

```
document.getElementById("para1").firstChild.nodeValue;
```

This will return the text from the opening paragraph tag to the following span tag.

As well as accessing the properties of nodes we can access attributes using the 'getAttribute' method, which takes an attribute name as a parameter. To access the 'id' attribute for the first 'div' element, for example, we could use the following expression:

```
document.getElementById("heading1").getAttribute("id");
```

If you add the following script to the body of the XHTML page previously described, you can test out some of the expressions we have introduced in this section:

```
<script type="text/javascript">
  <!--
  document.write("Paragraph 1 is node name " +
    document.getElementById("para1").nodeName);
  document.write("<br />Paragraph 1 is node type " +
    document.getElementById("para1").nodeType);
  document.write("<br />The text node inside paragraph 1 is " +
    document.getElementById("para1").firstChild.nodeValue);
  document.write("<br />The attribute value of the first div is " +
    document.getElementById("heading1").getAttribute("id") );
  // -->
</script>
```

You should be aware that if you want to navigate the DOM in your script you cannot put the script in the head element, because it will execute before the body has loaded and the DOM will not yet be built! Therefore this particular script needs to be in the body.

 NOTE In fact, you should never put scripts in the header that write content to the document, unless they are in functions, because they will write their output before the document body has been loaded.

The output from the script should include the information shown in Figure 7.1.

FIGURE 7.1   Displaying node types, names and values using the DOM

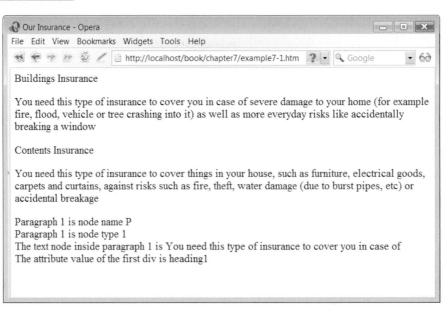

Changing values in the DOM

As well as reading node properties, JavaScript and the DOM can be used to change the content of parts of a document. In the next example, we are going to use a text field to display the time by setting its value inside a script. The text field is given a unique id of 'clock' so that we can access it easily using the 'getElementById' method. It is also set to be read only (using the 'read-only' attribute), since it is only intended for display purposes and not for user input:

```
<input type="text" size="6" id="clock" readonly="readonly"/>
```

The following JavaScript function ('showClock') uses a newly created Date object to show the time that the page was loaded. It uses 'getElementById' to locate the text field within the document, using its 'id' attribute. It then sets the 'value' property of the text field (this is from the HTML part of the DOM) to a string comprising the hours and minutes from the Date object.

```
<!-- showclock.js -->
function showClock()
{
    var date=new Date();
    document.getElementById("clock").value =
        date.getHours() + ":" + date.getMinutes();
}
```

The following XHTML page invokes the 'showClock' function using a script in the body:

```
<?xml version="1.0"?>
<!DOCTYPE html PUBLIC "-//W3C//DTD XHTML 1.1//EN"
    "http://www.w3.org/TR/xhtml11/DTD/xhtml11.dtd">
<html xmlns="http://www.w3.org/1999/xhtml" xml:lang="en">
    <head>
        <meta http-equiv="Content-Script-Type" content="text/javascript"/>
        <title>JavaScript clock</title>
        <script type="text/javascript" src="showclock.js">
        </script>
    </head>
    <body>
        <!-- File: example7-2.htm -->
        <div>
            <input type="text" size="6" id="clock" readonly="readonly"/>
        </div>
        <script type="text/javascript">
            showClock();
        </script>
    </body>
</html>
```

Figure 7.2 shows the time displayed in a text field in a browser.

7.2 JavaScript events

So far, all our JavaScript code has been run as part of the XHTML page being loaded, triggered by script elements in the document body. However we do not always want

FIGURE 7.2 The time the page was loaded displayed in a text field

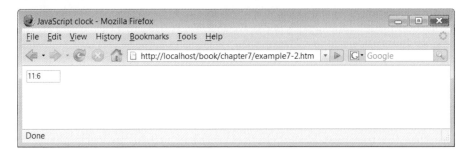

JavaScript, particularly functions, to be run only when the document loads. To give us more control over the running of our scripts, and make our browser-based applications more interactive, we can use various types of event to trigger the running of JavaScript code. These events include the document being loaded in the browser (the 'onload' event), the mouse moving over a component of the page ('onmouseover') or a button being pressed ('onclick'). Event handlers enable JavaScript objects and functions to respond to these events.

The 'onload' event

In our next example, instead of adding a script element to the body of the document, we will invoke the 'showClock' function from the 'onload' event, which is triggered when the document body is loaded.

```
<body onload="showClock()">
```

This approach means that we can have a JavaScript function run as soon as the document is loaded without using a script element in the document body.

 NOTE Note that 'onload' here is all in lower case. You will see examples from other sources of this event referred to as 'onLoad'. However, because the event appears as an attribute of the body tag, using any upper case letters will mean your pages are not valid XHTML.

This script shows an XHTML page that invokes the 'showClock' function using the 'onload' event:

```
<?xml version="1.0"?>
<!DOCTYPE html PUBLIC "-//W3C//DTD XHTML 1.1//EN"
  "http://www.w3.org/TR/xhtml11/DTD/xhtml11.dtd">
<html xmlns="http://www.w3.org/1999/xhtml" xml:lang="en">
  <head>
    <meta http-equiv="Content-Script-Type" content="text/javascript"/>
    <title>JavaScript clock</title>
    <script type="text/javascript" src="showclock.js">
    </script>
  </head>
```

```
<body onload="showClock()">
  <! -- File: example7-3.htm -- >
  <div>
  <input type="text" size="6" id="clock" readonly="readonly"/>
  </div>
</body>
</html>
```

Timer events

As we saw in the previous example, using the 'onload' event has the same effect as triggering a JavaScript function from a script in the document body. In the case of our clock, this is not really very helpful, since the time will soon (in no more than a minute) be wrong. We can, however, solve this problem using a JavaScript timer event. The 'setTimeOut' method can be used to set a timer that will call a function after a given interval, specified in milliseconds. In this modified version of the original 'showClock' function (called 'showTimer'), we add a 'setTimeOut' event to recursively call the 'showTimer' function approximately every 1000 milliseconds (every second). To see this working more easily, the seconds, as well as the minutes and hours, are written to the text field.

```
// File: showtimer.js
function showTimer()
{
   var date=new Date();
   document.getElementById("clock").value=date.getHours() + ":" +
     date.getMinutes() + ":" + date.getSeconds();
   setTimeout("showTimer()", 1000);
}
```

The page to call this function only needs to be modified in two places, first to call the new function in the header, and second to call the new function with the 'onload' event. Therefore the only changes are to the name of the '.js' file being used and the name of the function being called:

```
<?xml version = "1.0"?>
<!DOCTYPE html PUBLIC "-//W3C//DTD XHTML 1.1//EN"
   "http://www.w3.org/TR/xhtml11/DTD/xhtml11.dtd">
<html xmlns="http://www.w3.org/1999/xhtml" xml:lang="en">
  <head>
    <meta http-equiv="Content-Script-Type" content="text/javascript"/>
    <title>JavaScript clock</title>
    <script type="text/javascript"src="showtimer.js">
    </script>
  </head>
  <body onload="showTimer()">
    <!-- File: example7-4.htm -->
    <div>
      <input type="text" size="6" id="clock" readonly="readonly"/>
    </div>
  </body>
</html>
```

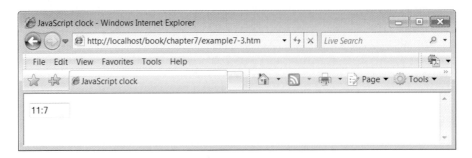

Figure 7.3 shows the modified text field, with the function showing the time in hours, minutes and seconds.

innerHTML and the DOM

In the previous examples, we used a text field to display the current time. An alternative approach to displaying content in a specific part of the browser is to write to a node of the document. One way of doing this is to use the interfaces of the DOM, but this can be quite complex and different browsers can react in different ways to the same scripts. Another way is to use the 'innerHTML' property of HTML elements. This enables us to access text nodes directly and update their contents.

The 'innerHTML' property is not part of the formal HTML DOM specification, and was introduced by Microsoft in Internet Explorer 4 in 1997. However due to its popularity it has been incorporated into other browsers, despite not being included in any public standard, and is therefore quite reliable in terms of cross-browser support. There has been much debate about whether using 'innerHTML' is wise or not. However, it is simple to use and has been used in many Ajax implementations. One of the objections to the use of 'innerHTML' is that it can be used to include structural elements (i.e. mark-up) inside the processes of client-side scripts, which is a poor separation of concerns. It is therefore preferable to restrict the use of 'innerHTML' to the manipulation of content rather than using it to dynamically generate mark-up.

In the next example, we modify the 'showTimer' function to use the 'innerHTML' property. The changes are relatively simple. First, we replace the text input field with a suitable document node, in this case a simple 'div' element that contains no text.

```
<div id="clock"></div>
```

Then all we have to do in the JavaScript function is modify the 'div' element, accessed using the 'getElementById' method, by setting the value of its 'innerHTML' property:

```
// File: showinnertimer.js
function showTimer()
{
    var date=new Date();
    document.getElementById("clock").innerHTML=date.getHours() + ":" +
```

```
        date.getMinutes() + ":" + date.getSeconds();
    setTimeout("showTimer()", 1000);
}
```

Otherwise everything looks, and works, pretty much the same as before, except that the time appears in the browser simply as text, and not in a text field component. Here is the full XHTML page, with the 'div' element used by the function.

```
<?xml version="1.0"?>
<!DOCTYPE html PUBLIC "-//W3C//DTD XHTML 1.1//EN"
    "http://www.w3.org/TR/xhtml11/DTD/xhtml11.dtd">
<html xmlns="http://www.w3.org/1999/xhtml" xml:lang="en">
    <head>
        <meta http-equiv="Content-Script-Type" content="text/javascript"/>
        <title>JavaScript clock</title>
        <script type="text/javascript" src="showinnertimer.js">
        </script>
    </head>
    <body onload="showTimer()">
        <!-- File: example7-5.htm -->
        <div id="clock"></div>
    </body>
</html>
```

Figure 7.4 shows the output in the browser. The time is no longer in a text field but simply a text node of the document.

Responding to button events

The events we have used so far, the 'onload' event and timer events, are not related to user activity. However, if we want to make web pages more dynamic we need to be able to respond to the user's actions in the page. One way of doing this is to trigger JavaScript functions with user-instigated events such as buttons being pressed. HTML button components can be linked to JavaScript functions by using their 'onclick' event. In our next example, we use button events to call the window object's 'resizeTo' method, which sets the browser window to a specified width and height. The values for the width and height appear in parentheses after the method name, separated by a comma. This example would set the window size to 400 pixels wide and 200 pixels high:

```
window.resizeTo(400,200);
```

FIGURE 7.4   The current time displayed in a browser using the 'innerHTML' property

Our next script example shows button events being used to resize the window. It also shows how a JavaScript function can be called from more than one place in a script. The function we use is called 'resizeWindow', takes two parameters for the width and the height, and sets the size of the window accordingly:

```
// File: resize.js
function resizeWindow(width, height)
{
    window.resizeTo(width,height);
}
```

In the body of the document, there are two buttons, both of which use the 'onclick' event to call the 'resizeWindow' function. The first button (labelled 'shrink window') sets the window to be 400 by 300 pixels. The second uses two properties of the screen ('availWidth' and 'availHeight') to set the window size to the maximum available. The 'screen' object is a property of the window object.

```
<?xml version="1.0"?>
<!DOCTYPE html PUBLIC "-//W3C//DTD XHTML 1.1//EN"
    "http://www.w3.org/TR/xhtml11/DTD/xhtml11.dtd">
<html xmlns="http://www.w3.org/1999/xhtml" xml:lang="en">
<head>
    <meta http-equiv="Content-Script-Type" content="text/javascript"/>
    <title>JavaScript window resize</title>
    <script type="text/javascript" src="resize.js">
    </script>
</head>
<body>
    <!-- File: example7-6.htm -->
    <div>
    <input type="button" onclick="resizeWindow(400,300)"
      value="shrink window"/>
    <input type="button"
        onclick="resizeWindow(window.screen.availWidth,
        window.screen.availHeight)" value="restore window"/>
    </div>
</body>
</html>
```

Figure 7.5 shows the window in Mozilla Firefox 2 before the 'shrink window' button has been pressed.

 NOTE | Different browsers may give you slightly different behaviours using this function. For example, Opera 9 will only resize the window if it is detached, not if it is part of a tabbed window.

FIGURE 7.5   The window before resizing using a button 'onclick' event

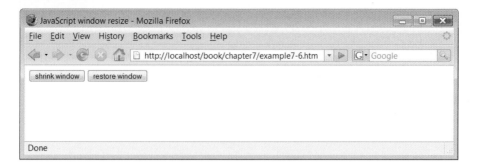

JavaScript URLs

In the previous example we saw how button events can be used to invoke JavaScript functions. Another approach to triggering JavaScript code from user actions is to use JavaScript URLs, which are preceded by a 'javascript:' prefix. This special protocol type can be used anywhere that a regular URL can be used, for example in hypertext anchors or form actions. We can follow this protocol with any JavaScript code, including function calls. This approach works well if we want to use an anchor to trigger a script or function. For example, this fragment of code shows an HTML anchor element where the URL is a JavaScript function called 'openWindow' that takes the name of an HTML page as a parameter:

```
<a href="javascript:openWindow('about.htm')">open window</a>
```

When the anchor is clicked in the browser, the 'openWindow' function is invoked. Here is the 'openWindow' function implementation, which uses the 'open' method of the window object.

```
// File: openwindow.js
function openWindow(url)
{
   window.open(url);
}
```

Here is an XHTML page that includes the JavaScript URL, which invokes the function when the user clicks on the hyperlink:

```
<?xml version="1.0"?>
<!DOCTYPE html PUBLIC "-//W3C//DTD XHTML 1.1//EN"
   "http://www.w3.org/TR/xhtml11/DTD/xhtml11.dtd">
<html xmlns="http://www.w3.org/1999/xhtml" xml:lang="en">
   <head>
      <meta http-equiv="Content-Script-Type" content="text/javascript"/>
      <title>JavaScript open window</title>
      <script type="text/javascript" src="openwindow.js">
      </script>
   </head>
```

7

```
<body>
  <!-- File: example7-7.htm -->
  <div>
  <a href="javascript:openWindow('about.htm')">open window</a>
  </div>
  </body>
</html>
```

The effect of clicking the hyperlink in the page varies from browser to browser. In some cases, a new window is created and in others a new tab appears. Figure 7.6 shows how Internet Explorer 7 responds to the function, opening a new window.

7.3 Dynamic style sheets

As well as interacting with the DOM, another important feature of DHTML is the use of style sheets to dynamically change the presentation of the document. A commonly used example of this technique is to apply JavaScript and style sheets to show or hide parts of a page. This technique can be used, for example, to add expandable menus to web pages. To interact with styles inside our scripts, we can use the 'style' property of the elements in the DOM to dynamically apply styles to parts of the document. The CSS style property that we can use to show or hide parts of the page is 'display', which can have the value 'block' to make the content visible, or 'none' to make it invisible. The following function uses an 'if' statement to switch the display style of an element between 'none' and 'block'. In this example, 'element' is a variable that references an element node from the current document, identified by its 'id' attribute.

FIGURE 7.6   The effect of the 'openWindow' function in Internet Explorer 7, triggered by a JavaScript URL

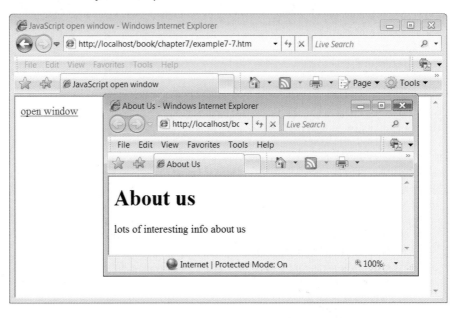

```
// File: changedisplay.js
function changeDisplay(id)
{
   var element=document.getElementById(id);
   if(element.style.display=='none')
   {
      element.style.display='block';
   }
   else
   {
      element.style.display = 'none';
   }
}
```

So far in this chapter we have looked at how we can use JavaScript to navigate to nodes in the DOM and to access the properties of these nodes, including the 'style' property. We have also looked at the use of events to trigger JavaScript functions. In the next example, we draw all of these techniques together into a DHTML page that shows and hides parts of a page when a JavaScript URL is clicked. The page consists of two sections with titles 'JavaScript' and 'DHTML (Dynamic HTML)' that are in anchors that use JavaScript URLs. When either of these titles is clicked, the detail text (enclosed in 'div' tags with unique ids) switches between shown and hidden. The ids of the 'div' elements are passed to the 'changeDisplay' function in order to switch their state.

We need to be able to invoke this function in two ways. First, we need to invoke it when the page is loaded, to set the initial state of the page, using the 'onload' event. To call more than one function from the 'onload' event or, as in this case, to call the same function more than once, the function calls can be put into a comma-separated list, like this:

```
<body onload="changeDisplay('jsdetail'), changeDisplay('dhtmldetail')">
```

Since the display state of the two 'div' elements has not been set initially, the first time it is called for a particular element, the function executes the 'else' block and sets the display state to 'none'. From that point onwards, the JavaScript URLs invoke the function when either one of them is clicked and switches the display state. Here is one example of these two URLs:

```
<a href="javascript:changeDisplay('jsdetail')">JavaScript</a>
```

Note how it passes the id of one of the 'div' elements to the function. Here is the complete XHTML page:

```
<?xml version="1.0"?>
<!DOCTYPE html PUBLIC "-//W3C//DTD XHTML 1.1//EN"
   "http://www.w3.org/TR/xhtml11/DTD/xhtml11.dtd">
<html xmlns="http://www.w3.org/1999/xhtml" xml:lang="en">
   <head>
      <meta http-equiv="Content-Script-Type" content="text/javascript"/>
      <title>DHTML show and hide</title>
      <script type="text/javascript" src="changedisplay.js">
      </script>
   </head>
   <body onload="changeDisplay('jsdetail'), changeDisplay('dhtmldetail')">
         <!-- File: example7-8.htm -->
         <div>
```

```
        <a href="javascript:changeDisplay('jsdetail')">JavaScript</a>
      </div>
      <div id="jsdetail">
JavaScript is a scripting language that can be run inside the browser to enable
client-side processes.
      </div>
      <div>
        <a href="javascript:changeDisplay('dhtmldetail')">
        DHTML (Dynamic HTML)</a>
      </div>
      <div id="dhtmldetail">
DHTML is a label given to techniques that use JavaScript, CSS and the DOM to make
web pages more dynamic and interactive.
      </div>
  </body>
</html>
```

Figure 7.7 shows the page once it has been initially loaded into the browser, with both div element styles in the 'none' display state.

Figure 7.8 shows how the page looks if both the 'div' element styles are in the 'block' state (i.e. visible).

FIGURE 7.7   The 'div' elements hidden by setting the display property of the style to 'none'

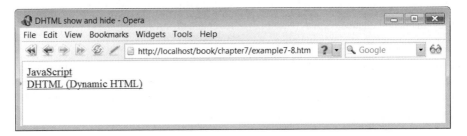

FIGURE 7.8   The 'div' elements made visible by setting the display property of the style to 'block'

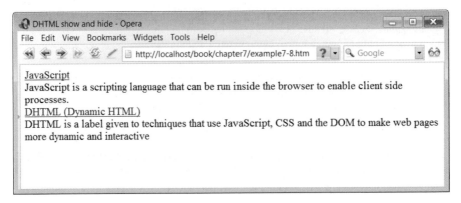

7.4 Client-side form validation

One of the most useful roles that JavaScript can perform in a web application is client-side validation of the data that users enter into web page forms. We can only provide *surface validation* on the client. For example, we can check that a credit card number matches the correct format for credit card numbers, or check that a particular type of card, such as a Visa card, starts with the correct numbers for that type, but we could not actually check the validity of the credit card itself in the browser. That would have to be done by a server-side process. Surface validation includes checking for empty fields, checking that selections have been made (for example from radio buttons or drop-down lists) rather than leaving empty defaults, checking that numeric, date, email or credit card fields contain the right types of characters, and so on.

Functions that process forms

With a normal HTML form, pressing the 'submit' button posts the HTTP request to the URI defined by the form element's 'action' attribute. For example, this simple form contains input fields for a user ID and a password and submits to a server-side application called 'customerLogin':

```
<form action="customerLogin" method="post">
  <table>
    <tr>
      <td><label for="loginid">Login Name:</label></td>
      <td><input type="text" id="loginid"/></td>
    </tr>
    <tr>
      <td><label for="pword">Password:</label></td>
      <td><input type="password" id="pword"/></td>
    </tr>
    <tr>
      <td></td>
      <td><input type="submit" value="Login"/>
      <input type="reset" value="Clear form"/></td>
    </tr>
  </table>
</form>
```

Once the form is submitted to the server, it is too late to validate any of the form data in the browser. Therefore, JavaScript provides us with a special 'onsubmit' event that lets us invoke a function when the button is pressed, rather than submitting directly to the server. We can use the function to validate the form and return either 'true' or 'false' depending on whether the contents of the form are valid or not. If it returns 'true', then the form data is submitted to the server-side application. If it returns 'false', then the submission is cancelled and we can give the user the opportunity to correct the data they have entered.

There are two ways that the JavaScript function can access the components of the form in order to check their validity:

- The function can use the DOM to access the form's components via the document object.
- The form can be passed as a parameter to the function.

As an example of the first approach, this form tag includes the 'onsubmit' event handler, invoking a JavaScript method called 'validate' that takes no parameters

```
<form action="customerLogin" method="post" onsubmit="return validate()">
```

If a reference to the form is not passed to the function, the 'getElementById' method of the DOM can be used to locate the input fields of the form, as long as they have 'id' attributes. In this example, the function accesses the 'loginid' text field using the DOM, checking if it is an empty field (using double speech marks with nothing in between represents an empty string, which would be the contents of an empty text input field).

```
function validate()
{
    if(document.getElementById("loginid").value==""
    . . .
```

In contrast, this version of the form element takes the second approach, passing the form to the 'validate' method as a parameter. The form is referred to using the reserved word 'this', (i.e. pass *this* form to the function):

```
<form action="customerLogin" method="post" onsubmit="return validate(this)">
```

If a reference to the form is passed as a parameter to the function, the form controls can be accessed as sub-elements of the parameter object. In this example, we navigate to the same text field ('loginid') but via the form, rather than the document object.

```
function validate(loginForm)
{
    if(loginForm.loginid.value=="")
    . . .
```

Which one of these approaches you use is up to you, but passing the form to the function seems to be more commonly used in validation routines.

Pop-up dialogs

So far in this section we have looked at some JavaScript code that checks the state of the components in a form, but what do we do if we want to indicate to the user that there is a problem? We could use the technique that we have already introduced to write to the page using the DOM, but a more common approach to indicating problems occurring in an application is to display a pop-up dialog box. JavaScript provides three types of pop-up dialog, the *alert*, *confirm* and *prompt* dialogs. These are modal dialogs, which means that you cannot do anything else in the browser until you have closed them. They are invoked by using the 'alert', 'confirm' and 'prompt' methods of the window object.

An alert is used simply to show a message to the user. The only button on an alert is an 'OK' button, which makes the dialog disappear when it is clicked. Creating an alert is very simple; we just pass the text we want to display as a parameter (in parentheses) to the alert function:

```
alert("message");
```

The confirm dialog is similar to the alert in that it will contain some type of message. However it has two buttons, 'OK' and 'Cancel'. If the user clicks 'OK', the box returns true. If the user clicks 'Cancel', the box returns false.

```
confirm("message");
```

Unlike the other two dialogs, the prompt dialog asks the user to enter a value. As well as a text entry field, it contains 'OK' and 'Cancel' buttons. If the user clicks 'OK' the box returns the input value, but if the user clicks 'Cancel' the box returns *null*. A null value in JavaScript means that the variable has no value.

```
var returnValue=prompt("prompt text", "default value");
```

Here is a simple JavaScript function that creates all three of these dialog types in turn. When the function is called, the dialogs appear one after the other.

```
// File: showdialogs.js
function showDialogs()
{
   alert("This is an alert");
   confirm("This message wants confirmation");
   prompt("Please enter something in the text area", "I'm a default");
}
```

Here is an XHTML page that calls this function when it loads:

```
<?xml version="1.0"?>
<!DOCTYPE html PUBLIC "-//W3C//DTD XHTML 1.1//EN"
   "http://www.w3.org/TR/xhtml11/DTD/xhtml11.dtd">
<html xmlns="http://www.w3.org/1999/xhtml" xml:lang="en">
   <head>
      <meta http-equiv="Content-Script-Type" content="text/javascript"/>
      <title>JavaScript Dialogs</title>
      <script type="text/javascript" src="showdialogs.js">
      </script>
   </head>
   <body onload="showDialogs()">
      <!-- File: example7-9.htm -->
   </body>
</html>
```

Figure 7.9 shows how the three dialogs look when displayed by the Mozilla Firefox 2 browser. They look a little different in other browsers but the content and buttons are very much the same.

Using dialogs in validation routines

All three of these dialog types could be used in validation routines. However, perhaps the simplest approach is to use an alert to inform the user if there errors in the form data.

Here is a complete 'validate' function, using a form parameter and an alert. The function checks if either the username or password text fields in the login form are empty. In each

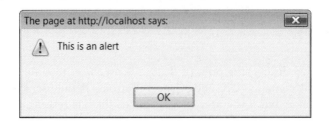

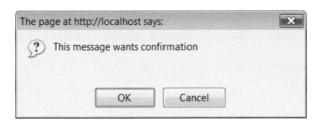

case, the value of the text field is compared to an empty string (""). If the field is empty, some error text is added to the 'strErrorMessage' variable and the value of the 'booValid' variable is set to 'false'. After both fields have been checked, if the 'booValid' variable is 'false' then an alert is displayed showing the error messages, and the form is not submitted, as the method itself returns 'false'.

```javascript
// File: validateform.js
function validate(loginForm)
{
    var booValid=true;
    var strErrorMessage="";
    if(loginForm.loginid.value=="")
    {
        strErrorMessage +="user name field cannot be empty\n";
        booValid=false;
    }
    if(loginForm.pword.value=="")
```

```
    {
       strErrorMessage +="password field cannot be empty";
       booValid=false;
    }
    if(!booValid)
    {
       alert(strErrorMessage);
    }
    return booValid;
}
```

Here is an XHTML page that calls the 'validate' function using the 'onsubmit' event of the form:

```
<?xml version="1.0"?>
<!DOCTYPE html PUBLIC "-//W3C//DTD XHTML 1.1//EN"
   "http://www.w3.org/TR/xhtml11/DTD/xhtml11.dtd">
<html xmlns="http://www.w3.org/1999/xhtml" xml:lang="en">
   <head>
      <title>Customer Login</title>
      <script type="text/javascript" src="validateform.js">
      </script>
   </head>
   <body>
   <!-- File: example7-10.htm -->
      <form action="customerLogin" method="post"
        onsubmit="return validate(this)">
        <table>
           <tr>
           <td><label for="loginid">Login Name:</label></td>
           <td><input type="text" id="loginid"></td>
           </tr>
           <tr>
              <td><label for="pword">Password:</label></td>
              <td><input type="password" id="pword"></td>
           </tr>
           <tr>
              <td></td>
              <td><input type="submit" value="Login">
                 <input type="reset" value="Clear form">
              </td>
           </tr>
        </table>
      </form>
   </body>
</html>
```

Figure 7.10 shows both the form and the alert that appears if both of the fields are empty. If only one field is empty, then only one message appears in the alert. If both fields have some content then the form data is submitted to the server.

FIGURE 7.10 The form and the alert that appears if both fields are left empty, running in Internet Explorer 7

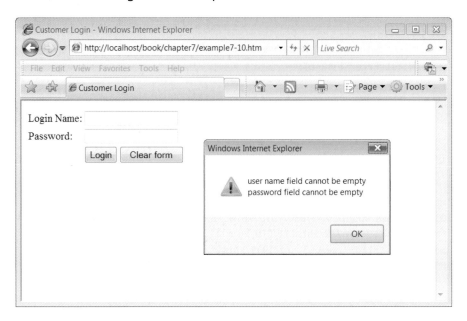

Validating other types of form component

In addition to checking if text fields contain characters, a common process for mandatory fields, we can do other types of check. For example we can see if the user has made a selection from a select list, or see if a radio button or check box has been checked.

It is useful to add an empty option to a 'select' component to confirm that the user has made a choice. If they accept the default (i.e. nothing selected) then we can flag that as an error using the JavaScript validation function. In this select, for example, the first option is empty. This means we can ensure that the user specifically chooses either 'Administrator' or 'User' from the list by validating that the zero-indexed selection (the empty one) has not been selected.

```
<select id="loginoptions" size="1">
   <option></option>
   <option>Administrator</option>
   <option>User</option>
</select>
```

In our JavaScript validation function, we can check the index of the selected option using the 'selectedIndex' property. If the index is zero then we can do some error notification.

```
if(loginForm.loginoptions.selectedIndex == 0 )
{
   strErrorMessage += "you must select your Login role\n";
   booValid=false;
}
```

In this example, we have radio buttons in the form.

```
<input type="radio" name="action" value="view"/> View settings
<input type="radio" name="action" value="update"/> Update settings
```

By not providing a default checked button, we can force the user to select one of these buttons specifically, and again check that they have done so using JavaScript validation. In this part of the 'validate' function, we see if the 'checked' property of both of the radio buttons is false. If neither button is checked, we flag an error.

```
if( (!loginForm.action[0].checked) && (!loginForm.action[1].checked) )
{
   strErrorMessage +="You must select View or Update settings\n";
   booValid=false;
}
```

Another possible form of validation is to check that different choices made within the same form are consistent with one another, for example in our login form it may be that only administrators are able to update the settings. This means that anyone attempting to log on as a user, but also selecting the 'change settings' radio button would be making an invalid choice. In this part of the 'validate' method, we combine these conditions together.

```
if( (loginForm.action[1].checked) &&
(loginForm.loginoptions.selectedIndex !=1) )
{
   strErrorMessage +=
      "You cannot update settings unless you are an administrator\n";
   booValid=false;
}
```

Here is the complete 'validate' function (in a different file to separate it from the previous version).

```
// File: validateloginform.js
function validate(loginForm)
{
   var booValid = true;
   var strErrorMessage = "";
   if(loginForm.loginid.value == "")
   {
      strErrorMessage += "user name field cannot be empty\n";
      booValid=false;
   }
   if(loginForm.pword.value == "")
   {
      strErrorMessage += "password field cannot be empty\n";
      booValid=false;
   }
   if(loginForm.loginoptions.selectedIndex == 0 )
   {
      strErrorMessage += "you must select your Login role\n";
      booValid=false;
```

```
    }
    if( (!loginForm.action[0].checked) && (!loginForm.action[1].checked) )
    {
        strErrorMessage += "You must select View or Update settings\n";
        booValid=false;
    }
    if( (loginForm.action[1].checked) &&
    (loginForm.loginoptions.selectedIndex != 1) )
    {
        strErrorMessage += "You cannot update settings unless you are
        an administrator\n";
        booValid=false;
    }
    if(!booValid)
    {
        alert(strErrorMessage);
    }
        return booValid;
}
```

The following XHTML page contains the various form components that are validated by
the JavaScript 'validate' function.

```
<?xml version="1.0"?>
<!DOCTYPE html PUBLIC "-//W3C//DTD XHTML 1.1//EN"
    "http://www.w3.org/TR/xhtml11/DTD/xhtml11.dtd">
<html xmlns="http://www.w3.org/1999/xhtml" xml:lang="en">
    <head>
        <title>Customer Login</title>
        <script type="text/javascript" src="validateloginform.js">
        </script>
    </head>
    <body>
<!-- File: example7-11.htm -->
        <form action="customerlogin" method="post"
        onsubmit="return validate(this)">
            <table>
                <tr>
                    <td><label for="loginid">Login Name:</label></td>
                    <td><input type="text" id="loginid"/></td>
                </tr>
                <tr>
                    <td><label for="pword">Password:</label></td>
                    <td><input type="password" id="pword"/></td>
                </tr>
                <tr>
                    <td><label for="loginoptions">Select Login role:</label></td>
                    <td><select id="loginoptions" size="1">
                        <option></option>
                        <option>Administrator</option>
                        <option>User</option>
```

```
                </select>
              </td>
            </tr>
            <tr>
              <td>Select Action:</td>
              <td>
                <input type="radio" name="action" value="view"/> View settings
                <input type="radio" name="action" value="update"/> Update
settings
              </td>
            </tr>
            <tr>
              <td></td>
              <td><input type = "submit" value = "Login"/>
                  <input type = "reset" value = "Clear form"/>
              </td>
            </tr>
          </table>
        </form>
      </body>
    </html>
```

Figure 7.11 shows what the alert looks like if a user name and password has been entered
but the user has attempted to log in as a user (rather than an administrator) and selected
'update' settings.

FIGURE 7.11   An alert displayed by the 'validate' function that cross-references two
of the controls in the form

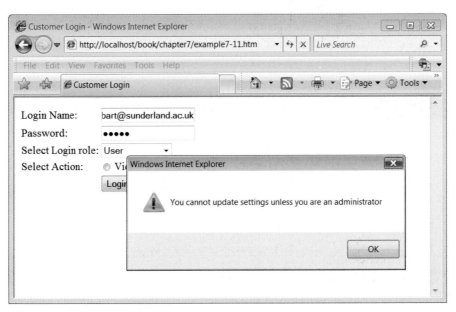

7.5 The emergence of Ajax

One of the big talking points around web application development in 2005 was the emergence of Ajax as a way of bringing some aspects of the desktop application experience into browser-based applications. Ajax is not a particularly new concept, following on as it does from a longer tradition of client-side processing that includes JavaScript, Java applets and DHTML. However the significant difference between Ajax and previous approaches is the concept of the 'one-page web application', whereby page content is updated asynchronously from the server without the whole page being rebuilt. An early example of this approach was Google Suggest, which was able to dynamically populate a search text box with suggestions for search terms as characters were typed into it, providing, of course, that the browser was able to support it. The most important component of an Ajax application is the 'XMLHttpRequest' component, which was first introduced by Microsoft into Outlook Web Access 2000 and later into Internet Explorer 5.0. Other browsers have since followed with their own implementations of the 'XMLHttpRequest'. This component enables browser-hosted applications to send requests to the server and receive responses without replacing or fully refreshing the current web page. Instead, the response that is returned from the server, which may be an XML document or a simple stream of characters, can be handled by a client-side script and used to update parts of the page using the DOM. Figure 7.12 shows the general architecture of Ajax-based systems. The key to this architecture is that the Ajax engine mediates between the user interface and the server, processing on the client where possible (using DHTML) and, where necessary, sending asynchronous HTTP requests and receiving XML data (or indeed data in any other suitable format) that it renders in the browser via the DOM.

Equally importantly, this processing can take place asynchronously. This means that the user does not have to wait for the server to respond in order to continue interacting with the application. Instead, the application is able to continue serving the user while at the same time handling the server response as and when it arrives. Figure 7.13 shows the general idea. User activity in the browser continues even while the Ajax engine is submitting XMLHttpRequests to the server and waiting for responses. The Ajax engine is responsible for handling events associated with getting back the server response but the user does not have to wait for it. Ajax applications do not have to be asynchronous, however. In some cases it might be appropriate to wait for the server's response before continuing with the current process.

FIGURE 7.12   Ajax architecture, adapted from (Garrett 2005)

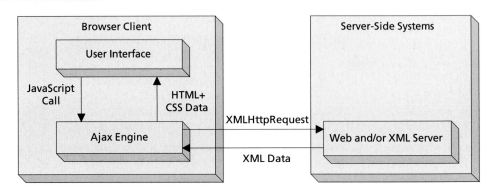

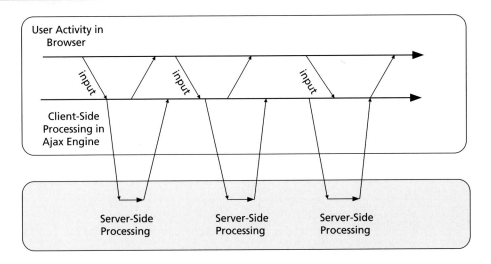

Ajax itself is not a technology but a label, applied by Garrett (2005), to a way of building web applications that uses the 'XMLHttpRequest' object within client-side scripts to seamlessly update web pages. Garrett summarized Ajax as a combination of:

- Standards-based presentation using XHTML and CSS
- Dynamic display and interaction using the document object model
- Data interchange and manipulation using XML and eXtensible Stylesheet Language Transformations (XSLT)
- Asynchronous data retrieval using the 'XMLHttpRequest'
- JavaScript binding everything together

Of course the technologies listed by Garrett are not the only way to provide one-page applications on the web; alternative technologies, such as Flash, can be used to similar effect.

Writing Ajax code with JavaScript

There are basically two approaches to writing an Ajax application. One is to build your own Ajax code using standard JavaScript. The other is to use some kind of API and/or development tool that encapsulates the underlying Ajax code, for example, the Google Ajax API (though this is just one example of many). In this chapter, we focus on using standard JavaScript to develop relatively simple Ajax applications. However, for more complex systems it may be more appropriate to look at using Ajax development tools.

If you are writing Ajax applications without using a tool or framework, one of the most important things to build is a JavaScript function that is able to acquire the appropriate type of 'XMLHttpRequest' object, depending on which browser the script is running in. The main choice to be made is between older Microsoft browsers and newer Microsoft, or non-Microsoft, browsers. This is because Microsoft has, over time, developed different implementations of the 'XMLHttpRequest' component. In earlier versions (used in

Internet Explorer 5 and 6), they used an ActiveX object to implement the 'XMLHttpRequest' as part of Microsoft XML Core Services (MSXML), and even within these Microsoft browser versions there are slightly different types of ActiveX objects. However, from Internet Explorer 7.0 onwards, the implementation is based on native scripting and works in a similar way to other browsers. Therefore in order to make sure we get the right type of 'XMLHttpRequest' object in our JavaScript, we need to write a function that tries to access these different implementations in turn until it finds a match. There are various ways of doing this, including the following simple example (Dutta 2006). It uses properties of the window object to identify which type of 'XMLHttpRequest' is available. For more recent versions of Internet Explorer and other browsers, there will be an 'XMLHttpRequest' property. If this is not present, then the browser may be an older version of Internet Explorer, in which case the window should have an 'ActiveXObject' property. Of course, if both of these tests return 'false' then the browser is not capable of supporting Ajax.

```
if(window.XMLHttpRequest)
{
    // If IE7, Mozilla, Safari, etc: Use native object
    var xmlHttp = new XMLHttpRequest();
}
else
{
    if(window.ActiveXObject)
    {
        // otherwise, use the ActiveX control for IE5.x and IE6
        var xmlHttp = new ActiveXObject("Microsoft.XMLHTTP");
    }
}
```

A slightly more detailed approach is described by (Zakas *et al.* 2006), which takes into account the several different versions of the ActiveX object that have been implemented. It also uses JavaScript exception handling as well as 'if' statements. Exception handling code uses the reserved words 'try' and 'catch'. Code that may throw an exception (i.e. an error condition) is put inside a block of code labelled with 'try', and code that can handle that exception, if it occurs, is put into a following 'catch' block. The code in the 'catch' block is only executed if an exception is thrown. Otherwise only the code in the 'try' block is executed. This is the basic structure of a 'try ... catch' block:

```
try
{
    // Attempt to execute some code here
}
catch(e)
{
    // If it throws an exception, handle it here
}
```

Here is an 'if' statement (as part of a function) that also includes a 'try ... catch' block. It attempts to create an 'XMLHttpRequest' object and return it to the caller of the function, but if this fails, an exception is thrown, which is handled by the catch block. In this case, we do not do anything other than allow the code to continue executing, because the next step is to look for the correct type of ActiveX object.

```
if(window.XMLHttpRequest)
{
   // If IE7, Mozilla, Safari, etc: Use native object
   try
   {
      xhrequest = new XMLHttpRequest();
      return xhrequest;
   }
   catch(exception)
   {
      // OK, just carry on looking
   }
}
```

There are five different versions of the ActiveX object that we may be able to identify in some versions of Internet Explorer. A useful way of checking for each of them is to put their various names into an array and then iterate through them using a 'for' loop until a match is found. The array needs to contain the names of the various objects starting with the most recent, because the more recent ActiveX components are likely to perform better than the older ones. Here is an array containing the relevant names of the various ActiveX objects:

```
var IEControls = ["MSXML2.XMLHttp.5.0", "MSXML2.XMLHttp.4.0", "MSXML2.XMLHttp.3.0",
"MSXML2.XMLHttp", "Microsoft.XMLHttp" ];
```

Here is a complete function, 'getXMLHttpRequest', which uses the various techniques and methods that we have introduced:

```
function getXMLHttpRequest()
{
   var xhrequest = null;
   if(window.XMLHttpRequest)
   {
   // If IE7, Mozilla, Safari, etc: Use native object
   try
   {
      xhrequest = new XMLHttpRequest();
      return xhrequest;
   }
   catch(exception)
   {
      // OK, just carry on looking
   }
}
   else if(window.ActiveXObject)
   {
   // ... otherwise, use the ActiveX control for IE5.x and IE6
      var IEControls=["MSXML2.XMLHttp.5.0", "MSXML2.XMLHttp.4.0",
         "MSXML2.XMLHttp.3.0", "MSXML2.XMLHttp", "Microsoft.XMLHttp"];
      for(var i=0; i < IEControls.length; i++)
```

```
        {
          try
          {
            xhrequest = new ActiveXObject(IEControls[i]);
            return xhrequest;
          }
          catch(exception)
          {
          // OK, just carry on looking
          }
        }
      }
      // if we got here we didn't find any matches
      throw new Error("Cannot create an XMLHttpRequest");
      }
    }
```

Once we have an 'XMLHttpRequest' object, we can open a connection to a server URL with it, using the 'open' method. This takes at least three parameters (it can take more, if a username and password are required for the connection). The first is the HTTP method for the connection (usually 'GET' or 'POST'), the second is the URL of the server-side application that we want to connect to, and the third parameter is a Boolean value that specifies if we want to make an asynchronous (true) or a synchronous (false) connection. Since one of the basic concepts behind Ajax is that we make asynchronous connections, the third parameter would normally be set to 'true', unless there was a good reason for waiting for the response before continuing.

```
    xhrequest.open("GET", url, true);
```

The URL string comprises the name of the server-side program that will deal with the request. In many cases, where the request type is 'GET', it also includes request parameters from the current page.

Once the connection to the server has been made, we have to have some way of knowing when, and if, a successful response has been received from the server.

Perhaps the most important aspect therefore of the 'XMLHttpRequest' object is its 'onreadystatechange' event, which is triggered when the request changes state. We can respond to this state change by assigning the name of a function to the event, so that the function is called when there is a state change.

```
    xhrequest.onreadystatechange = nameoffunction;
```

It is important to note that the name of the function that is associated with the 'onreadystatechange' is *not* followed by parentheses in this line of code. Parentheses are only used if the function is anonymous, and declared in-line, in other words the function definition appears as part of the same statement, like this:

```
    xhrequest.onreadystatechange = function()
    {
      // body of in-line function here
    };
```

Note the use of the reserved word 'function', and the semicolon at the end of the closing brace. In our first example, we use a function that is declared separately, called 'processResponse', so the assignment of the function name looks like this:

```
xhrequest.onreadystatechange = processResponse;
```

There are five possible states that the request can be in:

0 = uninitialized
1 = loading
2 = loaded
3 = interactive
4 = complete

The 'onreadystatechange' event is triggered every time the state changes, which means that our function is called several times as it works though the various stages from 0 to 4. However we do not usually want to respond to these events until the state has reached 4 (complete), at which point we have successfully received a server response and can process it accordingly. The function associated with the 'onreadystatechange' event has to be written to check the state before it continues processing and handle any problems. Even if we got a response back, it may not be the one we were expecting, for example we may get an HTTP response code back that is something other than 200 (the 'OK' response.) Therefore we also need to check that the response is OK before attempting to process it. Here is an outline of a function that checks the status of the 'XMLHttpRequest' and the HTTP status code.

```
function processResponse()
{
    if(xhrequest.readyState == 4 && xhrequest.status == 200)
    {
        // now we can do something with the response
    }
}
```

Once everything else is in place, we need to open a connection to the server using the 'open' method (as we have already described) and then send our request using the 'send' method, which may simply send the request or also send some data, perhaps as a string of data to be posted to the server (this may be necessary if we are not appending query parameters to the URL as a get request) or it may be an XML document. If we are not sending either of these data items then the parameter value can be set to null.

```
xhrequest.send(null);
```

Once the request has been sent to the server, and there is a function able to respond to the 'onreadystatechange' event, the next step is to be able to process the response. Depending on how the server-side implementation works, the data that comes back as a response could be either a simple string of data or an XML document. If the response is string data, then the appropriate property to use to handle it is 'responseText'. If the response is in the form of an XML document, then the appropriate property to use is 'responseXML'.

Tables 7.1 and 7.2 summarize the properties and methods of the 'XMLHttpRequest' object.

TABLE 7.1	'XMLHttpRequest' object properties

Property	Description
onreadystatechange	Event handler for an event that fires at every change in the readyState
readyState	The status of the request, which can be in the following states: 0 = uninitialized 1 = loading 2 = loaded 3 = interactive 4 = complete
responseText	Data returned from the server as a string
responseXML	Data returned from the server as an XML document
status	HTTP status code, for example 200 (OK), 404 (not found)
statusText	Message string describing the status code

TABLE 7.2	'XMLHttpRequest' object methods

Method	Description
abort()	Aborts the current request
getAllResponseHeaders()	Returns all headers (names and values) as a single string
getResponseHeader (*headerName*)	Returns the value of the specified header
open (*method, URL, asyncFlag, username, password*)	Opens a connection and retrieves a response from the specified URL. The method is usually either GET or POST; optionally, there can be a username and password for secure sites
send (*content*)	Sends the request to the server (can include data as a string or DOM object if it is a post request)
setRequestHeader(*name, value*)	Assigns the given value to the named header

Using Ajax and RSS

Later in this book, we see how to build Ajax applications where we connect from our JavaScript client to our own server-side applications. However, as a first example, we see how to create an Ajax application that connects to server-side data sources that are available from web sites in the public domain. There are many types of data on the web that we could potentially connect to using an Ajax application, but one of the simplest would be an RSS feed. RSS feeds were first introduced in 1999 and have become increasingly popular. During this time, increasing standardisation has been applied to try to ensure interoperability. RSS is an acronym that has some confused roots, standing variously for Really Simple Syndication, Rich Site Summary or RDF Site Summary. However they all

FIGURE 7.14 The standard RSS feed icon

have much the same intent: to provide a way of aggregating frequently updated content into web applications so that content can be syndicated. Increasingly, the standard 'feed' icon is becoming used across web applications to indicate the availability of RSS content (Figure 7.14).

The format of an RSS feed is basically a simple XML document that has a root element called 'rss'. Inside this element is a single 'channel' element, which describes the content of the channel and contains a series of item elements. Here are some of the main elements in RSS version 2.0 documents.

```
<?xml version="1.0"?>
<rss version="2.0">
  <channel>
    <title>...</title>
    <link>...</link>
    <description>...</description>
    . . .
    <item>
      <title>...</title>
      <link>...</link>
      <description>...</description>
      <pubDate>...</pubDate>
      <guid>...</guid>
    </item>
    <item>
    . . .
    </item>
  </channel>
</rss>
```

Security issues with the 'XMLHttpRequest'

One of the security issues with the 'XMLHttpRequest' is that browsers guard against cross domain requests, meaning that they either warn against, or disallow, any attempt to send an 'XMLHttpRequest' to a domain other than the one that the web page came from. This means, in fact, that using the 'XMLHttpRequest' as part of an RSS reader is perhaps not an ideal solution, since we then have to start looking into issues such as signing our scripts with security certificates. When we are connecting to our own test server this is not going to cause any problems, because we either create our own RSS feeds or use our server as a proxy between the browser and the original source of the RSS feed. Unfortunately, however, the security restrictions also apply to HTML pages that are loaded as local files. In order to test the Ajax examples in this chapter as local files, we have had to use Internet Explorer 7.0, because there are some browsers (for example, Firefox and Opera) that do not allow you to access the RSS content using 'XMLHttpRequest'. Of course, once we start to deploy our own web applications, this will no longer be an issue.

Connecting to a server using an 'XMLHttpRequest'

Because there are a number of different aspects to using Ajax, our first example simply tries to make a connection to a server using an 'XMLHttpRequest' and shows an alert if the connection is successful. The following function ('processResponse') simply checks that the ready state of the request is '4' and the HTTP status code is '200' (OK). If so, an alert is shown. The 'xhrequest' variable shown here is declared elsewhere as a global variable:

```
// File: processresponse.js
function processResponse()
{
    if(xhrequest.readyState == 4 && xhrequest.status == 200)
    {
        alert("Got Response!");
    }
}
```

Here is an XHTML page that uses the 'getXMLHttpRequest' function (in 'getxmlhttprequest.js') to get hold of an 'XMLHttpRequest' object. If it is successful, it uses the 'processResponse' function (in 'processresponse.js') to show the alert. The two functions are in separate files because the 'getXMLHttpRequest' function is generic and can be reused across many different pages, whereas the 'processResponse' function is specific to this example. The URL used here is for the Yahoo RSS news feed, but since we are just testing to see if we have made a connection, any valid URL can be used instead.

```
<?xml version="1.0"?>
<!DOCTYPE html PUBLIC "-//W3C//DTD XHTML 1.1//EN"
    "http://www.w3.org/TR/xhtml11/DTD/xhtml11.dtd">
<html xmlns="http://www.w3.org/1999/xhtml" xml:lang="en">
    <head>
        <title>Ajax RSS Reader</title>
        <script type="text/javascript" src="getxmlhttprequest.js">
        </script>
        <script type="text/javascript" src="processresponse.js">
        </script>
    </head>
    <body>
    <!-- File: example7-12.htm -->
        <script type="text/javascript">
        // no 'var', so this is a global variable!
            xhrequest = null;
```

```
        try
        {
            xhrequest = getXMLHttpRequest();
        }
        catch(error)
        {
            document.write("Cannot run Ajax code using this browser");
        }
        if(xhrequest != null)
        {
            xhrequest.onreadystatechange = processResponse
            xhrequest.open("GET", "http://rss.news.yahoo.com/rss/topstories", true);
            xhrequest.send(null);
        }
    </script>
  </body>
</html>
```

Figure 7.15 shows the alert that appears if you make a successful connection using the 'XMLHttpRequest'.

Reading XML data using the 'XMLHttpRequest'

For our final example, we build on the code that makes an Ajax connection and retrieve some data from an RSS feed into a web page. The first thing that we need is something on

FIGURE 7.15 The alert that appears if a successful connection to the server is made using the 'XMLHttpRequest'

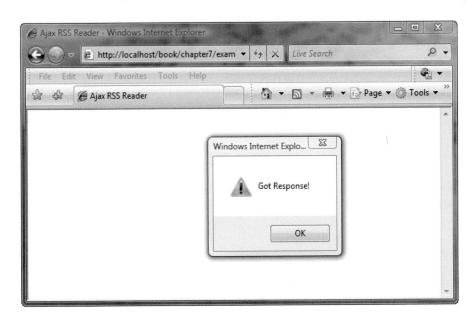

7

the page to display the content we are reading from the server. In our example, we use a 'div' with the id of 'feed':

```
<div id="feed"></div>
```

This is where we write the content to when we get the response.

The other main change that we need to make is to provide a function that does more than just show an alert when it makes a connection. We need instead to navigate the DOM of the RSS XML document. You will note from the structure of RSS documents that there is a 'description' element inside the 'channel' element, and another inside each 'item' element. In the following function we use the 'getElementsByTagName' method to get a collection of all the description elements. Then we navigate to the first of the item descriptions using the index '1' (since the first index, 0, would be the channel description). We then set the 'innerHTML' property of the 'div' to the value of the content of the element. When we connect to the Yahoo news feed, the content is a set of anchors that link to HTML content.

```
// File: processnewsfeed.js
function processYahooNewsFeed()
{
    if(xhrequest.readyState == 4 && xhrequest.status == 200)
    {
        var descriptions=xhrequest.responseXML.getElementsByTagName('description');
        var firstItemDescription=descriptions[1];
        feed.innerHTML=firstItemDescription.firstChild.nodeValue;
    }
}
```

Here is the web page that retrieves the content and displays it. It is similar to the last example, except that it includes the div tag and calls the 'processYahooNewsFeed' function.

```
<?xml version="1.0"?>
<!DOCTYPE html PUBLIC "-//W3C//DTD XHTML 1.1//EN"
    "http://www.w3.org/TR/xhtml11/DTD/xhtml11.dtd">
<html xmlns="http://www.w3.org/1999/xhtml" xml:lang="en">
    <head>
        <title>Ajax RSS Reader</title>
        <script type="text/javascript" src="getxmlhttprequest.js">
        </script>
        <script type="text/javascript" src="processnewsfeed.js">
        </script>
    </head>
    <body>
    <!-- File: example7-13.htm -->
        <h1>Yahoo News Feed</h1>
        <div id="feed"></div>
        <script type="text/javascript">
            // no 'var', so this is a global variable!
            xhrequest=null;
```

```
    try
    {
       xhrequest = getXMLHttpRequest();
    }
    catch(error)
    {
       document.write("Cannot run Ajax code using this browser");
    }
    if(xhrequest != null)
    {
       xhrequest.onreadystatechange = processYahooNewsFeed;
       xhrequest.open("GET", "http://rss.news.yahoo.com/rss/topstories", true);
       xhrequest.send(null);
    }
    </script>
  </body>
</html>
```

Figure 7.16 shows how the page looks when it has retrieved the first item from the feed. Of course the actual content changes on a daily basis.

FIGURE 7.16   Part of the Yahoo news feed included in a web page using Ajax

Exercises

7.1 Using the document in 'example7-1.htm', write a JavaScript function (in a separate '.js' file) that uses appropriate DOM properties and methods to locate the 'span' elements with the ids 'risk' and 'items'. Using the DOM (you can assign the values either to the 'nodeValue' property of the element's 'firstChild' or the 'innerHTML' property), replace the text in these spans with 'domestic disaster' and 'your possessions' respectively.

Invoke the function using the 'onload' event of the document body. The resulting page should appear as in Figure 7.17.

7.2 Modify the validation function in the file 'validateform.js', which currently just checks that the login id and password fields are not empty, to include these additional validations:

- Login IDs should be based on an email address, so the input must contain the '@' character.
- Passwords must be at least 5 characters long, but have no more than 10 characters.

Add an appropriate message to the alert if either of these conditions is not met.

You can use the length property of strings to check the length of the password.

To check for the '@' character (substring) in the login id, you can use the 'string.indexOf( )' function. If the function returns −1, it means the substring you are searching for is not in the string:

```
if(loginid.indexOf("@") == -1)
{
    // not there!
```

7.3 There is no need to write all your own validation code since there are many JavaScript validation routines available to download on the web. Find one of these

---

FIGURE 7.17   The expected result from Question 1

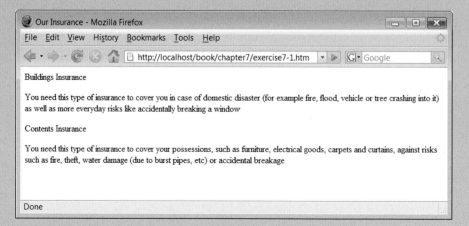

and use it to validate a form containing fields such as credit card numbers, dates and floating point numbers.

7.4 In an external file called 'mouseover.js', write two JavaScript functions to animate the WebHomeCover logo by using two different versions of the logo and switching between them when the mouse passes over the logo position. Here is an XHTML page that includes an anchor that uses the 'onmouseover' and 'onmouseout' events to trigger JavaScript functions.

```
<?xml version="1.0"?>
<!DOCTYPE html PUBLIC
    "-//W3C//DTD XHTML 1.1//EN"
    "http://www.w3.org/TR/xhtml11/DTD/xhtml11.dtd">
<html xmlns="http://www.w3.org/1999/xhtml" xml:lang="en">
    <head>
        <meta http-equiv="Content-Script-Type" content="text/javascript"/>
        <title>Mouse over logo</title>
        <script type="text/javascript" src ="mouseover.js"></script>
    </head>
    <body>
        <!-- File: Exercise7-4.htm -->
        <h2>WebHomeCover Logo</h2>
        <div>
            <a href="http://www.webhomecover.com" onmouseover="mouseOver()"
            onmouseout="mouseNotOver()">
            <img src="webhomecoverlogo.gif" alt="WebHomeCover logo"
                id="logo"/>
            </a>
        </div>
    </body>
</html>
```

You will need to implement the 'mouseOver' and 'mouseNotOver' functions. In these functions, use the getElementByID method to navigate to the 'logo' (the 'img' element) and set the name of the 'src' attribute to one of the two image file names (one in each function). The two files (supplied on the CD) are 'webhome coverlogo.gif' and 'webhomecoverinverted.gif'.

7.5 Write an Ajax function called 'processWeatherFeed' that accesses the first title element and second description element of an RSS document, concatenates them together and writes their content to an element of an XHTML document. You can use the URIs of various RSS weather feeds. Yahoo, for example, provides a simple RSS URI for weather feeds where you append a 'p' request parameter that has the value of a location. For example, the following URI would get the weather in London, UK.

```
http://weather.yahooapis.com/forecastrss?p=UKXX0085
```

You can find out the code for any global weather location by navigating from the main Yahoo weather page:

```
http://weather.yahoo.com/
```

There are other weather feeds that you can also use, for example RSSWeather.com. Here is the URL for accessing the weather in London using their RSS feed

```
http://www.rssweather.com/icao/EGLC/rss.php
```

You will find other feeds on the web that you may be able to connect to, depending on how they are configured. Remember that all RSSfeeds use the same XML document structure, so you can create a generic function that is able to read data from any RSS feed, not just news or weather as we have done so far.

SUMMARY

In this chapter, we built on the basics of JavaScript syntax introduced previously to explore some aspects of DHTML, form validation and Ajax. We began the chapter by describing some features of JavaScript that let us navigate to parts of an XHTML document using the DOM and dynamically change their state. We then looked at an important aspect of JavaScript, which is client-side validation. We concluded the chapter by looking at some fundamental aspects of Ajax, which uses JavaScript to communicate with the server and change the content of the current page without needing to reload it.

References and further reading

Dutta, S. (2006) *Native XMLHTTPRequest object*. http://blogs.msdn.com/ie/archive/2006/01/23/516393.aspx

Garrett, J.J. (2005) *Ajax: A New Approach to Web Applications*. http://www.adaptivepath.com/publications/essays/archives/000385.php

Zakas, N., McPeak, J. and Fawcett, J. (2006) *Professional Ajax*. Wrox/Wiley 2006

CHAPTER 8

Introduction to PHP

LEARNING OBJECTIVES

- Be aware of the PHP language and understand what it can be used for

- Understand that PHP can be embedded within (X)HTML documents using tags to denote the start and end of PHP code

- Understand how it is possible to jump in and out of PHP within a document and what the PHP parser does when it interprets a document

- Understand and be able to use the echo construct effectively

- Understand how PHP instructions should be separated

- Understand why you should comment your PHP scripts and be able to do so

- Understand the different PHP types that are supported and how to use PHP variables

- Understand what a PHP constant and a predefined variable are and be able to use them

- Understand what an expression is, the role of operators and operands and operator precedence

INTRODUCTION

Welcome to the PHP scripting language. In this chapter, we begin by introducing you to the PHP language. We explain what PHP is and how it works by introducing you to your first PHP script and show you how you can view the output that it generates within a Web browser.

We shall provide an introduction to script syntax and explain how and why it is important for you to comment your PHP scripts carefully. We shall introduce the concept of variables and describe how you use them. We shall examine the different types of data which a variable can store and the differences between them. We will also examine PHP operands and operators and explain how these go together to form expressions.

In conclusion, we cover all the basic fundamental PHP constructs and syntax you need to know before you can start doing some of the really interesting and powerful things we cover in later chapters. By the end of this chapter, you will be familiar with creating PHP scripts, saving them and viewing their output using a browser of your choice. It is worthwhile pointing out that PHP is widely supported by a large community of developers and you will find a comprehensive annotated manual online at http://www.php.net/manual/en/ if there are some PHP language concepts we introduce that you would like to investigate further. Anyway, we have a lot to get through, so let's get started.

8.1 Welcome to PHP

According to the PHP web site (www.php.net) 'PHP is a widely-used general-purpose scripting language that is especially suited for Web development and can be embedded into HTML'.

PHP is a scripting language which can be combined within (X)HTML documents to enable the creation of dynamic web systems. By doing this you can overcome one of the more serious limitation of (X)HTML documents – they are static in nature. What we mean by this

FIGURE 8.1   How PHP works

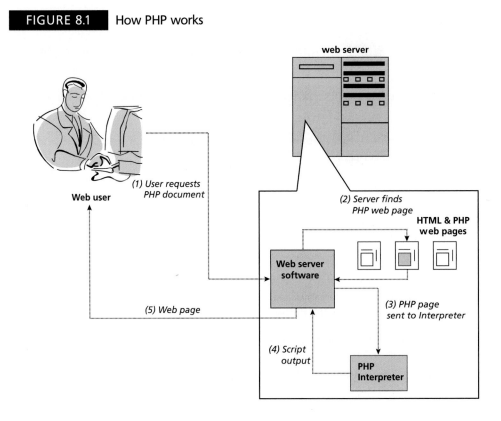

is that a standard (X)HTML document is stored on a server and, when requested, displayed to a user via a web browser. The document that is displayed does not change. It might have some clever JavaScript or plug-in which provides a degree of user interaction but it cannot change the fundamental content it contains nor interface with a database to reflect new dynamic up-to-date content each time it is loaded. By using PHP, you can accomplish all of these things.

PHP is a hypertext pre-processor (it's where the name PHP comes from) which means that it processes the hypertext document before it is served to the browser. PHP is therefore a server-side scripting language and all the work is done at the server before it is sent to the client (your web browser). Figure 8.1 illustrates how PHP works.

If you look closely at Figure 8.1, you see that a user has requested a PHP document from a web server. If the document had been a simple (X)HTML document, the server would have simply sent it to the client web browser. Because the document is a PHP document, the server passes the document to the PHP interpreter. This parses through the document searching for any PHP commands. When it finds any it removes them and replaces them with any output that the PHP commands generate. When it has finished parsing the document, the resulting document with the PHP removed is sent to the user's browser. It sounds complex but it is easier if you see it working for yourself.

8.2 Your first PHP script

Welcome to your first PHP script, which is commonly known as a 'hello world' application, as all it does is display the words 'Hello, World':

```
<!DOCTYPE html PUBLIC "-//W3C//DTD XHTML 1.1//EN"
   "http://www.w3.org/TR/xhtml11/DTD/xhtml11.dtd">

<html xmlns="http://www.w3.org/1999/xhtml" xml:lang="en">
<head>
<title>PHP Script</title>
<meta http-equiv="Content-Type" content="text/html; charset=ISO-8859-1" />
</head>
<body>
<?php
echo "<p>Hello, World</p>";
?>
</body>
</html>
```

Okay, this does look very complicated for an introductory script but that is because we have chosen to embed the PHP script into an (X)HTML document which conforms to the W3C recommendations and standards. This is a very good thing to do as it ensures the quality and consistency of web documents, but it does make things a little complex for the beginner.

Don't worry about understanding the script at the moment but type the script into your chosen editor and save it as 'example8–1.php' in your web server directory. Exactly how you do this depends on the editor you are using, the web server and the PHP environment

FIGURE 8.2 Your first PHP script

you have on your computer. We shall assume that you have installed the WAMP environment and that your web server directory is located at:

```
C:\wamp\www\
```

You may wish to create sub-directories below the 'www' directory in which to store your scripts for each chapter but that is up to you. If you have saved your script as 'example8–1.php' in the directory above then you can view the output from the script by typing:

```
localhost/example8–1.php
```

into the location bar of your browser and pressing return.

 NOTE It is important that PHP scripts are saved with a filename extension of .php. If you omit to do this then the web server may not recognize that your file contains PHP script and therefore it will not work as intended.

Figure 8.2 illustrates the output from the script when viewed using a web browser.

8.3 Simplifying your first PHP script

We can simplify this script by stripping away all of the (X)HTML elements before and after the PHP script to allow us to focus on the PHP script itself. We shall therefore for the sake of clarify remove the following lines from the start of the script:

```
<!DOCTYPE html PUBLIC "-//W3C//DTD XHTML 1.1//EN"
   "http://www.w3.org/TR/xhtml11/DTD/xhtml11.dtd">
   <html xmlns="http://www.w3.org/1999/xhtml" xml:lang="en">
<head>
<title>PHP Script</title>
   <meta http-equiv="Content-Type" content="text/html; charset=ISO-8859-1" />
</head>
<body>
```

and the following lines from the end of the script:

```
</body>
</html>
```

NOTE Unfortunately, by removing these XHTML elements before and after the PHP script we are not producing documents which conform to the XHTML standard. However, all of these examples and the solutions to the exercise are available for dowload at the publishers' web site and have been written to be XHTML 1.1 compliant.

Removing these lines from our 'example8–1.php' script results in the following lines being left behind:

```
<?php
echo '<p>Hello, World</p>';
?>
```

This script is a far simpler example to both explain and understand. The PHP code is enclosed within special start and end tags which denote the start and end of the PHP script:

```
<?php
?>
```

In this example the PHP code itself consists of a single instruction which displays the text 'Hello, World' on the web browser:

```
echo "<p>Hello, World</p>";
```

You should note that in the above example we are also outputting some (X)HTML paragraph tags (<p></p>) as well as the text 'Hello, World'. We use the echo construct to output this information. The echo construct is part of the PHP language and outputs all parameters passed to it. The following is another example of an echo construct outputting a simple string of characters:

```
echo 'These characters will be output';
```

We use the echo construct a lot as it is one of the primary ways of injecting output from a PHP script into a PHP document. We shall explore this concept further very shortly.

8.4 Jumping in and out of PHP

PHP code is often embedded in (X)HTML documents. It can also be used as a stand-alone programming language and we will be using it as the latter.

Within a document, PHP code is identified through some special tags which denote the start and end of the PHP code. We mentioned previously that when a browser requests a document which contains some PHP script the server passes the document to the PHP interpreter. Let us look at this process a little more clearly.

The interpreter parses the document line by line, producing as output a file which is identical to the input document unless it detects a PHP start tag. It interprets the code it finds after the tag and outputs any echo construct data to the output file until an end PHP tag is detected. It then continues parsing through the document copying any remaining lines to the output file.

All this happens at the server before the parsed document (with the PHP removed) is sent to the user's browser for display). This process is illustrated in Figure 8.3.

To illustrate this more clearly consider this slightly modified 'Hello, World!' script:

```
<body>
<?php
echo '<p>Hello, World!</p>';
?>
</body>
```

The only difference between this script and the cut-down version of the previous 'example8–1.php' is that we have included a <body> </body> element around the PHP script. After the script is parsed the output produced and sent to the web browser is as follows:

```
<body>
<p>'Hello, World!'</p>
</body>
```

You can prove to yourself that this is true by typing and saving the above script as 'example8–2.php' and viewing the output using a browser, by typing the following into your browser location bar:

```
localhost/example8–2.php
```

All you will see displayed is the text 'Hello, World!', as the <body> </body> tags are not visible on a web page. However, if you right click on the web page and select View Page (in FireFox) or View Source in Internet Explorer source then a window will appear, as shown in Figure 8.4, illustrating the complete output generated by the PHP parser.

FIGURE 8.3   A parsed PHP document

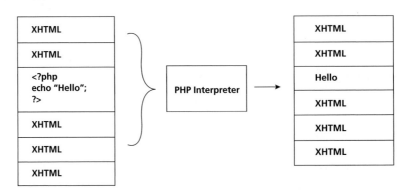

FIGURE 8.4   PHP parser output

FIGURE 8.4   PHP parser output

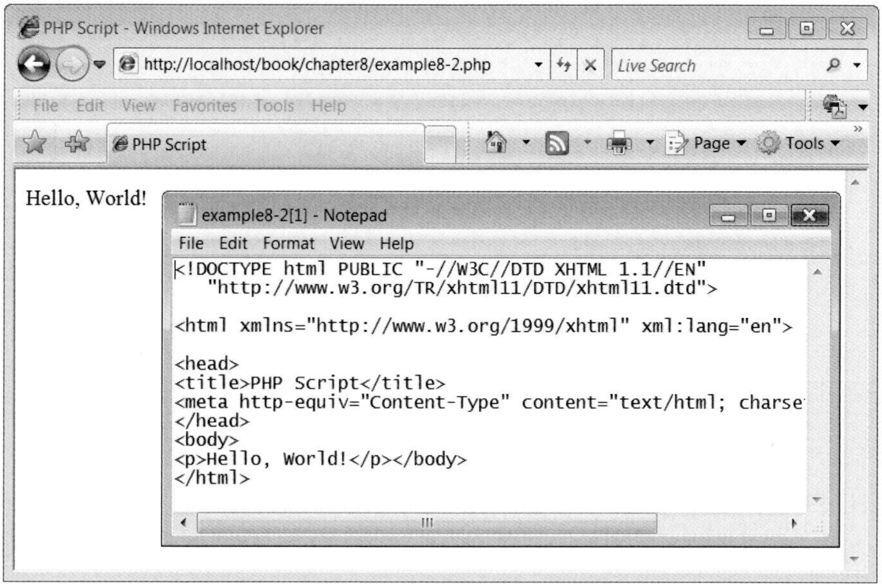

You can embed PHP start and end tags and code at many points in a (X)HTML document. Consider the following example:

```
<?php
echo '<p>This is PHP script generated.</p>';
?>
<p>This is not.</p>
<?php
echo '<p>This is also PHP script generated.</p>';
?>
```

This example (which can be saved as 'example8–3.php') illustrates two separate pairs of special start and end PHP tags, illustrating that within a document you can move from non-PHP script back to PHP script. The following output is generated after the above script has been parsed:

```
<p>This is PHP script generated.</p>
<p>This is not.</p>
<p>This is also PHP script generated.</p>
```

The output of this script is illustrated in Figure 8.5.

8.5 Separating PHP instructions

Let us look again at the simple Hello, World PHP ('example8–1.php') script:

```
<?php
echo '<p>Hello, World!</p>';
?>
```

FIGURE 8.5   Jumping in and out of PHP

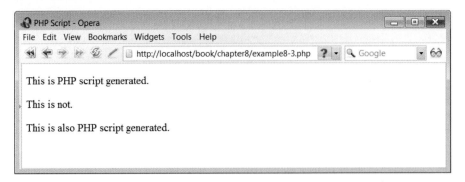

In this script there is only one instruction:

```
echo '<p>Hello, World!</p>';
```

PHP requires instructions to be terminated with a semicolon at the end of each statement. Here is an example of a PHP script (you can save this as 'example8–4.php') with two instructions:

```
<?php
echo '<p>Hello, World!</p>';
echo '<p>Hello, World!</p>';
?>
```

8.6 Commenting your scripts

Comments are human-readable text which is ignored by the PHP interpreter but are included to provide useful reminders or instructions to the developer or future code reader. PHP supports a number of different styles of comments, from C-style single-line comments like this:

```
// this is a single line comment
```

To shell-script single-line comments, which look like this:

```
# this is a shell-style comment
```

And also multi-line comments, like this:

```
/* this comment is an example of
a multi-line comment */
```

 NOTE Comments become very useful in large and complex scripts where it is difficult to work out what is happening. A well-written comment can help a designer remember or help a new developer understand what the original writer had implemented.

The following script illustrates a rather useless use of comments to help the reader follow what the script is doing. It is useless because the script is so simple that the comments just add clutter and do nothing to further understanding:

```php
<?php
// File: example8–5.php

/* This script will display the text "Hello, World!" twice on
separate lines of the web browser */

echo '<p>Hello, World!</p>'; // This is the first "Hello, World!"
echo '<p>Hello, World!</p>'; // This is the second.
?>
```

You should be careful not to 'nest' multi-line comments. For example, the following will cause a problem:

```php
/*
echo 'Hello';
/* this comment will cause problems */
*/
```

Why does this cause a problem? Well, because the parser determines the end of the comment when the first */ tag is reached. In the example above the parser will report an error because it finds a second */ tag.

We shall use comments from now on to indicate the filename of the script example we have created, for example in the above script:

```php
// File: example8–5.php
```

8.7 Basic variables

Variables can be thought of as containers which hold data. The data held by a variable can change during the execution of a PHP script, hence the name 'variable'. PHP variables can hold different types of information and we will consider this in a little more detail later. For now let us take a look at what a variable looks like in PHP and how to create them.

Variables in PHP are represented by a $ symbol followed by the name of the variable. Here is an example variable:

```php
$name='Simon';
```

The variable is called 'name' and it has been assigned the value 'Simon'.

8

 NOTE PHP variable names are case-sensitive. Therefore the variable $name is a different variable to $Name. Be careful!

There is a set of rules which need to be considered in naming your variables. A valid variable name can start with a letter or an underscore character, followed by any number of letters, numbers or underscores. The following script illustrates some example valid variables:

```php
<?php
// File: example8-6.php

$var= 'Elizabeth';
$_var= 56;
$Var= 'Hall';

echo "<p>$var $Var $_var</p>";
?>
```

The following variables are invalid:

```php
var = 'Simon'; // Invalid – does not start with a $ symbol
$2var = 'Simon'; // Invalid – name starts with a number.
```

8.8 Variable types

Variable data is stored in the computer's memory but the computer needs to know in what format the data should be stored as different types of data take up different amounts of space. The format of a piece of data is known as its data type and PHP supports eight primitive types, which are listed in Table 8.1.

We shall examine each of these types in turn and describe the data they can contain.

 NOTE The type of a variable is actually determined by PHP at the run time of the script depending on how the variable is being used. Such programming languages are known as weakly typed. In other programming languages, the variable type is determined by the programmer and these are known as strongly typed programming languages.

TABLE 8.1 PHP primitive data types

Description	Type
Scalar Types	Boolean
	Integer
	Float
	String
Compound Types	Array
	Object
Special Types	Resource
	NULL

TABLE 8.2   Variable type naming

Type	Variable name
Boolean	boo
Integer	int
Float	flo
String	str
Array	arr
Object	obj

Previously we described the rules for variable naming. However, it is useful when programming to use variable names which indicate the type of data which the variable is storing. Table 8.2 lists the different variable types and the three-letter code which can be used at the start of a variable name to indicate the type of data which the variable is storing.

 NOTE   The types Resource and NULL are special types and we have chosen not to give these a variable naming code.

The following illustrates two variable names:

```
$strName='Elizabeth';
$intAge=34;
```

The first variable, $strName, is designed to store a person's name, which is a string of characters, in this case 'Elizabeth', and uses the first three characters 'str' to indicate it is storing a string. The second variable, $intAge, is designed to store a person's age, which is an integer number, and uses the first three characters, 'int', to indicate that it is storing an integer.

We shall now examine each of the variable types briefly, describing their use and providing an example of what they look like.

Boolean

A Boolean type expresses a truth value. It can either be TRUE or FALSE. Here is an example of a variable holding a Boolean value:

```
$booAnswer=True;
```

Integer

An integer value is a number from the set:

$$Z = \{\ldots, -2, -1, 0, 1, 2, \ldots\}$$

Integer numbers are sometimes called whole numbers as they do not have a fractional part. Here are some examples of variables assigned to hold an integer value:

```php
$intNumber = 5;
$intAnotherNumber = -5;
```

 NOTE The size of an integer is platform-dependent, although you can usually assume that a maximum value would be two billion. If you specify a number beyond the size boundary of an integer then PHP interprets this number as a float.

Float

Floating point numbers are also known as floats, doubles or real numbers and are numbers which can contain a fractional part. Here is an example of a variable assigned to hold a floating point value:

```php
$floNumber = 1.234;
```

Floating point values can also be expressed using the following format:

```php
$floAnotherNumber=1.2e3;
```

 NOTE The size of a float is platform-dependent, although you can usually assume a maximum value of approximately 1.8 to the power of 308.

String

A string is a series of characters. We have used strings in our previous PHP examples but it is now time to explain that PHP has three different ways in which strings can be specified. The first and simplest is to use single quotation marks (') to denote the start and end of the string characters, for example:

```php
'This is a simple string'
```

We can assign strings to variables and output them using the echo construct:

```php
<?php

// File: example8-7.php
$strName = 'Elizabeth';
echo '<p>';
echo $strName;
echo '</p>';
?>
```

Because the string uses the single quote characters to specify its start and end we need a special means of including a single quote if we want to have this character as part of our string. For example, consider the following text:

```
Hello I'm Simon
```

If we were to simply enclose this in single quotes the PHP interpreter would not know which single quote indicated the end of the string:

```
'Hello I'm Simon'
```

To overcome this problem PHP uses a backslash (\) character known as 'escape' to allow us to include single quotations within our strings. Therefore the above string would look like this:

```
'Hello I\'m Simon'
```

 NOTE | Strings in PHP can be very large. You don't need to worry about using long strings!

If you look back over some of our previous examples you will note that we have used strings which are enclosed in double quotes ("). When a string is enclosed in double quotes, PHP understands a few more escape characters than it does with single quotes. These escape characters are listed in Table 8.3.

However, the addition of some extra escape characters is not the end of the story as the most important feature of a double-quoted string is that it expands any variable names which are included. Consider the following example:

```php
<?php
// File: example8–8.php

$strName='Elizabeth';

echo '<p>$strName</p>';
?>
```

TABLE 8.3 Escape characters

Escape sequence	Description
\n	Insert a line feed character
\r	Insert a carriage return character
\t	Insert a tab character
\\	Insert a backslash character
\$	Insert a dollar sign
\"	Insert a double quote character

8

In the above example the string displayed by echo will be:

```
<p>$strName</p>
```

However, if we amend the script so that the echo construct has a double-quoted string, like this:

```
<?php
// File: example8–9.php

$strName='Elizabeth';

echo "<p>$strName</p>";
?>
```

Then the output from the script will be:

```
<p>Elizabeth</p>
```

We shall return to strings in a later chapter and illustrate some of the PHP functions which allow us to manipulate them.

Array

Arrays in PHP are an ordered map, essentially a data type which maps values to keys. Arrays are very powerful and we shall explain them in Chapter 11.

Object

The object type is an instance of a class. The whole concept of object orientation and classes and objects is explained in Chapter 16 so you can forget about this type for the moment.

Resource

A resource is a special variable type which holds a reference (also called a handler) to an external item, such as a database, a text file or an image which is being created. Resource types are generated by special functions and we shall highlight them when we encounter them in later chapters.

NULL

The data type NULL is used to specify a variable that contains no value. A variable is considered to be NULL if it has been assigned the type NULL or has been defined but not set any value, for example:

```
$var = NULL;
```

8.9 Constants

A constant is a name for a simple value. Unlike a variable, a constant (as the name implies) does not change during script execution. A PHP constant follows the same naming conventions as PHP variables. A valid name can begin with a letter or underscore character followed by any number of letters, numbers or underscores.

 NOTE Constants are case-sensitive but, by default, are always written in upper case.

A constant is defined using the 'define( )' function. PHP contains many different functions to help make your programming life easier and also allows you to create your own functions (more on this in Chapter 13). The syntax for the use of the 'define( )' function is:

```
define (string name, mixed value)
```

What the above means is that when you create a constant you provide the 'define( )' function with its name followed by its value. Here is an example:

```php
<?php
// File: example8-10.php
define ("AUTHOR", "Simon Stobart");
echo '<p>';
echo AUTHOR;
echo '</p>';
?>
```

 NOTE PHP provides a number of predefined constants to a running script. The majority of these are created by the various PHP language extensions and are only available when these extensions are installed.

8.10 Expressions

Expressions are the building blocks of PHP and are so important that we could have begun this lesson by introducing them. In fact, all of the PHP examples we have used so far have included expressions. The fact that we didn't introduce them sooner is that we felt it was better to get you using some expressions without actually knowing what they were called. The best definition of an expression in PHP is 'anything that has a value', or, put another way, 'anything which expresses a value'.

The simplest types of expressions are constants and variables. Consider the following:

```
$intVar = 23;
```

The above variable declaration and assignment is an expression. However, when we look more closely we can see there is a little bit more to this than meets the eye. Firstly, we can see that the constant value 23 obviously has the value 23. We can say the 23 expresses the value 23 and is therefore an expression itself. When assigned to the variable $intVar, this variable now contains a value (23) and it too is an expression in its own right. The assignment character (=) is known as an operator. Variables and constants are known as operands. Operators and operands are the building blocks of all expressions in PHP.

8

An operator is something which, when given a value, will produce another value. The operator is said to operate upon the first value, which is where it gets its name. Operands are the things that operators operate upon. PHP has three different types of operator: unary operators which only operate on a single value, binary operators which operate on two values (these are the latest group of operators which PHP supports) and ternary operators which require three values. We shall examine each of the operators supported in PHP.

Arithmetic operators

Arithmetic operators perform basic arithmetic and are listed in Table 8.4.

The following script illustrates the outputs obtained from using the above operators:

```php
<?php
// File: example8-11.php

$intA = 5;
$intB = 4;

$intC = $intA + $intB;
echo "<p>$intA + $intB = $intC</p>";
$intC = $intA - $intB;
echo "<p>$intA - $intB = $intC</p>";
$intC = $intA * $intB;
echo "<p>$intA * $intB = $intC</p>";
$intC = $intA / $intB;
echo "<p>$intA / $intB = $intC</p>";
$intC = -$intA;
echo "<p>$intA minus = $intC</p>";
$intC = $intA % $intB;
echo "<p>$intA % $intB = $intC</p>";
?>
```

 NOTE The division operator returns a floating point value even if the two operands are integers.

The output from the above script is illustrated in Figure 8.6.

TABLE 8.4 Arithmetic operators

Operator	Name	Example	Result
+	Addition	$a + $b	The sum of $a and $b
−	Subtraction	$a − $b	The difference of $a and $b
*	Multiplication	$a * $b	The product of $a and $b
/	Division	$a / $b	The quotient of $a divided by $b
−	Negation	-$a	The negative of $a
%	Modulus	$a % $b	The remainder of $a divided by $b

FIGURE 8.6   Output from arithmetic operators

Assignment operators

The assignment operator is ' = ' We have used this operator in our previous examples where we assign a value to a variable, for example:

```
$intYear = 2005;
```

Most people wrongly think of the assignment operator as meaning 'equal to', as variable $intYear is equal to 2005, however this is wrong. You should think of the assignment operator as meaning 'assigned the value', as in variable $intYear is assigned the value 2005. In addition to the simple assignment operator there are also some combination operators which allow the combining of both arithmetic and assignment operations. Table 8.5 illustrates these assignment operators.

The following script illustrates the outputs obtained from using the above operators:

```php
<?php
// File: example8–12.php
$intA = 5;
$intB = 4;
$intA + = $intB;
echo "<p>5 + $intB = $intA</p>";
$intA = 5;
$intA -= $intB;
echo "<p>5 – $intB = $intA</p>";
$intA = 5;
$intA * = $intB;
echo "<p>5 * $intB = $intA</p>";
$intA = 5;
$intA / = $intB;
echo "<p>5 / $intB = $intA</p>";
$intA = 5;
$intA % = $intB;
echo "<p>5 % $intB = $intA</p>";
?>
```

The output from the above script is illustrated in Figure 8.7.

TABLE 8.5   Assignment operators

Operator	Name	Example	Result
=	Assign	$a = $b	Assign
+=	Add and assign	$a += $b	Assign the sum of $a and $b to $a
-=	Subtract and assign	$a -= $b	Assign the difference of $a and $b to $a
*=	Multiply and assign	$a *= $b	Assign the product of $a and $b to $a
/=	Divide and assign	$a /= $b	Assign the quotient of $a and $b to $a
%=	Get the remainder and assign	$a %= $b	Assign the remainder of $a divided by $b to $a

FIGURE 8.7   Assignment operators

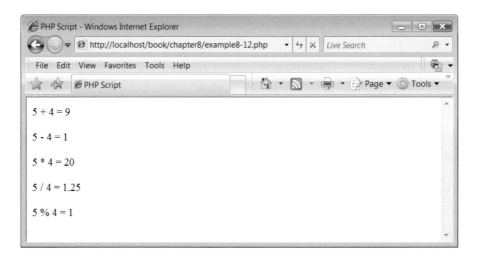

Bitwise operators

Bitwise operators, also known as bit manipulation operators, allow you to switch individual bits within an integer on or off. Table 8.6 illustrates the different bitwise operators which are available.

The following script illustrates the outputs obtained from using the above operators:

```php
<?php
// File: example8-13.php

$intA = 7;
$intB = 2;

$intC = $intA & $intB;
echo "<p>$intA & $intB = $intC</p>";
$intC = $intA | $intB;
echo "<p>$intA | $intB = $intC</p>";
$intC = $intA ^ $intB;
echo "<p>$intA ^ $intB = $intC</p>";
```

TABLE 8.6	Bitwise operators		
Operator	Name	Example	Result
&	And	$a & $b	Set bits to 1 where bits in both operands are set to 1
|	Or	$a | $b	Set bits to 1 where bits in either operand are set to 1
^	Xor	$a ^ $b	Set bits to 1 where bits in either operand are set to 1 but not when both are set.
~	Not	~$a	Bits which are set in $a are not set and vice versa (the high b it is set for negative numbers).
<<	Shift left	$a << $b	Shift the bits in $a to the left $b steps. Each step is the same as multiplying by two.
>>	Shift right	$a >> $b	Shift the bits in $a to the right $b steps. Each step is the same as dividing by two.

FIGURE 8.8 Output from bitwise operators

```php
$intC = ~$intA;
echo "<p>~$intA = $intC</p>";
$intC = $intA << $intB;
echo "<p>$intA << $intB = $intC</p>";
$intC = $intA >> $intB;
echo "<p>$intA >> $intB = $intC</p>";
?>
```

The output from the above script is illustrated in Figure 8.8.

Bitwise operators often cause the beginner a few problems but the great news is that they are not used frequently and so if you don't fully understand them don't worry about it and move along. We haven't got the space to include detailed examples of all of the operators, but Figure 8.9 illustrates how 7 ^ 2 works.

FIGURE 8.9   How to calculate 7 ^ 2

7

128	64	32	16	8	4	2	1
0	0	0	0	0	1	1	1

2

128	64	32	16	8	4	2	1
0	0	0	0	0	0	1	0

^

128	64	32	16	8	4	2	1
0	0	0	0	0	1	0	1

TABLE 8.7   Comparison operators

Operator	Name	Example	Result
==	Equal	$a == $b	True if $a is equal to $b
===	Identical	$a === $b	True if $a is equal to $b and they are the same type
!=	Not equal	$a != $b	True if $a is not equal to $b
<>	Not equal	$a <> $b	True if $a is not equal to $b
!==	Not identical	$a !== $b	True if $a is not equal to $b or they are not of the same type
<	Less than	$a < $b	True if $a is less than $b
>	Greater than	$a > $b	True if $a is greater than $b
<=	Less than or equal to	$a <= $b	True if $a is less than or equal to $b
>=	Greater than or equal to	$a >= $b	True if $a is greater than or equal to $b

In Figure 8.9, we see what the numbers 7 and 2 look like when they are stored in their binary form – as a byte. The Xor operator checks each bit in each of the two bytes and where they are both zero or where they are both one it stores a zero in the generated byte. In the case where one bit is a zero and the other a one then the value one is stored. The result creates the value five.

Comparison operators

Comparison operators allow you to compare two values. Table 8.7 illustrates the comparison operators.

We will provide examples of the use of these operators in Chapter 9 when we introduce the 'if' statement.

Ternary operator

The ternary operator (or conditional operator) requires three operands. Its syntax is:

```
(expr1) ? (expr2) : (expr3)
```

The operator evaluates to expr2 if expr1 is true or expr3 if expr1 is false. Here is a clearer example:

```
$strStockText = ($intStock > 0) ? "In stock" : "Out of stock";
```

In the above example the value of variable $strStockText is assigned the string 'In stock' if the variable $intStock is greater than 0, otherwise it is assigned the string 'Out of stock'.

String operators

PHP supports two string operators which are listed in Table 8.8.

The following script illustrates the use of these operators:

```php
<?php
// File: example8-14.php
$strFirstname = "Simon";
$strSurname = "Stobart";
$strFullname = $strFirstname . $strSurname;
echo "<p>$strFirstname joined with $strSurname is $strFullname</p>";

$strFullname = $strFirstname . " " . $strSurname;
echo "<p>$strFirstname joined with $strSurname with a space is $strFullname</p>";

$strFullname = $strFirstname;
$strFullname .= " ";
$strFullname .= $strSurname;
echo "<p>$strFirstname joined with $strSurname with a space is $strFullname</p>";
?>
```

The output from the above script is shown in Figure 8.10.

NOTE	If an integer or a float is concatenated to a string then it is converted to a string. Therefore, the following is perfectly valid:
	
	`$intAge = 56;`
	`$strName = "Simon's Age is";`
	
	`$strText = $strName . " " . $intAge;`
	`echo $strText;`

Incrementing and decrementing operators

PHP supports pre-and post-increment and -decrement operators and these are listed in Table 8.9.

TABLE 8.8	String operators		
Operator	Name	Example	Result
.	Concatenate	$a . $b	Returns $a concatenated with $b
.=	Concatenate and assign	$a .=$b	Concatenates $b to the end of $a

FIGURE 8.10 String operators

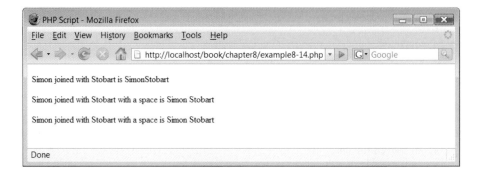

TABLE 8.9	Increment and decrement operators		
Operator	Name	Example	Result
++	Pre-increment	++$a	Increments $a by one and then returns $a
++	Post-increment	$a++	Returns $a and then increments $a by one
−	Pre-decrement	−$a	Decrements $a by one and then returns $a
−	Post-decrement	$a −	Returns $a and then decrements $a by one

The following script illustrates the differences between these operators:

```php
<?php
// File: example8-15.php
$intA = 3;
echo '<p>$intA begins as ' . $intA . "</p>";
echo '<p>$intA++ ' . $intA++ . "</p>";
echo '<p>$intA is now really ' . $intA . "</p>";
echo '<p>++$intA ' . ++$intA . "</p>";
echo '<p>$intA-- ' . $intA-- . "</p>";
echo '<p>$intA is now really ' . $intA . "</p>";
echo '<p> --$intA ' . --$intA . "</p>";
?>
```

The output from the above script is shown in Figure 8.11.

FIGURE 8.11   Incrementing and decrementing operators

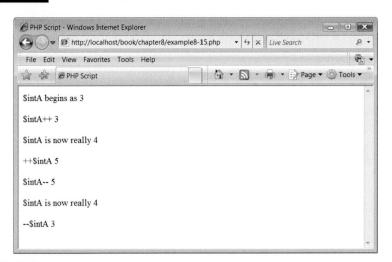

TABLE 8.10   Logical operators

Operator	Name	Example	Result
And	And	$a and $b	True if $a and $b are true
Or	Or	$a or $b	True if either $a or $b is true
Xor	Xor	$a xor $b	True if either $a or $b is true but not both.
!	Not	!$a	True is $a is not true
&&	And	$a && $b	True if $a and $b are true
||	Or	$a || $b	True if either $a or $b is true

The confusing output is a result of the post-increment and post-decrement operators returning the value to the echo construct (which then displays it) before the value in the variable is either incremented or decremented.

NOTE	The pre- and post-decrement and -increment operators use exactly the same characters but are pre- or post-depending on whether they come before or after the expression.

Logical operators

PHP supports six logical operators as shown in Table 8.10.

We shall provide examples of the use of these operators in Chapter 9 when the flow of control is introduced.

NOTE	The reason why we have different variations of 'and' and 'or' is because they operate at different precedences. This is shown in Table 8.11.

8

Error control operator

PHP supports the error control operator (@). When this operator is prepended to an expression any error messages that might be generated by that expression are ignored. The following script illustrates its use:

```php
<?php
// File: example8-16.php

$intA = 7;
$intB = 0;

@$intC = $intA / $intB;
echo "<p>$intA / $intB = $intC</p>";
?>
```

Try removing the @ operator to view the error message.

Array operators

PHP supports a number of array operators and we shall leave introducing these until Chapter 11.

Operator precedence

The precedence of an expression indicates the order in which the various operators in the expression are evaluated. Consider the following expression:

```
2 + 4 * 3
```

TABLE 8.11 Operator precedence

Operators	Associativity	Type
[	Left	Array
++ −	Non-Associative	Increment / decrement
! ~ @	Non-Associative	Types
* / %	Left	Arithmetic
+ −	Left	Arithmetic and String
<< >>	Left	Bitwise
< <= > >=	Non-Associative	Comparison
== != === !==	Non-Associative	Comparison
&	Left	Bitwise
^	Left	Bitwise
|	Left	Bitwise
&&	Left	Logical
||	Left	Logical
?:	Left	Ternary
= += -= *= /=.= %= &= |= ^= <<= >>=	Right	Assignment
And	Left	Logical
Xor	Left	Logical
Or	Left	Logical
,	Left	Many uses

Now, the answer to this expression could be 2 added to 4 giving 6 which is then multiplied by 3 giving 18. Or it could be 4 multiplied by 3 giving 12 added to 2 giving 14. In fact, the answer is 14 because the multiplication operator (*) has a higher precedence than the addition operator (+). Of course we could use parentheses to force precedence, for example:

```
(2 + 4) * 3
2 + (4 * 3)
```

However, PHP has a precedence table which lists the order of precedence of its operators (see Table 8.11). The highest precedence operators are at the top of the table. Operators on the same line of the table have equal precedence and in which case the associativity column of the table is used to determine the order in the expression from right to left or left to right that the operators are evaluated.

8.11 Predefined variables

PHP provides a large number of predefined variables to any script which is running. Many of these are platform and server-dependent and therefore cannot be easily documented here. PHP provides these predefined variables in a set of predefined arrays. These arrays are known as superglobals as they are available from anywhere in the script. Although we haven't yet described arrays, we provide an example of accessing a predefined variable in the following script to illustrate what they look like:

```php
<?php
// File: example8-17.php

echo "<p>" . $_SERVER['DOCUMENT_ROOT'] . "</p>";
?>
```

The predefined variable DOCUMENT_ROOT stores the location of the root server documents. On a windows WAMP server this should be:

```
C:/wamp/www
```

We shall return to predefined variables in Chapter 12 but, for now, if you examine Table 8.12 you can see the names of the arrays.

Don't worry if you don't fully understand the above table, we shall introduce the predefined variables and explain how to access them where appropriate.

8

TABLE 8.12	Predefined variable superglobals

Predefined arrays of variables	Descriptions
$GLOBALS	Contains a reference to all variables which are currently available
$_SERVER	Contains the predefined variables which are set by the web server
$_GET	Contains the predefined variables which are provided to the script by a URL query string
$_POST	Contains the predefined variables which are provided to the script via HTTP POST
$_COOKIE	Contains the predefined variables which are provided by cookies
$_FILES	Contains the predefined variables which are provided via HTTP post file uploads
$_ENV	Contains the predefined variables which are provided to the script via the environment
$_REQUEST	Contains the predefined variables which are provided to the script via the GET, POST and COOKIE mechanisms
$_SESSION	Contains the predefined variables which are currently registered to a script's session

Exercises

8.1 Consider the following variable names. For each one determine if they are valid or invalid:

```php
$var = 5;
$_var = 5;
$_var_ = 5;
$v3ar = 5;
$5var = 5;
$_5var = 5;
```

8.2 What will be displayed by the following script?

```php
<?php
echo '<p>Hello I\'m Simon</p>';
?>
```

8.3 What three characters do we suggest you start your variable names with to indicate the type of data the variable is storing for each of the following types?

```
Boolean
Integer
Float
String
Array
Object
```

8.4 What will be displayed by the following script?

```php
<?php
define ("NAME", "Hayley");

echo "<p>";
echo "NAME";
echo 'NAME';
echo NAME;
echo '</p>';
?>
```

8.5 What will be displayed by the following script?

```php
<?php
$strName = "Simon";

echo "<p>";
echo '$strName';
echo "</p>";
?>
```

8.6 What will be displayed by the following script?

```php
<?php
echo "<p>";
echo 2 + 4 * 4;
echo "</p>";
?>
```

SUMMARY

In this chapter we began by introducing the PHP language and describing what it was designed to do. We explained how the PHP interpreter replaces PHP commands embedded within an (X)HTML document with whatever output is produced from PHP echo constructs. We have shown how to create simple PHP scripts, save them and then view their output from a web browser.

We have introduced you to the echo construct and explained that this is the primary method of injecting information into your (X)HTML document. We have explained comments and their role as a human-readable aid to understanding scripts. We then introduced variables and their types as well as predefined variables and constants. We concluded by covering expressions and the multitude of operands and operators which PHP supports.

References and further reading

PHP manual http://www.php.net/manual/en/
PHP web site-www.php.net

Flow of Control

INTRODUCTION

In this chapter, we learn about flow of control. Flow of control is a term which is applied to the order in which a script's or program's statements are executed.

In all of our PHP scripts in Chapter 8, the individual statements were executed sequentially. What this means is that the interpreter began processing the first statement of the script, followed by the next statement until the end of the script was reached. Each statement was executed in the order in which it appeared in the script. Sequential execution of statements is illustrated in Figure 9.1.

However if all a scripting language like PHP could do was to process its statements in sequence then the sophistication of the scripts we could create would be quite limit. Luckily for us that the designers of PHP were rather more forward-thinking and included a number of statements which can be employed in order to change the order of execution of the statements within a script.

In the remainder of this chapter, we introduce the statements which are available to enable us to affect the flow of control of our PHP scripts and we illustrate these with some simple examples.

9.1 The 'if' construct

The 'if' construct is one of the most powerful features of the PHP language and it allows for conditional execution of code statements. In other words, the 'if' construct evaluates an expression and if it is found to be true then the statement following the 'if' condition is executed. The structure of the 'if' construct is as follows:

```
if ( expression )
    statement to be executed if expression is true
```

Figure 9.2 illustrates the structure of the 'if' construct.

The following is a simple example of the use of the 'if' construct:

```php
<?php
// File: example9-1.php

$intA = 5;
$intB = 3;

if ($intA > $intB)
    echo "<p>$intA is greater than $intB</p>";
?>
```

FIGURE 9.1   Sequential execution

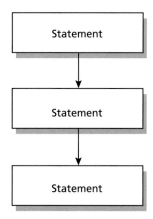

FIGURE 9.2   The 'if' construct

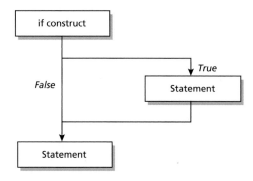

In the script above we define two variables and assign them the values 5 and 3. The if construct includes a simple conditional expression (see Section 8.10) which evaluates to either true or false. In this case, the value of variable $intA is larger than $intB and thus the statement following the 'if' construct is executed. The output from the above script is:

```
5 is greater than 3
```

 NOTE Because the variables $intA and $intB are fixed this script always produces the same output. You need to manually edit and then re-run the script to change the values of the variables to show that nothing is displayed if $intA is not greater than $intB.

Sometimes we may wish to have more than one statement executed conditionally. We could do this by including separate 'if' constructs around every statement we wanted to evaluate, for example:

```php
<?php
// File: example9-2.php

$strColor = "green";

if ($strColor == "green")
    echo "<p>The color is green</p>";
if ($strColor == "green")
    echo "<p>Green is a nice color</p>";
if ($strColor == "green")
    echo "<p>We have the color of grass</p>";
?>
```

Luckily we do not have to do this and there is a far easier way of accomplishing this. All we need to do is to use the open and close brace characters, '{'and'}', to group all statements that you wish to execute conditionally into a statement group, for example:

```php
<?php
// File: example9-3.php

$strColor = "green";
if ($strColor = = "green") {
    echo "<p>The color is green</p>";
    echo "<p>Green is a nice color</p>";
    echo "<p>We have the color of grass</p>";
}
?>
```

FIGURE 9.3 Output from the 'if' construct

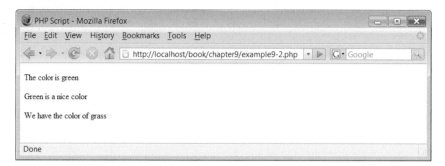

	NOTE	Using the brace characters we can specify any number of statements that we wish to execute conditionally.

The output from the above two scripts is shown in Figure 9.3.

	NOTE	Braces can be formatted so that they appear like the example above:
		
		`if ( expression ) {`
		    `. . .`
		`}`
		
		Alternatively they can appear on separate lines:
		
		`if ( expression )`
		`{`
		    `. . .`
		`}`

The 'else' statement

Sometimes you may wish to execute a certain statement if a condition is met and another statement if it is not. This is accomplished using the 'else' statement which extends the 'if' construct. The structure of the 'if–else' construct is as follows:

```
if ( expression )
    statement to be executed if expression is true
else
    statement to be executed if expression is false
```

Figure 9.4 illustrates the 'if–else' construct.

The following is a simple example of the use of the 'if–else' construct:

```php
<?php
// File: example9–4.php

$intA = 5;
$intB = 3;
```

```php
if ($intA > $intB)
    echo "<p>$intA is greater than $intB</p>";
else
    echo "<p>$intA is less than or equal to $intB</p>";
?>
```

You can alter the values of $intA and $intB to prove that the 'if–else' construct works correctly.

 NOTE | The 'else' construct cannot be used independently of the 'if' construct.

In the same way as the 'if' construct, the 'if–else' construct employs braces to group together multiple statements for conditional execution, for example:

```php
<?php
// File: example9-5.php

$strColor="blue";

if ($strColor == "green") {
    echo "<p>The color is green</p>";
    echo "<p>Green is a nice color</p>";
    echo "<p>We have the color of grass</p>";
}
else {
    echo "<p>We don't know what colour we have</p>";
    echo "<p>Other than it is not green</p>";
}
?>
```

The output from the above script is illustrated in Figure 9.5.

FIGURE 9.4   'if–else' construct

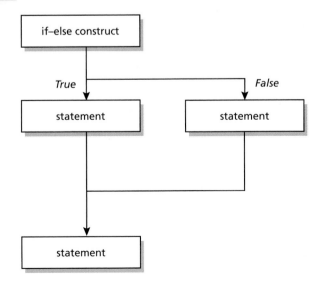

	NOTE	You can only use one 'else' statement with an 'if' construct.

The 'elseif' statement

The 'elseif' construct is a combination of 'else'and 'if'. It operates in a similar way to the 'else' construct, in that it extends the 'if' construct to execute a different statement if the 'if' expression evaluates to false. However it differs in that it will execute the alternative expression only if the 'elseif' expression is true. The syntax for the 'elseif' construct is:

```
if ( expression1 )
    statement to be executed if expression1 is true
elseif ( expression2 )
    statement to be executed if expression2 is true
```

Figure 9.6 illustrates the 'elseif' construct combined with an 'else' construct.

FIGURE 9.5   Output from the 'if–else' construct

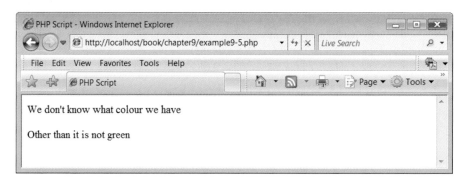

FIGURE 9.6   The 'if–elseif' construct

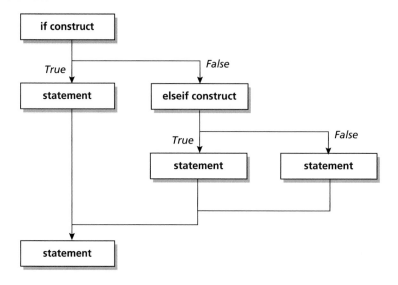

Figure 9.6 illustrates that an elseif construct can be followed by an else construct, so the true syntax depicted in the diagram is as follows:

```
if ( expression1 )
    statement to be executed if expression1 is true
elseif ( expression2 )
    statement to be executed if expression2 is true
else
    statement to be executed if expression2 is false
```

 NOTE 'If' constructs can be combined with multiple 'else' and 'elseif' constructs to make very complex conditional structures.

The following script illustrates the use of the 'elseif' construct:

```php
<?php
// File: example9-6.php

$intNumber1 = 100;
$intNumber2 = 80;

if ($intNumber1 > $intNumber2) {
    echo "<p>$intNumber1 is larger than $intNumber2</p>";
}
elseif ($intNumber1 == $intNumber2) {
    echo "<p>$intNumber1 is equal to $intNumber2</p>";
1}
else {
    echo "<p>$intNumber1 is smaller than $intNumber2</p>";
}
?>
```

 NOTE The 'elseif' construct cannot be used independently of the 'if' construct.

9.2 The 'switch' construct

The 'switch' construct is similar to a series of 'if' statements acting on the same conditional expression. The 'switch' construct is used when you wish to compare a variable against a number of different values and execute different code statements depending on the variables value. The syntax of the 'switch' construct is:

```
switch ( expression ) {
    case constant expression : statement
    case constant expression : statement
    . . .
default : statement
}
```

FIGURE 9.7 The 'switch' construct

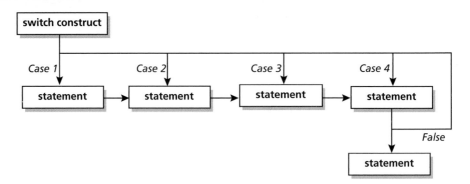

The 'switch' construct consists of a 'switch' component in which an expression is evaluated. The result of the expression is then compared in turn to a list of 'case' statements. The first 'case' value which matches to the expression determines which associated statements are executed.

 NOTE While you can implement the 'switch' construct using a number of 'if' statements the code can become complex and difficult to understand.

Figure 9.7 illustrates the 'switch' construct.

 NOTE Note the use of the braces to surround the 'switch' structure.

The following script illustrates the use of the 'switch' construct:

```php
<?php
// File: example9-7.php

$strName = "Elizabeth";

switch ($strName) {
case "Simon":
   echo "<p>Hello Simon</p>";
case "Elizabeth":
   echo "<p>Hello Elizabeth</p>";
case "Hayley":
   echo "<p>Hello Hayley</p>";
case "Alan":
   echo "<p>Hello Alan</p>";
}
?>
```

In the above example there are four cases which display a message depending on the value of variable $strName. The output from the above script is shown in Figure 9.8. Interestingly, the output may not be what you were expecting. Instead of simply displaying the text

FIGURE 9.8 Output from the 'switch' construct

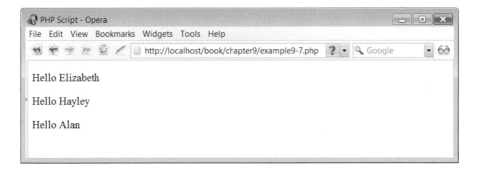

'Hello Elizabeth', the script has displayed this and all other 'echo' statement messages which were associated with all of the case statements following that for 'Elizabeth'.

The output shown in Figure 9.8 is not an error; it is working exactly according to how the PHP 'switch' statement is supposed to work. However, to accomplish the output we would really like we need to introduce a new statement.

Switch and break

The 'break' statement can be used to end the current execution of a 'switch' statement. It can also be used to end the execution of the loop constructs we shall examine later but for now let us look at it in our 'switch' example:

```php
<?php
// File: example9-8.php

$strName = "Elizabeth";

switch ($strName) {
case "Simon":
   echo "<p>Hello Simon</p>";
   break;
case "Elizabeth":
   echo "<p>Hello Elizabeth</p>";
   break;
case "Hayley":
   echo "<p>Hello Hayley</p>";
   break;
case "Alan":
   echo "<p>Hello Alan</p>";
}
?>
```

In the above script, we have included the 'break' statement as the last statement in each case of the 'switch' construct (except the last). When the 'break' statement is encountered the interpreter jumps to the end of the 'switch' construct. The result of this is that only the text output by the 'echo' statement within the case which matches the switch

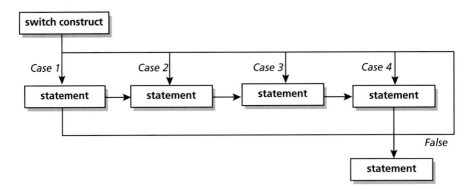

FIGURE 9.9   The 'switch' construct with 'breaks' statements

condition is output. Therefore in this example the text output is:

"Hello Elizabeth"

Figure 9.9 illustrates the 'switch' construct with 'break' statements.

 NOTE   Take a closer look at the diagram in Figure 9.9 and compare this to the one in Figure 9.7. Note how the arrows in Figure 9.9 indicate that the 'break' statements force the exit from the 'switch' construct after each case.

Using the 'break' statement lets us do some more complex things with the 'switch' construct. For example, 'if' we leave some of the 'case' statements empty and include a strategically placed 'break' statement we can show the power of the 'switch' statement:

```php
<?php
// File: example9-9.php

$intTotal = 3;

switch ($intTotal) {
case 0:
case 1:
case 2:
case 3:
case 4:
    echo "<p>$intTotal is less than or equal to four!</p>";
    break;
case 5:
    echo "<p>$intTotal is greater than four!</p>";
}
?>
```

In the above example, the values 0 to 3 have no associated statements and therefore, if the 'case' is true, then it simply passes control onto the next 'case' statement in the list. Therefore, if the value of $intTotal is between 0 and 4, the 'echo' statement associated with case 4 is executed followed by the 'break' statement which forces the 'switch' statement to end. Therefore the output produced in this script with the value of $intTotal being 3 is:

```
3 is less than or equal to four!
```

The 'default' statement

Another special case of the 'switch' statement is the 'default' case. The 'default' case will match against anything that wasn't matched by any of the other cases and thus should always be the last statement. The following script illustrates its use:

```php
<?php
// File: example9-10.php

$intTotal = 6;

switch ($intTotal) {
case 0:
case 1:
case 2:
case 3:
case 4:
   echo "<p>$intTotal is less than or equal to four!</p>";
   break;
case 5:
   echo "<p>$intTotal is equal to five!</p>";
   break;
default:
   echo "<p>$intTotal is greater than five!</p>";
}
?>
```

The output from the above script is illustrated in Figure 9.10.

 NOTE Try adjusting the value contained in the $intTotal variable to check that the other cases within the 'switch' construct work as expected.

FIGURE 9.10   Output from the 'default' case of the 'switch' statement

9.3 The 'while' loop construct

'while' loops are the simplest type of loop in PHP, however that is not to say that they are not powerful. The basic syntax of the 'while' loop is:

```
while ( expression )
statement
```

Like the 'if' construct, 'while' loops can use braces to group multiple statements within them. The syntax for this is:

```
while ( expression ) {
    statement

    . . .
}
```

The 'while' loop can use an alternative syntax to denote the statements it has grouped:

```
while ( expression ) :
    statement

    . . .
endwhile;
```

The meaning of a 'while' statement is simple. It tells PHP to execute the statements nested within the loop repeatedly, as long as the 'while' expression evaluates to true. During each iteration, the value of the expression is checked at the beginning of the loop. If the expression is true then the loop contents are executed. If false, then control jumps to the statement following the loop construct. If the 'while' expression evaluates to false on the first iteration; the statement(s) within the loop are not executed. Figure 9.11 illustrates a 'while' loop construct.

The following script illustrates a simple 'while' loop:

```php
<?php
// File: example9-11.php

$intCount = 1;

while ($intCount <= 10) {
    echo "<p>Iteration $intCount</p>";
    $intCount++;
}
?>
```

FIGURE 9.11 The 'while' loop construct

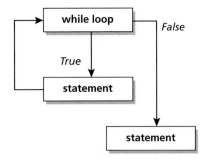

In this example, a variable $intCount is assigned the value 1. The 'while' loop expression checks to see if the value in $intCount is less than or equal to 10 and if so the statements within the loop are executed. Within the loop, an 'echo' construct outputs the value of variable $intCount, which is then incremented by 1. The output from the above script is illustrated is Figure 9.12.

 NOTE Because the statements within a 'while' loop may never execute, may execute only once or may execute many times the 'while' loop is known as a zero, one or many loop.

While loops usually use a variable which is incremented or decremented within the loop to control the number of loop iterations. If you don't take care to control the number of times the loop iterates you could end up with a problem, for example:

```php
<?php
// File: example9–12.php

$intCount = 1;

while (1) {
    echo "<p>Iteration $intCount</p>";
    $intCount++;
}
?>
```

FIGURE 9.12 Output from a 'while' loop

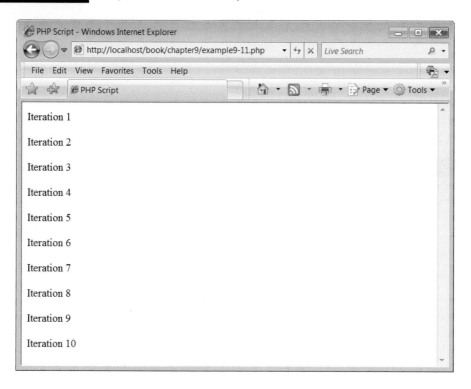

In this example, the conditional expression that the loop uses to determine whether or not to iterate once more is simply '1'. As this expression is always 1, it always evaluates to true and therefore the loop will continue for ever, or until the server forces a stop.

9.4 The 'do–while' loop construct

The 'do–while' loop is similar to the 'while' loop. The difference is where and when the loop expression is checked. In a 'while' loop, we have shown that the loop expression is checked at the start of the loop. Therefore, if the expression is false at the start, none of the statements within the loop are executed. With a 'do–while' loop the expression is evaluated at the end of the loop, after the statements within the loop have been executed at least once.

The syntax of the loop is:

```
do
    statement
while ( expression );
```

Figure 9.13 illustrates the syntax of the 'do–while' loop.

Like the other flow-of-control constructs previously, braces can be used to group multiple statements to be executed within the loop:

```
do {
    statement
    statement
    . . .
}
while ( expression );
```

FIGURE 9.13   The 'do–while' loop construct

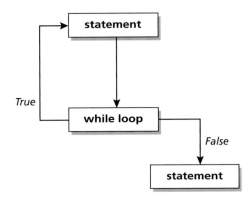

The following script illustrates an example of the 'do–while' loop:

```php
<?php
// File: example9-13.php
$intCount = 1;

do {
   echo "<p>Iteration $intCount</p>";
   $intCount++;
} while ($intCount < = 10);
?>
```

The output from the above script is exactly the same as that shown in Figure 9.12.

 NOTE Note that the 'while' statement has a semi colon at the end to indicate the end of the 'do–while' statement.

The main difference with a 'do–while' loop is that the statements within the loop are always executed at least once. Consider the following script:

```php
<?php
// File: example9-14.php

$intCount = 1;

do {
   echo "<p>Iteration $intCount</p>";
   $intCount++;
} while ($intCount < 1);
?>
```

In the above example, the 'do–while' loop conditional expression evaluates the value of $intCount to check that it is less than 1. However as $intCount is initialized to 1 and then incremented to 2 within the loop, the loop expression is never true. However, the output produced is:

```
Iteration 1
```

If the conditional expression were implemented within a 'while' loop then no output would be produced.

 NOTE A 'do–while' loop is known as a one or many iterative loop, as the statements within it are executed at least once and perhaps many times.

9.5 The 'for' loop construct

The 'for' loop is another commonly used loop. At first glance, they appear to be a little more complex than the 'while' and 'do–while' loops as they have three expressions incorporated into the condition. The syntax for the loop is:

```
for (expression1; expression2; expression3)
   statement
```

As with the previous loops, braces can be used to group statements within the loop construct:

```
for (expression1; expression2; expression3) {
   statement
   statement

   . . .
}
```

The first expression is used to set a start point for the loop, the second one is the main expression to control how many times the loop will be repeated and the third one is normally used to increment the variable which controls the number of iterations around the loop. Consider the example 'for' loop script:

```
<?php
// File: example9-15.php
for($intCount = 1; $intCount <= 10; $intCount++)
   echo "<p>Iteration $intCount</p>";
?>
```

Figure 9.14 illustrates the 'for' loop.

The above script produces the same output as the while loop illustrated in Figure 9.12. The 'for' loop looks complicated because it contains three expressions as part of its syntax, but in fact it is basically the same as the while loop, just that the 'for' loop gathers together in one place the expressions we use in different places within the 'while' loop. This is illustrated in Figure 9.15 which compares the 'while' loop script with the 'for' loop script and illustrates where each of the expressions occur.

	NOTE	Because the statements within a 'for' loop may never execute, may execute only once or may execute many times the 'for' loop is known as a zero, one or many loop.

FIGURE 9.14 The 'for' loop construct

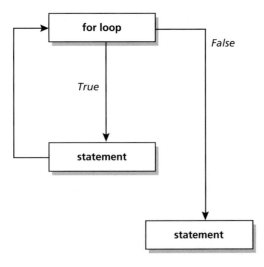

FIGURE 9.15   Comparison of 'while' and 'for' loops

```
<?php                                    <?php
// while loop                            // for loop
$intCount = 1;                           for ($intCount = 1; $intCount <= 10; $intCount ++)

while ($intCount <= 10) {                        echo "<p>Iteration $intCount</p>";
                                         ?>
    echo "<p>Iteration $intCount</p>";
    $intCount ++;

}
?>
```

9.6 The 'foreach' loop construct

PHP supports a special loop construct for accessing the contents of arrays. We shall examine this loop in Chapter 11.

9.7 Nested loops

Loops in PHP can be nested, which means that a loop can be placed inside another loop. With a nested loop, the first iteration of the outer loop is begun and then when the inner loop is encountered the iteration of the inner loop continues until its conditional expression forces it to stop. At this point the second iteration of the outer loop begins, followed by the iteration of the inner loop. The nested loop structure iteration completes with the final iteration of the outer loop.

Any combination of loop types can be nested and any level of nesting is permitted. Nested loops allow quite sophisticated scripts to be written easily. Consider the following example:

```php
<?php
// File: example9-16.php

$booBlackWhite = 0;
echo "<table border = '1'>";
for($intRows = 1; $intRows < = 8; $intRows++) {
    $intColumns = 1;
    echo "<tr>";
    while ($intColumns < = 8) {
        if ($booBlackWhite)
            echo "<td><img src='graphics/blackSquare.gif' width='30'
            height='30' alt='blackSquare' align='top'/></td>";
        else
            echo "<td><img src='graphics/whiteSquare.gif' width='30' height='30'
            alt='whiteSquare' align='top'/></td>";
        $intColumns++;
        if ($booBlackWhite == 1)
            $booBlackWhite = 0;
```

```
        else
            $booBlackWhite = 1;
    }
    echo "</tr>";
    if ($booBlackWhite == 1)
        $booBlackWhite = 0;
    else
        $booBlackWhite = 1;
    }
    echo "</table>";
    ?>
```

The above script uses a 'while' loop nested within a 'for' loop to produce a chess board pattern on the web page. The pattern is a table, the rows and columns of which are controlled by the two loops. Two separate 'if' statements control the switching from the black to the white images.

The black and white squares are produced using two simple gif images. These images have been placed in a subdirectory:

```
graphics/
```

below the location in which the PHP scripts are saved. You need to create your own gif images (30 x 30 pixels) or download them from the publisher's web site.

NOTE	When nesting loop constructs, it is important that both the start and end part of the loop construct are nested within the outer loop. Failure to ensure this will cause problems!

The output from the above script is illustrated in Figure 9.16.

9.8 Breaking out of loops

We introduced the 'break' statement in the 'switch' construct showing that it could be used to break out of the construct at a particular case. The 'break' statement can also be used to terminate the processing of a loop. Remember we showed an example of an 'infinite while loop' earlier? Well, here it is again, slightly modified so that it makes use of a 'break' statement to terminate processing:

```
<?php
// File: example9-17.php

$intCount = 1;

while (1) {
    echo "<p>Iteration $intCount</p>";
    $intCount++;
    if ($intCount > 6)
        break;
}
?>
```

In the above script, an 'if' construct is used to determine the value contained with $intCount. If this is greater than 6 then the break statement is executed, causing the loop iterations to be terminated. The output from this script is illustrated in Figure 9.17.

FIGURE 9.16   A chess board produced by nested loops

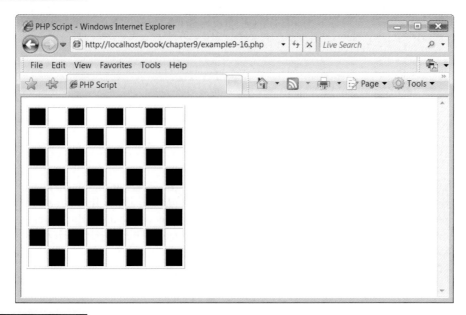

FIGURE 9.17   An infinite loop stopped with a 'break' statement

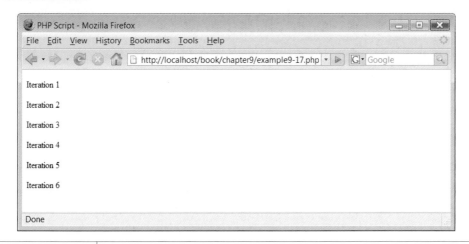

    NOTE   If a 'break' statement is used inside a loop which is nested within another then the 'break' statement will only stop the iteration of the inner loop and not the outer one. A 'break' statement can be used to break out of more than one nested loop by including an optional numeric argument which informs the interpreter how many nested loops are to be broken out of. The syntax looks like this:

```
break num;
```

9.9 Continuing a loop

Complementing the 'break' statement is the 'continue' statement. The 'continue' statement is used within a loop to skip the remainder of the statements within the current iteration and jump to the next iteration. Consider the example below:

```php
<?php
// File: example9-18.php

for($intCount = 1; $intCount<10; $intCount++){
    if ($intCount % 2)
        continue;
    echo "<p>$intCount is even.</p>";
}
?>
```

The above script uses a 'for' loop to iterate nine times. During each iteration an 'if' construct is used to determine if the value of $intCount is odd or even. If odd, a 'continue' statement is invoked causing processing to jump to the start of the loop, thus forcing a new iteration. If even, then a message to this effect is displayed. The output from the script is illustrated in Figure 9.18.

FIGURE 9.18   Continue statement

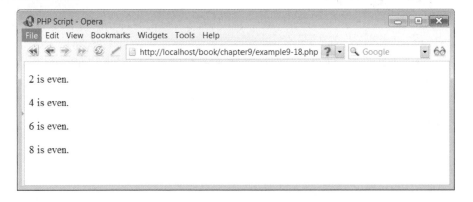

Exercises

9.1 Write a script which uses a 'while' loop to display the two times table:

```
2 x 1 = 2
2 x 2 = 4
2 x 3 = 6
2 x 4 = 8
2 x 5 = 10
2 x 6 = 12
2 x 7 = 14
2 x 8 = 16
2 x 9 = 18
2 x 10 = 20
```

Make sure that your script is flexible enough so that simply changing the value stored in a single variable, for example $intTable would allow it to correctly display a different times table.

9.2 Write a script which can display an XHTML table with a numeric value displayed in each table cell. For example, for a 3 x 4 table the table, should look like this:

1	2	3
4	5	6
7	8	9
10	11	12

The script should use a nested loop construct and should be able, by changing the values of two variables (for example, $intWidth and $intHeight), to adjust the size of the table. Therefore, if changed to a 4 x 2 table the output would look like this:

1	2	3	4
5	6	7	8

9.3 Write a script which defines a value of pence in a variable, for example $intNumberOfPence. It then calculates the minimum number of £2, £1, 50p, 20p, 10p, 5p, 2p and 1p coins that are required to represent that amount. For example if the value of $intNumberOfPence was 97 then the outout from the script would be:

The minimum number of coins required to make up 97p exactly is:

```
1 x 50p
2 x 20p
1 x 5p
1 x 2p
```

9.4 Using loop constructs, produce a script which will output a calendar. You will need to define variables to contain the start day of the month (Sunday, Monday, etc.) and the number of days in the month. The output from a month beginning on a Tuesday and with 30 days should look like this:

S	M	T	W	T	F	S
		1	2	3	4	5
6	7	8	9	10	11	12
13	14	15	16	17	18	19
20	21	22	23	24	25	26
27	28	29	30			

9.5 Write a script which will convert an Arabic format date, for example, 2005, into Roman numerals. To do this you will need to know the rules for Arabic to Roman numeral conversion:

Numeral	Usage
I	I = 1 II = 2 III = 3
V	IV = 4 (This means 5–1) V = 5 VI = 6 VII = 7 VIII = 8
X	IX = 9 (This means 10–1) X = 10 . . .
L	XL = 40 (This means 50–10) L = 50 LI = 51 . . .
C	XC = 90 (This means 100–10) C = 100 CI = 101 . . .
D	CD = 400 (This means 500–100) D = 500 DI = 501
M	CM = 900 (This means 1000–100) M = 1000 MI = 1001 . . .

Here are some dates for you to check your script with:

1900 = MCM
1975 = MCMLXXV
1998 = MCMXCVIII
2000 = MM
2067 = MMLXVII

9

SUMMARY

In this chapter, we began by describing the concept of flow of control and explained that PHP has a number of constructs which can be employed by the programmer to alter the flow of control through the script statements. The first flow of control statement which we examined was the 'if' statement. This was enhanced through the use of the 'else' and 'elseif' constructs. Following this, the 'switch' statement was described, which is essentially a different form of 'if' construct. The use of the 'break' statement was explained to control some of the processing within the 'switch' construct. Following this, the different forms of loop constructs, namely the 'while', 'do–while' and 'for' loops were examined. The chapter concluded by providing some examples of nested loops, breaking out of and continuing the iteration of various loop constructs.

References and further reading

Imagenation, PHP Documentation Group. *PHP Flow of Control Overview.*
    http://theopensourcery.com/phpcontrol.htm
Newman, C. (2005) *PHP's Flow Control: Conditional statements.* http://www.informit.com/
    articles/article.asp?p=381922&rl=1
Wikipedia. *Flow of Control.* http://en.wikipedia.org/wiki/Control_flow

Form Interaction

INTRODUCTION

In this chapter we are going to examine the way in which the user can interact with a PHP script. In all of our previous scripts, interaction with the computer user has been one way: the script runs and the user can view the output. Apart from directly editing the script, the user cannot alter the way in which the statements function. However, unless we have a means to alter what a script does or change the data a script uses dynamically during run time, our PHP scripts are always going to be a bit limited.

Luckily for us, PHP is able to interact with a user via a web page by using forms. Forms are part of (X)HTML and not part of PHP. However, PHP can be used to access data entered into the form and use this data within the script.

In this chapter, we begin by explaining how form interaction works. We examine how form field data can be accessed by a PHP script and why it is often better to combine a form and its accompanying script into a single file. We examine each of the form field types and illustrate how the data from each of them can be accessed. We conclude the chapter by examining form validation and how to retain data on a form so that the user doesn't have to retype it.

10.1 PHP and form interaction

As previously mentioned, PHP can use forms to allow a script to interact with the user. But how does this work and why would we want to do this? Well, in Chapter 9, we set a few exercises where user interaction would have allowed us to produce a far more interesting and useful script. Consider the Arabic to Roman date conversion problem. Because we were unable to interact with the script we were unable to alter the date that we wished to convert without modifying the original script. While this is slightly annoying in a development environment, it has far more serious consequences for any scripts we may wish to make available online to the Web community.

Consider the security implications that would surround allowing everyone access to your server to make changes to your PHP scripts! Apart from allowing access to the inner workings of your code (which you may not wish to do for confidentiality reasons), you would have to trust everyone who modified your script to do this properly and in an orderly fashion. Basically, this is not going to work and so a mechanism to allow users to specify the data that they wish to input to the script needs to be implemented and this is where forms come in.

By using an XHTML form, we can provide an interface (the form itself) to allow, for example, a user to enter the date they wish to convert. This date can then be transferred

FIGURE 10.1   Using forms to interact with PHP

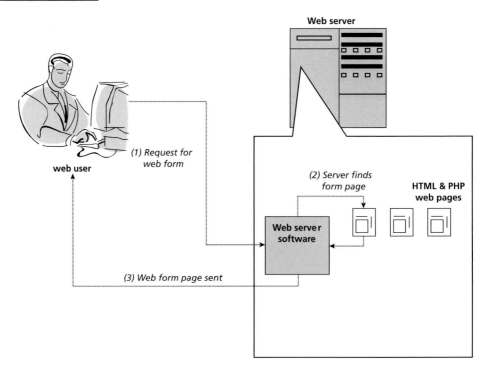

FIGURE 10.2   Using forms to interact with PHP

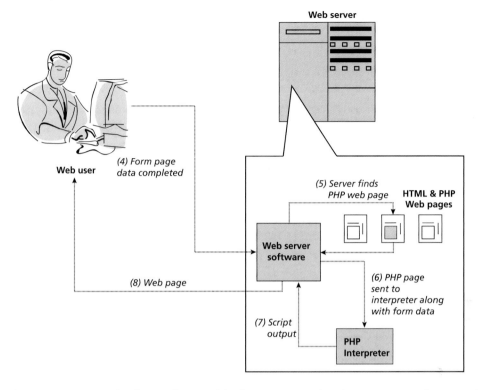

to the PHP script in the form of a variable for processing by the statements forming the script. This simple use of forms is illustrated in Figure 10.1.

In Figure 10.1, we see a web user request the form from the web server. This is located on the server and sent to the user's client computer to be displayed in the web browser. Figure 10.2 continues the story.

Figure 10.2 illustrates that the user completes the form by entering the required data. The form is then returned to the web server which locates the appropriate PHP script and the script and form data are passed to the PHP interpreter. The output from the interpreter is then sent back to the client browser to be viewed by the user.

10.2   A simple form

Since we are using forms to interact with PHP the best place to start is by creating an XHTML web form like the one shown here:

```
<! -- File: example10-1.htm -->

<h2>Please enter your personal details:</h2>
<form action="example10-1.php" method="post">

<p>
<label for="strFirstname">Firstname: </label>
```

```
<input type="text" name="strFirstname" id="strFirstname"/>
</p><p>
<label for="strSurname">Surname: </label>
<input type="text" name="strSurname" id="strSurname"/>
</p><p>
<label for="strUsername">Username: </label>
<input type="text" name="strUsername" id="strUsername"/>
</p><p>
<label for="strPassword">Password: </label>
<input type="password" name="strPassword" id="strPassword"/>
</p><p>
<input type="submit"/>
</p>
</form>
```

You should be familiar with XHTML forms but let us take a quick moment to examine the elements which make up the script.

 NOTE Note that the example web form script is an XHTML document and should be saved with the extension .htm.

The 'form' element consists of open and close tags and surround all other elements within the form:

```
< form action="filename" method="type">
. . .
</form>
```

The start form tag contains two attributes which specify the action to take when the form is submitted (this is normally the name of the script to invoke, in our case, a PHP script called 'example10–1.php') and the method by which the data should be sent to the script. PHP supports the *post* method and so the element looks like this:

```
<form action="example10–1.php" method="post">
. . .
</form>
```

Don't worry about exactly what is meant by the post method; we shall explain how to access data sent by the post method shortly. The great thing is that you don't need to understand the underlying mechanism to get some good results.

Within the 'form' element are a number of other elements. In this case, these are mostly pairs of 'label' elements denoting a text label and linking the label to a particular form input field:

```
<label for="inputFieldId">textLabel</label>
```

The labels are followed by 'input' elements and have the following syntax:

```
<input type="type" name="fieldname" id="inputFieldId"/>
```

The 'input' element contains a 'type' attribute where the type of the form input field is specified, a 'name' attribute where the unique name of the data held within the field is specified and an 'id' attribute to which the 'label' element refers. Each pair of form elements is surrounded by a 'paragraph' element to ensure that the 'form' elements appear on separate lines of the web page:

```
<p></p>
```

Our form fields look like this:

```
<p>
<label for="strFirstname">Firstname: </label>
<input type="text" name="strFirstname" id="strFirstname"/>
</p><p>
<label for="strSurname">Surname: </label>
<input type="text" name="strSurname" id="strSurname"/>
</p><p>
<label for="strUsername">Username: </label>
<input type="text" name="strUsername" id="strUsername"/>
</p><p>
<label for="strPassword">Password: </label>
<input type="password" name="strPassword" id="strPassword"/>
</p>
```

The above 'input' elements are simple input fields on the form where the user can type a free-form answer. To help guide the user on what to enter some accompanying text is used to label the input elements.

 NOTE Input elements have more attributes than we have mentioned above and you should consult an XHTML guide if you are unsure what they are and how to use them.

Our final input element is of type 'submit' and this allows the form data to be submitted. It displays as a clickable button on the form:

```
<input type='submit' />
```

As the 'submit' button isn't transmitting any relevant data in this example, we have chosen not to provide a 'name' attribute.

 NOTE Note that we have specified both 'text' and 'password' fields. The only difference is that with a password field, the text is hidden when the user types anything into the field.

The 'example10–1.htm' form is shown in Figure 10.3 when loaded into a web browser. There is no point clicking the form's submit button just yet as we haven't produced the PHP script to process the submitted form data.

The next thing to do is to create the PHP script which the (X)HTML form invokes. This is shown below:

```php
<?php
// File: example10–1.php

$strFirstname = $_POST["strFirstname"];
$strSurname = $_POST["strSurname"];
$strUsername = $_POST["strUsername"];
$strPassword = $_POST["strPassword"];

echo "<p>Greetings $strFirstname $strSurname</p>";
echo "<p>Your username is $strUsername and your password is $strPassword</p>";
?>
```

Accessing form data is essentially very easy. When a form is created an associated array of variables is created. This array is called $_POST. Each HTML form element that has a unique name is stored in the array and can be accessed by the PHP script. The $_POST syntax is as follows:

```php
$_POST["name"];
```

name is the name of the form value we wish to access. In our example we have assigned the contents of each of our form fields into variables of the same name:

```php
$strFirstname = $_POST["strFirstname"];
$strSurname = $_POST["strSurname"];
$strUsername = $_POST["strUsername"];
$strPassword = $_POST["strPassword"];
```

The values of these variables are then displayed using a couple of 'echo' statements.

FIGURE 10.3 An (X)HTML form

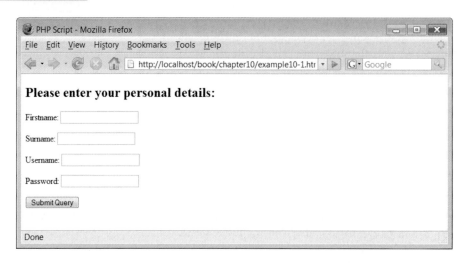

Now we have mentioned arrays before and have done so again above with the $_POST array and we still haven't explained them in any detail. Please bear with us – we do so in Chapter 11. It is just that they can be a little complex and for now you can access them without having to worry about how they work.

Figure 10.4 illustrates the output produced by the PHP script when the values 'Simon', 'Stobart', 'myusername' and 'mypassword' are entered into the form fields and the submit button is clicked.

To illustrate the scripts we have built and the interactions that can occur we are going to introduce a diagramming convention. The diagram is made up of two symbols: boxes which represent web pages or scripts and arrows which indicate actions. Figure 10.5 Illustrates

FIGURE 10.4 Displaying PHP form data

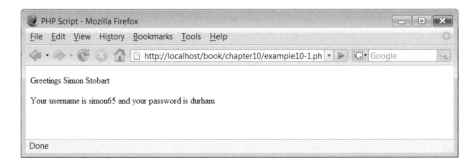

FIGURE 10.5 Separate (X)HTML and PHP scripts

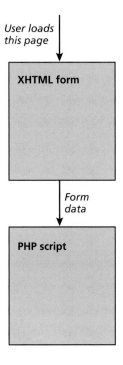

FIGURE 10.6   An (X)HTML form and PHP script combined

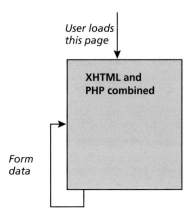

our two-script design, with the top box representing the (X)HTML form which invokes the PHP script, passing the relevant form data (indicated by the arrow). However, separating the (X)HTML form and the PHP script this way is not actually the best way of doing things. The problem comes if you want to be able to use the PHP script to check that the form data is correct and if not display a message next to any field where there is a problem.

If the PHP script is separate from the (X)HTML form, it cannot alter it easily and therefore the way forward is to combine the (X)HTML form and the PHP script into a single file.

10.3 Combining PHP and forms

What we are going to do is to combine our (X)HTML form and PHP script into a single document. When the form submit button is clicked the form invokes itself and processes the PHP script within it. This is illustrated in Figure 10.6.

In Figure 10.6, there is a single script represented by the box and an arrow representing the submission of data back to the script.

Why would we need to submit the form data back to the script if the script is already running? Well, because the data you entered into the form is only accessible to the PHP script after the submit button is clicked and the form data is submitted to the web server.

Let's look at an example script which combines the PHP and (X)HTML form:

```
<h2>Please enter your personal details:</h2>
<form action='example10-2.php' method='post'>
<p>
<label for="strFirstname">Firstname: </label>
<input type="text" name="strFirstname" id="strFirstname"/>
</p><p>
<label for="strSurname">Surname: </label>
<input type="text" name="strSurname" id="strSurname"/>
</p><p>
```

```
<label for="strUsername">Username: </label>
<input type="text" name="strUsername" id="strUsername"/>
</p><p>
<label for="strPassword">Password: </label>
<input type="password" name="strPassword" id="strPassword"/>
</p><p>
<input type="submit"/>
</p>
</form>

<?php
// File: example10-2.php
$strFirstname = $_POST["strFirstname"];
$strSurname = $_POST["strSurname"];
$strUsername = $_POST["strUsername"];
$strPassword = $_POST["strPassword"];

echo "<p>Greetings $strFirstname $strSurname</p>";
echo "<p>Your username is $strUsername and your password is $strPassword</p>";
?>
```

The above script is a combination of the (X)HTML form and the PHP script introduced previously. However, while syntactically correct and generating no errors the output produced by the script is not exactly what is required, as illustrated in Figure 10.7.

In Figure 10.7, we see that when the page is viewed for the first time the output from the PHP script is visible and as no form data has been sent the variables are not defined and an incomplete message is displayed.

FIGURE 10.7 Combined (X)HTML and PHP problem

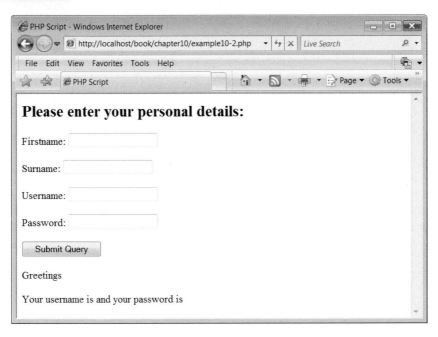

Furthermore, you might get some warning notices like this displayed:

```
Notice: Undefined index: strFirstname in C:\wamp\www\PHPLessonExamples\Lesson10\
example10-2.php on line 35
Notice: Undefined index: strSurname in C:\wamp\www\PHPLessonExamples\Lesson10\
example10-2.php on line 36
Notice: Undefined index: strUsername in C:\wamp\www\PHPLessonExamples\Lesson10\
example10-2.php on line 37
Notice: Undefined index: strPassword in C:\wamp\www\PHPLessonExamples\Lesson10\
example10-2.php on line 38
```

These are informing you, when the script runs for the first time, that these variables have not been created. By default these warnings are switched off and so you might not see them displayed on your computer. However, this is not good programming practice (as described further in Chapter 20) and so we need a means of determining if the form data was submitted or not.

```html
<h2>Please enter your personal details:</h2>
<form action='example10-3.php' method='post'>
<p>
<label for="strFirstname">Firstname: </label>
<input type="text" name="strFirstname" id="strFirstname"/>
</p><p>
<label for="strSurname">Surname: </label>
<input type="text" name="strSurname" id="strSurname"/>
</p><p>
<label for="strUsername">Username: </label>
<input type="text" name="strUsername" id="strUsername"/>
</p><p>
<label for="strPassword">Password: </label>
<input type="password" name="strPassword" id="strPassword"/>
</p><p>
<input type="submit" name="submit"/>
</p>
</form>

<?php
// File: example10-3.php

if (isset($_POST["submit"]) ) {
   $strFirstname = $_POST["strFirstname"];
   $strSurname = $_POST["strSurname"];
   $strUsername = $_POST["strUsername"];
   $strPassword = $_POST["strPassword"];

   echo "<p>Greetings $strFirstname $strSurname</p>";
   echo "<p>Your username is $strUsername and your password is
$strPassword</p>";
}
?>
```

If we examine the above script for changes, we find that there are only two. The first adds a 'name' attribute to the 'submit' input type to allow us to refer to it from within the PHP script:

```
<p><input type="submit" name="submit"/>
```

The second change is to associate all of the PHP statements within an 'if' construct. The expression to be evaluated within the 'if' construct is:

```
if (isset($_POST["submit"]) ) {
    . . .
}
```

The 'if' statement contains a function, isset(). The function returns true if a variable has been set and false if it has not and that variable in this case is $_POST["submit"]. The value of $_POST["submit"] is true if the submit button has been clicked. This means that the PHP statements within the 'if' construct are only invoked after the form's submit button is clicked. Therefore, the first time the script is executed no spurious text is output. The output from the above script is illustrated in Figure 10.8.

10.4 Invoking the correct script

In our previous examples, we have 'hard coded' into our form the name of the script to be invoked when the form is submitted, for example:

```
<form action='example10-3.php' method='post'>
```

FIGURE 10.8 Working form with combined PHP and XHTML

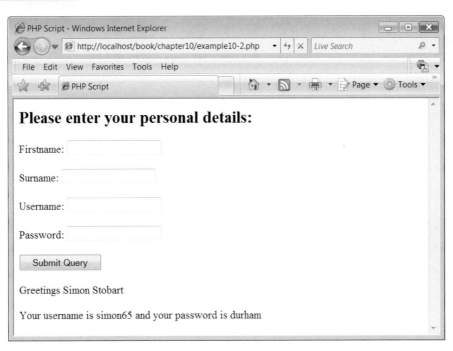

However, it would be great if we could write a script which always knew its name and would invoke that script automatically.

There is a server variable (we mentioned these in Lesson 1) which contains the name of the current script. It is:

```
$_SERVER["PHP_SELF"]
```

If we were to echo its contents as part of the form element this would ensure that the script would always call itself, no matter what name it had been saved as. The form element would look like this:

```
<form action='<?php echo $_SERVER["PHP_SELF"]; ?>' method='post'>
```

 NOTE We shall be using $_SERVER ["PHP_SELF"] in all form scripts from this point on.

10.5 An example form

It's about time we put our knowledge of forms being able to interact with PHP scripts to some good use. What we have below is a revised version of the answer to the Arabic to Roman date converter script which was the subject of Exercises:

```php
<h2>Please enter a date in Arabic numerals:</h2>
<form action='<?php echo $_SERVER["PHP_SELF"]; ?>' method='post'>
<p>
<label for="intDate">Date: </label>
<input type="text" name="intDate" id="intDate"/></p>
<p><input type="submit" name="SubmitQuery"/></p>
</form>
<?php
// File: example10-4.php
if (isset($_POST["intDate"]) ) {
   $intDate = $_POST["intDate"];

   echo "<p>$intDate is written ";
   while ($intDate >= 1000) {
      echo "M";
      $intDate -= 1000;
   }
   if ($intDate >= 900) {
      echo ("CM");
      $intDate -= 900;
   }
   if ($intDate >= 500) {
```

```php
        echo "D";
        $intDate -= 500;
    }
    if ($intDate >= 400) {
        echo ("XD");
        $intDate -= 400;
    }
    while ($intDate >= 100) {
        echo "C";
        $intDate -= 100;
    }
    if ($intDate >= 90) {
        echo ("XC");
        $intDate -= 90;
    }
    if ($intDate >= 50) {
        echo "L";
        $intDate -= 50;
    }
    if ($intDate >= 40) {
        echo ("XL");
        $intDate -= 40;
    }
    while ($intDate >= 10) {
        echo "X";
        $intDate -= 10;
    }
    if ($intDate >= 9) {
        echo ("IX");
        $intDate -= 9;
    }
    if ($intDate >= 5) {
        echo "V";
        $intDate -= 5;
    }
    if ($intDate >= 4) {
        echo ("IV");
        $intDate -= 4;
    }
    while ($intDate >= 1) {
        echo "I";
        $intDate -= 1;
    }
    echo " in Roman numerals</p>";
}
?>
```

Figure 10.9 illustrates the output from the above script.

The above script is an improvement on the previous model solution because the form allows the user to repeatedly change the date they wish to convert without changing the

FIGURE 10.9   Arabic to Roman numeral conversion

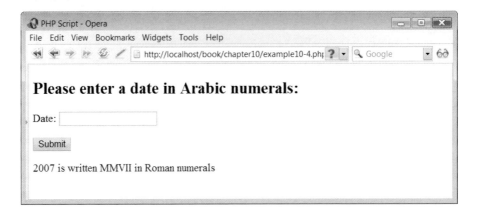

script itself. Let's take a look at what the script is doing:

```
<form action='<?php echo $_SERVER["PHP_SELF"]; ?>' method='post'>
<p>
<label for="intDate">Date: </label>
<input type="text" name="intDate" id="intDate"/></p>
<p><input type="submit" name="SubmitQuery"/></p>
</form>
```

The form component is actually very simple compared to our last script in that it only contains a single input text field and a submit button.

Next, an 'if' construct checks to see if we have an intDate form data field:

```
if (isset($_POST["intDate"]) ) {
```

If so, then the form data field value is assigned to a variable:

```
$intDate = $_POST["intDate"];
```

The remainder of the script consists of a number of sets of 'while' and 'if' constructs. Each one performs exactly the same function for each of the Roman numerals. Consider the first 'while' and 'if' construct pair:

```
while ($intDate >= 1000) {
    echo "M";
    $intDate -= 1000;
}
if ($intDate >= 900) {
    echo ("CM");
    $intDate -= 900;
}
```

The first 'while' loop iterates displaying the value 'M' and subtracting 1000 from the value of $intDate until the value of $intDate is below 1000. Next, the 'if' construct checks to see if the remaining value of $intDate is greater or equal to 900. We need to check this for the special case of placing a 'C' in front of the 'M', to indicate 900. If the value of $intDate is greater than 900 then the value 'CM' is displayed and the value of $intDate is reduced by 900. A number of 'while' and 'if' constructs repeat the processing of the date for each Roman numeral down to 'I'.

 NOTE If you think that the script design looks wasteful and that there should be a cleaner and better way of coding this script then you would be right. We shall return to this example later, in Chapter 12.

10.6 Accessing form elements

So far we have illustrated how to access form data entered in input text fields. Input password field data is accessed in exactly the same way. We shall continue by examining how to access data from the various other form elements we can use.

Radio buttons

The radio entry type is another form field we can interact with. It does not allow the user to enter any text but provides a series of 'radio buttons' from which the user can make a selection. Only one of the buttons grouped together can be selected. An example of the radio type is shown in the script below:

```
<h2>Please select your favourite color:</h2>
<form action='<?php echo $_SERVER["PHP_SELF"]; ?>' method='post'>
<p>
<label for="strBlue">Blue: </label>
<input type='radio' name='strColor' value='blue' id='strBlue'/>
<label for="strGreen">Green: </label>
<input type='radio' name='strColor' value='green' id='strGreen'/>
<label for="strYellow">Yellow: </label>
<input type='radio' name='strColor' value='yellow' id='strYellow'/>
<label for="strRed">Red: </label>
<input type = 'radio' name = 'strColor' value = 'red' id = 'strRed'/>
</p>
<p><input type = 'submit' name = 'submit'/></p></form>
<?php
// File: example10-5.php

if (isset($_POST["submit"]) ) {
   $strColour=$_POST["strColor"];
   echo "<p>Your favourite color is $strColor</p>";
}
?>
```

The script outputs a simple form which contains a series of labels and radio buttons:

```
<label for="strBlue">Blue: </label>
<input type='radio' name='strColor' value='blue' id='strBlue'/>
```

```
<label for="strGreen">Green: </label>
<input type='radio' name='strColor' value='green' id='strGreen'/>
<label for="strYellow">Yellow: </label>
<input type='radio' name='strColor' value='yellow' id='strYellow'/>
<label for="strRed">Red: </label>
<input type='radio' name='strColor' value='red' id='strRed'/>
```

Note that each of the radio buttons has a different value assigned to it but all the names are the same.

The PHP script which processes the form data assigns the value of the radio button field into variable $strColor:

```
if (isset($_POST["submit"]) ) {
    $strColour= $_POST["strColor"];
    echo "<p>Your favorite color is $strColor</p>";
}
```

A simple echo statement is then used to output the user's selected color. The output from the above script is shown in Figure 10.10.

Checkboxes

Checkbox fields enable the user to select as many options as they like from a form. Each checkbox is given a unique name. An example of the use of the checkbox form field is

FIGURE 10.10 Accessing radio button data

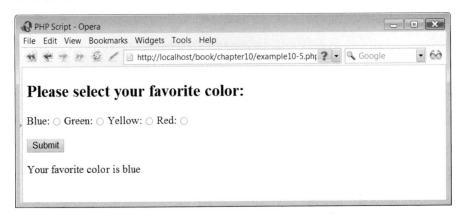

shown in the script below:

```
<h2>Please select your favourite colors:</h2>
<form action='<?php echo $_SERVER["PHP_SELF"]; ?>' method='post'>
<p>Blue <input type='checkbox' name='strColorBlue' value='blue'/>
Green <input type='checkbox' name='strColorGreen' value='green'/>
Yellow <input type='checkbox' name='strColorYellow' value='yellow'/>
Red <input type='checkbox' name='strColorRed' value='red'/></p>
<p><input type='submit' name='SubmitQuery/></p>
</form>
<?php
// File: example10-6.php
if (isset($_POST["submit"]) ) {
   $strColorBlue = $_POST["strColorBlue"];
   $strColorGreen = $_POST["strColorGreen"];
   $strColorYellow = $_POST["strColorYellow"];
   $strColorRed = $_POST["strColorRed"];
   echo "<p>Your favourite colors are $strColorBlue $strColorGreen $strColorYellow
$strColorRed</p>";
}
?>
```

The above script outputs a form which consists of four label and checkbox fields:

```
<label for="strBlue">Blue: </label>
<input type='checkbox' name='strColorBlue' value='blue' id='strBlue'/>
<label for="strGreen">Green: </label>
<input type='checkbox' name='strColorGreen' value='green' id='strGreen'/>
<label for="strYellow">Yellow: </label>
<input type='checkbox' name='strColorYellow' value='yellow' id='strYellow'/>
<label for="strRed">Red: </label>
<input type='checkbox' name='strColorRed' value='red' id='strRed'/></p>
```

Because the user can select any and all checkboxes then the PHP script must ensure that all data values stored in each checkbox are accessed. This is done here:

```
$strColourBlue = $_POST["strColorBlue"];
$strColourGreen = $_POST["strColorGreen"];
$strColourYellow = $_POST["strColorYellow"];
$strColourRed = $_POST["strColorRed"];
```

Figure 10.11 illustrates the output produced from this script.

Selections

The form selection construct is different from those form elements which we have introduced so far that use the input element. The selection construct actually uses two separate (X)HTML elements, the select element and the option element. The format for the

FIGURE 10.11 Acessing checkbox data

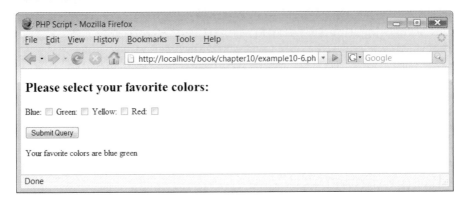

selection construct is:

```
<select name='name'>
<option>option</option>
   . . .
</select>
```

An example of the use of this element is shown in the following script:

```
<h2>Please select your title:</h2>
<form action='<?php echo $_SERVER["PHP_SELF"]; ?>' method='post'>
<p><select name='strTitle'>
     <option>Mr</option>
     <option>Miss</option>
     <option>Ms</option>
     <option>Mrs</option>
     <option>Dr</option>
</select></p>
<p><input type='submit' name='SubmitQuery'/></p>
</form>
<?php
// File: example10-7.php
if (isset($_POST["submit"]) ) {
     $strTitle = $_POST["strTitle"];
     echo "<p>Your title is $strTitle</p>";
}
?>
```

The above script outputs a form selection construct as follows:

```
<p><select name='strTitle'>
     <option>Mr</option>
     <option>Miss</option>
     <option>Ms</option>
     <option>Mrs</option>
     <option>Dr</option>
</select></p>
```

FIGURE 10.12 Accessing selection data

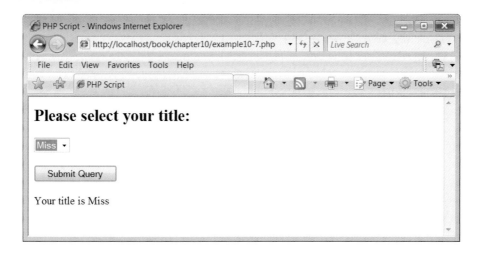

Note that in this example there are five option elements encompassed within the selection element. Accessing the value of the selected data item is the same as for previous scripts:

```
$strTitle = $_POST["strTitle"];
```

The output from the above script is illustrated in Figure 10.12.

Textareas

Another form element is the textarea, a text box of a certain number of rows and columns into which the user can enter text. The format of the element is:

```
<textarea name='name' rows='num' cols='num'>
</textarea>
```

Any text which is surrounded by the start and end tag of the 'textarea' element is displayed in the field when the form is displayed.

The following script illustrates the use of the 'textarea' element:

```
<h2>Please enter your address:</h2>
<form action='<?php echo $_SERVER["PHP_SELF"]; ?>' method='post'>
<p><textarea name='strAddress' rows='5' cols='30'></textarea></p>
<p><input type='submit' name='submit'/></p>
</form>
<?php
// File: example10-8.php
if (isset($_POST["submit"]) ) {
    $strAddress = $_POST["strAddress"];
    echo "<p>Your address is $strAddress</p>";
}
?>
```

FIGURE 10.13 Accessing 'textarea' data

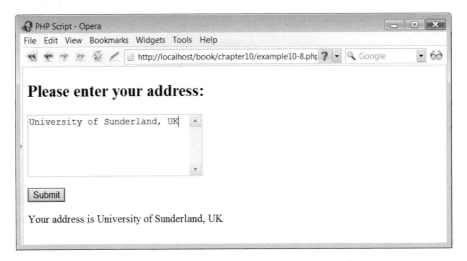

FIGURE 10.14 Four shapes as an 'input' element

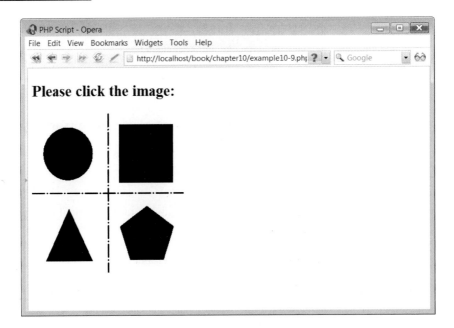

The script displays a textarea field of 30 columns by five rows:

```
<p><textarea name='strAddress' rows='5' cols='30'''></textarea></p>
```

The address entered into the field is accessed in the same way as with other form elements:

```
$strAddress = $_POST["strAddress"];
```

Figure 10.13 illustrates the use of the 'textarea' field.

Image fields

Forms can process images as input fields. While, this may at first seem strange consider the image illustrated in Figure 10.14. This image consists of four shapes and has been saved with the filename 'fourshapes.gif'. The form's 'input' element can be specified as an image type with the following syntax:

```
<input type='image' src='image' name='name'/>
```

When clicked, the image element returns the X and Y coordinates of the mouse click to the form script. These coordinates are returned as two separate data items names, 'name_x' and 'name_y' where 'name' is the name given to the image element. The (0,0) position of the image is the top left corner. The image is 300 by 300 pixels in size so the bottom right corner coordinates are (300,300).

The following script illustrates an example of the use of this form element:

```php
<h2>Please click the image:</h2>
<form action='<?php echo $_SERVER["PHP_SELF"]; ?>' method='post'>
<p><input type='image' src='graphics/fourshapes.gif'
name='intImage'/></p>
</form>
<?php
// File: example10-9.php
if (isset($_POST["intImage_x"]) ) {
   $intImageX = $_POST["intImage_x"];
   $intImageY = $_POST["intImage_y"];
   if ($intImageY < 150 && $intImageX < 150)
      echo "<p>You clicked on or near the Circle</p>";
   if ($intImageY < 150 && $intImageX >= 150)
      echo "<p>You clicked on or near the Square</p>";
   if ($intImageY >= 150 && $intImageX < 150)
      echo "<p>You clicked on or near the Triangle</p>";
   if ($intImageY >= 150 && $intImageX >= 150)
      echo "<p>You clicked on or near the Pentagon</p>";
}
?>
```

The above script includes a single 'image' input type in the form:

```php
<p><input type='image' src='graphics/fourshapes.gif'
name='intImage'/></p>
```

No submit button is needed as the form is submitted when the image is clicked, so the check for the submit button needs to be replaced with one which checks for either X or Y coordinates:

```php
if (isset($_POST["intImage_x"]) ) {
```

The X and Y coordinates are copied into two separate variables:

```php
$intImageX = $_POST["intImage_x"];
$intImageY = $_POST["intImage_y"];
```

Four 'if' statements are used to determine which shape was clicked by determining the returned X and Y coordinates:

```
if ($intImageY < 150 && $intImageX < 150)
    echo "<p>You clicked on or near the Circle</p>";
if ($intImageY < 150 && $intImageX >= 150)
    echo "<p>You clicked on or near the Square</p>";
if ($intImageY >= 150 && $intImageX < 150)
    echo "<p>You clicked on or near the Triangle</p>";
if ($intImageY >= 150 && $intImageX >= 150)
    echo "<p>You clicked on or near the Pentagon</p>";
```

 NOTE Because the form is returned when the image is clicked, there is no need for a submit button to be included as part of the form.

10.7 File uploads

Forms can employ an element that allows the user to select a file from the local computer and upload this to the server for access by the PHP script. This is a complex process and is covered in some detail in Chapter 12.

10.8 Form validation and data retention

When interacting with the user, it is important to ensure that the data that you think the user has entered is in fact what you want. Users are notorious for not typing what you expect and thus form data validation is very important. If an error in the data entered on the form is detected, then the form should be redisplayed to the user for correction. However, it would be very annoying if the user had to re-enter all of the form data, even that which was correct in the first instance. Therefore, a means of retaining and redisplaying form data is required.

Present or absent?

One of the simplest forms of validation is to determine if the user has entered anything in the form field or not. Checking that a text or password field contains data is a simple case of checking that the variable created from the form field is not of zero length. This can be done in most cases by using a simple 'if' statement such as:

```
if (formvariable == NULL)
```

In addition to simply checking if a field contains data or not, a suitable error message should be generated next to the form field to indicate to the user where the problem is.

In the case of a select form field things are a little different. By default, the first item on the menu is automatically selected. If the user does not want to select the default, you need a way to tell if they have forgotten to enter it. One way around this problem is to include a 'false' menu item at the top of the menu list. You can then check the variable for this value and thus reject the entry if it is found.

The following script illustrates whether certain form fields contain data or not:

```php
<?php
// File: example10-10.php
$booTitle = 0;
$booFirstname = 0;
$booSurname = 0;
if (isset($_POST["submit"]) ) {
    if($_POST["strTitle"] == "Select ... ")
        $booTitle = 1;
    if($_POST["strFirstname"] == NULL)
        $booFirstname = 1;
    if($_POST["strSurname"] == NULL)
        $booSurname = 1;
}
?>
<h2>Please select your title and name:</h2>
<form action='<?php echo $_SERVER["PHP_SELF"]; ?>' method='post'>
<p>
<label for="strTitle">Title: </label>
<select name='strTitle' id='strTitle'>
     <option>Select ... </option>
     <option>Mr</option>
     <option>Miss</option>
     <option>Ms</option>
     <option>Mrs</option>
     <option>Dr</option>
</select>
<?php if ($booTitle) echo "Please select a title!" ?>
</p>
<p>
<label for="strFirstname">Firstname: </label>
<input type='text' name='strFirstname' id='strFirstname'/>
<?php if ($booFirstname) echo "Please enter a firstname!" ?>
</p>
<p>
<label for="strSurname">Surname: </label>
<input type='text' name='strSurname' id='strSurname'/>
<?php if ($booSurname) echo "Please enter a surname!" ?>
</p>
<p><input type='submit' name='submit'/></p>
</form>
<?php
if (!($booTitle + $booFirstname + $booSurname) && isset($_POST["submit"]) )
    echo  "<p>All  is  well,  you  are  " . $_POST["strTitle"] . " " " .
$_POST["strFirstname"] . " " . $_POST["strSurname"] . "</p>";
?>
```

Quite a number of new things have been introduced to the script to allow us to perform validation of data. We shall go through each of these in turn. The first thing to note is that there is some PHP script before the XHTML form as we need to determine if the form has any missing fields before it is redisplayed. The following three variables are initialized to zero:

```
$booTitle = 0;
$booFirstname = 0;
$booSurname = 0;
```

Next, an 'if' construct determines if the form has been submitted:

```
if (isset($_POST["submit"]) ) {
```

The variables are used to record whether the form data items contain a value or not. As we have three form fields, we have three variables. Next, three 'if' constructs determine if the values of the form elements contain a value or not and if not set the value of the corresponding variable to 1:

```
if($_POST["strTitle"] == "Select ... ")
    $booTitle = 1;
if($_POST["strFirstname"] == NULL)
    $booFirstname = 1;
if($_POST["strSurname"] == NULL)
    $booSurname = 1;
```

The next part of the script outputs the (X)HTML form. Embedded within the form is the PHP script which will display the 'error messages' if the form field is null. The PHP scripts are:

```
<?php if ($booTitle) echo "Please select a title!" ?>
<?php if ($booFirstname) echo "Please enter a firstname!" ?>
<?php if ($booSurname) echo "Please enter a surname!" ?>
```

Finally, after the (X)HTML form we have some further PHP script which determines if the form has any missing data and if not displays a message that all is well:

```
if (!($booTitle + $booFirstname + $booSurname) &&
isset($_POST["submit"]) )
    echo "<p>All is well, you are " . $_POST["strTitle"] . " " .
$_POST["strFirstname"] . " " . $_POST["strSurname"] . "</p>";
```

The output from the above script is shown in Figure 10.15.

Retaining form data

The previous script works well, however it is far from perfect. You will note that, when you fail to complete one of the form fields and an error message is generated, all the data

FIGURE 10.15 Simple form validation

you entered in the other fields is lost. Obviously, it would be far better if this data was retained so that the user doesn't have to re-enter or reselect this information. Luckily there is a way of accomplishing this in PHP.

The following script illustrates how PHP can retain the data entered onto a form with the select and text elements:

```php
<?php
// File: example10–11.php
$booTitle = 0;
$booFirstname = 0;
$booSurname = 0;
$strTitle = "";
$strFirstname = "";
$strSurname = "";

if (isset($_POST["submit"]) ) {
   if($_POST["strTitle"] == "Select . . .")
      $booTitle = 1;
   else
      $strTitle = $_POST["strTitle"];
   if($_POST["strFirstname"] == NULL)
      $booFirstname = 1;
   else
      $strFirstname = $_POST["strFirstname"];
   if($_POST["strSurname"] == NULL)
      $booSurname = 1;
   else
      $strSurname = $_POST["strSurname"];
```

```
    }
    ?>
    <h2>Please select your title and name:</h2>
    <form action='<?php echo $_SERVER["PHP_SELF"]; ?>' method='post'>
    <p>
    <label for="strTitle">Title: </label>
    <select name='strTitle' id='strTitle'>
    <option>Select ... </option>
        <option <?php if($strTitle == "Mr") echo "Selected"
    ?>>Mr</option>
        <option <?php if($strTitle == "Miss") echo "Selected"
    ?>>Miss</option>
        <option <?php if($strTitle == "Ms") echo "Selected"
    ?>>Ms</option>
        <option <?php if($strTitle == "Mrs") echo "Selected"
    ?>>Mrs</option>
        <option <?php if($strTitle == "Dr") echo "Selected"
    ?>>Dr</option></select>
    <?php if ($booTitle) echo "Please select a title!" ?>
    </p>
    <p>
    <label for="strFirstname">Firstname: </label>
    <input type='text' name='strFirstname' value='<?php echo $strFirstname ?>'
    id='strFirstname'/>
    <?php if ($booFirstname) echo "Please enter a firstname!" ?>
    </p>
    <p>
    <label for="strSurname">Surname: </label>
    <input type='text' name='strSurname' value='<?php echo $strSurname ?>'
    id='strSurname'/>
    <?php if ($booSurname) echo "Please enter a surname!" ?>
    </p>
    <p><input type='submit' name='submit'/></p>
    </form>
    <?php
    if (!($booTitle + $booFirstname + $booSurname) && isset($_POST["submit"]) )
    echo "<p>All is well, you are " . $_POST["strTitle"] . " " . $_POST["strFirstname"]
    . " " . $_POST["strSurname"] . "</p>";
    ?>
```

The above script is a modification of the previous script, example10–10.php, with the data retention included.

Three new variables are defined and assigned to null:

```
    $strTitle = "";
    $strFirstname = "";
    $strSurname = "";
```

These variables are used to hold the values of their corresponding form fields.

When the form is submitted, a number of 'if' constructs set variables either to indicate that no field data has been received or to hold the value of the data received:

```php
if (isset($_POST["submit"]) ) {
    if($_POST["strTitle"] == "Select . . .")
        $booTitle = 1;
    else
        $strTitle = $_POST["strTitle"];
    if($_POST["strFirstname"] == NULL)
        $booFirstname = 1;
    else
        $strFirstname = $_POST["strFirstname"];
    if($_POST["strSurname"] == NULL)
        $booSurname = 1;
    else
        $strSurname = $_POST["strSurname"];
}
```

10

To indicate that a particular option has been selected, the keyword 'selected' needs to be included in the opening option tag:

```html
<option selected>
```

This means that we need to check each option element to determine if the option was previously selected and if so output the text "selected":

```php
<option <?php if($_POST["strTitle"] == "Mr") echo "Selected"
?>>Mr</option>

<option <?php if($_POST["strTitle"] == "Miss") echo "Selected"
?>>Miss</option>
<option <?php if($_POST["strTitle"] == "Ms") echo "Selected"
?>>Ms</option>
<option <?php if($_POST["strTitle"] == "Mrs") echo "Selected"
?>>Mrs</option>
<option <?php if($_POST["strTitle"] == "Dr") echo "Selected"
?>>Dr</option>
```

This can be quite a problem if you have a lot of select options! Luckily things are much easier with input text fields. They simply require a new attribute called value which is set to the value you wish to be displayed:

```html
<input type='text' name='name' value='value'>
```

 NOTE Data retention with 'password' form elements is exactly the same as input text elements.

FIGURE 10.16 Retaining form field data in select and text fields

The PHP which does this is shown here:

```
<input type='text' name='strFirstname' value='<?php
echo $_POST["strFirstname"] ?>' id="strFirstname"/>
<input type='text' name='strSurname' value='<?php
echo $_POST["strSurname"] ?>' id="strSurname"/>
```

Figure 10.16 illustrates the script retaining the form field data even after an error message of missing data in one of the fields is produced.

Retaining form data entered into a textarea field is slightly different and is illustrated in the following script:

```
<?php
// File: example10–12.php
$booAddress = 0;
$booFirstname = 0;
$booSurname = 0;
$strAddress = "";
$strFirstname = "";
$strSurname = "";
if (isset($_POST["submit"]) ) {
    if($_POST["strAddress"] == NULL)
        $booAddress = 1;
    else
        $strAddress = $_POST["strAddress"];
    if($_POST["strFirstname"] == NULL)
        $booFirstname = 1;
```

```php
            else
        $strFirstname = $_POST["strFirstname"];
    if($_POST["strSurname"] == NULL)
            $booSurname = 1;
            else
        $strSurname = $_POST["strSurname"];
    }
    ?>
    <h2>Please enter your name and address:</h2>
    <form action='<?php echo $_SERVER["PHP_SELF"]; ?>' method='post'>
    <p>
    <label for="strFirstname">Firstname: </label>
    <input type='text' name='strFirstname' value='<?php echo $strFirstname ?>'
    id='strFirstname'/>
    <?php if ($booFirstname) echo "Please enter a firstname!" ?>
    </p>
    <p>
    <label for="strSurname">Surname: </label>
    <input type='text' name='strSurname' value='<?php echo $strSurname ?>'
    id='strSurname'/>
    <?php if ($booSurname) echo "Please enter a surname!" ?>
    </p>
    <p>
    <label for="strAddress">Address: </label>
    <textarea name='strAddress' rows='5' cols='30' id='strAddress'><?php echo
    $strAddress ?></textarea>
    <?php if ($booAddress) echo "Please enter an address!" ?>
    </p>
    <p><input type='submit' name='submit'/></p>
    </form>
    <?php
    if (!($booAddress + $booFirstname + $booSurname) && isset($_POST["submit"]) )
        echo "<p>All is well, you are " . $_POST["strFirstname"] . " " .
    $_POST["strSurname"] . " and you live here: " . $_POST["strAddress"] . "</p>";
    ?>
```

The above script illustrates how data within the textarea field can be retained. The great news is that this is easy to accomplish and you simply need to output the value between the start and end textarea elements:

```
<textarea>data</textarea>
```

This is accomplished above with the line:

```
<textarea name='strAddress' rows='5' cols = '30' id='strAddress'><?php echo
$strAddress ?></textarea>
```

The output from the above script is illustrated in Figure 10.17.

In the case of radio buttons and checkbox fields, their settings are retained using the attribute 'checked' as part of the input type:

```
<input type='radio' name='name' value='value' checked />
```

FIGURE 10.17 Textarea data retention

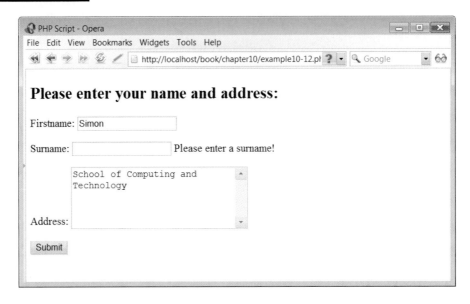

```
<input type='checkbox' name='name' value='value' checked />
```

10.9 Hidden data

Forms can be used to pass data that you don't want the user to see. This is achieved through the use of the form element type of 'hidden'. Why would you want to do this? Well, you might want to pass some information from one script to another or back to the same script via a form but you don't want the user to see what this data is and or be able to interfere with it. Let's create an example script to illustrate what we mean:

```php
<?php
// File: example10-13.php
if (isset($_POST["submit"]) ) {
    $intCount = $_POST["intCount"];
        $intCount++;
}
else
        $intCount = 1;
?>
<h2>The number of times this form has been submitted is: <?php echo($intCount) ?></h2>
<form action='<?php echo($_SERVER["PHP_SELF"]) ?>' method='post'>
<p><input type='hidden' name='intCount' value='<?php echo($intCount) ?>'/>
<input type='submit' name='submit'/></p>
</form>
```

The above script counts the number of times the submit button has been pressed. It does this by passing a hidden form field with a value set to the number of times the form has been submitted:

```
<p><input type='hidden' name='intCount' value='<?php echo($intCount) ?>'/>
```

This form field is hidden from the user but is essential in allowing the PHP script to 'remember' the total number of form submissions. The value of $intCount is incremented at the beginning of the script:

```
if (isset($_POST["submit"]) ) {
$intCount = $_POST["intCount"];
$intCount++;
}
else
$intCount = 1;
```

The output from this script is illustrated in Figure 10.18.

FIGURE 10.18   Passing hidden form data

Exercises

10.1 Write a script which includes a form containing the following elements:

> Title (select element)
> First name (text element)
> Surname (text element)
> Username (text element)
> Password (password element)
> Password Again (password element)

The PHP script should output all the values entered on the form.

10.2 Write a script which modifies the solution to Exercise 10.1. Your PHP script should now ensure that all form fields contain data.

10.3 Write a script which modifies the solution to Exercise 10.2. Your PHP script should now ensure that all form fields are retained if any errors are detected.

10.4 Write a script which modifies the solution to Exercise 10.3. Your PHP script should now perform the following additional validation:

a. Ensure that both password fields are the same.
b. Ensure that the username is not the same as either the first or surname.
c. Ensure that the password is not the same as the first, surname or username.

10.5 Write a script which uses a form to provide the value to the minimum number of coins exercise you did (Exercise 9.3).

SUMMARY

In this chapter we began by introducing simple forms and illustrating how the data entered by a user on a form can be accessed by a PHP script. Next we considered whether or not a PHP script should be kept separate from a form and also how to ensure that a form always invokes itself, whatever name it is saved as. We examined in some detail how the data from different form elements can be accessed. Finally, we finished the chapter by examining form validation, data retention and hidden data.

References and further reading

Refsnes Data. HTML Forms and Input. http://www.w3schools.com/html/html_forms.asp
World Wide Web Consortium. Forms in HTML documents. http://www.w3.org/TR/html4/interact/forms.html
Wikipedia. Web Forms. http://en.wikipedia.org/wiki/Form_(web)

CHAPTER 11

Strings and Arrays

LEARNING OBJECTIVES

- **To understand the concept of the variable type 'string' and its usefulness in a PHP application**

- **To be able to access the individual characters in a string**

- **To be able to calculate the length of a string**

- **To be able to use various predefined string functions**

- **To understand the concept of the variable type 'array' and its usefulness in a PHP application**

- **To be able to implement one-dimensional arrays**

- **To be able to use the 'foreach' loop construct**

- **To be able to create and use a multi-dimensional array**

- **To be able to pass an array within a form using the implode and explode functions**

- **To be able to determine the size of an array and to add and remove items from the array**

INTRODUCTION

In this chapter, we are going to concentrate on two of the most important data types within the PHP language. These are strings and arrays. We have in fact introduced strings previously and we have used them in all of our PHP examples this far, however PHP has quite a powerful set of string manipulation functions which we can use to help us manipulate our strings fairly easily. We have also mentioned arrays before and have included a few scripts which make use of arrays. However, we have not until now actually explained what arrays really are and shown how you can create your own and why they are so powerful.

We begin this chapter by re-examining strings and demonstrate how we can manipulate them. We illustrate how we can access an individual string's characters, determine the length of a string and find and replace strings within strings. We examine how to reverse a string, change its case and encrypt it.

We introduce the concept of arrays and illustrate how to create simple arrays in PHP. We examine how PHP supports arrays that can use non-numeric keys and how the 'foreach' loop can be used to access the contents of an array. We examine how to create multi-dimensional arrays and what they can be used for. We illustrate the way in which arrays have to undergo a conversion process to be passed as part of a form. Finally, we examine some of the functions in the standard PHP library which enable us to manipulate arrays, such as counting the number of occurrences of data within an array, sorting the array and implementing a stack.

11.1 Strings – a refresher

We have used strings a lot in our previous examples but we want to go over some of the key features which you should be familiar with just in case you missed them the first time around. A string is a series of characters encompassed within single or double quotes to denote the start and end of the string and they can be assigned to variables:

```
$strFirstname = "Simon";
$strSurname = 'Stobart';
```

Strings can be output to the browser using the 'echo' construct:

```
echo $strFirstname;
```

The echo construct can be used to output a string variable inside another string:

```
echo "$strFirstname";
```

In the above example the value 'Simon' is displayed. However, if the variable was enclosed in single quotes, like this:

```
echo '$strFirstname';
```

then the output would be $strFirstname as the string name would be displayed not its contents.

String concatenation

Strings can be concatenated together using the dot operator:

```
$strFirstname . $strSurname;
```

If the above was output using the 'echo' construct, like this:

```
echo $strFirstname . $strSurname;
```

then the output would be 'SimonStobart'. To include a space between the first name and surname, we can use the dot operator to insert a space like this:

```
echo $strFirstname . " " . $strSurname;
```

or alteratively we can do this:

```
echo "$strFirstname $strSurname";
```

String character access

Strings in PHP consist of zero or more characters. We can refer to the individual characters in a string by specifying the zero-based offset of the character we want within curly braces, for example:

```
$strName = "Simon";
$strTheSecondCharacter = $strName{1};
```

The above example stores the value 'i' in variable $strTheSecondCharacter, but why? Well, to understand this you need to understand how the string is stored and referenced. Consider Figure 11.1 which illustrates how our string is stored.

Figure 11.1 illustrates that string characters are stored consecutively with the first character being referenced at position 0 and the second at position 1, etc.

Consider the following script which outputs a string in a table and numbers the character offsets:

```
<?php
// File: example11–1.php

$strName = "Simon Stobart";

echo "<table border='1' width='300'>";
echo "<tr align='center'>";
```

FIGURE 11.1 Character references in a string

0	1	2	3	4
S	i	m	o	n

```
for ($intLetter=0;$intLetter<13;$intLetter++)
   echo "<td>$intLetter</td>";
echo "</tr>";
echo "<tr>";
for ($intLetter=0;$intLetter<13;$intLetter++)
   echo "<td align='center'>" . $strName{$intLetter} . "</td>";
echo "</tr>";
echo "</table>";
?>
```

The above script uses two loops to output two rows of a table. The first outputs the character offset numbers from 0 to 12:

```
for ($intLetter=0;$intLetter<13;$intLetter++)
   echo "<td>$intLetter</td>";
```

The second outputs the string characters:

```
for ($intLetter=0;$intLetter<13;$intLetter++)
   echo "<td align='center'>" . $strName{$intLetter} . "</td>";
```

All the rest of the script contains mainly 'echo' statements which form the XHTML table. Consider the 'echo' statement:

```
echo "<td align='center'>" . $strName{$intLetter} . "</td>";
```

We had to use the dot operator to concatenate the output as string character references cannot be expanded automatically inside of a double-quoted string. The following would not work:

```
echo "<td align='center'> $strName{$intLetter} </td>";
```

The output from the above script is illustrated in Figure 11.2.

Calculating the length of a string

In the above example, note that we included the length of the string as a constant value as part of the 'for' loop. This is no use if we have implemented a form to obtain a string from the user

---

FIGURE 11.2 String character output

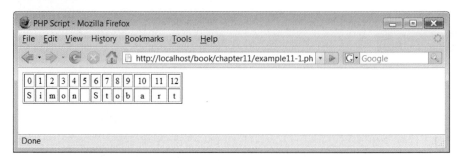

as we would not know the length of the string in advance. To overcome this, PHP has a function called 'strlen' (string length) which returns the number of characters in a string:

```
length = strlen(string);
```

We are going to explain how to create our own functions in Chapter 13, but for now it is probably worth explaining what a PHP function is and how we can use some of those prewritten and provided with the language. A function is an associated group of statements which, when invoked, executes those statements. Functions can be written to receive values which they then process and affect the result produced by the associated statements. Functions can return a single piece of data, such as an integer or string. Figure 11.3 illustrates graphically that a function can be viewed as a 'black box' with data being sent to it and the result being returned.

NOTE	Exactly how the function performs its 'magic' within the box is not known to the user.

In the case of the 'strlen' function, it can accept a single string value and return the length of the string. The use of the function is shown in the following script:

```php
<?php
// File: example11-2.php

$strName = "Simon Stobart";

$intStringLength = strlen($strName);
echo "<p>The string is $intStringLength characters long</p>";
?>
```

In the above script, the value of $strName is passed to the function and the resulting string length is stored in variable $intStringLength. The output from the script is:

```
The string is 13 characters long
```

FIGURE 11.3 A function

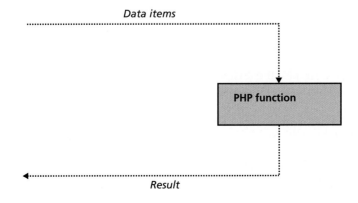

Finding a string within a string

The strstr() function can be used to find a specific part of a string inside another string, the function looks like this:

```
outputString=strstr(searchString, lookingForString)
```

Function strstr() requires two parameters to work. The first is the string which we are going to search and the second is what we are looking for. The function returns the remainder of the input string from the point at which it finds what we were looking for. Consider the following example script:

```php
<?php
// File: example11-3.php

$strName = "Simon Stobart";

$strOutput = strstr($strName, "St");
echo "<p>The result is $strOutput</p>";
?>
```

The script searches the variable $strName for the string 'St'. The output from the above script is:

```
The result is Stobart
```

Replacing part of a string

You may wish to replace part of a string with another string. The str_replace() function can assist you to do this. The function looks like this:

```
outputString=str_replace (lookingForString, replaceString, searchString)
```

Here is an example of the function being used:

```php
<?php
// File: example11-4.php

$strSentence = "The use of italics can be useful to highlight certain
words";

$strOutput = str_replace( "italics", "italics", $strSentence);
echo "<p>The string now looks like: '$strOutput'</p>";
?>
```

The above script searches the $strSentence string and replaces the text 'italics' with '<i>italics<i>'. The output from the script is:

```
The string now looks like: 'The use of italics can be useful to
highlight certain words'
```

Function str_replace() replaces all occurrences of the string it is looking for found within the search string with the replace string.

Reversing a string

Function strrev() reverses the characters of a string. It looks like this:

```
reversedString = strrev(startingString);
```

The function receives a single parameter which is the starting string and returns the string in reverse order. Following is a script illustrating its use:

```php
<?php
// File: example11-5.php

$strName = "Simon Stobart";

$strReversed = strrev($strName);
echo "<p>$strName backwards is $strReversed</p>";
?>
```

The above script reverses the string 'Simon Stobart' and displays it. The output from the script is:

```
Simon Stobart backwards is trabotS nomiS
```

Changing the case of a string

Sometimes we want to change the case of some strings we use in our scripts. The following functions are very useful as they help us change the case of the words in our strings or alter the first character of each word in the string:

```
upperString strtoupper (inputString);
lowerString strtolower (inputString);
upperFirstString ucfirst (inputString);
upperFirstWordsString ucwords (inputString);
```

The following script illustrates the use of these functions:

```php
<?php
// File: example11-6.php

$strUpper = strtoupper("simon stobart");
$strLower = strtolower("SIMON STOBART");
$strUpperFirst = ucfirst("simon stobart");
$strUpperFirstWords = ucwords("simon stobart");

echo "<p>simon stobart strtoupper = $strUpper</p>";
echo "<p>SIMON STOBART strtolower = $strLower</p>";
echo "<p>simon stobart ucfirst = $strUpperFirst</p>";
echo "<p>simon stobart ucwords = $strUpperFirstWords</p>";
?>
```

The output from the above script is illustrated in Figure 11.4.

FIGURE 11.4   Manipulating the case of a string

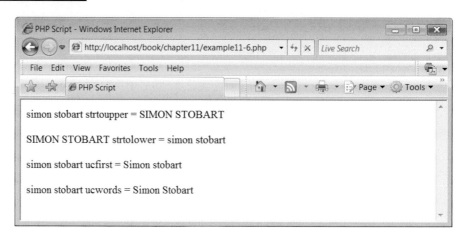

simon stobart strtoupper = SIMON STOBART

SIMON STOBART strtolower = simon stobart

simon stobart ucfirst = Simon stobart

simon stobart ucwords = Simon Stobart

Encrypting a string

Sometimes it is a very good idea to encrypt a string for storage in a file or database for example. Examples of when you may want to do this would be someone's password for example. PHP provides a function called MD5 which encrypts a string using the MD5 encryption algorithm. The function looks like this:

```
encryptedString = md5(unencryptedString)
```

A script illustrating the use of the function is given below:

```php
<?php
// File: example11-7.php

$strPassword = "secretsquirrel";
$strEncryptedPassword = md5($strPassword);
echo "<p>$strPassword encrypted is $strEncryptedPassword</p>";
?>
```

The output from the above script is:

```
secretsquirrel encrypted is d7d9771884d6a6c4a859faa9f7f4dd05
```

  NOTE   Note that MD5 encryption is one way and thus you cannot recover the original string from the encrypted form (not easily, that is).

Other string functions

There are many other string functions provided with the PHP language but unfortunately we do not have the time or space to examine each and every one. A quick look through the PHP manual (http://www.php.net/manual/en/) will provide you with a complete list of the functions that are available. However, we must now move onto a subject which we have been promising to get to for some time – arrays.

11.2 Creating arrays

An array in PHP is an ordered map, where a map is a type which maps values to keys. Because PHP stores its arrays as maps it means that they can be used for a whole variety of different data structures such as lists, trees, stacks, etc. Arrays are used to collect together data, such as people's names and perform operations on this data as easily as possible. PHP supports both single and multi-dimensional arrays, but for now let's look at creating a very simple array.

A simple array

Arrays are created using the array construct:

```
theArray = array (arrayItem1, arrayItem2, ...);
```

Here is an actual example:

```
$arrColors = array ("Red", "Green", "Blue", "Yellow", "White");
```

This creates an array called $arrColors which contains five elements storing various color names. We can refer to the elements within the array by using a subscript to the array name. Because the index defaults to numbering the array index from 0, we can access the first element of the array by the following statement:

```
$arrColors[0];
```

and the last element of the array by:

```
$arrColors[4];
```

This is illustrated in the following script:

```
<?php
// File: example11–8.php

$arrColors = array ("Red", "Green", "Blue", "Yellow", "White");

for($intCount=0;$intCount<5;$intCount++)
    echo "<p>" . $arrColors[$intCount] . "</p>";
?>
```

The above script uses a 'for' loop to access each element of the array. The output from the script is shown in Figure 11.5.

 NOTE The use of the [ ] to access the various elements of the array is similar to the use of braces { } to access string characters.

FIGURE 11.5   Array output

An array with a key

We can create an array and specify our own index key at the same time.:

```
$arrColors = array (0=>"Red", 1=>"Green", 2=>"Blue", 3=>"Yellow",
4=>"White");
```

A key index is specified using the operator =>. In the above example, the index has been specified exactly as the default index would: a numerical index starting from 0 and incremented by one each time. But what if we put the index items in a different order and even missed out an index number, for example:

```
$arrColors = array (0=>"Red", 2=>"Green", 3=>"Blue", 5=>"", 1=>"Yellow",
4=>"White");
```

In the above example, the index has not been created in numerical order and in addition a blank index key, number 5, has been included. If we use the above array with a slightly modified version of our simple 'for' loop example, we can see what is displayed when we cycle through the array:

```
<?php
// File: example11-9.php

$arrColors = array (0=>"Red", 2=>"Green", 3=>"Blue", 5=>"", 1=>"Yellow",
4=>"White");

for($intCount = 0;$intCount<6;$intCount++)
    echo "<p>$intCount " . $arrColors[$intCount] . "</p>";
?>
```

Note that the for loop now uses the expression <6 to determine the last item in the array as we have included an extra key. The output from the script is shown in Figure 11.6.

 NOTE   Note that the array elements are output in key order not the order in which they were defined in the 'array' construct.

FIGURE 11.6 Array key output

Foreach

PHP includes a loop construct specifically designed for iterating through arrays. This loop construct is known as the 'foreach' loop and there are two syntaxes. The first form is:

```
foreach (array as value) statement
```

The foreach loop will iterate through the array provided by 'array'. The value in the current index is assigned to 'value'. The array index is then incremented by one so the next iteration of the loop accesses the next element of the array. An example of this loop has been included in the following script:

```php
<?php
// File: example11–10.php

$arrColors = array (0=>"Red", 2=>"Green", 3=>"Blue", 5=>"", 1=>"Yellow",
4=>"White");
$intCount = 0;
foreach($arrColors as $strColour)
    echo "<p>" . $intCount++ . " $strColour</p>";
?>
```

The output from the above script is illustrated in Figure 11.7.

 NOTE Note that the output of the colors is in the order in which they were declared, not in the numerical index order as with the 'for' loop.

The second form of the 'foreach' loop is:

```
foreach (array as key=> value) statement
```

FIGURE 11.7 Arrays and the 'foreach' loop

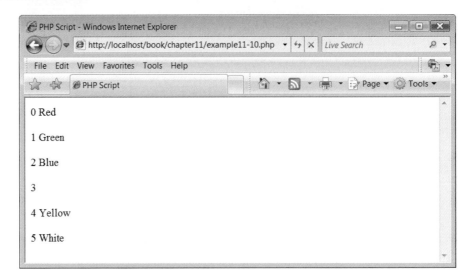

FIGURE 11.8 Output from another form of the 'foreach' loop

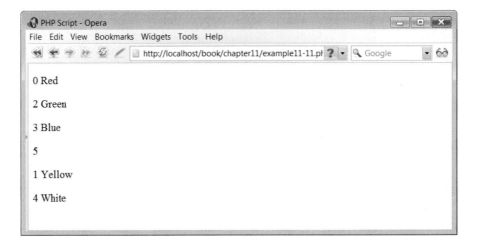

This foreach statement is similar to the previous example but in addition assigns the value of the current element's index to the key. This is shown in the following script:

```php
<?php
// File: example11-11.php
$arrColors = array (0=>"Red", 2=>"Green", 3=>"Blue", 5=>"", 1=>"Yellow",
4=>"White");
foreach($arrColors as $intKey=>$strColor)
   echo "<p>$intKey $strColor</p>";
?>
```

The output from the above script is shown in Figure 11.8.

FIGURE 11.9 Non-numerical keys

Arrays and Non-numerical Keys

Arrays don't have to have a numerical key, for example:

```
$arrColors = array ("red"=> "Red", "green"=>"Green", "blue"=>"Blue",
"yellow"=>"Yellow", "white"=>"White");
```

The following script illustrates the use of such an array:

```
<?php
// File: example11-12.php

$arrColors = array ("red"=>"Red", "green"=>"Green", "blue"=>"Blue",
"yellow"=>"Yellow", "white"=>"White");
foreach($arrColors as $strKey=>$strColor)
   echo "<p>$strKey $strColor</p>";
?>
```

The output from the above script is illustrated in Figure 11.9.

Using one-dimensional arrays

Okay, we are now going to examine how we can use the power of arrays to help us in our PHP scripting. All of the arrays we have introduced so far are what we term single-dimensional arrays as they have only one dimension of values. In the following example, we use a single-dimensional array to help us check if a username and password is correct. We build an array of usernames and passwords, where username is the key and password is the data element. We can then check if the username and password supplied matches those that we know. Here is the script:

```
<?php
// File: example11-13.php

$arrUsernamePassword = array ("simon"=>"sunderland1345", "alan"=>"stockton526",
"ian"=>"belmont32", "craig"=>"durham412");

$strEnteredUsername = "alan";
$strEnteredPassword = "stockton526";
```

```
$strStoredPassword = $arrUsernamePassword[$strEnteredUsername];

if (!$strStoredPassword)
   echo "<p>Invalid Username!</p>";
elseif ($strStoredPassword == $strEnteredPassword)
   echo "<p>Username and Password match!</p>";
else
   echo "<p>Invalid Password!</p>";
?>
```

The above script defines an array which uses keys to represent usernames and data elements to store passwords:

```
$arrUsernamePassword = array ("simon"=>"sunderland1345",
"alan"=>"stockton526", "ian"=>"belmont32", "craig"=>"durham412");
```

Two variables hold the 'entered' username and password:

```
$strEnteredUsername = "alan";
$strEnteredPassword = "stockton526";
```

Using the entered username, the array password value is obtained:

```
$strStoredPassword = $arrUsernamePassword[$strEnteredUsername];
```

If the entered username was not valid then the array returns a null password and thus the following is displayed:

```
if (!$strStoredPassword)
   echo "<p>Invalid Username!</p>";
```

The rest of the 'if' construct outputs appropriate messages depending on whether the password matches or not:

```
elseif ($strStoredPassword == $strEnteredPassword)
   echo "<p>Username and Password match!</p>";
else
   echo "<p>Invalid Password!</p>";
```

In the above example we output the messages 'Invalid Username!' and 'Invalid Password!'. In a real world application it is often better to simply output a more generic message 'Invalid Username and/or Password' in order that someone who is trying to break into a system is unaware if they have correctly guessed the username or password specifically.

Multi-dimensional arrays

PHP supports multi-dimensional arrays in addition to single-dimensional ones. Multi-dimensional arrays are arrays of single-dimensional arrays. Figure 11.10 illustrates a multi-dimensional array. The array consists of rows storing the car make, the color and the number in stock.

The array illustrated in Figure 11.10 can be constructed in PHP using the following syntax:

```
$arrCars = array (array ("Ford", "Mazda", "Renault", "Vauxhall", "Toyota"),
                  array("Blue", "Black", "Red", "Green", "Red"),
                  array(4,4,2,3,2)
      );
```

FIGURE 11.10   Multi-dimensional array

	0	1	2	3	4
0	Ford	Mazda	Renault	Vauxhall	Toyota
1	Blue	Black	Red	Green	Red
2	4	4	2	3	2

The above 'array' construct consists of the overall array called $arrCars and within this are three single-dimensional arrays, which have no names. Each of these single-dimensional arrays holds separately the make, color and quantity of car.

The different arrays can be accessed using a subscripted value as we did with the single-dimensional array. As this array has two dimensions then we need to use two subscripts. For example:

```php
$arrCars[1][0]
```

The above will access the element 'Blue'. The following script illustrates the use of this array:

```php
<?php
// File: example11-14.php

$arrCars = array (array("Ford", "Mazda", "Renault", "Vauxhall", "Toyota"),
            array("Blue", "Black", "Red", "Green", "Red"),
            array(4,4,2,3,2)
);
for ($intCount=0;$intCount<5;$intCount++) {
    $strMake = $arrCars[0][$intCount];
    $strColor = $arrCars[1][$intCount];
    $intQuantity = $arrCars[2][$intCount];
    echo "<p>Make: $strMake Color: $strColor Quantity: $intQuantity</p>";
}
?>
```

The output from the above script is shown in Figure 11.11.

Using non-numerical keys with multi-dimensional arrays

In our previous multi-dimensional array examples we have not specified any indexes and so the array defaulted to a numerical integer index. We can however specify our own numerical index or even use strings. For example:

```php
$arrCars = array ("Make" => array("Ford", "Mazda", "Renault", "Vauxhall", "Toyota"),
    "Color"=> array("Blue", "Black", "Red", "Green", "Red"),
    "Quantity"=> array(4,4,2,3,2)
);
```

FIGURE 11.11 Multi-dimensional array

Let's rewrite our previous script so it now uses a 'foreach' loop to access the array and also the new keys. Here is the script:

```php
<?php
// File: example11–15.php

$arrCars = array ("Make" => array("Ford", "Mazda", "Renault", "Vauxhall", "Toyota"),
    "Color" => array("Blue", "Black", "Red", "Green", "Red"),
    "Quantity" => array(4,4,2,3,2)
);

foreach($arrCars["Make"] as $strKey=>$strMake){
    $strColor = $arrCars["Color"][$strKey];
    $intQuantity = $arrCars["Quantity"][$strKey];
    echo "<p>Make: $strMake Color: $strColor Quantity:
$intQuantity</p>";
}
?>
```

The output produced is the same as shown in Figure 11.11.

11.3 Using arrays with forms

In Chapter 10, we illustrated how we can use forms to communicate with the form user and that variable data can be retained and hidden within the form. At the time, we did not discuss arrays and forms as we hadn't shown you how to create and use your own arrays. Another reason is that arrays have to be treated slightly differently from other types when passing them from form to form. You see you might think that you can include an array as a hidden data entry in a form, however this doesn't work. Consider the following example script:

```php
<?php
// File: example11–16.php

if (isset($_POST["submit"]) ) {
```

```
      echo("<p>The array contains:</p>");
      $arrNames = $_POST['arrNames'];
      for($intCount=0;$intCount<4;$intCount++)
         echo"<p>" . $arrNames[$intCount] . "</p>";
   }
   else
      $arrNames = array("Simon","Liz","Gemma","Hayley");
   ?>

   <h2>A Hidden Array Example</h2>

   <form action='<?php echo $_SERVER["PHP_SELF"]; ?>' method='post'>
   <p><input type='hidden' name='arrNames' value='<?php echo $arrNames
   ?>'/>
   <input type='submit' name='submit'/></p>
   </form>
```

The script begins by checking if the form has been submitted and if so displays the contents of the array:

```
if (isset($_POST["submit"]) ) {
   echo("<p>The array contains:</p>");
   $arrNames = $_POST['arrNames'];
   for($intCount=0;$intCount<4;$intCount++)
      echo"<p>" . $arrNames[$intCount] . "</p>";
}
```

If it hasn't been submitted then this must be the first time the script has been run and therefore the array is defined:

```
else
   $arrNames = array("Simon","Liz","Gemma","Hayley");
```

The form includes the hidden array and a submit button to post the array data:

```
<form action='<?php echo $_SERVER["PHP_SELF"]; ?>' method='post'>
<p><input type='hidden' name='arrNames' value='<?php echo $arrNames
?>'/>
<input type='submit' name='submit'/></p>
</form>
```

All this looks well, until we submit the form and we get the output illustrated in Figure 11.12. What has happened to your array data? Well, unfortunately, you cannot pass arrays between forms in this way and the data is lost.

There is however a method we can use to get around this problem and that is by using two special functions called explode and implode.

The way to get around the fact that we cannot send arrays as form data elements is to convert them into something we can send. In this case, a string. The explode and implode functions can be used to convert an array to a string and a string to an array.

The format for the explode function is:

```
array = explode(separator, string);
```

FIGURE 11.12   An array not working with a forms

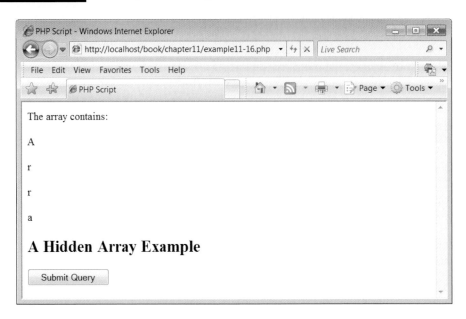

The function accepts two parameters, the first a string indicating what characters it will use to search the string to separate it into individual array elements. The second parameter is the string itself. The function returns an array.

The format of the implode function is:

```
string = implode(separator, array);
```

The implode function accepts two parameters, the first a string indicating what characters it will use to separate each element of the array and the second an array. The function returns a string. The following script is a rewrite of 'example11–16.php' but now using the explode and implode functions to pass the array via the form as a string:

```php
<?php
// File: example11–17.php
if (isset($_POST["submit"]) ) {
    echo("<p>The array contains:</p>");
    $strNames = $_POST['strNames'];
    $arrNames = explode("|",$strNames);
    for($intCount=0;$intCount<4;$intCount++)
        echo"<p>" . $arrNames[$intCount] . "</p>";
}
else {
    $arrNames = array("Simon","Liz","Gemma","Hayley");
    $strNames = implode("|",$arrNames);
}
?>

<h2>A Hidden Array Example</h2>

<form action='<?php echo $_SERVER["PHP_SELF"]; ?>' method='post'>
```

```
<p><input type='hidden' name='strNames' value='<?php echo $strNames
?>'/>
<input type='submit' name='submit'/></p>
</form>
```

The script begins by checking if the form has been submitted. If so, the string of names is obtained and converted to an array using the explode function. The array contents are then displayed:

```
if (isset($_POST["submit"]) ) {
    echo("<p>The array contains:</p>");
    $strNames = $_POST['strNames'];
    $arrNames = explode("|",$strNames);
    for($intCount=0;$intCount<4;$intCount++)
        echo"<p>" . $arrNames[$intCount] . "</p>";
}
```

If it hasn't been submitted then this must be the first time the script has been run and therefore the array is defined. Note that the array is turned into a string with the implode function:

```
else {
    $arrNames = array("Simon","Liz","Gemma","Hayley");
    $strNames = implode("|",$arrNames);
}
```

The form includes the hidden string:

```
<form action='<?php echo $_SERVER["PHP_SELF"]; ?>' method='post'>
<p><input type='hidden' name='strNames' value='<?php echo $strNames
?>'/>
<input type='submit' name='submit'/></p>
</form>
```

The output from the above script is illustrated in Figure 11.13.

11.4 Manipulating arrays

In the same way as with strings, the PHP function library contains a large number of functions to help you manipulate your arrays easily. In the remainder of this chapter, we introduce some of these functions and illustrate how they can be used to assist you in your programming.

Counting array elements

The function count() can be used to determine the size of an array (i.e. the number of data elements it contains). The format of the function is:

size = count(*array*)

FIGURE 11.13 Explode and implode functions at work

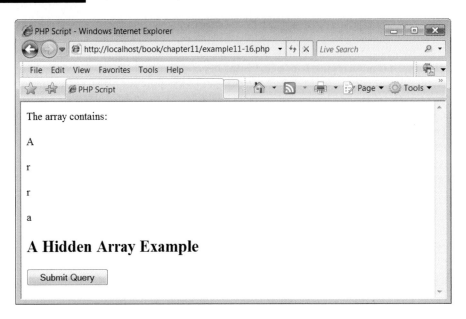

The function requires an array and returns the size of the array.

The following script illustrates the use of the count function:

```php
<?php
// File: example11–18.php

$arrColors = array (0=>"Red", 2=>"Green", 3=>"Blue", 1=>"Yellow",
4=>"White");

$intSize  = count($arrColors);

for($intCount=0;$intCount<$intSize;$intCount++)
   echo "<p>$intCount " . $arrColors[$intCount] . "</p>";
?>
```

The above script obtains the size of the array using the count function. This value is then used to control the number of iterations made by the 'for' loop, thus eliminating the need to include a constant value representing the size of the array.

Replacing an array element

You can replace the contents of an array element by simply assigning a new value to the array element, using the following syntax:

```
array[key] = element;
```

Therefore, consider the following script:

```php
<?php
// File: example11-19.php

$arrColors = array (0=>"Red", 2=>"Green", 3=>"Blue", 1=>"Yellow",
4=>"White");

$intSize = count($arrColors);

echo "<p>";
for($intCount=0;$intCount<$intSize;$intCount++)
   echo $arrColors[$intCount] . " ";
echo "</p>";
$arrColors[3]="Purple";
echo "<p>";
for($intCount=0;$intCount<$intSize;$intCount++)
   echo $arrColors[$intCount] . " ";
echo "</p>";
?>
```

The above example creates an array and using a for loop displays its contents:

```php
$arrColors = array (0=>"Red", 2=>"Green", 3=>"Blue", 1=>"Yellow",
4=>"White");

$intSize = count($arrColors);

echo "<p>";
for($intCount=0;$intCount<$intSize;$intCount++)
   echo $arrColors[$intCount] . " ";
echo "</p>";
```

Then the color in element position three is changed and the array is once again displayed:

```php
$arrColors[3]  = "Purple";
echo "<p>";
for($intCount=0;$intCount<$intSize;$intCount++)
   echo $arrColors[$intCount] . " ";
echo "</p>";
```

You should note that the color has changed from blue to purple, as illustrated in Figure 11.14.

Adding elements to the end of an array

Once an array has been created you may wish to add new elements to the end of it. One method of accomplishing this is as follows:

array[]=element;

FIGURE 11.14   Changing an array element

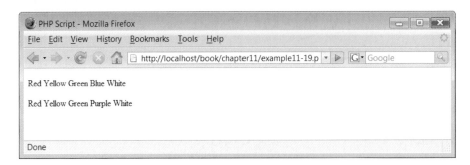

The above illustrates that if you wish to add a new element to an existing array you do this as though you were replacing elements but instead you do not specify the key of the array. This is illustrated in the following script:

```php
<?php
// File: example11-20.php

$arrColors = array (0=>"Red", 2=>"Green", 3=>"Blue", 1=>"Yellow",
4=>"White");

$intSize = count($arrColors);
echo "<p>";
for($intCount=0;$intCount<$intSize;$intCount++)
    echo $arrColors[$intCount] . " ";
echo "</p>";
$arrColors[] = "Purple";
$arrColors[] = "Brown";
$arrColors[] = "Grey";
$intSize = count($arrColors);
echo "<p>";
for($intCount=0;$intCount<$intSize;$intCount++)
    echo $arrColors[$intCount] . " ";
echo "</p>";
?>
```

The above script creates an array and outputs it as the previous one did:

```php
$arrColors = array (0=>"Red", 2=>"Green", 3=>"Blue", 1=>"Yellow",
4=>"White");

$intSize = count($arrColors);
echo "<p>";
for($intCount=0;$intCount<$intSize;$intCount++)
    echo $arrColors[$intCount] . " ";
echo "</p>";
```

However, next the script adds three colors to the end of the array. Note that it also recalculates the size of the array as this is now changed:

```php
$arrColors[] = "Purple";
$arrColors[] = "Brown";
```

FIGURE 11.15   New elements added to the end of an array

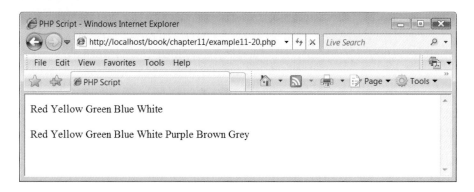

```
$arrColors[] = "Grey";
$intSize = count($arrColors);
```

The array is then redisplayed:

```
echo "<p>";
for($intCount=0;$intCount<$intSize;$intCount++)
    echo $arrColors[$intCount] . " ";
echo "</p>";
```

The output from the above script is illustrated in Figure 11.15.

Walking the array

PHP supports five functions, which are useful for 'walking an array'. Walking an array is a term used to describe a programming requirement where each element of the array is accessed and used in some way. The 'foreach' loop is an example of a construct which allows us to walk an array. However the loop only enables us to walk the array in a single direction, from start to end. The reset(), next(), prev(), current() and end() functions allow us to move from element to element easily. The format of these functions is as follows:

```
element next (array)
element prev (array)
element current (array)
element end (array)
element reset (array)
```

The next() function returns the array element in the next place pointed to by the array's internal array pointer. At the end of the array, a value of null is returned. When the element is returned, the value of the array pointer is advanced by one. The prev() function returns the previous element pointed to by the array's internal pointer. If the start of the array is reached, a value of null is returned. Function current() returns the array element currently pointed to by the array pointer and does not move the internal pointer. Function end() moves the internal array pointer to the end of the array and returns the last array element. Function reset() moves the internal pointer to the start of the array and returns the value of the first element.

The following script illustrates an example of the use of these functions:

```php
<?php
// File: example11-21.php

$arrColors = array (0=>"Red", 2=>"Green", 3=>"Blue", 1=>"Yellow",
4=>"White");

echo "<p>";
$strColour = reset($arrColors);
echo "$strColor ";
$strColor = next($arrColors);
echo "$strColor ";
$strColor = next($arrColors);
echo "$strColor ";
$strColor = prev($arrColors);
echo "$strColor ";
$strColor = current($arrColors);
echo "$strColor ";
$strColor = end($arrColors);
echo "$strColor ";
echo "</p>";
?>
```

The script simply jumps around the array using the different functions displaying the element value for each time. The output produced by the script is:

```
Red Green Blue Green Green White
```

Pushing and popping – creating a stack

What we often need to be able to do is to implement an array which will allow us to add and remove data to and from the end of the array. This is known as implementing a stack. Adding data to the end of the stack is known as pushing and removing data is known as popping. PHP has two functions which enable you to push and pop data, the format of these are:

```
element array_pop(array)
numberStored array_push(array, element)
```

Function array_pop() requires an array as a parameter. It returns the value stored in the last element in the array and reduces the array size by one. Function array_push() requires an array and the data you wish to add to the array as parameters. The array is increased in size by one element and the data is stored in this element. The function returns the number of elements stored in the array.

The following script illustrates the use of these functions:

```php
<?php
// File: example11-22.php

$arrColors = array ("Red", "Green", "Blue", "Yellow", "White");
```

```php
echo "<p>";
foreach($arrColors as $strColor)
    echo "$strColor ";
echo "</p>";

$strColour = array_pop($arrColors);
echo "<p>$strColor</p>";
$strColour = array_pop($arrColors);
echo "<p>$strColor</p>";

echo "<p>";
foreach($arrColors as $strColor)
    echo "$strColor ";
echo "</p>";

array_push($arrColors, "Grey");
echo "<p>";
foreach($arrColors as $strColor)
    echo "$strColor ";
echo "</p>";
?>
```

The script first displays the contents of the array:

```php
echo "<p>";
foreach($arrColors as $strColor)
    echo "$strColor ";
echo "</p>";
```

It then pops off two elements from the end of the array:

```php
$strColor = array_pop($arrColors);
echo "<p>$strColor</p>";
$strColor = array_pop($arrColors);
echo "<p>$strColor</p>";
```

The array is once again displayed:

```php
echo "<p>";
foreach($arrColors as $strColor)
    echo "$strColor ";
echo "</p>";
```

Finally, a new color is pushed onto the array and the array is displayed again in full:

```php
array_push($arrColors, "Grey");
echo "<p>";
foreach($arrColors as $strColor)
    echo "$strColor ";
echo "</p>";
```

The output from the script is illustrated in Figure 11.16.

Implementing a stack

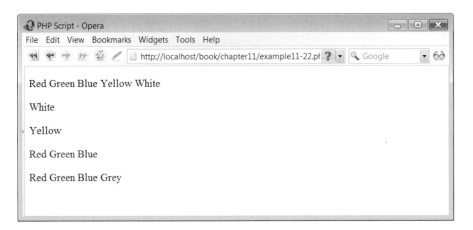

Counting occurrences

If an array contains a number of identical elements you may wish to count the numbers of each of them. Function array_count_values() can be used to do this and it looks like this:

```
array array_count_values(array)
```

The function requires an array as a parameter and returns an array of the results. The following script illustrates the use of the function:

```php
<?php
// File: example11-23.php
$arrColors = array ("Red", "Green", "Blue", "Yellow", "White",
                    "Yellow", "Green", "Blue", "Yellow", "Grey",
                    "Red", "Yellow", "Blue", "Yellow", "White");
$arrCount = array_count_values($arrColors);

foreach($arrCount as $strColor=>$intCount)
   echo "<p>$strColor occurs $intCount times</p>";
?>
```

The above script declares and populates an array:

```php
$arrColors = array ("Red", "Green", "Blue", "Yellow", "White",
                    "Yellow", "Green", "Blue", "Yellow", "Grey",
                    "Red", "Yellow", "Blue", "Yellow", "White");
```

The array_count_values() function is invoked creating a new array indexed on the number of occurances:

```php
$arrCount = array_count_values($arrColors);
```

The new array is then displayed:

```php
foreach($arrCount as $strColor=>$intCount)
   echo "<p>$strColor occurs $intCount times</p>";
```

The output produced from the above script is illustrated in Figure 11.17.

FIGURE 11.17   Counting occurrences in an array

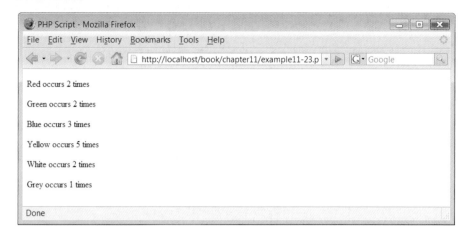

Sorting simple arrays

Functions sort( ) and rsort( ) are used to sort an array. Function sort( ) is used to sort an array in numerical or alphabetical order from lowest to highest. Function rsort( ) sorts the array from highest to lowest. The format of these functions is:

```
sort(array)
rsort(array)
```

Both functions require an array as a parameter and return the original array sorted. The following script illustrates the use of these functions:

```php
<?php
// File: example11–24.php

$arrColors = array ("Red", "Green", "Blue", "Yellow", "White");

echo "<p>";
foreach($arrColors as $strColor)
   echo "$strColor ";
echo "</p>";

sort($arrColors);
echo "<p>";
foreach($arrColors as $strColor)
   echo "$strColor ";
echo "</p>";

rsort($arrColors);
echo "<p>";
foreach($arrColors as $strColor)
   echo "$strColor ";
echo "</p>";
?>
```

The above script creates an array and displays it:

```
$arrColors = array ("Red", "Green", "Blue", "Yellow", "White");

echo "<p>";
foreach($arrColors as $strColor)
    echo "$strColor ";
echo "</p>";
```

The array is then sorted and then redisplayed:

```
sort($arrColors);
echo "<p>";
foreach($arrColors as $strColor)
    echo "$strColor ";
echo "</p>";
```

The array is then reverse sorted and redisplayed:

```
rsort($arrColors);
echo "<p>";
foreach($arrColors as $strColor)
    echo "$strColor ";
echo "</p>";
```

The output from the above script is illustrated in Figure 11.18.

Sorting multi-dimensional arrays

If you need to sort a multi-dimensional array, you can use the array_multisort() function, which looks like:

```
result array_multisort (array, flags)
```

The array_multisort() function returns true or false depending on whether the sort was accomplished successfully or not. It requires the array to sort and can also accept some flag parameters to affect how the sort is performed.

FIGURE 11.18   Output from sorting an array

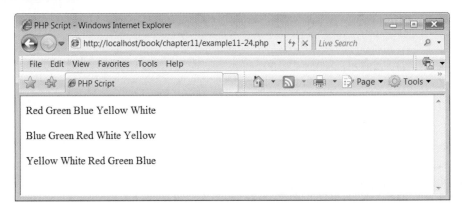

These flags are:

```
SORT_ASC – sort in ascending order
SORT_DESC – sort in descending order
SORT_REGULAR – compare items normally
SORT_NUMERIC – compare items numerically
SORT_STRING – compare items as strings
```

The following script illustrates the use of the array_multisort() function:

```php
<?php
// File: example11–25.php

$arrCars = array(array("Ford","Mazda","Renault","Vauxhall","Toyota"),
                 array("Blue", "Black", "Red", "Green", "Red"),
                 array(4,4,2,3,3)
);

echo "<h1>Unsorted</h1>";

for ($intCount=0;$intCount<5;$intCount++) {
    $strMake  = $arrCars[0][$intCount];
    $strColor = $arrCars[1][$intCount];
    $intQuantity = $arrCars[2][$intCount];
    echo "<p>Make: $strMake Color: $strColor Quantity:
            $intQuantity</p>";
}

echo "<h1>Sorted</h1>";

array_multisort($arrCars[0],SORT_ASC, SORT_STRING,
                $arrCars[1],SORT_ASC, SORT_STRING,
                $arrCars[2],SORT_NUMERIC);
for ($intCount=0;$intCount<5;$intCount++) {
    $strMake = $arrCars[0][$intCount];
    $strColor = $arrCars[1][$intCount];
    $intQuantity = $arrCars[2][$intCount];
    echo "<p>Make: $strMake Color: $strColor Quantity:
            $intQuantity</p>";
}
?>
```

The above script firstly creates the array and displays it in its unsorted form:

```php
$arrCars = array(array("Ford","Mazda","Renault","Vauxhall","Toyota"),
                 array("Blue", "Black", "Red", "Green", "Red"),
                 array(4,4,2,3,3)
);

echo "<h1>Unsorted</h1>";

for ($intCount=0;$intCount<5;$intCount++) {
    $strMake = $arrCars[0][$intCount];
    $strColor = $arrCars[1][$intCount];
    $intQuantity = $arrCars[2][$intCount];
```

```
    echo "<p>Make: $strMake Color: $strColour Quantity:
$intQuantity</p>";
    }
```

Next, the array_multisort() function is used to sort the array. The array is sorted on make, model and then quantity. The make and model are sorted in ascending order and are treated as strings. The quantity element is treated as numbers:

```
array_multisort($arrCars[0],SORT_ASC, SORT_STRING,
               $arrCars[1],SORT_ASC, SORT_STRING,
               $arrCars[2],SORT_NUMERIC);
```

Finally, the sorted array is displayed:

```
for ($intCount=0;$intCount<5;$intCount++) {
    $strMake = $arrCars[0][$intCount];
    $strColor = $arrCars[1][$intCount];
    $intQuantity = $arrCars[2][$intCount];
    echo "<p>Make: $strMake Color: $strColor Quantity:
            $intQuantity</p>";
}
```

The output from the above script is illustrated in Figure 11.19.

FIGURE 11.19 A sorted multi-dimensional array

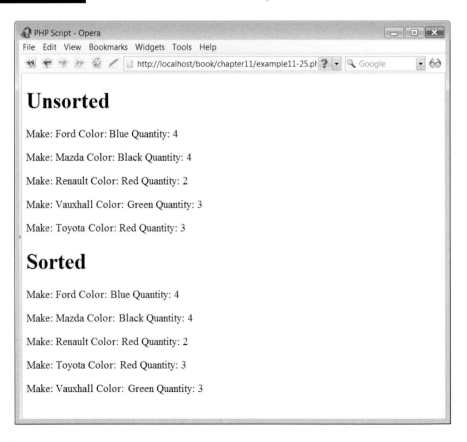

Exercises

11.1 Write a script which uses a form to allow the user to enter a string and then display each of the string characters in a single row table with the correct string character reference above it. Therefore with the string 'Simon', the output generated would look like this:

0	1	2	3	4
S	i	m	o	n

11.2 Write a script which uses a form to allow the user to enter in a password string. Your script should have an encrypted password as a constant value stored within a variable. You should determine if the newly entered password is the same as the encrypted one.

11.3 Write a script which amends the solution to Exercise 11.2 example above so that it uses a form to allow the user to enter their username and password which can then be checked against an array holding the names and passwords.

11.4 Write a script which uses a form to collect sales figures for an unknown number of sales people. The form should contain the following fields:

Sales person name
Monday
Tuesday
Wednesday
Thursday
Friday

The user can enter a sales person's data on the form and then click the submit button to enter another sales person's details. The form should also have a 'calculate' button which, when clicked, displays a table showing the weekly sales figures. Assuming there were three sales people called Simon, Joe and Lynn (the table below shows random sales data) the table might look this:

Day / Person	Simon	Joe	Lynn
Monday	34	54	12
Tuesday	3	145	76
Wednesday	56	24	45
Thursday	45	35	24
Friday	32	36	24

SUMMARY

In this chapter we began by re-examining strings and how they can be manipulated. We illustrated a variety of standard library functions which enable string manipulation, such as reversing a string or encrypting it.

We then introduced the concept of arrays and illustrated how to create simple arrays and multi-dimensional arrays in PHP. We examined how arrays need to be converted into strings to pass them via a form and finished by examining some of the functions in the standard PHP library which enable us to manipulate arrays, such as counting the number of occurrences of data within an array, sorting the array and implementing a stack.

References and further reading

Refsnes Data. PHP String Functions. http://www.w3schools.com/php/php_ref_string.asp
Tizag.com PHP Tutorial: Arrays. http://www.tizag.com/phpT/arrays.php

CHAPTER 12

Files, Cookies, Sessions and Email

LEARNING OBJECTIVES

- **To understand what a file is and how to open and close one**

- **To understand how to read data from a file**

- **To understand how to create a new file**

- **To understand how to use cookies**

- **To understand how to use sessions**

- **To understand how to upload files from a form to a server**

- **To understand how to generate email messages from within the PHP language**

- **To understand how to generate an (X)HTML email message**

INTRODUCTION

In this chapter, we concentrate on all things to do with 'files'. We begin by explaining what a file is and how they can be created. We illustrate how data in files can be read and how files can be a useful means of storing information in the long term. We also introduce how to manipulate simple files and examine some of the functions which PHP provides to make this easier to do. Then we investigate the role of cookies and sessions within the PHP environment and explain that while these are files they have very specific and important roles.

We examine how files can be uploaded to the server using a form interface. File uploading is very important if you want to implement a form-based, remote-document-sharing system. Next we introduce the concept of emails and how to create them in PHP. While you may not think of an email as a file, it is a document which is created and stored outside the PHP script and thus we felt it appropriate to include email in this chapter.

12.1 Files

Physically, a file is a sequential collection of characters which can be manipulated. Computers use files for all sorts of different things and so logically a file might be viewed as a collection of data records, a computer program, an email or a word document. Mostly, computers use files for storing information on a storage device such as a disk drive to access later. PHP includes a large collection of functions for the manipulation and creation of files. We begin by looking at how to open and close a file.

Opening and Closing a File

Before we can read the contents of a file or change or add data to it we need to open the file. Opening a file forms a link between the PHP script and the file itself. This link is maintained through a special type known as a resource. PHP uses a function called fopen() to open a file:

```
filestream = fopen (filename, mode);
```

The fopen() function requires the name of the file to open and a string indicating the mode in which to open the file. The function returns a file stream resource pointing to the opened file. Files can be open in a number of different modes and these are listed in Table 12.1.

Okay, but what is a file pointer? A file pointer is stored in the resource stream which is returned when a file is opened. The pointer 'points' to a location in the file. For example, when a file is opened to read its contents, the file pointer is at the start of the file and moves through the file with each successive read. In the case of a file which is opened for writing at the end, the file pointer points to the end of the file as that is normally where new data is written.

PHP allows you to open a file on the local machine as well as on a remote machine (if security permissions allow). Remote files can be accessed via HTTP or FTP connections.

TABLE 12.1   File open modes

Mode	Description
r	Open for reading only; place the file pointer at the beginning of the file.
r+	Open for reading and writing; place the file pointer at the beginning of the file.
w	Open for writing only; place the file pointer at the beginning of the file and truncate the file to zero length; if the file does not exist, attempt to create it.
w+	Open for reading and writing; place the file pointer at the beginning of the file and truncate the file to zero length; if the file does not exist, attempt to create it.
a	Open for writing only; place the file pointer at the end of the file; if the file does not exist, attempt to create it.
a+	Open for reading and writing; place the file pointer at the end of the file; if the file does not exist, attempt to create it.
x	Create and open for writing only; place the file pointer at the beginning of the file; if the file already exists, the fopen() function call fails.
X+	Create and open for reading and writing; place the file pointer at the beginning of the file; if the file already exists, the fopen() function call fails.

FIGURE 12.1   File pointers

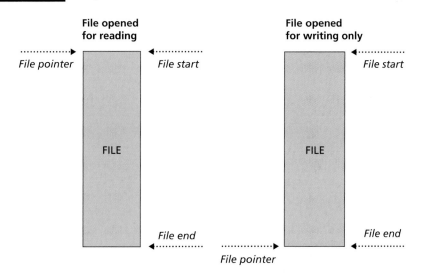

If the filename begins with http:// then an HTTP connection to the specified server is opened and a pointer to the requested file is returned.

Figure 12.1 illustrates the concept of a file pointer with files open in two modes.

Once you have finished accessing a file, you should close it to free up memory and inform the operating system that you have finished with the file. In PHP, the function fclose() is used to close a file:

```
fclose (filestream);
```

The fclose() function requires the resource stream of the file to close and returns true or false depending on whether it was able to close the file or not. The following script illustrates the use of these two functions in what is at the moment a rather useless example (we will improve it a little later):

```php
<?php
// File: example12-1.php

$fileTextFile = fopen ("text.txt",'a');

if (!fclose($fileTextFile) )
   echo "<p>Error closing file!</p>";
else
   echo "<p>File Closed</p>";
?>
```

There is no output from the above script (unless there is a problem with opening or closing the file).

NOTE   If you are running on a UNIX system then you need to ensure that you have the correct permissions in the directory to which you are writing.

Reading from a file

Single characters can be read from a file using the fgetc( ) function. This function has the following syntax:

```
character = fgetc (filestream);
```

The fgetc( ) function receives the file stream resource of the file to read and returns the character read from the file.

Before we go any further, let us create a text file to use in our examples. Create a simple text file containing the following text and save it as 'text.txt' in a sub-directory called 'files':

1. The quick brown fox jumped over the lazy dog.
2. The quick brown fox jumped over the lazy dog.
3. The quick brown fox jumped over the lazy dog.
4. The quick brown fox jumped over the lazy dog.

The following script uses the fgetc() function to read and display the first character of the 'text.txt' file:

```php
<?php
// File: example12-2.php

$fileTextFile = fopen ("files/text.txt",'r');

$strChar = fgetc($fileTextFile);
echo "<p>$strChar</p>";

if (!fclose($fileTextFile) )
    echo "<p>Error closing file!</p>";
?>
```

The output from the above script is:

1

To read the whole file we need to implement a loop construct. We also need some way of determining the end of the file. The feof() function can be used to check if the file pointer is at the end of the file. The function looks like this:

```
feof (filestream);
```

The function requires a file stream parameter and returns true or false depending on whether the end of the file has been reached. Let's modify our previous script to make use of this function and read the entire file:

```php
<?php
// File: example12-3.php

$fileTextFile = fopen ("files/text.txt",'r');
```

```
echo "<p>";
while (!feof($fileTextFile) ) {
    $strChar = fgetc($fileTextFile);
    echo "$strChar";
}
echo "</p>";

if (!fclose($fileTextFile) )
    echo "<p>Error closing file!</p>";
?>
```

In the above example, note the use of the 'while' loop and feof() function to control the iteration through the file:

```
while (!feof($fileTextFile) ) {
```

The output from the above script is shown in Figure 12.2.

'Ah, but' we hear you cry, 'why is the output in the browser not formatted with each line of the file on a separate line?' Well, the simple answer is that you haven't formatted the output in that way. In order to do this you should read a whole line of the file and output this with XHTML <br/> elements so that each line of the file appears on a separate line of the browser. The easiest way to do this is with another function, fgets():

```
string = fgets (filestream, length);
```

Function fgets() requires one parameter, but can accept two. The first parameter is the file stream to read and the second is an integer indicating the maximum number of characters to read in one go. The function reads into a string a number of characters up to the size of length, or until a newline character is read or the end of file marker is encountered. The function returns a string of the characters it has read.

 NOTE If the length parameter is not specified then the length defaults to 1 kB, or 1024 bytes.

FIGURE 12.2   Contents of a file

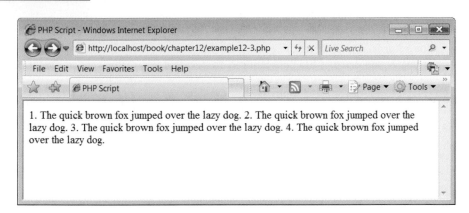

FIGURE 12.3 Formatted contents of a file

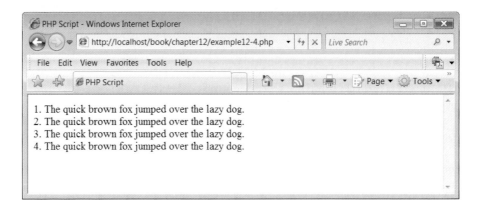

The following script is a modification of the previous one that uses the fgets( ) function and formats the output of the file to the browser:

```php
<?php
// File: example12–4.php
$fileTextFile = fopen ("files/text.txt",'r');

echo "<p>";
while (!feof($fileTextFile) ) {
   $strLine = fgets($fileTextFile);
   echo "$strLine<br/>";
}
echo "</p>";

if (!fclose($fileTextFile) )
   echo "<p>Error closing file!</p>";
?>
```

The output from the above script is illustrated in Figure 12.3.

Getting the size of a file

The size of a file in bytes can be easily found by using the filesize( ) function:

```php
filesize = filesize (filename);
```

The function returns an integer of the size of the file in bytes. This function is useful if you want to determine the size of a file, for example, to decide if you really want to read it or not.

Reading an entire file

You can read an entire file by using the fread( ) function:

```php
string = fread (filestream, length);
```

The fread( ) function consists of two parameters, the first of which is the file stream and the second is the number of characters to read. If this is set to the length of the file then the whole file is read in one go. The function returns a string of the file contents. The following script illustrates the use of this function:

```php
<?php
// File: example12–5.php

$fileTextFile = fopen ("files/text.txt",'r');

$intSize = filesize ("files/text.txt");
$strFile = fread($fileTextFile, $intSize);
echo "<p>$strFile</p>";

if (!fclose($fileTextFile) )
    echo "<p>Error closing file!</p>";
?>
```

The output from the above script is the same as that in Figure 12.3.

Creating a new file

So far, the examples have shown that files can be read and displayed. However, using PHP file-handling facilities you can also write data to files. The function fwrite() allows strings to be written to a file; its syntax is:

```php
fwrite(filestream, stringToWrite);
```

The fwrite() function requires two parameters, the first is the file stream and the second is the data to write to the file. The following script illustrates the use of this function:

```php
<?php
// File: example12–6.php

$fileTextFile = fopen ("files/newtext.txt",'w');

$strDataOne = "Simon";
$strDataTwo = "Elizabeth";

fwrite($fileTextFile, $strDataOne);
fwrite($fileTextFile, $strDataTwo);

if (!fclose($fileTextFile) )
    echo "<p>Error closing file!</p>";
else
    echo "<p>Closed Successfully</p>";
?>
```

The above script opens a new file for writing:

```php
$fileTextFile = fopen ("files/newtext.txt",'w');
```

Two variables are declared to hold strings which are going to be written to the file:

```php
$strDataOne = "Simon";
$strDataTwo = "Elizabeth";
```

FIGURE 12.4   Contents of the 'newtext.txt' file

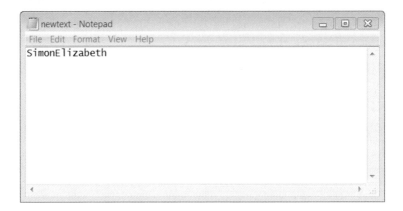

The two strings are written to the file:

```
fwrite($fileTextFile, $strDataOne);
fwrite($fileTextFile, $strDataTwo);
```

There is no browser output from the script but if you check the 'files' sub-directory, you should find a new file called 'newtext.txt' and when viewed should contain the data shown in Figure 12.4.

If you want the data 'records' you write to a file to appear on separate lines, you need to include the escaped characters '\r\n' at the end of each line. This is illustrated in the following script which is a simple modification of the one above:

```
<?php
// File: example12–7.php

$fileTextFile = fopen ("files/newertext.txt",'w');

$strDataOne = "Simon\r\n";
$strDataTwo = "Elizabeth";

fwrite($fileTextFile, $strDataOne);
fwrite($fileTextFile, $strDataTwo);

if (!fclose($fileTextFile) )
    echo "<p>Error closing file!</p>";
?>
```

The file should now contain the data formatted as shown in Figure 12.5.

Adding to an existing file

We can also add records to an existing file using the fwrite() function. Consider the following script:

```
<?php
// File: example12–8.php
```

```
$fileTextFile = fopen ("files/text.txt",'a');

$strDataOne = "Simon\r\n";
$strDataTwo = "Elizabeth\r\n";

fwrite($fileTextFile, $strDataOne);
fwrite($fileTextFile, $strDataTwo);

if (!fclose($fileTextFile) )
   echo "<p>Error closing file!</p>";
?>
```

After running this script, the 'text.txt' file should contain the data formatted as shown in Figure 12.6.

 NOTE If your file doesn't look exactly the same as the example in Figure 12.6, this could be because there wasn't an extra carriage return and new line on the last line of the original file.

FIGURE 12.5 Formatted contents of the 'newtext.txt' file

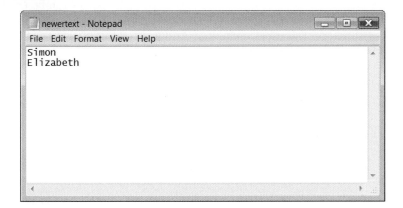

FIGURE 12.6 Amended contents of the 'text.txt' file

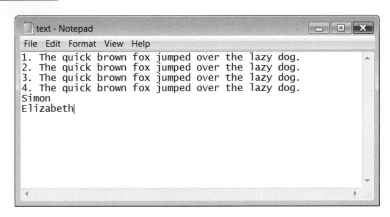

Checking if a file exists

To check a file exists, we use the file_exists() function:

```php
file_exists (filename);
```

The file_exists() function requires the name of the file to check for and returns true or false depending on whether the file is found. The following is a simple script to check if a file is present:

```php
<?php
// File: example5-9.php

if (!file_exists("files/text.txt") )
   echo "<p>File Doesn't exist!</p>";
else
   echo "<p>File Exists!</p>";
?>
```

12.2 Cookies

Cookies are a mechanism for a browser to store data on the client computer. Because the cookie is available the next time the web page is visited, cookies can be used to track or identify returning users to a web page. The important thing to remember about cookies is that they are stored on the client computer, as illustrated in Figure 12.7. Cookies are a type of file which is why we have included them in this chapter.

Browsers can control whether cookies can be written and thus you cannot guarantee that they are allowed. This is a major problem with cookies.

Creating a cookie

To create a cookie we need to use the setcookie() function:

```php
setcookie (name, value, expire, path, domain, secure)
```

FIGURE 12.7 Cookies are stored on the client computer

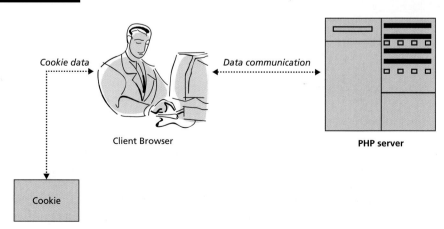

Cookie data

Data communication

Client Browser

PHP server

Cookie

Mode	Description
	TABLE 12.2 The setcookie() function parameters

Mode	Description
Name	Name of the cookie file
Value	Data to be stored in cookie file
Expire	Date string that defines the valid life time of the cookie
Path	Subset of URLs in a domain for which the cookie is valid
Domain	The domain for which the cookie is available
Secure	If set to '1' the cookie is only transmitted if the communications channel with the host is secure (https)

With the setcookie( ) function, all the arguments except 'name' are optional. If only the 'name' argument is present, a cookie by that name is deleted from the client. You may also replace any argument with an empty string ("") in order to skip that argument. Table 12.2 lists the setcookie( ) function arguments and describes their use.

The setcookie( ) function returns true or false depending on whether the cookie was successfully created.

When using cookies you need to know the following:

- Cookies do not become visible until the next loading of a page for which the cookie is visible. To test if a cookie was successfully set, check for the cookie on a next loading page before the cookie expires. Expiry time is set via the 'expire' parameter.
- Cookies must be deleted with the same parameters with which they were set.
- Cookie names can be set as array names and are available to your PHP scripts as arrays but separate cookies are stored on the user's system. You may wish to consider using the explode( ) or serialize( ) functions to set one cookie with multiple names and values.

The following script illustrates the use of the setcookie( ) function:

```php
<?php
// File: example12-10.php

$strValue = "Hello, this is a cookie";

setcookie ("TestCookie", $strValue);

echo "<p>Cookie Set</p>";
?>
```

The above script declares a string variable which it writes to a cookie called 'TestCookie'. There is no obvious output from the script so to see if we have successfully created a cookie and if we can read its data, then we need to know how to look at and access a cookie.

Cookie creation is part of the HTTP header which defines the (X)HTML script and so the setcookie( ) function must be called before any output is sent to the browser. If you are creating your script with all the valid (X)HTML document information, you may think that your script should look like this:

```
<!DOCTYPE html PUBLIC "-//W3C//DTD XHTML 1.1//EN"
    "http://www.w3.org/TR/xhtml11/DTD/xhtml11.dtd">

<html xmlns="http://www.w3.org/1999/xhtml" xml:lang="en">

<head>
<title>PHP Script</title>
<meta http-equiv="Content-Type" content="text/html; charset=ISO-8859-1" />
</head>
<body>
<?php
// File: example12-11.php
$strValue = "Hello, this is a cookie";
setcookie ("TestCookie", $strValue);
echo "<p>Cookie Set</p>";
?>
</body>
</html>
```

Unfortunately, the above script returns an error:

```
Warning: Cannot modify header information – headers already sent by (output
started at
/home/cs0sst/public_html/PHPLessonExamples/Lesson12/example12-11.php:11) in
/home/cs0sst/public_html/PHPLessonExamples/Lesson12/example12-11.php on line 14
```

This error indicates that the setcookie() function was not output before information was sent to the browser. This is indeed the case as all of the document header information was sent. In order to correctly produce a valid (X)HTML document with a cookie you need to set the cookie before the heading elements, like so:

```
<?php
// File: example12-12.php

$strValue = "Hello, this is a cookie";
setcookie ("TestCookie", $strValue);
?>

<!DOCTYPE html PUBLIC "-//W3C//DTD XHTML 1.1//EN"
    "http://www.w3.org/TR/xhtml11/DTD/xhtml11.dtd">

<html xmlns="http://www.w3.org/1999/xhtml" xml:lang="en">

<head>
<title>PHP Script</title>
<meta http-equiv="Content-Type" content="text/html; charset=ISO-8859-1" />
</head>
<body>
<?php
```

12

```php
echo "<p>Cookie Set</p>";
?>
</body>
</html>
```

In order to reduce space, we shall show the simple script forms.

Reading a cookie

Viewing and accessing cookies is easy. We mentioned previously that cookie variables could be accessed using the predefined $_COOKIE array and this is exactly how we shall access them. Remember that cookies do not become visible until the next loading of a page. To test if a cookie was successfully set, we need to check for the cookie on the next load of the page before the cookie expires. The script below illustrates checking for our cookie:

```php
<?php
// File: example12-13.php

$strCookieData = $_COOKIE["TestCookie"];

echo "<p>$strCookieData</p>";
?>
```

The output from the above script is:

```
Hello, this is a cookie
```

Deleting a cookie

Cookies can be deleted by simply using the setcookie( ) function with only the name of the cookie, for example:

```php
setcookie ("TestCookie");
```

Storing multiple data items in a cookie

One way of storing multiple variable data items within a cookie is to create a string with all preferred information stored within it and pass it as a single value to the cookie. We can then use the explode() function to extract all the information from the cookie. The following script illustrates the creation of the cookie's data:

```php
<?php
// File: example12-14.php

$strAddress = $_SERVER['REMOTE_ADDR'];
$strBrowser = $_SERVER['HTTP_USER_AGENT'];
$strOs = $_ENV['OS'];

$strInfo = "$strAddress::$strBrowser::$strOs";
setcookie ("AnotherCookie", $strInfo);
?>
```

The script obtains three predefined variables which hold the address of the client, the browser being used and the operating system:

```php
$strAddress = $_SERVER['REMOTE_ADDR'];
$strBrowser = $_SERVER['HTTP_USER_AGENT'];
$strOs = $_ENV['OS'];
```

These are combined and written to the cookie:

```php
$strInfo = "$strAddress::$strBrowser::$strOs";
setcookie ("AnotherCookie", $strInfo);
```

The next script illustrates the retrieving of the data from the cookie:

```php
<?php
// File: example12-15.php

$strReadCookie = $_COOKIE["AnotherCookie"];
$arrList = explode ("::", $strReadCookie);

echo "<p>IP Address: $arrList[0] </p>";
echo "<p>Client Browser: $arrList[1] </p>";
echo "<p>Operating System: $arrList[2] </p>";
?>
```

The above script reads the cookie data and 'explodes' the obtained string into an array:

```php
$strReadCookie = $_COOKIE["AnotherCookie"];
$strList = explode ("::", $strReadCookie);
```

Each element of the array is then displayed:

```php
echo "<p>IP Address: $arrList[0] </p>";
echo "<p>Client Browser: $arrList[1] </p>";
echo "<p>Operating System: $arrList[2] </p>";
```

The output from the above script is illustrated in Figure 12.8.

FIGURE 12.8   Multiple data from a cookie

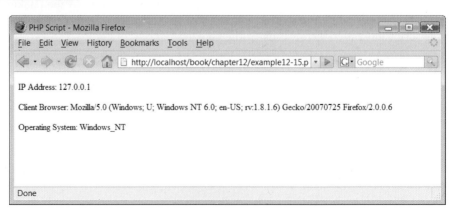

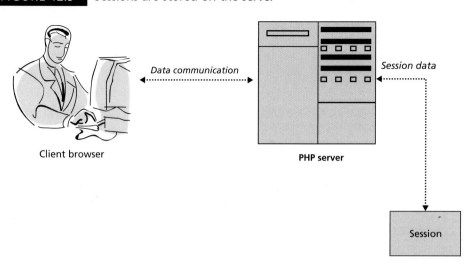

FIGURE 12.9   Sessions are stored on the server

Data communication

Session data

Client browser

PHP server

Session

12.3   Sessions

Sessions are similar to cookies in that they serve basically the same purpose – to preserve some data between pages on a web site. However, sessions differ from cookie in that they are stored on the server (see Figure 12.9) and are thus more secure as there is no data being passed back and forth between the client and the server. Furthermore, sessions work even if a user has disabled cookies on the client browser.

Essentially, sessions allow variables and their values to be stored for each and every user. The values of these variables can be different for every user and thus enable different users to be assigned different preferences. Sessions work by assigning a visitor a unique id, known as a session id. This is stored in a cookie by the user or is embedded as part of the URL. A session id looks something like this:

```
sess_f231be97d46fb1ca96c1323e88f4523f
```

On the server, a session file is created with the same name. This file is used to store the values of the variables assigned to the session. The contents of a session file may look like this:

```
intCount|i:18;strName|s:5:"Simon";
```

In the above example, 'intCount' is a variable, which has been stored in the session. Variable 'intCount' is of type integer and contains the value 18. 'strName' is a variable of type string and contains the value 'Simon'.

Starting a session

To create a session the first thing that we need to do is to invoke the session_start( ) function:

```
session_start ()
```

The session_start( ) function checks whether a session has been created for this user and, if not, creates one. If a session exists then all variables and their values are retrieved and are available for use. The function always returns true.

Session variables are registered using the $_SESSION associative array. For example:

```php
$_SESSION["intCount"] = 0;
```

The above line of code registers a variable called 'intCount' with the session. The following script provides an example of the use of a session variable:

```php
<?php
// File: example12-16.php

session_start();
if (!$_SESSION["intCount"])
    $_SESSION["intCount"] = 1;
else
    $_SESSION["intCount"]++;

echo "<p>You have accessed this page " . $_SESSION["intCount"] . "
times.</p>";
?>
```

The above script invokes the session_start() function to either create a new session or access an existing one:

```php
session_start();
```

If a variable 'intCount' has not been registered with the session, it is registered and set to 1:

```php
if (!$_SESSION["intCount"])
    $_SESSION["intCount"] = 1;
```

If the variable 'intCount' already exists, it is incremented by one:

```php
else
    $_SESSION["intCount"]++;
```

The value of the variable is displayed on the page, as shown in Figure 12.10.

12

FIGURE 12.10   Using a session

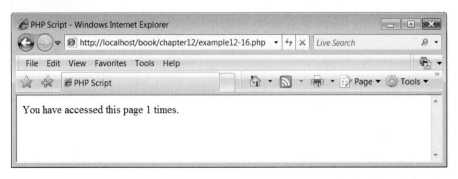

The effect of this script is to create a user-specific counter that records the number of accesses to the page that a particular user has made.

Session are like cookies in that they are part of the HTTP header, so the session-start( ) function must be called before any output is sent to the browser. If you were to include all of the correct DOCTYPE and header information in the above script, the creation of the cookie still needs to come before it. Therefore the full 'standard conforming' script looks like this:

```php
<?php
// File: example12–17.php

session_start();

if (!$_SESSION["intCount"])
   $_SESSION["intCount"] = 1;
else
   $_SESSION["intCount"]++;
?>

<!DOCTYPE html PUBLIC "-//W3C//DTD XHTML 1.1//EN"
   "http://www.w3.org/TR/xhtml11/DTD/xhtml11.dtd">

<html xmlns="http://www.w3.org/1999/xhtml" xml:lang="en">

<head>
<title>PHP Script</title>
<meta http-equiv="Content-Type" content="text/html; charset=ISO-8859–1" />
</head>
<body>
<?php
echo "<p>You have accessed this page " . $_SESSION["intCount"] . "
times.</p>";
?>
</body>
</html>
```

Using a session to set the page color

The following script illustrates the use of sessions to enable a user to set the colors used to display a web page. These colors remain the same until the user alters them:

```php
<?php
// File: example12–18.php

session_start();

if (!$_SESSION['strBgCol'])
   $_SESSION['strBgCol'] = "blue";
```

```php
    if (!$_SESSION['strTextCol'])
       $_SESSION['strTextCol'] = "yellow";

    if (isset($_POST["submit"]) ) {
       $strBgCol = $_POST["strNewBgCol"];
       $strTextCol = $_POST["strNewTextCol"];
       $_SESSION['strBgCol'] = $strBgCol;
       $_SESSION['strTextCol'] = $strTextCol;
    }
    else {
       $strBgCol = $_SESSION['strBgCol'];
       $strTextCol = $_SESSION['strTextCol'];
    }

    ?>
    <head>
    <style type="text/css">
    body {background-color: <?php echo $strBgCol ?>}
    p {color: <?php echo $strTextCol ?>}
    h2 {color: <?php echo $strTextCol ?>}
    </style>
    </head>
    <body>
    <h2>What Colors would you like?</h2>
    <form action='<?php echo $_SERVER["PHP_SELF"] ?>' method='post'>
    <p>
    <label for="strNewBgCol">Background Color: </label>
    <select name='strNewBgCol' id='strNewBgCol'>
       <option>red</option>
       <option>green</option>
       <option>blue</option>
       <option>cyan</option>
       <option>yellow</option>
    </select></p>
    <p>
    <label for="strNewTextCol">Text Color: </label>
    <select name='strNewTextCol' id='strNewTextCol'>
       <option>red</option>
       <option>green</option>
       <option>blue</option>
       <option>cyan</option>
       <option>yellow</option>
    </select>
    <input type='submit' name='submit'/>
    </p>
    </form>
    </body>
```

The script begins by registering a session:

```php
session_start();
```

Next, the two session variables are checked to see if they exist and, if not, two default values are created:

```
if (!$_SESSION['strBgCol'])
   $_SESSION['strBgCol'] = "blue";
if (!$_SESSION['strTextCol'])
   $_SESSION['strTextCol'] = "yellow";
```

If a form has been submitted (in other words, the user has altered the page's colors), then they are obtained:

```
if (isset($_POST["submit"]) ) {
   $strBgCol = $_POST["strNewBgCol"];
   $strTextCol = $_POST["strNewTextCol"];
   $_SESSION['strBgCol'] = $strBgCol;
   $_SESSION['strTextCol'] = $strTextCol;
}
```

Otherwise, the values stored in the session variables are obtained:

```
else {
   $strBgCol = $_SESSION['strBgCol'];
   $strTextCol = $_SESSION['strTextCol'];
}
```

Inside the header section of the page, a style is defined:

```
<head>
<style type="text/css">
```

Styles are set for the background color of the page and the text colour of the 'paragraph' and 'heading level 2' elements:

```
body {background-color: <?php echo $strBgCol ?>}
p {color: <?php echo $strTextCol ?>}
h2 {color: <?php echo $strTextCol ?>}
</style>
</head>
```

The remainder of the script outputs the form which allows the user to change the page colors. The output from the script is illustrated in Figure 12.11.

Un-registering session variables

Session variables can be unregistered. You may wish to do this to ensure that the session you have created is completely clear of any variable values. The unset() function clears a variable currently registered with the session and has the following format:

```
unset(variableName);
```

FIGURE 12.11   Changing a page color

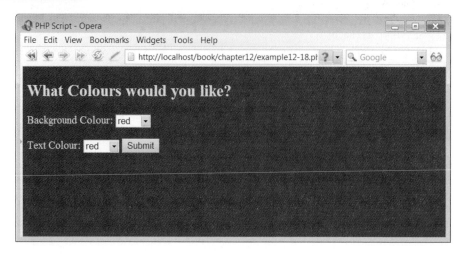

12.4 Uploading files from forms

We have shown in Chapter 10 that forms can be used to interact with the user. We introduced the various form field elements which we can use in this interaction. However, at that time we omitted to mention that there is an input 'file' type of element which allows users to submit an entire file from their local computer along with any form data. Being able to upload entire forms in this way is very powerful as it allows you to build dynamic web pages in which users from any location on the web can submit a document to your web server. What you do with this document when you have received it is up to you.

Creating the upload form

In addition to this extra input field type there are a few other changes we need to make to our 'form' construct in order to perform file uploads. Firstly we must insert the attribute 'enctype' into the form element with the value 'multipart/form-data'. This informs the server that the form may contain an uploaded file:

```
<form enctype='multipart/form-data' action='script' method='post'>
```

The input 'file' field should be included to create an input field in which we can browse for and select a file on the local machine to upload to the server. The format of this element is as follows:

```
<input type='file' name='myFileName'/>
```

Finally, it is good practice to include the maximum file size in bytes using a hidden field. In this field, the system variable MAX_FILE_SIZE is set to a certain value, thus limiting the maximum size of files which can be uploaded. An example of this is shown below:

```
<input type='hidden' name='MAX_FILE_SIZE' value='size' />
```

12

An example of a form with a file upload field is shown below:

```
<!--example12-19.htm -->

<form enctype='multipart/form-data' action='example12-19.php' method='post'>
<p><input type='hidden' name='MAX_FILE_SIZE' value='100000' />
<label for='strFile'>Document File: </label>
<input name='strFile' type='file' id = 'strFile'/>
<input type='submit' name='SubmitQuery' /></p>
</form>
```

NOTE Note that the above script contains no PHP and thus is saved with the extension .htm.

The output from the above script is illustrated in Figure 12.12.

You can enter the name and location of the file to upload in the form field, or you can click the Browse button to open a 'choose a file window' and locate and select the file to upload. This window is shown in Figure 12.13.

However, clicking on the submit button simply causes an error at this time as we haven't written the PHP script to handle the receipt of the file.

Creating the PHP upload script

There are many potential risks with scripts which access uploaded files. The potential for viruses and other malicious programs exists. In an attempt to overcome this, PHP file uploads have to undergo a number of steps to ensure their authenticity. Figure 12.14 illustrates these steps.

When a file is uploaded via a form, the file is stored in a temporary location. This location depends on your computer operating system. The file is stored using a temporary name created by PHP. A couple of environment variables are created to store the temporary

FIGURE 12.12   File upload form

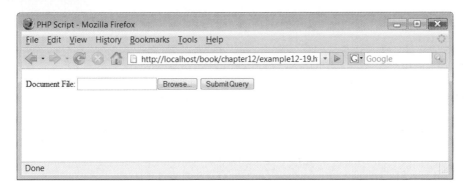

FIGURE 12.13   File browser window

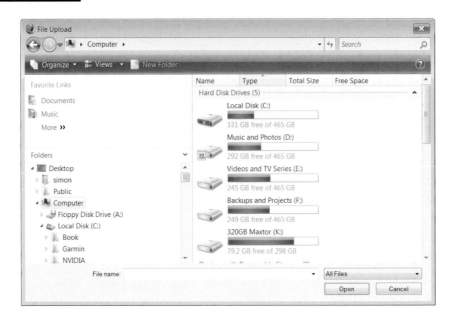

FIGURE 12.14   Uploading a file with PHP

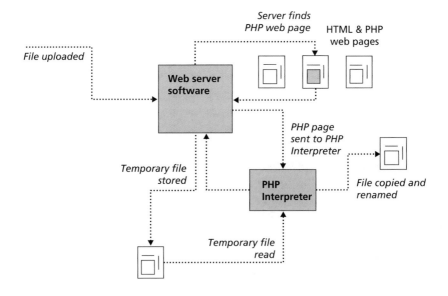

name of the file and the real name of the file. PHP contains some functions which enable you to determine if the temporary file was indeed uploaded via a PHP form and if so allow you to move the file to its final resting place with its original name.

We shall now examine the PHP statements which we need to implement to ensure that these steps are performed correctly. When the file is uploaded, the name assigned to the form field (in the previous example it was 'strFile') is used to store the temporary and real names of the files in an environment variable array called $_FILES.

The temporary file name and real file name can be accessed like this:

```
$strFilename = $_FILES['strFile']['tmp_name'];
$strRealname = $_FILES['strFile']['name'];
```

It is important to access this information as we need to use it to check whether this is a genuine file, which was uploaded correctly. To do this we use the is_uploaded_file() function:

```
is_uploaded_file(filename);
```

The is_uploaded_file() function returns a value of 1 if the file is a valid uploaded file, otherwise it returns a zero. If the file is genuine then it can be moved and renamed using the move_uploaded_file() function:

```
move_uploaded_file(filename, destination);
```

This function requires two parameters, which specify the temporary filename followed by the location to move the file and the name to store it as. Let us examine a simple example to show that these functions work as expected:

```
<?php
// File: example12-20.php

$strFilename = $_FILES['strFile']['tmp_name'];
$strRealname = $_FILES['strFile']['name'];

if (is_uploaded_file($strFilename) )
    if (move_uploaded_file($strFilename, "uploaded/$strRealname") )
        echo "<p>File uploaded successfully</p>";
    else
        echo "<p>Error: File not moved successfully!</p>";
else
    echo "<p>Error: Not an uploaded file!</p>";
?>
```

The script begins by assigning the name of the temporary file name to $strFilename and its original real file name to $strRealname:

```
$strFilename = $_FILES['strFile']['tmp_name'];
$strRealname = $_FILES['strFile']['name'];
```

Next, an 'if' statement is used in conjunction with the is_loaded_file() function to check if the file is a valid upload or not:

```
if (is_uploaded_file($strFilename) )
```

If the file is not a valid upload then the following message is displayed:

```
else
    echo "<p>Error: Not an uploaded file!</p>";
```

Otherwise another 'if' statement combined with the move_uploaded_file() function moves the file from the temporary location to its permanent location along with its original file name:

```
if (move_uploaded_file($strFilename, "uploaded/$strRealname") )
```

If the file could not be moved for whatever reason then an error message is displayed:

```
else
    echo "<p>Error: File not moved successfully!</p>";
```

Okay, so how do we access the file when we have copied it up? Well, we can browse to its location and view the file or we could write a small script to access the uploaded file.

 NOTE | If you are uploading to a UNIX computer then your upload path is likely to be different to that shown above.

Viewing the uploaded file

To allow us to view the files we have uploaded we are first going to amend our previous PHP script so that in addition to moving the file into the 'uploaded' sub-directory, we also record in a simple text file the name of the file which has been uploaded. We shall use this information in our viewing script. Here is the amended script:

```php
<?php
// File: example12-21.php

$strFilename = $_FILES['strFile']['tmp_name'];
$strRealname = $_FILES['strFile']['name'];

if (is_uploaded_file($strFilename) )
    if (move_uploaded_file($strFilename, "uploaded/$strRealname") ) {
        echo "<p>File uploaded successfully</p>";
        $fileTextFile = fopen ("uploadedfiles.txt",'a');
        fwrite($fileTextFile, "$strRealname\r\n");
        if (!fclose($fileTextFile) )
            echo "<p>Error closing file!</p>";
    }
else
    echo "<p>Error: File not moved successfully!</p>";
else
    echo "<p>Error: Not an uploaded file!</p>";
?>
```

You will need to change script 'example12–19.htm' so that the form calls this script ('example12–21.php') in order for this to work correctly.

The amendments to the script are all within the 'if' construct which checks to see if the file has been successfully moved. A file is opened for appending and the name of the uploaded file is written before the file is closed:

```php
$fileTextFile = fopen ("uploadedfiles.txt",'a');
fwrite($fileTextFile, "$strRealname\r\n");
if (!fclose($fileTextFile) )
   echo "<p>Error closing file!</p>";
```

The script now provides us with a list of files which have been uploaded. We can now write a simple script which allows us to see and view the files:

```php
<?php
// File: example12-22.php

$fileTextFile = fopen ("uploadedfiles.txt",'r');

echo "<h1>The following files have been uploaded</h1>";
while (!feof($fileTextFile) ) {
   $strLine = fgets($fileTextFile);
   echo "<p><a href='uploaded/$strLine'>$strLine</a></p>";
}

if (!fclose($fileTextFile) )
   echo "<p>Error closing file!</p>";
?>
```

The script is very simple. It opens the 'uploadedfiles.txt' file:

```php
$fileTextFile = fopen ("uploadedfiles.txt",'r');
```

Using a 'while' construct, it displays all the files uploaded:

```php
while (!feof($fileTextFile) ) {
   $strLine = fgets($fileTextFile);
   echo "<p><a href='uploaded/$strLine'>$strLine</a></p>";
}
```

The output from the above script looks something like that shown in Figure 12.15. Try clicking on the uploaded file links to see what happens.

FIGURE 12.15 File upload viewer

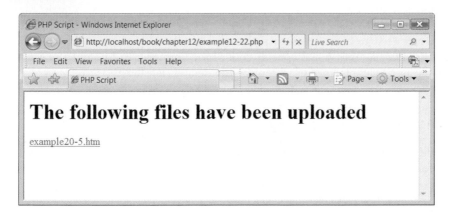

12.5 Emailing users

Email has become one of the key means of electronic communication. PHP includes function support for email creation and interactivity. In this section, we introduce the mail( ) function which is widely used within PHP scripts in order to send raw text, HTML and mime-type messages to one or more recipients at the same time. E-mail messages can be thought of as data streams (or files, if you like) and that is why we have included them in this lesson.

In addition to demonstrating how to use this function in its basic form, we shall also examine some of the mail( ) function's more advanced features.

Sending e-mail with PHP is very simple. In order to do it, we use the mail( ) function. This allows us to transmit the message from a source mail server to a target email account on the same or another mail server. In order to successfully use this function you must have access to a mail server.

The mail client that is to be used is defined within the php.ini file. By default the section of the php.ini file appropriate to mail is follows:

```
[mail function]
; For Win32 only.
SMTP = localhost
```

Depending on whether your PHP server is running on a UNIX or a Windows environment determines how you should configure this file. In the case of a Windows user, you must configure the location of your SMTP mail server and your email address. If you have a Google mail account then the address of your SMTP server is:

```
smtp.gmail.com
```

If you have a UK Yahoo! mail account it is:

```
smtp.mail.yahoo.co.uk
```

Change the php.ini file so that the SMTP is changed from 'localhost' to your SMTP mail server and save the file.

UNIX users need to enter the location of their sendmail application which is normally '/usr/bin/sendmail'. You should consult your service provider to find out the settings you need for your SMTP mail server to replace the default 'localhost'.

Sending a simple mail message

The mail( ) function can be used to construct a simple mail message. The format of the mail( ) function is as follows:

```
mail (to, subject, message, headers)
```

The mail( ) function consists of four attributes. The first attribute is used to specify the destination mail account where the message should be sent. The second attribute is the text which appears in the subject line of the message. The third attribute is the text which appears in the body of the message. Finally, the fourth attribute can be used to specify additional headers. Multiple extra headers are separated with carriage return and new-line characters (\r\n). The two main headers which concern us are the 'From:' header which specifies the real email address of the message we wish to send. Secondly, the 'Reply-To:' header specifies the reply address shown when the recipient clicks on the email message to send a reply. The following script illustrates the use of the mail function:

```php
<?php
// File: example12–23.php

$strEmail = "simon.stobart@sunderland.ac.uk";
$strSubject = "Hello";
$strMessage = "Hello Simon, how are you?";

$strHeaders = "From: simon.stobart@sunderland.ac.uk\r\n";
$strHeaders . = "Reply-To: simon.stobart@sunderland.ac.uk";

mail($strEmail, $strSubject, $strMessage, $strHeaders);
echo "<p>Message sent</p>";
?>
```

The script begins by defining the recipient of the email, its subject and the message:

```php
$strEmail = "simon.stobart@sunderland.ac.uk";
$strSubject = "Hello";
$strMessage = "Hello Simon, how are you?";
```

It then defines two headers which specify the from and reply-to parts of the email:

```php
$strHeaders = "From: simon.stobart@sunderland.ac.uk\r\n";
$strHeaders .= "Reply-To: simon.stobart@sunderland.ac.uk";
```

Finally, invoking the mail( ) function creates the email and sends it on its way:

```php
mail($strEmail, $strSubject, $strMessage, $strHeaders);
```

The output from the above script generated on the web page is:

```
Message sent
```

However, illustrated in Figure 12.16 is the email that is produced.

Sending (X)HTML email messages

PHP allows us to create more complex emails which, instead of simply including raw text, allow us to insert (X)HTML code into the message part of the email. Inserting (X)HTML allows us to have far greater control over the look and feel of the e-mail which is sent. However, it is important to note that not all email clients support (X)HTML emails and even for those that do, many individuals choose to turn off this facility.

FIGURE 12.16   A simple email

Simply including (X)HTML elements in the message body is not the end of the story however. To make this work we also need to include some additional header information, like this:

```
$headers = "MIME-Version: 1.0\r\n";
$headers .= "Content-type: text/html; charset=iso-8859-1\r\n";
```

MIME stands for multipurpose Internet mail extensions. MIME extends the format of Internet mail to allow more sophisticated non-text-based e-mail messages. The e-mail client needs to know what version of MIME we are using so the MIME header defines the MIME version. The Content-type header is a mandatory header which specifies the format of the message body (in this case text and html) and the character set being used. The following script illustrates an example of a script creating an (X)HTML email message:

```php
<?php
// File: example12-24.php

$strEmail = "simon.stobart@sunderland.ac.uk";
$strSubject = "Sales Figures";
$strMessage = "
<html>
<head>
<style type='text/css'>
body {background-color: white}
tr {color: white;
   background-color: blue}
h1 {color: black}
</style>
</head>

<body>
<div align=\"center\">
```

```
<h1>Weekly Sales Figures</h1>
<table width=\"385\">
    <tr>
      <td>Mon</td><td>Tue</td><td>Wed</td><td>Thu</td><td>Fri</td>
    </tr>
    <tr>

<td>£100,000</td><td>£89,000</td><td>£67,000</td><td>£120,400</td><td>
£101,800</td>
    </tr>
  </table>
</div>
</body>
</html>
";

$strHeaders = "MIME-Version: 1.0\r\n";
$strHeaders .= "Content-type: text/html; charset=iso-8859-1\r\n";
$strHeaders .= "From: simon.stobart@sunderland.ac.uk\r\n";
$strHeaders .= "Reply-To: simon.stobart@sunderland.ac.uk";
echo "<p>Message sent</p>";
mail($strEmail, $strSubject, $strMessage, $strHeaders);
?>
```

The above script begins by defining the recipient of the email and the email subject:

```
$strEmail = "simon.stobart@sunderland.ac.uk";
$strSubject = "Sales Figures";
```

The message is created with (X)HTML elements:

```
$strMessage = "
<html>
<head>
<style type='text/css'>
body {background-color: white}
tr {color: white;
    background-color: blue}
h1 {color: black}
</style>
</head>

<body>
<div align=\"center\">
<h1>Weekly Sales Figures</h1>
<table width=\"385\">
    <tr>
      <td>Mon</td><td>Tue</td><td>Wed</td><td>Thu</td><td>Fri</td>
    </tr>
    <tr>

<td>£100,000</td><td>£89,000</td><td>£67,000</td><td>£120,400</td><td>
```

```
£101,800</td>
      </tr>
    </table>
</div>
</body>
</html>
";
```

Next, the special MIME headers are included:

```
$strHeaders = "MIME-Version: 1.0\r\n";
$strHeaders .= "Content-type: text/html; charset=iso-8859-1\r\n";
```

These are followed by the from and reply-to headers:

```
$strHeaders .= "From: simon.stobart@sunderland.ac.ukr\n";
$strHeaders .= "Reply-To: simon.stobart@sunderland.ac.uk";
```

Finally, the message is sent:

```
mail($strEmail, $strSubject, $strMessage, $strHeaders);
```

The output from the above script generated on the web page is:

```
Message sent
```

However, illustrated in Figure 12.17 is the email that is produced.

Exercises

12.1 Write a script which reads a text file, character by character, and write these characters to a new file, thus making a copy of the original.

12.2 Write a script which amends 'example12-19.php' so that it uses a form interface for the user to supply the name and location of the file to check for its existence.

12.3 Write a script which uses sessions to allow the user to control the percentage size of the 'paragraph' and 'heading level 2' text. The script should use a form to allow the user to select 50%, 75%, 100%, 125% and 150% text font sizes.

12.4 Write a script which allows users to upload word-processed documents to a directory and then allows users to view the list of uploaded documents. You can assume that a word-processed document has the extension .'doc' and you need to check for this.

SUMMARY

In this chapter, we began by introducing the concept of files. We explained what a file is and how they can be created. We illustrated how data in files can be read and how files can be a useful means of storing information in the long term. Next we introduced cookies and sessions within the PHP environment and explained that, while these are files, they have very specific and important roles. We examined how files can be uploaded to the server using a form interface. We concluded by examining how e-mails can be created from with PHP.

12

References and further reading

Brain, M. Cookies. http://www.howstuffworks.com/cookie.htm
Ratschiller, T. (2000) Session Handling with PHP4. http://devzone.zend.com/node/view/id/1312
Yank, K. (2002) Advanced Email in PHP http://www.sitepoint.com/article/advanced-email-php
Wikipedia. Computer Files. http://en.wikipedia.org/wiki/Computer_file

CHAPTER 13

Functions, Dates and Times and Redirection

LEARNING OBJECTIVES

- **To understand what functions are and how to create them**

- **To understand the concept of variable scope**

- **To be able to pass arguments to functions**

- **To be able to use default arguments with functions**

- **To be able to return a value from a function**

- **To understand the difference between passing by value and passing by reference**

- **To understand what 'includes' and 'requires' allow you to achieve**

- **To be able to obtain the time and date**

- **To be able to produce and use a random number**

- **To understand how to check a page's referral page**

- **To understand how to redirect a user to a new page**

INTRODUCTION

In this chapter, we firstly examine how to create our own functions. In many of our previous script examples we have used functions which have been written by someone else and provided as part of the PHP function library. It is now time for us to learn how to create our own and see some examples of why they are so powerful. Next we look at file includes. These allow us to divide up a PHP script into separate parts and include only those we wish to use in the current situation.

Then we introduce dates, times and random numbers and explain why they are so powerful and assist us in developing creative and useful scripts. Next, we examine how to check the name of the web page which is invoking the new script. This is a very important security feature as we can ensure that login security is not easily bypassed. Finally, we learn how to redirect a user from one web page to another.

13.1 Functions

A function is a block of script which is invoked only when the function is called. If the function is never invoked, the script associated with the function is never executed. Functions are very powerful as they allow us to break up our code into modular chunks and thus aid script design. As a function can be invoked as many times as you wish from any point in your script they also help reduce the amount of code required to be written for an application as the code within a function can be 'reused' time and time again within the script. We have used functions before throughout many of our examples previously, but these were functions written by others for us to use. We are going to learn how to create our own functions. The great thing is that they operate in exactly the same way as the functions you have been using and, once written, you can share them with others to make their programming life easier in the same way that the PHP developers shared their function library with you.

We know that all functions can receive a number of arguments which are passed to the function for processing. We also know from our past use of defined functions that a function can return us a single function. This is illustrated in Figure 13.1.

Functions do not have to receive any arguments nor do they have to return a value. They can simply consist of user-defined PHP statements.

User-defined functions

When we wish to define our own function we need to do this using the 'function' keyword and the following syntax:

```
function name (arguments . . .) {
   . . .
   . . .
}
```

A function is defined with the keyword 'function' followed by the unique name of the function. Every function has to have a unique name. The function name is then followed

FIGURE 13.1 Function invocation

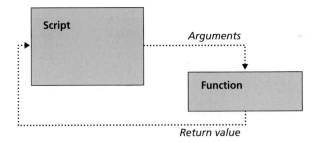

by a pair of parentheses which enclose a comma-separated list of arguments (if there are any). The script statements making up the function are enclosed within braces.

 NOTE — Even if there are no arguments to a function then the parentheses still need to be included.

We shall examine how functions 'return' a value a little later. However, for now let us examine how to create a function:

```php
<?php
// File: example13-1.php

echo "<p>Fahrenheit To Celsius</p>";

function fahrenheitToCelsius() {
    $floFahrenheit = 212;
    $floCelsius = (5/9)*($floFahrenheit-32);
    echo "<p>$floFahrenheit<sup>o</sup>F = $floCelsius<sup>o</sup>C</p>";
}
?>
```

The above script defined a function called fahrenheitToCelsius() which receives no arguments. The associated script within the function converts a Fahrenheit temperature value into a Celsius one. However, when we run the script, the code within the function is not processed. The reason is that we haven't invoked the function. In the above script, we would do this with the call:

```php
fahrenheitToCelsius();
```

So, for example:

```php
<?php
// File: example13-2.php

echo "<p>Fahrenheit To Celsius</p>";

function fahrenheitToCelsius() {
    $floFahrenheit = 212;
    $floCelsius = (5/9)*($floFahrenheit-32);
    echo "<p>$floFahrenheit<sup>o</sup>F = $floCelsius<sup>o</sup>C</p>";
}

fahrenheitToCelsius();
?>
```

The output from the above script is:

```
212°F = 100°C
```

 NOTE — In PHP, it doesn't matter if the function is defined before or after the function invocation!

13

Variables and scope

You will note that the example function declares the value of $floFahrenheit within the function. This is not very practical as the function will always perform the same calculation. What we need is to define the value of $floFahrenheit outside the function so that we can adjust it, for example like this:

```php
<?php
// File: example13-3.php

echo "<p>Fahrenheit To Celsius</p>";

function fahrenheitToCelsius() {
    $floCelsius = (5/9)*($floFahrenheit-32);
    echo "<p>$floFahrenheit<sup>o</sup>F = $floCelsius<sup>o</sup>C</p>";
}

$floFahrenheit = 212;
fahrenheitToCelsius();
?>
```

In the above example the value of $floFahrenheit is defined outside the function:

```php
$floFahrenheit = 212;
fahrenheitToCelsius();
```

Unfortunately the output from the function doesn't work as it gives a weird:

$$^oF = -17.7777777778^oC$$

You may also get a couple of warning notices like this:

```
Notice: Undefined variable: floFahrenheit in
C:\wamp\www\PHPLessonExamples\Lesson13\example13-3.php
```

You can try moving the variable declaration and function call before the function like this:

```php
<?php
// File: example13-4.php

echo "<p>Fahrenheit To Celsius</p>";

$floFahrenheit = 212;
fahrenheitToCelsius();

function fahrenheitToCelsius() {
    $floCelsius = (5/9)*($floFahrenheit-32);
    echo "<p>$floFahrenheit<sup>o</sup>F = $floCelsius<sup>o</sup>C</p>";
}
?>
```

Unfortunately it still doesn't work and more warning notices may appear! The reason for this is the way functions have been designed to work. Functions are designed to be isolated from the rest of the script. Variables which are declared outside a function are not visible

13

inside a function. This is known as a variable's scope. Interestingly, a variable defined inside a function is not available outside the function either!

 NOTE Variables have a scope and this is generally inside a function or outside one!

Consider the following script:

```php
<?php
// File: example13-5.php

echo "<p>Fahrenheit To Celsius</p>";
function fahrenheitToCelsius() {
   $floFahrenheit = 212;
   $floCelsius = (5/9)*($floFahrenheit-32);
}

fahrenheitToCelsius();
echo "<p>$floFahrenheit<sup>o</sup>F = $floCelsius<sup>o</sup>C</p>";
?>
```

In the above script we have modified our previous example so that the echo statement displaying the conversion is outside the function. However, both the original value of $floFahrenheit and the calculated value of $floCelsius are within the function and so it should be of no surprise that the output is:

^{o}F = ^{o}C

Yes, you have guessed it, the script still doesn't work and warning notices may appear! In fact variable scope means that we can do things like this:

```php
<?php
// File: example13-6.php

echo "<p>Fahrenheit To Celsius</p>";

function fahrenheitToCelsius() {
    $fltFahrenheit = 212;
    $fltCelsius = (5/9)*($fltFahrenheit-32);
    echo "<p>$fltFahrenheit<sup>o</sup>F = $fltCelsius<sup>o</sup>C</p>";
}

$fltFahrenheit = 100;
fahrenheitToCelsius();
echo "<p>$fltFahrenheit<sup>o</sup>F </p>";
?>
```

In the above example we declare a variable $fltFahrenheit and assign it the value 100:

```php
$fltFahrenheit = 100;
```

We then invoke the function fahrenheitToCelsius():

```
fahrenheitToCelsius();
```

Finally, we display the value of $fltFahrenheit:

```
echo "<p>$fltFahrenheit<sup>o</sup>F </p>";
```

The output from the above script is illustrated in Figure 13.2. What this shows us is that although we have a variable called $fltFahrenheit declared outside the function and a variable with the same name declared inside a function they are treated as two completely separate variables and each has its values maintained.

In order to advance the use of functions, we need some means to allow functions to see variable values from outside the function. The method for accomplishing this is through the use of function arguments.

Creating a function with an argument

Arguments are used to pass values to functions. These can either be constants or variables declared outside of the function. Here is an example of our script modified to include an argument:

```
<?php
// File: example13-7.php

echo "<p>Fahrenheit To Celsius</p>";

function fahrenheitToCelsius($floFahrenheit) {
    $floCelsius = (5/9)*($floFahrenheit-32);
    echo "<p>$floFahrenheit<sup>o</sup>F = $floCelsius<sup>o</sup>C</p>";
}
fahrenheitToCelsius(100);
?>
```

There are two main differences to be aware of in the above script. The first is in the function definition, where the parentheses now surround the name of a variable called

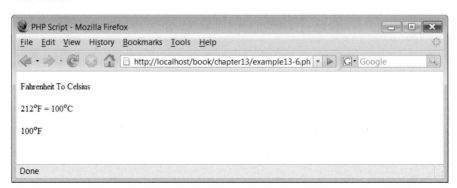

FIGURE 13.2 Variable scope

$floFahrenheit. This indicates that the function expects to receive a value when it is invoked, which it will store in the variable $floFahrenheit:

```php
function fahrenheitToCelsius($floFahrenheit) {
```

The second difference is the function invocation which now includes a constant value to pass to the function:

```php
fahrenheitToCelsius(100);
```

The result of the above script is a correct:

```
100°F = 37.7777777778°C
```

We can rewrite the script slightly to prove that we can pass a variable value:

```php
<?php
// File: example13-8.php

echo "<p>Fahrenheit To Celsius</p>";

function fahrenheitToCelsius($floFahrenheit) {
    $floCelsius = (5/9)*($floFahrenheit-32);
    echo "<p>$floFahrenheit<sup>o</sup>F = $floCelsius<sup>o</sup>C</p>";
}

$floFahrenheitOne = 100;
fahrenheitToCelsius($floFahrenheitOne);
?>
```

The above script illustrates two important things. Firstly that we can pass a variable directly to a function:

```php
fahrenheitToCelsius($floFahrenheitOne);
```

However, it also indicates that the name of a variable passed to a function doesn't have to be the same as the argument the function receives:

```php
function fahrenheitToCelsius($floFahrenheit) {
```

 NOTE When a function receives a value, it copies this into its argument and so it doesn't matter what name it is given.

Multiple arguments

Functions can be written to accept multiple arguments. The following script illustrates this by making our temperature conversion function a little more flexible. The function is now able to accept two arguments and make conversions either way between Celsius and Fahrenheit:

```php
<?php
// File: example13-9.php

echo "<p>Temperature Converter</p>";
```

```php
        function temperatureConvert($floTemp, $strType) {
            if ($strType == "F") {
                $floCelsius = (5/9)*($floTemp-32);
                echo "<p>$floTemp<sup>o</sup>F = $floCelsius<sup>o</sup>C</p>";
            }
            else {
                $floFahrenheit = (9/5)*$floTemp+32;
                echo "<p>$floTemp<sup>o</sup>C = $floFahrenheit<sup>o</sup>F</p>";
            }
        }
        temperatureConvert(100, "F");
        temperatureConvert(100, "C");
        ?>
```

The above script contains a function which is designed to receive two arguments. The first is the temperature value to be converted and the second a string indicating the type of temperature value being passed:

```php
function temperatureConvert($floTemp, $strType) {
```

If the temperature value is 'F' then the conversion to Celsius is performed:

```php
if ($strType == "F") {
    $floCelsius = (5/9)*($floTemp-32);
    echo "<p>$floTemp<sup>o</sup>F =
            $floCelsius<sup>o</sup>C</p>";
}
```

Otherwise the conversion to Fahrenheit is performed:

```php
else {
    $floFahrenheit = (9/5)*$floTemp+32;
    echo "<p>$floTemp<sup>o</sup>C = $floFahrenheit<sup>o</sup>F</p>";
}
```

The output from the above script is illustrated in Figure 13.3.

FIGURE 13.3 Multi-argument function

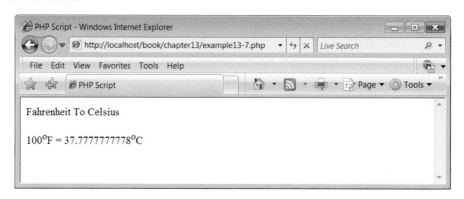

We can adapt the above script to illustrate that we can invoke functions from within a loop construct:

```php
<?php
// File: example13-10.php

function temperatureConvert($floTemp, $strType) {
    if ($strType == "F") {
        $floCelsius = (5/9)*($floTemp-32);
        echo "<p>$floTemp<sup>o</sup>F = $floCelsius<sup>o</sup>C</p>";
    }
    else {
        $floFahrenheit = (9/5)*$floTemp+32;
        echo "<p>$floTemp<sup>o</sup>C = $floFahrenheit<sup>o</sup>F</p>";
    }
}

echo "<h2>Some nice holiday temperatures:</h2>";
for($intCount=25;$intCount<40;$intCount++)
    temperatureConvert($intCount, "C");
?>
```

The output from the above script is illustrated in Figure 13.4.

Default arguments

Sometimes it is useful if functions have default arguments. This allows us to invoke a function without the need to pass all the arguments to it if we don't want to. Default arguments are assigned in the function declaration. Consider the following script which modifies our previous temperature conversion function. The modification assumes that if only the temperature is sent then the temperature type is Celsius.

```php
<?php
// File: example13-11.php

function temperatureConvert($floTemp, $strType = "C") {
    if ($strType == "F") {
        $floCelsius = (5/9)*($floTemp-32);
        echo "<p>$floTemp<sup>o</sup>F =
                        $floCelsius<sup>o</sup>C</p>";
    }
    else {
        $floFahrenheit = (9/5)*$floTemp+32;
        echo "<p>$floTemp<sup>o</sup>C =
                        $floFahrenheit<sup>o</sup>F</p>";
    }
}
echo "<h2>Some nice holiday temperatures:</h2>";
for($intCount=25;$intCount<40;$intCount++)
    temperatureConvert($intCount);
?>
```

Note that only one of the function arguments has a default value:

```php
function temperatureConvert($floTemp, $strType = "C") {
```

FIGURE 13.4   Functions in loops

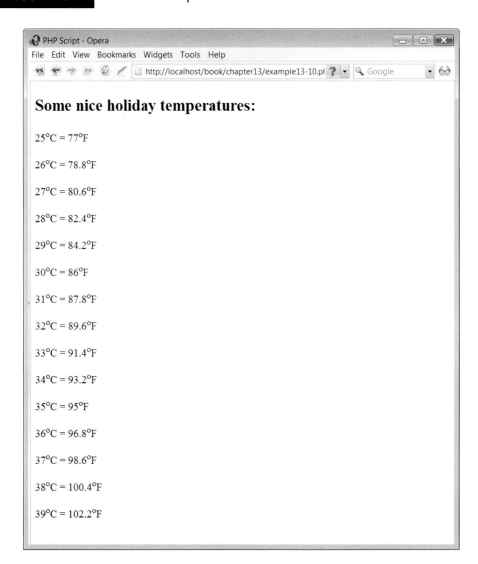

Also, note that the function invocation no longer specifies the temperature type:

```
temperatureConvert($intCount);
```

The output for the above script is the same as that shown in Figure 13.4. In some of our examples of user-defined functions, we have shown that we can pass values to the function and these can be used to affect the functionality of the function itself. What we have not yet seen is how we can return a value from a function.

Returning a value

The keyword 'return' is used to return a value from a function:

```
return value;
```

The function returns control to the location where it was invoked from when the keyword 'return' is encountered. Let us modify our script to illustrate a function return:

```php
<?php
// File: example13-12.php

function temperatureConvert($floTemp, $strType = "C") {
    if ($strType == "F")
        $floAnswer = (5/9)*($floTemp-32);
    else
            $floAnswer = (9/5)*$floTemp+32;
    return $floAnswer;
}

echo "<h2>Some nice holiday temperatures:</h2>";
for($intCount=25;$intCount<40;$intCount++) {
    $floFahrenheit = temperatureConvert($intCount);
    echo "<p>$intCount<sup>o</sup>C =
                $floFahrenheit<sup>o</sup>F</p>";
}
?>
```

The above script is a rewrite of the temperatureConvert() function so that it uses the keyword 'return' to return the answer to the temperature conversion:

```php
return $floAnswer;
```

The 'for' loop invoking the function is also slightly modified so that the value returned from the function is stored in a variable $floFahrenheit:

```php
for($intCount = 25;$intCount<40;$intCount++) {
    $floFahrenheit = temperatureConvert($intCount);
    echo "$intCount<sup>o</sup>C = $floFahrenheit<sup>o</sup>F</br>";
}
```

The output from the above script is the same as that in Figure 13.4.

 NOTE When the function has executed the flow of control of the program it returns to the point in the script immediately after where it was called.

It is possible to directly output the value returned from a function. Consider this modification to the above script:

```php
<?php
// File: example13-13.php

function temperatureConvert($floTemp, $strType = "C") {
    if ($strType =  = "F")
        $floAnswer = (5/9)*($floTemp-32);
    else
        $floAnswer = (9/5)*$floTemp+32;
```

```
        return $floAnswer;
    }
    echo "<h2>Some nice holiday temperatures:</h2>";
    for($intCount=25;$intCount<40;$intCount++)
        echo "<p>$intCount<sup>o</sup>C = " . temperatureConvert($intCount) .
                "<sup>o</sup>F</p>";
?>
```

The only difference between the above script and 'example13-12.php' is that the echo construct and function call have been combined:

```
echo "$intCount<sup>o</sup>C = " . temperatureConvert($intCount) .
"<sup>o</sup>F</br>";
```

Returning more than one value

We mentioned previously that functions within PHP cannot return more than one value. What is more correct is that they can return only a single type. Arrays can be used to 'get around' the issue of functions being able to return a single value.

The following script illustrates the use of an array to return more than one 'item' from a function:

```
<?php
// File: example13-14.php

function temperatureConvert($floTemp, $strType = "C") {
        if ($strType == "F")
            $floAnswer = (5/9)*($floTemp-32);
        else
            $floAnswer = (9/5)*$floTemp+32;

        $arrResult = array();
        $arrResult[] = $floAnswer;
        $arrResult[] = $strType;
        return $arrResult;
    }
    echo "<h2>Some nice holiday temperatures:</h2>";
    $floCelsius = 99.9;
    $arrResult = temperatureConvert($floCelsius);
    echo "<p>$floCelsius<sup>o</sup>" . $arrResult[1] . " = " .
                $arrResult[0] . "<sup>o</sup>F</p>";
?>
```

In this script the function temperatureConvert declares an array and assigns into the array the values of $floAnswer and $strType. The array is then returned from the function:

```
$arrResult = array();
$arrResult[] = $floAnswer;
$arrResult[] = $strType;
return $arrResult;
```

FIGURE 13.5   'Multiple' return values

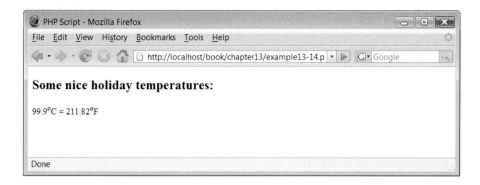

The function invocation receives the returned value from the function (which is an array) and accesses each of the values within the array:

```
$arrResult = temperatureConvert($floCelsius);
echo "<p>$floCelsius<sup>o</sup>" . $arrResult[1] . " = " .
$arrResult[0] . "<sup>o</sup>F</p>";
```

The output from the above script is illustrated in Figure 13.5.

Arguments passed by value

All of our examples of passing arguments to functions thus far are examples of passing by value. This means that a copy of the variable is passed. If that value is changed in the function, the value of the variable outside the function remains unchanged. Therefore this script:

```
<?php
// File: example13-15.php

function reverseIt($strString) {
    $strString = strrev($strString);
}

$strName = "Simon";
echo "<p>$strName ";
reverseIt($strName);
echo "reversed is $strName</p>";
?>
```

doesn't work as intended and produces the output:

```
Simon reversed is Simon
```

Arguments passed by reference

PHP supports passing a variable to a function 'by reference'. To pass a variable by reference, we simply include the character & before the variable name in the function definition. The passing of variables by reference permits the function to modify the original variable value. Consider the example below:

```php
<?php
// File: example13-16.php

function reverseIt(&$strString) {
        $strString = strrev($strString);
}
$strName = "Simon";
echo "<p>$strName ";
reverseIt($strName);
echo "reversed is $strName</p>";
?>
```

The above script outputs the following:

```
Simon reversed is nomiS
```

Calling functions within functions

Functions can invoke functions from within themselves. Consider the following script:

```php
<?php
// File: example13-17.php
function decimal($floNum) {
        $intNum = round($floNum, 2);
                return $floNum;
}
function multiply($floNumber) {
                $floNumber *= 3.12;
                echo "<p>$floNumber</p>";
                $floNumber = decimal($floNumber);
                echo "<p>$floNumber</p>";
}
$floNumber = 5.2234;
multiply($floNumber);
?>
```

In this script a floating point number is defined and passed to function multiply():

```php
$floNumber = 5.2234;
multiply($floNumber);
```

The function multiplies the number by 3.12 and then displays its current value:

```php
        $floNumber *= 3.12;
echo "<p>$floNumber</p>";
```

13

FIGURE 13.6 Output from a function calling another function

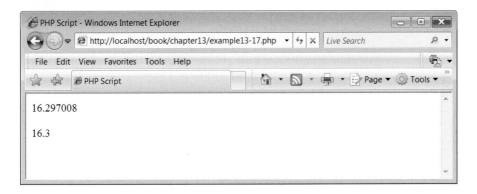

It then invokes function decimal(), passing it the value of $floNumber and assuming that the value is returned. Finally the number is displayed:

```php
$floNumber = decimal($floNumber);
echo "$floNumber";
```

Function decimal() receives the variable and using a predefined function round() rounds the value to two decimal places and returns this value:

```php
function decimal($floNum) {
    $floNum = round($floNum, 2);
        return $floNum;
}
```

The output from the above script is illustrated in Figure 13.6.

Recursive functions

A recursive function is one which calls itself. Recursive functions are useful in evaluating certain types of mathematical functions. The following example is a recursive function used to calculate whether a number is a power of 2:

```php
<?php
// File: example13-18.php

function isPowerOfTwo($intNumber) {
   if ($intNumber == 1)
     return "<p>yes</p>";
   elseif ($intNumber%2 == 1)
     return "<p>no</p>";
   else {
      $intNumber /= 2;
      return isPowerOfTwo($intNumber);
   }
}

echo isPowerOfTwo(256) ;
?>
```

13

In this example, the number 256 is checked to see if it is a power of two or not by passing it to the isPowerOfTwo() function:

```
echo isPowerOfTwo(256) ;
```

When the function is invoked an if statement checks to see if the number is equal to one. If so the value 'yes' is displayed. If not then another if statement is used to check if the remainder of dividing the current value of $n by 2 is equal to 1. If this is true then the value 'no' is displayed:

```
if ($intNumber == 1)
    return "<p>yes</p>";
elseif ($intNumber%2 == 1)
    return "<p>no</p>";
```

If the number does not satisfy either of these statements then it is divided by 2 and the function calls itself (by using the return keyword) and the process is repeated:

```
$intNumber /= 2;
return isPowerOfTwo($intNumber);
```

In this example the output generated is:

```
yes
```

13.2 Separating source files

Functions allow us to divide up our code into manageable pieces; however another way of dividing up code is to separate up a large PHP script into several smaller ones. This allows you to share and reuse parts of your scripts more easily.

Consider the following script:

```php
<?php
// File: example13-19.php

function temperatureConvert($floTemp, $strType = "C") {
    if ($strType == "F") {
        $floCelsius = (5/9)*($floTemp-32);
        echo "<p>$floTemp<sup>o</sup>F =
                      $floCelsius<sup>o</sup>C</p>";
    }
    else {
        $floFahrenheit = (9/5)*$floTemp+32;
        echo "<p>$floTemp<sup>o</sup>C =
                      $floFahrenheit<sup>o</sup>F</p>";
    }
}
?>
```

The above script is simply the temperatureConvert() function from a previous example. Now consider:

```php
<?php
// File: example13-20.php

include_once ("example13-19.php");

echo "<h2>Some nice holiday temperatures:</h2>";
for($intCount=25;$intCount<40;$intCount++)
    temperatureConvert($intCount);
?>
```

The above script uses the 'include_once' statement to include a copy of the 'example13-19.php' script at the point indicated. The output from this script is the same as shown in Figure 13.4.

 NOTE The difference between 'include' and 'include_once' is that 'include_once' will only include the file once even if asked to include it a second time.

The 'require' and 'require-once' statements operate in exactly the same way as the 'include' and 'include_once' statements operate. The only difference is in how they handle failure. With 'require' and 'require_once', if a file is not located then a fatal error is generated and execution of the script is terminated.

13.3 Getting the time and date

Being able to access the system time and date is a very useful ability. Dates and times can be used for a variety of tasks, from the simple activity of being able to display the correct date and time on your web page to creating a time stamp of when a database record was created.

Both the date and time can be accessed through a single function called getdate():

```php
array=getdate();
```

The getdate() function returns an array containing the current date and time. The array is a string-indexed array and the index values are described in Table 13.1.

The following script illustrates accessing the date using the getdate() function:

```php
<?php
// File: example13-21.php

$arrDate = getdate();

$intSeconds = $arrDate['seconds'];
$intMinutes = $arrDate['minutes'];
```

```
$intHours = $arrDate['hours'];
$intMonthDay = $arrDate['mday'];
$intWeekDay = $arrDate['wday'];
$intMonth = $arrDate['mon'];
$intYear = $arrDate['year'];
$intYearDays = $arrDate['yday'];
$strWeekDay = $arrDate['weekday'];
$strMonth = $arrDate['month'];

echo "<p>The time is $intHours:$intMinutes:$intSeconds</p>";
echo "<p>The date is $intMonthDay/$intMonth/$intYear</p>";
echo "<p>The month is $strMonth and the day of the week is $strWeekDay </p>";
echo "<p>It is day $intWeekDay out of 6 this week (with Sunday being 0)</p>";
echo "<p>There have been $intYearDays days so far this year.</p>";
?>
```

The above script invokes the getdate() function and then assigns each of the returned array elements into separate variables for the sake of clarity. These are then displayed on the web page, as illustrated in Figure 13.7.

NOTE	The time and date displayed on your computer will be different from those above, and depends on when you run the script.

Getting a more accurate time

The getdate() function returns the current time to the nearest second. While this is useful, you may need to get a more accurate time stamp and this can be achieved through the microtime() function:

```
timeString = microtime ()
```

TABLE 13.1   Contents of the date array

Index	Description
seconds	The seconds part of the current time
minutes	The minutes part of the current time
hours	The hours part of the current time
mday	Day of the month
wday	Numerical day of the week (Sunday = 0)
mon	Numerical month
year	Numerical year
yday	Numerical day of the year, e.g. 312
weekday	Textual day of the week, e.g. 'Monday'
month	Textual month of the year, e.g. 'May'

FIGURE 13.7   Date function

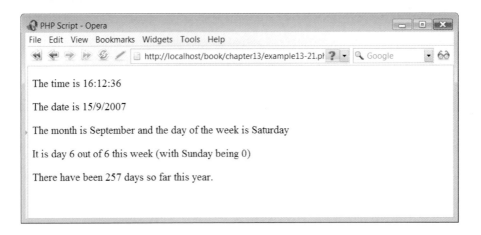

This function returns a string consisting of two parts:

```
'msec sec'
```

The value of 'sec' is the number of seconds, which have passed since midnight on 1st January 1970. The 'msec' part of the string is the microseconds fraction of the current second. Here is the function in a script:

```php
<?php
// File: example13-22.php

$strSecs = microtime();
echo "<p>$strSecs</p>";
?>
```

At the time of execution the output from the above script was:

```
0.29059500  1131475671
```

While we realize that the microtime() function does not seem very impressive it is actually very useful. We shall return to this function later in the chapter when we come to generate random numbers.

Checking for a valid date

Sometimes a user is required to enter a date via a form. It is good practice to check that the date is in fact valid although it is not immediately obvious, for example, which of the following dates are valid:

6,29,2005
13,19,2005
2,28,2005
2,29,2000

In actual fact the answer is:

Valid – 6,29,2005
Invalid – 13,19,2005
Valid – 2,28,2005
Valid – 2,29,2000

Luckly, the checkdate() function exists which returns true value if the date passed to it is valid and a value of false if it is not. The format of this function is:

```
checkdate (month, day, year);
```

The function receives three integer parameters, which represent the month, day and year of the date and returns true if the date is valid or false if it is not.

```php
<?php
// File: example13-23.php

$booDate = checkdate(2,29,1402);
if($booDate)
    echo "<p>This is a valid date!</p>";
else
    echo "<p>This is an invalid date</p>";
?>
```

The above script outputs the text:

```
This is an invalid date
```

NOTE	Note that the checkdate() function requires the date to be presented in the format of month, day, year.

13.4 Random numbers

In PHP there are two steps to generating a random number. The first concerns the seeding of the random number generator using the srand() function, the format of which is:

```
srand (seed);
```

The srand() function is used to set the random number generator to a random position before we start obtaining our random numbers. Failure to do this will result in a predictable set of random numbers To seed the random number generator, we need a large random number to begin with! One way of achieving this is to use the microtime() function to obtain the microseconds part of its output and multiply this to a large number (we told you that we would return to this function). We can do this with the statement:

```
srand( (double) microtime() * 1000000);
```

The above randomly seeds the random number generator with a random number produced from when the current time is obtained from the microtime() function. We are now ready to obtain random numbers and the function rand() enables us to do this. The format of this function is:

```
number = rand ();
```

The rand() function can be invoked without any parameters and this returns a random number, the maximum and minimum values of which are outside your control. However, you can limit the range of random numbers produced by including start and end parameters, like this:

```
number = rand (start, end);
```

The following script illustrates generating a random number between 1 and 6. This script could be therefore used to represent the role of a dice:

```php
<?php
// File: example13–24.php

srand( (double) microtime() * 1000000);
$intRandVal = rand(1,6);
echo "<p>Random Number: $intRandVal</p>";
?>
```

13.5 Fruit-machine example

We are going to put together the knowledge we have learned on the subject of functions and random numbers to create a fruit-machine script. The script uses some simple images to represent the fruits in our fruit machine. These are illustrated in Figure 13.8.

These images are stored in the 'graphics' sub-directory below where the script is stored:

```php
<?php
// File: example13–25.php

$arrFruits = array (1=>"apple", 2=>"orange", 3=>"lemon", 4=>"plum");

function randomNumber ($intStart, $intEnd) {
    srand( (double) microtime() * 1000000);
    $intRandVal = rand($intStart,$intEnd);
    return $intRandVal;
}

$strFirst = $arrFruits[randomNumber(1,4)];
$strSecond = $arrFruits[randomNumber(1,4)];
$strThird = $arrFruits[randomNumber(1,4)];

echo "<h2>Try your luck at the fruit machine &ellipsis;. . . </h2>";
echo "<table width='450'><tr>";
echo "<td><img src='graphics/$strFirst.gif' alt='$strFirst'/></td>";
```

```php
echo "<td><img src='graphics/$strSecond.gif' alt='$strSecond'/></td>";
echo "<td><img src='graphics/$strThird.gif' alt='$strThird'/></td>";
echo "</tr></table>";

if ($strFirst == $strSecond && $strFirst == $strThird)
    echo "<h2>You Win!</h2>";
?>
<form action='<?php echo $_SERVER["PHP_SELF"]; ?>' method='post'>
<p><input type='submit' value='spin'/></p>
</form>
```

The script begins by declaring an array of fruits:

```php
$arrFruits = array (1=>"apple", 2=>"orange", 3=>"lemon", 4=>"plum");
```

Function randomNumber() is defined to generate random numbers:

```php
function randomNumber ($intStart, $intEnd) {
    srand( (double) microtime() * 1000000);
    $intRandVal = rand($intStart,$intEnd);
    return $intRandVal;
}
```

Three random numbers between 1 and 4 are generated from invoking function randomNumber() and the corresponding array item is stored in its corresponding variable:

```php
$strFirst=$arrFruits[randomNumber(1,4)];
$strSecond=$arrFruits[randomNumber(1,4)];
$strThird=$arrFruits[randomNumber(1,4)];
```

The fruit images are output inside a simple table:

```php
echo "<h2>Try your luck at the fruit machine . . . </h2>";
echo "<table width='450'><tr>";
echo "<td><img src='graphics/$strFirst.gif' alt='$strFirst'/></td>";
echo "<td><img src='graphics/$strSecond.gif' alt='$strSecond'/></td>";
echo "<td><img src='graphics/$strThird.gif' alt='$strThird'/></td>";
echo "</tr></table>";
```

An 'if' construct checks if the fruits are the same:

```php
if ($strFirst == $strSecond && $strFirst == $strThird)
    echo "<h2>You Win!</h2>";
```

FIGURE 13.8 Fruit machine images

orange

lemon

apple

plum

FIGURE 13.9 Fruit machine

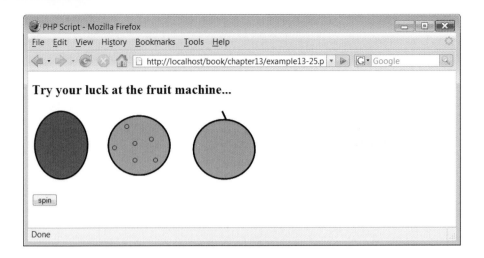

A simple form is used to allow the user to 'spin' the fruits again:

```
<form action='<?php echo $_SERVER["PHP_SELF"]; ?>' method='post'>
<p><input type='submit' value='spin'/></p>
</form>
```

The output from the above script is illustrated in Figure 13.9.

13.6 Page redirection and referral

Quite often you may wish to build a secure web page. You may create a login form and require that a user enters their username and password. You may check that these are correct by comparing them to a file or database (we shall show you how to do this later). If the username and password are valid then you may wish to direct the user to a new page for them to access. Otherwise the user will remain on the username and password form page.

User redirection can be performed using the 'Location:' string in the header() function:

```
header ("Location: webpage");
```

This basic form of web security is illustrated in Figure 13.10.

 NOTE Header functions, like those of cookies, must be called before any output is sent to the browser.

FIGURE 13.10   Simple login and redirection

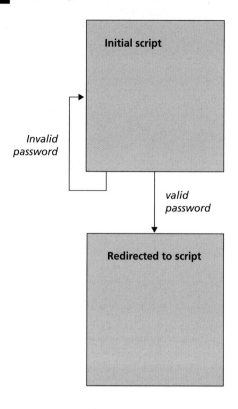

Let's create a simple page to illustrate redirection:

```php
<?php
// File: example13-26.php
if(isset($_POST["submit"]) ) {
    $strUserPass = array ( "john" => "red",
                           "simon" => "green",
                           "liz" => "blue",
                           "david" => "yellow");
        if (array_key_exists($_POST["strUsername"], $strUserPass) )
            if ($strUserPass[$_POST["strUsername"] ] ==
                    $_POST["strPassword"])
                header("location: example13-27.php");
            else
                echo "<h1>Incorrect Username and/or password!</h1>";
}
?>
<form name="form1" method="post" action="">
<p>
<label for="strUsername">Username: </label>
<input type="text" name="strUsername" id="strUsername"/></p>
<p>
<label for="strPassword">Password: </label>
```

```
<input type="password" name="strPassword" id="strPassword"/></p>
<p><input type="submit" name="submit" /></p>
</form>
```

The above script determines if a form has been submitted and if so defines an array of user-name and passwords:

```
if(isset($_POST["submit"]) ) {
    $strUserPass = array ( "john" => "red",
                           "simon" => "green",
                           "liz" => "blue",
                           "david" => "yellow");
```

Next function array_key_exists() is used to check if the username key is present in the array. The function looks like this:

```
trueFalse = array_key_exists(Arraykey, Array)
```

In the script we write:

```
if (array_key_exists($_POST["strUsername"], $strUserPass) )
```

It then checks to see if the entered username and passwords match and if so redirects the user to a new page:

```
if ($strUserPass[$_POST["strUsername"] ] == $_POST["strPassword"])
header("location: example13–28.php");
```

Otherwise an error message is generated and the form is redisplayed:

```
else
echo "<h1>Incorrect Username and/or password!</h1>";
```

The output from the above script for an incorrect username and password is illustrated in Figure 13.11.

We shall also need to create a simple page to be redirected to:

```
<?php
// File: example13-27.php

echo "<h1>Well done, you are correctly logged in!</h1>";
?>
```

The output from the above script is shown in Figure 13.12.

All appears to be working well, however consider what happens if a user simply bypasses the login script and loads 'example13-27.php' directly. It works and the user has bypassed our security.

FIGURE 13.11   Incorrect username and password

FIGURE 13.12   Correct username and password

The solution to this problem is to ensure that your script checks the 'referrer' of the page, the name of the web page or script which passed the data to your script. If it is not the name you were expecting then you can ignore the data. The page referrer is the address of the web page or script which called the new script and its value can be found in this server variable:

```
$_SERVER["HTTP_REFERER"]
```

Because we know the name of the script from which the page should have come ('example13-26.php'), we can amend our 'example13-27.php' script to check for this:

```php
<?php
// File: example13-28.php

if (!$_SERVER["HTTP_REFERER"] != "http://localhost/example13-26.php")
    header("location: example13-26.php");
echo "<h1>Well done, you are correctly logged in!</h1>";
?>
```

Header redirects are like cookies and sessions in that they are part of the HTTP header, so the header( ) function must be called before any output is sent to the browser. If you were to include all of the correct DOCTYPE and header information in the above script the creation of a cookie still needs to come before this. Therefore the full 'standard conforming' script looks like this:

```php
<?php
// File: example13-28.php

if ($_SERVER["HTTP_REFERER"]
! = "http://localhost/book/chapter13/example13-26.php")
   header("location: example13-26.php");
?>
<!DOCTYPE html PUBLIC "-//W3C//DTD XHTML 1.1//EN"
   "http://www.w3.org/TR/xhtml11/DTD/xhtml11.dtd">

<html xmlns="http://www.w3.org/1999/xhtml" xml:lang="en">
<head>
<title>PHP Script</title>
<meta http-equiv="Content-Type" content="text/html; charset=ISO-8859-1" />
</head>
<body>
<h1>Well, done you are correctly logged in!</h1>
</body>
</html>
```

Exercises

13.1 Write a script to implement a function which will convert centimetres to inches and inches to centimetres. The formula for conversion is:

1 centimeter = 0.393700787 inches

13.2 Rewrite the Roman to Arabic date conversion program that you were presented with in an earlier lesson so that it makes use of functions.

13.3 Create a script which implements the 'Drunk on a Bridge' problem. Basically the drunk starts in the middle of the bridge and randomly staggers to the left or right until he reaches the left or right hand side of the bridge. The size of the bridge is up to you.

The drunk and bridge graphics can be very simple:

FIGURE 13.13 Drunk on a bridge

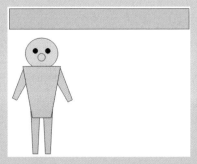

13.4 Write a script which amends 'example13–26.php' so that the username and passwords are stored in and read from a file.

SUMMARY

In this chapter we began by examining how to create our own user-defined functions. We introduced the concept of variable scope and illustrated how functions can receive arguments and return a value. Following this we introduced file 'include' statements and illustrated how they can be used to divide up complex scripts and assist in component reuse. We then introduced dates, times and random numbers and explained why they are useful. We concluded the chapter by examining how to check the referrer web page and how to redirect a web page to another automatically.

References and further reading

Gilfillan, I. (2002) Date and Time in PHP http://www.wdvl.com/Authoring/Languages/PHP/ Date_Time/

Hioxindia.com. Dates and Time in PHP http://www.hscripts.com/tutorials/php/dateAndTime.php

Wikipedia. Subroutines (Functions) http://en.wikipedia.org/wiki/Subroutine

CHAPTER 14

Databases

LEARNING OBJECTIVES

- **To understand what a relational database is and what tables and fields are**

- **To understand the different types that a field can be set to in MySQL**

- **To be able to create a database using PhpMyAdmin**

- **To understand the concept of database keys**

- **To be able to create a table using PhpMyAdmin**

- **To be able to populate and edit a table of data using PhpMyAdmin**

- **To be able to export a database backup dump file**

INTRODUCTION

So far we have learned quite a lot about the PHP language but we have not examined one of PHP's greatest strengths – its ability to interface to a database management system. In doing this a PHP script is able to extract, store, amend and delete data in a database. Being able to link a dynamic scripting language such as PHP to a database unlocks a huge amount of power in the PHP language and allows us to create very powerful web-enabled applications.

However, before we can illustrate how PHP interacts with a database, we first need to introduce the database management system we are going to use and explain how to interact with it in order to setup a database that PHP can access. In this chapter, we introduce the concept of databases and show you how to create a database which we use in Chapter 15.

14.1 Databases

What is a database?

A database is a structured collection of data. Databases occurred in the real world before computers were invented. Examples of real-world databases include:

- guide to TV programme times
- Filing cabinet of documents
- Telephone directory

A computer-based database is used to store structured information which can be retrieved and examined quickly and easily. Examples of computer-based databases are:

- DVLA – Driver and Vehicle Licensing Agency, which stores information of all vehicles registered within the UK.
- HOLMES – Home Office Large Major Enquiry System, which stores data on offenders and suspects involved with current and previous police investigations.

A database is essentially a much more sophisticated implementation of the flat files, which we introduced in Chapter 12. What makes a database so convenient is that the database manages the storage and retrieval of data to and from the database and hides the complexity of what is actually going on from the database user. The thing which manages the interface between the data in the database and the user is known as the database management system.

The database management system (DBMS) is the software that facilitates the creation and maintenance of a computerized database. In general, the DBMS enables:

- The management of large amounts of data.
- Access to the data using a query language.
- Provision of some form of security to the data.
- Multiple database access for users.
- Access to multiple databases.

We are going to use a database management system called MySQL. MySQL is a very powerful database management system and works extraordinarily well with PHP. You can find all about MySQL at http://www.mysql.com.

MySQL is, in fact, a relational database management system. A relational database stores data in separate tables instead of one single store. In theory, this provides a faster, more flexible database system.

Relational database fields and tables

In relational database systems such as MySQL, data is organized into tables. A database table is very similar to a table inserted into a word-processed document as a database table

14

consists of both rows and columns. Columns are often referred to as 'fields' and are used to delimit the data structure into the correct order. The rows in a database table are where the records are stored. A database table also has a unique name assigned to it within a specific database. A simple database table is illustrated in Figure 14.1.

If we look at Figure 14.1, we see that it contains a table called Customers. This table consists of three column fields of data entitled Title, Surname and Firstname. The data (there is none at the moment) will be inserted into each of these fields forming a number of record rows within the table. These rows are referred to as the table records. Figure 14.2 illustrates our database table populated with some records.

Relational databases can contain many different tables of data. For example, Figure 14.3 illustrates a Products table with some records.

One thing to note from Figure 14.3 is that the number of fields in each table within a database can vary. In the Products table we have four fields: name, description, quantity and cost.

FIGURE 14.1 Customers table

Customers		
Title	Surname	Firstname

FIGURE 14.2 Customers table with records

Customers		
Title	Surname	Firstname
Mrs	Smith	Lynne
Miss	Jones	Ann
Mr	Brown	Simon
Mr	Smith	David
Mr	Bell	Peter
Ms	Hall	Liz
Mr	Smith	Kevin
Mr	Jones	Jack
Mr	Green	William
Mrs	Smith	Lynne
Mr	Bell	Simon
Mr	Brown	Ian

FIGURE 14.3 Products table with records

Products			
Name	Description	Quantity	Cost
Beer Glass	600 ml Beer Glass	345	3.99
Wine Glass	125 ml Wine Glass	236	2.99
Wine Glass	175 ml Wine Glass	436	3.50
Shot Glass	50 ml Small Glass	132	1.50
Spirit Glass	100 ml Short Glass	489	2.50
Long Glass	200 ml Tall Glass	263	2.50
Beer Glass	300 ml Beer Glass	247	2.99
Wine Glass	225 ml Wine Glass	96	3.99

TABLE 14.1 Text field types

Type	Maximum Length	Description
varchar	255 characters	Variable-length text field type
char	255 characters	Fixed-length text field type
tinytext	255 characters	Variable-length text field type
text	65,535 characters	Variable-length text field type
mediumtext	16,777,215 characters	Variable-length text field type
longtext	4,294,967,295 characters	Variable-length text field type
enum	65,535 characters	Potential values of a text field

Database field types

Database fields are what defines the structure of the data within a table. Like variables, database fields can be defined as being of different types. To make things a little more complex, the types that the database fields can be defined as are not always the same as the programming language being used to access the database. In the MySQL database management system, quite a few field types can be defined. These are listed in Tables 14.1, 14.2 and 14.3.

Looking back to our Customers and Products tables, we can think about what types we should assign to each of our database fields. In the case of the Customers table, we would recommend the following types:

Title   varchar (10)
Surname   varchar (100)
Firstname   varchar (100)

In the case of the Products table:

Name   varchar (255)
Description text
Quantity   int
Cost   float

14

TABLE 14.2   Numeric field types

Type	Maximum Length	Description
int	4,294,967,295	Signed or unsigned numeric field type
tinyint	255	Signed or unsigned numeric field type
mediumint	16,777,215	Signed or unsigned numeric field type
bigint	18,446,744,073,709	Signed or unsigned numeric field type
float	-	Signed floating-point numeric field type
double	-	Signed floating-point numeric field type
decimal	-	Signed numeric field type (numbers stored as characters)

TABLE 14.3   Date and time field types

Type	Range	Description
date	1001-01-01 to 9999-12-31	Date format: YYYY-MM-DD
time	-838:59:59 to 838:59:59	Time format
datetime	1001-01-01 00:00:00 to 9999-12-31 23:59:59	Date–time format: YYYY-MM-DD HH:MM:SS
timestamp	2 to 14 digits	Numeric values to represent different types of Unix timestamp
year	1901 to 2155	Four digits (or two digits) to represent a year.

The numbers in parentheses after the varchar field types define the maximum number of characters which can be stored in that field. Therefore in the case of the Title field only 10 characters is specified as we will only store data such as 'Mr', 'Mrs', 'Doctor' and 'Professor' for example. However, in the case of Surname, a total of 100 characters is specified as we wish to store customer's surnames, some of which could be quite long.

14.2 phpMyAdmin interface

MySQL is a very powerful database management system and we will only just scratch the surface of it in these chapters. MySQL can be controlled through a simple command-line interface, however to make life more easy for us we are going to use a graphical user interface which is accessible through a web browser. This interface is known as phpMyAdmin (because it is written in PHP) and is illustrated in Figure 14.4.

More information on phpMyAdmin can be found at http://www.phpmyadmin.net/home_page/index.php. The phpMyAdmin interface is a very powerful tool in its own right. It has to be, as it is forming an interface to the MySQL database management system and that has a large number of facilities to which phpMyAdmin is providing access. You can

FIGURE 14.4   phpMyAdmin interface

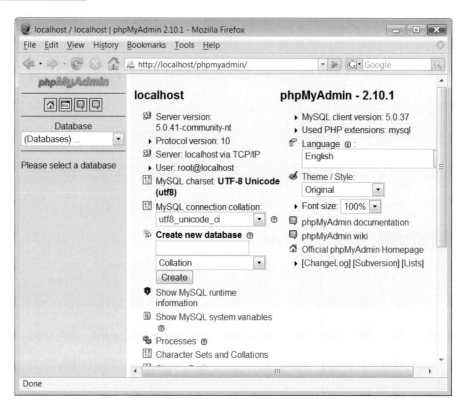

access phpMyAdmin by clicking your wamp icon on the tool bar and then choosing phpMyAdmin from the menu which appears. If you have installed wamp then another way of running phpMyAdmin is by typing:

```
http://localhost/
```

into your browser navigation window and then clicking phpMyadmin from the tools menu which appears in the browser window, as shown in Figure 14.5.

A web browser should launch shortly displaying the phpMyAdmin application, as shown in Figure 14.4.

By default, phpMyAdmin doesn't have a password set for the root account to which you default. This is a serious security issue which needs to be addressed if you wish to run your PHP scripts and MySQL database on a live web site. However, all good service providers will have secured their MySQL database systems which means that when the initial phpMyAdmin screen appears you will be prompted for a username and password. However, for now don't worry about the lack of root password if you are developing on your own computer.

Creating a database

To create a new database, you simply type the name you wish to call your database, for example 'glassesRus' into the form field on the home page of the phpMyAdmin system and click the 'Create' button, as illustrated in Figure 14.6.

FIGURE 14.5 Selecting the phpMyAdmin application

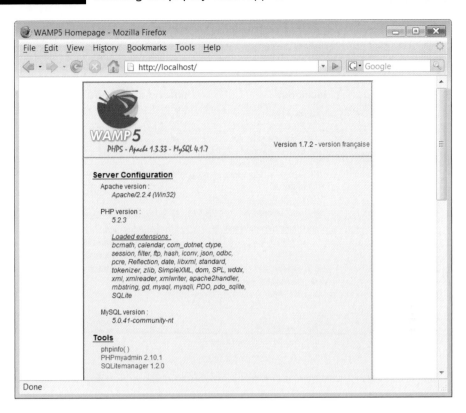

When you click the 'Create' button, you should get a message indicating that the database has been correctly created, as shown in Figure 14.7.

Viewing a database

phpMyAdmin provides access to all the databases you have created (or which have been created for you) via a simple drop-down menu system on the left of the application window. To view the databases you have available, click the button next to '(Databases)' on the left of the screen. A drop-down menu of the databases that you have available should appear. Figure 14.8 illustrates the databases which are available on our test computer. As you can see, we have rather a lot as we have been developing various projects over a number of years. However, if you look closely you can see that in the list is a database called 'glassesRus'. We are going to select this one by clicking on it.

When we have selected our database, we should see a screen with a message 'No tables found in database.', as shown in Figure 14.9.

This is fine as we haven't created any just yet. However, before we start creating some database tables, it is time to learn some more things about tables and database records.

FIGURE 14.6 Creating a database

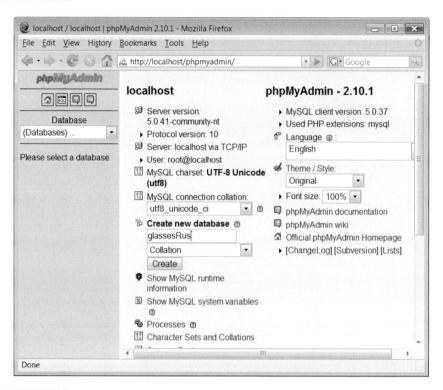

FIGURE 14.7 A successfully created database

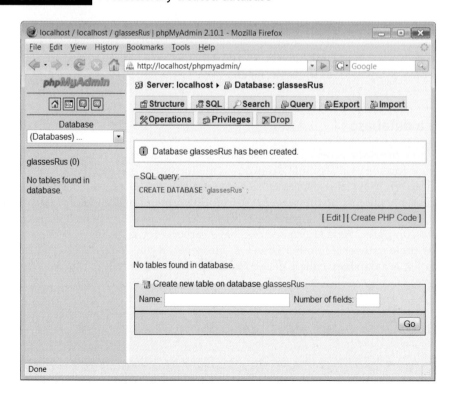

FIGURE 14.8 Available databases

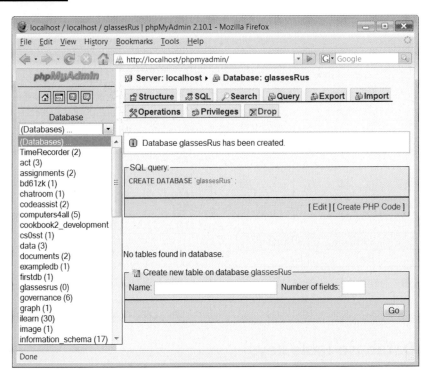

FIGURE 14.9 Database with no tables

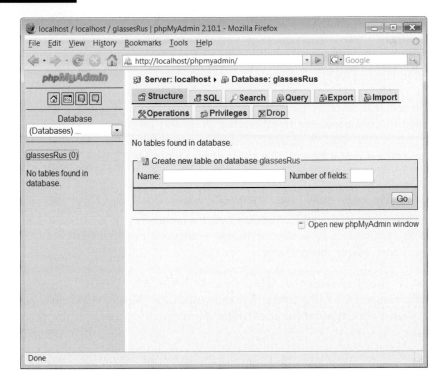

FIGURE 14.10   Obtaining a specific person's record

| Customers | | |
Title	Surname	Firstname
Mrs	Smith	Lynne
Miss	Jones	Ann
Mr	Brown	Simon
Mr	Smith	David
Mr	Bell	Peter
Ms	Hall	Liz
Mr	Smith	Kevin
Mr	Jones	Jack
Mr	Green	William
Mrs	Smith	Lynne
Mr	Bell	Simon
Mr	Brown	Ian

Title	Surname	Firstname
Ms	Hall	Liz

14.3 Database table keys

Take another look at the Customers table in Figure 14.2. Suppose we ask the database management system to search that table of records for a specific person, say 'Ms Liz Hall', the database is able to return us a single record for that person, as shown in Figure 14.10.

However, if we want to search for 'Mrs Lynne Smith', we have a potential problem, as illustrated in Figure 14.11.

The problem is that there are two Mrs Lynne Smiths and with our current table design we are not able to distinguish one from another. Now this might not be a problem for the moment, but if you want to charge Mrs Lynne Smith for a purchase that she has just made then you has better be sure that the correct Mrs Lynne Smith is charged.

The easy solution around the problem of potentially having identical data is to create a unique data field (called a key). Because the key field is always unique we can always identify one record from another. Figure 14.12 illustrates what a unique key field can look like. We have amended the Customers table so that it now contains a new field called Id. This field contains a simple unique integer value.

Figure 14.12 also illustrates that when we search for 'Ms Liz Hall' things work perfectly well. Figure 14.13 illustrates that the search for 'Mrs Lynne Smith' returns us the two records but the unique identifiers allow us to distinguish one record from another.

We can also create a unique key in the Products table, as illustrated in Figure 14.14.

FIGURE 14.11   Problem with obtaining a specific person's record

Customers		
Title	Surname	Firstname
Mrs	Smith	Lynne
Miss	Jones	Ann
Mr	Brown	Simon
Mr	Smith	David
Mr	Bell	Peter
Ms	Hall	Liz
Mr	Smith	Kevin
Mr	Jones	Jack
Mr	Green	William
Mrs	Smith	Lynne
Mr	Bell	Simon
Mr	Brown	Ian

Title	Surname	Firstname
Mrs	Smith	Lynne
Mrs	Smith	Lynne

FIGURE 14.12   Unique identifier field

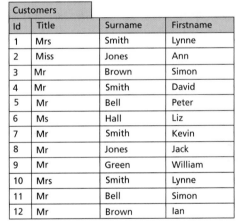

Customers			
Id	Title	Surname	Firstname
1	Mrs	Smith	Lynne
2	Miss	Jones	Ann
3	Mr	Brown	Simon
4	Mr	Smith	David
5	Mr	Bell	Peter
6	Ms	Hall	Liz
7	Mr	Smith	Kevin
8	Mr	Jones	Jack
9	Mr	Green	William
10	Mrs	Smith	Lynne
11	Mr	Bell	Simon
12	Mr	Brown	Ian

Id	Title	Surname	Firstname
6	Ms	Hall	Liz

NOTE	Note that our unique key fields can have the same name and values in different database tables.

The types for each of the fields in our Customers table now look like this:

```
Id          int
Title       varchar (10)
Surname     varchar (100)
Firstname   varchar (100)
```

FIGURE 14.13 Unique identifier field with multiple records

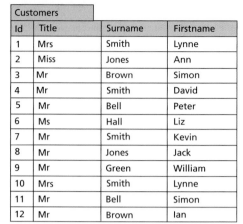

Customers			
Id	Title	Surname	Firstname
1	Mrs	Smith	Lynne
2	Miss	Jones	Ann
3	Mr	Brown	Simon
4	Mr	Smith	David
5	Mr	Bell	Peter
6	Ms	Hall	Liz
7	Mr	Smith	Kevin
8	Mr	Jones	Jack
9	Mr	Green	William
10	Mrs	Smith	Lynne
11	Mr	Bell	Simon
12	Mr	Brown	Ian

Id	Title	Surname	Firstname
1	Mrs	Smith	Lynne
10	Mrs	Smith	Lynne

FIGURE 14.14 Products table with Id field

Products				
Id	Name	Description	Quantity	Cost
1	Beer Glass	600 ml Beer Glass	345	3.99
2	Wine Glass	125 ml Wine Glass	236	2.99
3	Wine Glass	175 ml Wine Glass	436	3.50
4	Shot Glass	50 ml Small Glass	132	1.50
5	Spirit Glass	100 ml Short Glass	489	2.50
6	Long Glass	200 ml Tall Glass	263	2.50
7	Beer Glass	300 ml Tall Glass	247	2.99
8	Wine Glass	225 ml Wine Glass	96	3.99

And in the case of the Products table:

Id	int
Name	varchar (255)
Description	text
Quantity	int
Cost	float

We are now ready to create and populate these tables in our database using the phpMyAdmin tool.

14.4 Working with data in phpMyAdmin

Creating tables

To create a new table in phpMyAdmin, you simply type the name of the table you wish to create into the Name: field and the number of fields into the create table form. This form is illustrated in Figure 14.15. In the case of the Customers table we type 'Customers' and 4 and click the Go button.

After the Go button has been clicked, the screen changes to display the form field form! This is illustrated in Figure 14.16. The form looks quite difficult at first but the great thing is that we can ignore many of the options and things will work just fine.

The first thing to note is that we have four rows of the form to complete as the table has four fields. The first column, 'Field' is where the names of our fields are inserted. The next column, 'Type' is a drop-down list of the different types that MySQL supports. We have already determined which type each of our fields is going to be so there is no problem here. The third column, 'Length/Values' is where you specify the length of a field where applicable. For example, the Title field is a varchar type and we have specified that it has a maximum size of 10, so we would insert the value 10 in this column.

The remaining columns allow us to specify special attributes for our field. These are described in Table 14.4.

FIGURE 14.15 Creating a new table

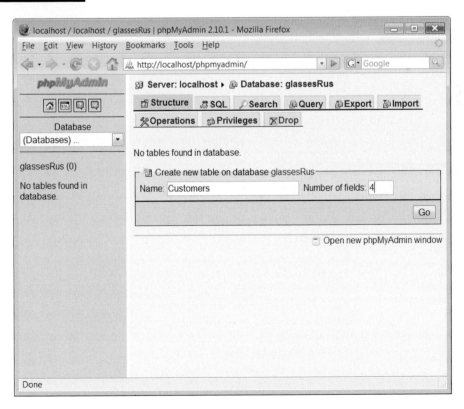

FIGURE 14.16 Table form field form

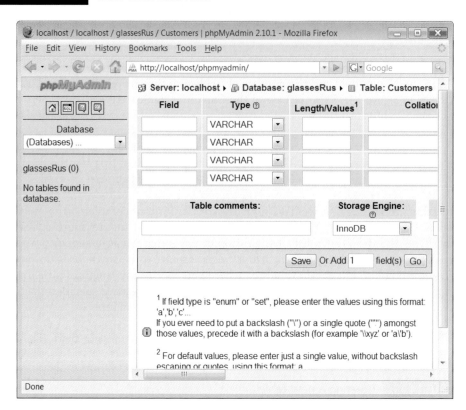

TABLE 14.4 Special field attributes

Field	Description
Collation	Specifies the character set of the data to be stored in the table. We will not be using this option.
Attributes	Unsigned: A numeric value is to be unsigned. Unsigned zero fill: A numeric value is to be unsigned and zeros will be placed before the start of the number to pad out the field to its specified maximum size. We will not be using this option.
Null	Not Null: The database field cannot be blank. If it is then an error is generated. Null: The database field can be blank.
Default	Specifies a value to which the field will be set if no data value is supplied.
Extra	Auto–increment: The field value is automatically generated when a new record is created. This is used mainly to ensure that a unique field value is created as the value produced is one larger than the last one produced. Primary, Indexed and Unique: Specifies how the table is indexed. We will be using primary key indexing with our key fields. Specifies that the field contains full text. We will not be using this option.

14

The great news is that in most cases we can simply ignore these extra columns. However, in the case of the first table field, Id we need to ensure that in addition to entering 'Id' in the Field column and selecting 'INT' in the Type column, we need to ensure that 'auto_increment' is selected in the Extra column and that the 'Primary' radio button is selected. The 'auto_increment' option instructs the database to create the data value stored in the Id field when a new record is added to the table. The data value is the value of the previously stored Id incremented by one. This option guarantees a unique primary key for each record and is typically used when a primary key is required.

The other three fields in the Customers table, require only the Field, Type and Length/Values columns to be entered. This is illustrated in Figure 14.17.

When the table has been completed the Save button can be clicked. The screen will then display a message that the Customers table has been created and provide a complex means of amending and altering the table if required. This screen is shown in Figure 14.18.

On the left of the screen, the drop-down Databases menu now has a (1) next to the database name. This indicates that the database has one table. Also note that below the drop-down database list is the name of the database which we are currently editing and the name of the first (and, currently, only) table within the database.

Now, this text is not simply information presented here but a clever data access system. If you click on the name of the database below the drop down list you will be taken to the

FIGURE 14.17   Completed field information for the customers table

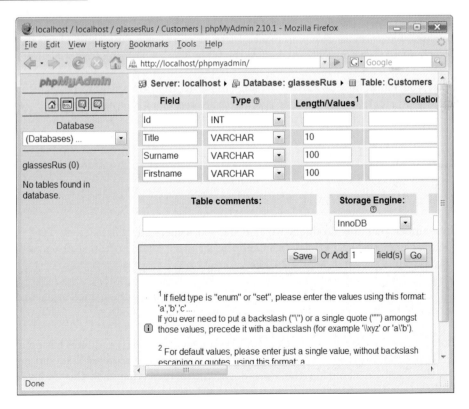

FIGURE 14.18 Customers table screen

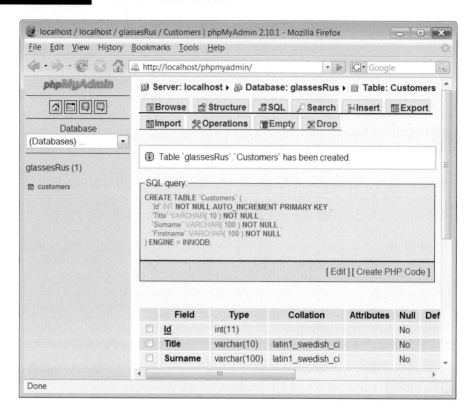

'Create new table' form, as shown in Figure 14.15. If you click on the name of the database table 'Customers' then you will be taken to the table edit screen as shown in Figure 14.18.

Now that you know how to create a table, move to the 'Create new table form' and create the Products table. Remember that there are five field types and they are:

Id	int
Name	varchar (255)
Description	text
Quantity	int
Cost	float

Also, remember that the Products Id, like the Customers Id, will need to have 'auto_increment' selected in the Extra column and the 'Primary' radio button also selected. The completed form is shown in Figure 14.19.

When the Save button is clicked, you should be taken to a screen indicating that the Products table has been correctly created, as shown in Figure 14.20.

You should also note that on the left of the screen a second table (products) has now been inserted below the previous, customers, one. Furthermore, the number 2 should now be next to the database name on the drop-down menu indicating that the database has two tables.

FIGURE 14.19 Completed field information for the Products table

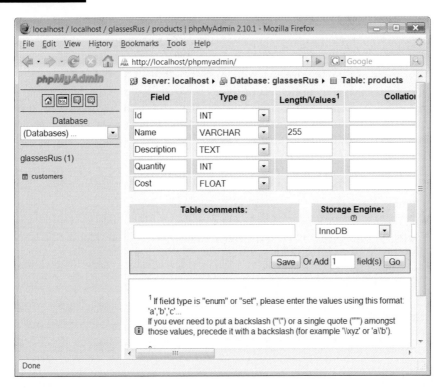

FIGURE 14.20 Products table screen

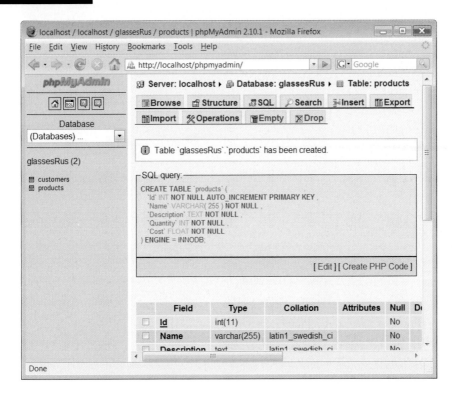

We are making progress. The next step is to populate these tables with the data shown in Figure 14.2 and Figure 14.3.

Adding data

To add data records to a table in phpMyAdmin, you first click on the table to which you wish to add records in the list on the left of the web page below the database name. If you click on customers, you should see a screen like that shown in Figure 14.18. To begin adding records, click the Insert tab near the middle top of the screen and you should see a screen similar to that in Figure 14.21.

The records we wish to insert into this table are shown in Figure 14.2. Our first record is:

Mrs Smith Lynne

You should type this data into the corresponding Value fields on the right of the top form. You can ignore the bottom form fields.

 NOTE | Do NOT enter a value for ID. When we created the table, we selected the auto-increment setting which means that this value will be created automatically for us.

FIGURE 14.21   Insert customer records screen

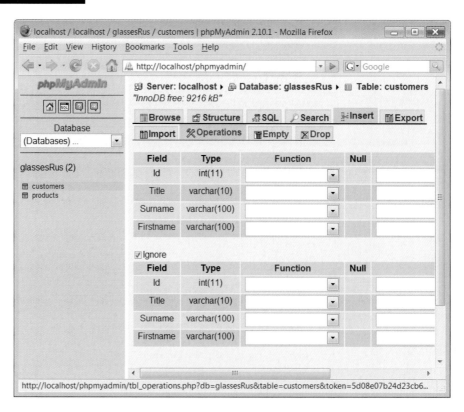

FIGURE 14.22 Completed customer records screen

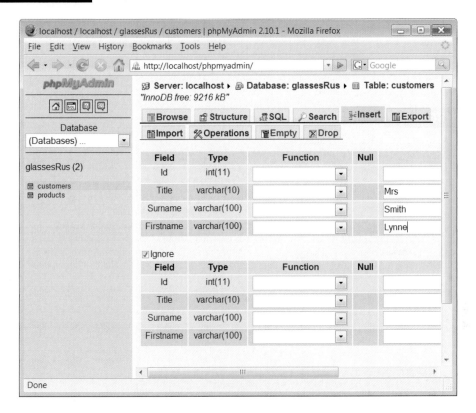

Because we have a number of records to insert, click the 'Insert another new row' button at the bottom of the screen. Your screen should look like that shown in Figure 14.22 just before you click the Go button.

After clicking the Go button, you should be taken to a screen which informs you that the row has been correctly inserted and presents you with a new form to insert the next row record. Insert all the records shown in Figure 14.2 into the table.

When you have finished, click the products table link on the left of the screen under the database name. Then select the Insert tab and insert all of the record rows for the Products table as shown in Figure 14.3.

NOTE   Remember not to insert the ID values for the records as these will be inserted automatically.

Viewing records

We can view the records we have entered to ensure that they are correct by clicking the icon to the left of the table names, as shown in Figure 14.23.

FIGURE 14.23 View records symbol

FIGURE 14.24 Customer table contents

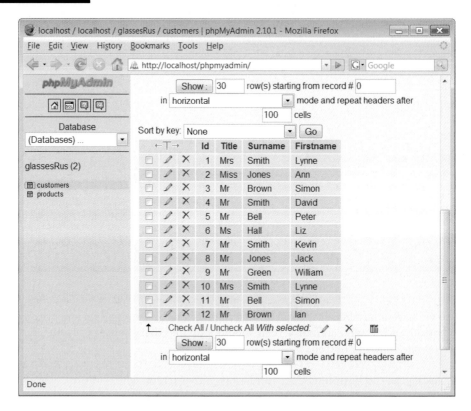

Clicking the symbol next to the Customers table name results in the display of the screen shown in Figure 14.24.

Clicking the same symbol next to 'products' will result in the display of the record rows inserted for the Products table. Take a close look at the 12 records you have inserted into the Customers table. Note that the Id record field has been automatically filled with the values 1 to 12. Also note that there are two graphical symbols next to each record row. The first is a pencil and allows us to edit the data within the row. The second symbol is a cross and enables us to delete the record.

Editing a record

To edit a record you need to click the pencil icon next to it. We are going to edit record number 6:

6 Ms Hall Liz

14

FIGURE 14.25 Editing a record screen

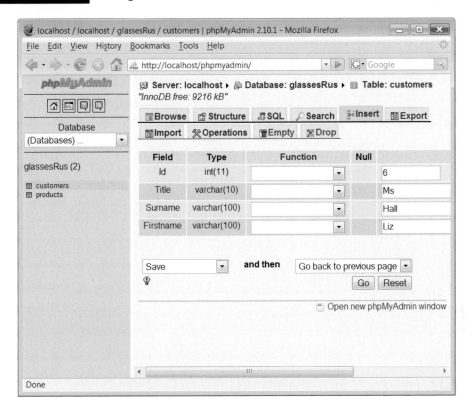

This customer has now decided that she wishes to be known by her full name, 'Elizabeth' and so we need to correct the record. After clicking the pencil icon we are taken to a screen like that shown in Figure 14.25.

In the values column of the form, delete the name 'Liz' and replace it with 'Elizabeth'. Clicking the Go button will return you to the previous screen.

 NOTE Check that all of the other records are correct in both the Customers and the Products tables and make any changes required before progressing to the next stage.

Backing up a database

While our MySQL database will remain perfectly okay for the moment, it is a good idea to make a copy of the database for security reasons. This will allow us to restore our database if anything goes wrong and also it will allow us to install the database on another MySQL database management system on another computer without the need to enter in all the data tables and records which we have done so far.

To make a database backup we first need to click on the database name on the left of the screen. The screen should now display the information shown in Figure 14.26.

FIGURE 14.26 Database information screen

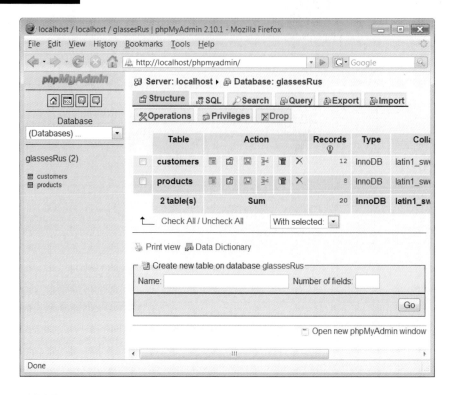

FIGURE 14.27 Export database screen

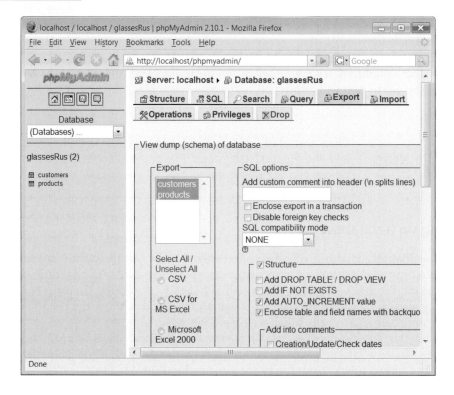

14

FIGURE 14.28   Save database to file

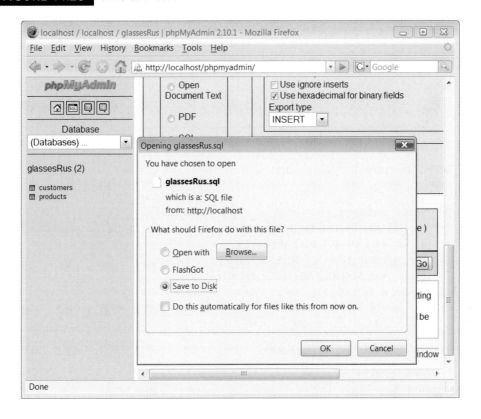

Next, we need to select the Export tab near the middle top of the screen. The screen should now look like Figure 14.27.

To back up your database to a file simply click the 'Save as file' checkbox and then click the Go button. A pop up dialogue box as shown in Figure 14.28 will appear allowing you to save the database to a local file.

Click the button and a file with the same name as your database and the extension .sql will be produced.

	NOTE	This is an SQL dump file of your database. It is not really a backup of the database but a file from which the database can be recreated on any MySQL system.

If you open the database .sql file in a text editor, you will see that its contents look like this:

```
-- phpMyAdmin SQL Dump
-- version 2.6.1-p13
-- http://www.phpmyadmin.net
```

```
--
-- Host: localhost
-- Generation Time: Nov 12, 2005 at 03:05 PM
-- Server version: 4.1.10
-- PHP Version: 5.0.4
--
-- Database: `glassesrus`
--

-- ------------------------------------------------------


--
-- Table structure for table `customers`
--

CREATE TABLE `customers` (
  `Id` int(11) NOT NULL auto_increment,
  `Title` varchar(10) NOT NULL default '',
  `Surname` varchar(100) NOT NULL default '',
  `Firstname` varchar(100) NOT NULL default '',
  PRIMARY KEY (`Id`)
) ENGINE = InnoDB DEFAULT CHARSET = latin1 AUTO_INCREMENT = 13 ;

--
-- Dumping data for table `customers`
--

INSERT INTO `customers` VALUES (1, 'Mrs', 'Smith', 'Lynne');
INSERT INTO `customers` VALUES (2, 'Miss', 'Jones', 'Ann');
INSERT INTO `customers` VALUES (3, 'Mr', 'Brown', 'Simon');
INSERT INTO `customers` VALUES (4, 'Mr', 'Smith', 'David');
INSERT INTO `customers` VALUES (5, 'Mr', 'Bell', 'Peter');
INSERT INTO `customers` VALUES (6, 'Ms', 'Hall', 'Elizabeth');
INSERT INTO `customers` VALUES (7, 'Mr', 'Smith', 'Kevin');
INSERT INTO `customers` VALUES (8, 'Mr', 'Jones', 'Jack');
INSERT INTO `customers` VALUES (9, 'Mr', 'Green', 'William');
INSERT INTO `customers` VALUES (10, 'Mrs', 'Smith', 'Lynne');
INSERT INTO `customers` VALUES (11, 'Mr', 'Bell', 'Simon');
INSERT INTO `customers` VALUES (12, 'Mr', 'Brown', 'Ian');

-- ------------------------------------------------------


--
-- Table structure for table `products`
--

CREATE TABLE `products` (
  `Id` int(11) NOT NULL auto_increment,
  `Name` varchar(255) NOT NULL default '',
  `Decription` text NOT NULL,
  `Quantity` int(11) NOT NULL default '0',
  `Cost` float NOT NULL default '0',
```

```
    PRIMARY KEY (`Id`)
) ENGINE=InnoDB DEFAULT CHARSET=latin1 AUTO_INCREMENT=9 ;


--
-- Dumping data for table `products`
--
INSERT INTO `products` VALUES (1, 'Beer Glass', '600 ml Beer Glass',
345, 3.99);
INSERT INTO `products` VALUES (2, 'Wine Glass', '125 ml Wine Glass',
236, 2.99);
INSERT INTO `products` VALUES (3, 'Wine Glass', '175 ml Wine Glass',
436, 3.5);
INSERT INTO `products` VALUES (4, 'Shot Glass', '50 ml Small Glass',
132, 1.5);
INSERT INTO `products` VALUES (5, 'Spirit Glass', '100 ml Short
Glass', 489, 2.5);
INSERT INTO `products` VALUES (6, 'Long Glass', '200 ml Tall Glass',
263, 2.5);
INSERT INTO `products` VALUES (7, 'Beer Glass', '300 ml Beer Glass',
247, 2.99);
INSERT INTO `products` VALUES (8, 'Wine Glass', '225 ml Wine Glass',
96, 3.99);
```

Keep this file safe: you can create your database on any MySQL system with it.

Deleting tables

If you ever need to delete a database's tables you can do this by first selecting the database from the drop-down menu.

To delete the tables from the database, you simply click the checkboxes on the far left next to each of the tables shown. Then you select the drop-down menu below the list of tables and select the Drop option. The screen displayed should look like that shown in Figure 14.29.

A screen will appear confirming that you want to delete the selected tables (see Figure 14.30). Clicking 'Yes' will delete the tables.

Restoring a database

To restore a database's tables, you first select the database you wish to restore from your drop-down menu list or create a new blank database. Next, click on the database name on the left of the screen and then select the Import tab from the top of the screen. Your screen should look something like that shown in Figure 14.31.

Click the Browse button and locate the .sql file that you created earlier. Clicking the Go button will result in the database tables being correctly loaded and a screen similar to that shown in Figure 14.32 should appear.

FIGURE 14.29 Deleting database tables

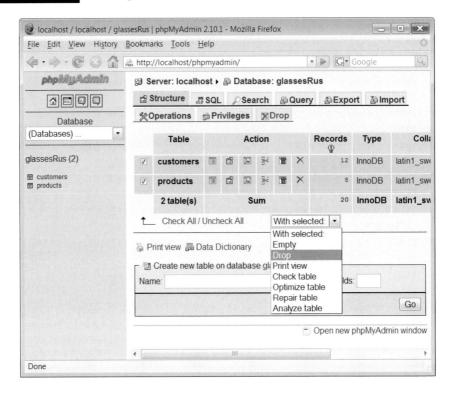

FIGURE 14.30 Deleting tables confirmation screen

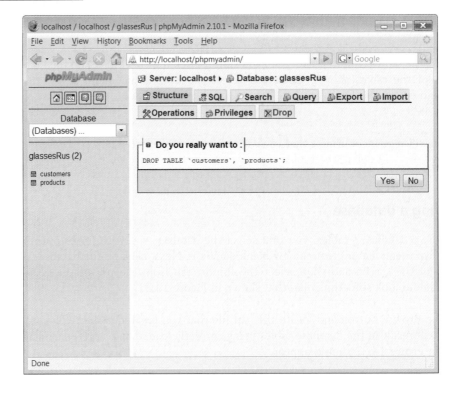

FIGURE 14.31 Restoring a database from an SQL file

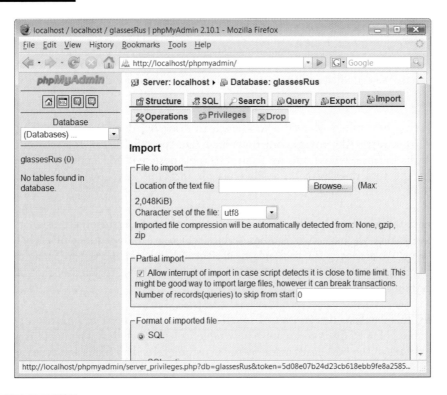

FIGURE 14.32 Recreating tables

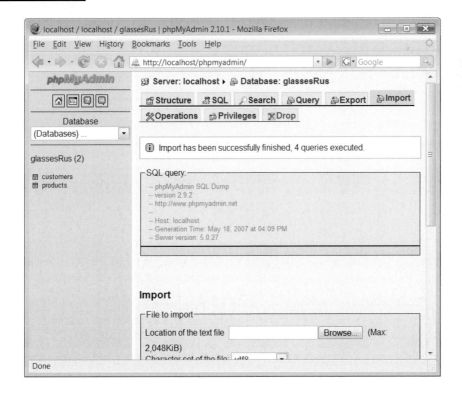

14.5 Extending our database

Our design

It's time now to consider our database design. Currently we have two tables: Customers and Products. We can illustrate them graphically using a database design notation as shown in Figure 14.33.

I have used a tool called MySQL Workbench to draw my database design. The tool is available from http://dev.mysql.com/downloads/gui-tools/5.0.html. It is currently only in an Alpha release which means that it is not designed for commercial projects. However, the tool does provide a good insight into the next generation of database design tools.

How to use the MySQL Workbench is outside the scope of this tutorial but what we can clearly see is that we have two database tables which are independent of each other at the moment. We are using the tool only to illustrate the new tables we are going to create and the relationships between them. We shall show how to create the tables in phpMyAdmin shortly.

Currently, this database design isn't of much use to us so we need to improve its design. What we are going to do is to create a new table called Purchases. This table is going to hold the details of the purchases made by each customer. Its data fields and types are going

FIGURE 14.33   Current database design in MySQL Workbench

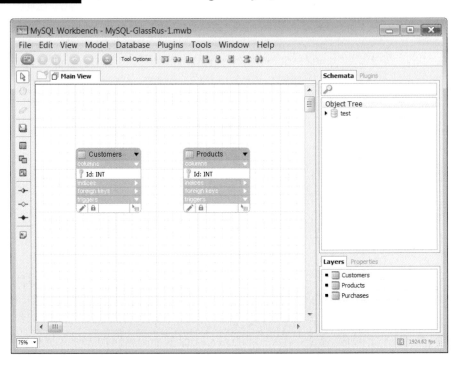

to be as follows:

Id   Integer
customers_Id   Integer
Day   Integer
Month   Integer
Year   Integer

The customers_Id field is the same as the id field in the Customers table and it allows us to form a relationship between the Customers table and the Purchases table as we need to be able to know when reading the Purchases table which customer made the purchase. Our database design now looks like that shown in Figure 14.34.

Now the Purchases table holds its own unique Id as well as the Id of the customer who made the purchase. It also has three fields to store the date that the purchase was made. We could have used a single date field but it will be easier for us later if we keep these as three separate integer fields. However, the design doesn't yet allow us to store which products were purchased at that time. To do this we need to create a new table called purchaseProducts. The purchaseProducts table will contain the following data fields and types:

products_Id   Integer
purchases_Id Integer
Quantity   Integer
Cost   Float

The products_Id field is the Id field from the Products table; it allows us to determine which product was bought. The purchase_Id is the Id field from the Purchases table.

FIGURE 14.34   Revised database design

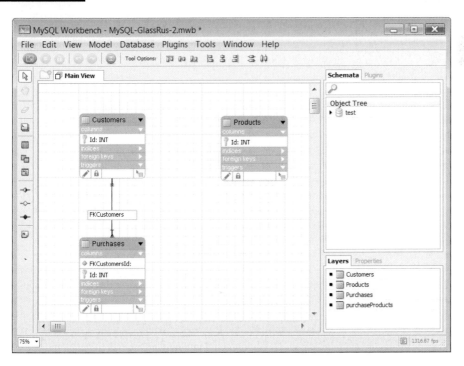

The Quantity field stores how many products were purchased and the Cost field is the price. We have included the cost field in this table as well as in the Products table as it is possible that the cost of a product may change over time but we would want to record the cost for which it was actually purchased, hence why this field is included in the purchaseProducts table. Our database design is now as shown in Figure 14.35.

It is time to create these new tables in our MySQL database using phpMyAdmin. Click on the database name on the left of the screen and, as shown in Figure 14.7, enter the name of the first new table. This will be purchaseProducts and it contains the four fields mentioned above. This table doesn't have its own primary index but it does have two indexes from other tables. These are the products_Id and purchases_Id fields. To indicate these we need to ensure that the 'Index' radio button is selected. This is the second radio button along on the far right of the screen. This radio button should be selected for both of these fields as indicated in Figure 14.36. After you have entered the data as shown, click the Save button to create the table.

Next we create the Purchases table by clicking on the database name of the left of the screen and entering the name 'Purchases' along with the value 5 for the number of fields.

Clicking the Go button will display the create table screen for the Purchases. This is completed as shown in Figure 14.37.

NOTE   Note that the Id field is auto_increment and is a Primary key. Also, that customer_Id is an Index.

FIGURE 14.35   purchaseProducts table added to design

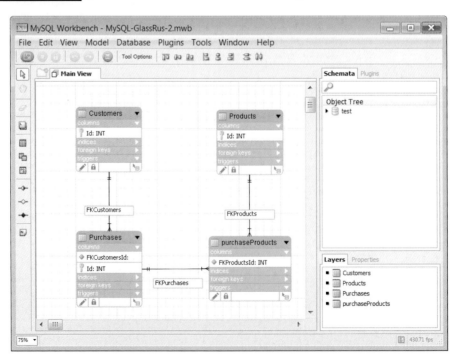

FIGURE 14.36   Adding the purchaseProducts table

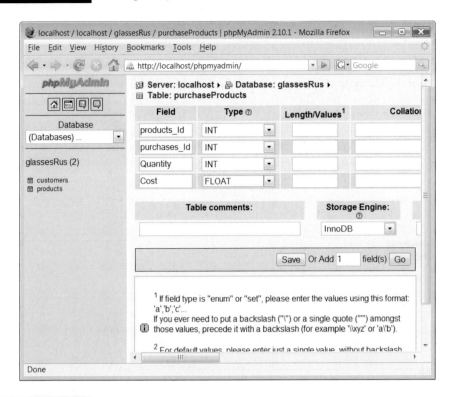

FIGURE 14.37   Adding the Purchases table

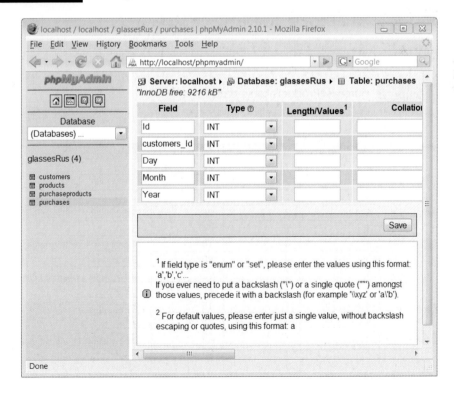

We have now finished creating our database structure and can add some data to these new fields.

Our data

The next step in our database creation is to include some new records for the tables we have just created. The data to be entered into the Purchases table is shown in Figure 14.38 and the data to be entered into the purchaseProducts table in Figure 14.39. Enter all of this data into the correct database tables.

That's it, we have now completed our database structure and data content. In the next lesson we shall learn how to use PHP scripts to interact with the MySQL database and extract and manipulate this data.

FIGURE 14.38 Purchases table data

Purchases

Id	customers_Id	Day	Month	Year
1	2	3	9	2006
2	4	6	9	2006
3	6	13	9	2006
4	2	22	9	2006
5	1	28	9	2006
6	9	1	10	2006
7	7	1	10	2006

FIGURE 14.39 purchaseProducts table data

purchaseProducts

products_Id	purchase_ID	Quantity	Cost
2	1	20	2.99
3	2	10	3.50
8	2	30	4.50
6	3	25	2.50
3	4	10	3.50
4	4	100	1.50
5	4	40	3.00
1	5	22	3.99
1	6	6	3.99
3	7	15	3.50
4	7	25	2.00
5	7	10	2.50
7	7	55	2.50
8	7	1	3.99

Exercises

14.1 Back up your completed database to a .sql file and keep this safe.

SUMMARY

In this chapter, we began by introducing the concept of databases. We described the concept of database tables and their fields. We examined the different field types that a database such as MySQL supports. Next we introduced the phpMyAdmin tool and illustrated how this can be used to manipulate MySQL databases. We showed the creation of a database through the creation of the 'glassesrus' database. We examined how records can be added, amended and deleted and how the database can be backed up to a dump file. Finally, we illustrated the MySQL Workbench tool and extended our database.

References and further reading

MySQL. Home Page. http://www.mysql.com/
MySQL. Documentation. http://dev.mysql.com/doc/
Php editors.com. Learning SQL using phpMyAdmin http://www.php-editors.com/articles/
   sql_phpmyadmin.php
phpMyAdmin. Home Page. http://www.phpmyadmin.net/home_page/index.php
Wikipedia. Databases. http://en.wikipedia.org/wiki/Database

14

Linking PHP to a Database

INTRODUCTION

In Chapter 14, we introduced the MySQL relational database management system. We showed that using the phpMyAdmin interface to MySQL we were able to create new databases. Within these databases we created tables and specified the field names and types which hold the data we included within the tables. We needed to undertake these tasks because this was preparation for what we are about to learn in this chapter.

We are now going to see how PHP can interact with the database we have created, extracting information from the database as well as updating it. We shall show how easy it is to do this and how the database can assist us in producing truly dynamic and useful web-enabled applications.

15.1 Connecting to a MySQL DBMS

In order for a PHP script to access a database we need to form a connection from the script to the database management system (DBMS). Connecting a PHP script to a DBMS is a multi-phased activity. We shall examine each of these activities separately. The first thing we need to do in our script is to form a connection from the local script to the DBMS we want to access. To do this we use the mysql_connect( ) function:

```
resourceId = mysql_connect(server, username, password);
```

The mysql_connect( ) function requires three parameters. The first is the name of the server, the second is your username and the third your password. The mysql_connect( ) function returns a resource-identifier type, which is the same type as was returned when we formed a connection to a file.

If you are developing on your own standalone computer the format of this function may look like this with the value of server set to be 'localhost', the username as 'root' and whatever password you have set:

```
$dbLocalhost = mysql_connect("localhost", "root", "password")
```

| NOTE | If you have no password you will still need to include the parameter but leave it blank like this: "". |

A PHP script can connect to a DBMS anywhere in the world, so long as it is connected to the Internet. The DBMS doesn't need to be on the same computer as that running the script. Furthermore, a script can connect to more than one DBMS at the same time. However, to keep things simple we shall connect to a single DBMS for now.

Having created a link to the DBMS we wish to access, the next stage is to select the database that we wish to use. This is done using the function mysql_select_db( ) which allows us to specify which database at the location defined in the mysql_connect( ) function we wish to access:

```
mysql_select_db(databasename, resourceId)
```

The mysql_connect( ) function requires two parameters. The first is the name of the database you wish to access and the second is the resourceId which was returned from invoking the previous mysql_connect( ) function. The function returns 'true' if the database selection worked or 'false' if not. The following is an example of invoking the function:

```
mysql_select_db("glassesrus", $dbLocalhost)
```

Next we need to mention the function die( ) which is an alias of exit( ).The die( ) function stops execution of the script if the previous database connection could not be formed, it looks like this:

```
die ("Error Message")
```

Function die( ) has a single parameter which is a message which is displayed before execution is stopped. It is common practice to combine the use of function die( ) with that of function mysql_error( ) which returns the text of the error message from the previous MySQL operation. The mysql_error( ) function looks like this:

```
mysql_error( )
```

15

The mysql_error( ) function requires no parameters and returns an error message string. Combining function die( ) and function mysql_error( ) looks like this:

```
die("Could not connect: " . mysql_error() )
```

Combining the die( ) function with the mysql_connect( ) function requires us to use the 'or' construct like this:

```
$dbLocalhost = mysql_connect("localhost", "root", "")
    or die("Could not connect: " . mysql_error() );
```

The above code fragment should now be read as 'form a mysql connection to localhost and if this doesn't work stop the script'.

We are now ready to form these functions together into our first PHP script and here it is:

```
<?php
// File: example15-1.php

$dbLocalhost = mysql_connect("localhost", "root", "")
    or die("Could not connect: " . mysql_error() );

mysql_select_db("glassesrus", $dbLocalhost)
    or die("Could not find database: " . mysql_error() );
echo "<h1>Connected To Database</h1>";
?>
```

The above script opens a connection to the DBMS server and then attempts to select database 'glassesrus' the database we created in Chapter 14. If something goes wrong in either operation an error message is generated and the script terminates. If all goes well, the output from running the above script will appear to be nothing.

15.2 Reading from a database

The next step in linking PHP to a database is to get it to send a Structured Query Language (SQL) statement to the database in order to begin to retrieve data records. To do this we need to introduce a new function that of mysql_query( ):

```
resourceRecords = mysql_query (query, resourceId);
```

Function mysql_query( ) requires two parameters; the first is an SQL query string (more on this in a minute) and the second is the database resource identifier returned from the mysql_connect( ) function. The function returns a resource identifier to the returned data.

NOTE	Function mysql_query( ) will fail and return 'false' if table(s) referenced by the query do not exist.

The following is an example of a valid use of the function:

```
$dbRecords = mysql_query("SELECT * FROM customers", $dbLocalhost)
```

If we modify our PHP script to include this function call we now end up with:

```php
<?php
// File: example15-2.php

$dbLocalhost = mysql_connect("localhost", "root", "")
    or die("Could not connect: " . mysql_error() );

mysql_select_db("glassesrus", $dbLocalhost)
    or die("Could not find database: " . mysql_error() );

$dbRecords = mysql_query("SELECT * FROM customers", $dbLocalhost)
    or die("Problem reading table: " . mysql_error() );
echo "<h1>Connected To Database</h1>";
?>
```

If all goes well the output from running the above script will appear to be nothing.

It is worth having a closer look at the SQL statement which we have used in the above function. Figure 15.1 illustrates what the components of this SQL statement actually mean.

The mysql_query( ) function returns us a resource pointer to all the records which match the SQL statement we supplied. This could be zero, one or many records. What we need is a function which returns the contents of one record cell from the record set. This function is called mysql_result( ):

```
fielddata = mysql_result (resourceRecords, row, field);
```

The mysql_query( ) function requires three parameters. The first is the resource pointer to the records returned by the mysql_query( ) function. The second is the number indicating which record to return, with 0 being the first record, 1 the second, and so on. The third parameter is the name of the database field to return. The function returns the data stored in the field. Here is an example of the function:

```
$strSurname = mysql_result($dbRecords, 0, "surname");
```

FIGURE 15.1 SQL select statement

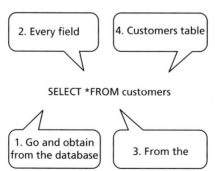

FIGURE 15.2 Customers table

Customers			
Id	Title	Surname	Firstname
1	Mrs	Smith	Lynne
2	Miss	Jones	Ann
3	Mr	Brown	Simon
4	Mr	Smith	David
5	Mr	Bell	Peter
6	Ms	Hall	Liz
7	Mr	Smith	Kevin
8	Mr	Jones	Jack
9	Mr	Green	William
10	Mrs	Smith	Lynne
11	Mr	Bell	Simon
12	Mr	Brown	Ian

The above function will retrieve from the database pointed to by the $dbRecords resource the first surname from the table. Adding this function into our script gives us:

```php
<?php
// File: example15-3.php

$dbLocalhost = mysql_connect("localhost", "root", "")
    or die("Could not connect: " . mysql_error() );

mysql_select_db("glassesrus", $dbLocalhost)
    or die("Could not find database: " . mysql_error() );

$dbRecords = mysql_query("SELECT * FROM customers", $dbLocalhost)
    or die("Problem reading table: " . mysql_error() );

$strSurname = mysql_result($dbRecords, 0, "Surname");
echo "<p>$strSurname</p>";
?>
```

The first time we run this script we get some output, which is:

```
Smith
```

Why Smith? Well, 'Smith' is the first surname in our customers table as shown in Figure 15.2.

15.3 Separating the database connection

Before we go any further with our scripts it is worth separating the database connectivity part from our scripts and placing this in a separate file. The actual lines of code to which I am referring are:

```php
<?php
// File: database.php
```

```php
$dbLocalhost = mysql_connect("localhost", "root", "")
    or die("Could not connect: " . mysql_error() );

mysql_select_db("glassesrus", $dbLocalhost)
    or die("Could not find database: " . mysql_error() );
?>
```

We suggest that you save these in a separate PHP file called 'database.php'. The main script will now need a require_once( ) function to include the 'database.php' script:

```php
require_once("database.php");
```

Our script now looks like this:

```php
<?php
// File: example15-4.php

require_once("database.php");

$dbRecords = mysql_query("SELECT * FROM customers", $dbLocalhost)
    or die("Problem reading table: " . mysql_error() );

$strSurname = mysql_result($dbRecords, 0, "Surname");
echo "<p>$strSurname</p>";
?>
```

 NOTE Don't include any of the XHTML declarations in 'database.php' or 'database2.php' which we will come to shortly, as these would be included in the main PHP script into which the files will be included.

The reason for separating the database connectivity section is that it provides a convenient means of moving your scripts from one database platform to another. Consider the following script:

```php
<?php
// File: database2.php

$strLocation = "Home";
//$strLocation = "Work";

if ($strLocation == "Home") {
    $dbLocalhost = mysql_connect("localhost", "root", "")
        or die("Could not connect: " . mysql_error() );

    mysql_select_db("glassesrus", $dbLocalhost)
        or die("Could not find database: " . mysql_error() );
}
else {

    $dbLocalhost = mysql_connect("localhost", "username", "password")
        or die("Could not connect: " . mysql_error() );
```

15

```
    mysql_select_db("anotherdatabase", $dbLocalhost)
    or die("Could not find database: " . mysql_error() );
  }
  ?>
```

The above script has been written to allow the user to simply change the value of $strLocation to be either 'Home' or 'Work'. The 'if' construct checks the value of this variable and makes the appropriate connection to the DBMS server. By keeping the 'database2.php' (in this case) file separate, the developer only needs to make this one change when moving the scripts from one development computer to another.

 NOTE It also has the advantage of keeping the scripts slightly shorter in our examples!

15.4 Viewing records

Viewing a whole record

Returning to our previous script where we were able to display a single field within a record, we should be able to deduce that we can display all the fields of the record by accessing each field like this:

```php
<?php
// File: example15-5.php

require_once("database2.php");

$dbRecords = mysql_query("SELECT * FROM customers", $dbLocalhost)
    or die("Problem reading table: " . mysql_error() );

$strSurname = mysql_result($dbRecords, 0, "Surname");
$strTitle = mysql_result($dbRecords, 0, "Title");
$strFirstname = mysql_result($dbRecords, 0, "Firstname");
$intId = mysql_result($dbRecords, 0, "Id");

echo "<p>$intId $strTitle $strFirstname $strSurname</p>";
?>
```

The output from the above script is:

```
1 Mrs Lynne Smith
```

While this is useful what we may want to do is display all the records easily.

Viewing all returned records

To display all the records which are returned from mysql_query( ) we need to introduce a new function called mysql_fetch_row( ):

```
array = mysql_fetch_row(resourceRecords);
```

The function requires a single parameter which is the resource identifier returned from the mysql_result( ) function. It returns an array containing the database record. When this new function is combined with a loop construct we can access and display all of the records returned. Here is an example of it working:

```php
<?php
// File: example15-6.php

require_once("database2.php");

$dbRecords = mysql_query("SELECT * FROM customers", $dbLocalhost)
    or die("Problem reading table: " . mysql_error() );

while ($arrRecord = mysql_fetch_row($dbRecords) ) {
    echo "<p>" . $arrRecord[0] . " ";
    echo $arrRecord[1] . " ";
    echo $arrRecord[2] . " ";
    echo $arrRecord[3] . "</p>";
}
?>
```

The above script invokes the mysql_fetch_row( ) function from within the 'while' loop construct. This function returns a single database record and stores this in the array

FIGURE 15.3   Displaying all customer records

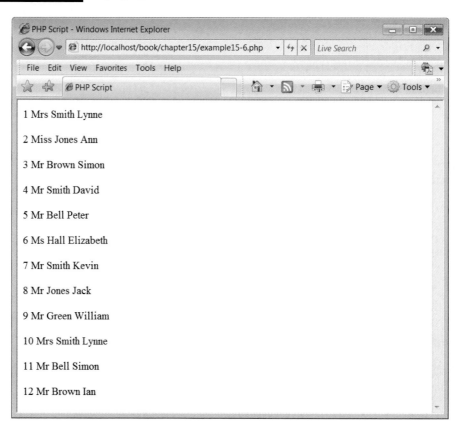

$arrRecord. When the last record has been returned, mysql_fetch_row( ) returns false and the loop stops iterating. Within the loop, a number of 'echo' statements are used to display the fields. The fields are stored within the $arrRecord array and are accessed through each array element, 0, 1, 2 and 3.

The output from the above script is illustrated in Figure 15.3. While the mysql_fetch_row( ) function can be used to access and display the database records it has a small fault. As you can see the script has to refer to the separate fields using array numbers. This does not make the code very easy to read and mistakes can be introduced. The function mysql_fetch_array( ) is an extended version of function mysql_fetch_row( ):

```
array = mysql_fetch_array(resourceRecords);
```

Like the mysql_fetch_row( ) function, the mysql_fetch_array( ) function requires a single parameter which is the resource identifier returned from the mysql_result( ) function. It returns an array containing the database record. The one thing that does differ from the mysql_fetch_row( ) function is that we can refer to the database fields by name. Here is an example:

```php
<?php
// File: example15-7.php

require_once("database2.php");

$dbRecords = mysql_query("SELECT * FROM customers", $dbLocalhost)
    or die("Problem reading table: " . mysql_error() );

while ($arrRecords = mysql_fetch_array($dbRecords) ) {
    echo "<p>" . $arrRecords["Id"] . " ";
    echo $arrRecords["Title"] . " ";
    echo $arrRecords["Surname"] . " ";
    echo $arrRecords["Firstname"] . "</p>";
}
?>
```

The above script works exactly the same as the previous one and the output is identical. The only difference is that the code is more readable as we are able to refer to the data record fields by name.

15.5 Limiting the records returned

Selecting only certain records

So far we have introduced a single SQL statement which allows us to obtain all of the records from a table. However, as you have probably guessed, SQL is far more powerful than that. Consider the following SQL statement:

```
SELECT Surname FROM customers
```

This enhancement of the SELECT statement replaces the * symbol which retrieves all fields with a list if the fields to retrieve. In this example only the 'Surname' is obtained.

FIGURE 15.4   Displaying only surnames

We can modify our previous script to use this SQL statement for example:

```php
<?php
// File: example15-8.php

require_once("database2.php");

$dbRecords = mysql_query("SELECT Surname FROM customers", $dbLocalhost)
    or die("Problem reading table: " . mysql_error() );
while ($arrRecords = mysql_fetch_array($dbRecords) ) {
    echo "<p>" . $arrRecords["Id"] . " ";
    echo $arrRecords["Title"] . " ";
    echo $arrRecords["Surname"] . " ";
    echo $arrRecords["Firstname"] . "</p>";
}
?>
```

Now when this script is run the output obtained is illustrated in Figure 15.4.

You will see that only the 'Surname' is displayed even though we have attempted to access the array contents of 'Title' and 'Firstname'. However, as only the 'Surname' was obtained by the SQL statement, these do not exist and thus they contain no value and are not displayed.

	NOTE	If you wish to obtain more than one field you can do so by listing them in the SQL statement separated by a comma, for example:
		`SELECT Surname,Firstname FROM customers`

Selecting a certain number of records

We can also modify the SELECT statement so that it uses the LIMIT option. We can use LIMIT to select a certain number of records from a table:

```
SELECT * FROM customers LIMIT 3,4
```

The LIMIT option has two parameters: the first one represents the starting row (where 0 is the first row) and the second represents the number of records to be selected after the starting row. So in the above example, the first record retrieved will be the fourth record and only four will be obtained from that point. Here is the statement in a script:

```php
<?php
// File: example15-9.php

require_once("database2.php");

$dbRecords = mysql_query("SELECT * FROM customers LIMIT 3,4", $dbLocalhost)
    or die("Problem reading table: " . mysql_error() );

while ($arrRecords = mysql_fetch_array($dbRecords) ) {
    echo "<p>" . $arrRecords["Id"] . " ";
    echo $arrRecords["Title"] . " ";
    echo $arrRecords["Surname"] . " ";
    echo $arrRecords["Firstname"] . "</p>";
}
?>
```

The output from the above script is illustrated in Figure 15.5.

FIGURE 15.5 Limiting the records retrieved

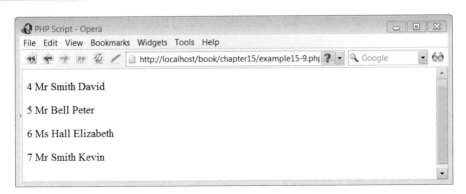

15

Searching for matching records

The SELECT statement can be further modified to obtain only records which match certain criteria. The WHERE attribute is used for this, for example:

```
SELECT * FROM customers WHERE Title = 'Mr'
```

The WHERE attribute can be used to specify what to search for within the database records. In the above example, only records which have a title of 'Mr' will be returned. This is implemented in the following script:

```php
<?php
// File: example15-10.php

require_once("database2.php");
$dbRecords = mysql_query("SELECT * FROM customers WHERE Title =
                         'Mr' ", $dbLocalhost)
   or die("Problem reading table: " . mysql_error() );
while ($arrRecords = mysql_fetch_array($dbRecords) ) {
   echo "<p>" . $arrRecords["Id"] . " ";
   echo $arrRecords["Title"] . " ";
   echo $arrRecords["Surname"] . " ";
   echo $arrRecords["Firstname"] . "</p>";
}
?>
```

The output from the above script is illustrated in Figure 15.6.

The WHERE attribute can also be combined with the AND attribute, for example:

```
SELECT * FROM customers WHERE Title = 'Mr' AND Surname = 'Smith'
```

FIGURE 15.6   Obtaining only records containing 'Mr'

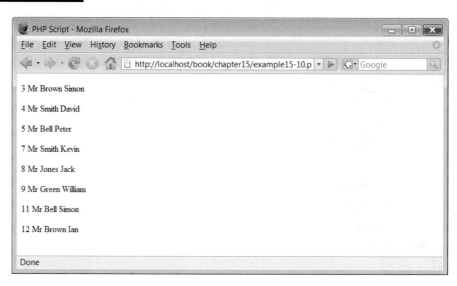

Here only those records who have the title 'Mr' and the surname 'Smith' are returned. Furthermore the OR attribute can also be used:

```
SELECT * FROM customers WHERE Title = 'Mr' OR Title = 'Mrs'
```

In the above example the records with a title of 'Mr' or 'Mrs' are returned. Finally, the use of AND and OR can be combined, for example:

```
SELECT * FROM customers WHERE Title = 'Mr' AND Surname = 'Smith'
OR Title = 'Mrs'
```

This SELECT statement will obtain all records with the surname of 'Smith' and the title of 'Mr' or the title of 'Mrs'. The above SELECT statement has been implemented in the following script:

```php
<?php
// File: example15-11.php

require_once("database2.php");

$dbRecords = mysql_query("SELECT * FROM customers WHERE Title = 'Mr' AND
Surname = 'Smith' OR Title = 'Mrs' ", $dbLocalhost)
    or die("Problem reading table: " . mysql_error() );
while ($arrRecords = mysql_fetch_array($dbRecords) ) {
    echo "<p>" . $arrRecords["Id"] . " ";
    echo $arrRecords["Title"] . " ";
    echo $arrRecords["Surname"] . " ";
    echo $arrRecords["Firstname"] . "</p>";
    }
?>
```

The output from the above script is illustrated in Figure 15.7.

FIGURE 15.7   Records that meet the WHERE criteria

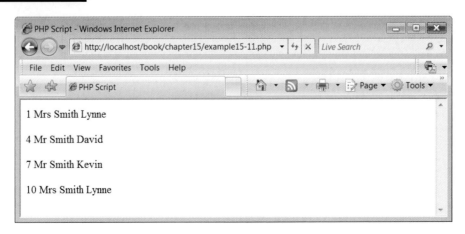

Sorting records

The ORDER BY attribute can be used to sort the order in which records are obtained, for example:

```
SELECT * FROM customers ORDER BY Surname DESC
```

The ORDER BY attribute is followed by the data field on which to sort the record. In the above example, this is Surname. The attributes DESC or ASC can be specified to indicate whether the sort should be in ascending or descending order. In other words from high to low or low to high.

The following script illustrates the use of the ORDER BY attribute:

```php
<?php
// File: example15-12.php

require_once("database2.php");

$dbRecords = mysql_query("SELECT * FROM customers WHERE Title = 'Mr'
ORDER BY Surname DESC", $dbLocalhost)
   or die("Problem reading table: " . mysql_error() );

while ($arrRecords = mysql_fetch_array($dbRecords) ) {
   echo "<p>" . $arrRecords["Id"] . " ";
   echo $arrRecords["Title"] . " ";
   echo $arrRecords["Surname"] . " ";
   echo $arrRecords["Firstname"] . "</p>";
}
?>
```

FIGURE 15.8 Sorted output

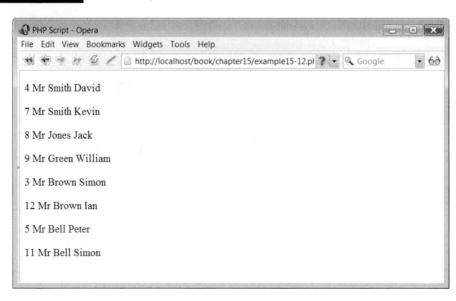

Closer examination of the script reveals that it also uses a WHERE attribute to obtain only the records with the title 'Mr'. Furthermore, the records have been sorted in DESCending order. The output from the above script is illustrated in Figure 15.8.

 NOTE The LIMIT, WHERE and ORDER BY attributes can be combined into a single SELECT statement.

15.6 Accessing multiple tables

Viewing data from multiple tables

So far, all of our examples have concerned a single table, Customers. However, there is no reason why we cannot access more than one table at the same time. Consider the following script:

```php
<?php
// File: example15-13.php

require_once("database2.php");

$dbRecords = mysql_query("SELECT * FROM customers WHERE Title = 'Mrs' ",
                          $dbLocalhost)
   or die("Problem reading table: " . mysql_error() );
echo "<p>Customers:</p>";

while ($arrRecords = mysql_fetch_array($dbRecords) ) {
   echo "<p>" . $arrRecords["Id"] . " ";
   echo $arrRecords["Title"] . " ";
   echo $arrRecords["Surname"] . " ";
   echo $arrRecords["Firstname"] . "</p>";
}
$dbRecords = mysql_query("SELECT * FROM products WHERE Name = 'Wine
Glass' ", $dbLocalhost)
   or die("Problem reading table: " . mysql_error() );

echo "<p>Products:</p>";

while ($arrRecords = mysql_fetch_array($dbRecords) ) {
   echo "<p>" . $arrRecords["Id"] . " ";
   echo $arrRecords["Name"] . " ";
   echo $arrRecords["Description"] . " ";
   echo $arrRecords["Quantity"] . " ";
   echo $arrRecords["Cost"] . "</p>";
}
?>
```

The above script obtains all the records from the customer table where the title is 'Mrs' and displays them. It follows this by obtaining all the records from the product table where the name is 'Wine Glass' and displays these. The output is shown in Figure 15.9.

15

FIGURE 15.9   Obtaining more than one table's data

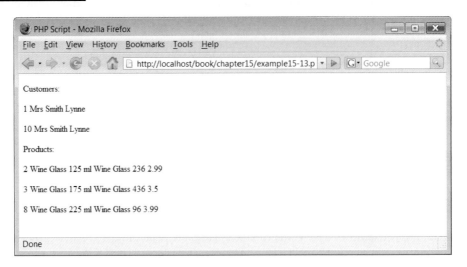

While this may be useful, what would be really useful is if we could read a table of customers and then find out which customers actually bought products and display those.

Using records to read another table

We know from Chapter 14 that our database has the following tables:

- Customer
- Products
- Purchases
- purchaseProducts

What we are going to create now is a script which reads a customer record and then shows the products that customer has purchased. Here is the script:

```php
<?php
// File: example15-14.php

require_once("database2.php");

$strSurname = "Jones";
$dbCustRecords = mysql_query("SELECT * FROM customers WHERE Surname =
                              '$strSurname' ", $dbLocalhost)
    or die("Problem reading table: " . mysql_error() );

while ($arrCustRecords = mysql_fetch_array($dbCustRecords) ) {
    $intId = $arrCustRecords["Id"];
    echo "<p>Customer: ";
    echo $arrCustRecords["Title"] . " ";
    echo $arrCustRecords["Surname"] . " ";
    echo $arrCustRecords["Firstname"] . "</p>";
```

```
$dbPurRecords = mysql_query("SELECT * FROM purchases WHERE
                            customers_Id = '$intId' ", $dbLocalhost)
    or die("Problem reading table: " . mysql_error() );

while ($arrPurRecords = mysql_fetch_array($dbPurRecords) ) {
    $intPurId = $arrPurRecords["Id"];
    echo "<p>Purchased On: ";
    echo $arrPurRecords["Day"] . "/";
    echo $arrPurRecords["Month"] . "/";
    echo $arrPurRecords["Year"] . "</p>";

    $dbProRecords = mysql_query("SELECT * FROM purchaseProducts WHERE
                                purchases_Id = '$intPurId' ", $dbLocalhost)
        or die("Problem reading table: " . mysql_error() );

while ($arrProRecords = mysql_fetch_array($dbProRecords) ) {
    $intProductId = $arrProRecords["products_Id"];
    echo "<p>" . $arrProRecords["Quantity"] . " ";

    $dbProductRecords = mysql_query("SELECT * FROM products WHERE
                                    Id = '$intProductId' ", $dbLocalhost)
        or die("Problem reading table: " . mysql_error() );

    $arrProductRecord = mysql_fetch_array($dbProductRecords);
    echo $arrProductRecord["Name"] . " (" .
        $arrProductRecord["Description"] . ") at &#163;";
    echo $arrProRecords["Cost"] . " each.</p>";
    }
  }
}
?>
```

The script begins by declaring a variable $strSurname which is set to the value 'Jones'. This is the surname of the person we are going to search for:

```
$strSurname = "Jones";
```

A database query ensures that all customers with a surname equal to 'Jones' are stored in resource $dbCustRecords:

```
$dbCustRecords = mysql_query("SELECT * FROM customers WHERE Surname =
                            '$strSurname' ", $dbLocalhost)
    or die("Problem reading table: " . mysql_error() );
```

15

A 'while' loop fetches each of these customer records and displays the customer details. The customer Id key is copied into variable $intId for use later:

```
while ($arrCustRecords = mysql_fetch_array($dbCustRecords) ) {
    $intId = $arrCustRecords["Id"];
    echo "<p>Customer: ";
    echo $arrCustRecords["Title"] . " ";
    echo $arrCustRecords["Surname"] . " ";
    echo $arrCustRecords["Firstname"] . "</p>";
```

Within the 'while' loop, another database query selects all purchases which match the customer Id stored in $intId:

```
$dbPurRecords = mysql_query("SELECT * FROM purchases WHERE
                            customers_Id = '$intId' ", $dbLocalhost)
    or die("Problem reading table: " . mysql_error() );
```

A 'while' loop fetches these purchases and displays when they were purchased. The purchase id key is stored in a variable $intPurId:

```
while ($arrPurRecords = mysql_fetch_array($dbPurRecords) ) {
    $intPurId = $arrPurRecords["Id"];
    echo "<p>Purchased On: ";
    echo $arrPurRecords["Day"] . "/";
    echo $arrPurRecords["Month"] . "/";
    echo $arrPurRecords["Year"] . "</p>";
```

Within the 'while' loop, another database query selects all purchaseProducts which match the purchase Id stored in $intPurId:

```
$dbProRecords = mysql_query("SELECT * FROM purchaseProducts
                            WHERE purchases_Id = '$intPurId' ", $dbLocalhost)
    or die("Problem reading table: " . mysql_error() );
```

A 'while' loop fetches these purchase products and displays them. The products_Id field is stored in $intProductId:

```
while ($arrProRecords = mysql_fetch_array($dbProRecords) ) {
    $intProductId = $arrProRecords["products_Id"];
    echo "<p>" . $arrProRecords["Quantity"] . " ";
```

Within the 'while' loop, yet another database query obtains all the products which match the key stored in $intProductId (there is only one):

```
$dbProductRecords = mysql_query("SELECT * FROM products WHERE
                                Id = '$intProductId' ", $dbLocalhost)
    or die("Problem reading table: " . mysql_error() );
```

Because there is only one product record which matches the product id key then there is no need for yet another loop and a simple mysql_fetch_array() function call returns all fields of the record for display:

```
$arrProductRecord = mysql_fetch_array($dbProductRecords);
echo $arrProductRecord["Name"] . " (" .
    $arrProductRecord["Description"] . ") at &#163;";
        echo $arrProRecords["Cost"] . " each.</p>";
```

The output from the above script is illustrated in Figure 15.10.

Examination of Figure 15.10 reveals that Miss Ann Jones purchased one product on 3/9/2006 and three products on 22/9/2006. However, Mr Jack Jones did not purchase anything.

FIGURE 15.10   Output from multiple tables

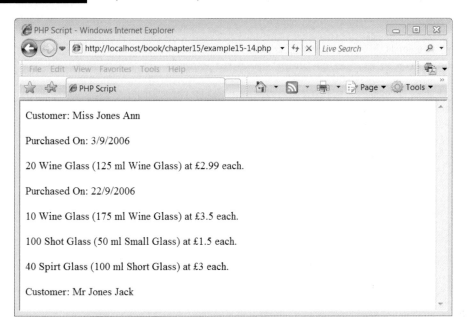

Inserting records

All of our examples thus far have illustrated reading and displaying database information. It is now time to examine how we can create new database records. To do this we need to introduce a new SQL statement, the INSERT INTO statement which looks like this:

```
INSERT INTO table (field1, field2, ... ) VALUES ('value1', 'value2', ... )
```

With the above statement the name of the table into which we are going to insert some data is specified after the INSERT INTO keywords. Next, each of the table field names into which we are going to insert are specified, separated by commas and enclosed in parentheses. Following this, the keyword VALUES is followed by the values to be placed in the field names, also separated by commas and enclosed in parentheses.

The above statement looks a little complex, however, we are able to simplify it a little like so:

```
INSERT INTO table VALUES ('value1', 'value2', ... )
```

The above INSERT INTO statement inserts the provided values into each database field in the order in which they have been provided. The following script provides an example of this:

```php
<?php
// File: example15-15.php

require_once("database2.php");
```

15

```
$dbProdRecords = mysql_query("INSERT INTO products VALUES ('', 'Beer
Mug', '600 ml Beer Mug', '100', '5.99')", $dbLocalhost)
    or die("Problem writing to table: " . mysql_error( ) );

$dbProdRecords = mysql_query("SELECT * FROM products", $dbLocalhost)
    or die("Problem reading table: " . mysql_error( ) );

while ($arrProdRecords = mysql_fetch_array($dbProdRecords) ) {
    echo "<p>" . $arrProdRecords["Id"] . " ";
    echo $arrProdRecords["Name"] . " ";
    echo $arrProdRecords["Description"] . " ";
    echo $arrProdRecords["Quantity"] . " ";
    echo $arrProdRecords["Cost"] . "</p>";
}
?>
```

The above script invokes a mysql_query( ) function with the SQL statement:

```
INSERT INTO products VALUES ('', 'Beer Mug', '600 ml Beer Mug', '100', '5.99')
```

This SQL statement creates a new data record in the Products table. The script also reads the Products table and displays the output, as illustrated in Figure 15.11.

NOTE	Note that the INSERT INTO data values included a blank data value as the first data item. This is blank because the actual value inserted into the data field is automatically incremented and handled by the MySQL DBMS.

FIGURE 15.11   Added a new record

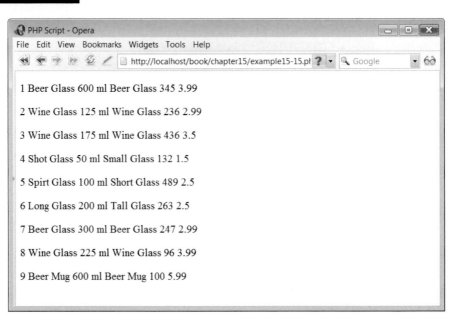

Deleting records

We can delete records from tables using the mysql_query( ) function using the DELETE FROM statement:

```
DELETE FROM table WHERE field='value'
```

The DELETE FROM query requires the name of the database table to be provided as well as the field and its value which we are looking to delete. So for example if we wished to delete customer Simon Brown, who has customer Id '3' then we could write:

```
DELETE FROM customers WHERE Id='3'
```

 NOTE Before you start running scripts which delete database records it would be a good time to export the database and make a backup of its data!

This SQL statement is illustrated in the following script:

```php
<?php
// File: example15-16.php

require_once("database2.php");

$dbCustRecords = mysql_query("DELETE FROM customers WHERE Id = '3' ",
                             $dbLocalhost)
  or die("Problem writing to table: " . mysql_error() );

$dbCustRecords = mysql_query("SELECT * FROM customers", $dbLocalhost)
  or die("Problem reading table: " . mysql_error() );

while ($arrCustRecords = mysql_fetch_array($dbCustRecords) ) {
  echo "<p>" . $arrCustRecords["Id"] . " ";
  echo $arrCustRecords["Title"] . " ";
  echo $arrCustRecords["Surname"] . " ";
  echo $arrCustRecords["Firstname"] . "</p>";
}
?>
```

The above script deletes from the Customers table the record with Id = '3'. The contents of the table after the deletion is then displayed. You can see illustrated in Figure 15.12 that the record Id with a value of 3 is now missing.

 NOTE Note that we selected this customer carefully as they have made no purchases. If they had made some purchases we would have to ensure that we tidied up the Purchases and purchaseProducts tables to ensure that there were no key references to a customer who no longer exists!

FIGURE 15.12   After deleting a record

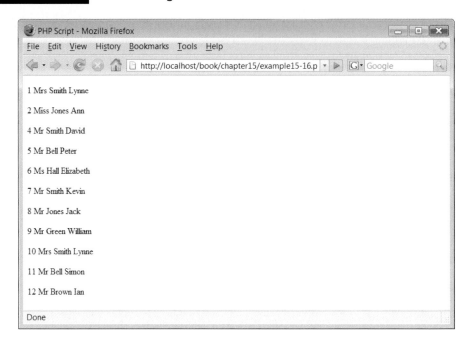

It is possible to delete all records from a table using the following syntax:

```
DELETE FROM table
```

Deleting the records from an entire database table is illustrated in the following script:

```php
<?php
// File: example15-17.php

require_once("database2.php");

$dbCustRecords = mysql_query("DELETE FROM customers", $dbLocalhost)
    or die("Problem writing to table: " . mysql_error() );

$dbCustRecords = mysql_query("SELECT * FROM customers", $dbLocalhost)
    or die("Problem reading table: " . mysql_error() );

while ($arrCustRecords = mysql_fetch_array($dbCustRecords) ) {
    echo "<p>" . $arrCustRecords["Id"] . " ";
    echo $arrCustRecords["Title"] . " ";
    echo $arrCustRecords["Surname"] . " ";
    echo $arrCustRecords["Firstname"] . "</p>";
}
echo "<p>Nothing There!</p>";
?>
```

NOTE	Make sure you back up your database before deleting an entire table!

Amending records

The SQL UPDATE statement is used to modify the contents of an existing database record.

```
UPDATE table SET field1='value1', field2='value2' ... WHERE
field='value'
```

The UPDATE statement requires you to specify the name of the table in which to update, provide a list of the fields and their updated values and finally indicate which records should be updated with these values. The following script illustrates updating a single record:

```php
<?php
// File: example15-18.php

require_once("database2.php");

$dbCustRecords = mysql_query("UPDATE products
SET Description = '250 ml Tall Glass' WHERE Id = '6' ", $dbLocalhost)
    or die("Problem updating table: " . mysql_error() );

$dbProdRecords = mysql_query("SELECT * FROM products", $dbLocalhost)
    or die("Problem reading table: " . mysql_error() );

while ($arrProdRecords = mysql_fetch_array($dbProdRecords) ) {
    echo "<p>" . $arrProdRecords["Id"] . " ";
    echo $arrProdRecords["Name"] . " ";
    echo $arrProdRecords["Description"] . " ";
    echo $arrProdRecords["Quantity"] . " ";
    echo $arrProdRecords["Cost"] . "</p>";
}
?>
```

In the above script the following SQL query is sent to the database:

```
UPDATE products SET Description = '250 ml Tall Glass' WHERE Id = '6'
```

This alters the description of record 6 in the Products table. The output from the script is illustrated in Figure 15.13.

You can of course produce an SQL statement which causes a number of records to be updated, consider this script:

```php
<?php
// File: example15-19.php

require_once("database2.php");

$dbCustRecords = mysql_query("UPDATE products SET Name = 'Beer and Lager Glass'
                            WHERE Name = 'Beer Glass' ", $dbLocalhost)
    or die("Problem updating table: " . mysql_error() );

$dbProdRecords = mysql_query("SELECT * FROM products", $dbLocalhost)
    or die("Problem reading table: " . mysql_error() );
```

FIGURE 15.13 Updating a single record

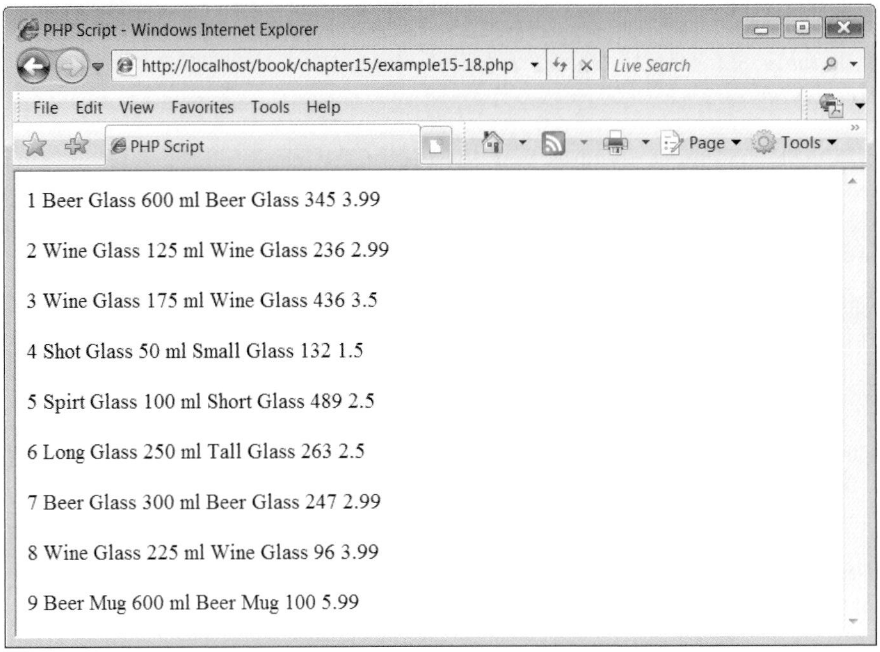

```
while ($arrProdRecords = mysql_fetch_array($dbProdRecords) ) {
    echo "<p>" . $arrProdRecords["Id"] . " ";
    echo $arrProdRecords["Name"] . " ";
    echo $arrProdRecords["Description"] . " ";
    echo $arrProdRecords["Quantity"] . " ";
    echo $arrProdRecords["Cost"] . "</p>";
}
?>
```

The script updated all product records where the Name is "Beer Glass" to read "Beer and Lager Glass". The output from the above script is illustrated in Figure 15.14.

15.8 Counting records and checking existence

How many records are there?

The mysql_num_rows( ) function can be used to count the number of records in a table. It looks like this:

```
numberRecords = mysql_num_rows (resourceQuery);
```

The function requires a resource handler returned from a mysql_query( ) function and returns an integer of the number of records returned. Here is an example of the function

FIGURE 15.14 Updating more than one record

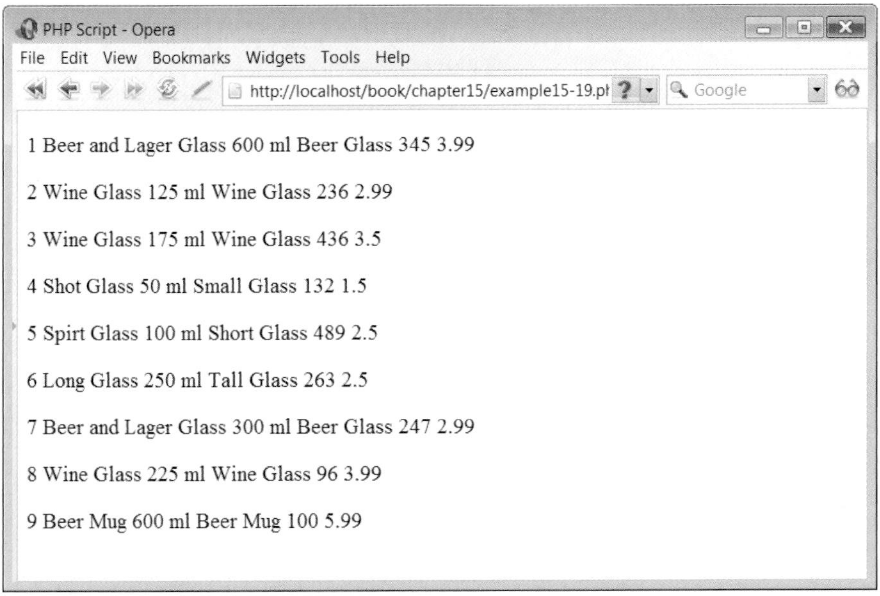

```
PHP Script - Opera
File   Edit   View   Bookmarks   Widgets   Tools   Help
http://localhost/book/chapter15/example15-19.ph   ?   Google   60

1 Beer and Lager Glass 600 ml Beer Glass 345 3.99

2 Wine Glass 125 ml Wine Glass 236 2.99

3 Wine Glass 175 ml Wine Glass 436 3.5

4 Shot Glass 50 ml Small Glass 132 1.5

5 Spirt Glass 100 ml Short Glass 489 2.5

6 Long Glass 250 ml Tall Glass 263 2.5

7 Beer and Lager Glass 300 ml Beer Glass 247 2.99

8 Wine Glass 225 ml Wine Glass 96 3.99

9 Beer Mug 600 ml Beer Mug 100 5.99
```

in a script:

```php
<?php
// File: example15-20.php

require_once("database2.php");

$dbProdRecords = mysql_query("SELECT * FROM products", $dbLocalhost)
    or die("Problem reading table: " . mysql_error() );

$intProductCount = mysql_num_rows($dbProdRecords);

echo "<p>We currently have $intProductCount products</p>";

while ($arrProdRecords = mysql_fetch_array($dbProdRecords) ) {
    echo "<p>" . $arrProdRecords["Id"] . " ";
    echo $arrProdRecords["Name"] . " ";
    echo $arrProdRecords["Description"] . " ";
    echo $arrProdRecords["Quantity"] . " ";
    echo $arrProdRecords["Cost"] . "</p>";
}
?>
```

The output from the above script is illustrated in Figure 15.15.

FIGURE 15.15   Counting records

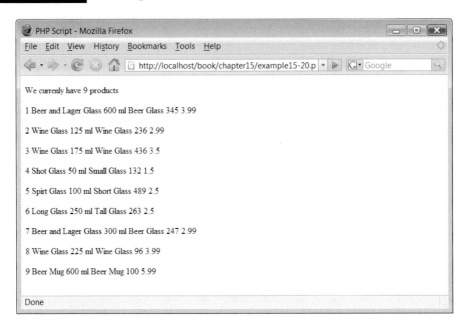

We currenly have 9 products

1 Beer and Lager Glass 600 ml Beer Glass 345 3.99

2 Wine Glass 125 ml Wine Glass 236 2.99

3 Wine Glass 175 ml Wine Glass 436 3.5

4 Shot Glass 50 ml Small Glass 132 1.5

5 Spirt Glass 100 ml Short Glass 489 2.5

6 Long Glass 250 ml Tall Glass 263 2.5

7 Beer and Lager Glass 300 ml Beer Glass 247 2.99

8 Wine Glass 225 ml Wine Glass 96 3.99

9 Beer Mug 600 ml Beer Mug 100 5.99

Does a record exist?

The mysql_num_rows( ) function can also be used to determine if a record exists in the database. Consider the following script:

```php
<?php
// File: example15-21.php

require_once("database2.php");

$dbProdRecords = mysql_query("SELECT * FROM products WHERE Name = 'Shot Glass' ",
                             $dbLocalhost)
   or die("Problem reading table: " . mysql_error() );

$intProductCount = mysql_num_rows($dbProdRecords);

if ($intProductCount > 0)
   echo "<p>Yes we have a Shot Glass</p>";
else
   echo "<p>No, we have no Shot Glasses</p>";
?>
```

The script invokes a mysql_query( ) function to return all products which have the name 'Shot Glass':

```php
$dbProdRecords = mysql_query("SELECT * FROM products WHERE Name = 'Shot Glass' ",
                             $dbLocalhost)
   or die("Problem reading table: " . mysql_error() );
```

The number of records returned are counted:

```php
$intProductCount = mysql_num_rows($dbProdRecords);
```

15

A simple if construct outputs an appropriate message:

```
if ($intProductCount > 0)
    echo "<p>Yes we have a Shot Glass</p>";
else
    echo "<p>No, we have no Shot Glasses</p>";
```

The output from the above script is:

```
Yes, we have a Shot Glass
```

15.9 Select and substring

The SUBSTRING attribute of the SELECT statement can be used to obtain records which match the substring parameters, for example:

```
SELECT * FROM products WHERE substring(Name,1,4) = 'Wine'
```

In the above example, the SELECT statement returns all records from the Products table where the first four characters in the Name field equal 'Wine'.

The following script illustrates the use of this command:

```
<?php
// File: example15-22.php

require_once("database2.php");

$dbProdRecords = mysql_query("SELECT * FROM products WHERE
                    substring(Name,1,4) = 'Wine' ", $dbLocalhost)
    or die("Problem reading table: " . mysql_error() );

echo "<p>Products:</p>";
while ($arrRecords = mysql_fetch_array($dbProdRecords) ) {
    echo "<p>" . $arrRecords["Id"] . " ";
    echo $arrRecords["Name"] . " ";
    echo $arrRecords["Description"] . " ";
    echo $arrRecords["Quantity"] . " ";
    echo $arrRecords["Cost"] . "</p>";
}
?>
```

The SELECT statement returns any and all records in the Products table where the Name field begins with the value 'Wine'. The output from this script is illustrated in Figure 15.16.

FIGURE 15.16   Records selected by a substring

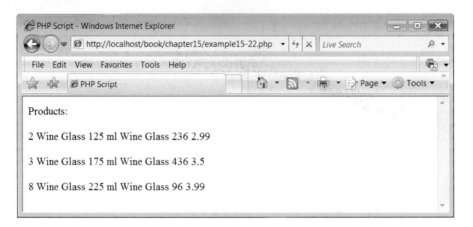

Products:

2 Wine Glass 125 ml Wine Glass 236 2.99

3 Wine Glass 175 ml Wine Glass 436 3.5

8 Wine Glass 225 ml Wine Glass 96 3.99

Exercises

15.1 Write a script which amends 'example15-13.php' so that a form interface allows the user to enter a surname to search for.

15.2 Write a script which amends 'example15-14.php' so that appropriate messages are displayed if no records are found at any stage. For example 'No purchases made.'

15.3 Write a script which amends 'example15-13.php' so that instead of searching for a customer, it searches for a particular product and then determines who has purchased it.

SUMMARY

In this chapter, we began by explaining how to form a connection between a PHP script and a MySQL database management system. We explained how to select a particular database served by the management system and how to access the records stored in the tables within the database. In addition to examining how to read database records, we explained how to insert, delete and amend records to the database. We concluded the chapter by explaining how to check if a record exists, determine the number of records which conform to a selection and how to use the substring function to find partial record matches.

References and further reading

astonishinc.com (2001) MySQL PHP Web Database Tutorial. http://blazonry.com/scripting/linksdb/index.php

Brown, K. Web-based Databases Using PHP. http://www.keithjbrown.co.uk/vworks/php/

Refdev.com. PHP Database Tutorials. http://www.refdev.com/tutorials/PHP/Databases/

15

Introducing Object Orientation

INTRODUCTION

Many modern programming languages now support the object-oriented paradigm and PHP is no exception. Over the years, support for the object-oriented paradigm has improved and now, in PHP 5, there is a new object model where the handling of objects has been completely rewritten, allowing for better performance and more implemented features. Within the object-oriented paradigm, programmers model things known as classes and use them within a program by creating instances of these classes known as objects.

In this chapter, we describe the concept of object orientation and provide some examples of what aspects of the paradigm PHP supports.

16.1 What is object orientation?

Object orientation is a paradigm that encourages and helps to enable code reuse. Object orientation also aims to minimize the impact of any programming changes, through a technique known as encapsulation. We have used a traditional structured programming technique to solve the problems and to explain many of the ideas introduced in previous chapters. With structured programming, we break a solution down into simple easy to program functions and group these functions together within the program to perform the task required of the program.

While the structured programming (also known as functional) technique has proven successful, it is not perfect. For example, while it does help programmers reuse their code to some extent, it doesn't fundamentally help protect data from accidental change. You see, with a functional approach local data may be declared within a function, but this may be required as a parameter to another function to enable further processing. If the data structures being passed from function to function are large and complex then it is easy for a programmer to accidentally misuse some data which could result in data being altered when it should not be.

The object-oriented paradigm takes a different approach to the design of data and their associated functions. In an object-oriented design, data variables (known as data members) and functions (known as methods) are wrapped up in what is known as a class. Collectively, the methods and data members of a class are referred to as class members, which can be confusing if you are not careful.

Data members cannot normally be accessed from outside the class (and neither can certain types of methods) protecting them from the rest of the script and other classes. This 'protection of class members' is known as encapsulation. Usually, only the methods associated with the class can access and alter values held within data members and the methods form an 'interface' to the class data members. Invoking methods in this way is known as sending a message to the class. This is illustrated in Figure 16.1.

The object-oriented paradigm also encourages software reuse as it provides a means for programmers to define new classes which are very similar to existing ones. The great thing is that the programmer only needs to specify what the differences are between the new class and the existing one. Data members and methods which are not defined as being private to a class are automatically accessible by the new class. This is known as inheritance and is an extremely powerful and useful programming tool.

FIGURE 16.1 Data members encapsulated by class methods

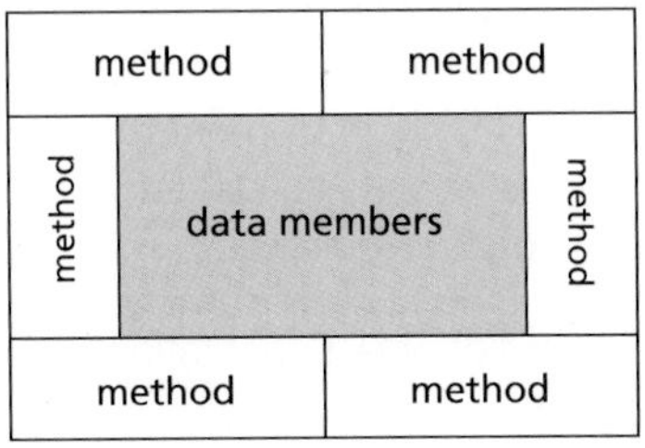

The object-oriented paradigm also supports the concept of polymorphism. Polymorphism is a concept where a number of related classes all have a method, which shares the same name. For example, we could have created a number of classes, which draw different shapes on the screen. All of the shapes have a method called draw ( ) which allows them to display themselves. The programmer can invoke the draw ( ) method in any of the classes knowing that it will result in the shape being displayed. However, the resulting image produced will be different depending on the shape class from which the message is sent.

Creating classes is not the end of the story. Classes are in effect templates, which define what information can be held and what things they can do. Classes are essentially sophisticated 'variable types'. In the same way that variables are designed to hold data of a specific type and you can do certain things with a particular variable, we can build classes which can contain certain data (held in the data members) and have associated with them certain methods which allow that data to be manipulated in different ways. However, before you can use a variable you need to create an instance of one and the same is true with classes. The class is the template and to use it you must create an instance of the class with some specific data. An instance of a class is known as an object.

Most object-oriented programming languages will implement the features described previously. However, depending on the programming language you are using, the terminology used differs. For example, class methods, functions and procedures are all used to describe the same thing. Likewise, data members, fields and variables are terms used to mean the same thing.

16.2 PHP and object orientation

PHP keeps things simple and consistent with the other aspects of the PHP language. In defining a class, the programmer specifies the data members and methods (variables and functions), which are encompassed within the class. Instances of classes will be referred to as objects.

Creating a class

The keyword used to define a class is 'class'. This is followed by a class name, which can be any name that isn't a reserved word in PHP. The name is followed by a pair of curly braces, which contain the definition of the class's data members and methods:

```
class name {

}
```

If we were to create a class called person then we would begin with:

```
class person {

}
```

This class doesn't do anything just yet because we haven't assigned any methods or data members to the class. Before we can do that we need to know about data member and method visibility.

Visibility

The visibility of a method or data member can be defined by prefixing the declaration with the keywords:

```
public
protected
private
```

'Public' items can be accessed everywhere, both within and outside of the class. 'Protected' limits access to classes which inherit from the class and also the original class in which the item was defined. 'Private' limits the visibility of the method or data member only to the class that defines the item.

If we include some data members in our class it is usual for them to be private as we want to make use of the encapsulation feature of the object-oriented paradigm.

Class data members and methods

The following script illustrates our class with some data members defined. All class members must be placed inside the class definition, i.e. between the start and end braces:

```
class person {
    private $strFirstname = "Simon";
    private $strSurname = "Stobart";
}
```

Classes can also have methods associated with them. Each class method is defined in exactly the same way as a function defined outside of the class. Class methods must be defined as public, private, or protected.

Consider our class with two member functions included:

```
class person {
    private $strFirstname = "Simon";
    private $strSurname = "Stobart";

    function getFirstname() {
    }
    function getSurname() {
    }
}
```

 NOTE Class members without any visibility specified in their declaration are defined as public. That is why the two methods in the example above appear not to have any visibility but they are, in fact, public.

These functions don't do anything at the moment as they contain no code. What we would like them to do is return the values of data members $strFirstname and $strSurname

16

respectively. You would think that we could simply include a return statement like this in method getFirstname( ):

```
function getFirstname() {
    return $strFirstname;
}
```

Unfortunately this will not work. The above code fragment would be fine if we had defined variable $strFirstname as part of the getFirstname( ) method. However it is not, it is a data member (defined within the class but outside any class method). To solve this problem we need to introduce a new pseudo-variable called $this.

$this

Pseudo-variable $this is a reference to the calling object (usually the object to which the method or data member belongs). To access a data member of the class, we use $this, followed by the operator -> followed by the variable name, for example:

```
$this->strFirstname;
```

 NOTE Note that the $ symbol is in front of 'this' and not immediately in front of the name of the data member.

We can now amend our class methods to make correct use of the $this pseudo-variable, like this:

```
class person {
    private $strFirstname = "Simon";
    private $strSurname = "Stobart";

    function getFirstname() {
        return $this->strFirstname;
    }
    function getSurname() {
        return $this->strSurname;
    }
}
```

We now have a class which contains two data members and has two methods. These methods have been designed to return the values of the respective data members. However, if you were to view the output from the above script in a browser you would be very disappointed as nothing would appear. This is because while we have correctly created a class we have not used it. What we need to do now is to create an instance of this class, known as an object.

Using a class

16

To make use of our person class we need to create an object of that class. To do this we need to use the keyword new. A new object must be created and assigned to a variable:

```
variable = new class
```

So for our example class we could write:

```
$objSimon = new person();
```

The above is essentially saying we wish to create a variable called $objSimon which is of the type "person". This is the same as creating a new variable:

```
$strName;
```

Now, if you remember our class has two methods: getFirstname( ) and getSurname( ). To invoke these methods, we use the syntax:

```
objectName->methodName()
```

Therefore, with our example class, we write either of the following:

```
$objSimon->getFirstname();
$objSimon->getSurname();
```

In order to access the values returned by the methods we need to echo the result or copy the returned values into variables. The following script contains our completed class, created object and object method calls:

```php
<?php
// File: example16-1.php

class person {
    private $strFirstname = "Simon";
    private $strSurname = "Stobart";

    function getFirstname() {
        return $this->strFirstname;
    }
    function getSurname() {
        return $this->strSurname;
    }
}
$objSimon = new person;
echo "<p>Firstname: " . $objSimon->getFirstname() . "</p>";
echo "<p>Surname: " . $objSimon->getSurname() . "</p>";
?>
```

The output from the above script is illustrated in Figure 16.2.

So that works. If we want to alter the values of data members, $strFirstname and $strSurname, we can try to write something like:

```
$objSimon->strFirstname = "Tim";
```

Unfortunately this will result in an error message being generated because the data member strFirstname is defined as private and is therefore not available for access outside of the class. What we need to do in order to allow us to alter an object's data member values is to write some methods to allow us to do this.

FIGURE 16.2   Object output

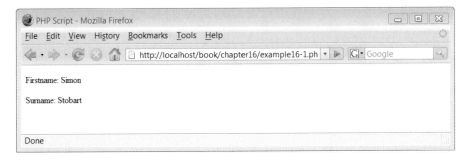

FIGURE 16.3   Setting an object's members

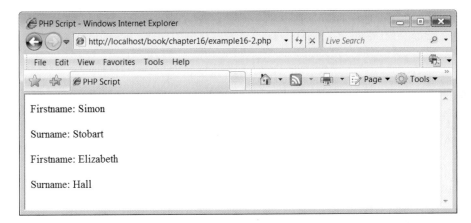

 NOTE   If you were to change the visibility of the data member strFirstname to be public then the above script would work correctly.

To do this we need to create a method like this:

```php
function setFirstname($strSurname) {
    $this->strFirstname = $strSurname;
}
```

This method receives as an argument a variable containing a new surname and then assigns this value to the data member $this->strFirstname. Consider the following script which defines two methods to allow the value of the data member to be altered and illustrates this working:

```php
<?php
// File: example16-2.php

class person {
    private $strFirstname = "Simon";
    private $strSurname = "Stobart";
```

16

```php
    function getFirstname() {
        return $this->strFirstname;
    }

    function getSurname() {
        return $this->strSurname;
    }

    function setFirstname($strFirstname) {
        $this->strFirstname = $strFirstname;
    }

    function setSurname($strSurname) {
        $this->strSurname = $strSurname;
    }

}

$objSimon = new person;
echo "<p>Firstname: " . $objSimon->getFirstname() . "</p>";
echo "<p>Surname: " . $objSimon->getSurname() . "</p>";

$objSimon->setFirstname("Elizabeth");
$objSimon->setSurname("Hall");

echo "<p>Firstname: " . $objSimon->getFirstname() . "</p>";
echo "<p>Surname: " . $objSimon->getSurname() . "</p>";
?>
```

The output from the above script is illustrated in Figure 16.3.

Multiple object instances

Once a class has been created, any number of object instances of that class can be created. This is exactly like having many variables of type integer within a script. Consider the following example:

```php
<?php
// File: example16-3.php

class person {
    private $strFirstname;
    private $strSurname;

    function getFirstname() {
        return $this->strFirstname;
    }

    function getSurname() {
        return $this->strSurname;
    }

    function setFirstname($strFirstname) {
        $this->strFirstname = $strFirstname;
    }
```

```
    function setSurname($strSurname) {
        $this->strSurname = $strSurname;
    }
}

$objSimon = new person;
$objSimon->setFirstname("Simon");
$objSimon->setSurname("Stobart");
echo "<p>Firstname: " . $objSimon->getFirstname() . "</p>";
echo "<p>Surname: " . $objSimon->getSurname() . "</p>";

$objLiz = new person;
$objLiz->setFirstname("Liz");
$objLiz->setSurname("Hall");
echo "<p>Firstname: " . $objLiz->getFirstname() . "</p>";
echo "<p>Surname: " . $objLiz->getSurname() . "</p>";
?>
```

The above example creates a new person object called $objSimon and sets the firstname and surname member values which it then displays through invoking the two methods. It then creates a second person object called $objLiz and repeats the process for this new object. The output produced is the same as that illustrated in Figure 16.3.

Invoking methods of a class from within the same class

Class methods can invoke other class methods. To do this they use the $this pseudo-variable again with the syntax:

```
$this->functionName();
```

Consider the following script which illustrates this:

```
<?php
// File: example16-4.php

class person {
    private $strFirstname;
    private $strSurname;

    function getFirstname() {
        return $this->strFirstname;
    }

    function getSurname() {
        return $this->strSurname;
    }

    function setFirstname($strFirstname) {
        $this->strFirstname = $strFirstname;
    }

    function setSurname($strSurname) {
        $this->strSurname = $strSurname;
    }
```

16

```
    private function display() {
       echo "<p>Firstname: " . $this->strFirstname . "</p>";
       echo "<p>Surname: " . $this->strSurname . "</p>";
    }
    function setDisplayFirstnameSurname($strFirstname, $strSurname) {
       $this->setFirstname($strFirstname);
       $this->setSurname($strSurname);
       $this->display();
    }
}

$objSimon = new person;
$objSimon->setDisplayFirstnameSurname("Simon", "Stobart");
?>
```

The above script creates a new method called display( ), which displays the values of the two data members:

```
private function display() {
    echo "<p>Firstname: " . $this->strFirstname . "</p>";
    echo "<p>Surname: " . $this->strSurname . "</p>";
}
```

Note that the display( ) method is declared as private, which stops it being invoked from outside with a call such as this:

```
$objSimon->display();
```

 NOTE There is no real reason to define this method as private other than to illustrate the use of a private method.

The script also creates a new method called setDisplayFirstnameSurname( ):

```
function setDisplayFirstnameSurname($strFirstname, $strSurname) {
    $this->setFirstname($strFirstname);
    $this->setSurname($strSurname);
    $this->display();
}
```

This method receives both the firstname and surname as arguments. It then invokes the setFirstname( ) and setSurname( ) methods to assign the appropriate values to the class data members. Finally it invokes method display( ) to output the current values of these data members. The output produced is the same as shown in Figure 16.2.

16

Creating multiple classes

In addition to creating multiple instances of a class, you can also create multiple classes and then multiple instances of each of these. Consider the following script:

```php
<?php
// File: example16-5.php

class person {
    private $strFirstname;
    private $strSurname;

    function getFirstname() {
        return $this->strFirstname;
    }

    function getSurname() {
        return $this->strSurname;
    }

    function setFirstname($strFirstname) {
        $this->strFirstname = $strFirstname;
    }

    function setSurname($strSurname) {
        $this->strSurname = $strSurname;
    }

    private function display() {
        echo "<p>Firstname: " . $this->strFirstname . "</p>";
        echo "<p>Surname: " . $this->strSurname . "</p>";
    }

    function setDisplayFirstnameSurname($strFirstname, $strSurname)
    {
        $this->setFirstname($strFirstname);
        $this->setSurname($strSurname);
        $this->display();
    }
}

    class vehicle {
    private $strDescription;

    function getDescription() {
        return $this->strDescription;
    }

    function setDescription($strDescription) {
        $this->strDescription = $strDescription;
    }
}
```

```
$objSimon = new person;
$objSimon->setDisplayFirstnameSurname("Simon", "Stobart");
$objBike = new vehicle;
$objBike->setDescription("Bicycle");
echo "<p>Vehicle: " . $objBike->getDescription() . "</p>";
?>
```

The above script creates the same person class as before but in addition also creates a vehicle class:

```
class vehicle {
   private $strDescription;
   function getDescription() {
      return $this->strDescription;
   }

   function setDescription($strDescription) {
      $this->strDescription = $strDescription;
   }
}
```

The vehicle class contains a single data member called strDescription which holds a description of the vehicle. It also contains two methods which allow the data member to be set and retrieved from outside the class.

After the person object is created and displayed a vehicle object is created:

```
$objBike = new vehicle;
$objBike->setDescription("Bicycle");
echo "<p>Vehicle: " . $objBike->getDescription() . "</p>";
```

The output from the above script is illustrated in Figure 16.4.

16.3 Multiple source files

You should notice that, even with these rather simple examples, the scripts are getting quite long. To solve this problem many developers writing object-oriented applications create one PHP source file per class definition. This aids class reuse and script clarity.

FIGURE 16.4   Output from multiple classes

A series of includes or requires can be used to load the classes which are required. If we split up our script to do this, we end up with the 'person.php' script for the person class:

```php
<?php
// File: person.php

class person {
    private $strFirstname;
    private $strSurname;

    function getFirstname() {
        return $this->strFirstname;
    }

    function getSurname() {
        return $this->strSurname;
    }

    function setFirstname($strFirstname) {
        $this->strFirstname = $strFirstname;
    }

    function setSurname($strSurname) {
        $this->strSurname = $strSurname;
    }

    private function display() {
        echo "<p>Firstname: " . $this->strFirstname . "</p>";
        echo "<p>Surname: " . $this->strSurname . "</p>";
    }

    function setDisplayFirstnameSurname($strFirstname, $strSurname) {
        $this->setFirstname($strFirstname);
        $this->setSurname($strSurname);
        $this->display();
    }
}
?>
```

Then the 'vehicle.php' script contains the vehicle class:

```php
<?php
// File: vehicle.php

class vehicle {
    private $strDescription;

    function getDescription() {
        return $this->strDescription;
    }
```

```php
    function setDescription($strDescription) {
        $this->strDescription = $strDescription;
    }
}
?>
```

Finally, the following script creates the object instances of the classes, which requires the inclusion of the two scripts above:

```php
<?php
// File: example16-6.php

require_once("person.php");
require_once("vehicle.php");

$objSimon = new person;
$objSimon->setDisplayFirstnameSurname("Simon", "Stobart");
$objBike = new vehicle;
$objBike->setDescription("Bicycle");
echo "<p>Vehicle: " . $objBike->getDescription() . "</p>";
?>
```

The output from the above script is the same as shown in Figure 16.4.

However, while this is really useful it does have one annoying feature: you have to write a long list of includes or requires statements at the beginning of each script (one for each class). In PHP 5, this is no longer necessary. You may define an __autoload function which is automatically called in case you are trying to use a class which hasn't been defined yet. The function looks like this:

```php
function __autoload($class_name) {
    require_once $class_name . '.php';
}
```

The function is invoked each time a class is required but hasn't been defined. We can insert this function into our script:

```php
<?php
// File: example16-7.php

function __autoload($class_name) {
    require_once $class_name . '.php';

}

$objSimon = new person;
$objSimon->setDisplayFirstnameSurname("Simon", "Stobart");
$objBike = new vehicle;
$objBike->setDescription("Bicycle");
echo "<p>Vehicle: " . $objBike->getDescription() . "</p>";
?>
```

The output from the above script is the same as Figure 16.4.

16.4 Constructors and destructors

Constructors

You will have noticed by now that creating an object is a two-stage process. First we create a new object then we call a function that populates that object with data, for example:

```
$objSimon = new person;
$objSimon->setDisplayFirstnameSurname("Simon", "Stobart");
```

There is however a way to perform these two operations in one. In order to do so, we need to create a constructor. A constructor is a function, which is automatically called when you create a new object and it looks like this:

```
void function __construct (various)
```

 NOTE For backwards compatibility, if PHP 5 cannot find a __construct() function for a given class, it will search for the old-style constructor function, by the name of the class.

Let's create a constructor function for our person class. It looks like this:

```
function __construct ($strFirstname, $strSurname) {
    $this->setFirstname($strFirstname);
    $this->setSurname($strSurname);
    $this->display();
}
```

The constructor function receives two arguments which are the values of firstname and surname and assigns these to the appropriate data members. Our complete person class, which we have now renamed to revisedperson now looks like this:

```
<?php
// File: revisedperson.php

class revisedperson {
    private $strFirstname;
    private $strSurname;

    function __construct ($strFirstname, $strSurname) {
        $this->setFirstname($strFirstname);
        $this->setSurname($strSurname);
        $this->display();
    }

    function getFirstname() {
        return $this->strFirstname;
    }
```

```
        function getSurname() {
            return $this->strSurname;
        }

        function setFirstname($strFirstname) {
            $this->strFirstname = $strFirstname;
        }

        function setSurname($strSurname) {
            $this->strSurname = $strSurname;
        }

    private function display() {
        echo "<p>Firstname: " . $this->strFirstname . "</p>";
        echo "<p>Surname: " . $this->strSurname . "</p>";
    }

    function setDisplayFirstnameSurname($strFirstname, $strSurname) {
        $this->setFirstname($strFirstname);
        $this->setSurname($strSurname);
        $this->display();
    }
  }
?>
```

We can create a constructor for the vehicle class also:

```
function __construct ($strDescription) {
    $this->strDescription = $strDescription;
}
```

Having created a constructor we can now combine the creation of the object and the population of data with the syntax:

```
new class (various);
```

So in our main script we now have the following:

```
<?php
// File: example16-8.php

function __autoload($class_name) {
    require_once $class_name . '.php';
}

$objSimon = new revisedperson("Simon", "Stobart");

$objBike = new vehicle("Bicycle");
echo "<p>Vehicle: " . $objBike->getDescription() . "</p>";
?>
```

Note that, because our person script has a display( ) method which is invoked from the constructor, there is still not a need (unlike with the vehicle class) to invoke a method to

16

obtain the value of the object members. The output from the above script is the same as in Figure 16.4.

Destructors

PHP 5 introduces a destructor concept similar to that of other object-oriented languages, such as C++. The destructor method is called as soon as all references to a particular object are removed or when the object is explicitly destroyed. The syntax of the method is:

```
void function __destruct (void)
```

An example of a destructor function is:

```
function __destruct() {
    echo "<p>Destroying Class</p>";
}
```

The above example doesn't really do anything useful but tell us at what point the object has been deleted. Destructors can be useful to include code to free up memory that the object has been using, for example.

16.5 Arrays and objects

Objects that have been created can be treated in the same way as you would variables. Therefore, you can easily create an array of objects, for example:

```
<?php
// File: example16-9.php

function __autoload($class_name) {
    require_once $class_name . '.php';
}

$objSimon = new revisedperson("Simon", "Stobart");
$objLiz = new revisedperson("Liz", "Hall");
$objIan = new revisedperson("Ian", "Walker");
$objBilly = new revisedperson("Billy", "Lee");
$objHayley = new revisedperson("Hayley", "West");
$arrPeople = array($objSimon, $objLiz, $objIan, $objBilly, $objHayley);
foreach($arrPeople as $objThePerson)
    echo($objThePerson->display() );
?>
```

The above script creates five objects of type 'revisedperson':

```
$objSimon = new revisedperson("Simon", "Stobart");
$objLiz = new revisedperson("Liz", "Hall");
$objIan = new revisedperson("Ian", "Walker");
$objBilly = new revisedperson("Billy", "Lee");
$objHayley = new revisedperson("Hayley", "West");
```

It then puts them in an array and uses a foreach loop to cycle through the array and display the contents of the object using the display( ) method:

```
$arrPeople = array($objSimon, $objLiz, $objIan, $objBilly, $objHayley);
foreach($arrPeople as $objThePerson)
    echo($objThePerson->display() );
```

To allow the above script to work as intended we must change the visibility of the display( ) method in the person class back to public so it looks like this:

```
function display() {
    echo "Firstname: " . $this->strFirstname;
    echo "<br/>Surname: " . $this->strSurname . "<br/>";
}
```

We also removed the invocation to the display( ) method from within the constructor, so that the constructor of the person class now looks like this:

```
function __construct ($strFirstname, $strSurname) {
    $this->setFirstname($strFirstname);
    $this->setSurname($strSurname);
}
```

The output from the above script is illustrated in Figure 16.5.

FIGURE 16.5   Objects and arrays

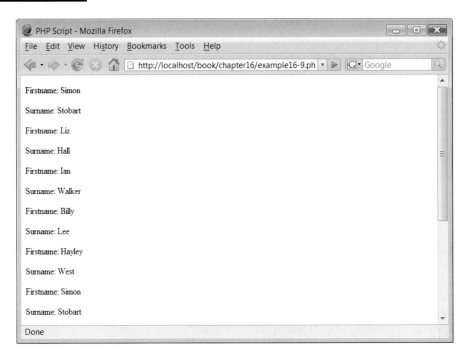

16.6 Functions and objects

Objects can be passed to functions in the same way as variables. The following script illustrates something to be wary of however:

```php
<?php
// File: example16-10.php

function __autoload($class_name) {
    require_once $class_name . '.php';
}

function change($objPerson){
    $objPerson->setFirstname("Tim");
}

$objSimon = new revisedperson("Simon", "Stobart");
change($objSimon);
$objSimon->display();
?>
```

In this example, you find a simple function called change( ) which receives a person object and changes its firstname to 'Tim':

```php
function change($objPerson){
    $objPerson->setFirstname("Tim");
}
```

Next an object is created, the member values are set to 'Simon' and 'Stobart' and the object contents are displayed through the call to function display( ) within the constructor:

```php
$objSimon = new revisedperson("Simon", "Stobart");
```

Finally, function change( ) is invoked, passing the object, and then function display( ) is invoked once more:

```php
change($objSimon);
$objSimon->display();
```

'Okay', I hear you cry, 'I know the answer to this, the object is passed by value and therefore function change( ) is going to simply change a copy of the object and so the original object when displayed the second time will still be as it was when it was first displayed'. Well, the output from this script is illustrated in Figure 16.6.

If you thought that the object was going to be unchanged you were be wrong. In fact, objects in PHP 5 are very special creatures and are passed around by reference without the need for any special & characters.

16

NOTE	Objects in versions of PHP prior to version 5 are passed by value and therefore behave like any other kind of variable.

FIGURE 16.6   Objects and function output

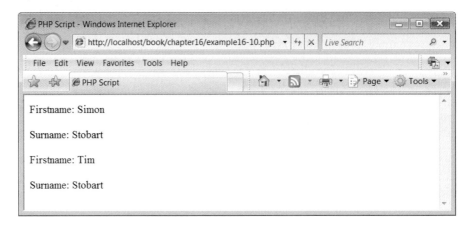

This makes programming easier but you need to be aware that objects are handled differently from other data types.

16.7 Default arguments

Class functions, like their non-class counterparts, can include default argument values. This allows a function to be called with an argument or without, knowing that if it is missing the default value will be set. The constructor function in class revisedperson has been rewritten to include default arguments:

```php
function __construct ($strFirstname = "Simon", $strSurname = "Stobart") {
    $this->setFirstname($strFirstname);
    $this->setSurname($strSurname);
}
```

We shall call this new class 'revisedagainperson'. Consider the following script:

```php
<?php
// File: example16-11.php

function __autoload($class_name) {
    require_once $class_name . '.php';
}

$objSimon = new revisedagainperson("Simon", "Stobart");
$objSimon->display();

$objAnotherSimon = new person();
$objAnotherSimon->display();
?>
```

Here an object called $objSimon is constructed using the arguments 'Simon' and 'Stobart'. Then, an object called $objAnotherSimon is constructed without any arguments but the default values are used. The output from the above script is illustrated in Figure 16.7.

FIGURE 16.7   Default method values

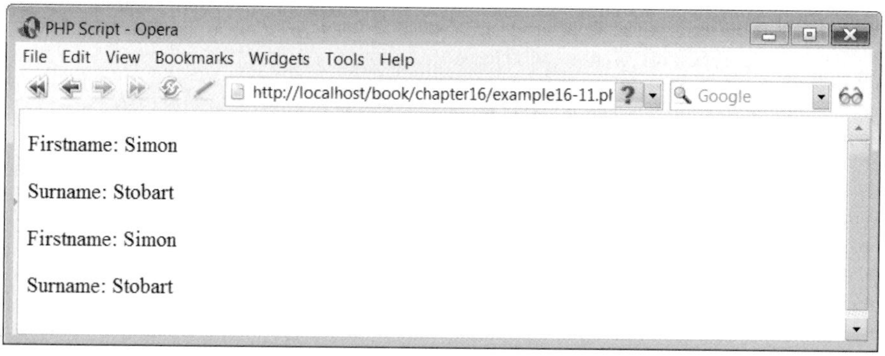

```
PHP Script - Opera
File  Edit  View  Bookmarks  Widgets  Tools  Help
                     http://localhost/book/chapter16/example16-11.ph  ?  ▼  Google  ▼  6∂

Firstname: Simon

Surname: Stobart

Firstname: Simon

Surname: Stobart
```

16.8 An object invoking another

An object may wish to interact with another object. To illustrate this consider the following script which implements a 'bucket':

```php
<?php
// File: bucket.php

class bucket {
   private $intMaxVolume;
   private $intCurrentVolume;
   private $strName;

   function __construct ($strName, $intMaxVol, $intCurrentVol) {
      $this->strName = $strName;
      $this->intMaxVolume = $intMaxVol;
      $this->intCurrentVolume = $intCurrentVol;
      $this->display();
   }

   function addLiquid($intVolume){
      $this->intCurrentVolume = $this->intCurrentVolume + $intVolume;
   }

   function getName(){
      return $this->strName;
   }

   function getRemainingSpace() {
      return $this->intMaxVolume - $this->intCurrentVolume;
   }

   function emptyDownDrain() {
      $this->intCurrentVolume = 0;
      echo "<p>Emptying the " . $this->strName . "</p>";
   }

   function fillFromTap() {
      $this->intCurrentVolume = $this->intMaxVolume;
```

```
        echo "<p>Filling " . $this->strName . "</p>";
    }

    function display() {
        echo "<p>The " . $this->strName . " contains " .
$this->intCurrentVolume . " litres out of a maximum of " .
$this->intMaxVolume . " litres</p>";
    }

    function transfer($objOtherBucket) {
        $intSpace = $objOtherBucket->getRemainingSpace();
        if ($intSpace > $this->intCurrentVolume) {
            $objOtherBucket->addLiquid($this->intCurrentVolume);

            echo "<p>Pouring " . $this->intCurrentVolume .
                    " litres from the " . $this->strName . " into the " .
                    $objOtherBucket->getName() . "</p>";
            $this->intCurrentVolume = 0;
        }
        else {
            $objOtherBucket->addLiquid($intSpace);
            $this->intCurrentVolume = $this->intCurrentVolume - $intSpace;
            echo "<p>Pouring " . $intSpace . " litres from the "
                $this->strName . " into the " . $objOtherBucket->getName() .
                "</p>";
        }
        $this->display();
        $objOtherBucket->display();
    }
}
?>
```

The above script implements a bucket class. It contains three data members which store the maximum volume of water the bucket can hold, its current volume and the name of the bucket:

```
class bucket {
    private $intMaxVolume;
    private $intCurrentVolume;
    private $strName;
```

A constructor function is used to create the bucket and invokes a display( ) function to show the bucket's status:

```
function __construct ($strName, $intMaxVol, $intCurrentVol) {
    $this->strName = $strName;
    $this->intMaxVolume = $intMaxVol;
    $this->intCurrentVolume = $intCurrentVol;
    $this->display();
}
```

Function addLiquid( ) allows for additional liquid to be added to the bucket's content:

```
function addLiquid($intVolume){
```

```
    $this->intCurrentVolume = $this->intCurrentVolume + $intVolume;
}
```

Function getName( ) returns the name of the bucket:

```
function getName(){
    return $this->strName;
}
```

Function getRemainingSpace( ) calculates the amount of liquid that can be added to the bucket:

```
function getRemainingSpace() {
    return $this->intMaxVolume - $this->intCurrentVolume;
}
```

Function emptyDownDrain( ) empties the contents of the bucket:

```
function emptyDownDrain() {
    $this->intCurrentVolume = 0;
    echo "<p>Emptying the " . $this->strName . "</p>";
}
```

Function fillFromTap( ) fills the bucket completely:

```
function fillFromTap() {
    $this->intCurrentVolume = $this->intMaxVolume;
    echo "<p>Filling " . $this->strName . "</p>";
}
```

Function display( ) displays the current status of the bucket:

```
function display() {
    echo "<p>The " . $this->strName . " contains " . $this->intCurrentVolume . "
        litres out of a maximum of " . $this->intMaxVolume . " litres</p>";
}
```

Function transfer( ) is the most complex function of the class. It receives as an argument another bucket object:

```
function transfer($objOtherBucket) {
```

The remaining space in the other bucket is calculated:

```
$intSpace = $objOtherBucket->getRemainingSpace();
```

If the amount of space the other bucket can hold is greater than the current bucket's content then the contents of this bucket are added to the other one, a message is displayed and the current volume of this bucket is set to zero:

```
if ($intSpace > $this->intCurrentVolume) {
    $objOtherBucket->addLiquid($this->intCurrentVolume);
    echo "<p>Pouring " . $this->intCurrentVolume .
    "litres from the " . $this->strName . " into the " .
    $objOtherBucket->getName() . "</p>";
    $this->intCurrentVolume = 0;
}
```

FIGURE 16.8 Two buckets

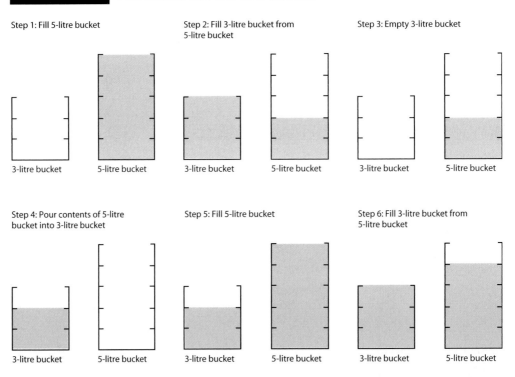

3-litre bucket   5-litre bucket

FIGURE 16.9   Two buckets and four litres solution

Step 1: Fill 5-litre bucket

Step 2: Fill 3-litre bucket from
5-litre bucket

Step 3: Empty 3-litre bucket

3-litre bucket   5-litre bucket

3-litre bucket   5-litre bucket

3-litre bucket   5-litre bucket

Step 4: Pour contents of 5-litre
bucket into 3-litre bucket

Step 5: Fill 5-litre bucket

Step 6: Fill 3-litre bucket from
5-litre bucket

3-litre bucket   5-litre bucket

3-litre bucket   5-litre bucket

3-litre bucket   5-litre bucket

Otherwise, the maximum amount of liquid that the other bucket can hold is passed, the current volume of this bucket is reduced by that amount and a message detailing this is output:

```
else {
    $objOtherBucket->addLiquid($intSpace);
    $this->intCurrentVolume = $this->intCurrentVolume &ndash; $intSpace;
    echo "<p>Pouring " . $intSpace . "litres from the " . $this->strName . "
        into the " . $objOtherBucket->getName() . "</p>";
}
```

Finally, the display methods in both the current bucket and the other bucket are invoked:

```
$this->display();
$objOtherBucket->display();
```

16

Now suppose we want to create two bucket objects, one of 3 litres and the other of 5 litres, so they look like those illustrated in Figure 16.8.

We can create them via the following statements:

```php
$objFiveBucket = new bucket("Five-litre bucket",5,5);
$objThreeBucket = new bucket("Three-litre bucket",3,0);
```

Having got these two buckets we can use our script to implement an old problem: 'If you have a 3-litre bucket and a 5-litre bucket, how using only the buckets and a tap for water can you end up with exactly four litres of water in the 5-litre bucket?'. Have a go at trying to solve this problem yourself, but if you get stuck the solution to the problem is illustrated in Figure 16.9.

This is what the solution looks like when implemented in a script:

```php
<?php
// File: example16-12.php

function __autoload($class_name) {
    require_once $class_name . '.php';
}

$objFiveBucket = new bucket("Five-litre bucket",5,5);
$objThreeBucket = new bucket("Three-litre bucket",3,0);
$objFiveBucket->transfer($objThreeBucket);
$objThreeBucket->emptyDownDrain();
$objFiveBucket->transfer($objThreeBucket);
$objFiveBucket->fillFromTap();
$objFiveBucket->transfer($objThreeBucket);
?>
```

The output from the above script is illustrated in Figure 16.10.

16.9 Objects within objects

An object can be embedded within another object as part of the class definition. Consider the following script:

```php
<?php
// File: lock.php

class lock {
    private $strLockStatus;

    function __construct ($strLockStatus) {
        $this->strLockStatus = $strLockStatus;
    }

    function display() {
        echo " and the lock is " . $this->strLockStatus . "</p>";
    }
}
?>
```

FIGURE 16.10   Output from bucket class

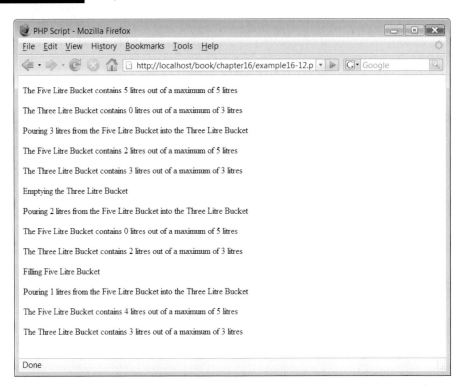

This script implements a class called lock which has one data member, the status (locked or unlocked) of the lock:

```
class lock {
    private $strLockStatus;
```

A constructor creates the object:

```
function __construct ($strLockStatus) {
    $this->strLockStatus = $strLockStatus;
}
```

A method called display( ) outputs the status of the lock:

```
function display() {
        echo " and the lock is " . $this->strLockStatus . "</p>";
    }
}
?>
```

Next, consider the following script:

```
<?php
// File: door.php
```

```
class door {

    private $strdoorStatus;
    private $objLock;

    function __construct($strDoorStatus,$strLockStatus){
       $this->strDoorStatus = $strDoorStatus;
       $this->objLock = new lock($strLockStatus);
       $this->display();
    }

    function display(){
       echo "<p>The door is " . $this->strDoorStatus;
       $this->objLock->display();
    }
  }
?>
```

The above script implements a door class:

```
class door {
```

The class consists of two data members: $strDoorStatus which stores the status of the door (open or closed) and $objLock which is a lock object (as defined previously):

```
private $strDoorStatus;
private $objLock;
```

A constructor function constructs the door status data member as well as creating a new lock object. The constructor also invokes the display( ) method:

```
function __construct($strDoorStatus,$strLockStatus){
   $this->strDoorStatus = $strDoorStatus;
   $this->objLock = new lock($strLockStatus);
   $this->display();
}
```

The display( ) method displays the status of the door. It also invokes the lock object's display method:

```
    function display(){
       echo "<p>The door is " . $this->strDoorStatus;
       $this->objLock->display();
    }
  }
?>
```

NOTE   Note the use of the $this->objLock->display() syntax to invoke the display method, which belongs to the objLock object, which is part of this object.

The following script instantiates two doors with locks:

```php
<?php
// File: example16-13.php

function __autoload($class_name) {
    require_once $class_name . '.php';
}
$objDoor = new door("Closed","Locked");
$objDoor = new door("Open","Unlocked");
?>
```

The output from the above script is illustrated in Figure 16.11.

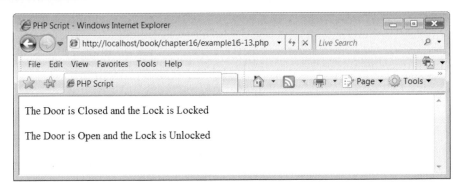

Exercises

16.1 Write a script which expands the functionality of the door and lock classes:

- A door can only be opened if the lock is unlocked.
- When a door is opened, a lock can be in the locked or unlocked position. However a door cannot be closed if a lock is currently locked.

You can assume that when a door and lock are first created it is closed but unlocked.

16.2 Write a script which creates a class 'electriccar'. The class should include two other classes called engine and gearbox:

- The engine can be started or stopped.
- The gearbox can select forward, neutral and reverse.
- The electriccar class has a function speedup( ), which increases the car's speed by 5 mph each time it is invoked if the engine is switched on and the gearbox is not in neutral.
- A function slowdown( ) reduces the speed of the car by 5 mph when invoked.
- If the gearbox is in neutral, the engine just revs, assuming that the car is switched on of course!

SUMMARY

In this chapter, we introduced the concept of object orientation. We examined how to create classes in PHP and how to use these classes by creating objects. We illustrated how classes could be created as separate source files and what advantages this brings. We introduced the concept of constructors and destructors which can make creating objects simpler. We concluded by illustrating how one object can invoke another and also how one object can consist of another.

References and further reading

Berard, E. (1998) Basic Object-Oriented Concepts. http://www.toa.com/pub/oobasics/oobasics.htm

Developer Shed (2003) Beginning OO Programming in PHP. http://www.codewalkers.com/c/a/Programming-Basics/Beginning-Object-Oriented-Programming-in-PHP/

Hathaway, R. (2003) Object FAQ. http://www.objectfaq.com/oofaq2/

Wikipedia. Object Orientation. http://en.wikipedia.org/wiki/Object-oriented_programming

CHAPTER 17

Object-Oriented Inheritance and Polymorphism

LEARNING OBJECTIVES

- **To understand how to create and be able to read class diagrams**

- **To understand the concept of class inheritance**

- **To understand and be able to use the scope resolution operator**

- **To understand the concept of class abstraction**

- **To understand the concept of polymorphism**

- **To understand and use static members and methods**

- **To understand class contents and type hinting**

- **To be able to compare objects and understand the different comparison operators**

- **To understand the use of the Final keyword**

- **To understand the concept of object interfaces**

INTRODUCTION

In this chapter, we are going to further our exploration of the object-oriented paradigm. We are going to continue where we left off in Chapter 16 and examine mainly the concepts of inheritance and polymorphism. We shall conclude the chapter by looking at some of the new object-oriented features that have been included in the latest release of the PHP language.

17.1 Diagramming classes

Before we continue by introducing more aspects of the object-oriented paradigm, it is best that we introduce a simple diagramming convention which we use in some of the following examples to help illustrate the class design which we are using. The diagramming notation illustrates classes as shown in Figure 17.1.

Figure 17.1 illustrates a simple rectangle which has been divided into three sections. In the top section is the name of the class which the rectangle represents. In the middle section are listed the data members which belong to the class. Finally, in the bottom section are the methods which form part of the class. Figure 17.2 shows a class being represented in this form.

Figure 17.2 illustrates the bucket class from Chapter 16. There are a number of things that are worthy of note before continuing. Firstly, that the different sections of the rectangle have been 'stretched' to accommodate the various numbers of items which have been included in each section. The top section indicates the class name, bucket. The middle section lists all three data members of the class. Finally, the bottom section lists the methods. Note that the constructor method has been omitted for clarity (actually they are often missed off anyway in the commercial world!). Where the methods receive arguments these are specified and if a value is returned then the type of the value is specified.

While you may not think that such diagrams are all that useful, we hope you will appreciate their use when we introduce the concept of inheritance.

FIGURE 17.1 A class diagram

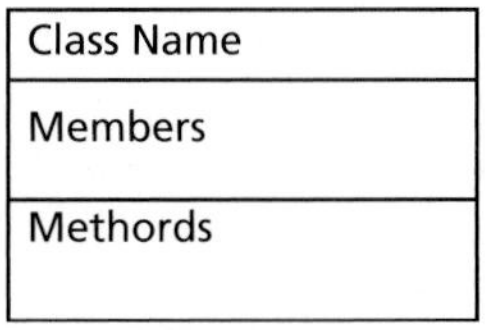

Class Name
Members
Methords

FIGURE 17.2 An example class

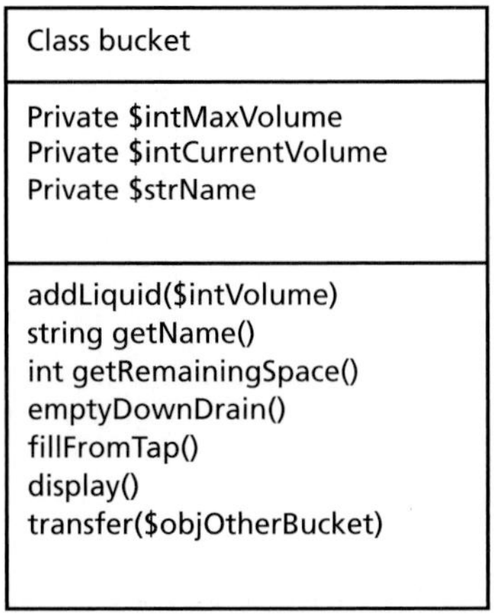

Class bucket
Private $intMaxVolume Private $intCurrentVolume Private $strName
addLiquid($intVolume) string getName() int getRemainingSpace() emptyDownDrain() fillFromTap() display() transfer($objOtherBucket)

17.2 Inheritance

A key strength of object orientation which we haven't yet introduced is a class's ability to inherit properties from other classes. This ability saves the programmer time, reduces the complexity of the solution and helps raise quality by reducing code duplication and thus error introduction. We illustrate inheritance on our diagram through the use of an arrow, as illustrated in Figure 17.3.

In Figure 17.3 we can see two classes. The first is called class 'shape'. The second class is called 'rectangle'. The arrow from rectangle to shape indicates that rectangle 'is a' kind of shape.

With inheritance, a class which inherits from another is able to access all the members and methods of the class from which it inherits (if the class allows it) and is also able to add and amend class members of its own.

The keyword 'extends' is used in a class definition to indicate that a class inherits from another:

```
class className extends otherClassName
```

Therefore in the example in Figure 17.3, we would write the following to define our 'rectangle' class:

```
class rectangle extends shape {

}
```

Our 'shape' class is defined simply as:

```
class shape {

}
```

FIGURE 17.3   Inheritance – 'Is A'

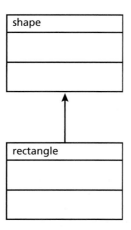

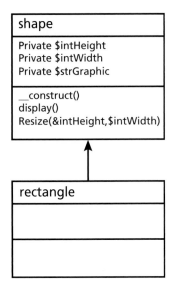

FIGURE 17.4   Expanded shape and rectangle classes

Let's begin by building these two classes. The shape class is going to contain the data members, $intHeight, $intWidth and $strGraphic to store the width, height and graphical image used to represent the shape. The shape class is also going to contain three methods: a constructor, a display() method, which will display the shape, and a resize() method which will allow the shape to be resized. This is illustrated in Figure 17.4.

 NOTE   Note that we have included the __construct() function in the list because of what we will be doing later. However, to keep things simple we have removed the constructor's arguments.

In PHP then, our shape class looks like this and should be saved as 'shape.php':

```php
<?php
// File: shape.php

class shape {
    private $intHeight;
    private $intWidth;
    private $strGraphic;

    function __construct($intHeight, $intWidth, $strGraphic){
        $this->intHeight = $intHeight;
        $this->intWidth = $intWidth;
        $this->strGraphic = $strGraphic;
    }
```

```php
    function display(){
        $intHeight = $this->intHeight;
        $intWidth = $this->intWidth;
        $strGraphic = $this->strGraphic;
        echo "<p><img src='graphics/$strGraphic' width='$intWidth'
                    height='$intHeight' alt='$strGraphic'/></p>";
    }

    function resize($intHeight, $intWidth) {
        $this->intHeight = $intHeight;
        $this->intWidth = $intWidth;
    }
  }
?>
```

And our rectangle class is a very simple and should be saved as 'rectangle.php':

```php
<?php
// File: rectangle.php

class rectangle extends shape {
}
?>
```

We need to create some images which we are going to use in this example and these are listed in Figure 17.5.

Note that the square and rectangle images are both square. We stretch the rectangle to the required shape in our script.

We can write a small script to use the classes:

```php
<?php
// File: example17-1.php

function __autoload($class_name) {
    require_once $class_name . '.php';
}

$objRectangle = new rectangle(100,50, "rectangle.gif");
$objRectangle->display();
$objRectangle->resize(50,100);
$objRectangle->display();
?>
```

FIGURE 17.5 Graphical shape images

square.gif   rectangle.gif   triangle.gif   ellipse.gif

FIGURE 17.6   Rectangle object

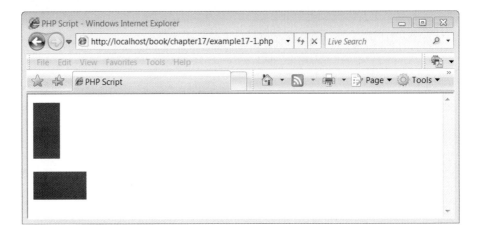

The above script uses the __autoload function introduced in Chapter 16 to load all classes as required. It also refines an object of type rectangle and invokes the display() method:

```php
$objRectangle = new rectangle(100,50, "rectangle.gif");
$objRectangle->display();
```

Next it resizes the object and redisplays it:

```php
$objRectangle->resize(50,100);
$objRectangle->display();
```

The output from the above script is illustrated in Figure 17.6.

> **ⓘ NOTE** Note that the rectangle object worked just fine in both displaying and resizing itself. This is because although the methods are not part of the rectangle class, they are part of the shape class and the rectangle inherited their use.

The next thing that we are going to do is create a new class called 'square'. We could define this as inheriting from shape, but squares and rectangles are very similar, the only difference being that a square's width and height are the same. We shall therefore build a class called 'square' which inherits from 'rectangle', but only requires a single value to specify its width and height. Because of this we are going to need to rewrite both the constructor and resize methods. This is illustrated in Figure 17.7.

The following script illustrates our square class, which should be saved as square.php:

```php
<?php
// File: square.php

class square extends rectangle {
```

FIGURE 17.15 Comparing objects

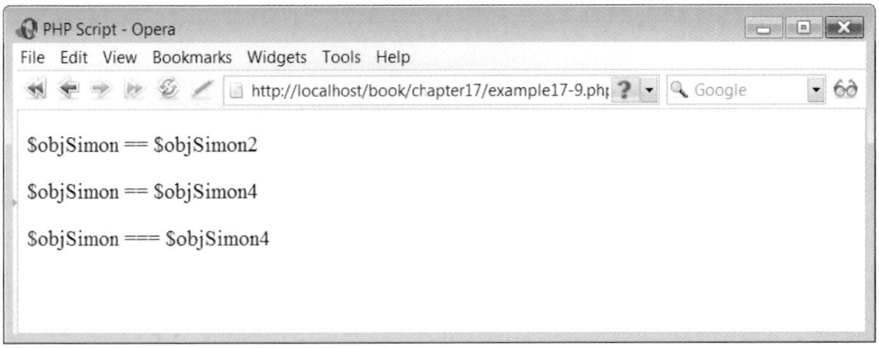

The output from the above script is illustrated in Figure 17.15.

17.10 The 'final' keyword

The 'final' keyword can be prefixed before a class method and prevents a child class from overriding the method. Consider the following example:

```php
<?php
// File: example17-10.php

class Person {

   private $strName;

   function __construct ($strName) {
      $this->strName = $strName;
   }

   final function showName() {
      echo "<p>" . $this->strName . "</p>";
   }
}
class Student extends Person {

   function showName() {

   }
}
?>
```

The above example creates a Person class with a constructor and showName() method which has the prefixed keyword final:

```php
class Person {

   private $strName;

   function __construct ($strName) {
      $this->strName = $strName;
   }
```

FIGURE 17.7   Adding a square

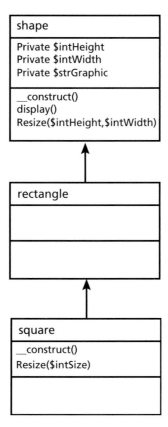

```
    function __construct($intSize, $strGraphic){
        __construct($intSize, $intSize, $strGraphic);
    }

    function resize($intSize) {
        resize($intSize, $intSize);
    }
}
?>
```

The above script consists of two methods, the first is the constructor which receives the square size and the graphical image of the square as arguments. However, we run into a small problem which is that the dimensions of the square and the graphical image are held within the shape class not the square class. However, to get around that problem all the constructor does is invoke the constructor of the parent class (shape) passing it the size of the square twice (for its width and height) followed by the graphic string. Likewise the resize method does a similar thing invoking the parent resize method passing it the value of size twice as arguments.

Unfortunately, we have run into a problem: this doesn't work. It doesn't have anything to do with the fact that the parent class is rectangle not shape as we would expect the language to keep on looking up the inheritance hierarchy until we found a matching method, but simply the fact that we don't yet know what the syntax is for referring to a parent's methods. To do this we need to introduce the scope resolution operator.

17.3 Scope resolution operator

The scope resolution operator (also called Paamayim Nekudotayim) or in simpler terms, the double colon(::), is a token that allows access to static, constant and overridden members or methods of a class. We shall come back to this later. However, combined with the keywords 'self' and 'parent' it allows specific access to members and methods.

 NOTE Paamayim Nekudotayim means 'double colon' in Hebrew by the way, we didn't just make this up!

For example, we hit upon a snag of how to refer to a specific parent's function which has the same name as one in the current class. To specifically refer to the parent class we would write:

```
parent::
```

before the member or method name. So applying this to our square class above we end up with:

```php
<?php
// File: square.php

class square extends rectangle {

    function __construct($intSize, $strGraphic){
        parent::__construct($intSize, $intSize, $strGraphic);
    }

    function resize($intSize) {
        parent::resize($intSize, $intSize);
    }
}
?>
```

We can show the square class works by amending our script which creates the instances of the classes:

```php
<?php
// File: example17-2.php

function __autoload($class_name) {
    require_once $class_name . '.php';
}

$objRectangle = new rectangle(100,50, "rectangle.gif");
$objRectangle->display();
$objRectangle->resize(50,100);
$objRectangle->display();

$objSquare = new square(100, "square.gif");
$objSquare->display();
?>
```

FIGURE 17.8 Square output

The above script now creates a square object as well as a rectangle and the output produced is illustrated in Figure 17.8.

We can continue to show the power of inheritance by adding some more shapes to our inheritance tree. These are shown in Figure 17.9. We have created two new shapes: a triangle and an ellipse. The script for these is currently very simple:

```php
<?php
// File: ellipse.php

class ellipse extends shape {

}
?>
```

```php
<?php
// File: triangle.php

class triangle extends shape {

}
?>
```

We can amend our script which creates the instances of the classes:

```php
<?php
// File: example17-3.php

function __autoload($class_name) {
    require_once $class_name . '.php';
}

$objRectangle = new rectangle(100,50, "rectangle.gif");
$objRectangle->display();
```

```
$objRectangle->resize(50,100);
$objRectangle->display();

$objSquare = new square(100, "square.gif");
$objSquare->display();

$objTriangle = new triangle(50,100, "triangle.gif");
$objTriangle->display();

$objEllipse = new ellipse(50,100, "ellipse.gif");
$objEllipse->display();
$objEllipse->resize(100,50);
$objEllipse->display();
?>
```

In addition to creating our square and rectangle and displaying those as before the script creates and displays a triangle:

```
$objTriangle = new triangle(50,100, "triangle.gif");
$objTriangle->display();
```

It then creates an ellipse, displays it, resizes it and displays it again:

```
$objEllipse = new ellipse(50,100, "ellipse.gif");
$objEllipse->display();
$objEllipse->resize(100,50);
$objEllipse->display();
```

FIGURE 17.9   Triangle and ellipse classes

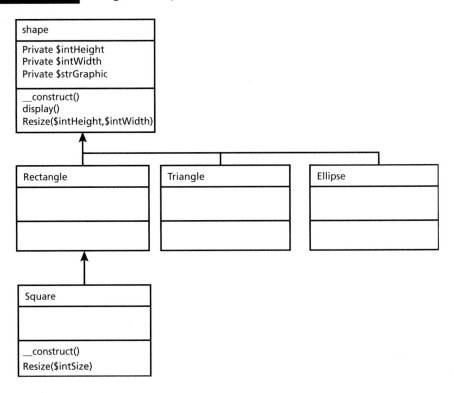

The output from the above script is illustrated in Figure 17.10.

We have now reached the stage where we have an inheritance structure consisting of four different shapes. It is now time to add a new method, one which is able to calculate the area of the shape in question. We cannot simply include a single method in the shape class as the formula to calculate a shape's area differs from shape to shape. We are going to have to include a method for each of our shapes. Table 17.1 lists the formulae for calculating the area of our shapes.

FIGURE 17.10   Triangles, ellipses and more

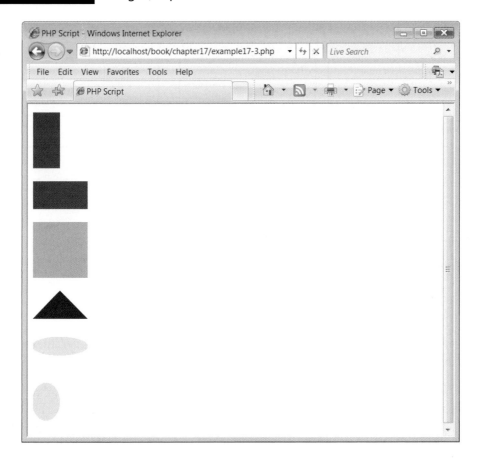

TABLE 17.1   Shape area calculations

Shape	Formula	Code
Rectangle	Width * Height	$intArea = $intWidth * $intHeight;
Square	As for rectangle	Can inherit from rectangle
Triangle	Width * Height/2	$intArea = $intWidth * $intHeight/2;
Ellipse	π* Width/2 * Height/2	round(Pi() * ($intWidth/2) * ($intHeight/2));

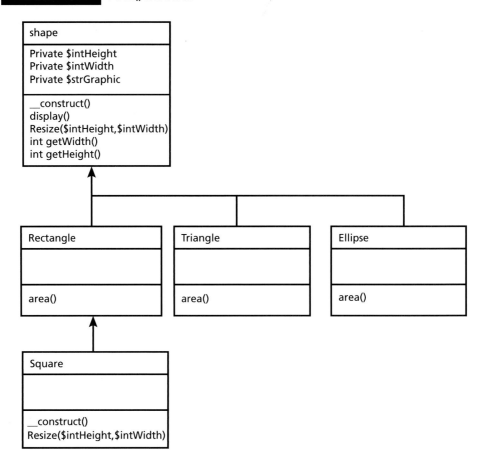

FIGURE 17.11   Area() methods

Figure 17.11 illustrates where our area() methods are going to be included in our class hierarchy.

An examination of Figure 17.11 will reveal that not only has the area() method been included in the rectangle, triangle and ellipse classes but also that two new methods, getWidth and getHeight, have been included in the shape class. These are required as the area() methods need to be able to access the values of $intWidth and $intHeight which are part of the shape class.

Let's have a look at the script, beginning with the shape class:

```php
<?php
// File: shape.php

class shape {

    private $intHeight;
    private $intWidth;
    private $strGraphic;
```

```php
    function getHeight(){
        return $this->intHeight;
    }

    function getWidth(){
        return $this->intWidth;
    }

    function __construct($intHeight, $intWidth, $strGraphic){
        $this->intHeight = $intHeight;
        $this->intWidth = $intWidth;
        $this->strGraphic = $strGraphic;
    }
function display(){
    $intHeight = $this->intHeight;
    $intWidth = $this->intWidth;
    $strGraphic = $this->strGraphic;
    echo "<p><img src = 'graphics/$strGraphic' width = '$intWidth'
            height = '$intHeight' alt = '$strGraphic'/></p>";
}
function resize($intHeight, $intWidth) {
    $this->intHeight = $intHeight;
    $this->intWidth = $intWidth;
    }
}
?>
```

An examinination of the script will reveal the two methods getHeight() and getWidth() which return the values of data members $intHeight and $intWidth:

```php
function getHeight(){
    return $this->intHeight;
}

function getWidth(){
    return $this->intWidth;
}
```

The rectangle class now includes an area() method:

```php
<?phpF
// File: rectangle.php

class rectangle extends shape {

    function area() {
        $intWidth = parent::getWidth();
        $intHeight = parent::getHeight();
        $intArea = $intWidth * $intHeight;
        echo "<p>Area is $intArea</p>";
    }
}
?>
```

As does the triangle class:

```php
<?php
// File: triangle.php

class triangle extends shape {

    function area() {
        $intWidth = parent::getWidth();
        $intHeight = parent::getHeight();
        $intArea = $intWidth * $intHeight/2;
        echo "<p>Area is $intArea</p>";
    }
}
?>
```

So does the ellipse class:

```php
<?php
// File: ellipse.php

class ellipse extends shape {

    function area() {
        $intWidth = parent::getWidth();
        $intHeight = parent::getHeight();
        $intArea = round(Pi() * ($intWidth/2) * ($intHeight/2) );
        echo "<p>Area is $intArea</p>";
    }
}
?>
```

Our example script can now be modified to invoke this method:

```php
<?php
// File: example17-4.php

function __autoload($class_name) {
    require_once $class_name . '.php';
}

$objRectangle = new rectangle(100,50, "rectangle.gif");
$objRectangle->display();
$objRectangle->resize(50,100);
$objRectangle->display();
$objRectangle->area();

$objSquare = new square(100, "square.gif");
$objSquare->display();

$objTriangle = new triangle(50,100, "triangle.gif");
$objTriangle->display();
$objTriangle->area();
```

```
$objEllipse = new ellipse(50,100, "ellipse.gif");
$objEllipse->display();
$objEllipse->area();
?>
```

The output from the above script is illustrated in Figure 17.12.

17.4 Class abstraction

Sometimes we want to define a class which is used purely to help with the inheritance structure, but we don't want programmers to be able to create instances of that class. The shape class is a good illustration. Currently someone could do this:

```
$objThing = new shape(100,100, "thing.gif");
```

We don't want someone to be able to create an instance of shape as it doesn't have an area() method for example and it will cause us all sorts of problems. However, help is at

FIGURE 17.12 Areas of shapes

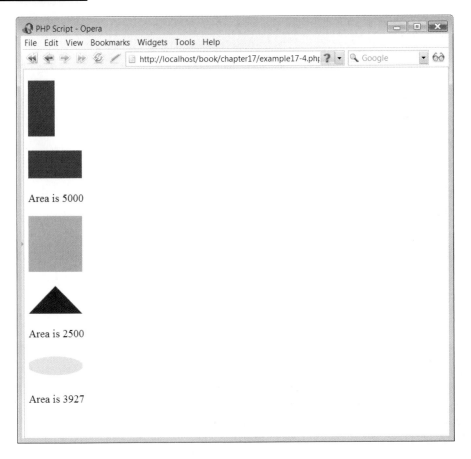

hand as PHP allows us to define a class as being abstract:

```
abstract class className {

}
```

We amend our shape class so that it reads:

```
abstract class shape {

}
```

This will prevent anyone trying to create instances of the shape class.

17.5 Polymorphism

Polymorphism is Greek and it means 'Many forms'. We have actually implemented polymorphic methods in our previous inheritance example but may not have actually realized this or what potential they have. Polymorphic functions are those which have the same name in a class inheritance structure but are redefined from class to class, thus enabling the behaviour of that class to be different. In our example, the area() method exhibits polymorphism as it has the same name and attributes from class to class, but uses a different formula to calculate the area of the shape concerned.

The power of polymorphic methods can be seen in the following example:

```php
<?php
// File: example17-5.php

function __autoload($class_name) {
    require_once $class_name . '.php';
}

$objRectangle = new rectangle(100,50, "rectangle.gif");
$objSquare = new square(100, "square.gif");
$objTriangle = new triangle(50,100, "triangle.gif");
$objEllipse = new ellipse(50,100, "ellipse.gif");

$arrShapes = array
    ($objRectangle,$objSquare,$objTriangle,$objEllipse);
foreach ($arrShapes as $objShape){
    $objShape->display();
    $objShape->area();
}
?>
```

The above script creates four different shape objects:

```php
$objRectangle = new rectangle(100,50, "rectangle.gif");
$objSquare = new square(100, "square.gif");
$objTriangle = new triangle(50,100, "triangle.gif");
$objEllipse = new ellipse(50,100, "ellipse.gif");
```

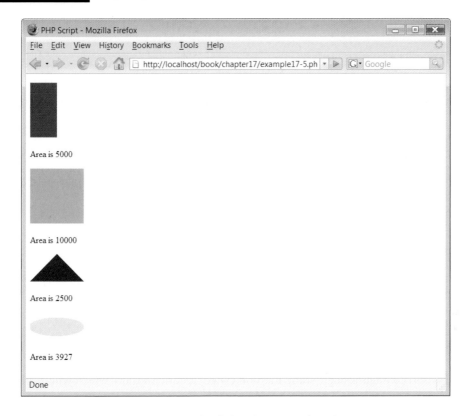

FIGURE 17.13 Polymorphism

It then creates an array and places each of the objects within the array:

```
$arrShapes = array
    ($objRectangle,$objSquare,$objTriangle,$objEllipse);
```

A foreach loop is then used to iterate around the array extracting each object one at a time. The display() and area() methods of the object are invoked:

```
foreach ($arrShapes as $objShape){
    $objShape->display();
    $objShape->area();
}
```

The foreach loop works flawlessly with the output from the display() and area() methods being displayed, as illustrated in Figure 17.13. The polymorphic method properties mean that the programmer doesn't have to worry about which object is being returned from the array as they know that simply invoking the method will result in the correct display() and area() method being performed.

17.6 Static members and methods

Declaring class members or methods as static makes them accessible without needing an instantiation of the class. A member declared as static cannot be accessed with an instantiated class object (though a static method can). Consider the following script:

```php
<?php
// File: example17-6.php

class noInstancesRequiredClass {

    public static $strName = "Simon Stobart";
    public static function aStaticMethod() {
        echo "<p>" . self::$strName . "</p>";
    }

}
echo "<p>" . noInstancesRequiredClass::$strName . "</p>";
noInstancesRequiredClass::aStaticMethod();

$objExample = new noInstancesRequiredClass;
$objExample->aStaticMethod();

?>
```

The above script defines a class called 'noInstancesRequiredClass' and within this creates a static member variable called $strName:

```php
class noInstancesRequiredClass {
    public static $strName = "Simon Stobart";
```

The class also contains a single static method called 'aStaticMethod' which will display the value of the static member:

```php
public static function aStaticMethod() {
    echo "<p>" . self::$strName . "</p>";
}
```

Note that the method uses the self:: scope operator to access the member.

 NOTE Because static methods are callable without an instance of the object created, the pseudo-variable *$this* is not available inside the method declared as static.

Outside the class the scope operator is used to access the value of the static member without any need to instantiate the class:

```php
echo "<p>" . noInstancesRequiredClass::$strName . "</p>";
```

It addition the static method is also invoked in a similar way:

```php
noInstancesRequiredClass::aStaticMethod();
```

Finally, the class is instantiated then a call to aStaticMethod is made to illustrate that this also works:

```
$objExample = new noInstancesRequiredClass;
$objExample->aStaticMethod();
```

 NOTE Static properties cannot be accessed through the object using the arrow operator ->.

The output from the above script is:

Simon Stobart
Simon Stobart
Simon Stobart

17.7 Class constants

PHP classes support the inclusion of constant values. Once defined these remain the same and are unchangeable. Constants differ from normal data members in that you don't use the $ symbol to declare or use them. Consider the following script:

```
<?php
// File: example17-7.php

class constantClass {

   const strName = "Simon Stobart";

   function showConstant() {
      echo "<p>" . self::strName . "</p>";
   }
}
echo "<p>" . constantClass::strName . "</p>";

$objExample = new constantClass;
$objExample->showConstant();
?>
```

In the above script, constantClass is defined and a const member is created:

```
class constantClass {

   const strName = "Simon Stobart";
```

 NOTE Constant members do not use the $ symbol to define them.

A method showConstant( ) is defined and outputs the value of the constant. Note that the self:: scope operator is used to access the constant member as the -> operator will not work:

```
function showConstant() {
    echo "<p>" . self::$strName . "</p>";
}
```

Outside the class, the scope operator is used to access the value of the constant member without any need to instantiate the class:

```
echo "<p>" . constantClass::strName . "</p>";
```

Finally, the class is instantiated then a call to method showConstant( ) is made to illustrate that this also works:

```
$objExample = new constantClass;
$objExample->showConstant();
```

The output from the above script is:

Simon Stobart
Simon Stobart

17.8 Type hinting

PHP 5 introduces the concept of type hinting. Functions can force parameters to be objects (by specifying the name of the class in the function prototype) or arrays. Consider the following script:

```
<?php
// File: example17-8.php

class typeHintingClass {

    private $arrNames = array();

    function __construct(array $arrNames) {
        $this->arrNames = $arrNames;
    }

    function showContents() {
        foreach ($this->arrNames as $arrItem)
            echo "<p>$arrItem</p>";
    }

    function showOtherClass(typeHintingClass $objOther) {
        $objOther->showContents();
    }
}

$arrNames = array("Simon","Alan","Fred");
$arrColours = array("Red","Green","Blue","Yellow");

$objNames = new typeHintingClass($arrNames);
$objNames->showContents();
```

```
$objColours = new typeHintingClass($arrColours);
$objNames->showOtherClass($objColours);
?>
```

 NOTE Type hints can only be of the object and array (since PHP 5.1) types. If your computer is not running PHP 5.1 or newer, the above script will not work.

The script begins by creating a class called typeHintingClass, which contains a single data member array:

```
class typeHintingClass {
   private $arrNames = array();
```

A constructor function populates the array member:

```
function __construct(array $arrNames) {
   $this->arrNames = $arrNames;
}
```

Method showContents() displays the contents of the array:

```
function showContents() {
   foreach ($this->arrNames as $arrItem)
      echo "<p>$arrItem</p>";
}
```

Method showOtherClass() receives an object and then invokes method showContents() to display its members' contents. Type hinting is used in the method argument to specify that the method is expecting a typeHintingClass object to be received:

```
function showOtherClass(typeHintingClass $objOther) {
   $objOther->showContents();
}
```

Two arrays are created:

```
$arrNames = array("Simon","Alan","Fred");
$arrColours = array("Red","Green","Blue","Yellow");
```

An object is created and its contents displayed:

```
$objNames = new typeHintingClass($arrNames);
$objNames->showContents();
```

Another object is created and then the previous object is passed the new object for display:

```
$objColours = new typeHintingClass($arrColours);
$objNames->showOtherClass($objColours);
}
```

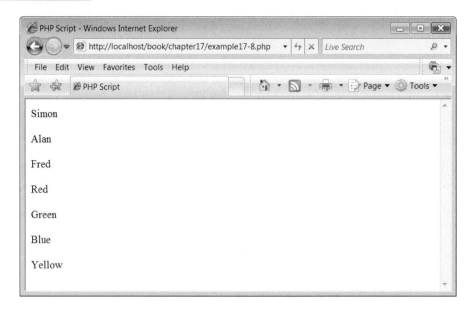

FIGURE 17.14 Type hinting

You can illustrate the type hinting aspect of this code by trying to insert the following line of script:

```
$objNames->showOtherClass("Not an object!");
```

This will cause an error as it is a string, not an array which is being passed.

The output from the above script is illustrated in Figure 17.14.

17.9 Comparing objects

In PHP 5, object comparison is more complicated than in previous versions of the language. Objects can be compared in two different ways. Firstly, when using the comparison operator (==), two object instances are equal if they have the same attributes and values and are instances of the same class. Secondly, when using the identity operator (===), object variables are identical if and only if they refer to the same instance of the same class. Consider the following example:

```php
<?php
// File: example17-9.php

class Person {

    public $strName;

    function __construct ($strName) {
        $this->strName = $strName;
    }
}
```

```
   }

class AnotherPerson {

   public $strName;

   function __construct ($strName) {
      $this->strName = $strName;
   }
}

$objSimon = new Person("Simon");
$objSimon2 = new Person("Simon");
$objSimon3 = new AnotherPerson("Simon");
$objSimon4 = $objSimon;

if ($objSimon == $objSimon2)
   echo '<p>$objSimon == $objSimon2</p>';

if ($objSimon == $objSimon3)
   echo '<p>$objSimon == $objSimon3</p>';

if ($objSimon == $objSimon4)
   echo '<p>$objSimon == $objSimon4</p>';

if ($objSimon === $objSimon2)
   echo '<p>$objSimon === $objSimon2</p>';

if ($objSimon === $objSimon3)
   echo '<p>$objSimon === $objSimon3</p>';

if ($objSimon === $objSimon4)
   echo '<p>$objSimon === $objSimon4</p>';
?>
```

This script begins by creating a Person class, which contains a single data member $strName and a constructor function:

```
class Person {

   public $strName;

   function __construct ($strName) {
      $this->strName = $strName;
   }
}
```

Another class called AnotherPerson is created which contains exactly the same data members as the Person class:

```
class AnotherPerson {

   public $strName;

   function __construct ($strName) {
```

```
            $this->strName = $strName;
        }
    }
```

Four objects are created. The first and second are of class Person:

```
$objSimon = new Person("Simon");
$objSimon2 = new Person("Simon");
```

The third is of class AnotherPerson:

```
$objSimon3 = new AnotherPerson("Simon");
```

The fourth is of type Person as it is created from an instance already created:

```
$objSimon4 = $objSimon;
```

$objSimon and $objSimon2 are compared using the comparison operator (==) and the result is true:

```
if ($objSimon == $objSimon2)
    echo '<p>$objSimon == $objSimon2</p>';
```

$objSimon and $objSimon3 are compared using the comparison operator (==) and the result is false as the classes are not the same:

```
if ($objSimon == $objSimon3)
    echo '<p>$objSimon == $objSimon3</p>';
```

$objSimon and $objSimon4 are compared using the comparison operator (==) and the result is true:

```
if ($objSimon == $objSimon4)
    echo '<p>$objSimon == $objSimon4</p>';
```

$objSimon and $objSimon2 are compared using the identity operator (===) and the result is false as they are not the same instance of the object:

```
if ($objSimon === $objSimon2)
    echo '<p>$objSimon === $objSimon2</p>';
```

$objSimon and $objSimon3 are compared using the identity operator (===) and the result is false as they are not the same instance of the object:

```
if ($objSimon === $objSimon3)
    echo '<p>$objSimon === $objSimon3</p>';
```

$objSimon and $objSimon4 are compared using the identity operator (===) and the result is true:

```
if ($objSimon === $objSimon4)
    echo '<p>$objSimon === $objSimon4</p>';
?>
```

```
final function showName() {
    echo $this->strName;
  }
}
```

A second class Student extends Person and includes a showName() method:

```
class Student extends Person {

  function showName() {

  }
```

However, the following error message is generated as the final keyword prevents the showName() method from being overridden:

Fatal error: `Cannot override final method Person::showName()` in **c:\wamp\www\lesson 1\example17-10.php** on line **22**

 NOTE If the final keyword is placed before the class keyword, like this:

```
final class Person {
}
```

then the class itself cannot be extended.

17.11 Object interfaces

An object interface is a means to enable you to create a script which specifies the methods a class must have but without the need to define exactly how these methods are to be built. Interfaces are defined using the interface keyword, in the same way as a basic class but differ in that none of the methods have their contents defined.

 NOTE All of the methods declared in an interface must be public.

Consider the following script:

```
interface iPerson {

  public function showName();
  public function setSurname($strSurname);
  public function setFirstname($strFirstname);
```

The above script specifies an interface called iPerson and specifies that its implementation should contain three member methods. The script doesn't actually do anything at the moment.

To implement an interface, the *implements* operator is used. All methods in the interface must be implemented within a class otherwise an error is produced.

The following script enhances the previous one by adding an implementation of the interface class:

```php
<?php
// File: example17-11.php

interface iPerson {
    public function showName();
    public function setSurname($strSurname);
    public function setFirstname($strFirstname);
}

class Person implements iPerson {

    private $strSurname;
    private $strFirstname;

    public function showName() {
        echo "<p>" . $this->strFirstname;
        echo " ";
        echo $this->strSurname . "</p>";
    }

    public function setSurname($strSurname) {
        $this->strSurname = $strSurname;
    }

    public function setFirstname($strFirstname) {
        $this->strFirstname = $strFirstname;
    }
}

$objSimon = new Person;
$objSimon->setSurname("Stobart");
$objSimon->setFirstname("Simon");
$objSimon->showName();
?>
```

The above script implements the interface like so:

```php
class Person implements iPerson {

    private $strSurname;
    private $strFirstname;

    public function showName() {
        echo "<p>" . $this->strFirstname;
        echo " ";
        echo $this->strSurname . "</p>";
    }

    public function setSurname($strSurname) {
        $this->strSurname = $strSurname;
```

```
        }
        public function setFirstname($strFirstname) {
           $this->strFirstname = $strFirstname;
        }
}
```

It then creates an instance of the class to illustrate that it works correctly:

```
$objSimon = new Person;
$objSimon->setSurname("Stobart");
$objSimon->setFirstname("Simon");
$objSimon->showName();
```

The output from the above script is:

Simon Stobart

Exercises

17.1 Add a new class to the shape class hierarchy called circle. This could inherit from ellipse. The area of a circle can be calculated by the formula:

$\pi * r^2$

We can replace this with:

$\pi * (\$intWidth * \$intWidth)$

17.2 Write a class inheritance structure which implements the following classes:

Vehicle
Car
Hybrid Car
Boat
Bicycle

Vehicle should be an abstract class. Car, Boat and Bicycle inherit from Vehicle. Hybrid Car inherits from car. A hybrid car is one which is capable of running on batteries and petrol. The following are various members; you will need to consider where they fit into the hierarchy:

intWeight
intLength
intTopSpeed
intDisplacement
intRemaingFuelLitres
intRemaingBatteryLife
strDescription

You should create a display() method which will display all details about the instantiated vehicle. You will need to create other support methods also, such as a constructor and some get member methods.

SUMMARY

In this chapter, we began by introducing inheritance and polymorphism.

We then examined some of the new object-oriented features that have been included in the latest release of the PHP language such as class constants, type hinting and the use of the 'final' keyword. We concluded the chapter by examining PHP implementation of object interfaces.

References and further reading

Day, D. (2005) The Practicality of OO PHP. http://www.onlamp.com/pub/a/php/2005/07/28/oo_php.html

Refdev.com PHP Object Oriented Tutorials. http://www.refdev.com/tutorials/PHP/Object_Oriented/

Yank, K. (2002) Object Oriented PHP: Paging Result Sets. http://www.sitepoint.com/article/php-paging-result-sets

CHAPTER 18

Combining Ajax and PHP – Making the Web More Dynamic

INTRODUCTION

In this chapter we are going to examine how PHP, JavaScript and Ajax technologies can be combined to enable the creation of dynamic web applications. Using this technology enables us to create systems which interface to databases and at the same time provide more responsive web applications.

We have already introduced JavaScript, in Chapter 6, and Ajax, in Chapter 7, and have subsequently delved into the world of PHP and its integration with databases. We are now ready to introduce how the three technologies can be easily integrated. The good news is that there is not a great deal of new technology to learn; the syntax and language constructs should already be familiar to you as we have introduced them all previously.

Support for PHP and Ajax is growing on the web and there are a growing number of articles and resources which may be of interest to you once you have mastered the basics. We have included links to some web sites in the further reading section of this chapter which you may find interesting.

We begin by revisiting the JavaScript/Ajax techniques and show how a simple PHP application can be invoked. After this we shall introduce some simple example applications in PHP to show what effects can be created using Ajax and PHP.

18.1 Implementing Ajax

Creating combined JavaScript, Ajax and PHP applications is relatively easy. In all of the following examples we use the same getXMLHttpRequest function to create an XMLHttpRequest object as we did in Chapter 7, shown again below:

```
// getxmlhttprequest.js
function getXMLHttpRequest()
{
  var xhrequest = null;
  if(window.XMLHttpRequest)
  {
  // If IE7, Mozilla, Safari, etc: Use native object
    try
    {
      xhrequest = new XMLHttpRequest();
      return xhrequest;
    }
    catch(exception)
    {
    // OK, just carry on looking
    }
  }
  else
  {

    //...otherwise, use the ActiveX control for IE5.x and IE6
      var IEControls =
          ["MSXML2.XMLHttp.5.0","MSXML2.XMLHttp.4.0","MSXML2.XMLHttp.3.0",
           "MSXML2.XMLHttp"];
      for(var i=0; i<IEControls.length; i++)
      {
        try
        {
          xhrequest = new ActiveXObject(IEControls[i]);
          return xhrequest;
        }
        catch(exception)
        {
        // OK, just carry on looking
        }
      }
    // if we got here we didn't find any matches
    throw new Error("Cannot create an XMLHttpRequest");
  }
}
```

For the sake of the readability and reuse we save this function as the JavaScript file:

```
getxmlhttprequest.js
```

We then load this function in each of our scripts with the JavaScript instruction:

```
<script type="text/javascript" src="getxmlhttprequest.js">
</script>
```

This means that once we have created this function, we can use it again and again in each of our examples without the need to recreate or change it in anyway. In addition to the 'getxmlhttprequest.js' file, each of the following examples also has a unique JavaScript file that contains the two functions that open a connection to the PHP script on the server, using an xhrequest.open( ) function, and process the response from the server. These two functions are stored in a single JavaScript file with a name appropriate to the example script, for instance:

```
example18-1.js
example18-2.js
. . .
example18-6.js
```

The PHP scripts which are invoked by the xhrequest.open( ) function are also given a file name appropriate to the example, for instance:

```
example18-1.php
example18-2.php
. . .
example18-6.php
```

and the (X)HTML file which wraps everything together and is what the user invokes to start the examples are named:

```
example18-1.htm
example18-2.htm
. . .
example18-6.htm
```

Therefore, each example consists of four files: two JavaScript files, a PHP server script and an (X)HTML file. We shall begin with our simplest example to illustrate how these files all work together.

18.2 A simple calculator

The following example implements a simple calculator. This calculator allows a user to type numbers into a couple of form fields and then, by selecting an operator (add, subject, multiply and divide) from a form select field, perform some basic mathematics on the entered numbers. The following is the (X)HTML script, named 'example18-1.htm' which the user invokes from the browser:

```
<!DOCTYPE html PUBLIC "-//W3C//DTD XHTML 1.1//EN"
   "http://www.w3.org/TR/xhtml11/DTD/xhtml11.dtd">
```

```
<html xmlns="http://www.w3.org/1999/xhtml" xml:lang="en">
<head>
<title>Calculator Script</title>
<meta http-equiv="Content-Type" content="text/html; charset=ISO-8859-1" />

<script type="text/javascript" src="getxmlhttprequest.js">
</script>
<script type="text/javascript" src="example18-1.js">
</script>
</head>
<body>
<!-- File: example18-1.htm -->

<h2>Simple Calculator:</h2>
<form action="" method="post">
<p>
<input type="text" name="intValue1" id="intValue1"
onchange="startJS();" />
<select name="strOperator" id="strOperator" onchange="startJS();">
<option value="1">+</option>
<option value="2">-</option>
<option value="3">/</option>
<option value="4">*</option>
</select>
<input type="text" name="intValue2" id="intValue2"
onchange="startJS();"/>
<input type="button" value="=" onclick="startJS();" />
<input type="text" name="intResult" id="intResult" />
</p>
</form>
</body>
</html>
```

After the initial document declaration and heading information the script begins by including the 'getxmlhttprequest.js' and 'example18-1.js' JavaScript files which are going to be used to form an XMLHttpRequest object and to process the user events (entering the numbers and selecting the operation to be performed):

```
<script type="text/javascript" src="getxmlhttprequest.js">
</script>
<script type="text/javascript" src="example18-1.js">
</script>
```

Next, a form is declared which consists of five form elements. These elements are the two input text fields where the user enters the numbers to use in the calculation, a select element to enable selection of a mathematical operator, an input button to force the calculation to be updated (by clicking on it) and an input text field where the sum of the calculation is displayed:

```
<form action="" method="post">
<p>
<input type="text" name="intValue1" id="intValue1"
onchange="startJS();" />
```

```
<select name="strOperator" id="strOperator" onchange="startJS();">
<option value="1">+</option>
<option value="2">-</option>
<option value="3">/</option>
<option value="4">*</option>
</select>
<input type="text" name="intValue2" id="intValue2"
onchange="startJS();"/>
<input type="button" value="=" onclick="startJS();" />
<input type="text" name="intResult" id="intResult" />
</p>
</form>
```

Note that three 'onchange' events have been included on certain form elements which invoke function startJS( ) whenever an input text field or select field is changed. An onclick event also invokes function startJS( ) if the button is clicked.

Function startJS( ) as well as another function changePage( ) are defined within the 'example18-1.js' file and are as follows:

```
function startJS() {
   xhrequest = null;
   try {
      xhrequest = getXMLHttpRequest();
   }
   catch(error) {
      document.write("Cannot run Ajax code using this browser");
   }

   if(xhrequest ! = null) {
   // get form values
      var intValue1 = document.getElementById("intValue1").value;
      var intValue2 = document.getElementById("intValue2").value;
      var strOperator = document.getElementById("strOperator").value;
      var strUrl = "example18-1.php?intValue1=" + intValue1 + "&intValue2=" +
            intValue2 + "&strOperator=" + strOperator;

         xhrequest.onreadystatechange = changePage;
         xhrequest.open("GET", strUrl, true);
         xhrequest.send(null);
      }
}


function changePage() {
   if (xhrequest.readyState == 4 && xhrequest.status == 200) {
      var intResponse = xhrequest.responseText;
      document.getElementById("intResult").value = intResponse;
   }
}
```

Function startJS( ) begins by determining whether the browser supports Ajax by trying to create a getXMLHttpRequest object by invoking the getXMLHttpRequest( ) function in the 'getsmlhttprequest.js' file. If an error is generated a message is displayed and the operation terminates:

```
xhrequest = null;
try {
xhrequest = getXMLHttpRequest();
}
catch(error) {
document.write("Cannot run Ajax code using this browser");
}
```

If all is well then the values in the two input text form field values and the operator from the select field are obtained and stored in separate variables:

```
if(xhrequest != null) {
    // get form values
    var intValue1 = document.getElementById("intValue1").value;
    var intValue2 = document.getElementById("intValue2").value;
    var strOperator = document.getElementById("strOperator").value;
```

Next, a string defining the connection to the PHP script on the server is created. This consists of the name of the script and the three variables created from the data obtained from the calculator form:

```
var strUrl = "example18-1.php?intValue1=" + intValue1 +
"&intValue2=" + intValue2 + "&strOperator=" + strOperator;
```

Finally, three methods of the XMLHttpRequest object are invoked:

```
xhrequest.onreadystatechange = changePage;
xhrequest.open("GET", strUrl, true);
xhrequest.send(null);
```

These methods define what function should be invoked when the PHP script has done something, open a connection to the PHP script and send the form data to the script. In this example, when the PHP script does something, this is handled by the JavaScript function changePage( ) which is also included within the 'example18-1.js' file:

```
function changePage() {
    if (xhrequest.readyState == 4 && xhrequest.status == 200) {
        var intResponse = xhrequest.responseText;
        document.getElementById("intResult").value = intResponse;
    }
}
```

Function changePage( ) simply determines if the PHP script has finished executing and if so stores the output from the script in variable intResponse. This value is then injected into the form text result field, thus displaying the answer to the calculation to the user.

FIGURE 18.1   Simple calculator

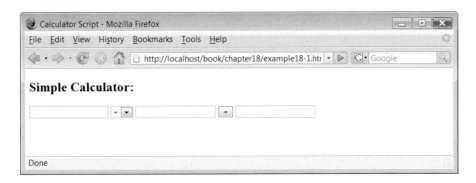

The PHP script, 'example18-1.php', which is invoked and does the calculation is as follows:

```php
<?php
// File: example18-1.php
$intValue1 = $_GET["intValue1"];
$intValue2 = $_GET["intValue2"];
$strOperator = $_GET["strOperator"];

switch ($strOperator){
    case 1: echo $intValue1 + $intValue2;
            break;
    case 2: echo $intValue1 - $intValue2;
            break;
    case 3: echo $intValue1 / $intValue2;
            break;
    case 4: echo $intValue1 * $intValue2;
}
?>
```

The script obtains the values of the three variables passed to it via the GET method and uses a 'switch' statement to output the result of the mathematical calculation using an 'echo' construct.

The output from the above example is illustrated in Figure 18.1.

So, to summarize, the example creates a simple web form and waits for a user to trigger an event. When an event is triggered, an Ajax connection is formed and a PHP script is invoked. When the PHP script finishes, the output from the script is displayed on the form.

18.3 A simple database stock example

This example illustrates a simple dynamic database stock check and demonstrates that Ajax can be used to run PHP scripts that obtain up-to-the-minute information stored on a database. The advantage of using Ajax for this example is that the database is queried when the user interacts with the application thus ensuring that the information displayed is accurate but the user is not inconvenienced by a page reload:

```
<!DOCTYPE html PUBLIC "-//W3C//DTD XHTML 1.1//EN"
    "http://www.w3.org/TR/xhtml11/DTD/xhtml11.dtd">
```

```
<html xmlns="http://www.w3.org/1999/xhtml" xml:lang="en">

<head>
<title>Stock Script</title>
<meta http-equiv="Content-Type" content="text/html; charset=ISO-8859-1" />

<script type="text/javascript" src="getxmlhttprequest.js">
</script>
<script type="text/javascript" src="example18-2.js">
</script>
</head>
<body>
<!-- File: example18-2.htm -->

<h2>Fruit Stock Information:</h2>
<form action="" method="post">
<p>
<label for="strStock">Stock Query: </label>
<input type="text" name="strStock" id="strStock"/></p>
<p>
<input type="button" value="Check" onclick="startJS();"/></p>
<div id="strStockResult"></div>
</form>
</body>
</html>
```

As in our previous example the 'getxmlhttprequest.js' file is loaded but this time the JavaScript file 'example18-2.js' is loaded:

```
<script type="text/javascript" src="getxmlhttprequest.js">
</script>
<script type="text/javascript" src="example18-2.js">
</script>
```

The remainder of the script creates a simple form consisting of two elements: an input text field where the user enters the database item they are searching for and a form submit button:

```
<form action="" method="post">
<p>
<label for="strStock">Stock Query: </label>
<input type="text" name="strStock" id="strStock"/></p>
<p>
<input type="button" value="Check" onclick="startJS();"/></p>
<div id="strStockResult"></div>
</form>
```

Note firstly that the form includes an empty 'div' element with the id 'strStockResult'. We use it to display the output from our PHP script later. Note secondly, that the form submit button includes an onclick event which invokes function startJS( ) when the button is clicked. Functions startJS( ) and changePage( ) are defined in the 'example18-2.js' file:

```
function startJS() {
    xhrequest = null;
    try {
```

```
        xhrequest = getXMLHttpRequest();
      }
      catch(error) {
        document.write("Cannot run Ajax code using this browser");
      }

      if(xhrequest != null) {
        // get form values
        var strStock = document.getElementById("strStock").value;

        var strUrl = "example18-2.php?strStock=" + strStock;
        xhrequest.onreadystatechange = changePage;
        xhrequest.open("GET", strUrl, true);
        xhrequest.send(null);
      }
    }

    function changePage() {
      if (xhrequest.readyState == 4 && xhrequest.status == 200) {
        var strResponse = xhrequest.responseText;
        document.getElementById("strStockResult").innerHTML = str Response;
      }
    }
```

As in our previous example, function startJS( ) checks to see if there is any problem creating an xmlhttprequest object and, if not, obtains the data entered on the form, opens a connection to the PHP script, passes the data to the script and defines function changePage( ) to process the output from the PHP script. Function changePage( ) obtains the data output from the PHP script and stores this in variable strResponse. This data is then injected into the strStockResult division defined previously using the innerHTML method.

Our PHP script which queries the database and outputs the corresponding records is as follows:

```
<?php
// File: example18-2.php

$strStock = $_GET["strStock"];

$dbLocalhost = mysql_connect("localhost", "root", "")
   or die("Could not connect: " . mysql_error() );

mysql_select_db("stock", $dbLocalhost)
   or die("Could not find database: " . mysql_error() );

$dbRecords = mysql_query("SELECT * FROM stock WHERE
                         Name='$strStock' ", $dbLocalhost)
   or die("Problem reading table: " . mysql_error() );

$intRecords = mysql_num_rows($dbRecords);

if ($intRecords == 0)
   echo "<p>Stock Item '$strStock' Unknown.</p>";
else {
   while ($arrRecords = mysql_fetch_array($dbRecords) ) {
```

```
                    $strDescription = $arrRecords["Description"];
                    $intQuantity = $arrRecords["Quantity"];
                    echo "<p>$strDescription: Currently we have $intQuantity
                            of boxes.</p>";
            }
        }
        ?>
```

The script begins by retrieving the data passed to it by the getXMLHttpRequest object and storing this in variable $strStock:

```
        $strStock = $_GET["strStock"];
```

Next it forms a connection to a database which we have created called stock:

```
        $dbLocalhost = mysql_connect("localhost", "root", "")
            or die("Could not connect: " . mysql_error() );

        mysql_select_db("stock", $dbLocalhost)
            or die("Could not find database: " . mysql_error() );
```

The database fields, types and the data stored within the database is illustrated in Table 18.1.

It is not really important what the data in the database actually is, nor the actual fields within the table, so long as there is something for the script to search for and display. The remainder of the script searches the database for any records matching the data received by the PHP script:

```
        $dbRecords = mysql_query("SELECT * FROM stock WHERE
                            Name = '$strStock' ", $dbLocalhost)
            or die("Problem reading table: " . mysql_error() );

        $intRecords = mysql_num_rows($dbRecords);

        if ($intRecords == 0)
            echo "<p>Stock Item '$strStock' Unknown.</p>";
        else {
            while ($arrRecords = mysql_fetch_array($dbRecords) ) {
                $strDescription = $arrRecords["Description"];
                $intQuantity = $arrRecords["Quantity"];
                echo "<p>$strDescription: Currently we have $intQuantity of boxes.</p>";
        }
```

TABLE 18.1 The stock database

Id (int)	Name (varchar 100)	Description (text)	Quantity (int)
1	Apples	English Granny Smith Apples	12
2	Apples	French Golden Apples	20
3	Pears	Italian Blushed Pears	23
4	Pears	English Conference Pears	104
5	Apples	French Pink Lady Apples	6
6	Oranges	Spanish Oranges Seedless	45

FIGURE 18.2   Stock database output

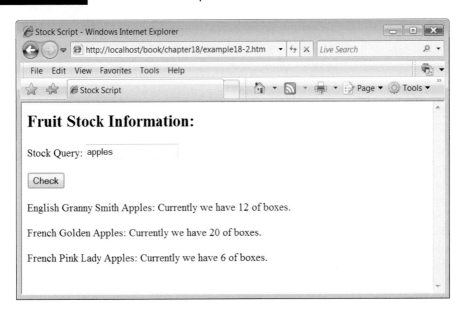

The output from the above example is illustrated in Figure 18.2.

18.4 A zooming photo thumbnail application

This example illustrates a zooming photo thumbnail application. The user is presented with a series of small thumbnails of photos. When they move the mouse over a photo then a larger image is displayed. This application could have been written using standard JavaScript and (X)HTML but this would have required either all the images to be downloaded when the page was requested initially, which would have resulted in a long download time, or a page refresh whenever the user moved the mouse over an image. The advantage of using Ajax is that only the images that the user wishes to zoom in on are downloaded and a full page refresh is avoided:

```
<!DOCTYPE html PUBLIC "-//W3C//DTD XHTML 1.1//EN"
    "http://www.w3.org/TR/xhtml11/DTD/xhtml11.dtd">

<html xmlns="http://www.w3.org/1999/xhtml" xml:lang="en">

<head>
<title>Picture Script</title>
<meta http-equiv="Content-Type" content="text/html; charset=ISO-8859-
1" />
<script type="text/javascript" src="getxmlhttprequest.js">
</script>
<script type="text/javascript" src="example18-3.js">
</script>
<style type="text/css">
#big {
```

```
        float: left;
           }
    #small {
        float: left;
        width: 320px;
           }

    </style>
    </head>
    <body>
    <!-- File: example18-3.htm -->

    <h2>Zooming Pictures:</h2>
    <div id = "small">
    <img src="graphics/1s.jpg" onmouseover="startJS(1);"
    alt="small picture"/>
    <img src="graphics/2s.jpg" onmouseover="startJS(2);"
    alt="small picture"/>
    <img src="graphics/3s.jpg" onmouseover="startJS(3);"
    alt="small picture"/>
    <img src="graphics/4s.jpg" onmouseover="startJS(4);"
    alt="small picture"/>
    <img src="graphics/5s.jpg" onmouseover="startJS(5);"
    alt="small picture"/>
    <img src="graphics/6s.jpg" onmouseover="startJS(6);"
    alt="small picture"/>
    <img src="graphics/7s.jpg" onmouseover="startJS(7);"
    alt="small picture"/>
    <img src="graphics/8s.jpg" onmouseover="startJS(8);"
    alt="small picture"/>
    <img src="graphics/9s.jpg" onmouseover="startJS(9);"
    alt="small picture"/>
    <img src="graphics/10s.jpg" onmouseover="startJS(10);"
    alt="small picture"/>
    <img src="graphics/11s.jpg" onmouseover="startJS(11);"
    alt="small picture"/>
    <img src="graphics/12s.jpg" onmouseover="startJS(12);"
    alt="small picture"/>
    </div>
    <div id="big"><img src="graphics/1l.jpg" width='600'
    alt="large picture"/></div>
    </body>
    </html>
```

The 'getxmlhttprequest.js' and 'example18-3.js' JavaScript files are loaded:

```
<script type="text/javascript" src="getxmlhttprequest.js">
</script>
<script type="text/javascript" src="example18-3.js">
</script>
```

An embedded CSS-style definition is included to define the style of the small thumbnail photos and the larger zoomed image:

```
<style type="text/css">
#big {
    float: left;
        }
#small {
    float: left;
    width: 320px;
        }
</style>
```

Next, each of the thumbnail images is displayed within a division with an id "small". Each thumbnail image has the file name 1s.jpg, 2s.jgp, ,3s.jpg . . . 11s.jpg:

```
<div id="small">
<img src="graphics/1s.jpg" onmouseover="startJS(1);"
alt="small picture"/>
<img src="graphics/2s.jpg" onmouseover="startJS(2);"
alt="small picture"/>
<img src="graphics/3s.jpg" onmouseover="startJS(3);"
alt="small picture"/>
<img src="graphics/4s.jpg" onmouseover="startJS(4);"
alt="small picture"/>
<img src="graphics/5s.jpg" onmouseover="startJS(5);"
alt="small picture"/>
<img src="graphics/6s.jpg" onmouseover="startJS(6);"
alt="small picture"/>
<img src="graphics/7s.jpg" onmouseover="startJS(7);"
alt="small picture"/>
<img src="graphics/8s.jpg" onmouseover="startJS(8);"
alt="small picture"/>
<img src="graphics/9s.jpg" onmouseover="startJS(9);"
alt="small picture"/>
<img src="graphics/10s.jpg" onmouseover="startJS(10);"
alt="small picture"/>
<img src="graphics/11s.jpg" onmouseover="startJS(11);"
alt="small picture"/>
<img src="graphics/12s.jpg" onmouseover="startJS(12);"
alt="small picture"/>
</div>
```

When the mouse is moved over the image an 'onmouseover' event triggers a call to the JavaScript function startJS( ) passing it a numerical value corresponding to the image the mouse has moved over. A 'div' element with the id 'big' is used to display the zoomed image. Large images have the same file name as their corresponding small thumbnails except that the character 's' is replaced with an 'l'. Image '1l.jpg' is displayed initially:

```
<div id="big"><img src="graphics/1l.jpg" width='600'
alt="large picture"/></div>
```

It doesn't matter what images you use in this example (the ones here are available for download from the book web site) but they must all be numbered, from 1 to 12 in this case, with the letter 's' appended to the filename. Likewise the corresponding large images should be labelled the same but with a letter 'l'.

Functions startJS( ) and changePage( ) are defined in file 'example18-3.js':

```
function startJS(intPicture) {
    xhrequest = null;
    try {
        xhrequest = getXMLHttpRequest();
    }
    catch(error) {
        document.write("Cannot run Ajax code using this browser");
    }

    if(xhrequest != null) {
        // get form values
        var strUrl = "example18-3.php?intPicture=" + intPicture;
        xhrequest.onreadystatechange = changePage;
        xhrequest.open("GET", strUrl, true);
        xhrequest.send(null);
    }
}

function changePage() {
    if (xhrequest.readyState == 4 && xhrequest.status == 200) {
        var strResponse = xhrequest.responseText;
        document.getElementById("big").innerHTML = strResponse;
    }
}
```

Function startJS( ) is slightly different from our previous examples as it contains a single parameter, intPicture. This variable contains a number representing the image the mouse has moved over. As before the function checks to see if there is any problem creating an xmlhttprequest object and if not opens a connection to the PHP script, passes the value of the image in intPicture to the script and defines function changePage( ) to process the output from the PHP script.

Function changePage( ) obtains the data output from the PHP script and stores this in variable strResponse. This data, which is a simple (X)HTML element pointing to the large image is then injected into the 'big' element using the innerHTML method.

The PHP script is very simple. It obtains the value of the image the mouse has moved over, passed via the GET method and stores it in a variable called $intPicture. It then outputs the (X)HTML element pointing to the corresponding large image:

```
<?php
// File: example18-3.php

$intPicture = $_GET["intPicture"];

echo "<img src='graphics/$intPicture" . "l.jpg' width='600' />";
?>
```

The output from the above example is illustrated in Figure 18.3.

18.5 A dynamic histogram

Consider that you may wish to create a web site which displays a graph showing in almost real time some data about your site. This data could be the number of users registered or online, or the number of transactions or sales processed in the last minute, for example. You may also wish to display this information as a histogram or bar-chart and by using Ajax you can minimize the effect that continually updating this graph will have on the users of your site.

FIGURE 18.3 Zoomed thumbnail image

```
<!DOCTYPE html PUBLIC "-//W3C//DTD XHTML 1.1//EN"
  "http://www.w3.org/TR/xhtml11/DTD/xhtml11.dtd">

<html xmlns="http://www.w3.org/1999/xhtml" xml:lang="en">

<head>
<title>Graph Script</title>
<meta  http-equiv="Content-Type"  content = "text/html;  charset=ISO-8859-1"
/>

<script type="text/javascript" src="getxmlhttprequest.js">
</script>
<script type="text/javascript" src="example18-4.js">
</script>
<style type="text/css">
#graphBars {
   float: left;
      }

#graphScale {
   float: left;
   width: 40px;
      }
</style>
</head>
<body onload="startJS();">
<!-- File: example18-4.htm -->

<h2>Graph:</h2>
<div id="graph">
</div>
</body>
</html>
```

The 'getxmlhttprequest.js' and 'example18-4.js' JavaScript files are loaded:

```
<script type="text/javascript" src="getxmlhttprequest.js">
</script>
<script type="text/javascript" src="example18-4.js">
</script>
```

An embedded CSS-style definition is included to define the style of the histogram bars and the scale which is going to be displayed:

```
<style type="text/css">
#graphBars {
   float: left;
      }
#graphScale {
   float: left;
   width: 40px;
      }
</style>
```

When the web page is loaded, an 'onload' event invokes function startJS( ):

```
<body onload="startJS();">
```

Next a division is created called "graph" where the histogram will be displayed:

```
<h2>Graph:</h2>
<div id="graph">
</div>
```

Functions startJS( ) and changePage( ) are defined in file 'example18-4.js':

```
    function startJS() {
    xhrequest = null;
    try {
       xhrequest = getXMLHttpRequest();
  }
  catch(error) {
     document.write("Cannot run Ajax code using this browser");
  }

  if(xhrequest != null) {
     var objDate = new Date();
     var intSecs = objDate.getTime();

     var strUrl = "example18-4.php?intSecs=" + intSecs;
     xhrequest.onreadystatechange = changePage;
     xhrequest.open("GET", strUrl, true);
     xhrequest.send(null);
     setTimeout("startJS()", 500);
     }
  }


  function changePage() {
     if (xhrequest.readyState == 4 && xhrequest.status == 200) {
        var strResponse = xhrequest.responseText;
        document.getElementById("graph").innerHTML = strResponse;
     }
  }
```

Function startJS( ) begins by checking to see if there is any problem creating an xmlhttprequest object:

```
  function startJS(intPicture) {
    xhrequest = null;
    try {
       xhrequest = getXMLHttpRequest();
    }
    catch(error) {
       document.write("Cannot run Ajax code using this browser");
    }
```

A date object is created and used to return the number of seconds since 1/1/1970 by using the getTime( ) method:

```
if(xhrequest != null) {
    var objDate = new Date();
    var intSecs = objDate.getTime();
```

We are going to use the value obtained to solve a caching problem with some browsers. Some browsers do not reload a web page if they think they have a perfectly good one stored in their local cache. This presents us with a problem as we want the graph script to automatically reload every few seconds and redisplay the graph. However, this does not work in some browsers as they simply redisplay the old cached page thus not obtaining and displaying any new graph bars. We can get around this problem by using the number of seconds value, as this is always growing and thus changing. If we append this value to the script invocation it fools the browser into thinking that we are calling a different script and thus not using the one stored in the cache.

If there is no problem, the script opens a connection to the PHP script passing the value of the number of seconds obtained previously. Function changePage( ) is defined to process the output produced from the PHP script.

```
var strUrl = "example18-4.php?intSecs=" + intSecs;
xhrequest.onreadystatechange = changePage;
xhrequest.open("GET", strUrl, true);
xhrequest.send(null);
```

Another difference from the startJS( ) functions in our previous examples is the inclusion of a setTimeOut( ) function call which is defined to call the startJS( ) function 500 milliseconds later:

```
setTimeout("startJS()", 500);
```

Function changePage( ) obtains the data output from the PHP script and stores this in variable strResponse. This data, which is the entire (X)HTML defining the histogram is then injected into the 'graph' element using the innerHTML method:

```
function changePage() {
    if (xhrequest.readyState == 4 && xhrequest.status == 200) {
        var strResponse = xhrequest.responseText;
        document.getElementById("graph").innerHTML = strResponse;
    }
}
```

The following PHP script generates the histogram graph and it is somewhat more complex than our previous examples:

```
<?php
// File: example18-4.php

$dbLocalhost = mysql_connect("localhost", "root", "")
    or die("Could not connect: " . mysql_error() );

mysql_select_db("graph", $dbLocalhost)
    or die("Could not find database: " . mysql_error() );
```

```
srand( (double) microtime() * 1000000);
$intPercentage = rand(0,99);

$dbWriteRecords = mysql_query("INSERT INTO percentageValues VALUES
                              ('', '$intPercentage')", $dbLocalhost)
   or die("Problem reading table: " . mysql_error() );

$dbRecords = mysql_query("SELECT * FROM percentageValues", $dbLocalhost)
   or die("Problem reading table: " . mysql_error() );
$intCount = mysql_num_rows($dbRecords);
if ($intCount > 20) {
    $intStart = $intCount - 20;
    $dbRecords = mysql_query("SELECT * FROM percentageValues LIMIT
                             $intStart,20", $dbLocalhost)
    or die("Problem reading table: " . mysql_error() );
}

$arrPercent = array (0,0,0,0,0,0,0,0,0,0,0,0,0,0,0,0,0,0,0,0);
$intSize = count($arrPercent);
$intCount = 0;

while ($arrRecords = mysql_fetch_array($dbRecords) ) {
   $arrPercent[$intCount++] = $arrRecords["Percentage"];
}
graph($arrPercent, $intSize);

function graph($arrData, $intSize) {
   $intBarWidth = 10;
   $intBarSpacing = 10;
   $intMultiplier = 1.5;

   $intSize=count($arrData);
   echo "<div id='graphScale'><img src='graphics/scale.gif'
              width='27' height='150' /></div>";
   echo "<div id='graphBars'>";
   echo "<img src='graphics/hiddenbar.gif' width='0'
              height=' " . 99 * $intMultiplier . "'>";
   for($intCount=0;$intCount<$intSize;$intCount++) {
      echo "<img src='graphics/redbar.gif' width='$intBarWidth'
         height=' " . $arrData[$intCount] * $intMultiplier . "'>";
      }
   echo "</div>";
}
?>
```

The script begins by forming a connection to database 'graph':

```
$dbLocalhost = mysql_connect("localhost", "root", "")
   or die("Could not connect: " . mysql_error() );

mysql_select_db("graph", $dbLocalhost)
   or die("Could not find database: " . mysql_error() );
```

The graph database has a single table called percentageValues which consists of just two integer fields: Id and Percentage. The contents of the table are generated by the PHP script. The next part of the script generates a random number between 0 and 99 and stores this in the graph database:

```
srand( (double) microtime() * 1000000);
$intPercentage = rand(0,99);

$dbWriteRecords = mysql_query("INSERT INTO percentageValues VALUES
('', '$intPercentage')", $dbLocalhost)
    or die("Problem reading table: " . mysql_error() );
```

Next, the contents of the database is read and the number of records in the database is stored in $intCount:

```
$dbRecords = mysql_query("SELECT * FROM percentageValues", $dbLocalhost)
    or die("Problem reading table: " . mysql_error() );
$intCount = mysql_num_rows($dbRecords);
```

If the number of records in the database is greater than 20 then the last 20 records are read:

```
if ($intCount > 20) {
  $intStart = $intCount - 20;
  $dbRecords = mysql_query("SELECT * FROM percentageValues LIMIT $intStart,20",
                           $dbLocalhost)
    or die("Problem reading table: " . mysql_error() );
}
```

An array is defined and the percentage values of the selected database records are stored in the array:

```
$arrPercent = array (0,0,0,0,0,0,0,0,0,0,0,0,0,0,0,0,0,0,0,0);
$intSize = count($arrPercent);
$intCount = 0;

while ($arrRecords = mysql_fetch_array($dbRecords) ) {
  $arrPercent[$intCount++] = $arrRecords["Percentage"];
}
```

Finally, function graph( ) is invoked passing it the array contents and the size of the array:

```
graph($arrPercent, $intSize);
```

Function graph( ) begins by specifying the width of the histogram bars, the spacing between them and a multiplier which affects the height of the bars:

```
function graph($arrData, $intSize) {
  $intBarWidth = 10;
  $intBarSpacing = 10;
  $intMultiplier = 1.5;
```

FIGURE 18.4   Dynamic histogram

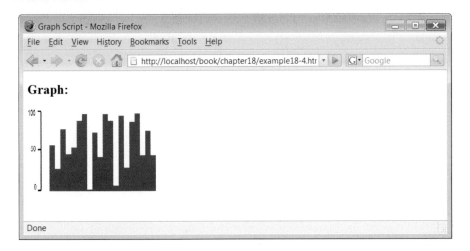

An image representing the scale of the histogram is displayed as well as a hidden image which fixes the maximum height of the bars:

```
$intSize=count($arrData);
echo "<div id='graphScale'><img src='graphics/scale.gif'
          width='27' height = '150' /></div>";
echo "<div id='graphBars'>";
echo "<img src='graphics/hiddenbar.gif' width='0'
          height=' " . 99 * $intMultiplier . "'>";
```

For each percentage value in the array an image representing a histogram bar is displayed in a 'div' element:

```
for($intCount=0;$intCount<$intSize;$intCount++) {
   echo "<img src='graphics/redbar.gif' width='$intBarWidth'
      height=' " . $arrData[$intCount] * $intMultiplier . "'>";
   }
   echo "</div>";
```

The output from the above example is illustrated in Figure 18.4.

18.6   A simple chat system

The following example illustrates a simple chat system. Users can post messages which are then visible to anyone viewing the chat system. The chat system also displays new messages automatically to all users as it receives them without the need to refresh the page:

```
<!DOCTYPE html PUBLIC "-//W3C//DTD XHTML 1.1//EN"
     "http://www.w3.org/TR/xhtml11/DTD/xhtml11.dtd">

<html xmlns="http://www.w3.org/1999/xhtml" xml:lang="en">
```

```
<head>
<title>Chatroom Script</title>
<meta http-equiv="Content-Type" content="text/html; charset = ISO-8859-
1" />

<script type="text/javascript" src="getxmlhttprequest.js">
</script>
<script type="text/javascript" src="example18-5.js">
</script>
<style type="text/css">
#chatroom {
   float: left;
   width: 300px;
      }

#messageform {
   float: left;
   width: 250px;
      }

</style>
</head>
<body onload="startJS(1);">

<!-- File: example18-5.htm -->

<h2>Chatroom:</h2>

<div id="chatroom">
</div>
<div id="messageform">
<form action="" method="post">
<p>UserId: <input type="text" name="strUserId" id="strUserId" /></p>
<p>Message: <input type="text" name="strMessage" id="strMessage" /></p>
<p><input type="button" value="Send Message" onclick="startJS(2);" /></p>
</form>
</div>
</body>
</html>
```

Firstly, the 'getxmlhttprequest.js' and 'example18-5.js' JavaScript files are loaded:

```
<script type="text/javascript" src="getxmlhttprequest.js">
</script>
<script type="text/javascript" src="example18-5.js">
</script>
```

An embedded CSS-style definition is included to define the styles of the message form, where the user enters new messages, and the chatroom, where the messages are displayed:

```
<style type="text/css">
#chatroom {
```

```
      float: left;
      width: 300px;
         }

   #messageform {
      float: left;
      width: 250px;
         }

   </style>
```

When the page first loads, function startJS( ) is invoked passing it the parameter 1, indicating the user has joined the chat system:

```
<body onload="startJS(1);">
```

A 'div' element defines the extent of the chatroom. This is used to display the chat messages:

```
<div id="chatroom">
</div>
```

Another 'div' element defines the message form, which consists of two text fields for the chat user to enter their id and the message to display:

```
<div id="messageform">
<form action="" method="post">
<p>UserId: <input type="text" name="strUserId" id="strUserId" /></p>
<p>Message: <input type="text" name="strMessage" id="strMessage" /></p>
<p><input type="button" value="Send Message" onclick="startJS(2);" /></p>
</form>
</div>
```

When the form button is clicked the onclick event invokes the startJS( ) function passing it the parameter 2, indicating a new message. Functions startJS( ) and changePage( ) are defined in file 'example18-5.js':

```
function startJS(intFlag) {
   xhrequest = null;
   try {
      xhrequest = getXMLHttpRequest();
   }
   catch(error) {
      document.write("Cannot run Ajax code using this browser");
   }

   if(xhrequest !=null) {
      // get form values
      var strUserId = document.getElementById("strUserId").value;
      var strMessage = document.getElementById("strMessage").value;

      var objDate = new Date();
      var intSecs = objDate.getTime();

      if (intFlag = = 2)
```

```
        strUrl = "example18-5.php?strUserId=" + strUserId +
                "&strMessage=" + strMessage;
    else {
        strUrl = "example18-5.php?intSecs = " + intSecs;
        xhrequest.onreadystatechange = changePage;
        xhrequest.open("GET", strUrl, true);
        xhrequest.send(null);
        setTimeout("startJS()", 500);
    }
}
function changePage() {
    if (xhrequest.readyState == 4 && xhrequest.status == 200) {
        var strResponse = xhrequest.responseText;
        document.getElementById("chatroom").innerHTML = strResponse;
    }
}
```

Function startJS( ) contains a single parameter, intFlag, which denotes whether a user has just launched a chat application or whether a message has been entered:

```
function startJS(intFlag) {
    xhrequest = null;
    try {
        xhrequest = getXMLHttpRequest();
    }
    catch(error) {
        document.write("Cannot run Ajax code using this browser");
    }
}
```

As before the function checks to see if there is any problem creating an xmlhttprequest object and, if not, obtains the user id and message from the form:

```
if(xhrequest != null) {
    // get form values
    var strUserId = document.getElementById("strUserId").value;
    var strMessage = document.getElementById("strMessage").value;
```

A date object is created and used to return the number of seconds since 1/1/1970 by using the getTime( ) method:

```
var objDate = new Date();
var intSecs = objDate.getTime();
```

We are going to use the value obtained to solve a caching problem with some browsers as in Section 18.5. Next, if the value of intFlag is equal to 2 then the data stored in the strUserId and strMessage variables are added to the PHP invocation, otherwise they are not and the value of intSecs is appended instead.

```
if (intFlag == 2)
    strUrl = "example18-5.php?strUserId=" + strUserId +
            "&strMessage = " + strMessage;
else
    strUrl = "example18-5.php?intSecs=" + intSecs;
```

18

Finally, a connection to the PHP script is opened and invoked. Function changePage( ) is defined to process the output from the PHP script. A setTimeout( ) function is defined to invoke the startJS( ) function in 500 milliseconds from now in order to check if any further messages have been posted by other users of the system:

```
xhrequest.onreadystatechange = changePage;
xhrequest.open("GET", strUrl, true);
xhrequest.send(null);
setTimeout("startJS()", 500);
```

The following PHP script processes the chatroom messages:

```php
<?php
// File: example18-5.php

$dbLocalhost = mysql_connect("localhost", "root", "")
      or die("Could not connect: " . mysql_error() );

mysql_select_db("chatroom", $dbLocalhost)
      or die("Could not find database: " . mysql_error() );

if (isset($_GET["strUserId"]) ) {
     $strUserId = $_GET["strUserId"];
     $strMessage = $_GET["strMessage"];
}
else {
   $strUserId = "";
   $strMessage = "";
}
   if (strlen($strMessage) > 0 && strlen($strUserId) > 0) {
      $dbWriteRecords = mysql_query("INSERT INTO messages VALUES ('',
                               '$strUserId', '$strMessage')", $dbLocalhost)
         or die("Problem reading table: " . mysql_error() );
}
   $dbRecords = mysql_query("SELECT * FROM messages", $dbLocalhost)
      or die("Problem reading table: " . mysql_error() );

while ($arrRecords = mysql_fetch_array($dbRecords) ) {
   echo "<p>[" . $arrRecords["UserId"] . "]: ";
   echo $arrRecords["Message"] . "</p>";
}
?>
```

The PHP script begins by forming a connection to the 'chatroom' database:

```php
$dbLocalhost = mysql_connect("localhost", "root", "")
   or die("Could not connect: " . mysql_error() );

mysql_select_db("chatroom", $dbLocalhost)
   or die("Could not find database: " . mysql_error() );
```

The chatroom database has a single table called chatroom consisting of just three fields: Id (int), UserId (varchar(50)) and Message (text). The contents of the database table are generated by the PHP script so we don't need to populate the database with any data.

Next, the values of the UserId and Message are checked to see if they exist and if so are stored in appropriately named variables:

```
if (isset($_GET["strUserId"]) ) {
    $strUserId = $_GET["strUserId"];
    $strMessage = $_GET["strMessage"];
}
else {
    $strUserId = "";
    $strMessage = "";
}
```

If the message and user Id fields are not blank then they are written to the database table:

```
if (strlen($strMessage) > 0 && strlen($strUserId) > 0) {
    $dbWriteRecords = mysql_query("INSERT INTO messages VALUES ('',
                                '$strUserId', '$strMessage')", $dbLocalhost)
        or die("Problem reading table: " . mysql_error() );
}
```

Finally, all messages are read from the database and output to the user's web page:

```
$dbRecords = mysql_query("SELECT * FROM messages", $dbLocalhost)
    or die("Problem reading table: " . mysql_error() );

while ($arrRecords = mysql_fetch_array($dbRecords) ) {
    echo "<p>[" . $arrRecords["UserId"] . "]: ";
    echo $arrRecords["Message"] . "</p>";
}
```

The output from the above example is illustrated in Figure 18.5.

FIGURE 18.5   Dual chat window

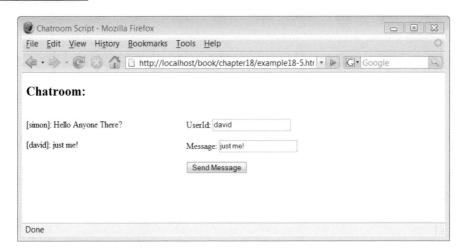

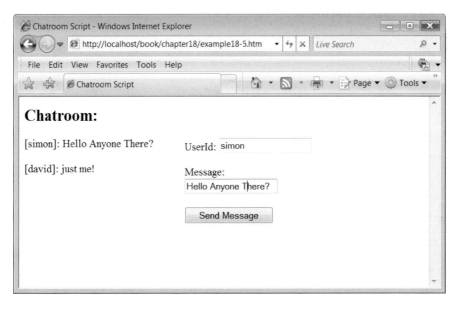

Exercises

18.1 Amend the simple calculator (example 18.1) so that it checks to see if there are numeric values in both fields and if not outputs the value 'error' in the result field.

18.2 Amend the dynamic histogram (example 18.4) so that a user is able to select the colour that the graph is displayed in, from red, blue, yellow and green. You should use a select field to provide these options to the user.

18.3 Create a dynamic expanding menu system. The menu should consist of a series of buttons with a '+' character displayed on them and some associated menu text, as shown in the screen shot below:

Clicking on any of the '+' buttons invokes an Ajax script which injects some menu data into that part of the menu. It should also change the '+' menu button into a '−' button as shown in the screen shot below:

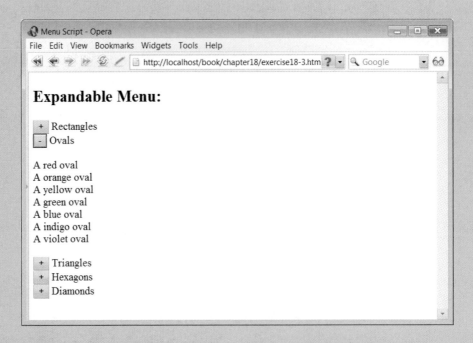

Clicking on the '−' button removes the injected menu text returning that part of the menu to its previous state (with the '+' button also displayed instead of the '−' one).

18.4 Create a script which displays an image and allows the user to enlarge or reduce it by clicking one of two form buttons.

SUMMARY

In this chapter we began by reviewing the JavaScript syntax for implementing Ajax applications. Next, we introduced our first PHP, Ajax enabled application a simple calculator and explained how the technologies were integrated together. We then introduced other examples which illustrated a simple database information retrieval, a zooming thumbnail application, a dynamic histogram and a simple chat system.

References and further reading

Babin, L. (2006) Beginning Ajax with PHP: From novice to professional. http://www.phpbuilder.com/columns/beginning_ajax20070104.php3

Hadlock, K. (2006) Database Enabled Ajax with PHP. http://www.webreference.com/programming/javascript/kh/

Walter, A. (2006) Using Ajax and PHP to build your mailing list. http://www.sitepoint.com/article/use-ajax-php-build-mailing-list

CHAPTER 19

Conformance to Standards and Accessibility

LEARNING OBJECTIVES

- Be aware of various web standards, their use and understand why writing web applications which conform to the standards is important

- Know where to go to obtain further information about the various web standards which are available

- Be aware of and be able to use various on-line conformance tools which help determine if your scripts meet the specific standard

- Understand the problems and pitfalls of using on-line standard conformance tools

- Understand the concept of web accessibility and why it is important to create web systems which are accessible

- Be aware of the different levels of accessibility which web systems can strive to address

- Be aware of and be able to use on-line tools to assist in validation that a web system meets basic accessibility guidelines

INTRODUCTION

In this chapter, we explore some of the different web standards which are available today and explain why it is important that you ensure that the web systems you create conform to one or more of these standards depending on what technologies you are using and what it is that you wish to achieve. We introduce the standards for the creation of (X)HTML documents and cascading style sheets (CSS). We examine how various on-line tools can be used to assist you in ensuring that your applications conform to your chosen standard. We then explore the concept of accessibility and explain why accessibility standards and guidelines are important in designing and building applications for the web. We examine various levels of accessibility and consider those tools which are available to help improve web system accessibility for as many individuals as possible.

19.1 Software standards and web standardisation

According to the Wikipedia (http://en.wikipedia.org), 'Software standards enable software to interoperate. Many things are (somewhat) arbitrary, so the important thing is that everyone agrees on what they are.' This is especially true for software engineers engaged with developing applications using web technology as it is a fast-changing and developing arena, with an ever-increasing number of applications interacting with one another, exchanging information and using different protocols and technologies. It is therefore vitally important if this is all going to work smoothly then the various applications should all ensure that they conform to the standards which have been agreed.

Standards are often owned and developed by private organisations, such as the standards Microsoft has created for how to design and create software which runs on its Windows operating systems. Other standards are developed by non-profit-making, public organisations. The main organisation responsible for developing and refining web standards is the World Wide Web Consortium (W3C), which in their own words ' . . . develops interoperable technologies (specifications, guidelines, software, and tools) to lead the Web to its full potential.' The W3C (http://www.w3.org) operates as a consortium of member organisations which in addition to developing various web standards, are actively involved with research, education and software development projects. Working alongside the W3C is the Internet Engineering Task Force (IETF) which is part of the Internet Society (http://www.isoc.org) which helps promote and develop the adoption of various web standards.

In this chapter, we examine the W3C's work on standards for (Extensible) HyperText Markup Language: (X)HTML, JavaScript and cascading style sheets (CSS). In addition, we examine the work on web accessibility content guidelines.

19.2 HTML and XHTML

The HyperText Markup Language (HTML) can trace its routes back to 1993 where it was originally published not as a full standard but as an IETF working draft. Over the years, HTML had been refined and developed leading to its final incarnation, version 4.01, published as a full standard in 1999, to which the last changes were made in 2001. The HTML 4.01 specification is available at the W3C web site, as shown in Figure 19.1.

Since the end of the development of the HTML 4.01 standard, the W3C has continued work on a successor to HTML, the eXtensible HTML language (XHTML). XHTML has been developed using the eXtensible Markup Language (XML) providing a standard which is not only less ambiguous than those developed previously but is also easier to extend and develop to cater for the next generation of web technologies. The latest version of the XHTML standard is version 1.1 (although version 2.0 is being developed as a draft) and the full standard is available at the W3C site, as shown in Figure 19.2.

FIGURE 19.1 HTML 4.01 Specification (http://www.w3.org/TR/html4/)

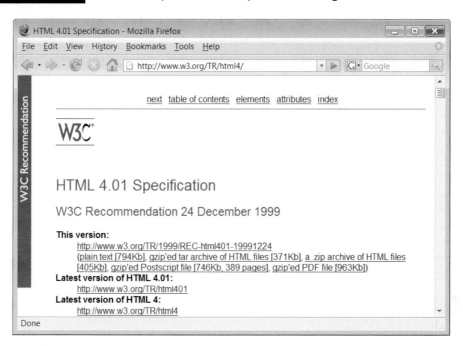

FIGURE 19.2 XHTML 1.1 Specification (http://www.w3.org/TR/xhtml11/)

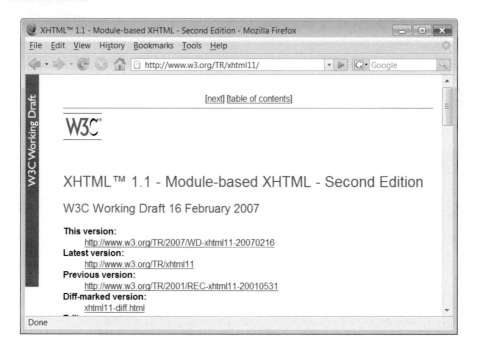

It is interesting to note that while XHTML may appear to be a newer and 'better' version of HTML than HTML 4.01, the W3C does not recommend that HTML 4.01 be deprecated with XHTML 1.1 and that both are currently W3C standards recommendations.

Strictly non-conforming documents

Due to the protracted development timescale, various standards and competing commercial interests, it is very easy to create an HTML document which will (in most web browsers) display the words 'Hello world!' and here it is:

```
Hello world!
```

Saving the above as a text file with the extension .htm and then viewing it using a web browser such as Firefox or Internet Explorer will result in the words being correctly displayed. However, while this works, the document doesn't conform to any HTML standard; it isn't actually HTML at all; it just works because the browser developers have provided a great deal of flexibility in the browsers' ability to process and render HTML documents. Great we hear you say, this is simple and if this works then I don't really need to know anything else. Well, just a minute, not so fast. Because the document has not been written correctly to the standard, the browser has to make a number of guesses when deciding how to display the document. In this case, because there is very little to display, it probably gets it correct but with larger, more sophisticated documents, the chances are that different browsers from different browser developers will guess slightly differently and the corresponding web document will look slightly different in one browser compared to another. This has been one of the main problems of web development for many years and still is to a large extent.

The primary reason for this is because historically we have been allowed to be very ambiguous about what we specify about our web documents. The standards are there to try and address this issue and ensure that the web applications that we create are of the highest quality possible and that the interoperability of web applications is increased.

 NOTE A good web developer never lets the browser 'guess' how to display something.

Strictly conforming HTML documents

The problem is that writing web documents which conform to standards is more difficult. Let us consider what we need to do to create a valid HTML 4.01 'Hello world!' document. To create a valid HTML document we need to:

1 Include a line specifying the document version information. The correct format for this for HTML 4.01 is:

```
<!DOCTYPE HTML PUBLIC "-//W3C//DTD HTML 4.01//EN"
   "http://www.w3.org/TR/html4/strict.dtd">
```

2 Include a header section, delimited by the <HEAD> element.

3 Within the header section, include a title, delimited by the <TITLE> element, for example:

```
<TITLE>HTML 4.01 Document</TITLE>
```

4 Within the header section, include a <META> element specifying what character set the document is using. An example of this is:

```
<META HTTP-EQUIV="Content-Type" CONTENT="text/html; charset=ISO-8859-1">
```

5 Include a body section which contains the document's content, delimited by the <BODY> element.

6 The body section needs to include a valid element, for example:

```
<P>Hello world!
```

7 The header and body sections should be delimited by the <HTML> element.

8 HTML elements should be written in upper case.

Combining all of the above, our correctly conforming HTML 4.01 document is now as follows:

```
<!DOCTYPE HTML PUBLIC "-//W3C//DTD HTML 4.01//EN"
"http://www.w3.org/TR/html4/strict.dtd".

<HTML>
     <HEAD>
        <TITLE>HTML 4.01 Document</TITLE>
        <META HTTP-EQUIV="Content-Type" CONTENT="text/html;
charset=ISO-8859-1">
     </HEAD>
     <BODY>
        <P>Hello world!
     </BODY>
</HTML>
```

It does seem a lot of effort for what appears to be little or no gain. However, this is a 'worse case' example as the same additional elements need to be added whether your document is a single line (as in this example) or 1000 lines.

Strictly conforming XHTML documents

Things are different again when writing to the XHTML standard, as we have been throughout this book. To create our 'Hello world!' document to conform to the XHTML 1.1 standard, we need to consider things a little differently:

1 The first line of the document must specify the document version information. The correct format for this for XHTML 1.1 is:

```
<!DOCTYPE html PUBLIC "-//W3C//DTD XHTML 1.1//EN"
   "http://www.w3.org/TR/xhtml11/DTD/xhtml11.dtd">
```

2 The next line of the document must be an <html> element and must designate the xhtml namespace (a means of qualifying names used in the document). A correct example of this is:

```
<html xmlns="http://www.w3.org/1999/xhtml" xml:lang="en">
```

3 The <html> element must include a header section, delimited by the <head> element.

4 The header section must include a title, delimited by the <title> element, for example:

```
<title>XHTML 1.1 Document</title>
```

5 The header section must include a <meta> element specifying what character set the document is using. An example of this is:

```
<meta http-equiv="Content-Type" content="text/html; charset=ISO-8859-1" />
```

6 The <html> element must include a body section which contains the document's content, delimited by the <body> element.

7 The body section must include a valid element, for example:

```
<p>Hello world!</p>
```

8 XHTML elements should be written in lower case.

9 Note that those elements, such as <p>, which could be used in HTML 4.01 and before without an end tag are required to have a closing tag: </p>.

10 Note that those elements, such as <meta>, which had no closing tag in HTML 4.01 and before now must ensure that the start tag ends with />.

Combining all of the above, our correctly conforming XHTML 1.1 document is now as follows:

```
<!DOCTYPE html PUBLIC "-//W3C//DTD XHTML 1.1//EN"
        "http://www.w3.org/TR/xhtml11/DTD/xhtml11.dtd">

<html xmlns="http://www.w3.org/1999/xhtml" xml:lang="en">
        <head>
            <title>XHTML 1.1 Document</title>
            <meta http-equiv="Content-Type" content="text/html;
charset=ISO-8859-1" />
        </head>
        <body>
        <p>Hello world!</p>
        </body>
</html>
```

Once again there is a lot of work here and you could easily forget or mistype something even though you wanted to ensure that you had produced a document which conforms exactly to the standard. Luckily there are tools available to help and one of the better ones is provided by the W3C itself.

19.3 The W3C Markup Validation Service

The W3C HTML and XHTML Markup Validation service is an online tool which allows you to check HTML and XHTML documents for conformance against W3C standards. It is illustrated in Figure 19.3.

| FIGURE 19.3 | W3C Markup Validation Service (http://validator.w3.org) |

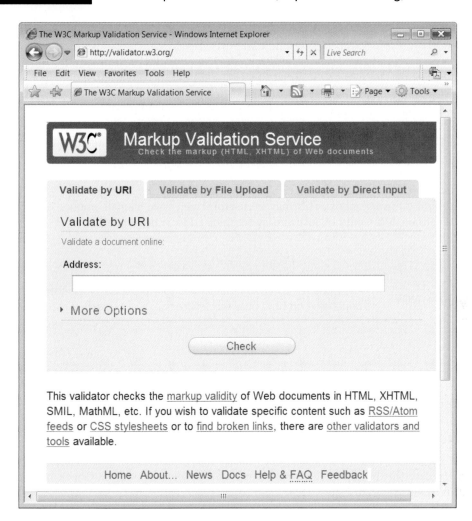

The free service allows you to specify the document that you wish to validate in one of three different ways, as illustrated in Figure 19.3.

The first method of validation is by simply entering the URL of the document you wish to validate, for example:

```
www.sunderland.ac.uk
```

Documents that you wish to validate by URL have to be available on-line to web users and you are not able to validate documents stored on a 'localhost' intranet in this way. However, it does allow you to validate any page currently on the web to determine if it conforms to a W3C standard.

The second method of validation is via file upload. In this case, you provide the location of a local file on your computer which you wish to validate. A browser form file and upload interface is provided to allow you to search for and locate the file you wish to upload and submit for validation, for example:

```
c:\wamp\www\chapter19\example19-1.htm
```

This method of validation is very useful for a developer who is creating web documents on a local computer and wishes to validate them before placing them on a publicly viewable web space. The problem is that uploading documents for validation in this way does not allow you to check scripts which use PHP to generate XHTML/HTML output as these scripts would need to be parsed through a PHP interpreter for the output to be generated. Such scripts would need to be uploaded to a web space and then validated by supplying the URL of the web document.

The final method of validation is by directly entering the file markup that you wish to validate into a form textbox. This may be useful if you have a small amount of script to validate, although it would be just as easy to upload a local document.

19

NOTE	The speed with which the on-line tool processes your script varies depending on how busy the service is.

Whichever way you choose to submit your document for validation the results can be one of only two outputs: either the document is valid or it is not. Let us begin by validating our simplest document:

```
Hello world!
```

If we validate this by typing it into the textarea box and clicking the Check button, the result is as illustrated in Figure 19.4.

We return to the initial validation screen and try validating the HTML 4.01 document we introduced earlier:

```
<!DOCTYPE HTML PUBLIC "-//W3C//DTD HTML 4.01//EN"
  "http://www.w3.org/TR/html4/strict.dtd">
<HTML>
  <HEAD>
    <TITLE>HTML 4.01 Document</TITLE>
    <META HTTP-EQUIV="Content-Type" CONTENT="text/html; charset=ISO-8859-1">
  </HEAD>
  <BODY>
    <P>Hello world!
  </BODY>
</HTML>
```

If we save this file and submit it via the file upload option, then the corresponding output is as illustrated in Figure 19.5.

FIGURE 19.4   W3C Markup Validation Service – invalid document

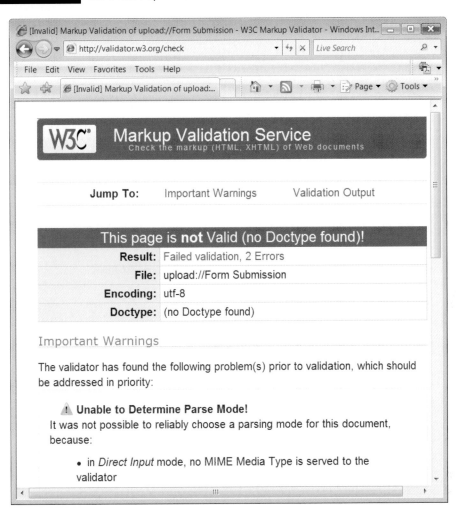

This page is valid and the service provides you with a graphic which you can include on your web page to show others that you have taken care to create an interoperable web page. The code required to include the graphic in the web page is also provided:

```
<p>
  <a href="http://validator.w3.org/check?uri=referer"><img
     src="http://www.w3.org/Icons/valid-html401"
     alt="Valid HTML 4.01 Strict" height="31" width="88"></a>
</p>
```

Different graphical icons are provided depending on the standard to which you have decided to write your web page and some of these are illustrated in Figure 19.6.

FIGURE 19.5 W3C Markup Validation Service – valid document

 NOTE All the examples in this book have been written so that they conform to the XHTML 1.1 Strict standard although, to save space, many of the PHP scripts have been included without the XHTML document information.

19.4 CSS validation

In addition to providing a tool which allows the user to freely check their (X)HTML documents for conformance to standards the W3C also provide a validation service which allows you to validate cascading style sheets (CSS) and (X)HTML documents with embedded style sheets, this is illustrated in Figure 19.7.

As with the (X)HTML validation service, the tool allows three forms of validation input: by URL, by file upload and by direct input. The following is a small CSS file which we can

FIGURE 19.6   W3C Markup Validation Service – icons for standards conformance

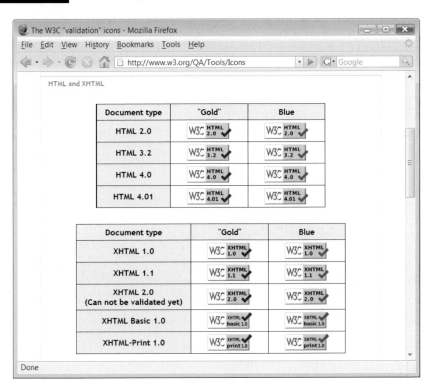

FIGURE 19.7   W3C CSS Validation Service (http://jigsaw.w3.org/css-validator)

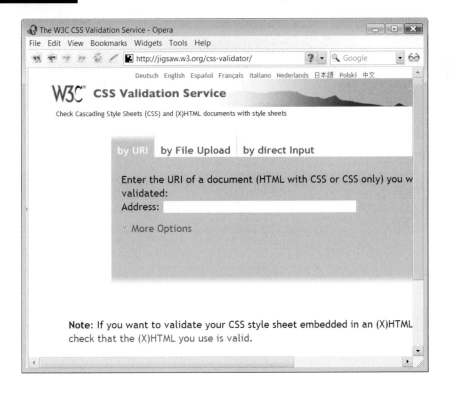

use to illustrate the use of this tool:

```css
body {
    background-color: white;
    color: black;
    font-family: arial;
    font-size: 80%;
}

div.page {
    background-colour: white;
}

div.formField {
    float: left;
    background-color: white;
    width: 12cm;
    padding-top: 0.5cm;
}
```

If we save the above CSS file as 'style.css' and then use the file upload option of the tool to locate and upload the CSS file for validation, the output produced is illustrated in Figure 19.8.

Unfortunately, the tool has found one error. Luckily it can easily be fixed:

```css
background-colour: white;
```

FIGURE 19.8   W3C CSS Validation errors

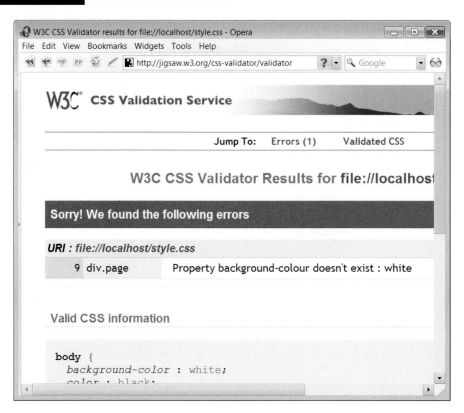

The property on line 9 needs to be spelt with the American spelling of 'color':

```
background-color: white;
```

 NOTE   Don't get tripped up by the differences in American and British spellings!

19.5 What do you get from conformance and validation?

Validation tools simply check for inaccuracies in the work you have produced. If the scripts you have written conform to the standards exactly then using a validation tool is not necessary. The point however is that human beings find writing scripts which conform to a set of complex rules difficult and often make simple errors which can be detected by validation tools.

Validating your (X)HTML and CSS files to ensure that the scripts you have created conform to the published standards simply confirms that your scripts are standards-compliant. Validation in this way doesn't mean that your scripts are correct, as validation tools are only currently able to check for typos and the incorrect application of script syntax rules. Validation doesn't teach you how to write good scripts, it simply checks that what you have written meets the rules. You can of course create a script which doesn't do what you really intended, but conforms precisely to the published rules, but what use is this?

Validation and conformance does have the benefit that you have a degree of certainty that your script has the best chance to work as intended with as many different types of web browsers and in as many different environments as possible both now and in the future. Creating scripts which do not conform to standards now but work as expected will provide you with considerably less certainty that in the future the script will continue to work as many browsers evolve to conform more closely to the published standards.

19.6 Web accessibility

In addition to ensuring that your web documents conform to the published standards, it is also extremely important to ensure that they are as accessible as possible to people with disabilities.

The term disability is sometimes misunderstood as meaning simply physical or mental disabilities in the traditional sense of the word. In the context of designing web documents, the meaning is broader than this. Web developers need to consider the different individuals who are accessing their web systems, the location from where they are accessing them and the technology they are using. With this in mind disabilities which can be considered are an individual's:

- Inability to differentiate easily between different color combinations.
- Difficulty in reading or understanding the text displayed.
- Difficulty in processing visually certain types of information such as images or in comprehending sounds.

- Inability to speak or understand the language the document is written.
- Location: a noisy work environment may affect their ability to interact with and understand the information presented to them, acting as a distraction.
- Technology which may not be the most up to date and thus not include the latest tools and technologies, including low resolution screens and limited graphical ability.
- Inability to communicate using keyboard or mouse.

In an attempt to remove as many of these problems the W3C has produced guidelines for developers to help them create accessible web systems.

 NOTE | The guidelines are quite detailed and complex. Don't give up on them because they look too much to read and digest.

Web content accessibility guidelines

The W3C web content accessibility guidelines (http://www.w3.org/TR/1999/WAI-WEB-CONTENT-19990505/#Guidelines) provide some essential reading and advice to the developer creating on-line web systems. The guidelines provide a number of key points to successful accessible design, summarized as:

- Separate the structure of your system from its design presentation.
- Always provide text as this is one of the most versatile items of data, which can be converted into many different forms, such as speech or Braille.
- Create systems which are understandable by users who cannot see or hear.
- Don't create systems which rely on one specific type of hardware. With today's technology, users are accessing web systems from portable wireless devices with smaller than standard screens and perhaps without a mouse to interact with.
- Ensure navigation between pages is simple and understandable. The use of frames, menus and image maps may allow for a slick user design but may not make for an easy-to-use and navigate system.
- Ensure that the content and language is clear and understandable.

Priorities and conformance

The W3C guidelines are arranged into 14 guidelines which help to address the accessibility issues raised previously. Each guideline has a number of checkpoints for the web system designer to consider. The checkpoints are graded against a three-level priority scale indicating the importance of the checkpoint's impact on accessibility, as listed in Table 19.1.

If a web document satisfies all priority 1 checkpoints then it is said to be at accessibility 'Conformance Level A'. If it satisfies all of priority 1 and priority 2 checkpoints then it is said to be at accessibility 'Conformance Level Double-A'. Finally, 'Conformance Level Triple-A' is said to be met when all priority level 1, 2 and 3 checkpoints are met. In a similar way to the way in which the W3C validation tool illustrated conformance to standards by providing a small image which could be included on a web site the same is true for conformance to the accessibility guidelines. The three images which can be included are illustrated in Figure 19.9.

TABLE 19.1	Priorities (taken from http://www.w3.org/TR/1999/ WAI-WEBCONTENT-19990505/#Guidelines)

Priority	Description
1	A web content developer **must** satisfy this checkpoint. Otherwise, one or more groups will find it impossible to access information in the document. Satisfying this checkpoint is a basic requirement for some groups to be able to use web documents.
2	A web content developer **should** satisfy this checkpoint. Otherwise, one or more groups will find it difficult to access information in the document. Satisfying this checkpoint will remove significant barriers to accessing web documents.
3	A web content developer **may** address this checkpoint. Otherwise, one or more groups will find it somewhat difficult to access information in the document. Satisfying this checkpoint will improve access to web documents.

FIGURE 19.9	W3C accessibility images (http://www.w3.org/WAI/WCAG1-Conformance.html)

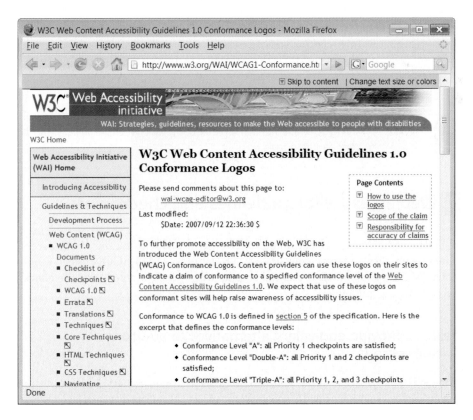

The W3C provides the (X)HTML script (http://www.w3.org/WAI/WCAG1-Conformance.html) to allow the images to be included on your web page:

Level A conformance script:

```
<a href="http://www.w3.org/WAI/WCAG1A-Conformance"
    title="Explanation of Level A Conformance">

<img height="32" width="88"
    src=http://www.w3.org/WAI/wcag1A
    alt="Level A conformance icon,
    W3C-WAI Web Content Accessibility Guidelines 1.0"></a>
```

Level Double-A conformance script:

```
<a href="http://www.w3.org/WAI/WCAG1AA-Conformance"
    title="Explanation of Level Double-A Conformance">

<img height="32" width="88"
    src="http://www.w3.org/WAI/wcag1AA"
    alt="Level Double-A conformance icon,
    W3C-WAI Web Content Accessibility Guidelines 1.0"></a>
```

Level Triple-A conformance script:

```
<a href="http://www.w3.org/WAI/WCAG1AAA-Conformance"
    title="Explanation of Level Triple-A Conformance">
<img height="32" width="88"
    src="http://www.w3.org/WAI/wcag1AAA"
    alt="Level Triple-A conformance icon,
    W3C-WAI Web Content Accessibility Guidelines 1.0"></a>
```

 NOTE Try to get your web pages to conform to Level A accessibility first. Trying to implement a Triple-A compliant web site initially can be a very daunting task.

19.7 Web accessibility guidelines and checkpoints

The following guidelines and checkpoints have been taken from the W3C accessibility guidelines web site: http://www.w3.org/TR/1999/WAI-WEBCONTENT-19990505/#Guidelines. Each guideline is presented and discussed, with a table listing the checkpoints associated with the guideline.

Guideline 1. Provide equivalent alternatives to auditory and visual content

While some individuals cannot see text and images and others cannot hear sounds, they can employ technologies which provide an equivalent view of this information. Such technologies include automatic text to speech translation and text to Braille reader conversion. Table 19.2 illustrates the associated checkpoints for this guideline and their priority ratings.

Guideline 2. Don't rely on color alone

If colored text or graphics are used to convey meaning you should ensure that the same meaning can be determined if the information is viewed without color. This ensures that the application is useable when viewed with a monochrome monitor. Furthermore, colors which are too similar in hue may prove difficult for individuals who suffer from color defects such as color blindness. Table 19.3 illustrates the associated checkpoints for this guideline and their priority ratings.

Guideline 3. Use markup and style sheets properly

As mentioned previously in this chapter, when creating applications and information for the web, you should ensure that your scripts and XHTML conform to the standards. This

TABLE 19.2 Guideline 1 checkpoints

Checkpoint	Description	Priority
1.1	Provide a text equivalent for every non-text element.	1
1.2	Provide redundant text links for each active region of a server-side image map.	1
1.3	Until user agents can automatically read aloud the text equivalent of a visual track, provide an auditory description of the important information of the visual track of a multimedia presentation.	1
1.4	For any time-based multimedia presentation (e.g., a movie or animation), synchronize equivalent alternatives (e.g., captions or auditory descriptions of the visual track) with the presentation.	1
1.5	Until user agents render text equivalents for client-side image-map links, provide redundant text links for each active region of a client-side image map.	3

TABLE 19.3 Guideline 2 checkpoints

Checkpoint	Description	Priority
2.1	Ensure that all information conveyed with color is also available without color, for example from context or markup.	1
2.2	Ensure that foreground and background color combinations provide sufficient contrast when viewed by someone having color deficits or when viewed on a black and white screen.	2 for images 3 for text

will help ensure that your applications are accessible to the widest possible audience across all platforms. Exploiting 'glitches' in the language to achieve special effects will inevitably cause problems in the future as these problems are resolved and removed from the next generation of web browsers. Table 19.4 illustrates the associated checkpoints for this guideline and their priority ratings.

Guideline 4. Clarify natural language usage

You should ensure that, as part of the document header information, you identify the main language used within the web page. You should also indicate when this language changes within a web page thus enabling automatic text-to-speech tools, for example, to automatically switch to the new language seamlessly. Furthermore, all acronyms and abbreviations should be provided in full at least once. Table 19.5 illustrates the associated checkpoints for this guideline and their priority ratings.

Guideline 5. Create tables that transform gracefully

The table element is designed to provide a neat tabular method for displaying data. It is not meant to enable web developers to layout the design of a web page. Doing so makes it

TABLE 19.4   Guideline 3 checkpoints

Checkpoint	Description	Priority
3.1	When an appropriate markup language exists, use markup rather than images to convey information.	2
3.2	Create documents that validate to published formal grammars.	2
3.3	Use style sheets to control layout and presentation.	2
3.4	Use relative rather than absolute units in markup language attribute values and style sheet property values.	2
3.5	Use header elements to convey the document structure and use them according to specification.	2
3.6	Mark up lists and list items properly.	2
3.7	Mark up quotations. Do not use quotation markup for formatting effects such as indentation.	2

TABLE 19.5   Guideline 4 checkpoints

Checkpoint	Description	Priority
4.1	Clearly identify changes in the natural language of a document's text and any text equivalents (e.g., captions).	1
4.2	Specify the expansion of each abbreviation or acronym in a document where it first occurs.	3
4.3	Identify the primary natural language of a document.	3

difficult for specialist screen readers to translate these pages into different formats (such as Braille). Table 19.6 illustrates the associated checkpoints for this guideline and their priority ratings.

Guideline 6. Ensure that pages featuring new technologies transform gracefully

While at the same time ensuring that your applications employ the latest technology, where appropriate it is also important that your applications and scripts work with older browsers as not everyone will want or is able to update their technology and keep pace with the latest developments. Table 19.7 illustrates the associated checkpoints for this guideline and their priority ratings.

TABLE 19.6   Guideline 5 checkpoints

Checkpoint	Description	Priority
5.1	For data tables, identify row and column headers.	1
5.2	For data tables that have two or more logical levels of row or column headers, use markup to associate data cells and header cells.	1
5.3	Do not use tables for layout unless the table makes sense when linearized. Otherwise, if the table does not make sense, provide an alternative equivalent (which may be a linearized version).	2
5.4	If a table is used for layout, do not use any structural markup for the purpose of visual formatting.	2
5.5	Provide summaries for tables.	3
5.6	Provide abbreviations for header labels.	3

TABLE 19.7   Guideline 6 checkpoints

Checkpoint	Description	Priority
6.1	Organize documents so they may be read without style sheets. For example, when an HTML document is rendered without associated style sheets, it must still be possible to read the document.	1
6.2	Ensure that equivalents for dynamic content are updated when the dynamic content changes.	1
6.3	Ensure that pages are usable when scripts, applets, or other programmatic objects are turned off or not supported. If this is not possible, provide equivalent information on an alternative accessible page.	1
6.4	For scripts and applets, ensure that event handlers are input device-independent.	2
6.5	Ensure that dynamic content is accessible or provide an alternative presentation or page.	2

Guideline 7. Ensure user control of time-sensitive content changes

The use of blinking, animated and scrolling feature on web pages can cause difficulties for certain individuals. Ensure that these features can be paused and that, when paused, the information they contain is clearly visible. Table 19.8 illustrates the associated checkpoints for this guideline and their priority ratings.

Guideline 8. Ensure direct accessibility of embedded user interfaces

Sometimes 'objects' are embedded into a web page. Examples of these include video players, flash animations and Java applets. If using such objects you should ensure that the interfaces that they use are also accessible to users. Table 19.9 illustrates the associated checkpoints for this guideline and their priority ratings.

Guideline 9. Design for device-independence

Device-independence refers to the ability of web applications to work successfully with a variety of different input devices, such as mouse, keyboard, tracker-ball, tablet. Requiring the specific use of a device, such as a mouse, will restrict the accessibility of the

TABLE 19.8   Guideline 7 checkpoints

Checkpoint	Description	Priority
7.1	Until user agents allow users to control flickering, avoid causing the screen to flicker.	1
7.2	Until user agents allow users to control blinking, avoid causing content to blink (i.e., change presentation at a regular rate, such as turning on and off).	2
7.3	Until user agents allow users to freeze moving content, avoid movement in pages.	2
7.4	Until user agents provide the ability to stop the refresh, do not create periodically auto-refreshing pages.	2
7.5	Until user agents provide the ability to stop auto-redirect, do not use markup to redirect pages automatically. Instead, configure the server to perform redirects.	2

TABLE 19.9   Guideline 8 checkpoints

Checkpoint	Description	Priority
8.1	Make programmatic elements such as scripts and applets directly accessible or compatible with assistive technologies.	1

application to certain individuals who may require to use a non-pointing device for example. Table 19.10 illustrates the associated checkpoints for this guideline and their priority ratings.

Guideline 10. Use interim solutions

Pop-up windows can be rather disorienting for a user and while newer browsers permit such events they should be avoided. Table 19.11 illustrates the associated checkpoints for this guideline and their priority ratings. It should be noted that it is expected that these checkpoints will not be required in the future as web technologies will automatically address them.

TABLE 19.10 Guideline 9 checkpoints

Checkpoint	Description	Priority
9.1	Provide client-side image maps instead of server-side image maps except where the regions cannot be defined with an available geometric shape.	1
9.2	Ensure that any element that has its own interface can be operated in a device-independent manner.	2
9.3	For scripts, specify logical event handlers rather than device-dependent event handlers.	2
9.4	Create a logical tab order through links, form controls, and objects.	3
9.5	Provide keyboard shortcuts to important links (including those in client-side image maps), form controls, and groups of form controls.	3

TABLE 19.11 Guideline 10 checkpoints

Checkpoint	Description	Priority
10.1	Until user agents allow users to turn off spawned windows, do not cause pop-ups or other windows to appear and do not change the current window without informing the user.	2
10.2	Until user agents support explicit associations between labels and form controls, for all form controls with implicitly associated labels, ensure that the label is properly positioned.	2
10.3	Until user agents (including assistive technologies) render side-by-side text correctly, provide a linear text alternative (on the current page or some other) for *all* tables that lay out text in parallel, word-wrapped columns.	3
10.4	Until user agents handle empty controls correctly, include default, place-holding characters in edit boxes and text areas.	3
10.5	Until user agents (including assistive technologies) render adjacent links distinctly, include non-link, printable characters (surrounded by spaces) between adjacent links.	3

Guideline 11. Use W3C technologies and guidelines

Where possible, use W3C technologies such as HTML and CSS to construct your applications. Other technologies such as PDF and Flash, for example, do not include the ability to build in accessibility functions and therefore may not be as accessible. When such technologies must be used, provide equivalent accessible pages as well. Table 19.12 illustrates the associated checkpoints for this guideline and their priority ratings.

Guideline 12. Provide context and orientation information

If you have a complex page then providing content and orientation information to help users understand the nature and structure of the web page is very useful. Table 19.13 illustrates the associated checkpoints for this guideline and their priority ratings.

TABLE 19.12   Guideline 11 checkpoints

Checkpoint	Description	Priority
11.1	Use W3C technologies when they are available and appropriate for a task and use the latest versions when supported.	2
11.2	Avoid deprecated features of W3C technologies.	2
11.3	Provide information so that users may receive documents according to their preferences (e.g., language, content type, etc.).	3
11.4	If, after best efforts, you cannot create an accessible page, provide a link to an alternative page that uses W3C technologies, is accessible, has equivalent information (or functionality), and is updated as often as the inaccessible (original) page.	1

TABLE 19.13   Guideline 12 checkpoints

Checkpoint	Description	Priority
12.1	Title each frame to facilitate frame identification and navigation.	1
12.2	Describe the purpose of frames and how frames relate to each other if it is not obvious by frame titles alone.	2
12.3	Divide large blocks of information into more manageable groups where natural and appropriate.	2
12.4	Associate labels explicitly with their controls.	2

Guideline 13. Provide clear navigation mechanisms

Ensure that you provide consistent and clear navigation mechanisms such as site maps, 'bread-crumbs', navigation bars, etc. Table 19.14 illustrates the associated checkpoints for this guideline and their priority ratings.

Guideline 14. Ensure that documents are clear and simple

Ensure that your web applications are clear and simple and the use of language is not ambiguous and that images are clear and obvious as to their function. Table 19.15 illustrates the associated checkpoints for this guideline and their priority ratings.

TABLE 19.14   Guideline 13 checkpoints

Checkpoint	Description	Priority
13.1	Clearly identify the target of each link.	2
13.2	Provide metadata to add semantic information to pages and sites.	2
13.3	Provide information about the general layout of a site (e.g., a site map or table of contents).	2
13.4	Use navigation mechanisms in a consistent manner.	2
13.5	Provide navigation bars to highlight and give access to the navigation mechanism.	3
13.6	Group related links, identify the group (for user agents) and, until user agents do so, provide a way to bypass the group.	3
13.7	If search functions are provided, enable different types of searches for different skill levels and preferences.	3
13.8	Place distinguishing information at the beginning of headings, paragraphs, lists, etc.	3
13.9	Provide information about document collections (i.e., documents comprising multiple pages).	3
13.10	Provide a means to skip over multi-line ASCII art.	3

TABLE 19.15   Guideline 14 checkpoints

Checkpoint	Description	Priority
14.1	Use the clearest and simplest language appropriate for a site's content.	1
14.2	Supplement text with graphic or auditory presentations where they will facilitate comprehension of the page.	3
14.3	Create a style of presentation that is consistent across pages.	3

19.8 Producing Triple-A accessible web sites

Having read through the W3C guidelines on accessibility you may have come to realise that most of the Priority 1 checkpoints are quite clear in their meaning and interpretation, for example:

1.1 Provide a text equivalent for every non-text element.

5.1 For data tables, identify row and column headers.

9.1 Provide client-side image maps instead of server-side image maps except where the regions cannot be defined with an available geometric shape.

However, some Priority 2 checkpoints are a little more difficult to conform to, consider:

11.1 Use W3C technologies when they are available and appropriate for a task and use the latest versions when supported.

Determining when and if a new technology is appropriate for a task can be problematic. For example, how often should you check for new technological improvements and at what point should you evaluate them and decide when it is correct to implement the technology? One developer may have decided that today is the correct day and therefore believe that all sites not using the new technology for the particular circumstances are no longer accessibility compliant.

13.4 Use navigation mechanisms in a consistent manner.

Some may argue that if you wish to implement certain navigational effects on a web page, such as automatic redirection to another page then it is impossible to have any other form of navigation as this would invalidate the 'consistent manner' checkpoint.

14.1 Use the clearest and simplest language appropriate for a site's content.

Exactly what 'simplest language' means is open to debate and argument. What one individual believes is a simple use of the language, another may not.

Things get even more difficult to conform to when it comes to some of the Priority 3 checkpoints:

11.3 Provide information so that users may receive documents according to their preferences (e.g., language, content type, etc.).

Does this mean that a user can request a document in any format and your system must be able to deliver it in that format otherwise the checkpoint is not met?

The point of this is to show that some of the checkpoints are very subjective in the way that they can be interpreted. Some developers claim that, in all but the simplest of systems, achieving a Triple-A standard web page would be very difficult indeed without leaving one open to criticism that the checkpoints were not being strictly adhered to. The higher the level of compliance claimed, the more difficult it is to claim that the system conforms (which indeed should be the case). However, while some of these checkpoints are difficult to achieve, the overarching concept of trying to attain a higher level of accessibility is obviously a highly important one. In Section 19.9, we introduce a tool which provides a degree of support determining the level of accessibility your web page has attained.

19.9 WatchFire WebXACT

The W3C does not currently provide an automated tool in order for you to check whether your documents or application is accessible or not and what level compliance you could claim. This is partly because many of the accessibility guidelines are subjective and are difficult to quantify. There is a free on-line service called WebXACT which allows you to check single web pages to see how accessible they are. WebXACT can be found at http://webxact.watchfire.com/ and its welcome page is shown in Figure 19.10.

 NOTE The WebXACT tool is very useful for assisting with your accessibility issues. However, don't think that it will do this all on its own. It will still need some thought and judgement from you.

FIGURE 19.10 WebXACT tool

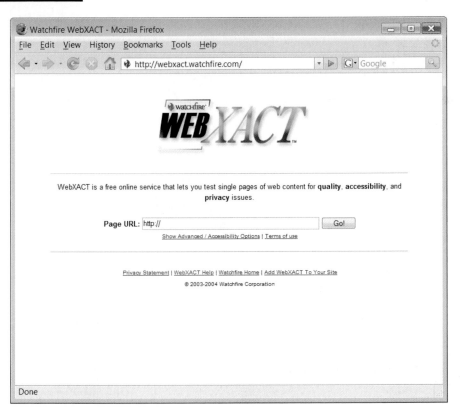

The WebXACT tool allows you to specify the location of a web page for it to analyse. Any web page that you wish to check must therefore be accessible on the Internet and you cannot, unlike in the case of the W3C tools, upload a page from your own computer's test environment.

In order to test WebXACT, we have chosen a web site at the following location:

```
http://www.cit.sunderland.ac.uk/
```

The web page is illustrated in Figure 19.11. It is the home of the Centre for Internet Technologies at the University of Sunderland and you will note that the site claims not only compliance to (X)HMTL 1.0 and CSS, but also that it is triple-A accessibility compliant!

Typing the URL of the site into WebXACT starts the tool. After a short while, the results page is displayed. This is divided into four sections which assess the following areas:

- General
- Quality
- Accessibility
- Privacy

FIGURE 19.11 Centre for Internet Technologies web site

Figure 19.12 illustrates the General output page and you should note that the tool found no quality issues it wanted to report.

The tool is also able to perform a number of automated checks on the accessibility of the web site. For those areas it cannot automatically check, it prompts the user to check themselves. Figure 19.13 illustrates the accessibility output from the WebXACT tool which indicates that all automatic tests have been passed and lists a number of manual checks for the user to perform.

The WebXACT tool is a very useful resource in checking simple accessibility errors and making you reconsider whether you really have met the accessibility guidelines or not. Whether you think that this site is actually triple-A compliant, we shall leave up to you to decide.

FIGURE 19.12   Centre for Internet Technologies: General

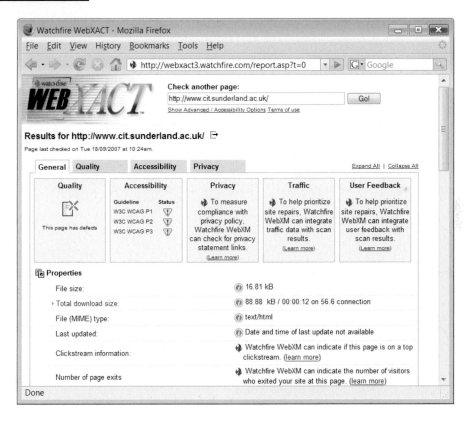

FIGURE 19.13   Centre for Internet Technologies: Accessibility

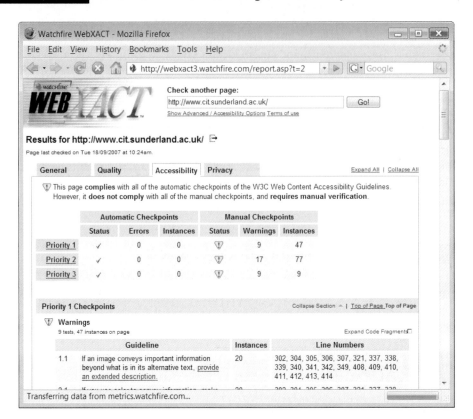

Exercises

19.1 Consider the following XHTML script. Using the W3C validation tool, amend the script so that it conforms correctly to its XHTML doctype.

```
<!DOCTYPE html PUBLIC "-//W3C//DTD XHTML 1.1//EN"
   "http://www.w3.org/TR/xhtml11/DTD/xhtml11.dtd">
<html xmlns="http://www.w3.org/1999/xhtml" xml:lang="en">

<head>
<title>PHP Script</title>
<meta http-equiv="Content-Type" content="text/html; charset=ISO-8859-1" />
</head>
<body>
<!-- File: exercsie19-1.htm -->

<h2>What Colors would you like?</h2>
<form action='processform.php' method='post'>
<p>
<label for="strNewBgCol">Background Color: </label>
<select name='strNewBgCol' id='strNewBgCol'>
   <option>red</option>
   <option>green</option>
   <option>blue</option>
   <option>cyan</option>
   <option>yellow</option>
</p>
<p>
<select name='strNewTextCol' id='strNewTextCol'>
   <option>red</option>
   <option>green</option>
   <option>blue</option>
   <option>cyan</option>
   <option>yellow</option>
</select>
<input type='submit' name='submit'>
</form>
</body>
</html>
```

19.2 Using the WatchFire WebXACT tool, take one of your favourite web sites and analyse the report generated from the tool. In your judgement, consider what level of accessibility the web page has attained. Is this different from the level that the web page claims (if any)?

SUMMARY

In this chapter, we began by explaining the different web standards, where they can be found and who created them. We have explained that while writing web systems which conform to the standards takes a little bit of effort, it is a good ideal as it provides some degree of insurance that your scripts will work on the largest diversity of platforms and browsers and will be future-proofed as much as possible. We also introduced some of the on-line validation tools which provide you with support in ensuring that your scripts conform to the documented standards.

The chapter then introduced the concept of accessibility. We began by explaining what accessibility could mean to different individuals. We introduced the W3C guidelines on accessibility and described the different checkpoints and their priority. We discussed the issues surrounding the interpretation and the subjective nature of the W3C guidelines. Finally, we introduced the WatchFire WebXACT tool and illustrated its use in determining the accessibility level of a web page.

References and further reading

Internet Engineering Task Force. Home Page. http://www.ietf.org/
Internet Society. Home page. http://www.isoc.org
Wikipedia. Home Page. http://en.wikipedia.org
World Wide Web Consortium. HomePage.http://www.w3.org
World Wide Web Consortium. Accessibility Guidelines. http://www.w3.org/TR/1999/
    WAI-WEBCONTENT-19990505/. Guidelines
World Wide Web Consortium. Accessibility Images. http://www.w3.org/WAI/WCAG1-
    Conformance.html
World Wide Web Consortium. CSS Validation Service. http://jigsaw.w3.org/css-vailidator/
World Wide Web Consortium. HTML 4.01 Specification. http://www.w3.org/TR/html4/
World Wide Web Consortium. HTML/XHTML Validation Service. http://validator.w3.org
World Wide Web Consortium. XHTML 1.1 Specification. http://www.w3.org/TR/xhtml11/

CHAPTER 20

Building More Secure and Robust Web Applications

INTRODUCTION

In this chapter, we examine some good practice in the development of PHP applications in order to ensure that they are as secure and robust as possible. PHP web applications, by their very nature, often tend to be accessible and visible to the world as a whole and that immediately brings with it a host of problems. Unfortunately, we live in a world where individuals seek to exploit loop-holes in web applications. These individuals and groups may break into on-line systems for a number of different reasons, ranging from wishing to profit through access to money or goods which are not their own, wishing to view confidential data for personal or political reasons or simply to cause disruption and inconvenience to the real users of the application in an attempt to show how clever they are.

Software developers have a professional duty to ensure that the web systems they create are hardened as much as possible against such malicious attacks. In order to accomplish this you need to be aware of some good programming practice which will help to ensure that your applications are well designed and written, and are not easily broken. In addition, you should be aware of the various security mechanisms which you can implement in order to fortify your applications. You should also be aware of the different forms of 'attack' which can be implemented and thus know how to defend against them.

20.1 Web application security and robustness

Hopefully, our earlier chapters have demonstrated that creating PHP applications is relatively easy but unfortunately that is not the end of the story. In Chapter 19, we introduced the concepts of ensuring that any (X)HTML and CSS scripts conform to W3C standards and that designing systems for accessibility should be considered right from the start. As PHP is used to generate (X)HTML output, these considerations are an integral part of the PHP script design and implementation phases. However, in addition to this, PHP developers need to consider other aspects of their design, namely the robustness of their software and the security of its data.

Because your web application has been installed on a secure web server is not enough to ensure that your application is as secure and robust as possible. You need to implement a strategy to raise the quality and security of your applications. This strategy consists of:

- Developing good programming practice to ensure your applications are well implemented.
- Being aware of the different forms of attack which could be ranged against your application and ensuring that you have defended against them.
- Ensuring you have authenticated a valid user and have implemented a good secure password mechanism.

We begin by examining some good PHP development practices.

20.2 Good PHP development practice

Report all errors

The first, and perhaps the most important, tip for good PHP development practice is to ensure that you are aware of all errors and warnings that the PHP interpreter generates. Interestingly, by default PHP does not do this and you need to edit the PHP configuration file, called 'php.ini', in order to change this.

The 'php.ini' file can be most easily accessed from the wamp icon on the Windows application bar, assuming this is how you installed PHP. If you did not, then you will need to search Windows for the 'php.ini' file. To access the 'php.ini' file through wamp, left click on the wamp icon on the right of the application bar at the bottom of your desktop and select 'config files'. Finally, from the menu that appears, click on 'php.ini'. The file is illustrated in Figure 20.1.

Notepad launches with a copy of the 'php.ini' file loaded ready for you to edit. The file is quite long and complex and in order to find the correct section to edit you need to scroll down until you come to the section labelled 'Error handling and logging', as

FIGURE 20.1   The 'php.ini' file

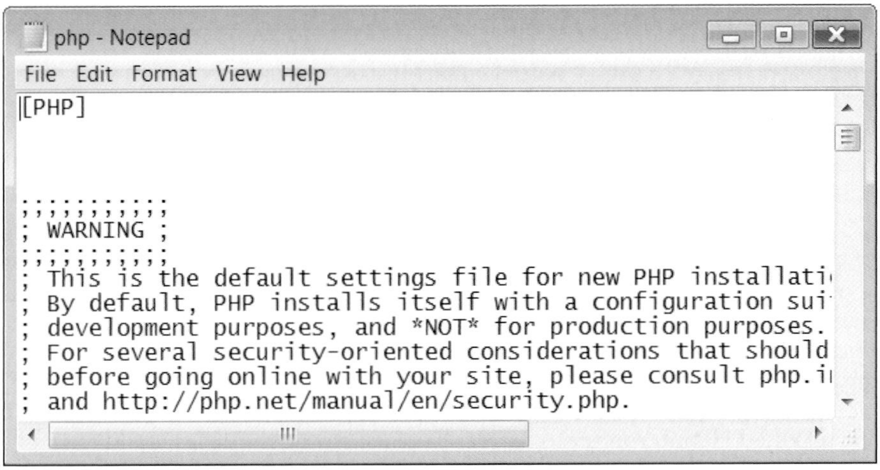

shown below:

```
;;;;;;;;;;;;;;;;;;;;;;;;;;;;;;;;
; Error handling and logging ;
;;;;;;;;;;;;;;;;;;;;;;;;;;;;;;;;

; error_reporting is a bit-field. Or each number up to get desired error
; reporting level
; E_ALL              - All errors and warnings
; E_ERROR            - fatal run-time errors
; E_WARNING          - run-time warnings (non-fatal errors)
; E_PARSE            - compile-time parse errors
; E_NOTICE           - run-time notices (these are warnings which often result
;                      from a bug in your code, but it's possible that it was
;                      intentional (e.g., using an uninitialised variable and
;                      relying on the fact it's automatically initialised to an
;                      empty string)
; E_STRICT           - run-time notices, enable to have PHP suggest changes
;                      to your code which will ensure the best interoperability
;                      and forward compatability of your code
; E_CORE_ERROR       - fatal errors that occur during PHP's initial startup
; E_CORE_WARNING     - warnings (non-fatal errors) that occur during PHP's
;                      initial startup
; E_COMPILE_ERROR    - fatal compile-time errors
; E_COMPILE_WARNING  - compile-time warnings (non-fatal errors)
; E_USER_ERROR       - user-generated error message
; E_USER_WARNING     - user-generated warning message
; E_USER_NOTICE      - user-generated notice message
;
; Examples:
;
;   - Show all errors, except for notices
;
```

```
;error_reporting = E_ALL & ~E_NOTICE
;
;    - Show only errors
;
;error_reporting = E_COMPILE_ERROR|E_ERROR|E_CORE_ERROR
;
;    - Show all errors except for notices and coding standards warnings
;
error_reporting = E_ALL & ~E_NOTICE & ~E_STRICT
```

This section of the 'php.ini' file allows you to adjust the level of error reporting and logging of these errors. The line which is of most importance to us here is the last line of the above fragment of 'php.ini' file:

```
error_reporting = E_ALL & ~E_NOTICE & ~E_STRICT
```

This line sets the PHP interpreter to report all errors, but not notices (a mild form of error) and any coding standards which it detects. We are going to replace this line with the following:

```
error_reporting = E_ALL
```

This line will turn on all error reporting, even the minor notice errors. Saving the 'php.ini' file and restarting wamp will activate the change. If you do not have access to the 'php.ini' file or are prevented from editing it you can force the level of error reporting in a script through the error_reporting( ) function, for example:

```
error_reporting(E_ALL);
```

To illustrate the difference error reporting can make consider the following example:

```php
<?php
// File: example20-1.php

$intNoValue;

if ($intNoValue == 0)
    echo "<p>Equals zero</p>";
?>
```

Here the script defines a variable called $intNoValue and then employs a simple 'if' statement to determine if the value is equal to zero or not and displays an appropriate message. By default, the above script runs without errors reported, with the output displayed being:

```
Equals zero
```

However, by changing the level of error reporting, to E_ALL we now find that a notice is generated:

```
Notice: Undefined variable: intNoValue in
C:\wamp\www\book\chapter20\example20-1.php on line 6
Equals zero
```

This notice informs us that the variable $intNoValue was undefined. In other words we have not assigned it a value before testing it in the 'if' statement. This is bad programming practice and should in fact be coded as:

```php
<?php
// File: example20-2.php
$intNoValue = 0;

if ($intNoValue == 0)
echo "<p>Equals zero</p>";
?>
```

When developing scripts, it is best to have the highest possible level of error checking to ensure that we trap all errors and ensure that our code is of the highest standard.

Do not use global variables

Historically, PHP automatically generated global variables for all GET, POST, COOKIE and SESSION variables you created. Defining global variables in this way was great for the programmer as the scripts were quite simple. Unfortunately this simplicity came at a price, as the global variables provided a means for a malicious user to try and break a script you created. Interestingly PHP still allows for global variables to be created, but only when you edit the 'php.ini' file and turn the facility on, something we would not recommend.

Searching the 'php.ini' file for the section on Data Handling reveals the following:

```
;;;;;;;;;;;;;;;;;
; Data Handling ;
;;;;;;;;;;;;;;;;;
;
; Note - track_vars is ALWAYS enabled as of PHP 4.0.3

; The separator used in PHP generated URLs to separate arguments.
; Default is "&".
;arg_separator.output = "&amp;"

; List of separator(s) used by PHP to parse input URLs into variables.
; Default is "&".
; NOTE: Every character in this directive is considered as separator!
;arg_separator.input = ";&"

; This directive describes the order in which PHP registers GET, POST, Cookie,
; Environment and Built-in variables (G, P, C, E & S respectively, often
; referred to as EGPCS or GPC). Registration is done from left to right, newer
; values override older values.
variables_order = "EGPCS"

; Whether or not to register the EGPCS variables as global variables. You may
; want to turn this off if you don't want to clutter your scripts' global scope
; with user data. This makes most sense when coupled with track_vars - in which
; case you can access all of the GPC variables through the $HTTP_*_VARS[],
; variables.
;
```

```
; You should do your best to write your scripts so that they do not require
; register_globals to be on; Using form variables as globals can easily lead
; to possible security problems, if the code is not very well thought of.
register_globals = Off
```

The last line of the 'php.ini' file should be edited to:

```
register_globals = On
```

when the 'php.ini' file is saved and PHP is restarted then the use of global variables is active.

 NOTE | Switching register_globals to 'on' is not considered a very good idea!

It may be that you do not have control of the 'php.ini' file and that your service provider has set the register_globals variable to 'On' to allow some historical code to function. However you should not be tempted by the lure of programming with global variables as the following example will illustrate:

```
<!-- File: example20-3.htm -->

<h2>Please enter your Username and Password:</h2>

<form action='example20-4.php' method='post'>
<p>
<label for="strUserName">Username: </label>
<input type="text" name="strUserName" id="intUserName"/>
</p>
<p>
<label for="strPassword">Password: </label>
<input type="password" name="strPassword" id="intPassword"/>
</p>
<p><input type="submit" name="submit"/></p>
</form>
```

The above script implements a simple HTML form which requires the user to enter a username and password. This data is then passed to the following script:

```
<?php
// File: example20-4.php

if (checkusernamepassword($strUserName, $strPassword) )
   $intOkay = 1;

if ($intOkay)
   echo "Valid User confirmed";

function checkusernamepassword($strUserName, $strPassword) {
   return false;
}
?>
```

This script attempts to authenticate the user by passing the username and password to a function checkusernamepassword(). The function simply returns a value of false and therefore the value of $strOkay should never be set to true. However, if someone were to create a new form script and include the following line:

```
<p><input type="hidden" name="intOkay" value="1"/></p>
```

For example:

```
<!-- File: example20-5.htm -->
<h2>Please enter your Username and Password:</h2>
<form action='example20-4.php' method='post'>
<p>
<label for="strUserName">Username: </label>
<input type="text" name="strUserName" id="intUserName"/>
</p>
<p>
<label for="strPassword">Password: </label>
<input type="password" name="strPassword" id="intPassword"/>
</p>
<p><input type="hidden" name="intOkay" value="1"/></p>
<p><input type="submit" name="submit"/></p>
</form>
```

Then, when 'example20-4.php' were invoked, although the value of $strOkay was never set to true within the script because it was not initialized, the value passed from the form would still be valid and the user would be cleared as a valid user. One way to overcome this would be to ensure that in this instance that the variable $intOkay was initialized at the start of the script, but this is an easy thing to miss. A better and more secure way would be to ensure that register_globals = off and to implement the code using the $_POST super-global associative arrays as shown in earlier chapters, for example:

```php
<?php
// File: example20-6.php

$intOkay=0;

if (isset($_POST["submit"]) ) {
    if (checkusernamepassword($_POST["strUserName"],
        $_POST["strPassword"]) )
        $intOkay = 1;
}
if ($intOkay)
    echo "Valid User confirmed";

function checkusernamepassword($strUserName, $strPassword) {
    return false;
}
?>
```

In the above script, the global variables have been replaced by the $_POST super-global associative arrays. The problem of the variable $intOkay being set by the form in the previous script does not occur as there are no global variables.

Loose typing is bad

As we described in an earlier chapter, PHP is not a strongly typed language and this can lead to some problems if you are not careful about what you are doing.

Consider the following script which has been adapted from an article on this subject online (http://www.onlamp.com/pub/a/php/2003/04/03/php_security.html):

```php
<?php
// File: example20-7.php

$arrUserPasswords = array(0=>"", 1=>"password1", 2=>"password2",
    3=>"password3");

// Setting username and password for the test
$intUserId = 1;
$strPassword = "password1";

// UserId within array range?
if ($intUserId < 0 || $intUserId > 3)
    die ("UserId out of range");

// UserId actually present?
if (!isset($intUserId) )
    die ("No UserId");

// Password actually present?
if ($intUserId ! = 0 && !isset($strPassword) )
    die ("No Password");

// Valid Password for everyone but guest?
if ($intUserId ! = 0 && $arrUserPasswords[$intUserId] ! = $strPassword)
    die ("Invalid Password");

if ($intUserId)
    echo "You are a valid User";
else
    echo "You are a Guest User";
?>
```

The script is part of a user authentication process (it has been simplified for the purposes of this example). It begins by creating an array of usernames and corresponding passwords. The usernames in this case are represented by integer values from 0 to 3. The 0 username is representative of a guest account and no password is required:

```php
$arrUserPasswords = array(0=>"", 1=>"password1", 2=>"password2",
3=>"password3");
```

The next part of the script creates the entered username (intUserId) and password (strPassword). In a real system these would be entered via some interface such as a form:

```
// Setting username and password for the test
$intUserId = 1;
$strPassword = "password1";
```

We can change the values stored in these variables manually to test our script. The next lines employ an 'if' construct to ensure that the value of our username (intUserId) is between 0 and 3 as these are the only valid accounts in the username and password array:

```
// UserId within array range?
if ($intUserId < 0 || $intUserId > 3)
    die ("UserId out of range");
```

If a valid username is not detected then the script terminates with the message 'UserId out of range'. The next lines of code check to ensure that the variable $intUserId is actually present and, if not, the script terminates with the message 'No UserId':

```
// UserId actually present?
if (!isset($intUserId) )
    die ("No UserId");
```

The password is checked to see if it is present, but only when the value of $intUserId is not 0:

```
// Password actually present?
if ($intUserId != 0 && !isset($strPassword) )
    die ("No Password");
```

Next, the script uses an 'if' statement to check whether $intUserId is equal to 0 otherwise it checks that the password in $strPassword matches that stored in the array. If not, the script terminates with a message 'Invalid Password':

```
// Valid Password for everyone but guest?
if ($intUserId != 0 && $arrUserPasswords[$intUserId] != $strPassword)
    die ("Invalid Password");
```

Finally, if the script makes it this far, an 'if' statement is used to display a message to indicate if the user is a valid user or a guest user.

```
if ($intUserId)
    echo "You are a valid User";
else
    echo "You are a Guest User";
```

So far so good. But now it's time to test our script by adjusting the values of $intUserId and $strPassword and ensuring that the output of the script is as expected.

Table 20.1 illustrates some simple test cases which we have devised. Test 1 begins with the values of 0 and '' for the username and password and this correctly outputs 'You are a Guest User'. Test 2 uses the values of 1 and 'password1' and correctly outputs 'You are a valid User'. Test 3 uses the values 2 and 'password1' and correctly determines that

TABLE 20.1 Username and password combinations and output

Test	Username	Password	Output	Comment
1	0	' '	You are a Guest User	Correct
2	1	password1	You are a valid User	Correct
3	2	password1	Invalid Password	Correct
4	0	42	You are a Guest User	Incorrect. Password should be.
5	a	password1	You are a valid User	Incorrect. Username is not valid.

this is an 'Invalid Password' for this username. Test 4 uses the values 0 and 42 and outputs the text 'You are a Guest User'. There is some debate whether this is correct: the password should be blank but whether it matters or not is questionable. Finally, test 5 uses the values 'a' and 'password1' and incorrectly outputs the text 'You are a valid User', as a username of 'a' is not valid. So why did this happen?

 NOTE Ensuring that you test your applications sufficiently is a good way of ensuring that programming loop-holes are discovered and can be fixed.

The problems with the script lies in the fact that information entered via a form element cannot be assumed to be anything other than alphanumeric (containing any characters) and not simply numeric. While we are simulating form data entry by assigning values with the lines:

```
// Setting username and password for the test
$intUserId = 1;
$strPassword = "password1";
```

We cannot assume that data entered is numeric, for example we can write:

```
$intUserId = 'a';
```

Moving further down the script, things start to go wrong at this expression:

```
if ($intUserId != 0 && $arrUserPasswords[$intUserId] != $strPassword)
```

In the above expression the value of $intUserId != 0 is evaluated to false in the case of $intUserId being equal to 'a' as 'a' doesn't equal 0. Because of this, the rest of the expression is ignored and we arrive at the 'if' expression:

```
if ($intUserId)
    echo "You are a valid User";
else
    echo "You are a Guest User";
```

Here the value of $intUserId is evaluated to 'true' as $intUserId contains a value other than 0. It should be noted that being more consistent and implementing all 'if' conditions in the same way, for example using:

```
if ($intUserId != 0)
```

in the last 'if' statement would have resulted in the output being 'You are a Guest User', which could be a less damaging breach to system access.

To overcome the problem of knowing if a variable contains an integer value we can use the is_int( ) function:

```
is_int( variabletocheckforint )
```

In our script the function looks like this:

```
// Is UserId an Int?
if (!is_int($intUserId) )
    die ("UserId not integer");
```

This ensures that values such as 'a' are not acceptable and ensures that we are not mixing types within a given variable. Implementing the function to check for type and ensuring that our 'if' expressions are all consistent, results in the following more robust script:

```
<?php
// File: example20-8.php

$arrUserPasswords = array(0=>"", 1=>"password1", 2=>"password2",
    3=>"password3");

// Setting username and passwords for the test
$intUserId = 'a';
$strPassword = "password1";

// Is UserId an Int?
if (!is_int($intUserId) )
    die ("UserId not integer");

// UserId within array range?
if ($intUserId < 0 || $intUserId > 3)
    die ("UserId out of range");

// UserId actually present?
if (!isset($intUserId) )
    die ("No UserId");

//Password actually present?
if ($intUserId != 0 && !isset($strPassword) )
    die ("No Password");

// Valid Password for everyone but guest?
if ($intUserId != 0 && $arrUserPasswords[$intUserId] != $strPassword)
    die ("Invalid Password");

if ($intUserId != 0)
    echo "You are a valid User";
```

```
else
    echo "You are a Guest User";
?>
```

Validate your form data

It sounds fairly obvious when you think about it but one of the key ways that malicious users can affect the workings of a script is through the primary interface which scripts use to communicate with users i.e. forms. Forms consist of various fields which require the user to input data but we cannot assume that the data entered by the user is in the form which we are expecting. To ensure that the data is in the format we expected, we need to correctly validate the data. Failure to do this can result in scripts which behave unexpectedly or even crash when they try to perform an operation using the invalid data.

Some form elements are easier to validate than others, for example the select, checkbox and radio button elements. They are easier to validate as their input is more restricted than, for example, input fields where the user has much more freedom on what they can enter.

Consider the following example script which illustrates a simple select menu:

```
<h2>Please select your title:</h2>

<form action='<?php echo $_SERVER["PHP_SELF"]; ?>' method='post'>
<p><select name='strTitle'>
    <option>Mr</option>
    <option>Miss</option>
    <option>Ms</option>
    <option>Mrs</option>
    <option>Dr</option>
</select></p>
<p><input type='submit' name='submit'/></p>
</form>

<?php
// File: example20-9.php
if (isset($_POST["submit"]) ) {
    $strTitle = $_POST["strTitle"];
    echo "<p>Your title is $strTitle</p>";
}
?>
```

In this script the user is presented with a form consisting of two elements, a select menu and a submit button. The user has only five choices to make from the menu and therefore it would appear that validation is not necessary in this case as the user has very restricted input.

There is however some improvements which can be made to increase the chance that the user has chosen the correct title. As the script stands at the moment the select menu defaults to the first item in the list, in this case 'Mr'. If the user forgets to select the correct title from the list and simply clicks the submit button, the value 'Mr' will be sent and assumed to be correct. This is illustrated in Figure 20.2.

FIGURE 20.2   Select menu with no null option

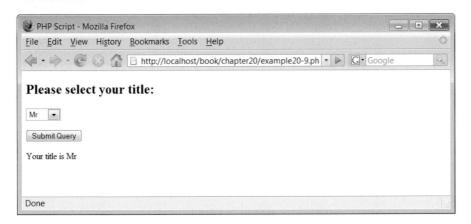

However, an improvement to our script would be to include a null value for the select menu, such as '———' as a default, for example:

```
<option> ———</option>
```

We could then check that the user has selected a title other than this, for example:

```
if ($_POST["submit"] == "———")
    echo "<p>Please select a title.</p>";
```

This would provide a degree of confidence that the user has made an informed choice and not simply clicked submit as a default. The completed script now looks like this:

```
<h2>Please select your title:</h2>

<form action='<?php echo $_SERVER["PHP_SELF"]; ?>' method='post'>
<p><select name='strTitle'>
   <option>———</option>
   <option>Mr</option>
   <option>Miss</option>
   <option>Ms</option>
   <option>Mrs</option>
   <option>Dr</option>
</select></p>
<p><input type='submit' name='submit'/></p>
</form>

<?php
// File: example20-10.php

if (isset($_POST["submit"]) ) {
   if ($_POST["submit"] == "———")
      echo "<p>Please select a title.</p>";
   else {
      $strTitle = $_POST["strTitle"];
      echo "<p>Your title is $strTitle</p>";
   }
}
?>
```

FIGURE 20.3   Select menu with null option

Figure 20.3 illustrates the revised form menu.

Other form elements allow the user more freedom in the data they can input and these include the text, password and textbox elements. The following script illustrates a simple login form consisting of three form elements, a username input field, a password input field and a submit button:

```
<h2>Please login:</h2>

<form action='<?php echo $_SERVER["PHP_SELF"]; ?>' method='post'>
<p>
<label for="intUsername">Username: </label>
<input type="text" name="intUsername" id="intUsername"/>
</p><p>
<label for="strPassword">Password: </label>
<input type="password" name="strPassword" id="strPassword"/>
</p>
<p><input type='submit' name='submit'/></p>
</form>

<?php
// File: example20-11.php

if (isset($_POST["submit"]) ) {
    $intUsername = $_POST["intUsername"];
    $strPassword = $_POST["strPassword"];
    echo "<p>Username: $intUsername Password: $strPassword</p>";
}
?>
```

At the moment all the script does is to display the values of intUsername and strPassword and performs no error checking. This is fine if the users always obey the rules which are:

- A username must be an 8-digit number beginning with the number 5 and containing no non-numeric characters.

- A password can be any combination of characters but must be a minimum of 6 characters long and a maximum of 12.

These validation criteria can be enforced in a number of different ways. First the length of the username can be limited to 8 characters using the maxlength attribute:

```
<input type="text" name="intUsername" id="intUsername" maxlength='8'/>
```

The maximum length of the password can be limited to 12 characters like this:

```
<input type="password" name="strPassword" id="strPassword"
maxlength='12'/>
```

To ensure the minimum length of the username, which is 8, and the password, 6, we need to implement some 'if' constructs and employ the strlen( ) function:

```
if (strlen($intUsername) < 8)
    echo "<p>Username less than 8 characters</p>";

if (strlen($strPassword) < 6)
    echo "<p>Password less than 6 characters</p>";
```

To check that the username begins with a number 5 we need to check its first character:

```
if ($intUsername{0} != "5")
    echo "<p>Username doesn't start with a 5</p>";
```

Finally, to check that the username is all numeric characters we can use the is_numeric() function:

```
is_numeric (variabletocheckfornumeric)
```

In our program this looks like this:

```
if (!is_numeric($intUsername) )
    echo "<p>Username needs to consist of only numbers</p>";
```

The complete script including a variable to keep count of the number of errors detected and then checked to see if a username and password should be displayed is as follows:

```
<h2>Please login:</h2>

<form action='<?php echo $_SERVER["PHP_SELF"]; ?>' method='post'>
<p>
<label for="intUsername">Username: </label>
<input type="text" name="intUsername" id="intUsername" maxlength='8'/>
</p><p>
<label for = "strPassword">Password: </label>
<input type="password" name="strPassword" id="strPassword"
maxlength='12'/>
</p>
<p><input type='submit' name='submit'/></p>
</form>
```

```php
<?php
// File: example20-12.php

if (isset($_POST["submit"]) ) {
    $intUsername = $_POST["intUsername"];
    $strPassword = $_POST["strPassword"];

$intErrorCount = 0;

    if (strlen($intUsername) < 8) {
        echo "<p>Username less than 8 characters</p>";
        $intErrorCount++;
    }
    if (strlen($strPassword) < 6) {
        echo "<p>Password less than 6 characters</p>";
        $intErrorCount++;
    }

    if ($intUsername{0} ! = "5") {
        echo "<p>Username doesn't start with a 5</p>";
    $intErrorCount++;
    }
    if (!is_numeric($intUsername) ) {
        echo "<p>Username needs to consist of only numbers</p>";
    $intErrorCount++;
    }

    if ($intErrorCount == 0)
        echo "<p>Username: $intUsername Password: $strPassword and all is well.</p>";
}
?>
```

Figure 20.4 illustrates the output from the script.

FIGURE 20.4 Form field detecting errors

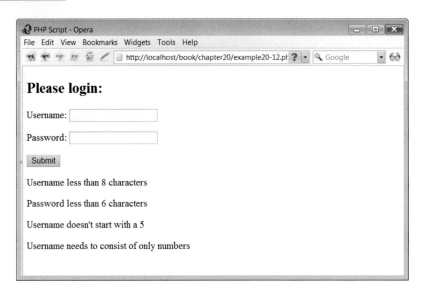

One other check we may need to implement is where the value of a data item in one form field affects the validation criteria of another. Consider the following script:

```
<h2>Please select your title:</h2>
<form action='<?php echo $_SERVER["PHP_SELF"]; ?>' method='post'>
<p>
<label for="strTitle">Title: </label>
<select name='strTitle' id='strTitle'>
    <option>Mr</option>
    <option>Miss</option>
    <option>Ms</option>
    <option>Mrs</option>
    <option>Dr</option>
    <option>Other</option>
</select>
<label for="strOther">Other: </label>
<input type="text" name="strOther" id="strOther"/>
</p>
<p><input type='submit' name='submit'/></p>
</form>

<?php
// File: example20-13.php

if (isset($_POST["submit"]) ) {
    echo "<p>Your title is $strTitle.</p>";
}
?>
```

The above script implements a simple form consisting of three elements: a select menu, a text field and a submit button. The select menu allows a user to select their title from the menu. What we would like to include is some script which detects if the option 'Other' is chosen and subsequently set the strTitle variable to contain the value entered in the $strOther text field. A further check is required that the length of the data in the $strOther field is a minimum of two characters. Here is the additional script:

```
if ($strTitle == "Other") {
    $strTitle = $strOther;
}

if (strlen($strTitle) < 2)
    echo "<p>Title must be greater than two characters</p>";
```

The completed script with the above validation checks incorporated is as follows:

```
<h2>Please select your title:</h2>
<form action='<?php echo $_SERVER["PHP_SELF"]; ?>' method='post'>
<p>
<label for="strTitle">Title: </label>
<select name='strTitle' id='strTitle'>
    <option>Mr</option>
    <option>Miss</option>
    <option>Ms</option>
    <option>Mrs</option>
```

```
          <option>Dr</option>
          <option>Other</option>
      </select>
      <label for="strOther">Other: </label>
      <input type="text" name="strOther" id="strOther"/>
   </p>
   <p><input type='submit' name='submit'/></p>
</form>

<?php
// File: example20-14.php

if (isset($_POST["submit"]) ) {
   $strTitle = $_POST["strTitle"];
   $strOther = $_POST["strOther"];

   if ($strTitle == "Other") {
      $strTitle = $strOther;
   }

   if (strlen($strTitle) < 2)
      echo "<p>Title must be greater than two characters</p>";
   else
      echo "<p>Your title is $strTitle.</p>";
}
?>
```

Figure 20.5 illustrates the output from the script.

20.3 Countering malicious data injection

Escaping HTML elements in text fields

Another security breach which can be overcome is that of injecting HTML elements into form text, password and textarea fields. This is closely related to the issue of form data

FIGURE 20.5 Cross-field validation

validation and once again concerns the subject of whether the data you have is what you expected. Consider the following script:

```
<h2>Please enter your message:</h2>
<form action='<?php echo $_SERVER["PHP_SELF"]; ?>' method='post'>
<p>
<label for="strMessage">Message: </label>
<textarea name="strMessage" id="strMessage"></textarea>
</p>
<p><input type='submit' name='submit'/></p>
</form>
<?php
// File: example20-15.php

if (isset($_POST["submit"]) ) {
    $strMessage = $_POST["strMessage"];

    echo "<p>Your message is $strMessage.</p>";
}
echo "<p>This is some text further down the web page.</p>";
?>
```

The above script displays a form consisting of two elements: a textarea and a submit button. A user is free to type a message in the textarea which, once submitted, is displayed on the web page. This is illustrated in Figure 20.6, where the message 'Isn't PHP great?' is displayed.

The problem comes when a user decides to enter a message which includes some (X)HTML elements. They are free to do this as (X)HTML is just text after all and this is known as (X)HTML injection. An example of this could be where a user enters '<h1>This is large!</h1>' as the message. In this case, the user's message is displayed as a level 1 heading. Worse than that, if a user enters only the first part of a multiple part element the whole display of the web page can be affected from that point onwards. Consider the message '<i>Hello, this is in italics'. The result of this displays the message in italic characters but also the text following the message. This is illustrated in Figure 20.7.

To overcome this vulnerability, you can use the PHP function htmlentities( ). In its simplest form, it looks like this:

```
htmlentities (string string)
```

The function translates '<' characters into the character entity '<' and '>' into the character entity '>'. These are displayed as the characters '<' and '>' respectively in a browser but a browser does not recognize them as being the start and end of an (X)HTML element and therefore does not parse the (X)HTML element. The following script illustrates

FIGURE 20.6   Displaying text messages

FIGURE 20.6   Displaying text messages

FIGURE 20.7   HTML injection

the incorporation of the function to prevent (X)HTML injection:

```
<h2>Please enter your message:</h2>
<form action='<?php echo $_SERVER["PHP_SELF"]; ?>' method='post'>
<p>
<label for="strMessage">Message: </label>
<textarea name="strMessage" id="strMessage"></textarea>
```

```
</p>
<p><input type='submit' name='submit'/></p>
</form>

<?php
// File: example20-16.php
if (isset($_POST["submit"])) {
    $strMessage = $_POST["strMessage"];

    echo "<p>" . htmlentities("Your message is " . $strMessage) . ".</p>";
}
echo "<p>This is some text further down the web page.</p>";
?>
```

The output from the above script is illustrated in Figure 20.8.

 NOTE | If you don't write your code to prevent HTML injection and your application allows such user input it will only be a matter of time until this occurs either deliberately or accidentally.

Escaping characters and SQL injection

Another form of character injection can be a little more sinister and this is known as SQL injection. To explain SQL injection we need to create a database and populate it with some data. We will create a database called 'users' with a single table called 'users'. The table fields and field types are shown in Table 20.2.

FIGURE 20.8 HTML injection prevented

TABLE 20.2	Table users: fields and types	
Field	Type	Other
Id	Int	Auto_increment, primary key
Username	Varchar (30)	
Password	Varchar (30)	

TABLE 20.3	Table users: data	
Id	Username	Password
1	Alan	Smith
2	David	Regan

And suppose that we populate this with the data shown in Table 20.3.

Now we can create a simple script to allow us to access the database:

```php
<?php
// File: example20-17.php

$strUsername = 'David';
$strPassword = 'Regan';

$dbLocalhost = mysql_connect("localhost", "root", "")
   or die("Could not connect: " . mysql_error() );

mysql_select_db("users", $dbLocalhost)
   or die("Could not find database: " . mysql_error() );
$dbRecords = mysql_query("SELECT * FROM users WHERE username = '$strUsername' ");

$arrRecords = mysql_fetch_array($dbRecords);
if ($strPassword != $arrRecords["Password"])
   echo "<p>Invalid Password/Username</p>";
else
   echo "<p>Password and Username match!</p>";
?>
```

The script is a basic username and password verification script. We start with a username and password which we can assume the user has entered (but for the sake of simplicity we have hard-coded into the script). We then check the database for the username, reporting an error if it is not present and finally check if the database stored password matches that supplied along with the username. You should find that the script works fine.

However, what if the username value of 'David' was replaced with:

```
"' OR '1 = 1";
```

To be clear the above value of $strUsername consists of the following characters:

```
Double-quote
Single-quote
Space character
OR
Space character
Single-quote
1
=
1
Double-quote
Semi-colon
```

$strPassword is set to blank:

```
$strPassword = '';
```

The script now looks like this:

```php
<?php
// File: example20-18.php

$strUsername = "' OR '1=1";
$strPassword = '';
$dbLocalhost = mysql_connect("localhost", "root", "")
    or die("Could not connect: " . mysql_error() );

mysql_select_db("users", $dbLocalhost)
    or die("Could not find database: " . mysql_error() );

$dbRecords = mysql_query("SELECT * FROM users WHERE username = '$strUsername' ");

$arrRecords = mysql_fetch_array($dbRecords);
echo $arrRecords["Password"];
if ($strPassword != $arrRecords["Password"])
    echo "<p>Invalid Password/Username</p>";
else
    echo "<p>Password and Username match!</p>";
?>
```

The problem is that when it now runs, the script returns the string 'Passwords and Usernames match!' and our security has been breached through changing the SQL statement. The above works because the SQL statement with the contents of $strUsername expanded now reads:

```
SELECT * FROM users WHERE username='' OR '1=1'
```

This actually returns no records and as the password is set to null, the 'if' statements comparing the passwords evaluates to true. Therefore the script thinks that the username and password matches.

SQL injection can be prevented through the use of the mysql_escape_string( ) function:

```
mysql_escape_string ( string unescaped_string )
```

This function escapes quotation characters in the SQL string so that, in our example, the query looks like this:

```
SELECT * FROM users WHERE username='\' OR \'1=1'
```

The escaped characters remove the danger of the quotes being interpreted incorrectly by the SQL parser. In addition, it is important to ensure that you include code which checks to see if any records have been returned from the database by your query. If you are expecting one and none are returned there is a potential problem. We can use the mysql_num_rows( ) function to do this, for example:

```php
if (mysql_num_rows($dbRecords) != 1)
    echo "<p>Username not found!</p>";
```

Our amended script now looks like this and removes the possibility that SQL injection will be able to circumvent our login security:

```php
<?php
// File: example20-19.php

$strUsername = "' OR '1=1";
$strPassword = '';

$dbLocalhost = mysql_connect("localhost", "root", "")
    or die("Could not connect: " . mysql_error() );

mysql_select_db("users", $dbLocalhost)
    or die("Could not find database: " . mysql_error() );

$strUsername = mysql_real_escape_string($strUsername);

$dbRecords = mysql_query("SELECT * FROM users WHERE username = '$strUsername' ");

$arrRecords = mysql_fetch_array($dbRecords);

if (mysql_num_rows($dbRecords) ! = 1)
    echo "<p>Username not found!</p>";
else {

    if ($strPassword != $arrRecords["Password"])
        echo "<p>Invalid Password/Username</p>";
    else
        echo "<p>Password and Username match!</p>";
}
?>
```

20.4 User authentication and passwords

Checking the referrer

We briefly introduced the concept of checking the referrer page in an earlier chapter, but here is a recap. Consider the following script:

```php
<?php
// File: example20-20.php
```

```
if(isset($_POST["submit"])) {
    $strUserPass = array ( "john" => "red",
                           "simon" => "green",
                           "liz" => "blue",
                           "david" => "yellow");

    if ($strUserPass[$_POST[" strUsername"] ] == $_POST["strPassword"])
            header("location: example20-21.php");

    echo "<h1>Incorrect Username and/or password!</h1>";
}
?>

<form method="post" action="">
<p>
<label for="strUsername">Username: </label>
<input type="text" name="strUsername" id="strUsername"/></p>
<p>
<label for="strPassword">Password: </label>
<input type="password" name="strPassword" id="strPassword"/></p>
<p><input type="submit" name="submit" /></p>
</form>
```

The above script outputs a form consisting of three elements: a text field, a password field and a submit button. The user enters a username and password and these are then checked against a simple array of usernames and passwords. If a match is found then the user is redirected to a new page like this:

```
<?php
// File: example20-21.php

if ($_SERVER["HTTP_REFERER"])
    if ($_SERVER["HTTP_REFERER"] != "http://localhost/Book/example20-20.php")
        header("location: example20-20.php");
?>
<h1>Well, done you are correctly logged in!</h1>
```

Obviously we don't want the user or some malicious person to be able to jump directly to the second page by typing into the browser the address of the second page and completely bypassing the security we have put in place, for example:

```
http://localhost/example20-21.php
```

To stop this we have included the following lines at the top of the second script:

```
if ($_SERVER["HTTP_REFERER"])
    if ($_SERVER["HTTP_REFERER"] != "http://localhost/Book/example20-20.php")
        header("location: example20-20.php");
```

These check the value 'HTTP_REFERER' which is held in the associative array $_SERVER. In this instance we need to check whether the value stored is equal to:

```
http://localhost/Book/example20-20.php
```

This value indicates the address of the page from which the current page was launched. If the user correctly completed the username and password login form then this will be set to the value above. If however they simply typed the address of the second page directly into the browser then this value will not be set correctly and we know that something is wrong. The script then uses the header( ) function to redirect the browser to the initial login form:

```php
header("location: example20-20.php");
```

Sessions for authentication

Sessions can also be used to enhance the security of a web application. Consider the following script:

```php
<?php
// File: example20-22.php

if(isset($_POST["submit"]) ) {
    $strUserPass = array ( "john"  => "red",
                           "simon" => "green",
                           "liz"   => "blue",
                           "david" => "yellow");

    if ($strUserPass[$_POST["strUsername"] ] == $_POST["strPassword"]) {
        session_start();
        $_SESSION['strUsername'] = $_POST["strUsername"];
        header("location: example20-23.php");
    }
        echo "<h1>Incorrect Username and/or password!</h1>";
}
?>

<form method="post" action = "">
<p>
<label for="strUsername">Username: </label>
<input type="text" name="strUsername" id="strUsername"/></p>
<p>
<label for="strPassword">Password: </label>
<input type="password" name="strPassword" id="strPassword"/></p>
<p><input type="submit" name="submit" /></p>
</form>
</body>
</html>
```

This script is similar to 'example20-20.php' except that, before it directs the browser to a new page, it starts a session and stores the value of username:

```php
session_start();
$_SESSION['strUsername'] = $_POST["strUsername"];
```

The script then calls script 'example20-23.php':

```php
<?php
// File: example20-23.php

session_start();
if (!isset($_SESSION['strUsername']))
```

```
      header("location: example20-22.php");

  unset($_SESSION['strUsername']);
  ?>
  <h1>Well, done you are correctly logged in!</h1>
```

This script starts a session and then checks to see if the session variable strUsername has been set:

```
  session_start();

  if (!isset($_SESSION['strUsername']) )
```

If it has not, then the script assumes that the user did not arrive at this current script via 'example20-22.php' and returns the user to this script.

 NOTE You can of course increase your security further by combining both session and referral checking in the same script.

Store passwords in encrypted form

You may wish to store a user's password in a database similar to the database example we used earlier in this chapter. Table 20.4 illustrates the database table structure we devised previously and can reuse.

This time however, instead of storing the passwords as text as we did previously, we are going to store them in encrypted form. The advantage of this is that if someone does breach the security of your database and gain access to the database records they will not gain access to the passwords for each of your users. We can use the md5( ) function to create an encrypted version of the password for storage.

Entering MD5 data in MySQL would appear to be hard but the designers of the PHPMyAdmin interface have made things easy. When you wish to store data in MD5 format you simply enter the data in unencrypted and then select the MD5 function as illustrated in Figure 20.9.

Doing this results in the database storing the passwords ('Smith' and 'Regan') as indicated in Table 20.5.

Finally, in order to access and check that the password entered via a form matches those in a database we need to convert the entered password to its encrypted form before

TABLE 20.4 Database user fields and types

Field	Type	Other
Id	Int	Auto_increment, primary key
Username	Varchar (30)	
Password	Varchar (30)	

FIGURE 20.9 Storing MD5 data in MySQL

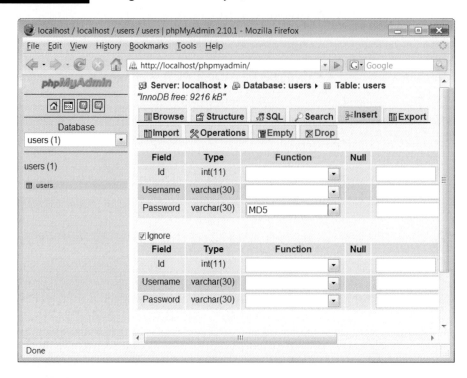

TABLE 20.5 Table users: data

Id	Username	Password
1	Alan	e95f770ac4fb91ac2e4873e4b2dfc0e6
2	David	09e9de9b75f2014dd8abe9dbe3a0d9fd

comparing it with that stored in the database, as shown here:

```php
// File: example20-24.php

$strUsername = 'David';
$strPassword = 'Regan';
$dbLocalhost = mysql_connect("localhost", "root", "")
    or die("Could not connect: " . mysql_error());

mysql_select_db("users", $dbLocalhost)
    or die("Could not find database: " . mysql_error());
$dbRecords = mysql_query("SELECT * FROM users WHERE username='$strUsername' ");

$arrRecords = mysql_fetch_array($dbRecords);
if (md5($strPassword) != $arrRecords["Password"])
    echo "<p>Invalid Password/Username</p>";
else
    echo "<p>Password and Username match!</p>";
?>
```

TABLE 20.6   Leet Speak letter translations

Letter	Leet Character
A	@ or 4
B	8
E	3 or &
H	#
I	1
L	1 or £
O	0 or *
P	9
S	5 or $
Z	2

Enforce strong passwords

The final security enhancement we can suggest in this chapter concerns the quality of passwords which you let your users select. Your system should advise your users on the strength of their password and enforce a minimum standard. For example a simple system could be to score 1 point for each of the following rules a user's password meets:

- a minimum length (no less than 6 characters)
- contains upper case letters
- contains lower case letters
- contains at least one number
- contains at least one other character, such as !£$%^&*@#+

A password such as 'simonstobart' would only score 1 point on the above scale and rightly so, as it would be quite easy to guess. A password such as 'Hy6^gDs3+' would score 5 points and is far more secure but is more difficult to remember.

One method to help make passwords secure but still memorable is to convert some of your letters into 'Leet Speak' (http://en.wikipedia.org/wiki/Leet). This is a form of English developed on-line where certain letters are replaced with numbers or other characters. The result is a word which looks similar to the original and is therefore memorable but is far more difficult to guess. Table 20.6 lists some letters and their Leet Speak translations.

 NOTE   Leet Speak is not yet standardized across the web and so different translations of characters and letters are widespread.

The following script is a simple tool to help you convert a memorable word into a more secure Leet Speak one:

```
<h2>Password suggestor:</h2>

<form action='<?php echo $_SERVER["PHP_SELF"]; ?>' method='post'>
```

```
<p>
<label for="strWord">Word: </label>
<input type="text" name="strWord" id="strWord"/>
</p>
<p><input type='submit' name='submit'/></p>
</form>

<?php
// File: example20-25.php

if (isset($_POST["submit"]) ) {
  $strPassword = generatePassword($_POST["strWord"]);
    echo "<p>$strPassword</p>";
}

function generatePassword($strWord) {
  $intWordLength = strlen($strWord);
  $strPassword = "";
  srand( (double) microtime() * 1000000);

for ($intLetter = 0;$intLetter<$intWordLength;$intLetter++) {
  if ($strWord{$intLetter} == 'o' || $strWord{$intLetter} == 'O')

     if (rand(0,1) )
       $strPassword .= '0';
     else
       $strPassword .= '*';
   elseif($strWord{$intLetter} == 'l' || $strWord{$intLetter} == 'L')
     if (rand(0,1) )
       $strPassword .= '£';
     else
       $strPassword .= '1';
   elseif($strWord{$intLetter} == 'i' || $strWord{$intLetter} == 'I')
       $strPassword .= '1';
   elseif($strWord{$intLetter} == 'z' || $strWord{$intLetter} == 'Z')
       $strPassword .= '2';
   elseif($strWord{$intLetter} == 'e' || $strWord{$intLetter} == 'E')
     if (rand(0,1) )
       $strPassword .= '&';
     else
       $strPassword .= '3';
   elseif($strWord{$intLetter} == 's' || $strWord{$intLetter} == 'S') {
     if (rand(0,1) )
       $strPassword .= '5';
     else
       $strPassword .= '$';
   }
   elseif($strWord{$intLetter} == 'b' || $strWord{$intLetter} == 'B')
       $strPassword .= '8';
   elseif($strWord{$intLetter} == 'p' || $strWord{$intLetter} == 'P')
       $strPassword .= '9';
   elseif($strWord{$intLetter} == 'a' || $strWord{$intLetter} == 'A') {
     if (rand(0,1) )
       $strPassword .= '@';
```

```
        else
            $strPassword .= '4';
    }
    elseif($strWord{$intLetter} == 'h' || $strWord{$intLetter} == 'H')
            $strPassword .= '#';
        else {
        if (rand(0,1) )
            $strPassword .= strtoupper($strWord{$intLetter});
        else
            $strPassword .= strtolower($strWord{$intLetter});
        }
    }
    return $strPassword;
}
?>
```

The script implements a function which parses each letter of the word you enter via the form and decides (in some case randomly) which letters to convert to numbers and characters and whether any remaining letters should be upper or lower case. Figure 20.10 illustrates the output from the above script in parsing the password 'simonstobart'. Remember the output from the script is random so you can get different output each time you run the script.

FIGURE 20.10   Generating Leet Speak passwords

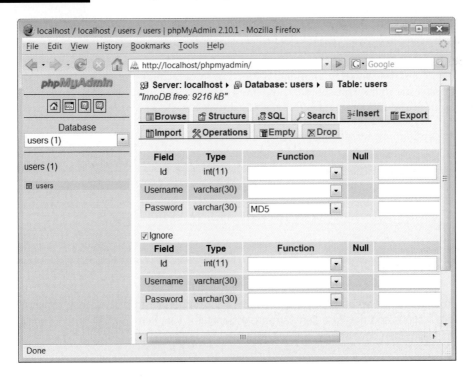

Exercises

20.1 Consider the following script, which is designed to display the surname of 'Alan' three times:

```php
<?php
$intCount;

$arrFirstSurnames = array(Simon =>"Jones", James =>"Smith",
                          Alan =>"Barclay", Gemma =>"West");

for ($intA=0;$intA<=$intCount;$intA++)
   echo $arrFirstSurnames[Alan] . " ";
?>
```

Determine what errors are included and correct them. If you have only found one error then you are not trying hard enough.

20.2 Write a script which validates the following form fields according to the following rules:

Day of Month
Month
Year

Day of Month
Month
Year

The two dates should both be checked to ensure they are valid dates.

The second date must be a minimum of 30 days greater than the first.

20.3 Write a script which implements a function to determine the strength of a generated password. Your script should score the strength of the password by adding 1 point for each of the following rules the password matches (to a total score of 5):

- a minimum length (no less than 6 characters)
- contains upper case letters
- contains lower case letters
- contains at least one number
- contains at least one other character, such as !£$%^&*@#+

SUMMARY

In this chapter, we began by explaining why it is important to build secure, robust PHP applications and that as a software professional it is vital that you pay due diligence to this fact when developing your web systems.

We have addressed the issue of building robust and secure web systems by addressing PHP web development from three angles. Firstly the issue of understanding and being able to apply good development practice was introduced. Secondly, we described some of the various hacking attacks which may be employed against your application and presented various means by which these can be countered. Finally, we discussed the issue of user authentication and why is it is a vitally important security issue. As part of this we discussed how to ensure the creation and subsequent protection of strong passwords.

References and further reading

Malcolm, C. (2003) Ten Security Checks for PHP, Part 2. http://www.onlamp.com/pub/a/php/2003/04/03/php_security.html

Wikipedia. Leetspeak. http://en.wikipedia.org/wiki/Leet

20

Using XMLSpy

INTRODUCTION

XMLSpy is an XML editor from Altova® GmbH that provides tools for modelling, editing, transforming and debugging XML technologies. Among its many features, it provides support for XML validation.

This appendix refers to the Altova® XMLSpy 2007 Enterprise Edition which is supplied with this book. The current version, along with an evaluation licence key, can be downloaded from http://www.altova.com/download. Altova are also able to provide special site licences for educational partners and extended evaluation licences for students enrolled on recognized courses. Enquiries by academic staff should be made to the Altova Partner program (partners@altova.com).

Why do we need XMLSpy?

Browsers such as Internet Explorer can check if XML and DTD documents are well formed. Figure 1 shows Internet Explorer 7 displaying an error message about an XML document that is not well formed.

Most browsers do not, however, validate XML documents without special tools being added. In addition, browsers offer little editing support for XML documents. Therefore it can be much more productive to edit and process XML documents using a dedicated tool like XMLSpy, which can, among other things:

- Check if XML documents are well-formed
- Validate XML documents against DTD
- Validate XML documents against an XML Schema
- Perform XSLT transformations
- Display HTML / XHTML

FIGURE 1

Internet Explorer 7 displaying an error message because an XML document is not well formed

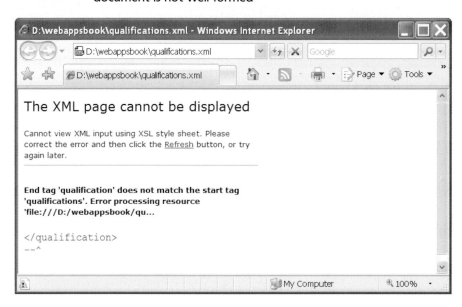

FIGURE 2

The XMLSpy windows and helpers

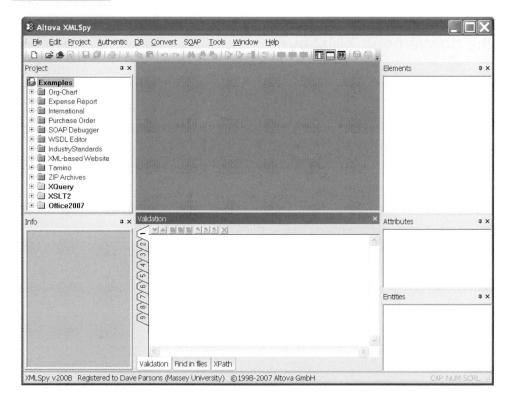

Using XMLSpy

To install XMLSpy, you will need to run the installation file, which is available both on the CD supplied with this book and from the Altova web site. Once the program has been installed, you will need to run it for the first time in order to enter your license details. These can be copied from the email that will be received from Altova once you have applied for an evaluation licence.

The XMLSpy environment comprises a number of windows and 'helpers' (Figure 2), which can be toggled on and off using the 'Window' menu item. The left hand view is the 'Project' window, but you do not have to use a project in XMLSpy. Documents can be created and manipulated independently of a project file. However a project is useful if you want to group multiple documents together for loading and saving as a unit, for example an XML file and its associated DTD.

Creating a New File

To create a new file, click on the 'File' menu and then select 'New'. A dialog box will appear similar to that shown in Figure 3. From here, you can choose the type of file you want to create, for example a new XML document.

If you choose to create a new XML document, another dialog will appear that asks you to choose either a DTD or an XML Schema to validate the document (Figure 4). If you do not yet have one of these, you can simply click the 'Cancel' button. Otherwise another dialog will appear that lets you browse for a DTD or an XML Schema to apply to the document.

Testing if XML Documents are Well-Formed and Valid.

FIGURE 3   The 'Create new document' dialog in XMLSpy

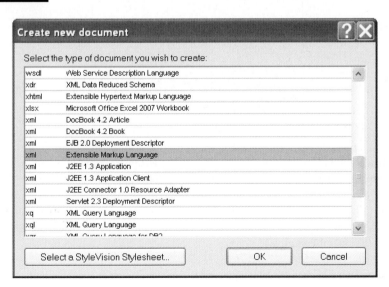

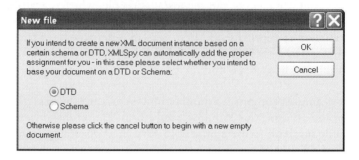

| FIGURE 5a | XMLSpy indicating that an XML document is not well-formed |

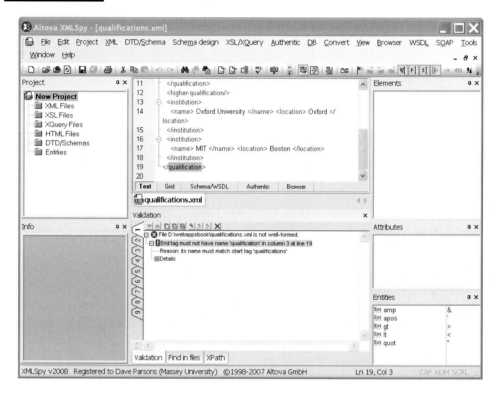

You can use XMLSpy to test if XML documents are both well-formed and valid. The XML source can be typed directly into editing the window, copied and pasted from an external editor or loaded from an external file (XMLSpy also provides a number of different editing views that make it easy to create and edit a document). To test if the XML document is well formed, select 'XML' from the main menu and then select 'Check well-formedness'. The result will appear in the output window at the bottom of the screen. Figure 5a shows an XML document that is not well formed, with an error message displayed in the output window.

Figure 5b shows the 'tick' icon that appears if the document is well formed.

XMLSpy indicating well-formed XML document

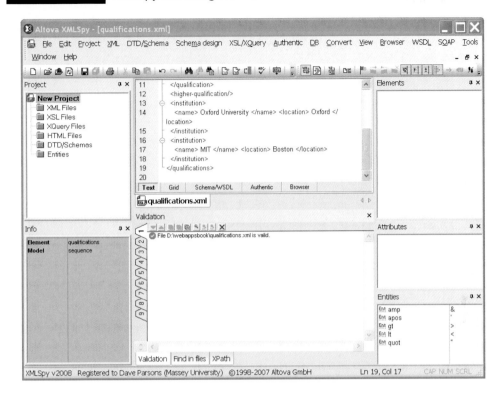

FIGURE 6

The dialog that enables you to browse for a validating document

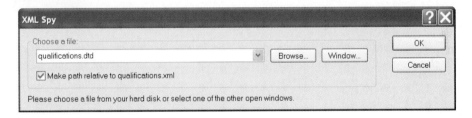

Validating XML

To validate an XML document you can assign either a DTD or an XML Schema. This assignment can either be done manually or by browsing for the validating document via the 'DTD/Schema' menu item. To assign a DTD, for example, select 'Assign DTD' from the 'DTD/Schema' menu and find the document in the file system (Figure 6).

Once a DTD has been assigned to an XML document, you can check if it is valid by selecting 'XML' from the top level menu and then selecting 'validate' from the menu. Figure 7 shows an error message being displayed by XMLSpy because an XML document has failed validation.

Figure 8 shows a valid document being checked by XMLSpy.

| FIGURE 7 | XMLSpy indicating that an XML document has failed validation |

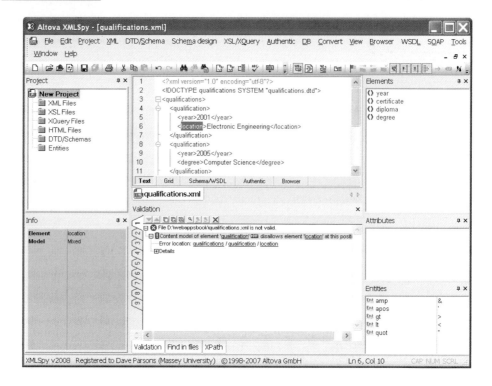

| FIGURE 8 | An XML document passing validation in XMLSpy |

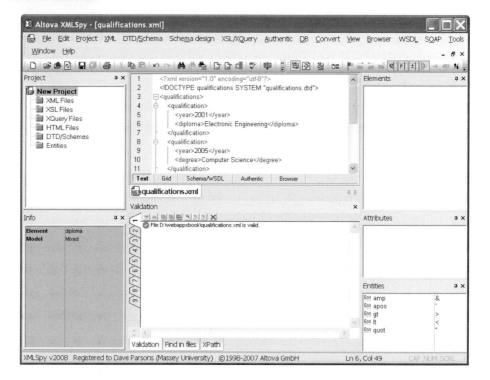

Further information

For further information about XMLSpy, refer to the Altova web site (http://www.altova.com) or the 'Help' facility within XMLSpy itself (accessible from the main menu bar).